W9-AVL-285

BARRON'S FINANCIAL GUIDES

Barron's Financial Tables for Better Money Management

Mortgage Payments

Third Edition

Stephen S. Solomon
M.S., Applied Mathematics

Clifford W. Marshall
Ph.D., Applied Mathematics
Professor of Mathematics
Polytechnic University

Martin Pepper
Master of Science, E.E.
Fellow, Society of Actuaries

BARRON'S

Great effort has been made to develop accurate tables;
however, no warranty of absolute accuracy is given.

All inquiries should be addressed to:
Barron's Educational Series, Inc.
250 Wireless Boulevard
Hauppauge, New York 11788
http://www.barronseduc.com

International Standard Book No. 0-7641-1801-3

Library of Congress Catalog Card No. 00-067466

Library of Congress Cataloging-in-Publication Data

Solomon, Stephen S.
     Mortgage payments / Stephen S. Solomon, Clifford W.
Marshall, Martin Pepper. — 3rd ed.
     p. cm. — (Barron's financial tables for better money
management)
     ISBN 0-7641-1801-3 (alk. paper)
     1. Loan amortization schedules. 2. Mortgage loans—
Tables. I. Marshall, Clifford W., 1928– II. Pepper, Martin.
III. Title. IV. Series.
HG1634.S65   2001
332.8′2′0212—dc21

                                                    00-067466

PRINTED IN THE UNITED STATES OF AMERICA

9 8 7 6 5 4 3 2 1

Contents

Introduction

The idea behind *Barron's Financial Tables for Better Money Management* is to provide assistance to anyone who invests, makes purchases, or borrows money. Since these guides require no financial or mathematical expertise, they can be used easily by the average investor or mortgage seeker. The tables are easy to read and are preceded by sample situations that show the nature and scope of the tables. Following each sample situation a short explanation tells how to use a particular table to find the desired answer and how to locate data on the table. After reading the situation and explanation you should be able to apply the same procedure to answer questions regarding your particular situation. If you spend time "walking through" all the situations given, you will better understand how to use the tables.

Because these tables are designed for the non-professional, no formulas or mathematical derivations are shown. Such derivations are not required for proper use of the tables.

Monthly Mortgage Payment Tables

Prospective home buyers must consider many important factors when purchasing a home. For most, the purchase of a home is the largest investment of their lives, and the financial arrangements are uppermost in their minds. Therefore, understanding the basis for mortgage financing is the most important factor in the entire undertaking.

The most common source of financing among home buyers is the conventional mortgage. A mortgage is an agreement between a buyer and a lender, usually a bank. Under the terms of the typical mortgage, in return for a loan the buyer agrees to make monthly payments to the lender for a specific number of years. Part of the monthly payment goes for repayment of a portion of the original loan principal and part goes for payment of an interest charge at a specified rate.

Several types of mortgage loans are available today. The tables in this book are for the type used most often by home buyers, under which monthly payments are constant over a fixed repayment period.

The tables that follow cover mortgage loans with interest rates between 5% and 21% and show the required monthly payment for loan amounts ranging from $100 to $600,000 with repayment periods of 1 to 40 years. Here are some illustrative situations to help you understand and use the tables:

Situation 1

Mr. Smith wants to buy a house that costs $60,000.00. He has a down payment of $10,000.00 and now seeks a 30-year conventional mortgage of $50,000.00 (after paying separately all required fees, service charges, etc.). If the stipulated interest rate is 13%, he can determine the required monthly mortgage payment by (1) locating the 13% pages of the monthly mortgage payment tables, (2) finding the vertical column that shows 30 years, (3) looking down the left column on the same page until he finds $50,000.00, and (4) looking across to the 30-year column, which shows a monthly payment of $553.10.

Situation 2

Ms. Green wishes to purchase a house for $110,000.00 and has a down payment of $30,000.00. A bank will give her an $80,000.00 mortgage for 25 years at $12^3/_4$%. Ms. Green can determine the monthly mortgage payment by locating the $12^3/_4$% pages and the 25-year column on the top of the appropriate page. After looking down the left side of the page for the loan amount of $80,000.00, she then must look across the line to the 25-year column, where she will find a monthly payment of $887.24.

5%

Monthly Payments

necessary to amortize a loan

AMOUNT	1 YEAR	2 YEARS	3 YEARS	4 YEARS	5 YEARS	6 YEARS	7 YEARS
100	8.56	4.39	3.00	2.30	1.89	1.61	1.41
200	17.12	8.77	5.99	4.61	3.77	3.22	2.83
500	42.80	21.94	14.99	11.51	9.44	8.05	7.07
1000	85.61	43.87	29.97	23.03	18.87	16.10	14.13
2000	171.21	87.74	59.94	46.06	37.74	32.21	28.27
5000	428.04	219.36	149.85	115.15	94.36	80.52	70.67
6000	513.64	263.23	179.83	138.18	113.23	96.63	84.80
7000	599.25	307.10	209.80	161.21	132.10	112.73	98.94
8000	684.86	350.97	239.77	184.23	150.97	128.84	113.07
9000	770.47	394.84	269.74	207.26	169.84	144.94	127.21
10000	856.07	438.71	299.71	230.29	188.71	161.05	141.34
15000	1284.11	658.07	449.56	345.44	283.07	241.57	212.01
20000	1712.15	877.43	599.42	460.59	377.42	322.10	282.68
25000	2140.19	1096.78	749.27	575.73	471.78	402.62	353.35
30000	2568.22	1316.14	899.13	690.88	566.14	483.15	424.02
35000	2996.26	1535.50	1048.98	806.03	660.49	563.67	494.69
40000	3424.30	1754.86	1198.84	921.17	754.85	644.20	565.36
45000	3852.34	1974.21	1348.69	1036.32	849.21	724.72	636.03
50000	4280.37	2193.57	1498.54	1151.46	943.56	805.25	706.70
55000	4708.41	2412.93	1648.40	1266.61	1037.92	885.77	777.36
60000	5136.45	2632.28	1798.25	1381.76	1132.27	966.30	848.03
65000	5564.49	2851.64	1948.11	1496.90	1226.63	1046.82	918.70
70000	5992.52	3071.00	2097.96	1612.05	1320.99	1127.35	989.37
75000	6420.56	3290.35	2247.82	1727.20	1415.34	1207.87	1060.04
80000	6848.60	3509.71	2397.67	1842.34	1509.70	1288.39	1130.71
85000	7276.64	3729.07	2547.53	1957.49	1604.05	1368.92	1201.38
90000	7704.67	3948.43	2697.38	2072.64	1698.41	1449.44	1272.05
95000	8132.71	4167.78	2847.24	2187.78	1792.77	1529.97	1342.72
100000	8560.75	4387.14	2997.09	2302.93	1887.12	1610.49	1413.39
105000	8988.79	4606.50	3146.94	2418.08	1981.48	1691.02	1484.06
110000	9416.82	4825.85	3296.80	2533.22	2075.84	1771.54	1554.73
120000	10272.90	5264.57	3596.51	2763.52	2264.55	1932.59	1696.07
130000	11128.97	5703.28	3896.22	2993.81	2453.26	2093.64	1837.41
140000	11985.05	6141.99	4195.93	3224.10	2641.97	2254.69	1978.75
150000	12841.12	6580.71	4495.63	3454.39	2830.69	2415.74	2120.09
160000	13697.20	7019.42	4795.34	3684.69	3019.40	2576.79	2261.43
170000	14553.27	7458.14	5095.05	3914.98	3208.11	2737.84	2402.76
180000	15409.35	7896.85	5394.76	4145.27	3396.82	2898.89	2544.10
190000	16265.42	8335.56	5694.47	4375.57	3585.53	3059.94	2685.44
200000	17121.50	8774.28	5994.18	4605.86	3774.25	3220.99	2826.78
210000	17977.57	9212.99	6293.89	4836.15	3962.96	3382.04	2968.12
220000	18833.65	9651.71	6593.60	5066.44	4151.67	3543.09	3109.46
230000	19689.72	10090.42	6893.31	5296.74	4340.38	3704.13	3250.80
240000	20545.80	10529.13	7193.02	5527.03	4529.10	3865.18	3392.14
250000	21401.87	10967.85	7492.72	5757.32	4717.81	4026.23	3533.48
260000	22257.95	11406.56	7792.43	5987.62	4906.52	4187.28	3674.82
270000	23114.02	11845.28	8092.14	6217.91	5095.23	4348.33	3816.16
280000	23970.09	12283.99	8391.85	6448.20	5283.95	4509.38	3957.49
290000	24826.17	12722.70	8691.56	6678.50	5472.66	4670.43	4098.83
300000	25682.24	13161.42	8991.27	6908.79	5661.37	4831.48	4240.17
310000	26538.32	13600.13	9290.98	7139.08	5850.08	4992.53	4381.51
320000	27394.39	14038.84	9590.69	7369.37	6038.79	5153.58	4522.85
330000	28250.47	14477.56	9890.40	7599.67	6227.51	5314.63	4664.19
340000	29106.54	14916.27	10190.11	7829.96	6416.22	5475.68	4805.53
350000	29962.62	15354.99	10489.81	8060.25	6604.93	5636.73	4946.87
400000	34242.99	17548.56	11988.36	9211.72	7548.49	6441.97	5653.56
450000	38523.37	19742.13	13486.90	10363.18	8492.06	7247.22	6360.26
500000	42803.74	21935.69	14985.45	11514.65	9435.62	8052.47	7066.95
550000	47084.11	24129.26	16483.99	12666.11	10379.18	8857.71	7773.65
600000	51364.49	26322.83	17982.54	13817.58	11322.74	9662.96	8480.35

Monthly Payments 5%
necessary to amortize a loan

AMOUNT	8 YEARS	9 YEARS	10 YEARS	11 YEARS	12 YEARS	13 YEARS	14 YEARS
100	1.27	1.15	1.06	0.99	0.92	0.87	0.83
200	2.53	2.30	2.12	1.97	1.85	1.75	1.66
500	6.33	5.76	5.30	4.93	4.62	4.37	4.14
1000	12.66	11.52	10.61	9.86	9.25	8.73	8.29
2000	25.32	23.03	21.21	19.73	18.50	17.46	16.58
5000	63.30	57.59	53.03	49.32	46.24	43.65	41.44
6000	75.96	69.10	63.64	59.19	55.49	52.38	49.73
7000	88.62	80.62	74.25	69.05	64.74	61.11	58.02
8000	101.28	92.14	84.85	78.92	73.99	69.84	66.31
9000	113.94	103.66	95.46	88.78	83.24	78.58	74.60
10000	126.60	115.17	106.07	98.64	92.49	87.31	82.89
15000	189.90	172.76	159.10	147.97	138.73	130.96	124.33
20000	253.20	230.35	212.13	197.29	184.98	174.61	165.77
25000	316.50	287.93	265.16	246.61	231.22	218.26	207.22
30000	379.80	345.52	318.20	295.93	277.47	261.92	248.66
35000	443.10	403.10	371.23	345.26	323.71	305.57	290.10
40000	506.40	460.69	424.26	394.58	369.96	349.22	331.55
45000	569.70	518.28	477.29	443.90	416.20	392.88	372.99
50000	633.00	575.86	530.33	493.22	462.45	436.53	414.44
55000	696.30	633.45	583.36	542.55	508.69	480.18	455.88
60000	759.60	691.04	636.39	591.87	554.93	523.84	497.32
65000	822.89	748.62	689.43	641.19	601.18	567.49	538.77
70000	886.19	806.21	742.46	690.51	647.42	611.14	580.21
75000	949.49	863.80	795.49	739.84	693.67	654.79	621.65
80000	1012.79	921.38	848.52	789.16	739.91	698.45	663.10
85000	1076.09	978.97	901.56	838.48	786.16	742.10	704.54
90000	1139.39	1036.55	954.59	887.80	832.40	785.75	745.98
95000	1202.69	1094.14	1007.62	937.13	878.65	829.41	787.43
100000	1265.99	1151.73	1060.66	986.45	924.89	873.06	828.87
105000	1329.29	1209.31	1113.69	1035.77	971.13	916.71	870.31
110000	1392.59	1266.90	1166.72	1085.09	1017.38	960.37	911.76
120000	1519.19	1382.07	1272.79	1183.74	1109.87	1047.67	994.64
130000	1645.79	1497.25	1378.85	1282.38	1202.36	1134.98	1077.53
140000	1772.38	1612.42	1484.92	1381.03	1294.85	1222.28	1160.42
150000	1898.99	1727.59	1590.98	1479.67	1387.34	1309.59	1243.31
160000	2025.59	1842.76	1697.05	1578.32	1479.82	1396.90	1326.19
170000	2152.19	1957.94	1803.11	1676.96	1572.31	1484.20	1409.08
180000	2278.79	2073.11	1909.18	1775.61	1664.80	1571.51	1491.97
190000	2405.38	2188.28	2015.24	1874.25	1757.29	1658.81	1574.85
200000	2531.98	2303.45	2121.31	1972.90	1849.78	1746.12	1657.74
210000	2658.58	2418.63	2227.38	2071.54	1942.27	1833.43	1740.63
220000	2785.18	2533.80	2333.44	2170.19	2034.76	1920.73	1823.52
230000	2911.78	2648.97	2439.51	2268.83	2127.25	2008.04	1906.40
240000	3038.38	2764.15	2545.57	2367.48	2219.74	2095.34	1989.29
250000	3164.98	2879.32	2651.64	2466.12	2312.23	2182.65	2072.18
260000	3291.58	2994.49	2757.70	2564.77	2404.72	2269.96	2155.06
270000	3418.18	3109.66	2863.77	2663.41	2497.20	2357.26	2237.95
280000	3544.78	3224.84	2969.83	2762.06	2589.69	2444.57	2320.84
290000	3671.38	3340.01	3075.90	2860.70	2682.18	2531.87	2403.73
300000	3797.98	3455.18	3181.97	2959.35	2774.67	2619.18	2486.61
310000	3924.58	3570.35	3288.03	3057.99	2867.16	2706.49	2569.50
320000	4051.17	3685.53	3394.10	3156.64	2959.65	2793.79	2652.39
330000	4177.77	3800.70	3500.16	3255.28	3052.14	2881.10	2735.27
340000	4304.37	3915.87	3606.23	3353.93	3144.63	2968.40	2818.16
350000	4430.97	4031.05	3712.29	3452.57	3237.12	3055.71	2901.05
400000	5063.97	4606.91	4242.62	3945.80	3699.56	3492.24	3315.48
450000	5696.96	5182.77	4772.95	4439.02	4162.01	3928.77	3729.92
500000	6329.96	5758.64	5303.28	4932.24	4624.45	4365.30	4144.35
550000	6962.96	6334.50	5833.60	5425.47	5086.90	4801.83	4558.79
600000	7595.95	6910.36	6363.93	5918.69	5549.34	5238.36	4973.22

5% Monthly Payments
necessary to amortize a loan

AMOUNT	15 YEARS	16 YEARS	17 YEARS	18 YEARS	19 YEARS	20 YEARS	21 YEARS
100	0.79	0.76	0.73	0.70	0.68	0.66	0.64
200	1.58	1.52	1.46	1.41	1.36	1.32	1.28
500	3.95	3.79	3.64	3.52	3.40	3.30	3.21
1000	7.91	7.58	7.29	7.03	6.80	6.60	6.42
2000	15.82	15.15	14.57	14.06	13.61	13.20	12.83
5000	39.54	37.88	36.43	35.15	34.01	33.00	32.09
6000	47.45	45.46	43.72	42.18	40.82	39.60	38.50
7000	55.36	53.04	51.01	49.21	47.62	46.20	44.92
8000	63.26	60.61	58.29	56.24	54.42	52.80	51.34
9000	71.17	68.19	65.58	63.27	61.22	59.40	57.75
10000	79.08	75.77	72.87	70.30	68.03	66.00	64.17
15000	118.62	113.65	109.30	105.46	102.04	98.99	96.26
20000	158.16	151.54	145.73	140.61	136.06	131.99	128.34
25000	197.70	189.42	182.16	175.76	170.07	164.99	160.43
30000	237.24	227.30	218.60	210.91	204.08	197.99	192.52
35000	276.78	265.19	255.03	246.06	238.10	230.98	224.60
40000	316.32	303.07	291.46	281.21	272.11	263.98	256.69
45000	355.86	340.96	327.89	316.37	306.12	296.98	288.77
50000	395.40	378.84	364.33	351.52	340.14	329.98	320.86
55000	434.94	416.72	400.76	386.67	374.15	362.98	352.95
60000	474.48	454.61	437.19	421.82	408.17	395.97	385.03
65000	514.02	492.49	473.63	456.97	442.18	428.97	417.12
70000	553.56	530.38	510.06	492.12	476.19	461.97	449.20
75000	593.10	568.26	546.49	527.28	510.21	494.97	481.29
80000	632.63	606.14	582.92	562.43	544.22	527.96	513.37
85000	672.17	644.03	619.36	597.58	578.24	560.96	545.45
90000	711.71	681.91	655.79	632.73	612.25	593.96	577.55
95000	751.25	719.80	692.22	667.88	646.26	626.96	609.63
100000	790.79	757.68	728.66	703.03	680.28	659.96	641.72
105000	830.33	795.57	765.09	738.19	714.29	692.95	673.80
110000	869.87	833.45	801.52	773.34	748.31	725.95	705.89
120000	948.95	909.22	874.39	843.64	816.33	791.95	770.06
130000	1028.03	984.99	947.25	913.94	884.36	857.94	834.23
140000	1107.11	1060.75	1020.12	984.25	952.39	923.94	898.41
150000	1186.19	1136.52	1092.98	1054.55	1020.42	989.93	962.58
160000	1265.27	1212.29	1165.85	1124.85	1088.44	1055.93	1026.75
170000	1344.35	1288.06	1238.71	1195.16	1156.47	1121.92	1090.92
180000	1423.43	1363.83	1311.58	1265.46	1224.50	1187.92	1155.09
190000	1502.51	1439.59	1384.45	1335.76	1292.53	1253.92	1219.27
200000	1581.59	1515.36	1457.31	1406.07	1360.56	1319.91	1283.44
210000	1660.67	1591.13	1530.18	1476.37	1428.58	1385.91	1347.61
220000	1739.75	1666.90	1603.04	1546.67	1496.61	1451.90	1411.78
230000	1818.83	1742.67	1675.91	1616.98	1564.64	1517.90	1475.95
240000	1897.90	1818.43	1748.77	1687.28	1632.67	1583.89	1540.12
250000	1976.98	1894.20	1821.64	1757.58	1700.69	1649.89	1604.30
260000	2056.06	1969.97	1894.50	1827.89	1768.72	1715.88	1668.47
270000	2135.14	2045.74	1967.37	1898.19	1836.75	1781.88	1732.64
280000	2214.22	2121.51	2040.23	1968.49	1904.78	1847.88	1796.81
290000	2293.30	2197.27	2113.10	2038.80	1972.81	1913.87	1860.98
300000	2372.38	2273.04	2185.97	2109.10	2040.83	1979.87	1925.16
310000	2451.46	2348.81	2258.83	2179.40	2108.86	2045.86	1989.33
320000	2530.54	2424.58	2331.70	2249.71	2176.89	2111.86	2053.50
330000	2609.62	2500.35	2404.56	2320.01	2244.92	2177.85	2117.67
340000	2688.70	2576.12	2477.43	2390.32	2312.94	2243.85	2181.84
350000	2767.78	2651.88	2550.29	2460.62	2380.97	2309.85	2246.02
400000	3163.17	3030.72	2914.62	2812.14	2721.11	2639.82	2566.87
450000	3558.57	3409.56	3278.95	3163.65	3061.25	2969.80	2887.73
500000	3953.97	3788.40	3643.28	3515.17	3401.39	3299.78	3208.59
550000	4349.36	4167.25	4007.60	3866.69	3741.53	3629.76	3529.45
600000	4744.76	4546.09	4371.93	4218.20	4081.67	3959.73	3850.31

Monthly Payments 5%

necessary to amortize a loan

AMOUNT	22 YEARS	23 YEARS	24 YEARS	25 YEARS	30 YEARS	35 YEARS	40 YEARS
100	0.63	0.61	0.60	0.58	0.54	0.50	0.48
200	1.25	1.22	1.19	1.17	1.07	1.01	0.96
500	3.13	3.05	2.98	2.92	2.68	2.52	2.41
1000	6.25	6.10	5.97	5.85	5.37	5.05	4.82
2000	12.51	12.21	11.94	11.69	10.74	10.09	9.64
5000	31.26	30.52	29.84	29.23	26.84	25.23	24.11
6000	37.52	36.62	35.81	35.08	32.21	30.28	28.93
7000	43.77	42.73	41.78	40.92	37.58	35.33	33.75
8000	50.02	48.83	47.75	46.77	42.95	40.38	38.58
9000	56.28	54.94	53.72	52.61	48.31	45.42	43.40
10000	62.53	61.04	59.69	58.46	53.68	50.47	48.22
15000	93.79	91.56	89.53	87.69	80.52	75.70	72.33
20000	125.06	122.08	119.38	116.92	107.36	100.94	96.44
25000	156.32	152.60	149.22	146.15	134.21	126.17	120.55
30000	187.58	183.12	179.07	175.38	161.05	151.41	144.66
35000	218.85	213.64	208.91	204.61	187.89	176.64	168.77
40000	250.11	244.16	238.76	233.84	214.73	201.88	192.88
45000	281.38	274.68	268.60	263.07	241.57	227.11	216.99
50000	312.64	305.20	298.45	292.30	268.41	252.34	241.10
55000	343.90	335.72	328.29	321.52	295.25	277.58	265.21
60000	375.17	366.24	358.14	350.75	322.09	302.81	289.32
65000	406.43	396.76	387.98	379.98	348.93	328.05	313.43
70000	437.70	427.28	417.83	409.21	375.78	353.28	337.54
75000	468.96	457.80	447.67	438.44	402.62	378.52	361.65
80000	500.22	488.32	477.52	467.67	429.46	403.75	385.76
85000	531.49	518.85	507.36	496.90	456.30	428.98	409.87
90000	562.75	549.37	537.21	526.13	483.14	454.22	433.98
95000	594.02	579.89	567.05	555.36	509.98	479.45	458.09
100000	625.28	610.41	596.90	584.59	536.82	504.69	482.20
105000	656.54	640.93	626.74	613.82	563.66	529.92	506.31
110000	687.81	671.45	656.59	643.05	590.50	555.16	530.42
120000	750.34	732.49	716.28	701.51	644.19	605.63	578.64
130000	812.86	793.53	775.97	759.97	697.87	656.09	626.86
140000	875.39	854.57	835.66	818.43	751.55	706.56	675.08
150000	937.92	915.61	895.35	876.89	805.23	757.03	723.29
160000	1000.45	976.65	955.04	935.34	858.91	807.50	771.51
170000	1062.98	1037.69	1014.73	993.80	912.60	857.97	819.73
180000	1125.51	1098.73	1074.42	1052.26	966.28	908.44	867.95
190000	1188.03	1159.77	1134.11	1110.72	1019.96	958.91	916.17
200000	1250.56	1220.81	1193.80	1169.18	1073.64	1009.38	964.39
210000	1313.09	1281.85	1253.48	1227.64	1127.33	1059.84	1012.61
220000	1375.62	1342.89	1313.17	1286.10	1181.01	1110.31	1060.83
230000	1438.15	1403.93	1372.86	1344.56	1234.69	1160.78	1109.05
240000	1500.67	1464.97	1432.55	1403.02	1288.37	1211.25	1157.27
250000	1563.20	1526.01	1492.24	1461.48	1342.05	1261.72	1205.49
260000	1625.73	1587.06	1551.93	1519.93	1395.74	1312.19	1253.71
270000	1688.26	1648.10	1611.62	1578.39	1449.42	1362.66	1301.93
280000	1750.79	1709.14	1671.31	1636.85	1503.10	1413.13	1350.15
290000	1813.31	1770.18	1731.00	1695.31	1556.78	1463.59	1398.37
300000	1875.84	1831.22	1790.69	1753.77	1610.46	1514.06	1446.59
310000	1938.37	1892.26	1850.38	1812.23	1664.15	1564.53	1494.81
320000	2000.90	1953.30	1910.07	1870.69	1717.83	1615.00	1543.03
330000	2063.43	2014.34	1969.76	1929.15	1771.51	1665.47	1591.25
340000	2125.95	2075.38	2029.45	1987.61	1825.19	1715.94	1639.47
350000	2188.48	2136.42	2089.14	2046.07	1878.88	1766.41	1687.69
400000	2501.12	2441.62	2387.59	2338.36	2147.29	2018.75	1928.79
450000	2813.76	2746.83	2686.04	2630.66	2415.70	2271.09	2169.88
500000	3126.40	3052.03	2984.49	2922.95	2684.07	2523.44	2410.98
550000	3439.04	3357.23	3282.94	3215.25	2952.52	2775.78	2652.08
600000	3751.68	3662.44	3581.39	3507.54	3220.93	3028.13	2893.18

5¼%   Monthly Payments
necessary to amortize a loan

AMOUNT	1 YEAR	2 YEARS	3 YEARS	4 YEARS	5 YEARS	6 YEARS	7 YEARS
100	8.57	4.40	3.01	2.31	1.90	1.62	1.43
200	17.14	8.80	6.02	4.63	3.80	3.24	2.85
500	42.86	21.99	15.04	11.57	9.49	8.11	7.13
1000	85.72	43.98	30.08	23.14	18.99	16.22	14.25
2000	171.44	87.97	60.17	46.29	37.97	32.44	28.50
5000	428.61	219.92	150.42	115.71	94.93	81.11	71.26
6000	514.33	263.90	180.50	138.86	113.92	97.33	85.51
7000	600.05	307.88	210.58	162.00	132.90	113.55	99.76
8000	685.78	351.87	240.67	185.14	151.89	129.77	114.01
9000	771.50	395.85	270.75	208.28	170.87	145.99	128.27
10000	857.22	439.83	300.83	231.43	189.86	162.21	142.52
15000	1285.83	659.75	451.25	347.14	284.79	243.32	213.78
20000	1714.44	879.67	601.67	462.85	379.72	324.42	285.03
25000	2143.05	1099.59	752.08	578.57	474.65	405.53	356.29
30000	2571.66	1319.50	902.50	694.28	569.58	486.63	427.55
35000	3000.27	1539.42	1052.91	809.99	664.51	567.74	498.81
40000	3428.88	1759.34	1203.33	925.71	759.44	648.85	570.07
45000	3857.49	1979.25	1353.75	1041.42	854.37	729.95	641.33
50000	4286.10	2199.17	1504.16	1157.14	949.30	811.06	712.58
55000	4714.71	2419.09	1654.58	1272.85	1044.23	892.16	783.84
60000	5143.33	2639.01	1805.00	1388.56	1139.16	973.27	855.10
65000	5571.94	2858.92	1955.41	1504.28	1234.09	1054.37	926.36
70000	6000.55	3078.84	2105.83	1619.99	1329.02	1135.48	997.62
75000	6429.16	3298.76	2256.25	1735.70	1423.95	1216.59	1068.88
80000	6857.77	3518.67	2406.66	1851.42	1518.88	1297.69	1140.13
85000	7286.38	3738.59	2557.08	1967.13	1613.81	1378.80	1211.39
90000	7714.99	3958.51	2707.49	2082.84	1708.74	1459.90	1282.65
95000	8143.60	4178.43	2857.91	2198.56	1803.67	1541.01	1353.91
100000	8572.21	4398.34	3008.33	2314.27	1898.60	1622.12	1425.17
105000	9000.82	4618.26	3158.74	2429.98	1993.53	1703.22	1496.43
110000	9429.43	4838.18	3309.16	2545.70	2088.46	1784.33	1567.68
120000	10286.65	5278.01	3609.99	2777.13	2278.32	1946.54	1710.20
130000	11143.87	5717.85	3910.83	3008.55	2468.18	2108.75	1852.72
140000	12001.09	6157.68	4211.66	3239.98	2658.04	2270.96	1995.23
150000	12858.31	6597.52	4512.49	3471.41	2847.90	2433.17	2137.75
160000	13715.53	7037.35	4813.32	3702.83	3037.76	2595.38	2280.27
170000	14572.76	7477.18	5114.16	3934.26	3227.62	2757.60	2422.79
180000	15429.98	7917.02	5414.99	4165.69	3417.48	2919.81	2565.30
190000	16287.20	8356.85	5715.82	4397.12	3607.34	3082.02	2707.82
200000	17144.42	8796.69	6016.65	4628.54	3797.20	3244.23	2850.34
210000	18001.64	9236.52	6317.49	4859.97	3987.06	3406.44	2992.85
220000	18858.86	9676.36	6618.32	5091.40	4176.92	3568.65	3135.37
230000	19716.08	10116.19	6919.15	5322.82	4366.78	3730.87	3277.89
240000	20573.30	10556.02	7219.98	5554.25	4556.64	3893.08	3420.40
250000	21430.52	10995.86	7520.82	5785.68	4746.50	4055.29	3562.92
260000	22287.74	11435.69	7821.65	6017.11	4936.36	4217.50	3705.44
270000	23144.96	11875.53	8122.48	6248.53	5126.22	4379.71	3847.95
280000	24002.19	12315.36	8423.32	6479.96	5316.08	4541.92	3990.47
290000	24859.41	12755.20	8724.15	6711.39	5505.94	4704.13	4132.99
300000	25716.63	13195.03	9024.98	6942.81	5695.80	4866.35	4275.50
310000	26573.85	13634.87	9325.81	7174.24	5885.65	5028.56	4418.02
320000	27431.07	14074.70	9626.65	7405.67	6075.51	5190.77	4560.54
330000	28288.29	14514.53	9927.48	7637.10	6265.37	5352.98	4703.05
340000	29145.51	14954.37	10228.31	7868.52	6455.23	5515.19	4845.57
350000	30002.73	15394.20	10529.14	8099.95	6645.09	5677.40	4988.09
400000	34288.84	17593.37	12033.31	9257.09	7594.39	6488.46	5700.67
450000	38574.94	19792.55	13537.47	10414.22	8543.69	7299.52	6413.26
500000	42861.05	21991.72	15041.64	11571.36	9492.99	8110.58	7125.84
550000	47147.15	24190.89	16545.80	12728.49	10442.29	8921.63	7838.42
600000	51433.25	26390.06	18049.96	13885.63	11391.59	9732.69	8551.01

8

Monthly Payments 5¼%

necessary to amortize a loan

AMOUNT	8 YEARS	9 YEARS	10 YEARS	11 YEARS	12 YEARS	13 YEARS	14 YEARS
100	1.28	1.16	1.07	1.00	0.94	0.89	0.84
200	2.56	2.33	2.15	2.00	1.87	1.77	1.68
500	6.39	5.82	5.36	4.99	4.69	4.43	4.21
1000	12.78	11.64	10.73	9.99	9.37	8.86	8.42
2000	25.56	23.28	21.46	19.98	18.75	17.72	16.84
5000	63.90	58.19	53.65	49.94	46.87	44.29	42.09
6000	76.68	69.83	64.38	59.93	56.25	53.15	50.51
7000	89.45	81.47	75.10	69.92	65.62	62.01	58.93
8000	102.23	93.11	85.83	79.91	75.00	70.87	67.34
9000	115.01	104.74	96.56	89.90	84.37	79.72	75.76
10000	127.79	116.38	107.29	99.89	93.75	88.58	84.18
15000	191.69	174.57	160.94	149.83	140.62	132.87	126.27
20000	255.59	232.77	214.58	199.78	187.50	177.16	168.36
25000	319.48	290.96	268.23	249.72	234.37	221.45	210.45
30000	383.38	349.15	321.88	299.66	281.24	265.74	252.54
35000	447.27	407.34	375.52	349.61	328.12	310.04	294.63
40000	511.17	465.53	429.17	399.55	374.99	354.33	336.72
45000	575.07	523.72	482.81	449.49	421.87	398.62	378.81
50000	638.96	581.91	536.46	499.44	468.74	442.91	420.90
55000	702.86	640.10	590.10	549.38	515.61	487.20	462.99
60000	766.76	698.30	643.75	599.33	562.49	531.49	505.07
65000	830.65	756.49	697.40	649.27	609.36	575.78	547.16
70000	894.55	814.68	751.04	699.21	656.24	620.07	589.25
75000	958.45	872.87	804.69	749.16	703.11	664.36	631.34
80000	1022.34	931.06	858.33	799.10	749.99	708.65	673.43
85000	1086.24	989.25	911.98	849.04	796.86	752.94	715.52
90000	1150.14	1047.44	965.63	898.99	843.73	797.23	757.61
95000	1214.03	1105.63	1019.27	948.93	890.61	841.52	799.70
100000	1277.93	1163.83	1072.92	998.88	937.48	885.82	841.79
105000	1341.82	1222.02	1126.56	1048.82	984.36	930.11	883.88
110000	1405.72	1280.21	1180.21	1098.76	1031.23	974.40	925.97
120000	1533.51	1396.59	1287.50	1198.65	1124.98	1062.98	1010.15
130000	1661.31	1512.97	1394.79	1298.54	1218.73	1151.56	1094.33
140000	1789.10	1629.36	1502.08	1398.43	1312.47	1240.14	1178.51
150000	1916.89	1745.74	1609.38	1498.31	1406.22	1328.72	1262.69
160000	2044.69	1862.12	1716.67	1598.20	1499.97	1417.30	1346.87
170000	2172.48	1978.50	1823.96	1698.09	1593.72	1505.89	1431.04
180000	2300.27	2094.89	1931.25	1797.98	1687.47	1594.47	1515.22
190000	2428.06	2211.27	2038.54	1897.86	1781.21	1683.05	1599.40
200000	2555.86	2327.65	2145.83	1997.75	1874.96	1771.63	1683.58
210000	2683.65	2444.03	2253.13	2097.64	1968.71	1860.21	1767.76
220000	2811.44	2560.42	2360.42	2197.53	2062.46	1948.79	1851.94
230000	2939.23	2676.80	2467.71	2297.41	2156.21	2037.38	1936.12
240000	3067.03	2793.18	2575.00	2397.30	2249.96	2125.96	2020.30
250000	3194.82	2909.56	2682.29	2497.19	2343.70	2214.54	2104.48
260000	3322.61	3025.95	2789.58	2597.08	2437.45	2303.12	2188.66
270000	3450.41	3142.33	2896.88	2696.96	2531.20	2391.70	2272.84
280000	3578.20	3258.71	3004.17	2796.85	2624.95	2480.28	2357.01
290000	3705.99	3375.09	3111.46	2896.74	2718.70	2568.87	2441.19
300000	3833.78	3491.48	3218.75	2996.63	2812.44	2657.45	2525.37
310000	3961.58	3607.86	3326.04	3096.51	2906.19	2746.03	2609.55
320000	4089.37	3724.24	3433.33	3196.40	2999.94	2834.61	2693.73
330000	4217.16	3840.62	3540.63	3296.29	3093.69	2923.19	2777.91
340000	4344.96	3957.01	3647.92	3396.18	3187.44	3011.77	2862.09
350000	4472.75	4073.39	3755.21	3496.06	3281.19	3100.35	2946.27
400000	5111.71	4655.30	4291.67	3995.50	3749.93	3543.26	3367.16
450000	5750.68	5237.22	4828.13	4494.94	4218.67	3986.17	3788.06
500000	6389.64	5819.13	5364.59	4994.38	4687.41	4429.08	4208.95
550000	7028.61	6401.04	5901.04	5493.81	5156.15	4871.99	4629.85
600000	7667.57	6982.95	6437.50	5993.25	5624.89	5314.89	5050.75

5¼%

Monthly Payments
necessary to amortize a loan

AMOUNT	15 YEARS	16 YEARS	17 YEARS	18 YEARS	19 YEARS	20 YEARS	21 YEARS
100	0.80	0.77	0.74	0.72	0.69	0.67	0.66
200	1.61	1.54	1.48	1.43	1.39	1.35	1.31
500	4.02	3.85	3.71	3.58	3.47	3.37	3.28
1000	8.04	7.71	7.42	7.17	6.94	6.74	6.56
2000	16.08	15.42	14.84	14.33	13.88	13.48	13.12
5000	40.19	38.55	37.10	35.83	34.70	33.69	32.79
6000	48.23	46.26	44.52	43.00	41.64	40.43	39.35
7000	56.27	53.96	51.94	50.16	48.58	47.17	45.90
8000	64.31	61.67	59.37	57.33	55.52	53.91	52.46
9000	72.35	69.38	66.79	64.49	62.46	60.65	59.02
10000	80.39	77.09	74.21	71.66	69.40	67.38	65.58
15000	120.58	115.64	111.31	107.49	104.10	101.08	98.36
20000	160.78	154.19	148.41	143.32	138.80	134.77	131.15
25000	200.97	192.73	185.52	179.15	173.50	168.46	163.94
30000	241.16	231.28	222.62	214.98	208.20	202.15	196.73
35000	281.36	269.82	259.72	250.81	242.90	235.85	229.52
40000	321.55	308.37	296.83	286.64	277.60	269.54	262.31
45000	361.74	346.92	333.93	322.47	312.30	303.23	295.09
50000	401.94	385.46	371.03	358.30	347.01	336.92	327.88
55000	442.13	424.01	408.14	394.13	381.70	370.61	360.67
60000	482.33	462.56	445.24	429.96	416.40	404.31	393.46
65000	522.52	501.10	482.34	465.79	451.11	438.00	426.25
70000	562.71	539.65	519.45	501.62	485.81	471.69	459.03
75000	602.91	578.20	556.55	537.45	520.51	505.38	491.82
80000	643.10	616.74	593.65	573.28	555.21	539.08	524.61
85000	683.30	655.29	630.75	609.11	589.91	572.77	557.40
90000	723.49	693.84	667.86	644.94	624.61	606.46	590.19
95000	763.68	732.38	704.96	680.77	659.31	640.15	622.98
100000	803.88	770.93	742.06	716.60	694.01	673.84	655.76
105000	844.07	809.47	779.17	752.43	728.71	707.54	688.55
110000	884.27	848.02	816.27	788.26	763.41	741.23	721.34
120000	964.65	925.11	890.48	859.92	832.81	808.61	786.92
130000	1045.04	1002.21	964.68	931.59	902.21	876.00	852.49
140000	1125.43	1079.30	1038.89	1003.25	971.61	943.38	918.07
150000	1205.82	1156.39	1113.10	1074.91	1041.01	1010.77	983.65
160000	1286.20	1233.48	1187.30	1146.57	1110.41	1078.15	1049.22
170000	1366.59	1310.58	1261.51	1218.23	1179.81	1145.54	1114.80
180000	1446.98	1387.67	1335.72	1289.89	1249.21	1212.92	1180.38
190000	1527.37	1464.76	1409.92	1361.55	1318.61	1280.30	1245.95
200000	1607.76	1541.86	1484.13	1433.21	1388.02	1347.69	1311.53
210000	1688.14	1618.95	1558.34	1504.87	1457.42	1415.07	1377.10
220000	1768.53	1696.04	1632.54	1576.53	1526.82	1482.46	1442.68
230000	1848.92	1773.13	1706.75	1648.19	1596.22	1549.84	1508.26
240000	1929.31	1850.23	1780.95	1719.85	1665.62	1617.23	1573.83
250000	2009.69	1927.32	1855.16	1791.51	1735.02	1684.61	1639.41
260000	2090.08	2004.41	1929.37	1863.17	1804.42	1751.99	1704.99
270000	2170.47	2081.51	2003.57	1934.83	1873.82	1819.38	1770.56
280000	2250.86	2158.60	2077.78	2006.49	1943.22	1886.76	1836.14
290000	2331.25	2235.69	2151.99	2078.15	2012.62	1954.15	1901.72
300000	2411.63	2312.78	2226.19	2149.81	2082.02	2021.53	1967.29
310000	2492.02	2389.88	2300.40	2221.47	2151.42	2088.92	2032.87
320000	2572.41	2466.97	2374.61	2293.13	2220.82	2156.30	2098.45
330000	2652.80	2544.06	2448.81	2364.79	2290.23	2223.69	2164.02
340000	2733.18	2621.16	2523.02	2436.45	2359.63	2291.07	2229.60
350000	2813.57	2698.25	2597.23	2508.11	2429.03	2358.45	2295.17
400000	3215.51	3083.71	2968.26	2866.42	2776.03	2695.38	2623.06
450000	3617.45	3469.18	3339.29	3224.72	3123.03	3032.30	2950.94
500000	4019.39	3854.64	3710.32	3583.02	3470.04	3369.22	3278.82
550000	4421.33	4240.10	4081.35	3941.32	3817.04	3706.14	3606.70
600000	4823.27	4625.57	4452.39	4299.62	4164.05	4043.06	3934.58

Monthly Payments 5¼%
necessary to amortize a loan

AMOUNT	22 YEARS	23 YEARS	24 YEARS	25 YEARS	30 YEARS	35 YEARS	40 YEARS
100	0.64	0.62	0.61	0.60	0.55	0.52	0.50
200	1.28	1.25	1.22	1.20	1.10	1.04	1.00
500	3.20	3.12	3.06	3.00	2.76	2.60	2.49
1000	6.39	6.25	6.11	5.99	5.52	5.21	4.99
2000	12.79	12.50	12.23	11.98	11.04	10.41	9.98
5000	31.97	31.24	30.57	29.96	27.61	26.04	24.94
6000	38.37	37.49	36.68	35.95	33.13	31.24	29.93
7000	44.76	43.73	42.80	41.95	38.65	36.45	34.92
8000	51.16	49.98	48.91	47.94	44.18	41.66	39.91
9000	57.55	56.23	55.03	53.93	49.70	46.87	44.90
10000	63.95	62.48	61.14	59.92	55.22	52.07	49.89
15000	95.92	93.71	91.71	89.89	82.83	78.11	74.83
20000	127.90	124.95	122.28	119.85	110.44	104.15	99.77
25000	159.87	156.19	152.85	149.81	138.05	130.19	124.72
30000	191.84	187.43	183.42	179.77	165.66	156.22	149.66
35000	223.82	218.67	213.99	209.74	193.27	182.26	174.60
40000	255.79	249.90	244.56	239.70	220.88	208.30	199.55
45000	287.77	281.14	275.13	269.66	248.49	234.33	224.49
50000	319.74	312.38	305.70	299.62	276.10	260.37	249.44
55000	351.71	343.62	336.27	329.59	303.71	286.41	274.38
60000	383.69	374.86	366.84	359.55	331.32	312.45	299.32
65000	415.66	406.09	397.41	389.51	358.93	338.48	324.27
70000	447.64	437.33	427.98	419.47	386.54	364.52	349.21
75000	479.61	468.57	458.55	449.44	414.15	390.56	374.15
80000	511.59	499.81	489.12	479.40	441.76	416.59	399.10
85000	543.56	531.05	519.69	509.36	469.37	442.63	424.04
90000	575.53	562.28	550.26	539.32	496.98	468.67	448.98
95000	607.51	593.52	580.83	569.29	524.59	494.71	473.93
100000	639.48	624.76	611.40	599.25	552.20	520.74	498.87
105000	671.46	656.00	641.97	629.21	579.81	546.78	523.81
110000	703.43	687.24	672.55	659.17	607.42	572.82	548.76
120000	767.38	749.71	733.69	719.10	662.64	624.89	598.64
130000	831.33	812.19	794.83	779.02	717.86	676.97	648.53
140000	895.27	874.67	855.97	838.95	773.09	729.04	698.42
150000	959.22	937.14	917.11	898.87	828.31	781.11	748.31
160000	1023.17	999.62	978.25	958.80	883.53	833.19	798.19
170000	1087.12	1062.09	1039.39	1018.72	938.75	885.26	848.08
180000	1151.07	1124.57	1100.53	1078.65	993.97	937.34	897.97
190000	1215.02	1187.05	1161.67	1138.57	1049.19	989.41	947.85
200000	1278.96	1249.52	1222.81	1198.50	1104.41	1041.49	997.74
210000	1342.91	1312.00	1283.95	1258.42	1159.63	1093.56	1047.63
220000	1406.86	1374.47	1345.09	1318.34	1214.85	1145.63	1097.51
230000	1470.81	1436.95	1406.23	1378.27	1270.07	1197.71	1147.40
240000	1534.76	1499.43	1467.37	1438.19	1325.29	1249.78	1197.29
250000	1598.70	1561.90	1528.51	1498.12	1380.51	1301.86	1247.18
260000	1662.65	1624.38	1589.65	1558.04	1435.73	1353.93	1297.06
270000	1726.60	1686.85	1650.79	1617.97	1490.95	1406.01	1346.95
280000	1790.55	1749.33	1711.93	1677.89	1546.17	1458.08	1396.84
290000	1854.50	1811.81	1773.07	1737.82	1601.39	1510.15	1446.72
300000	1918.45	1874.28	1834.21	1797.74	1656.61	1562.23	1496.61
310000	1982.39	1936.76	1895.35	1857.67	1711.83	1614.30	1546.50
320000	2046.34	1999.23	1956.49	1917.59	1767.05	1666.38	1596.39
330000	2110.29	2061.71	2017.64	1977.52	1822.27	1718.45	1646.27
340000	2174.24	2124.19	2078.78	2037.44	1877.49	1770.53	1696.16
350000	2238.19	2186.66	2139.92	2097.37	1932.71	1822.60	1746.05
400000	2557.93	2499.04	2445.62	2396.99	2208.81	2082.97	1995.48
450000	2877.67	2811.42	2751.32	2696.61	2484.92	2343.34	2244.92
500000	3197.41	3123.80	3057.02	2996.24	2761.02	2603.72	2494.35
550000	3517.15	3436.18	3362.73	3295.86	3037.12	2864.09	2743.79
600000	3836.89	3748.57	3668.43	3595.49	3313.22	3124.46	2993.22

5½%

Monthly Payments
necessary to amortize a loan

AMOUNT	1 YEAR	2 YEARS	3 YEARS	4 YEARS	5 YEARS	6 YEARS	7 YEARS
100	8.58	4.41	3.02	2.33	1.91	1.63	1.44
200	17.17	8.82	6.04	4.65	3.82	3.27	2.87
500	42.92	22.05	15.10	11.63	9.55	8.17	7.19
1000	85.84	44.10	30.20	23.26	19.10	16.34	14.37
2000	171.67	88.19	60.39	46.51	38.20	32.68	28.74
5000	429.18	220.48	150.98	116.28	95.51	81.69	71.85
6000	515.02	264.57	181.18	139.54	114.61	98.03	86.22
7000	600.86	308.67	211.37	162.80	133.71	114.37	100.59
8000	686.69	352.77	241.57	186.05	152.81	130.70	114.96
9000	772.53	396.86	271.76	209.31	171.91	147.04	129.33
10000	858.37	440.96	301.96	232.56	191.01	163.38	143.70
15000	1287.55	661.43	452.94	348.85	286.52	245.07	215.55
20000	1716.74	881.91	603.92	465.13	382.02	326.76	287.40
25000	2145.92	1102.39	754.90	581.41	477.53	408.45	359.25
30000	2575.10	1322.87	905.88	697.69	573.03	490.14	431.10
35000	3004.29	1543.35	1056.86	813.98	668.54	571.83	502.95
40000	3433.47	1763.83	1207.84	930.26	764.05	653.52	574.80
45000	3862.66	1984.30	1358.82	1046.54	859.55	735.20	646.65
50000	4291.84	2204.78	1509.80	1162.82	955.06	816.89	718.50
55000	4721.02	2425.26	1660.77	1279.11	1050.56	898.58	790.35
60000	5150.21	2645.74	1811.75	1395.39	1146.07	980.27	862.20
65000	5579.39	2866.22	1962.73	1511.67	1241.58	1061.96	934.05
70000	6008.57	3086.70	2113.71	1627.95	1337.08	1143.65	1005.90
75000	6437.76	3307.17	2264.69	1744.24	1432.59	1225.34	1077.75
80000	6866.94	3527.65	2415.67	1860.52	1528.09	1307.03	1149.60
85000	7296.13	3748.13	2566.65	1976.80	1623.60	1388.72	1221.45
90000	7725.31	3968.61	2717.63	2093.08	1719.10	1470.41	1293.30
95000	8154.49	4189.09	2868.61	2209.37	1814.61	1552.10	1365.15
100000	8583.68	4409.57	3019.59	2325.65	1910.12	1633.79	1437.00
105000	9012.86	4630.04	3170.57	2441.93	2005.62	1715.48	1508.85
110000	9442.05	4850.52	3321.55	2558.21	2101.13	1797.17	1580.70
120000	10300.41	5291.48	3623.51	2790.78	2292.14	1960.55	1724.41
130000	11158.78	5732.44	3925.47	3023.34	2483.15	2123.93	1868.11
140000	12017.15	6173.39	4227.43	3255.91	2674.16	2287.30	2011.81
150000	12875.52	6614.35	4529.39	3488.47	2865.17	2450.68	2155.51
160000	13733.89	7055.30	4831.34	3721.04	3056.19	2614.06	2299.21
170000	14592.25	7496.26	5133.30	3953.60	3247.20	2777.44	2442.91
180000	15450.62	7937.22	5435.26	4186.17	3438.21	2940.82	2586.61
190000	16308.99	8378.17	5737.22	4418.73	3629.22	3104.20	2730.31
200000	17167.36	8819.13	6039.18	4651.30	3820.23	3267.58	2874.01
210000	18025.72	9260.09	6341.14	4883.86	4011.24	3430.96	3017.71
220000	18884.09	9701.04	6643.10	5116.42	4202.26	3594.34	3161.41
230000	19742.46	10142.00	6945.06	5348.99	4393.27	3757.71	3305.11
240000	20600.83	10582.96	7247.02	5581.55	4584.28	3921.09	3448.81
250000	21459.20	11023.91	7548.98	5814.12	4775.29	4084.47	3592.51
260000	22317.56	11464.87	7850.93	6046.68	4966.30	4247.85	3736.21
270000	23175.93	11905.83	8152.89	6279.25	5157.31	4411.23	3879.91
280000	24034.30	12346.78	8454.85	6511.81	5348.33	4574.61	4023.61
290000	24892.67	12787.74	8756.81	6744.38	5539.34	4737.99	4167.31
300000	25751.04	13228.70	9058.77	6976.94	5730.35	4901.37	4311.01
310000	26609.40	13669.65	9360.73	7209.51	5921.36	5064.74	4454.71
320000	27467.77	14110.61	9662.69	7442.07	6112.37	5228.12	4598.41
330000	28326.14	14551.57	9964.65	7674.64	6303.38	5391.50	4742.11
340000	29184.51	14992.52	10266.61	7907.20	6494.40	5554.88	4885.81
350000	30042.87	15433.48	10568.57	8139.77	6685.41	5718.26	5029.51
400000	34334.71	17638.26	12078.36	9302.59	7640.46	6535.15	5748.02
450000	38626.55	19843.05	13588.16	10465.41	8595.52	7352.05	6466.52
500000	42918.39	22047.83	15097.95	11628.24	9550.58	8168.94	7185.02
550000	47210.23	24252.61	16607.75	12791.06	10505.64	8985.84	7903.52
600000	51502.07	26457.39	18117.54	13953.89	11460.70	9802.73	8622.03

Monthly Payments $5^{1}/_{2}\%$

necessary to amortize a loan

AMOUNT	8 YEARS	9 YEARS	10 YEARS	11 YEARS	12 YEARS	13 YEARS	14 YEARS
100	1.29	1.18	1.09	1.01	0.95	0.90	0.85
200	2.58	2.35	2.17	2.02	1.90	1.80	1.71
500	6.45	5.88	5.43	5.06	4.75	4.49	4.27
1000	12.90	11.76	10.85	10.11	9.50	8.99	8.55
2000	25.80	23.52	21.71	20.23	19.00	17.97	17.10
5000	64.50	58.80	54.26	50.57	47.51	44.93	42.74
6000	77.40	70.56	65.12	60.68	57.01	53.92	51.29
7000	90.30	82.32	75.97	70.80	66.51	62.91	59.84
8000	103.19	94.08	86.82	80.91	76.01	71.89	68.39
9000	116.09	105.84	97.67	91.03	85.52	80.88	76.93
10000	128.99	117.60	108.53	101.14	95.02	89.87	85.48
15000	193.49	176.40	162.79	151.71	142.53	134.80	128.22
20000	257.99	235.20	217.05	202.28	190.03	179.74	170.97
25000	322.48	294.00	271.32	252.85	237.54	224.67	213.71
30000	386.98	352.80	325.58	303.42	285.05	269.60	256.45
35000	451.48	411.60	379.84	353.99	332.56	314.54	299.19
40000	515.97	470.40	434.11	404.56	380.07	359.47	341.93
45000	580.47	529.20	488.37	455.13	427.58	404.41	384.67
50000	644.97	588.00	542.63	505.70	475.09	449.34	427.41
55000	709.46	646.80	596.89	556.27	522.59	494.27	470.15
60000	773.96	705.60	651.16	606.84	570.10	539.21	512.90
65000	838.46	764.40	705.42	657.41	617.61	584.14	555.64
70000	902.95	823.20	759.68	707.98	665.12	629.07	598.38
75000	967.45	882.00	813.95	758.54	712.63	674.01	641.12
80000	1031.95	940.80	868.21	809.11	760.14	718.94	683.86
85000	1096.44	999.60	922.47	859.68	807.65	763.88	726.60
90000	1160.94	1058.40	976.74	910.25	855.15	808.81	769.34
95000	1225.44	1117.20	1031.00	960.82	902.66	853.74	812.08
100000	1289.93	1176.00	1085.26	1011.39	950.17	898.68	854.83
105000	1354.43	1234.80	1139.53	1061.96	997.68	943.61	897.57
110000	1418.93	1293.60	1193.79	1112.53	1045.19	988.55	940.31
120000	1547.92	1411.20	1302.32	1213.67	1140.21	1078.41	1025.79
130000	1676.91	1528.80	1410.84	1314.81	1235.22	1168.28	1111.27
140000	1805.91	1646.40	1519.37	1415.95	1330.24	1258.15	1196.76
150000	1934.90	1764.00	1627.89	1517.09	1425.26	1348.02	1282.24
160000	2063.89	1881.60	1736.42	1618.23	1520.28	1437.89	1367.72
170000	2192.88	1999.20	1844.95	1719.37	1615.29	1527.75	1453.20
180000	2321.88	2116.80	1953.47	1820.51	1710.31	1617.62	1538.69
190000	2450.87	2234.40	2062.00	1921.65	1805.33	1707.49	1624.17
200000	2579.86	2352.00	2170.53	2022.79	1900.34	1797.36	1709.65
210000	2708.86	2469.60	2279.05	2123.93	1995.36	1887.22	1795.13
220000	2837.85	2587.20	2387.58	2225.07	2090.38	1977.09	1880.62
230000	2966.84	2704.80	2496.10	2326.20	2185.40	2066.96	1966.10
240000	3095.84	2822.40	2604.63	2427.34	2280.41	2156.83	2051.58
250000	3224.83	2940.00	2713.16	2528.48	2375.43	2246.70	2137.06
260000	3353.82	3057.60	2821.68	2629.62	2470.45	2336.56	2222.55
270000	3482.82	3175.20	2930.21	2730.76	2565.46	2426.43	2308.03
280000	3611.81	3292.80	3038.74	2831.90	2660.48	2516.30	2393.51
290000	3740.80	3410.40	3147.26	2933.04	2755.50	2606.17	2478.99
300000	3869.80	3528.00	3255.79	3034.18	2850.52	2696.04	2564.48
310000	3998.79	3645.60	3364.31	3135.32	2945.53	2785.90	2649.96
320000	4127.78	3763.20	3472.84	3236.46	3040.55	2875.77	2735.44
330000	4256.78	3880.80	3581.37	3337.60	3135.57	2965.64	2820.92
340000	4385.77	3998.40	3689.89	3438.74	3230.59	3055.51	2906.41
350000	4514.76	4116.00	3798.42	3539.88	3325.60	3145.37	2991.89
400000	5159.73	4704.00	4341.05	4045.57	3800.69	3594.71	3419.30
450000	5804.69	5292.00	4883.68	4551.27	4275.77	4044.05	3846.72
500000	6449.66	5880.00	5426.31	5056.97	4750.86	4493.39	4274.13
550000	7094.63	6468.00	5968.95	5562.66	5225.95	4942.73	4701.54
600000	7739.59	7056.00	6511.58	6068.36	5701.03	5392.07	5128.95

13

5½%

Monthly Payments
necessary to amortize a loan

AMOUNT	15 YEARS	16 YEARS	17 YEARS	18 YEARS	19 YEARS	20 YEARS	21 YEARS
100	0.82	0.78	0.76	0.73	0.71	0.69	0.67
200	1.63	1.57	1.51	1.46	1.42	1.38	1.34
500	4.09	3.92	3.78	3.65	3.54	3.44	3.35
1000	8.17	7.84	7.56	7.30	7.08	6.88	6.70
2000	16.34	15.69	15.11	14.61	14.16	13.76	13.40
5000	40.85	39.22	37.78	36.52	35.39	34.39	33.50
6000	49.03	47.06	45.34	43.82	42.47	41.27	40.20
7000	57.20	54.90	52.89	51.12	49.55	48.15	46.90
8000	65.37	62.74	60.45	58.43	56.63	55.03	53.60
9000	73.54	70.59	68.00	65.73	63.71	61.91	60.30
10000	81.71	78.43	75.56	73.03	70.79	68.79	67.00
15000	122.56	117.65	113.34	109.55	106.18	103.18	100.50
20000	163.42	156.86	151.12	146.06	141.58	137.58	133.99
25000	204.27	196.08	188.90	182.58	176.97	171.97	167.49
30000	245.13	235.29	226.68	219.09	212.37	206.37	200.99
35000	285.98	274.51	264.46	255.61	247.76	240.76	234.49
40000	326.83	313.72	302.24	292.13	283.15	275.15	267.99
45000	367.69	352.94	340.02	328.64	318.55	309.55	301.49
50000	408.54	392.15	377.80	365.16	353.94	343.94	334.99
55000	449.40	431.37	415.59	401.67	389.34	378.34	368.48
60000	490.25	470.58	453.37	438.19	424.73	412.73	401.98
65000	531.10	509.80	491.15	474.71	460.13	447.13	435.48
70000	571.96	549.01	528.93	511.22	495.52	481.52	468.98
75000	612.81	588.23	566.71	547.74	530.91	515.92	502.48
80000	653.67	627.44	604.49	584.25	566.31	550.31	535.98
85000	694.52	666.66	642.27	620.77	601.70	584.70	569.47
90000	735.38	705.87	680.05	657.28	637.10	619.10	602.97
95000	776.23	745.09	717.83	693.80	672.49	653.49	636.47
100000	817.08	784.30	755.61	730.32	707.89	687.89	669.97
105000	857.94	823.52	793.39	766.83	743.28	722.28	703.47
110000	898.79	862.73	831.17	803.35	778.67	756.68	736.97
120000	980.50	941.16	906.73	876.38	849.46	825.46	803.96
130000	1062.21	1019.60	982.29	949.41	920.25	894.25	870.96
140000	1143.92	1098.03	1057.85	1022.44	991.04	963.04	937.96
150000	1225.63	1176.46	1133.41	1095.47	1061.83	1031.83	1004.96
160000	1307.33	1254.89	1208.97	1168.51	1132.62	1100.62	1071.95
170000	1389.04	1333.32	1284.54	1241.54	1203.41	1169.41	1138.95
180000	1470.75	1411.73	1360.10	1314.57	1274.20	1238.20	1205.95
190000	1552.46	1490.18	1435.66	1387.60	1344.98	1306.99	1272.94
200000	1634.17	1568.61	1511.22	1460.63	1415.77	1375.77	1339.94
210000	1715.88	1647.04	1586.78	1533.66	1486.56	1444.56	1406.94
220000	1797.58	1725.47	1662.34	1606.70	1557.35	1513.35	1473.93
230000	1879.29	1803.90	1737.90	1679.73	1628.14	1582.14	1540.93
240000	1961.00	1882.33	1813.46	1752.76	1698.93	1650.93	1607.93
250000	2042.71	1960.76	1889.02	1825.79	1769.72	1719.72	1674.93
260000	2124.42	2039.19	1964.58	1898.82	1840.50	1788.51	1741.92
270000	2206.13	2117.62	2040.14	1971.85	1911.29	1857.30	1808.92
280000	2287.83	2196.05	2115.71	2044.89	1982.08	1926.08	1875.92
290000	2369.54	2274.48	2191.27	2117.92	2052.87	1994.87	1942.91
300000	2451.25	2352.91	2266.83	2190.95	2123.66	2063.66	2009.91
310000	2532.96	2431.34	2342.39	2263.98	2194.45	2132.45	2076.91
320000	2614.67	2509.77	2417.95	2337.01	2265.24	2201.24	2143.90
330000	2696.38	2588.20	2493.51	2410.04	2336.02	2270.03	2210.90
340000	2778.08	2666.63	2569.07	2483.08	2406.81	2338.82	2277.90
350000	2859.79	2745.06	2644.63	2556.11	2477.60	2407.61	2344.90
400000	3268.33	3137.22	3022.44	2921.27	2831.54	2751.55	2679.88
450000	3676.88	3529.37	3400.24	3286.42	3185.49	3095.49	3014.87
500000	4085.42	3921.52	3778.05	3651.58	3539.43	3439.44	3349.85
550000	4493.96	4313.67	4155.85	4016.74	3893.37	3783.38	3684.84
600000	4902.50	4705.82	4533.66	4381.90	4247.32	4127.32	4019.82

Monthly Payments 5¹/₂%
necessary to amortize a loan

AMOUNT	22 YEARS	23 YEARS	24 YEARS	25 YEARS	30 YEARS	35 YEARS	40 YEARS
100	0.65	0.64	0.63	0.61	0.57	0.54	0.52
200	1.31	1.28	1.25	1.23	1.14	1.07	1.03
500	3.27	3.20	3.13	3.07	2.84	2.69	2.58
1000	6.54	6.39	6.26	6.14	5.68	5.37	5.16
2000	13.08	12.79	12.52	12.28	11.36	10.74	10.32
5000	32.69	31.96	31.30	30.70	28.39	26.85	25.79
6000	39.23	38.36	37.57	36.85	34.07	32.22	30.95
7000	45.77	44.75	43.83	42.99	39.75	37.59	36.10
8000	52.31	51.14	50.09	49.13	45.42	42.96	41.26
9000	58.85	57.54	56.35	55.27	51.10	48.33	46.42
10000	65.38	63.93	62.61	61.41	56.78	53.70	51.58
15000	98.08	95.89	93.91	92.11	85.17	80.55	77.37
20000	130.77	127.86	125.22	122.82	113.56	107.40	103.15
25000	163.46	159.82	156.52	153.52	141.95	134.25	128.94
30000	196.15	191.79	187.83	184.23	170.34	161.10	154.73
35000	228.85	223.75	219.13	214.93	198.73	187.96	180.52
40000	261.54	255.72	250.44	245.63	227.12	214.81	206.31
45000	294.23	287.68	281.74	276.34	255.51	241.66	232.10
50000	326.92	319.64	313.04	307.04	283.89	268.51	257.89
55000	359.62	351.61	344.35	337.75	312.28	295.36	283.67
60000	392.31	383.57	375.65	368.45	340.67	322.21	309.46
65000	425.00	415.54	406.96	399.16	369.06	349.06	335.25
70000	457.69	447.50	438.26	429.86	397.45	375.91	361.04
75000	490.39	479.47	469.57	460.57	425.84	402.76	386.83
80000	523.08	511.43	500.87	491.27	454.23	429.61	412.62
85000	555.77	543.39	532.18	521.97	482.62	456.46	438.40
90000	588.46	575.36	563.48	552.68	511.01	483.31	464.19
95000	621.16	607.32	594.78	583.38	539.40	510.17	489.98
100000	653.85	639.29	626.09	614.09	567.79	537.02	515.77
105000	686.54	671.25	657.39	644.79	596.18	563.87	541.56
110000	719.23	703.22	688.70	675.50	624.57	590.72	567.35
120000	784.62	767.15	751.31	736.90	681.35	644.42	618.92
130000	850.00	831.07	813.92	798.31	738.13	698.12	670.50
140000	915.39	895.00	876.52	859.72	794.90	751.82	722.08
150000	980.77	958.93	939.13	921.13	851.68	805.52	773.66
160000	1046.16	1022.86	1001.74	982.54	908.46	859.23	825.23
170000	1111.54	1086.79	1064.35	1043.95	965.24	912.93	876.81
180000	1176.93	1150.72	1126.96	1105.36	1022.02	966.63	928.39
190000	1242.31	1214.65	1189.57	1166.77	1078.80	1020.33	979.96
200000	1307.70	1278.58	1252.18	1228.17	1135.58	1074.03	1031.54
210000	1373.08	1342.50	1314.79	1289.58	1192.36	1127.73	1083.12
220000	1438.47	1406.43	1377.40	1350.99	1249.14	1181.44	1134.69
230000	1503.85	1470.36	1440.00	1412.40	1305.91	1235.14	1186.27
240000	1569.24	1534.29	1502.61	1473.81	1362.69	1288.84	1237.85
250000	1634.62	1598.22	1565.22	1535.22	1419.47	1342.54	1289.43
260000	1700.01	1662.15	1627.83	1596.63	1476.25	1396.24	1341.00
270000	1765.39	1726.08	1690.44	1658.04	1533.03	1449.94	1392.58
280000	1830.78	1790.01	1753.05	1719.44	1589.81	1503.65	1444.16
290000	1896.16	1853.93	1815.66	1780.85	1646.59	1557.35	1495.73
300000	1961.55	1917.86	1878.27	1842.26	1703.37	1611.05	1547.31
310000	2026.93	1981.79	1940.88	1903.67	1760.15	1664.75	1598.89
320000	2092.32	2045.72	2003.48	1965.08	1816.92	1718.45	1650.46
330000	2157.70	2109.65	2066.09	2026.49	1873.70	1772.15	1702.04
340000	2223.09	2173.58	2128.70	2087.90	1930.48	1825.86	1753.62
350000	2288.47	2237.51	2191.31	2149.31	1987.26	1879.56	1805.20
400000	2615.40	2557.15	2504.36	2456.35	2271.16	2148.07	2063.08
450000	2942.32	2876.79	2817.40	2763.39	2555.05	2416.57	2320.97
500000	3269.25	3196.44	3130.44	3070.44	2838.95	2685.08	2578.85
550000	3596.17	3516.08	3443.49	3377.48	3122.84	2953.59	2836.74
600000	3923.09	3835.73	3756.53	3684.52	3406.73	3222.10	3094.62

5³/₄%

Monthly Payments
necessary to amortize a loan

AMOUNT	1 YEAR	2 YEARS	3 YEARS	4 YEARS	5 YEARS	6 YEARS	7 YEARS
100	8.60	4.42	3.03	2.34	1.92	1.65	1.45
200	17.19	8.84	6.06	4.67	3.84	3.29	2.90
500	42.98	22.10	15.15	11.69	9.61	8.23	7.24
1000	85.95	44.21	30.31	23.37	19.22	16.46	14.49
2000	171.90	88.42	60.62	46.74	38.43	32.91	28.98
5000	429.76	221.04	151.54	116.85	96.08	82.28	72.45
6000	515.71	265.25	181.85	140.22	115.30	98.73	86.93
7000	601.66	309.46	212.16	163.59	134.52	115.19	101.42
8000	687.61	353.66	242.47	186.96	153.73	131.64	115.91
9000	773.56	397.87	272.78	210.34	172.95	148.10	130.40
10000	859.52	442.08	303.09	233.71	192.17	164.55	144.89
15000	1289.27	663.12	454.63	350.56	288.25	246.83	217.34
20000	1719.03	884.16	606.18	467.41	384.34	329.10	289.78
25000	2148.79	1105.20	757.72	584.26	480.42	411.38	362.23
30000	2578.55	1326.24	909.26	701.12	576.50	493.65	434.67
35000	3008.30	1547.28	1060.81	817.97	672.59	575.93	507.12
40000	3438.06	1768.32	1212.35	934.82	768.67	658.21	579.56
45000	3867.82	1989.36	1363.90	1051.68	864.75	740.48	652.01
50000	4297.58	2210.40	1515.44	1168.53	960.84	822.76	724.45
55000	4727.33	2431.44	1666.98	1285.38	1056.92	905.03	796.90
60000	5157.09	2652.48	1818.53	1402.23	1153.01	987.31	869.34
65000	5586.85	2873.52	1970.07	1519.09	1249.09	1069.58	941.79
70000	6016.61	3094.56	2121.62	1635.94	1345.17	1151.86	1014.23
75000	6446.37	3315.60	2273.16	1752.79	1441.26	1234.13	1086.68
80000	6876.13	3536.64	2424.70	1869.65	1537.34	1316.41	1159.12
85000	7305.88	3757.68	2576.25	1986.50	1633.43	1398.69	1231.57
90000	7735.64	3978.72	2727.79	2103.35	1729.51	1480.96	1304.01
95000	8165.40	4199.76	2879.34	2220.21	1825.59	1563.24	1376.46
100000	8595.16	4420.80	3030.88	2337.06	1921.68	1645.51	1448.90
105000	9024.91	4641.84	3182.42	2453.91	2017.76	1727.79	1521.35
110000	9454.67	4862.89	3333.97	2570.76	2113.84	1810.06	1593.79
120000	10314.19	5304.97	3637.05	2804.47	2306.01	1974.62	1738.68
130000	11173.70	5747.05	3940.14	3038.18	2498.18	2139.17	1883.57
140000	12033.22	6189.13	4243.23	3271.88	2690.35	2303.72	2028.46
150000	12892.73	6631.21	4546.32	3505.59	2882.52	2468.27	2173.35
160000	13752.25	7073.29	4849.41	3739.29	3074.68	2632.82	2318.24
170000	14611.77	7515.37	5152.49	3973.00	3266.85	2797.37	2463.13
180000	15471.28	7957.45	5455.58	4206.70	3459.02	2961.92	2608.02
190000	16330.80	8399.53	5758.67	4440.41	3651.19	3126.48	2752.91
200000	17190.31	8841.61	6061.76	4674.12	3843.35	3291.03	2897.80
210000	18049.83	9283.69	6364.85	4907.82	4035.52	3455.58	3042.69
220000	18909.34	9725.77	6667.93	5141.53	4227.69	3620.13	3187.58
230000	19768.86	10167.85	6971.02	5375.24	4419.86	3784.68	3332.47
240000	20628.38	10609.93	7274.11	5608.94	4612.02	3949.23	3477.36
250000	21487.89	11052.01	7577.20	5842.65	4804.19	4113.78	3622.25
260000	22347.41	11494.09	7880.29	6076.35	4996.36	4278.33	3767.14
270000	23206.92	11936.17	8183.37	6310.06	5188.53	4442.89	3912.03
280000	24066.44	12378.25	8486.46	6543.76	5380.70	4607.44	4056.92
290000	24925.95	12820.33	8789.55	6777.47	5572.86	4771.99	4201.81
300000	25785.47	13262.41	9092.64	7011.17	5765.03	4936.54	4346.70
310000	26644.98	13704.49	9395.73	7244.88	5957.20	5101.09	4491.59
320000	27504.50	14146.58	9698.81	7478.59	6149.37	5265.64	4636.48
330000	28364.02	14588.66	10001.90	7712.29	6341.53	5430.19	4781.37
340000	29223.53	15030.74	10304.99	7946.00	6533.70	5594.74	4926.26
350000	30083.05	15472.82	10608.08	8179.70	6725.87	5759.30	5071.15
400000	34380.63	17683.22	12123.52	9348.23	7686.71	6582.05	5795.60
450000	38678.20	19893.62	13638.96	10516.76	8647.55	7404.81	6520.05
500000	42975.78	22104.02	15154.40	11685.29	9608.38	8227.57	7244.50
550000	47273.36	24314.43	16669.83	12853.82	10569.22	9050.32	7968.95
600000	51570.94	26524.83	18185.27	14022.35	11530.06	9873.08	8693.40

Monthly Payments 5³/₄%

necessary to amortize a loan

AMOUNT	8 YEARS	9 YEARS	10 YEARS	11 YEARS	12 YEARS	13 YEARS	14 YEARS
100	1.30	1.19	1.10	1.02	0.96	0.91	0.87
200	2.60	2.38	2.20	2.05	1.93	1.82	1.74
500	6.51	5.94	5.49	5.12	4.81	4.56	4.34
1000	13.02	11.88	10.98	10.24	9.63	9.12	8.68
2000	26.04	23.76	21.95	20.48	19.26	18.23	17.36
5000	65.10	59.41	54.88	51.20	48.15	45.58	43.40
6000	78.12	71.29	65.86	61.44	57.78	54.70	52.08
7000	91.14	83.18	76.84	71.68	67.41	63.82	60.76
8000	104.16	95.06	87.82	81.92	77.04	72.93	69.44
9000	117.18	106.94	98.79	92.16	86.67	82.05	78.12
10000	130.20	118.82	109.77	102.40	96.30	91.16	86.80
15000	195.30	178.24	164.65	153.60	144.44	136.75	130.20
20000	260.40	237.65	219.54	204.80	192.59	182.33	173.59
25000	325.50	297.06	274.42	256.00	240.74	227.91	216.99
30000	390.60	356.47	329.31	307.20	288.89	273.49	260.39
35000	455.70	415.89	384.19	358.40	337.04	319.08	303.79
40000	520.80	475.30	439.08	409.60	385.18	364.66	347.19
45000	585.90	534.71	493.96	460.80	433.33	410.24	390.59
50000	651.00	594.12	548.85	512.00	481.48	455.82	433.99
55000	716.10	653.54	603.73	563.20	529.63	501.41	477.39
60000	781.20	712.95	658.62	614.40	577.78	546.99	520.78
65000	846.30	772.36	713.50	665.60	625.93	592.57	564.18
70000	911.40	831.77	768.38	716.80	674.07	638.15	607.58
75000	976.50	891.19	823.27	768.00	722.22	683.74	650.98
80000	1041.60	950.60	878.15	819.20	770.37	729.32	694.38
85000	1106.70	1010.01	933.04	870.40	818.52	774.90	737.78
90000	1171.80	1069.42	987.92	921.60	866.67	820.48	781.18
95000	1236.90	1128.84	1042.81	972.80	914.81	866.07	824.58
100000	1302.00	1188.25	1097.69	1024.00	962.96	911.65	867.97
105000	1367.10	1247.66	1152.58	1075.20	1011.11	957.23	911.37
110000	1432.20	1307.07	1207.46	1126.41	1059.26	1002.81	954.77
120000	1562.40	1425.90	1317.23	1228.80	1155.55	1093.98	1041.57
130000	1692.61	1544.72	1427.00	1331.20	1251.85	1185.14	1128.37
140000	1822.81	1663.55	1536.77	1433.60	1348.15	1276.31	1215.16
150000	1953.01	1782.37	1646.54	1536.00	1444.44	1367.47	1301.96
160000	2083.21	1901.20	1756.31	1638.40	1540.74	1458.64	1388.76
170000	2213.41	2020.02	1866.08	1740.80	1637.04	1549.80	1475.56
180000	2343.61	2138.85	1975.85	1843.21	1733.33	1640.97	1562.35
190000	2473.81	2257.67	2085.62	1945.61	1829.63	1732.13	1649.15
200000	2604.01	2376.50	2195.38	2048.01	1925.92	1823.30	1735.95
210000	2734.21	2495.32	2305.15	2150.41	2022.22	1914.46	1822.75
220000	2864.41	2614.15	2414.92	2252.81	2118.52	2005.63	1909.54
230000	2994.61	2732.97	2524.69	2355.21	2214.81	2096.79	1996.34
240000	3124.81	2851.80	2634.46	2457.61	2311.11	2187.96	2083.14
250000	3255.01	2970.62	2744.23	2560.01	2407.40	2279.12	2169.94
260000	3385.21	3089.45	2854.00	2662.41	2503.70	2370.28	2256.73
270000	3515.41	3208.27	2963.77	2764.81	2600.00	2461.45	2343.53
280000	3645.61	3327.10	3073.54	2867.21	2696.29	2552.61	2430.33
290000	3775.81	3445.92	3183.31	2969.61	2792.59	2643.78	2517.13
300000	3906.01	3564.75	3293.08	3072.01	2888.89	2734.94	2603.92
310000	4036.21	3683.57	3402.85	3174.41	2985.18	2826.11	2690.72
320000	4166.41	3802.40	3512.62	3276.81	3081.48	2917.27	2777.52
330000	4296.61	3921.22	3622.38	3379.21	3177.77	3008.44	2864.31
340000	4426.81	4040.05	3732.15	3481.61	3274.07	3099.60	2951.11
350000	4557.01	4158.87	3841.92	3584.01	3370.37	3190.77	3037.91
400000	5208.02	4753.00	4390.77	4096.01	3851.85	3646.59	3471.90
450000	5859.02	5347.12	4939.61	4608.01	4333.33	4102.42	3905.88
500000	6510.02	5941.25	5488.46	5120.01	4814.81	4558.24	4339.87
550000	7161.02	6535.37	6037.31	5632.02	5296.29	5014.06	4773.86
600000	7812.02	7129.50	6586.15	6144.02	5777.77	5469.89	5207.85

5¾% Monthly Payments
necessary to amortize a loan

AMOUNT	15 YEARS	16 YEARS	17 YEARS	18 YEARS	19 YEARS	20 YEARS	21 YEARS
100	0.83	0.80	0.77	0.74	0.72	0.70	0.68
200	1.66	1.60	1.54	1.49	1.44	1.40	1.37
500	4.15	3.99	3.85	3.72	3.61	3.51	3.42
1000	8.30	7.98	7.69	7.44	7.22	7.02	6.84
2000	16.61	15.96	15.39	14.88	14.44	14.04	13.69
5000	41.52	39.89	38.46	37.21	36.10	35.10	34.22
6000	49.82	47.87	46.16	44.65	43.31	42.13	41.06
7000	58.13	55.85	53.85	52.09	50.53	49.15	47.90
8000	66.43	63.82	61.54	59.53	57.75	56.17	54.75
9000	74.74	71.80	69.24	66.98	64.97	63.19	61.59
10000	83.04	79.78	76.93	74.42	72.19	70.21	68.43
15000	124.56	119.67	115.39	111.63	108.29	105.31	102.65
20000	166.08	159.56	153.86	148.83	144.38	140.42	136.87
25000	207.60	199.45	192.32	186.04	180.48	175.52	171.08
30000	249.12	239.34	230.79	223.25	216.57	210.63	205.30
35000	290.64	279.23	269.25	260.46	252.67	245.73	239.52
40000	332.16	319.12	307.72	297.67	288.76	280.83	273.73
45000	373.68	359.01	346.18	334.88	324.86	315.94	307.95
50000	415.21	398.90	384.64	372.08	360.96	351.04	342.17
55000	456.73	438.79	423.11	409.29	397.05	386.15	376.38
60000	498.25	478.68	461.57	446.50	433.15	421.25	410.60
65000	539.77	518.57	500.04	483.71	469.24	456.35	444.82
70000	581.29	558.47	538.50	520.92	505.34	491.46	479.03
75000	622.81	598.36	576.97	558.13	541.43	526.56	513.25
80000	664.33	638.25	615.43	595.34	577.53	561.67	547.47
85000	705.85	678.14	653.90	632.54	613.63	596.77	581.68
90000	747.37	718.03	692.36	669.75	649.72	631.88	615.90
95000	788.89	757.92	730.82	706.96	685.82	666.98	650.12
100000	830.41	797.81	769.29	744.17	721.91	702.08	684.34
105000	871.93	837.70	807.75	781.38	758.01	737.19	718.55
110000	913.45	877.59	846.22	818.59	794.10	772.29	752.77
120000	996.49	957.37	923.15	893.00	866.29	842.50	821.20
130000	1079.53	1037.15	1000.07	967.42	938.49	912.71	889.64
140000	1162.57	1116.93	1077.00	1041.84	1010.68	982.92	958.07
150000	1245.62	1196.71	1153.93	1116.25	1082.87	1053.13	1026.50
160000	1328.66	1276.49	1230.86	1190.67	1155.06	1123.33	1094.94
170000	1411.70	1356.27	1307.79	1265.09	1227.25	1193.54	1163.37
180000	1494.74	1436.05	1384.72	1339.51	1299.44	1263.75	1231.80
190000	1577.78	1515.83	1461.65	1413.92	1371.63	1333.96	1300.24
200000	1660.82	1595.61	1538.58	1488.34	1443.82	1404.17	1368.67
210000	1743.86	1675.40	1615.51	1562.76	1516.01	1474.38	1437.10
220000	1826.90	1755.18	1692.43	1637.17	1588.21	1544.58	1505.54
230000	1909.94	1834.96	1769.36	1711.59	1660.40	1614.79	1573.97
240000	1992.98	1914.74	1846.29	1786.01	1732.59	1685.00	1642.40
250000	2076.03	1994.52	1923.22	1860.42	1804.78	1755.21	1710.84
260000	2159.07	2074.30	2000.15	1934.84	1876.97	1825.42	1779.27
270000	2242.11	2154.08	2077.08	2009.26	1949.16	1895.63	1847.70
280000	2325.15	2233.86	2154.01	2083.67	2021.35	1965.83	1916.14
290000	2408.19	2313.64	2230.94	2158.09	2093.54	2036.04	1984.57
300000	2491.23	2393.42	2307.86	2232.51	2165.74	2106.25	2053.01
310000	2574.27	2473.20	2384.79	2306.93	2237.93	2176.46	2121.44
320000	2657.31	2552.98	2461.72	2381.34	2310.12	2246.67	2189.87
330000	2740.35	2632.76	2538.65	2455.76	2382.31	2316.88	2258.31
340000	2823.39	2712.55	2615.58	2530.18	2454.50	2387.08	2326.74
350000	2906.44	2792.33	2692.51	2604.59	2526.69	2457.29	2395.17
400000	3321.64	3191.23	3077.15	2976.68	2887.65	2808.33	2737.34
450000	3736.85	3590.13	3461.80	3348.76	3248.60	3159.38	3079.51
500000	4152.05	3989.04	3846.44	3720.85	3609.56	3510.42	3421.68
550000	4567.26	4387.94	4231.09	4092.93	3970.51	3861.46	3763.84
600000	4982.46	4786.84	4615.73	4465.02	4331.47	4212.50	4106.01

Monthly Payments 5¾%
necessary to amortize a loan

AMOUNT	22 YEARS	23 YEARS	24 YEARS	25 YEARS	30 YEARS	35 YEARS	40 YEARS
100	0.67	0.65	0.64	0.63	0.58	0.55	0.53
200	1.34	1.31	1.28	1.26	1.17	1.11	1.07
500	3.34	3.27	3.20	3.15	2.92	2.77	2.66
1000	6.68	6.54	6.41	6.29	5.84	5.54	5.33
2000	13.37	13.08	12.82	12.58	11.67	11.07	10.66
5000	33.42	32.70	32.05	31.46	29.18	27.68	26.64
6000	40.10	39.24	38.46	37.75	35.01	33.21	31.97
7000	46.79	45.78	44.87	44.04	40.85	38.75	37.30
8000	53.47	52.32	51.28	50.33	46.69	44.28	42.63
9000	60.15	58.86	57.69	56.62	52.52	49.82	47.96
10000	66.84	65.40	64.09	62.91	58.36	55.35	53.29
15000	100.26	98.10	96.14	94.37	87.54	83.03	79.93
20000	133.68	130.80	128.19	125.82	116.71	110.70	106.58
25000	167.10	163.50	160.24	157.28	145.89	138.38	133.22
30000	200.51	196.20	192.28	188.73	175.07	166.05	159.87
35000	233.93	228.89	224.33	220.19	204.25	193.73	186.51
40000	267.35	261.59	256.38	251.64	233.43	221.40	213.16
45000	300.77	294.29	288.43	283.10	262.61	249.08	239.80
50000	334.19	326.99	320.47	314.55	291.79	276.75	266.44
55000	367.61	359.69	352.52	346.01	320.97	304.43	293.09
60000	401.03	392.39	384.57	377.46	350.14	332.10	319.73
65000	434.45	425.09	416.62	408.92	379.32	359.78	346.38
70000	467.87	457.79	448.66	440.37	408.50	387.45	373.02
75000	501.29	490.49	480.71	471.83	437.68	415.13	399.67
80000	534.70	523.19	512.76	503.29	466.86	442.80	426.31
85000	568.12	555.89	544.81	534.74	496.04	470.48	452.95
90000	601.54	588.59	576.85	566.20	525.22	498.15	479.60
95000	634.96	621.28	608.90	597.65	554.39	525.83	506.24
100000	668.38	653.98	640.95	629.11	583.57	553.50	532.89
105000	701.80	686.68	673.00	660.56	612.75	581.18	559.53
110000	735.22	719.38	705.04	692.02	641.93	608.85	586.18
120000	802.06	784.78	769.14	754.93	700.29	664.20	639.47
130000	868.89	850.18	833.23	817.84	758.64	719.55	692.75
140000	935.73	915.58	897.33	880.75	817.00	774.90	746.04
150000	1002.57	980.98	961.42	943.66	875.36	830.25	799.33
160000	1069.41	1046.37	1025.52	1006.57	933.72	885.60	852.62
170000	1136.25	1111.77	1089.61	1069.48	992.07	940.95	905.91
180000	1203.09	1177.17	1153.71	1132.39	1050.43	996.30	959.20
190000	1269.92	1242.57	1217.80	1195.30	1108.79	1051.65	1012.49
200000	1336.76	1307.97	1281.90	1258.21	1167.15	1107.00	1065.78
210000	1403.60	1373.37	1345.99	1321.12	1225.50	1162.35	1119.06
220000	1470.44	1438.76	1410.08	1384.03	1283.86	1217.70	1172.35
230000	1537.28	1504.16	1474.18	1446.94	1342.22	1273.05	1225.64
240000	1604.11	1569.56	1538.27	1509.86	1400.57	1328.40	1278.93
250000	1670.95	1634.96	1602.37	1572.77	1458.93	1383.75	1332.22
260000	1737.79	1700.36	1666.46	1635.68	1517.29	1439.10	1385.51
270000	1804.63	1765.76	1730.56	1698.59	1575.65	1494.45	1438.80
280000	1871.47	1831.15	1794.65	1761.50	1634.00	1549.80	1492.09
290000	1938.30	1896.55	1858.75	1824.41	1692.36	1605.15	1545.37
300000	2005.14	1961.95	1922.84	1887.32	1750.72	1660.50	1598.66
310000	2071.98	2027.35	1986.94	1950.23	1809.08	1715.85	1651.95
320000	2138.82	2092.75	2051.03	2013.14	1867.43	1771.20	1705.24
330000	2205.66	2158.15	2115.13	2076.05	1925.79	1826.55	1758.53
340000	2272.49	2223.55	2179.22	2138.96	1984.15	1881.90	1811.82
350000	2339.33	2288.94	2243.32	2201.87	2042.50	1937.25	1865.11
400000	2673.52	2615.94	2563.79	2516.43	2334.29	2214.00	2131.55
450000	3007.71	2942.93	2884.26	2830.98	2626.08	2490.75	2397.99
500000	3341.90	3269.92	3204.74	3145.53	2917.86	2767.50	2664.44
550000	3676.09	3596.91	3525.21	3460.09	3209.65	3044.25	2930.88
600000	4010.28	3923.90	3845.69	3774.64	3501.44	3321.00	3197.33

19

6%

Monthly Payments
necessary to amortize a loan

AMOUNT	1 YEAR	2 YEARS	3 YEARS	4 YEARS	5 YEARS	6 YEARS	7 YEARS
100	8.61	4.43	3.04	2.35	1.93	1.66	1.46
200	17.21	8.86	6.08	4.70	3.87	3.31	2.92
500	43.03	22.16	15.21	11.74	9.67	8.29	7.30
1000	86.07	44.32	30.42	23.49	19.33	16.57	14.61
2000	172.13	88.64	60.84	46.97	38.67	33.15	29.22
5000	430.33	221.60	152.11	117.43	96.66	82.86	73.04
6000	516.00	265.92	182.53	140.91	116.00	99.44	87.65
7000	602.47	310.24	212.95	164.40	135.33	116.01	102.26
8000	688.53	354.56	243.38	187.88	154.66	132.58	116.87
9000	774.60	398.89	273.80	211.37	174.00	149.16	131.48
10000	860.66	443.21	304.22	234.85	193.33	165.73	146.09
15000	1291.00	664.81	456.33	352.28	289.99	248.59	219.13
20000	1721.33	886.41	608.44	469.70	386.66	331.46	292.17
25000	2151.66	1108.02	760.55	587.13	483.32	414.32	365.21
30000	2581.99	1329.62	912.66	704.55	579.98	497.19	438.26
35000	3012.33	1551.22	1064.77	821.98	676.65	580.05	511.30
40000	3442.66	1772.82	1216.88	939.40	773.31	662.92	584.34
45000	3872.99	1994.43	1368.99	1056.83	869.98	745.78	657.38
50000	4303.32	2216.03	1521.10	1174.25	966.64	828.64	730.43
55000	4733.65	2437.63	1673.21	1291.68	1063.30	911.51	803.47
60000	5163.99	2659.24	1825.32	1409.10	1159.97	994.37	876.51
65000	5594.32	2880.84	1977.43	1526.53	1256.63	1077.24	949.56
70000	6024.65	3102.44	2129.54	1643.95	1353.30	1160.10	1022.60
75000	6454.98	3324.05	2281.65	1761.38	1449.96	1242.97	1095.64
80000	6885.31	3545.65	2433.75	1878.80	1546.62	1325.83	1168.68
85000	7315.65	3767.25	2585.86	1996.23	1643.29	1408.70	1241.73
90000	7745.98	3988.85	2737.97	2113.65	1739.95	1491.56	1314.77
95000	8176.31	4210.46	2890.08	2231.08	1836.62	1574.42	1387.81
100000	8606.64	4432.06	3042.19	2348.50	1933.28	1657.29	1460.86
105000	9036.98	4653.66	3194.30	2465.93	2029.94	1740.15	1533.90
110000	9467.31	4875.27	3346.41	2583.35	2126.61	1823.02	1606.94
120000	10327.97	5318.47	3650.63	2818.20	2319.94	1988.75	1753.03
130000	11188.64	5761.68	3954.85	3053.05	2513.26	2154.48	1899.11
140000	12049.30	6204.89	4259.07	3287.90	2706.59	2320.20	2045.20
150000	12909.96	6648.09	4563.29	3522.75	2899.92	2485.93	2191.28
160000	13770.63	7091.30	4867.51	3757.60	3093.25	2651.66	2337.37
170000	14631.29	7534.50	5171.73	3992.45	3286.58	2817.39	2483.45
180000	15491.96	7977.71	5475.95	4227.31	3479.90	2983.12	2629.54
190000	16352.62	8420.92	5780.17	4462.16	3673.23	3148.85	2775.63
200000	17213.29	8864.12	6084.39	4697.01	3866.56	3314.58	2921.71
210000	18073.95	9307.33	6388.61	4931.86	4059.89	3480.31	3067.80
220000	18934.61	9750.53	6692.83	5166.71	4253.22	3646.04	3213.88
230000	19795.28	10193.74	6997.05	5401.56	4446.54	3811.76	3359.97
240000	20655.94	10636.95	7301.26	5636.41	4639.87	3977.49	3506.05
250000	21516.61	11080.15	7605.48	5871.26	4833.20	4143.22	3652.14
260000	22377.27	11523.36	7909.70	6106.11	5026.53	4308.95	3798.22
270000	23237.94	11966.56	8213.92	6340.96	5219.86	4474.68	3944.31
280000	24098.60	12409.77	8518.14	6575.81	5413.18	4640.41	4090.40
290000	24959.26	12852.98	8822.36	6810.66	5606.51	4806.14	4236.48
300000	25819.93	13296.18	9126.58	7045.51	5799.84	4971.87	4382.57
310000	26680.59	13739.39	9430.80	7280.36	5993.17	5137.60	4528.65
320000	27541.26	14182.60	9735.02	7515.21	6186.50	5303.32	4674.74
330000	28401.92	14625.80	10039.24	7750.06	6379.82	5469.05	4820.82
340000	29262.59	15069.01	10343.46	7984.91	6573.15	5634.78	4966.91
350000	30123.25	15512.21	10647.68	8219.76	6766.48	5800.51	5112.99
400000	34426.57	17728.24	12168.77	9394.01	7733.12	6629.16	5843.42
450000	38729.89	19944.27	13689.87	10568.26	8699.76	7457.80	6573.85
500000	43033.21	22160.31	15210.97	11742.51	9666.40	8286.44	7304.28
550000	47336.54	24376.34	16732.07	12916.77	10633.04	9115.09	8034.70
600000	51639.86	26592.37	18253.16	14091.02	11599.68	9943.73	8765.13

Monthly Payments 6%
necessary to amortize a loan

AMOUNT	8 YEARS	9 YEARS	10 YEARS	11 YEARS	12 YEARS	13 YEARS	14 YEARS
100	1.31	1.20	1.11	1.04	0.98	0.92	0.88
200	2.63	2.40	2.22	2.07	1.95	1.85	1.76
500	6.57	6.00	5.55	5.18	4.88	4.62	4.41
1000	13.14	12.01	11.10	10.37	9.76	9.25	8.81
2000	26.28	24.01	22.20	20.73	19.52	18.49	17.62
5000	65.71	60.03	55.51	51.84	48.79	46.24	44.06
6000	78.85	72.03	66.61	62.20	58.55	55.48	52.87
7000	91.99	84.04	77.71	72.57	68.31	64.73	61.69
8000	105.13	96.05	88.82	82.94	78.07	73.98	70.50
9000	118.27	108.05	99.92	93.30	87.83	83.23	79.31
10000	131.41	120.06	111.02	103.67	97.59	92.47	88.12
15000	197.12	180.09	166.53	155.51	146.38	138.71	132.19
20000	262.83	240.11	222.04	207.34	195.17	184.94	176.25
25000	328.54	300.14	277.55	259.18	243.96	231.18	220.31
30000	394.24	360.17	333.06	311.01	292.76	277.42	264.37
35000	459.95	420.20	388.57	362.85	341.55	323.65	308.43
40000	525.66	480.23	444.08	414.68	390.34	369.89	352.49
45000	591.36	540.26	499.59	466.52	439.13	416.13	396.56
50000	657.07	600.29	555.10	518.35	487.93	462.36	440.62
55000	722.78	660.32	610.61	570.19	536.72	508.60	484.68
60000	788.49	720.34	666.12	622.02	585.51	554.83	528.74
65000	854.19	780.37	721.63	673.86	634.30	601.07	572.80
70000	919.90	840.40	777.14	725.69	683.10	647.31	616.87
75000	985.61	900.43	832.65	777.53	731.89	693.54	660.93
80000	1051.31	960.46	888.16	829.36	780.68	739.78	704.99
85000	1117.02	1020.49	943.67	881.20	829.47	786.01	749.05
90000	1182.73	1080.52	999.18	933.03	878.27	832.25	793.11
95000	1248.44	1140.55	1054.69	984.87	927.06	878.49	837.17
100000	1314.14	1200.57	1110.21	1036.70	975.85	924.72	881.24
105000	1379.85	1260.60	1165.72	1088.54	1024.64	970.96	925.30
110000	1445.56	1320.63	1221.23	1140.37	1073.44	1017.20	969.36
120000	1576.97	1440.69	1332.25	1244.04	1171.02	1109.67	1057.48
130000	1708.39	1560.75	1443.27	1347.71	1268.61	1202.14	1145.61
140000	1839.80	1680.80	1554.29	1451.38	1366.19	1294.61	1233.73
150000	1971.21	1800.86	1665.31	1555.06	1463.78	1387.09	1321.85
160000	2102.63	1920.92	1776.33	1658.73	1561.36	1479.56	1409.98
170000	2234.04	2040.98	1887.35	1762.40	1658.95	1572.03	1498.10
180000	2365.46	2161.03	1998.37	1866.07	1756.53	1664.50	1586.22
190000	2496.87	2281.09	2109.39	1969.74	1854.12	1756.97	1674.35
200000	2628.29	2401.15	2220.41	2073.41	1951.70	1849.45	1762.47
210000	2759.70	2521.21	2331.43	2177.08	2049.29	1941.92	1850.60
220000	2891.11	2641.26	2442.45	2280.75	2146.87	2034.39	1938.72
230000	3022.53	2761.32	2553.47	2384.42	2244.46	2126.86	2026.84
240000	3153.94	2881.38	2664.49	2488.09	2342.04	2219.34	2114.97
250000	3285.36	3001.44	2775.51	2591.76	2439.63	2311.81	2203.09
260000	3416.77	3121.49	2886.53	2695.43	2537.21	2404.28	2291.21
270000	3548.19	3241.55	2997.55	2799.10	2634.80	2496.75	2379.34
280000	3679.60	3361.61	3108.57	2902.77	2732.38	2589.23	2467.46
290000	3811.01	3481.67	3219.59	3006.44	2829.97	2681.70	2555.58
300000	3942.43	3601.72	3330.62	3110.11	2927.55	2774.17	2643.71
310000	4073.84	3721.78	3441.64	3213.78	3025.14	2866.64	2731.83
320000	4205.26	3841.84	3552.66	3317.45	3122.72	2959.12	2819.95
330000	4336.67	3961.90	3663.68	3421.12	3220.31	3051.59	2908.08
340000	4468.09	4081.95	3774.70	3524.79	3317.89	3144.06	2996.20
350000	4599.50	4202.01	3885.72	3628.46	3415.48	3236.53	3084.33
400000	5256.57	4802.30	4440.82	4146.81	3903.40	3698.89	3524.94
450000	5913.64	5402.59	4995.92	4665.17	4391.33	4161.25	3965.56
500000	6570.72	6002.87	5551.03	5183.52	4879.25	4623.62	4406.18
550000	7227.79	6603.16	6106.13	5701.87	5367.18	5085.98	4846.80
600000	7884.86	7203.45	6661.23	6220.22	5855.10	5548.34	5287.42

6% Monthly Payments
necessary to amortize a loan

AMOUNT	15 YEARS	16 YEARS	17 YEARS	18 YEARS	19 YEARS	20 YEARS	21 YEARS
100	0.84	0.81	0.78	0.76	0.74	0.72	0.70
200	1.69	1.62	1.57	1.52	1.47	1.43	1.40
500	4.22	4.06	3.92	3.79	3.68	3.58	3.49
1000	8.44	8.11	7.83	7.58	7.36	7.16	6.99
2000	16.88	16.23	15.66	15.16	14.72	14.33	13.98
5000	42.19	40.57	39.16	37.91	36.80	35.82	34.94
6000	50.63	48.69	46.99	45.49	44.16	42.99	41.93
7000	59.07	56.80	54.82	53.07	51.53	50.15	48.92
8000	67.51	64.92	62.65	60.65	58.89	57.31	55.91
9000	75.95	73.03	70.48	68.23	66.25	64.48	62.90
10000	84.39	81.14	78.31	75.82	73.61	71.64	69.89
15000	126.58	121.72	117.47	113.72	110.41	107.46	104.83
20000	168.77	162.29	156.62	151.63	147.22	143.29	139.77
25000	210.96	202.86	195.78	189.54	184.02	179.11	174.71
30000	253.16	243.43	234.93	227.45	220.82	214.93	209.66
35000	295.35	284.00	274.09	265.36	257.63	250.75	244.60
40000	337.54	324.58	313.24	303.26	294.43	286.57	279.54
45000	379.74	365.15	352.40	341.17	331.24	322.39	314.49
50000	421.93	405.72	391.55	379.08	368.04	358.22	349.43
55000	464.12	446.29	430.71	416.99	404.85	394.04	384.37
60000	506.31	486.86	469.86	454.90	441.65	429.86	419.31
65000	548.51	527.43	509.02	492.81	478.45	465.68	454.26
70000	590.70	568.01	548.17	530.71	515.26	501.50	489.20
75000	632.89	608.58	587.33	568.62	552.06	537.32	524.14
80000	675.09	649.15	626.48	606.53	588.87	573.14	559.09
85000	717.28	689.72	665.64	644.44	625.67	608.97	594.03
90000	759.47	730.29	704.79	682.35	662.47	644.79	628.97
95000	801.66	770.87	743.95	720.25	699.28	680.61	663.91
100000	843.86	811.44	783.10	758.16	736.08	716.43	698.86
105000	886.05	852.01	822.26	796.07	772.89	752.25	733.80
110000	928.24	892.58	861.41	833.98	809.69	788.07	768.74
120000	1012.63	973.73	939.72	909.79	883.30	859.72	838.63
130000	1097.01	1054.87	1018.03	985.61	956.91	931.36	908.51
140000	1181.40	1136.01	1096.34	1061.43	1030.52	1003.00	978.40
150000	1265.79	1217.16	1174.65	1137.24	1104.12	1074.65	1048.29
160000	1350.17	1298.30	1252.96	1213.06	1177.73	1146.29	1118.17
170000	1434.56	1379.44	1331.27	1288.88	1251.34	1217.93	1188.06
180000	1518.94	1460.59	1409.58	1364.69	1324.95	1289.58	1257.94
190000	1603.33	1541.73	1487.89	1440.51	1398.56	1361.22	1327.83
200000	1687.71	1622.88	1566.20	1516.32	1472.17	1432.86	1397.71
210000	1772.10	1704.02	1644.51	1592.14	1545.77	1504.51	1467.60
220000	1856.49	1785.16	1722.82	1667.96	1619.38	1576.15	1537.49
230000	1940.87	1866.31	1801.13	1743.77	1692.99	1647.79	1607.37
240000	2025.26	1947.45	1879.44	1819.59	1766.60	1719.43	1677.26
250000	2109.64	2028.59	1957.75	1895.41	1840.21	1791.08	1747.14
260000	2194.03	2109.74	2036.06	1971.22	1913.82	1862.72	1817.03
270000	2278.41	2190.88	2114.37	2047.04	1987.42	1934.36	1886.91
280000	2362.80	2272.03	2192.68	2122.85	2061.03	2006.01	1956.80
290000	2447.18	2353.17	2270.99	2198.67	2134.64	2077.65	2026.69
300000	2531.57	2434.31	2349.30	2274.49	2208.25	2149.29	2096.57
310000	2615.96	2515.46	2427.61	2350.30	2281.86	2220.94	2166.46
320000	2700.34	2596.60	2505.92	2426.12	2355.47	2292.58	2236.34
330000	2784.73	2677.74	2584.23	2501.94	2429.07	2364.22	2306.23
340000	2869.11	2758.89	2662.54	2577.75	2502.68	2435.87	2376.11
350000	2953.50	2840.03	2740.85	2653.57	2576.29	2507.51	2446.00
400000	3375.43	3245.75	3132.40	3032.65	2944.33	2865.72	2795.43
450000	3797.36	3651.47	3523.95	3411.73	3312.37	3223.94	3144.86
500000	4219.28	4057.19	3915.50	3790.81	3680.41	3582.16	3494.28
550000	4641.21	4462.91	4307.05	4169.89	4048.46	3940.37	3843.71
600000	5063.14	4868.63	4698.60	4548.97	4416.50	4298.59	4193.14

Monthly Payments 6%

necessary to amortize a loan

AMOUNT	22 YEARS	23 YEARS	24 YEARS	25 YEARS	30 YEARS	35 YEARS	40 YEARS
100	0.68	0.67	0.66	0.64	0.60	0.57	0.55
200	1.37	1.34	1.31	1.29	1.20	1.14	1.10
500	3.42	3.34	3.28	3.22	3.00	2.85	2.75
1000	6.83	6.69	6.56	6.44	6.00	5.70	5.50
2000	13.66	13.38	13.12	12.89	11.99	11.40	11.00
5000	34.15	33.44	32.80	32.22	29.98	28.51	27.51
6000	40.98	40.13	39.36	38.66	35.97	34.21	33.01
7000	47.82	46.82	45.92	45.10	41.97	39.91	38.51
8000	54.65	53.51	52.48	51.54	47.96	45.62	44.02
9000	61.48	60.20	59.04	57.99	53.96	51.32	49.52
10000	68.31	66.88	65.60	64.43	59.96	57.02	55.02
15000	102.46	100.33	98.40	96.65	89.93	85.53	82.53
20000	136.61	133.77	131.20	128.86	119.91	114.04	110.04
25000	170.77	167.21	163.99	161.08	149.89	142.55	137.55
30000	204.92	200.65	196.79	193.29	179.87	171.06	165.06
35000	239.08	234.10	229.59	225.51	209.84	199.57	192.57
40000	273.23	267.54	262.39	257.72	239.82	228.08	220.09
45000	307.38	300.98	295.19	289.94	269.80	256.59	247.60
50000	341.54	334.42	327.99	322.15	299.78	285.09	275.11
55000	375.69	367.87	360.79	354.37	329.75	313.60	302.62
60000	409.84	401.31	393.59	386.58	359.73	342.11	330.13
65000	444.00	434.75	426.39	418.80	389.71	370.62	357.64
70000	478.15	468.19	459.18	451.01	419.69	399.13	385.15
75000	512.31	501.64	491.98	483.23	449.66	427.64	412.66
80000	546.46	535.08	524.78	515.44	479.64	456.15	440.17
85000	580.61	568.52	557.58	547.66	509.62	484.66	467.68
90000	614.77	601.96	590.38	579.87	539.60	513.17	495.19
95000	648.92	635.40	623.18	612.09	569.57	541.68	522.70
100000	683.07	668.85	655.98	644.30	599.55	570.19	550.21
105000	717.23	702.29	688.78	676.52	629.53	598.70	577.72
110000	751.38	735.73	721.58	708.73	659.51	627.21	605.24
120000	819.69	802.62	787.17	773.16	719.46	684.23	660.26
130000	888.00	869.50	852.77	837.59	779.42	741.25	715.28
140000	956.30	936.39	918.37	902.02	839.37	798.27	770.30
150000	1024.61	1003.27	983.97	966.45	899.33	855.28	825.32
160000	1092.92	1070.16	1049.56	1030.88	959.28	912.30	880.34
170000	1161.23	1137.04	1115.16	1095.31	1019.24	969.32	935.36
180000	1229.53	1203.92	1180.76	1159.74	1079.19	1026.34	990.38
190000	1297.84	1270.81	1246.36	1224.17	1139.15	1083.36	1045.41
200000	1366.15	1337.69	1311.96	1288.60	1199.10	1140.38	1100.43
210000	1434.46	1404.58	1377.55	1353.03	1259.06	1197.40	1155.45
220000	1502.76	1471.46	1443.15	1417.46	1319.01	1254.42	1210.47
230000	1571.07	1538.35	1508.75	1481.89	1378.97	1311.44	1265.49
240000	1639.38	1605.23	1574.35	1546.32	1438.92	1368.46	1320.51
250000	1707.69	1672.12	1639.95	1610.75	1498.88	1425.47	1375.53
260000	1775.99	1739.00	1705.54	1675.18	1558.83	1482.49	1430.56
270000	1844.30	1805.89	1771.14	1739.61	1618.79	1539.51	1485.58
280000	1912.61	1872.77	1836.74	1804.04	1678.74	1596.53	1540.60
290000	1980.92	1939.66	1902.34	1868.47	1738.70	1653.55	1595.62
300000	2049.22	2006.54	1967.93	1932.90	1798.65	1710.57	1650.64
310000	2117.53	2073.43	2033.53	1997.33	1858.61	1767.59	1705.66
320000	2185.84	2140.31	2099.13	2061.76	1918.56	1824.61	1760.68
330000	2254.15	2207.20	2164.73	2126.19	1978.52	1881.63	1815.71
340000	2322.45	2274.08	2230.33	2190.62	2038.47	1938.65	1870.73
350000	2390.76	2340.97	2295.92	2255.05	2098.43	1995.66	1925.75
400000	2732.30	2675.39	2623.91	2577.21	2398.20	2280.76	2200.85
450000	3073.84	3009.81	2951.90	2899.36	2697.98	2565.85	2475.96
500000	3415.37	3344.24	3279.89	3221.51	2997.75	2850.95	2751.07
550000	3756.91	3678.66	3607.88	3543.66	3297.53	3136.04	3026.18
600000	4098.45	4013.08	3935.87	3865.81	3597.30	3421.14	3301.28

6¹/₄% Monthly Payments
necessary to amortize a loan

AMOUNT	1 YEAR	2 YEARS	3 YEARS	4 YEARS	5 YEARS	6 YEARS	7 YEARS
100	8.62	4.44	3.05	2.36	1.94	1.67	1.47
200	17.24	8.89	6.11	4.72	3.89	3.34	2.95
500	43.09	22.22	15.27	11.80	9.72	8.35	7.36
1000	86.18	44.43	30.54	23.60	19.45	16.69	14.73
2000	172.36	88.87	61.07	47.20	38.90	33.38	29.46
5000	430.91	222.17	152.68	118.00	97.25	83.46	73.64
6000	517.09	266.60	183.21	141.60	116.70	100.15	88.37
7000	603.27	311.03	213.75	165.20	136.14	116.84	103.10
8000	689.45	355.47	244.28	188.80	155.59	133.53	117.83
9000	775.63	399.90	274.82	212.40	175.04	150.22	132.56
10000	861.81	444.33	305.35	236.00	194.49	166.91	147.29
15000	1292.72	666.50	458.03	354.00	291.74	250.37	220.93
20000	1723.63	888.67	610.71	472.00	388.99	333.82	294.57
25000	2154.53	1110.83	763.38	590.00	486.23	417.28	368.22
30000	2585.44	1333.00	916.06	707.99	583.48	500.73	441.86
35000	3016.35	1555.17	1068.74	825.99	680.72	584.19	515.50
40000	3447.26	1777.33	1221.41	943.99	777.97	667.65	589.15
45000	3878.16	1999.50	1374.09	1061.99	875.22	751.10	662.79
50000	4309.07	2221.67	1526.77	1179.99	972.46	834.56	736.43
55000	4739.98	2443.83	1679.44	1297.99	1069.71	918.01	810.08
60000	5170.88	2666.00	1832.12	1415.99	1166.96	1001.47	883.72
65000	5601.79	2888.17	1984.80	1533.99	1264.20	1084.93	957.37
70000	6032.70	3110.33	2137.47	1651.99	1361.45	1168.38	1031.01
75000	6463.60	3332.50	2290.15	1769.99	1458.69	1251.84	1104.65
80000	6894.51	3554.67	2442.83	1887.99	1555.94	1335.29	1178.30
85000	7325.42	3776.83	2595.50	2005.98	1653.19	1418.75	1251.94
90000	7756.32	3999.00	2748.18	2123.98	1750.43	1502.20	1325.58
95000	8187.23	4221.17	2900.86	2241.98	1847.68	1585.66	1399.23
100000	8618.14	4443.33	3053.53	2359.98	1944.93	1669.12	1472.87
105000	9049.04	4665.50	3206.21	2477.98	2042.17	1752.57	1546.51
110000	9479.95	4887.67	3358.89	2595.98	2139.42	1836.03	1620.16
120000	10341.77	5332.00	3664.24	2831.98	2333.91	2002.94	1767.44
130000	11203.58	5776.33	3969.59	3067.98	2528.40	2169.85	1914.73
140000	12065.39	6220.67	4274.95	3303.97	2722.90	2336.76	2062.02
150000	12927.21	6665.00	4580.30	3539.97	2917.39	2503.67	2209.30
160000	13789.02	7109.34	4885.65	3775.97	3111.88	2670.58	2356.59
170000	14650.83	7553.67	5191.01	4011.97	3306.37	2837.50	2503.88
180000	15512.65	7998.00	5496.36	4247.97	3500.87	3004.41	2651.17
190000	16374.46	8442.34	5801.71	4483.97	3695.36	3171.32	2798.45
200000	17236.28	8886.67	6107.07	4719.96	3889.85	3338.23	2945.74
210000	18098.09	9331.00	6412.42	4955.96	4084.34	3505.14	3093.03
220000	18959.90	9775.34	6717.78	5191.96	4278.84	3672.05	3240.31
230000	19821.72	10219.67	7023.13	5427.96	4473.33	3838.97	3387.60
240000	20683.53	10664.00	7328.48	5663.96	4667.82	4005.88	3534.89
250000	21545.35	11108.34	7633.84	5899.95	4862.32	4172.79	3682.17
260000	22407.16	11552.67	7939.19	6135.95	5056.81	4339.70	3829.46
270000	23268.97	11997.00	8244.54	6371.95	5251.30	4506.61	3976.75
280000	24130.79	12441.34	8549.90	6607.95	5445.79	4673.52	4124.04
290000	24992.60	12885.67	8855.25	6843.95	5640.29	4840.43	4271.32
300000	25854.41	13330.00	9160.60	7079.95	5834.78	5007.35	4418.61
310000	26716.23	13774.34	9465.96	7315.94	6029.27	5174.26	4565.90
320000	27578.04	14218.67	9771.31	7551.94	6223.76	5341.17	4713.18
330000	28439.86	14663.00	10076.66	7787.94	6418.26	5508.08	4860.47
340000	29301.67	15107.34	10382.02	8023.94	6612.75	5674.99	5007.76
350000	30163.48	15551.67	10687.37	8259.94	6807.24	5841.90	5155.04
400000	34472.55	17773.34	12214.14	9439.93	7779.70	6676.46	5891.48
450000	38781.62	19995.01	13740.90	10619.92	8752.17	7511.02	6627.91
500000	43090.69	22216.67	15267.67	11799.91	9724.63	8345.58	7364.35
550000	47399.76	24438.34	16794.44	12979.90	10697.09	9180.13	8100.78
600000	51708.83	26660.01	18321.20	14159.89	11669.56	10014.69	8837.22

Monthly Payments 6¹/₄%
necessary to amortize a loan

AMOUNT	8 YEARS	9 YEARS	10 YEARS	11 YEARS	12 YEARS	13 YEARS	14 YEARS
100	1.33	1.21	1.12	1.05	0.99	0.94	0.89
200	2.65	2.43	2.25	2.10	1.98	1.88	1.79
500	6.63	6.06	5.61	5.25	4.94	4.69	4.47
1000	13.26	12.13	11.23	10.49	9.89	9.38	8.95
2000	26.53	24.26	22.46	20.99	19.78	18.76	17.89
5000	66.32	60.65	56.14	52.47	49.44	46.90	44.73
6000	79.58	72.78	67.37	62.97	59.33	56.27	53.68
7000	92.84	84.91	78.60	73.46	69.22	65.65	62.62
8000	106.11	97.04	89.82	83.96	79.11	75.03	71.57
9000	119.37	109.17	101.05	94.45	89.00	84.41	80.51
10000	132.63	121.30	112.28	104.95	98.88	93.79	89.46
15000	198.95	181.95	168.42	157.42	148.33	140.69	134.19
20000	265.27	242.60	224.56	209.90	197.77	187.58	178.92
25000	331.59	303.24	280.70	262.37	247.21	234.48	223.65
30000	397.90	363.89	336.84	314.85	296.65	281.37	268.38
35000	464.22	424.54	392.98	367.32	346.09	328.27	313.11
40000	530.54	485.19	449.12	419.80	395.53	375.16	357.84
45000	596.86	545.84	505.26	472.27	444.98	422.06	402.57
50000	663.17	606.49	561.40	524.75	494.42	468.95	447.31
55000	729.49	667.14	617.54	577.22	543.86	515.85	492.04
60000	795.81	727.79	673.68	629.70	593.30	562.74	536.77
65000	862.13	788.43	729.82	682.17	642.74	609.64	581.50
70000	928.44	849.08	785.96	734.65	692.19	656.53	626.23
75000	994.76	909.73	842.10	787.12	741.63	703.43	670.96
80000	1061.08	970.38	898.24	839.60	791.07	750.32	715.69
85000	1127.40	1031.03	954.38	892.07	840.51	797.22	760.42
90000	1193.71	1091.68	1010.52	944.55	889.95	844.11	805.15
95000	1260.03	1152.33	1066.66	997.02	939.39	891.01	849.88
100000	1326.35	1212.98	1122.80	1049.49	988.84	937.90	894.61
105000	1392.67	1273.62	1178.94	1101.97	1038.28	984.80	939.34
110000	1458.98	1334.27	1235.08	1154.44	1087.72	1031.69	984.07
120000	1591.62	1455.57	1347.36	1259.39	1186.60	1125.49	1073.53
130000	1724.25	1576.87	1459.64	1364.34	1285.49	1219.28	1162.99
140000	1856.89	1698.17	1571.92	1469.29	1384.37	1313.07	1252.45
150000	1989.52	1819.46	1684.20	1574.24	1483.26	1406.86	1341.92
160000	2122.16	1940.76	1796.48	1679.19	1582.14	1500.65	1431.38
170000	2254.79	2062.06	1908.76	1784.14	1681.02	1594.44	1520.84
180000	2387.43	2183.36	2021.04	1889.09	1779.91	1688.23	1610.30
190000	2520.06	2304.65	2133.32	1994.04	1878.79	1782.02	1699.76
200000	2652.70	2425.95	2245.60	2098.99	1977.67	1875.81	1789.22
210000	2785.33	2547.25	2357.88	2203.94	2076.56	1969.60	1878.68
220000	2917.97	2668.55	2470.16	2308.89	2175.44	2063.39	1968.14
230000	3050.60	2789.84	2582.44	2413.84	2274.32	2157.18	2057.60
240000	3183.24	2911.14	2694.72	2518.79	2373.21	2250.97	2147.06
250000	3315.87	3032.44	2807.00	2623.74	2472.09	2344.76	2236.53
260000	3448.51	3153.74	2919.28	2728.69	2570.98	2438.55	2325.99
270000	3581.14	3275.03	3031.56	2833.64	2669.86	2532.34	2415.45
280000	3713.78	3396.33	3143.84	2938.59	2768.74	2626.13	2504.91
290000	3846.41	3517.63	3256.12	3043.54	2867.63	2719.92	2594.37
300000	3979.05	3638.93	3368.40	3148.48	2966.51	2813.71	2683.83
310000	4111.68	3760.22	3480.68	3253.43	3065.39	2907.50	2773.29
320000	4244.32	3881.52	3592.96	3358.38	3164.28	3001.29	2862.75
330000	4376.95	4002.82	3705.24	3463.33	3263.16	3095.08	2952.21
340000	4509.59	4124.12	3817.52	3568.28	3362.05	3188.87	3041.67
350000	4642.22	4245.41	3929.80	3673.23	3460.93	3282.67	3131.14
400000	5305.40	4851.90	4491.20	4197.98	3955.35	3751.62	3578.44
450000	5968.57	5458.39	5052.60	4722.73	4449.77	4220.57	4025.75
500000	6631.75	6064.88	5614.00	5247.47	4944.18	4689.52	4473.05
550000	7294.92	6671.37	6175.41	5772.22	5438.60	5158.47	4920.36
600000	7958.10	7277.85	6736.81	6296.97	5933.02	5627.43	5367.66

6¼%

Monthly Payments
necessary to amortize a loan

AMOUNT	15 YEARS	16 YEARS	17 YEARS	18 YEARS	19 YEARS	20 YEARS	21 YEARS
100	0.86	0.83	0.80	0.77	0.75	0.73	0.71
200	1.71	1.65	1.59	1.54	1.50	1.46	1.43
500	4.29	4.13	3.99	3.86	3.75	3.65	3.57
1000	8.57	8.25	7.97	7.72	7.50	7.31	7.14
2000	17.15	16.50	15.94	15.45	15.01	14.62	14.27
5000	42.87	41.26	39.85	38.61	37.52	36.55	35.68
6000	51.45	49.51	47.82	46.34	45.02	43.86	42.81
7000	60.02	57.76	55.79	54.06	52.53	51.16	49.95
8000	68.59	66.02	63.76	61.78	60.03	58.47	57.08
9000	77.17	74.27	71.73	69.51	67.54	65.78	64.22
10000	85.74	82.52	79.70	77.23	75.04	73.09	71.35
15000	128.61	123.78	119.56	115.84	112.56	109.64	107.03
20000	171.48	165.04	159.41	154.46	150.08	146.19	142.71
25000	214.36	206.30	199.26	193.07	187.60	182.73	178.38
30000	257.23	247.56	239.11	231.69	225.12	219.28	214.06
35000	300.10	288.82	278.97	270.30	262.64	255.82	249.74
40000	342.97	330.08	318.82	308.92	300.16	292.37	285.41
45000	385.84	371.34	358.67	347.53	337.68	328.92	321.09
50000	428.71	412.60	398.52	386.15	375.20	365.46	356.77
55000	471.58	453.86	438.37	424.76	412.72	402.01	392.44
60000	514.45	495.12	478.23	463.38	450.24	438.56	428.12
65000	557.32	536.38	518.08	501.99	487.76	475.10	463.80
70000	600.20	577.64	557.93	540.61	525.28	511.65	499.47
75000	643.07	618.90	597.78	579.22	562.80	548.20	535.15
80000	685.94	660.16	637.64	617.83	600.32	584.74	570.83
85000	728.81	701.42	677.49	656.45	637.84	621.29	606.50
90000	771.68	742.67	717.34	695.06	675.36	657.84	642.18
95000	814.55	783.93	757.19	733.68	712.88	694.38	677.86
100000	857.42	825.19	797.05	772.29	750.40	730.93	713.53
105000	900.29	866.45	836.90	810.91	787.92	767.47	749.21
110000	943.17	907.71	876.75	849.52	825.44	804.02	784.89
120000	1028.91	990.23	956.45	926.75	900.48	877.11	856.24
130000	1114.65	1072.75	1036.16	1003.98	975.52	950.21	927.59
140000	1200.39	1155.27	1115.86	1081.21	1050.56	1023.30	998.95
150000	1286.13	1237.79	1195.57	1158.44	1125.60	1096.39	1070.30
160000	1371.88	1320.31	1275.27	1235.67	1200.64	1169.49	1141.65
170000	1457.62	1402.83	1354.98	1312.90	1275.68	1242.58	1213.01
180000	1543.36	1485.35	1434.68	1390.13	1350.72	1315.67	1284.36
190000	1629.10	1567.87	1514.39	1467.36	1425.76	1388.76	1355.71
200000	1714.85	1650.39	1594.09	1544.59	1500.80	1461.86	1427.07
210000	1800.59	1732.91	1673.80	1621.82	1575.84	1534.95	1498.42
220000	1886.33	1815.43	1753.50	1699.05	1650.88	1608.04	1569.77
230000	1972.07	1897.95	1833.20	1776.27	1725.92	1681.13	1641.13
240000	2057.81	1980.47	1912.91	1853.50	1800.96	1754.23	1712.48
250000	2143.56	2062.99	1992.61	1930.73	1876.00	1827.32	1783.83
260000	2229.30	2145.50	2072.32	2007.96	1951.04	1900.41	1855.19
270000	2315.04	2228.02	2152.02	2085.19	2026.08	1973.51	1926.54
280000	2400.78	2310.54	2231.73	2162.42	2101.12	2046.60	1997.89
290000	2486.53	2393.06	2311.43	2239.65	2176.15	2119.69	2069.25
300000	2572.27	2475.58	2391.14	2316.88	2251.19	2192.78	2140.60
310000	2658.01	2558.10	2470.84	2394.11	2326.23	2265.88	2211.95
320000	2743.75	2640.62	2550.55	2471.34	2401.27	2338.97	2283.31
330000	2829.50	2723.14	2630.25	2548.57	2476.31	2412.06	2354.66
340000	2915.24	2805.66	2709.95	2625.80	2551.35	2485.16	2426.01
350000	3000.98	2888.18	2789.66	2703.03	2626.39	2558.25	2497.37
400000	3429.69	3300.78	3188.18	3089.17	3001.59	2923.71	2854.13
450000	3858.40	3713.37	3586.70	3475.32	3376.79	3289.18	3210.90
500000	4287.11	4125.97	3985.23	3861.47	3751.99	3654.64	3567.67
550000	4715.83	4538.57	4383.75	4247.61	4127.19	4020.11	3924.43
600000	5144.54	4951.16	4782.27	4633.76	4502.39	4385.57	4281.20

Monthly Payments 6¼%

necessary to amortize a loan

AMOUNT	22 YEARS	23 YEARS	24 YEARS	25 YEARS	30 YEARS	35 YEARS	40 YEARS
100	0.70	0.68	0.67	0.66	0.62	0.59	0.57
200	1.40	1.37	1.34	1.32	1.23	1.17	1.14
500	3.49	3.42	3.36	3.30	3.08	2.94	2.84
1000	6.98	6.84	6.71	6.60	6.16	5.87	5.68
2000	13.96	13.68	13.42	13.19	12.31	11.74	11.35
5000	34.90	34.19	33.56	32.98	30.79	29.35	28.39
6000	41.88	41.03	40.27	39.58	36.94	35.22	34.06
7000	48.85	47.87	46.98	46.18	43.10	41.10	39.74
8000	55.83	54.71	53.69	52.77	49.26	46.97	45.42
9000	62.81	61.55	60.41	59.37	55.41	52.84	51.10
10000	69.79	68.39	67.12	65.97	61.57	58.71	56.77
15000	104.69	102.58	100.68	98.95	92.36	88.06	85.16
20000	139.59	136.77	134.24	131.93	123.14	117.42	113.55
25000	174.48	170.97	167.79	164.92	153.93	146.77	141.93
30000	209.38	205.16	201.35	197.90	184.72	176.12	170.32
35000	244.27	239.36	234.91	230.88	215.50	205.48	198.71
40000	279.17	273.55	268.47	263.87	246.29	234.83	227.10
45000	314.07	307.74	302.03	296.85	277.07	264.18	255.48
50000	348.96	341.94	335.59	329.83	307.86	293.54	283.87
55000	383.86	376.13	369.15	362.82	338.64	322.89	312.26
60000	418.76	410.32	402.71	395.80	369.43	352.25	340.64
65000	453.65	444.52	436.27	428.79	400.22	381.60	369.03
70000	488.55	478.71	469.82	461.77	431.00	410.95	397.42
75000	523.45	512.91	503.38	494.75	461.79	440.31	425.80
80000	558.34	547.10	536.94	527.74	492.57	469.66	454.19
85000	593.24	581.29	570.50	560.72	523.36	499.02	482.58
90000	628.14	615.49	604.06	593.70	554.15	528.37	510.97
95000	663.03	649.68	637.62	626.69	584.93	557.72	539.35
100000	697.93	683.87	671.18	659.67	615.72	587.08	567.74
105000	732.82	718.07	704.74	692.65	646.50	616.43	596.13
110000	767.72	752.26	738.30	725.64	677.29	645.78	624.51
120000	837.51	820.65	805.41	791.60	738.86	704.49	681.29
130000	907.31	889.04	872.53	857.57	800.43	763.20	738.06
140000	977.10	957.42	939.65	923.54	862.00	821.91	794.84
150000	1046.89	1025.81	1006.77	989.50	923.58	880.61	851.61
160000	1116.68	1094.20	1073.88	1055.47	985.15	939.32	908.38
170000	1186.48	1162.59	1141.00	1121.44	1046.72	998.03	965.16
180000	1256.27	1230.97	1208.12	1187.40	1108.29	1056.74	1021.93
190000	1326.06	1299.36	1275.24	1253.37	1169.86	1115.45	1078.71
200000	1395.86	1367.75	1342.35	1319.34	1231.43	1174.15	1135.48
210000	1465.65	1436.14	1409.47	1385.31	1293.01	1232.86	1192.25
220000	1535.44	1504.52	1476.59	1451.27	1354.58	1291.57	1249.03
230000	1605.23	1572.91	1543.71	1517.24	1416.15	1350.28	1305.80
240000	1675.03	1641.30	1610.83	1583.21	1477.72	1408.98	1362.57
250000	1744.82	1709.69	1677.94	1649.17	1539.29	1467.69	1419.35
260000	1814.61	1778.07	1745.06	1715.14	1600.86	1526.40	1476.12
270000	1884.41	1846.46	1812.18	1781.11	1662.44	1585.11	1532.90
280000	1954.20	1914.85	1879.30	1847.07	1724.01	1643.81	1589.67
290000	2023.99	1983.24	1946.41	1913.04	1785.58	1702.52	1646.44
300000	2093.78	2051.62	2013.53	1979.01	1847.15	1761.23	1703.22
310000	2163.58	2120.01	2080.65	2044.98	1908.72	1819.94	1759.99
320000	2233.37	2188.40	2147.77	2110.94	1970.30	1878.64	1816.77
330000	2303.16	2256.79	2214.89	2176.91	2031.87	1937.35	1873.54
340000	2372.96	2325.17	2282.00	2242.88	2093.44	1996.06	1930.31
350000	2442.75	2393.56	2349.12	2308.84	2155.01	2054.77	1987.09
400000	2791.71	2735.50	2684.71	2638.68	2462.87	2348.31	2270.96
450000	3140.68	3077.44	3020.30	2968.51	2770.73	2641.84	2554.83
500000	3489.64	3419.37	3355.89	3298.35	3078.59	2935.38	2838.70
550000	3838.60	3761.31	3691.48	3628.18	3386.44	3228.92	3122.57
600000	4187.57	4103.25	4027.06	3958.02	3694.30	3522.46	3406.44

6¹/₂%

Monthly Payments
necessary to amortize a loan

AMOUNT	1 YEAR	2 YEARS	3 YEARS	4 YEARS	5 YEARS	6 YEARS	7 YEARS
100	8.63	4.45	3.06	2.37	1.96	1.68	1.48
200	17.26	8.91	6.13	4.74	3.91	3.36	2.97
500	43.15	22.27	15.32	11.86	9.78	8.40	7.42
1000	86.30	44.55	30.65	23.71	19.57	16.81	14.85
2000	172.59	89.09	61.30	47.43	39.13	33.62	29.70
5000	431.48	222.73	153.25	118.57	97.83	84.05	74.25
6000	517.78	267.28	183.89	142.29	117.40	100.86	89.10
7000	604.07	311.82	214.54	166.00	136.96	117.67	103.95
8000	690.37	356.37	245.19	189.72	156.53	134.48	118.80
9000	776.67	400.92	275.84	213.43	176.10	151.29	133.64
10000	862.96	445.46	306.49	237.15	195.66	168.10	148.49
15000	1294.45	668.19	459.74	355.72	293.49	252.15	222.74
20000	1725.93	890.93	612.98	474.30	391.32	336.20	296.99
25000	2157.41	1113.66	766.23	592.87	489.15	420.25	371.24
30000	2588.89	1336.39	919.47	711.45	586.98	504.30	445.48
35000	3020.37	1559.12	1072.72	830.02	684.82	588.35	519.73
40000	3451.86	1781.85	1225.96	948.60	782.65	672.40	593.98
45000	3883.34	2004.58	1379.21	1067.17	880.48	756.45	668.22
50000	4314.82	2227.31	1532.45	1185.75	978.31	840.50	742.47
55000	4746.30	2450.04	1685.70	1304.32	1076.14	924.55	816.72
60000	5177.79	2672.78	1838.94	1422.90	1173.97	1008.60	890.97
65000	5609.27	2895.51	1992.19	1541.47	1271.80	1092.65	965.21
70000	6040.75	3118.24	2145.43	1660.05	1369.63	1176.70	1039.46
75000	6472.23	3340.97	2298.68	1778.62	1467.46	1260.74	1113.71
80000	6903.71	3563.70	2451.92	1897.20	1565.29	1344.79	1187.95
85000	7335.20	3786.43	2605.17	2015.77	1663.12	1428.84	1262.20
90000	7766.68	4009.16	2758.41	2134.35	1760.95	1512.89	1336.45
95000	8198.16	4231.89	2911.66	2252.92	1858.78	1596.94	1410.70
100000	8629.64	4454.63	3064.90	2371.50	1956.61	1680.99	1484.94
105000	9061.12	4677.36	3218.15	2490.07	2054.45	1765.04	1559.19
110000	9492.61	4900.09	3371.39	2608.64	2152.28	1849.09	1633.44
120000	10355.57	5345.55	3677.88	2845.79	2347.94	2017.19	1781.93
130000	11218.53	5791.01	3984.37	3082.94	2543.60	2185.29	1930.43
140000	12081.50	6236.48	4290.86	3320.09	2739.26	2353.39	2078.92
150000	12944.46	6681.94	4597.35	3557.24	2934.92	2521.49	2227.42
160000	13807.43	7127.40	4903.84	3794.39	3130.58	2689.59	2375.91
170000	14670.39	7572.86	5210.33	4031.54	3326.25	2857.69	2524.40
180000	15533.36	8018.33	5516.82	4268.69	3521.91	3025.79	2672.90
190000	16396.32	8463.79	5823.31	4505.84	3717.57	3193.89	2821.39
200000	17259.28	8909.25	6129.80	4742.99	3913.23	3361.99	2969.89
210000	18122.25	9354.71	6436.29	4980.14	4108.89	3530.09	3118.38
220000	18985.21	9800.18	6742.78	5217.29	4304.55	3698.18	3266.88
230000	19848.18	10245.64	7049.27	5454.44	4500.21	3866.28	3415.37
240000	20711.14	10691.10	7355.76	5691.59	4695.88	4034.38	3563.86
250000	21574.10	11136.56	7662.25	5928.74	4891.54	4202.48	3712.36
260000	22437.07	11582.03	7968.74	6165.89	5087.20	4370.58	3860.85
270000	23300.03	12027.49	8275.23	6403.04	5282.86	4538.68	4009.35
280000	24163.00	12472.95	8581.72	6640.19	5478.52	4706.78	4157.84
290000	25025.96	12918.41	8888.21	6877.34	5674.18	4874.88	4306.34
300000	25888.93	13363.88	9194.70	7114.49	5869.84	5042.98	4454.83
310000	26751.89	13809.34	9501.19	7351.64	6065.51	5211.08	4603.33
320000	27614.85	14254.80	9807.68	7588.78	6261.17	5379.18	4751.82
330000	28477.82	14700.26	10114.17	7825.93	6456.83	5547.28	4900.31
340000	29340.78	15145.73	10420.66	8063.08	6652.49	5715.38	5048.81
350000	30203.75	15591.19	10727.15	8300.23	6848.15	5883.48	5197.30
400000	34518.57	17818.50	12259.60	9485.98	7826.46	6723.97	5939.77
450000	38833.39	20045.81	13792.05	10671.73	8804.77	7564.47	6682.25
500000	43148.21	22273.13	15324.50	11857.48	9783.07	8404.96	7424.72
550000	47463.03	24500.44	16856.95	13043.22	10761.38	9245.46	8167.19
600000	51777.85	26727.75	18389.40	14228.97	11739.69	10085.96	8909.66

Monthly Payments 6½%
necessary to amortize a loan

AMOUNT	8 YEARS	9 YEARS	10 YEARS	11 YEARS	12 YEARS	13 YEARS	14 YEARS
100	1.34	1.23	1.14	1.06	1.00	0.95	0.91
200	2.68	2.45	2.27	2.12	2.00	1.90	1.82
500	6.69	6.13	5.68	5.31	5.01	4.76	4.54
1000	13.39	12.25	11.35	10.62	10.02	9.51	9.08
2000	26.77	24.51	22.71	21.25	20.04	19.02	18.16
5000	66.93	61.27	56.77	53.12	50.10	47.56	45.40
6000	80.32	73.53	68.13	63.74	60.12	57.07	54.49
7000	93.70	85.78	79.48	74.37	70.13	66.58	63.57
8000	107.09	98.04	90.84	84.99	80.15	76.10	72.65
9000	120.48	110.29	102.19	95.61	90.17	85.61	81.73
10000	133.86	122.55	113.55	106.24	100.19	95.12	90.81
15000	200.79	183.82	170.32	159.36	150.29	142.68	136.21
20000	267.72	245.09	227.10	212.48	200.38	190.24	181.62
25000	334.66	306.36	283.87	265.59	250.48	237.80	227.02
30000	401.59	367.64	340.64	318.71	300.58	285.36	272.43
35000	468.52	428.91	397.42	371.83	350.67	332.92	317.83
40000	535.45	490.18	454.19	424.95	400.77	380.48	363.24
45000	602.38	551.45	510.97	478.07	450.86	428.04	408.64
50000	669.31	612.73	567.74	531.19	500.96	475.60	454.05
55000	736.24	674.00	624.51	584.31	551.06	523.15	499.45
60000	803.17	735.27	681.29	637.43	601.15	570.71	544.86
65000	870.11	796.54	738.06	690.54	651.25	618.27	590.26
70000	937.04	857.82	794.84	743.66	701.34	665.83	635.67
75000	1003.97	919.09	851.61	796.78	751.44	713.39	681.07
80000	1070.90	980.36	908.38	849.90	801.54	760.95	726.48
85000	1137.83	1041.63	965.16	903.02	851.63	808.51	771.88
90000	1204.76	1102.91	1021.93	956.14	901.73	856.07	817.29
95000	1271.69	1164.18	1078.71	1009.26	951.83	903.63	862.69
100000	1338.62	1225.45	1135.48	1062.38	1001.92	951.19	908.10
105000	1405.55	1286.72	1192.25	1115.50	1052.02	998.75	953.50
110000	1472.49	1348.00	1249.03	1168.61	1102.11	1046.31	998.91
120000	1606.35	1470.54	1362.58	1274.85	1202.31	1141.43	1089.72
130000	1740.21	1593.09	1476.12	1381.09	1302.50	1236.55	1180.52
140000	1874.07	1715.63	1589.67	1487.33	1402.69	1331.67	1271.33
150000	2007.93	1838.18	1703.22	1593.57	1502.88	1426.79	1362.14
160000	2141.80	1960.72	1816.77	1699.80	1603.07	1521.90	1452.95
170000	2275.66	2083.27	1930.32	1806.04	1703.27	1617.02	1543.76
180000	2409.52	2205.81	2043.86	1912.28	1803.46	1712.14	1634.57
190000	2543.38	2328.36	2157.41	2018.52	1903.65	1807.26	1725.38
200000	2677.25	2450.90	2270.96	2124.75	2003.84	1902.38	1816.19
210000	2811.11	2573.45	2384.51	2230.99	2104.03	1997.50	1907.00
220000	2944.97	2695.99	2498.06	2337.23	2204.23	2092.62	1997.81
230000	3078.83	2818.54	2611.60	2443.47	2304.42	2187.74	2088.62
240000	3212.70	2941.08	2725.15	2549.70	2404.61	2282.86	2179.43
250000	3346.56	3063.63	2838.70	2655.94	2504.80	2377.98	2270.24
260000	3480.42	3186.17	2952.25	2762.18	2604.99	2473.09	2361.05
270000	3614.28	3308.72	3065.80	2868.42	2705.19	2568.21	2451.86
280000	3748.15	3431.26	3179.34	2974.65	2805.38	2663.33	2542.67
290000	3882.01	3553.81	3292.89	3080.89	2905.57	2758.45	2633.48
300000	4015.87	3676.35	3406.44	3187.13	3005.76	2853.57	2724.29
310000	4149.73	3798.90	3519.99	3293.37	3105.96	2948.69	2815.10
320000	4283.59	3921.44	3633.54	3399.61	3206.15	3043.81	2905.91
330000	4417.46	4043.99	3747.08	3505.84	3306.34	3138.93	2996.72
340000	4551.32	4166.54	3860.63	3612.08	3406.53	3234.05	3087.53
350000	4685.18	4289.08	3974.18	3718.32	3506.72	3329.17	3178.34
400000	5354.49	4901.81	4541.92	4249.51	4007.68	3804.76	3632.38
450000	6023.80	5514.53	5109.66	4780.70	4508.64	4280.36	4086.43
500000	6693.12	6127.26	5677.40	5311.88	5009.61	4755.95	4540.48
550000	7362.43	6739.98	6245.14	5843.07	5510.57	5231.55	4994.53
600000	8031.74	7352.71	6812.88	6374.26	6011.53	5707.14	5448.58

6½%

Monthly Payments
necessary to amortize a loan

AMOUNT	15 YEARS	16 YEARS	17 YEARS	18 YEARS	19 YEARS	20 YEARS	21 YEARS
100	0.87	0.84	0.81	0.79	0.76	0.75	0.73
200	1.74	1.68	1.62	1.57	1.53	1.49	1.46
500	4.36	4.20	4.06	3.93	3.82	3.73	3.64
1000	8.71	8.39	8.11	7.87	7.65	7.46	7.28
2000	17.42	16.78	16.22	15.73	15.30	14.91	14.57
5000	43.56	41.95	40.56	39.33	38.24	37.28	36.42
6000	52.27	50.34	48.67	47.19	45.89	44.73	43.70
7000	60.98	58.74	56.78	55.06	53.54	52.19	50.99
8000	69.69	67.13	64.89	62.92	61.19	59.65	58.27
9000	78.40	75.52	73.00	70.79	68.84	67.10	65.55
10000	87.11	83.91	81.11	78.66	76.49	74.56	72.84
15000	130.67	125.86	121.67	117.98	114.73	111.84	109.25
20000	174.22	167.82	162.22	157.31	152.97	149.11	145.67
25000	217.78	209.77	202.78	196.64	191.21	186.39	182.09
30000	261.33	251.72	243.34	235.97	229.46	223.67	218.51
35000	304.89	293.68	283.89	275.30	267.70	260.95	254.93
40000	348.44	335.63	324.45	314.62	305.94	298.23	291.35
45000	392.00	377.58	365.00	353.95	344.19	335.51	327.76
50000	435.55	419.54	405.56	393.28	382.43	372.79	364.18
55000	479.11	461.49	446.12	432.61	420.67	410.07	400.60
60000	522.66	503.45	486.67	471.94	458.91	447.34	437.02
65000	566.22	545.40	527.23	511.26	497.16	484.62	473.44
70000	609.78	587.35	567.78	550.59	535.40	521.90	509.85
75000	653.33	629.31	608.34	589.92	573.64	559.18	546.27
80000	696.89	671.26	648.90	629.25	611.88	596.46	582.69
85000	740.44	713.21	689.45	668.58	650.13	633.74	619.11
90000	784.00	755.17	730.01	707.91	688.37	671.02	655.53
95000	827.55	797.12	770.57	747.23	726.61	708.29	691.94
100000	871.11	839.08	811.12	786.56	764.86	745.57	728.36
105000	914.66	881.03	851.68	825.89	803.10	782.85	764.78
110000	958.22	922.98	892.23	865.22	841.34	820.13	801.20
120000	1045.33	1006.89	973.35	943.87	917.83	894.69	874.04
130000	1132.44	1090.80	1054.46	1022.53	994.31	969.25	946.87
140000	1219.55	1174.71	1135.57	1101.19	1070.80	1043.80	1019.71
150000	1306.66	1258.61	1216.68	1179.84	1147.28	1118.36	1092.54
160000	1393.77	1342.52	1297.79	1258.50	1223.77	1192.92	1165.38
170000	1480.88	1426.43	1378.91	1337.15	1300.26	1267.47	1238.22
180000	1567.99	1510.34	1460.02	1415.81	1376.74	1342.03	1311.05
190000	1655.10	1594.24	1541.13	1494.47	1453.23	1416.59	1383.89
200000	1742.21	1678.15	1622.24	1573.12	1529.71	1491.15	1456.73
210000	1829.33	1762.06	1703.35	1651.78	1606.20	1565.70	1529.56
220000	1916.44	1845.97	1784.47	1730.43	1682.68	1640.26	1602.40
230000	2003.55	1929.87	1865.58	1809.09	1759.17	1714.82	1675.23
240000	2090.66	2013.78	1946.69	1887.75	1835.65	1789.38	1748.07
250000	2177.77	2097.69	2027.80	1966.40	1912.14	1863.93	1820.91
260000	2264.88	2181.60	2108.91	2045.06	1988.63	1938.49	1893.74
270000	2351.99	2265.50	2190.03	2123.72	2065.11	2013.05	1966.58
280000	2439.10	2349.41	2271.14	2202.37	2141.60	2087.60	2039.42
290000	2526.21	2433.32	2352.25	2281.03	2218.08	2162.16	2112.25
300000	2613.32	2517.23	2433.36	2359.68	2294.57	2236.72	2185.09
310000	2700.43	2601.13	2514.48	2438.34	2371.05	2311.28	2257.93
320000	2787.54	2685.04	2595.59	2517.00	2447.54	2385.83	2330.76
330000	2874.65	2768.95	2676.70	2595.65	2524.02	2460.39	2403.60
340000	2961.77	2852.86	2757.81	2674.31	2600.51	2534.95	2476.43
350000	3048.88	2936.76	2838.92	2752.96	2677.00	2609.51	2549.27
400000	3484.43	3356.30	3244.48	3146.25	3059.42	2982.29	2913.45
450000	3919.98	3775.84	3650.04	3539.53	3441.85	3355.08	3277.63
500000	4355.54	4195.38	4055.61	3932.81	3824.28	3727.87	3641.81
550000	4791.09	4614.91	4461.17	4326.09	4206.71	4100.65	4006.00
600000	5226.64	5034.45	4866.73	4719.37	4589.14	4473.44	4370.18

Monthly Payments 6½%

necessary to amortize a loan

AMOUNT	22 YEARS	23 YEARS	24 YEARS	25 YEARS	30 YEARS	35 YEARS	40 YEARS
100	0.71	0.70	0.69	0.68	0.63	0.60	0.59
200	1.43	1.40	1.37	1.35	1.26	1.21	1.17
500	3.56	3.50	3.43	3.38	3.16	3.02	2.93
1000	7.13	6.99	6.87	6.75	6.32	6.04	5.85
2000	14.26	13.98	13.73	13.50	12.64	12.08	11.71
5000	35.65	34.95	34.33	33.76	31.60	30.21	29.27
6000	42.78	41.94	41.19	40.51	37.92	36.25	35.13
7000	49.91	48.93	48.06	47.26	44.24	42.29	40.98
8000	57.04	55.93	54.92	54.02	50.57	48.33	46.84
9000	64.16	62.92	61.79	60.77	56.89	54.37	52.69
10000	71.29	69.91	68.65	67.52	63.21	60.42	58.55
15000	106.94	104.86	102.98	101.28	94.81	90.62	87.82
20000	142.59	139.81	137.31	135.04	126.41	120.83	117.09
25000	178.23	174.77	171.64	168.80	158.02	151.04	146.36
30000	213.88	209.72	205.96	202.56	189.62	181.25	175.64
35000	249.53	244.67	240.29	236.32	221.22	211.45	204.91
40000	285.18	279.63	274.62	270.08	252.83	241.66	234.18
45000	320.82	314.58	308.94	303.84	284.43	271.87	263.46
50000	356.47	349.53	343.27	337.60	316.03	302.08	292.73
55000	392.12	384.49	377.60	371.36	347.64	332.28	322.00
60000	427.76	419.44	411.93	405.12	379.24	362.49	351.27
65000	463.41	454.39	446.25	438.88	410.84	392.70	380.55
70000	499.06	489.35	480.58	472.65	442.45	422.91	409.82
75000	534.70	524.30	514.91	506.41	474.05	453.12	439.09
80000	570.35	559.25	549.23	540.17	505.65	483.32	468.37
85000	606.00	594.20	583.56	573.93	537.26	513.53	497.64
90000	641.65	629.16	617.89	607.69	568.86	543.74	526.91
95000	677.29	664.11	652.22	641.45	600.46	573.95	556.18
100000	712.94	699.06	686.54	675.21	632.07	604.15	585.46
105000	748.59	734.02	720.87	708.97	663.67	634.36	614.73
110000	784.23	768.97	755.20	742.73	695.27	664.57	644.00
120000	855.53	838.88	823.85	810.25	758.48	724.99	702.55
130000	926.82	908.78	892.51	877.77	821.69	785.40	761.09
140000	998.11	978.69	961.16	945.29	884.90	845.82	819.64
150000	1069.41	1048.60	1029.81	1012.81	948.10	906.23	878.19
160000	1140.70	1118.50	1098.47	1080.33	1011.31	966.65	936.73
170000	1212.00	1188.41	1167.12	1147.85	1074.52	1027.06	995.28
180000	1283.29	1258.32	1235.78	1215.37	1137.73	1087.48	1053.82
190000	1354.58	1328.22	1304.43	1282.89	1200.93	1147.89	1112.37
200000	1425.88	1398.13	1373.09	1350.41	1264.14	1208.31	1170.91
210000	1497.17	1468.04	1441.74	1417.94	1327.34	1268.72	1229.46
220000	1568.47	1537.94	1510.39	1485.46	1390.55	1329.14	1288.00
230000	1639.76	1607.85	1579.05	1552.98	1453.76	1389.55	1346.55
240000	1711.05	1677.76	1647.70	1620.50	1516.96	1449.97	1405.10
250000	1782.35	1747.66	1716.36	1688.02	1580.17	1510.39	1463.64
260000	1853.64	1817.57	1785.01	1755.54	1643.38	1570.80	1522.19
270000	1924.94	1887.47	1853.67	1823.06	1706.58	1631.22	1580.73
280000	1996.23	1957.38	1922.32	1890.58	1769.79	1691.63	1639.28
290000	2067.52	2027.29	1990.97	1958.10	1833.00	1752.05	1697.82
300000	2138.82	2097.19	2059.63	2025.62	1896.20	1812.46	1756.37
310000	2210.11	2167.10	2128.28	2093.14	1959.41	1872.88	1814.92
320000	2281.40	2237.01	2196.94	2160.66	2022.62	1933.29	1873.46
330000	2352.70	2306.91	2265.59	2228.18	2085.82	1993.71	1932.01
340000	2423.99	2376.82	2334.25	2295.70	2149.03	2054.12	1990.55
350000	2495.28	2446.73	2402.90	2363.23	2212.24	2114.54	2049.10
400000	2851.76	2796.26	2746.17	2700.83	2528.27	2416.62	2341.83
450000	3208.23	3145.79	3089.44	3038.43	2844.31	2718.69	2634.56
500000	3564.69	3495.32	3432.71	3376.04	3160.34	3020.77	2927.28
550000	3921.16	3844.86	3775.98	3713.64	3476.37	3322.85	3220.01
600000	4277.63	4194.39	4119.26	4051.24	3792.41	3624.93	3512.74

6³/₄% Monthly Payments
necessary to amortize a loan

AMOUNT	1 YEAR	2 YEARS	3 YEARS	4 YEARS	5 YEARS	6 YEARS	7 YEARS
100	8.64	4.47	3.08	2.38	1.97	1.69	1.50
200	17.28	8.93	6.15	4.77	3.94	3.39	2.99
500	43.21	22.33	15.38	11.92	9.84	8.46	7.49
1000	86.41	44.66	30.76	23.83	19.68	16.93	14.97
2000	172.82	89.32	61.53	47.66	39.37	33.86	29.94
5000	432.06	223.30	153.81	119.15	98.42	84.65	74.85
6000	518.47	267.96	184.58	142.98	118.10	101.58	89.82
7000	604.88	312.62	215.34	166.81	137.78	118.50	104.80
8000	691.29	357.27	246.10	190.64	157.47	135.43	119.77
9000	777.70	401.93	276.87	214.47	177.15	152.36	134.74
10000	864.12	446.59	307.63	238.30	196.83	169.29	149.71
15000	1296.17	669.89	461.44	357.46	295.25	253.94	224.56
20000	1728.23	893.19	615.26	476.61	393.67	338.58	299.42
25000	2160.29	1116.48	769.07	595.76	492.09	423.23	374.27
30000	2592.35	1339.78	922.89	714.91	590.50	507.88	449.12
35000	3024.40	1563.08	1076.70	834.06	688.92	592.52	523.98
40000	3456.46	1786.37	1230.52	953.22	787.34	677.17	598.83
45000	3888.52	2009.67	1384.33	1072.37	885.76	761.81	673.68
50000	4320.58	2232.97	1538.15	1191.52	984.17	846.46	748.54
55000	4752.63	2456.26	1691.96	1310.67	1082.59	931.11	823.39
60000	5184.69	2679.56	1845.78	1429.83	1181.01	1015.75	898.25
65000	5616.75	2902.86	1999.59	1548.98	1279.42	1100.40	973.10
70000	6048.81	3126.15	2153.40	1668.13	1377.84	1185.04	1047.95
75000	6480.87	3349.45	2307.22	1787.28	1476.26	1269.69	1122.81
80000	6912.92	3572.75	2461.03	1906.43	1574.68	1354.34	1197.66
85000	7344.98	3796.04	2614.85	2025.59	1673.09	1438.98	1272.51
90000	7777.04	4019.34	2768.66	2144.74	1771.51	1523.63	1347.37
95000	8209.10	4242.64	2922.48	2263.89	1869.93	1608.28	1422.22
100000	8641.15	4465.93	3076.29	2383.04	1968.35	1692.92	1497.08
105000	9073.21	4689.23	3230.11	2502.19	2066.76	1777.57	1571.93
110000	9505.27	4912.53	3383.92	2621.35	2165.18	1862.21	1646.78
120000	10369.38	5359.12	3691.55	2859.65	2362.02	2031.51	1796.49
130000	11233.50	5805.71	3999.18	3097.96	2558.85	2200.80	1946.20
140000	12097.62	6252.31	4306.81	3336.26	2755.68	2370.09	2095.91
150000	12961.73	6698.90	4614.44	3574.56	2952.52	2539.38	2245.61
160000	13825.85	7145.49	4922.07	3812.87	3149.35	2708.67	2395.32
170000	14689.96	7592.09	5229.70	4051.17	3346.19	2877.97	2545.03
180000	15554.08	8038.68	5537.33	4289.48	3543.02	3047.26	2694.74
190000	16418.20	8485.27	5844.96	4527.78	3739.86	3216.55	2844.45
200000	17282.31	8931.87	6152.58	4766.09	3936.69	3385.84	2994.15
210000	18146.42	9378.46	6460.21	5004.39	4133.53	3555.13	3143.86
220000	19010.54	9825.05	6767.84	5242.69	4330.36	3724.43	3293.57
230000	19874.65	10271.65	7075.47	5481.00	4527.20	3893.72	3443.28
240000	20738.77	10718.24	7383.10	5719.30	4724.03	4063.01	3592.98
250000	21602.88	11164.83	7690.73	5957.61	4920.87	4232.30	3742.69
260000	22467.00	11611.43	7998.36	6195.91	5117.70	4401.60	3892.40
270000	23331.12	12058.02	8305.99	6434.22	5314.53	4570.89	4042.11
280000	24195.23	12504.61	8613.62	6672.52	5511.37	4740.18	4191.81
290000	25059.35	12951.21	8921.25	6910.82	5708.20	4909.47	4341.52
300000	25923.46	13397.80	9228.88	7149.13	5905.04	5078.76	4491.23
310000	26787.58	13844.39	9536.51	7387.43	6101.87	5248.06	4640.94
320000	27651.69	14290.99	9844.13	7625.74	6298.71	5417.35	4790.64
330000	28515.81	14737.58	10151.76	7864.04	6495.54	5586.64	4940.35
340000	29379.92	15184.17	10459.39	8102.35	6692.38	5755.93	5090.06
350000	30244.04	15630.77	10767.02	8340.65	6889.21	5925.22	5239.77
400000	34564.62	17863.73	12305.17	9532.17	7873.38	6771.69	5988.31
450000	38885.19	20096.70	13843.43	10723.69	8857.56	7618.15	6736.84
500000	43205.77	22329.66	15381.46	11915.21	9841.73	8464.61	7485.38
550000	47526.35	24562.63	16919.61	13106.74	10825.90	9311.07	8233.92
600000	51846.92	26795.60	18457.75	14298.26	11810.08	10157.53	8982.46

Monthly Payments 6¾%
necessary to amortize a loan

AMOUNT	8 YEARS	9 YEARS	10 YEARS	11 YEARS	12 YEARS	13 YEARS	14 YEARS
100	1.35	1.24	1.15	1.08	1.02	0.96	0.92
200	2.70	2.48	2.30	2.15	2.03	1.93	1.84
500	6.75	6.19	5.74	5.38	5.08	4.82	4.61
1000	13.51	12.38	11.48	10.75	10.15	9.65	9.22
2000	27.02	24.76	22.96	21.51	20.30	19.29	18.43
5000	67.55	61.90	57.41	53.77	50.76	48.23	46.08
6000	81.06	74.28	68.89	64.52	60.91	57.87	55.30
7000	94.57	86.66	80.38	75.27	71.06	67.52	64.52
8000	108.08	99.04	91.86	86.03	81.21	77.17	73.74
9000	121.59	111.42	103.34	96.78	91.36	86.81	82.95
10000	135.10	123.80	114.82	107.53	101.51	96.46	92.17
15000	202.64	185.70	172.24	161.30	152.27	144.69	138.25
20000	270.19	247.60	229.65	215.07	203.02	192.92	184.34
25000	337.74	309.50	287.06	268.84	253.78	241.15	230.42
30000	405.29	371.40	344.47	322.60	304.53	289.37	276.51
35000	472.84	433.30	401.88	376.37	355.29	337.60	322.59
40000	540.39	495.20	459.30	430.14	406.04	385.83	368.68
45000	607.93	557.10	516.71	483.91	456.80	434.06	414.76
50000	675.48	619.00	574.12	537.67	507.55	482.29	460.85
55000	743.03	680.90	631.53	591.44	558.31	530.52	506.93
60000	810.58	742.80	688.94	645.21	609.06	578.75	553.02
65000	878.13	804.70	746.36	698.98	659.82	626.98	599.10
70000	945.67	866.60	803.77	752.74	710.57	675.21	645.19
75000	1013.22	928.50	861.18	806.51	761.33	723.44	691.27
80000	1080.77	990.40	918.59	860.28	812.08	771.66	737.35
85000	1148.32	1052.30	976.00	914.05	862.84	819.89	783.44
90000	1215.87	1114.20	1033.42	967.81	913.59	868.12	829.52
95000	1283.42	1176.10	1090.83	1021.58	964.35	916.35	875.61
100000	1350.96	1238.00	1148.24	1075.35	1015.10	964.58	921.69
105000	1418.51	1299.90	1205.65	1129.12	1065.86	1012.81	967.78
110000	1486.06	1361.80	1263.07	1182.88	1116.61	1061.04	1013.86
120000	1621.16	1485.60	1377.89	1290.42	1218.12	1157.50	1106.03
130000	1756.25	1609.40	1492.71	1397.95	1319.63	1253.95	1198.20
140000	1891.35	1733.20	1607.54	1505.49	1421.14	1350.41	1290.37
150000	2026.45	1857.00	1722.36	1613.02	1522.65	1446.87	1382.54
160000	2161.54	1980.80	1837.19	1720.56	1624.16	1543.33	1474.71
170000	2296.64	2104.60	1952.01	1828.09	1725.67	1639.79	1566.88
180000	2431.74	2228.40	2066.83	1935.63	1827.18	1736.24	1659.05
190000	2566.83	2352.20	2181.66	2043.16	1928.70	1832.70	1751.22
200000	2701.93	2476.00	2296.48	2150.70	2030.21	1929.16	1843.39
210000	2837.02	2599.80	2411.31	2258.23	2131.72	2025.62	1935.56
220000	2972.12	2723.60	2526.13	2365.77	2233.23	2122.08	2027.72
230000	3107.22	2847.41	2640.95	2473.30	2334.74	2218.53	2119.89
240000	3242.31	2971.21	2755.78	2580.84	2436.25	2314.99	2212.06
250000	3377.41	3095.01	2870.60	2688.37	2537.76	2411.45	2304.23
260000	3512.51	3218.81	2985.43	2795.91	2639.27	2507.91	2396.40
270000	3647.60	3342.61	3100.25	2903.44	2740.78	2604.37	2488.57
280000	3782.70	3466.41	3215.08	3010.98	2842.29	2700.82	2580.74
290000	3917.80	3590.21	3329.90	3118.51	2943.80	2797.28	2672.91
300000	4052.89	3714.01	3444.72	3226.05	3045.31	2893.74	2765.08
310000	4187.99	3837.81	3559.55	3333.58	3146.82	2990.20	2857.25
320000	4323.08	3961.61	3674.37	3441.12	3248.33	3086.66	2949.42
330000	4458.18	4085.41	3789.20	3548.65	3349.84	3183.12	3041.59
340000	4593.28	4209.21	3904.02	3656.19	3451.35	3279.57	3133.76
350000	4728.37	4333.01	4018.84	3763.72	3552.86	3376.03	3225.93
400000	5403.86	4952.01	4592.96	4301.39	4060.41	3858.32	3686.77
450000	6079.34	5571.01	5167.09	4839.07	4567.96	4340.61	4147.62
500000	6754.82	6190.01	5741.21	5376.74	5075.51	4822.90	4608.47
550000	7430.30	6809.01	6315.33	5914.42	5583.06	5305.19	5069.31
600000	8105.78	7428.01	6889.45	6452.09	6090.62	5787.48	5530.16

6³/₄% **Monthly Payments**
necessary to amortize a loan

AMOUNT	15 YEARS	16 YEARS	17 YEARS	18 YEARS	19 YEARS	20 YEARS	21 YEARS
100	0.88	0.85	0.83	0.80	0.78	0.76	0.74
200	1.77	1.71	1.65	1.60	1.56	1.52	1.49
500	4.42	4.27	4.13	4.00	3.90	3.80	3.72
1000	8.85	8.53	8.25	8.01	7.79	7.60	7.43
2000	17.70	17.06	16.51	16.02	15.59	15.21	14.87
5000	44.25	42.65	41.27	40.05	38.97	38.02	37.17
6000	53.09	51.18	49.52	48.06	46.77	45.62	44.60
7000	61.94	59.72	57.77	56.07	54.56	53.23	52.03
8000	70.79	68.25	66.03	64.08	62.36	60.83	59.47
9000	79.64	76.78	74.28	72.09	70.15	68.43	66.90
10000	88.49	85.31	82.53	80.10	77.95	76.04	74.33
15000	132.74	127.96	123.80	120.14	116.92	114.05	111.50
20000	176.98	170.62	165.07	160.19	155.89	152.07	148.67
25000	221.23	213.27	206.33	200.24	194.86	190.09	185.84
30000	265.47	255.92	247.60	240.29	233.84	228.11	223.00
35000	309.72	298.58	288.86	280.34	272.81	266.13	260.17
40000	353.96	341.23	330.13	320.39	311.78	304.15	297.34
45000	398.21	383.89	371.40	360.43	350.75	342.16	334.50
50000	442.45	426.54	412.66	400.48	389.73	380.18	371.67
55000	486.70	469.19	453.93	440.53	428.70	418.20	408.84
60000	530.95	511.85	495.20	480.58	467.67	456.22	446.01
65000	575.19	554.50	536.46	520.63	506.65	494.24	483.17
70000	619.44	597.16	577.73	560.68	545.62	532.25	520.34
75000	663.68	639.81	618.99	600.72	584.59	570.27	557.51
80000	707.93	682.46	660.26	640.77	623.56	608.29	594.67
85000	752.17	725.12	701.53	680.82	662.54	646.31	631.84
90000	796.42	767.77	742.79	720.87	701.51	684.33	669.01
95000	840.66	810.43	784.06	760.92	740.48	722.35	706.18
100000	884.91	853.08	825.33	800.96	779.45	760.36	743.34
105000	929.15	895.73	866.59	841.01	818.43	798.38	780.51
110000	973.40	938.39	907.86	881.06	857.40	836.40	817.68
120000	1061.89	1023.70	990.39	961.16	935.35	912.44	892.01
130000	1150.38	1109.00	1072.92	1041.25	1013.29	988.47	966.35
140000	1238.87	1194.31	1155.46	1121.35	1091.24	1064.51	1040.68
150000	1327.36	1279.62	1237.99	1201.45	1169.18	1140.55	1115.01
160000	1415.86	1364.93	1320.52	1281.54	1247.13	1216.58	1189.35
170000	1504.35	1450.24	1403.06	1361.64	1325.07	1292.62	1263.68
180000	1592.84	1535.54	1485.59	1441.74	1403.02	1368.66	1338.02
190000	1681.33	1620.85	1568.12	1521.83	1480.96	1444.69	1412.35
200000	1769.82	1706.16	1650.65	1601.93	1558.91	1520.73	1486.69
210000	1858.31	1791.47	1733.19	1682.03	1636.85	1596.76	1561.02
220000	1946.80	1876.78	1815.72	1762.12	1714.80	1672.80	1635.35
230000	2035.29	1962.08	1898.25	1842.22	1792.75	1748.84	1709.69
240000	2123.78	2047.39	1980.78	1922.32	1870.69	1824.87	1784.02
250000	2212.27	2132.70	2063.32	2002.41	1948.64	1900.91	1858.36
260000	2300.76	2218.01	2145.85	2082.51	2026.58	1976.95	1932.69
270000	2389.26	2303.32	2228.38	2162.60	2104.53	2052.98	2007.03
280000	2477.75	2388.62	2310.91	2242.70	2182.47	2129.02	2081.36
290000	2566.24	2473.93	2393.45	2322.80	2260.42	2205.06	2155.69
300000	2654.73	2559.24	2475.98	2402.89	2338.36	2281.09	2230.03
310000	2743.22	2644.55	2558.51	2482.99	2416.31	2357.13	2304.36
320000	2831.71	2729.86	2641.05	2563.09	2494.25	2433.16	2378.70
330000	2920.20	2815.16	2723.58	2643.18	2572.20	2509.20	2453.03
340000	3008.69	2900.47	2806.11	2723.28	2650.15	2585.24	2527.37
350000	3097.18	2985.78	2888.64	2803.38	2728.09	2661.27	2601.70
400000	3539.64	3412.32	3301.31	3203.84	3117.82	3041.46	2973.37
450000	3982.09	3838.86	3713.97	3604.34	3507.55	3421.64	3345.04
500000	4424.55	4265.40	4126.63	4004.82	3897.27	3801.82	3716.72
550000	4867.00	4691.94	4539.30	4405.31	4287.00	4182.00	4088.39
600000	5309.46	5118.48	4951.96	4805.79	4676.73	4562.18	4460.06

34

Monthly Payments   6¾%
necessary to amortize a loan

AMOUNT	22 YEARS	23 YEARS	24 YEARS	25 YEARS	30 YEARS	35 YEARS	40 YEARS
100	0.73	0.71	0.70	0.69	0.65	0.62	0.60
200	1.46	1.43	1.40	1.38	1.30	1.24	1.21
500	3.64	3.57	3.51	3.45	3.24	3.11	3.02
1000	7.28	7.14	7.02	6.91	6.49	6.21	6.03
2000	14.56	14.29	14.04	13.82	12.97	12.43	12.07
5000	36.41	35.72	35.10	34.55	32.43	31.07	30.17
6000	43.69	42.86	42.12	41.45	38.92	37.28	36.20
7000	50.97	50.01	49.14	48.36	45.40	43.50	42.23
8000	58.25	57.15	56.17	55.27	51.89	49.71	48.27
9000	65.53	64.30	63.19	62.18	58.37	55.93	54.30
10000	72.81	71.44	70.21	69.09	64.86	62.14	60.34
15000	109.22	107.16	105.31	103.64	97.29	93.21	90.50
20000	145.62	142.88	140.41	138.18	129.72	124.28	120.67
25000	182.03	178.60	175.52	172.73	162.15	155.35	150.84
30000	218.43	214.32	210.62	207.27	194.58	186.42	181.01
35000	254.84	250.04	245.72	241.82	227.01	217.50	211.17
40000	291.24	285.77	280.83	276.36	259.44	248.57	241.34
45000	327.65	321.49	315.93	310.91	291.87	279.64	271.51
50000	364.05	357.21	351.04	345.46	324.30	310.71	301.68
55000	400.46	392.93	386.14	380.00	356.73	341.78	331.85
60000	436.86	428.65	421.24	414.55	389.16	372.85	362.01
65000	473.27	464.37	456.35	449.09	421.59	403.92	392.18
70000	509.67	500.09	491.45	483.64	454.02	434.99	422.35
75000	546.08	535.81	526.55	518.18	486.45	466.06	452.52
80000	582.48	571.53	561.66	552.73	518.88	497.13	482.69
85000	618.89	607.25	596.76	587.27	551.31	528.20	512.85
90000	655.29	642.97	631.86	621.82	583.74	559.27	543.02
95000	691.70	678.69	666.97	656.37	616.17	590.35	573.19
100000	728.11	714.41	702.07	690.91	648.60	621.42	603.36
105000	764.51	750.13	737.17	725.46	681.03	652.49	633.52
110000	800.92	785.86	772.28	760.00	713.46	683.56	663.69
120000	873.73	857.30	842.49	829.09	778.32	745.70	724.03
130000	946.54	928.74	912.69	898.18	843.18	807.84	784.36
140000	1019.35	1000.18	982.90	967.28	908.04	869.98	844.70
150000	1092.16	1071.62	1053.11	1036.37	972.90	932.12	905.04
160000	1164.97	1143.06	1123.31	1105.46	1037.76	994.27	965.37
170000	1237.78	1214.50	1193.52	1174.55	1102.62	1056.41	1025.71
180000	1310.59	1285.94	1263.73	1243.64	1167.48	1118.55	1086.04
190000	1383.40	1357.39	1333.94	1312.73	1232.34	1180.69	1146.38
200000	1456.21	1428.83	1404.14	1381.82	1297.20	1242.83	1206.71
210000	1529.02	1500.27	1474.35	1450.91	1362.06	1304.97	1267.05
220000	1601.83	1571.71	1544.56	1520.01	1426.92	1367.12	1327.39
230000	1674.64	1643.15	1614.76	1589.10	1491.78	1429.26	1387.72
240000	1747.45	1714.59	1684.97	1658.19	1556.64	1491.40	1448.06
250000	1820.26	1786.03	1755.18	1727.28	1621.50	1553.54	1508.39
260000	1893.07	1857.48	1825.38	1796.37	1686.36	1615.68	1568.73
270000	1965.88	1928.92	1895.59	1865.46	1751.21	1677.82	1629.06
280000	2038.69	2000.36	1965.80	1934.55	1816.07	1739.97	1689.40
290000	2111.70	2071.80	2036.01	2003.64	1880.93	1802.11	1749.73
300000	2184.32	2143.24	2106.21	2072.73	1945.79	1864.25	1810.07
310000	2257.13	2214.68	2176.42	2141.83	2010.65	1926.39	1870.41
320000	2329.94	2286.12	2246.63	2210.92	2075.51	1988.53	1930.74
330000	2402.75	2357.57	2316.83	2280.01	2140.37	2050.67	1991.08
340000	2475.56	2429.01	2387.04	2349.10	2205.23	2112.82	2051.41
350000	2548.37	2500.45	2457.25	2418.19	2270.09	2174.96	2111.75
400000	2912.42	2857.65	2808.28	2763.65	2594.39	2485.67	2413.43
450000	3276.47	3214.86	3159.32	3109.10	2918.69	2796.37	2715.11
500000	3640.53	3572.07	3510.36	3454.56	3242.99	3107.08	3016.78
550000	4004.58	3929.28	3861.39	3800.01	3567.29	3417.79	3318.46
600000	4368.63	4286.48	4212.43	4145.47	3891.59	3728.50	3620.14

7%

Monthly Payments
necessary to amortize a loan

AMOUNT	1 YEAR	2 YEARS	3 YEARS	4 YEARS	5 YEARS	6 YEARS	7 YEARS
100	8.65	4.48	3.09	2.39	1.98	1.70	1.51
200	17.31	8.95	6.18	4.79	3.96	3.41	3.02
500	43.26	22.39	15.44	11.97	9.90	8.52	7.55
1000	86.53	44.77	30.88	23.95	19.80	17.05	15.09
2000	173.05	89.55	61.75	47.89	39.60	34.10	30.19
5000	432.63	223.86	154.39	119.73	99.01	85.25	75.46
6000	519.16	268.64	185.26	143.68	118.81	102.29	90.56
7000	605.69	313.41	216.14	167.62	138.61	119.34	105.65
8000	692.21	358.18	247.02	191.57	158.41	136.39	120.74
9000	778.74	402.95	277.89	215.52	178.21	153.44	135.83
10000	865.27	447.73	308.77	239.46	198.01	170.49	150.93
15000	1297.90	671.59	463.16	359.19	297.02	255.74	226.39
20000	1730.53	895.45	617.54	478.92	396.02	340.98	301.85
25000	2163.17	1119.31	771.93	598.66	495.03	426.23	377.32
30000	2595.80	1343.18	926.31	718.39	594.04	511.47	452.78
35000	3028.44	1567.04	1080.70	838.12	693.04	596.72	528.24
40000	3461.07	1790.90	1235.08	957.85	792.05	681.96	603.71
45000	3893.70	2014.77	1389.47	1077.58	891.05	767.21	679.17
50000	4326.34	2238.63	1543.85	1197.31	990.06	852.45	754.63
55000	4758.97	2462.49	1698.24	1317.04	1089.07	937.70	830.10
60000	5191.60	2686.35	1852.63	1436.77	1188.07	1022.94	905.56
65000	5624.24	2910.22	2007.01	1556.51	1287.08	1108.19	981.02
70000	6056.87	3134.08	2161.40	1676.24	1386.08	1193.43	1056.49
75000	6489.51	3357.94	2315.78	1795.97	1485.09	1278.68	1131.95
80000	6922.14	3581.81	2470.17	1915.70	1584.10	1363.92	1207.41
85000	7354.77	3805.67	2624.55	2035.43	1683.10	1449.17	1282.88
90000	7787.41	4029.53	2778.94	2155.16	1782.11	1534.41	1358.34
95000	8220.04	4253.40	2933.32	2274.89	1881.11	1619.66	1433.80
100000	8652.67	4477.26	3087.71	2394.62	1980.12	1704.90	1509.27
105000	9085.31	4701.12	3242.10	2514.36	2079.13	1790.15	1584.73
110000	9517.94	4924.98	3396.48	2634.09	2178.13	1875.39	1660.19
120000	10383.21	5372.71	3705.25	2873.55	2376.14	2045.88	1811.12
130000	11248.48	5820.44	4014.02	3113.01	2574.16	2216.37	1962.05
140000	12113.74	6268.16	4322.79	3352.47	2772.17	2386.86	2112.98
150000	12979.01	6715.89	4631.56	3591.94	2970.18	2557.35	2263.90
160000	13844.28	7163.61	4940.34	3831.40	3168.19	2727.84	2414.83
170000	14709.55	7611.34	5249.11	4070.86	3366.20	2898.33	2565.76
180000	15574.81	8059.06	5557.88	4310.32	3564.22	3068.82	2716.68
190000	16440.08	8506.79	5866.65	4549.79	3762.23	3239.31	2867.61
200000	17305.35	8954.52	6175.42	4789.25	3960.24	3409.80	3018.54
210000	18170.62	9402.24	6484.19	5028.71	4158.25	3580.29	3169.46
220000	19035.88	9849.97	6792.96	5268.17	4356.26	3750.78	3320.39
230000	19901.15	10297.69	7101.73	5507.64	4554.28	3921.27	3471.32
240000	20766.42	10745.42	7410.50	5747.10	4752.29	4091.76	3622.24
250000	21631.69	11193.14	7719.27	5986.56	4950.30	4262.25	3773.17
260000	22496.95	11640.87	8028.05	6226.02	5148.31	4432.74	3924.10
270000	23362.22	12088.60	8336.82	6465.49	5346.32	4603.23	4075.02
280000	24227.49	12536.32	8645.59	6704.95	5544.34	4773.72	4225.95
290000	25092.76	12984.05	8954.36	6944.41	5742.35	4944.21	4376.88
300000	25958.02	13431.77	9263.13	7183.87	5940.36	5114.70	4527.80
310000	26823.29	13879.50	9571.90	7423.34	6138.37	5285.19	4678.73
320000	27688.56	14327.23	9880.67	7662.80	6336.38	5455.68	4829.66
330000	28553.83	14774.95	10189.44	7902.26	6534.40	5626.17	4980.58
340000	29419.09	15222.68	10498.21	8141.72	6732.41	5796.66	5131.51
350000	30284.36	15670.40	10806.98	8381.19	6930.42	5967.15	5282.44
400000	34610.70	17909.03	12350.84	9578.50	7920.48	6819.60	6037.07
450000	38937.04	20147.66	13894.69	10775.81	8910.54	7672.05	6791.71
500000	43263.37	22386.29	15438.55	11973.12	9900.60	8524.50	7546.34
550000	47589.71	24624.92	16982.40	13170.43	10890.66	9376.95	8300.97
600000	51916.05	26863.55	18526.26	14367.75	11880.72	10229.40	9055.61

Monthly Payments 7%
necessary to amortize a loan

AMOUNT	8 YEARS	9 YEARS	10 YEARS	11 YEARS	12 YEARS	13 YEARS	14 YEARS
100	1.36	1.25	1.16	1.09	1.03	0.98	0.94
200	2.73	2.50	2.32	2.18	2.06	1.96	1.87
500	6.82	6.25	5.81	5.44	5.14	4.89	4.68
1000	13.63	12.51	11.61	10.88	10.28	9.78	9.35
2000	27.27	25.01	23.22	21.77	20.57	19.56	18.71
5000	68.17	62.53	58.05	54.42	51.42	48.90	46.77
6000	81.80	75.04	69.67	65.30	61.70	58.68	56.12
7000	95.44	87.54	81.28	76.19	71.99	68.47	65.48
8000	109.07	100.05	92.89	87.07	82.27	78.25	74.83
9000	122.70	112.56	104.50	97.96	92.55	88.03	84.19
10000	136.34	125.06	116.11	108.84	102.84	97.81	93.54
15000	204.51	187.59	174.16	163.26	154.26	146.71	140.31
20000	272.67	250.13	232.22	217.68	205.68	195.61	187.08
25000	340.84	312.66	290.27	272.10	257.10	244.52	233.85
30000	409.01	375.19	348.33	326.52	308.51	293.42	280.62
35000	477.18	437.72	406.38	380.94	359.93	342.33	327.39
40000	545.35	500.25	464.43	435.36	411.35	391.23	374.16
45000	613.52	562.78	522.49	489.78	462.77	440.13	420.93
50000	681.69	625.31	580.54	544.21	514.19	489.04	467.70
55000	749.85	687.85	638.60	598.63	565.61	537.94	514.47
60000	818.02	750.38	696.65	653.05	617.03	586.84	561.24
65000	886.19	812.91	754.71	707.47	668.45	635.75	608.01
70000	954.36	875.44	812.76	761.89	719.87	684.65	654.78
75000	1022.53	937.97	870.81	816.31	771.29	733.56	701.55
80000	1090.70	1000.50	928.87	870.73	822.70	782.46	748.32
85000	1158.87	1063.03	986.92	925.15	874.12	831.36	795.09
90000	1227.03	1125.56	1044.98	979.57	925.54	880.27	841.86
95000	1295.20	1188.10	1103.03	1033.99	976.96	929.17	888.63
100000	1363.37	1250.63	1161.08	1088.41	1028.38	978.07	935.40
105000	1431.54	1313.16	1219.14	1142.83	1079.80	1026.98	982.17
110000	1499.71	1375.69	1277.19	1197.25	1131.22	1075.88	1028.94
120000	1636.05	1500.75	1393.30	1306.09	1234.06	1173.69	1122.48
130000	1772.38	1625.82	1509.41	1414.93	1336.90	1271.50	1216.02
140000	1908.72	1750.88	1625.52	1523.77	1439.73	1369.30	1309.56
150000	2045.06	1875.94	1741.63	1632.62	1542.57	1467.11	1403.10
160000	2181.39	2001.00	1857.74	1741.46	1645.41	1564.92	1496.64
170000	2317.73	2126.07	1973.84	1850.30	1748.25	1662.73	1590.18
180000	2454.07	2251.13	2089.95	1959.14	1851.09	1760.53	1683.72
190000	2590.41	2376.19	2206.06	2067.98	1953.92	1858.34	1777.26
200000	2726.74	2501.26	2322.17	2176.82	2056.76	1956.15	1870.80
210000	2863.08	2626.32	2438.28	2285.66	2159.60	2053.96	1964.34
220000	2999.42	2751.38	2554.39	2394.50	2262.44	2151.76	2057.88
230000	3135.75	2876.44	2670.50	2503.34	2365.28	2249.57	2151.42
240000	3272.09	3001.51	2786.60	2612.18	2468.11	2347.38	2244.96
250000	3408.43	3126.57	2902.71	2721.03	2570.95	2445.19	2338.50
260000	3544.77	3251.63	3018.82	2829.87	2673.79	2542.99	2432.04
270000	3681.10	3376.69	3134.93	2938.71	2776.63	2640.80	2525.58
280000	3817.44	3501.76	3251.04	3047.55	2879.47	2738.61	2619.12
290000	3953.78	3626.82	3367.15	3156.39	2982.31	2836.42	2712.66
300000	4090.12	3751.88	3483.25	3265.23	3085.14	2934.22	2806.20
310000	4226.45	3876.95	3599.36	3374.07	3187.98	3032.03	2899.74
320000	4362.79	4002.01	3715.47	3482.91	3290.82	3129.84	2993.28
330000	4499.13	4127.07	3831.58	3591.75	3393.66	3227.64	3086.82
340000	4635.46	4252.13	3947.69	3700.59	3496.50	3325.45	3180.36
350000	4771.80	4377.20	4063.80	3809.44	3599.33	3423.26	3273.90
400000	5453.49	5002.51	4644.34	4353.64	4113.52	3912.30	3741.60
450000	6135.17	5627.82	5224.88	4897.85	4627.71	4401.33	4209.30
500000	6816.86	6253.14	5805.42	5442.05	5141.91	4890.37	4677.00
550000	7498.54	6878.45	6385.97	5986.26	5656.10	5379.41	5144.70
600000	8180.23	7503.77	6966.51	6530.46	6170.29	5868.44	5612.40

7%

Monthly Payments
necessary to amortize a loan

AMOUNT	15 YEARS	16 YEARS	17 YEARS	18 YEARS	19 YEARS	20 YEARS	21 YEARS
100	0.90	0.87	0.84	0.82	0.79	0.78	0.76
200	1.80	1.73	1.68	1.63	1.59	1.55	1.52
500	4.49	4.34	4.20	4.08	3.97	3.88	3.79
1000	8.99	8.67	8.40	8.16	7.94	7.75	7.58
2000	17.98	17.34	16.79	16.31	15.88	15.51	15.17
5000	44.94	43.36	41.98	40.78	39.71	38.76	37.92
6000	53.93	52.03	50.38	48.93	47.65	46.52	45.51
7000	62.92	60.70	58.78	57.09	55.59	54.27	53.09
8000	71.91	69.38	67.17	65.24	63.54	62.02	60.68
9000	80.89	78.05	75.57	73.40	71.48	69.78	68.26
10000	89.88	86.72	83.97	81.55	79.42	77.53	75.85
15000	134.82	130.08	125.95	122.33	119.13	116.29	113.77
20000	179.77	173.44	167.93	163.10	158.84	155.06	151.69
25000	224.71	216.80	209.92	203.88	198.55	193.82	189.62
30000	269.65	260.16	251.90	244.65	238.26	232.59	227.54
35000	314.59	303.52	293.88	285.43	277.97	271.35	265.47
40000	359.53	346.88	335.86	326.20	317.68	310.12	303.39
45000	404.47	390.24	377.85	366.98	357.39	348.88	341.31
50000	449.41	433.60	419.83	407.75	397.10	387.65	379.24
55000	494.36	476.96	461.81	448.53	436.81	426.41	417.16
60000	539.30	520.32	503.80	489.30	476.52	465.18	455.08
65000	584.24	563.69	545.78	530.08	516.23	503.94	493.01
70000	629.18	607.05	587.76	570.85	555.93	542.71	530.93
75000	674.12	650.41	629.75	611.63	595.64	581.47	568.85
80000	719.06	693.77	671.73	652.40	635.35	620.24	606.78
85000	764.00	737.13	713.71	693.18	675.06	659.00	644.70
90000	808.95	780.49	755.69	733.95	714.77	697.77	682.62
95000	853.89	823.85	797.68	774.73	754.48	736.53	720.55
100000	898.83	867.21	839.66	815.50	794.19	775.30	758.47
105000	943.77	910.57	881.64	856.28	833.90	814.06	796.40
110000	988.71	953.93	923.63	897.05	873.61	852.83	834.32
120000	1078.59	1040.65	1007.59	978.60	953.03	930.36	910.17
130000	1168.48	1127.37	1091.56	1060.15	1032.45	1007.89	986.01
140000	1258.36	1214.09	1175.52	1141.70	1111.87	1085.42	1061.86
150000	1348.24	1300.81	1259.49	1223.25	1191.29	1162.95	1137.71
160000	1438.13	1387.53	1343.46	1304.80	1270.71	1240.48	1213.55
170000	1528.01	1474.25	1427.42	1386.35	1350.13	1318.01	1289.40
180000	1617.89	1560.97	1511.39	1467.90	1429.55	1395.54	1365.25
190000	1707.77	1647.70	1595.36	1549.45	1508.97	1473.07	1441.10
200000	1797.66	1734.42	1679.32	1631.00	1588.38	1550.60	1516.94
210000	1887.54	1821.14	1763.29	1712.55	1667.80	1628.13	1592.79
220000	1977.42	1907.86	1847.25	1794.10	1747.22	1705.66	1668.64
230000	2067.31	1994.58	1931.22	1875.65	1826.64	1783.19	1744.49
240000	2157.19	2081.30	2015.19	1957.21	1906.06	1860.72	1820.33
250000	2247.07	2168.02	2099.15	2038.76	1985.48	1938.25	1896.18
260000	2336.95	2254.74	2183.12	2120.31	2064.90	2015.78	1972.03
270000	2426.84	2341.46	2267.08	2201.86	2144.32	2093.31	2047.87
280000	2516.72	2428.18	2351.05	2283.41	2223.74	2170.84	2123.72
290000	2606.60	2514.90	2435.02	2364.96	2303.16	2248.37	2199.57
300000	2696.48	2601.62	2518.98	2446.51	2382.58	2325.90	2275.42
310000	2786.37	2688.34	2602.95	2528.06	2462.00	2403.43	2351.26
320000	2876.25	2775.07	2686.91	2609.61	2541.42	2480.96	2427.11
330000	2966.13	2861.79	2770.88	2691.16	2620.83	2558.49	2502.96
340000	3056.02	2948.51	2854.85	2772.71	2700.25	2636.02	2578.80
350000	3145.90	3035.23	2938.81	2854.26	2779.67	2713.55	2654.65
400000	3595.31	3468.83	3358.64	3262.01	3176.77	3101.20	3033.89
450000	4044.73	3902.44	3778.47	3669.76	3573.87	3488.85	3413.12
500000	4494.14	4336.04	4198.30	4077.51	3970.96	3876.49	3792.36
550000	4943.56	4769.64	4618.13	4485.26	4368.06	4264.14	4171.59
600000	5392.97	5203.25	5037.96	4893.01	4765.15	4651.79	4550.83

AMOUNT	22 YEARS	23 YEARS	24 YEARS	25 YEARS	30 YEARS	35 YEARS	40 YEARS
100	0.74	0.73	0.72	0.71	0.67	0.64	0.62
200	1.49	1.46	1.44	1.41	1.33	1.28	1.24
500	3.72	3.65	3.59	3.53	3.33	3.19	3.11
1000	7.43	7.30	7.18	7.07	6.65	6.39	6.21
2000	14.87	14.60	14.36	14.14	13.31	12.78	12.43
5000	37.17	36.50	35.89	35.34	33.27	31.94	31.07
6000	44.61	43.80	43.07	42.41	39.92	38.33	37.29
7000	52.04	51.09	50.24	49.47	46.57	44.72	43.50
8000	59.47	58.39	57.42	56.54	53.22	51.11	49.71
9000	66.91	65.69	64.60	63.61	59.88	57.50	55.93
10000	74.34	72.99	71.78	70.68	66.53	63.89	62.14
15000	111.51	109.49	107.66	106.02	99.80	95.83	93.21
20000	148.68	145.98	143.55	141.36	133.06	127.77	124.29
25000	185.86	182.48	179.44	176.69	166.33	159.71	155.36
30000	223.03	218.98	215.33	212.03	199.59	191.66	186.43
35000	260.20	255.47	251.22	247.37	232.86	223.60	217.50
40000	297.37	291.97	287.10	282.71	266.12	255.54	248.57
45000	334.54	328.46	322.99	318.05	299.39	287.49	279.64
50000	371.71	364.96	358.88	353.39	332.65	319.43	310.72
55000	408.88	401.46	394.77	388.73	365.92	351.37	341.79
60000	446.05	437.95	430.66	424.07	399.18	383.31	372.86
65000	483.23	474.45	466.54	459.41	432.45	415.26	403.93
70000	520.40	510.94	502.43	494.75	465.71	447.20	435.00
75000	557.57	547.44	538.32	530.08	498.98	479.14	466.07
80000	594.74	583.94	574.21	565.42	532.24	511.09	497.15
85000	631.91	620.43	610.10	600.76	565.51	543.03	528.22
90000	669.08	656.93	645.98	636.10	598.77	574.97	559.29
95000	706.25	693.42	681.87	671.44	632.04	606.91	590.36
100000	743.42	729.92	717.76	706.78	665.30	638.86	621.43
105000	780.60	766.42	753.65	742.12	698.57	670.80	652.50
110000	817.77	802.91	789.54	777.46	731.83	702.74	683.57
120000	892.11	875.90	861.31	848.14	798.36	766.63	745.72
130000	966.45	948.89	933.09	918.81	864.89	830.51	807.86
140000	1040.79	1021.89	1004.86	989.49	931.42	894.40	870.00
150000	1115.14	1094.88	1076.64	1060.17	997.95	958.28	932.15
160000	1189.48	1167.87	1148.42	1130.85	1064.48	1022.17	994.29
170000	1263.82	1240.86	1220.19	1201.52	1131.01	1086.06	1056.43
180000	1338.16	1313.85	1291.97	1272.20	1197.54	1149.94	1118.58
190000	1412.51	1386.85	1363.74	1342.88	1264.07	1213.83	1180.72
200000	1486.85	1459.84	1435.52	1413.56	1330.60	1277.71	1242.86
210000	1561.19	1532.83	1507.30	1484.24	1397.14	1341.60	1305.01
220000	1635.53	1605.82	1579.07	1554.91	1463.67	1405.48	1367.15
230000	1709.88	1678.81	1650.85	1625.59	1530.20	1469.37	1429.29
240000	1784.22	1751.81	1722.62	1696.27	1596.73	1533.26	1491.44
250000	1858.56	1824.80	1794.40	1766.95	1663.26	1597.14	1553.58
260000	1932.90	1897.79	1866.17	1837.63	1729.79	1661.03	1615.72
270000	2007.25	1970.78	1937.95	1908.30	1796.32	1724.91	1677.86
280000	2081.59	2043.77	2009.73	1978.98	1862.85	1788.80	1740.01
290000	2155.93	2116.77	2081.50	2049.66	1929.38	1852.68	1802.15
300000	2230.27	2189.76	2153.28	2120.34	1995.91	1916.57	1864.29
310000	2304.61	2262.75	2225.05	2191.02	2062.44	1980.45	1926.44
320000	2378.96	2335.74	2296.83	2261.69	2128.97	2044.34	1988.58
330000	2453.30	2408.73	2368.61	2332.37	2195.50	2108.23	2050.72
340000	2527.64	2481.73	2440.38	2403.05	2262.03	2172.11	2112.87
350000	2601.98	2554.72	2512.16	2473.73	2328.56	2236.00	2175.01
400000	2973.70	2919.68	2871.04	2827.12	2661.21	2555.43	2485.73
450000	3345.41	3284.64	3229.92	3180.51	2993.86	2874.85	2796.44
500000	3717.12	3649.60	3588.80	3533.90	3326.51	3194.28	3107.16
550000	4088.83	4014.56	3947.68	3887.29	3659.16	3513.71	3417.87
600000	4460.54	4379.52	4306.56	4240.68	3991.81	3833.14	3728.59

7¼% Monthly Payments
necessary to amortize a loan

AMOUNT	1 YEAR	2 YEARS	3 YEARS	4 YEARS	5 YEARS	6 YEARS	7 YEARS
100	8.66	4.49	3.10	2.41	1.99	1.72	1.52
200	17.33	8.98	6.20	4.81	3.98	3.43	3.04
500	43.32	22.44	15.50	12.03	9.96	8.58	7.61
1000	86.64	44.89	30.99	24.06	19.92	17.17	15.22
2000	173.28	89.77	61.98	48.12	39.84	34.34	30.43
5000	433.21	224.43	154.96	120.31	99.60	85.85	76.08
6000	519.85	269.32	185.95	144.37	119.52	103.02	91.29
7000	606.49	314.20	216.94	168.44	139.44	120.19	106.51
8000	693.14	359.09	247.93	192.50	159.35	137.35	121.72
9000	779.78	403.97	278.92	216.56	179.27	154.52	136.94
10000	866.42	448.86	309.92	240.62	199.19	171.69	152.15
15000	1299.63	673.29	464.87	360.94	298.79	257.54	228.23
20000	1732.84	897.72	619.83	481.25	398.39	343.39	304.30
25000	2166.05	1122.15	774.79	601.56	497.98	429.23	380.38
30000	2599.26	1346.58	929.75	721.87	597.58	515.08	456.46
35000	3032.47	1571.01	1084.70	842.18	697.18	600.93	532.53
40000	3465.68	1795.44	1239.66	962.50	796.77	686.77	608.61
45000	3898.89	2019.87	1394.62	1082.81	896.37	772.62	684.68
50000	4332.10	2244.30	1549.58	1203.12	995.97	858.47	760.76
55000	4765.31	2468.73	1704.53	1323.43	1095.56	944.31	836.84
60000	5198.52	2693.16	1859.49	1443.74	1195.16	1030.16	912.91
65000	5631.73	2917.59	2014.45	1564.06	1294.76	1116.00	988.99
70000	6064.94	3142.02	2169.41	1684.37	1394.36	1201.85	1065.06
75000	6498.15	3366.45	2324.36	1804.68	1493.95	1287.70	1141.14
80000	6931.36	3590.88	2479.32	1924.99	1593.55	1373.54	1217.21
85000	7364.57	3815.31	2634.28	2045.30	1693.15	1459.39	1293.29
90000	7797.78	4039.74	2789.24	2165.62	1792.74	1545.24	1369.37
95000	8230.99	4264.17	2944.20	2285.93	1892.34	1631.08	1445.44
100000	8664.20	4488.60	3099.15	2406.24	1991.94	1716.93	1521.52
105000	9097.41	4713.03	3254.11	2526.55	2091.53	1802.78	1597.59
110000	9530.62	4937.46	3409.07	2646.86	2191.13	1888.62	1673.67
120000	10397.04	5386.32	3718.98	2887.49	2390.32	2060.32	1825.82
130000	11263.47	5835.18	4028.90	3128.11	2589.52	2232.01	1977.97
140000	12129.89	6284.04	4338.81	3368.74	2788.71	2403.70	2130.13
150000	12996.31	6732.90	4648.73	3609.36	2987.90	2575.40	2282.28
160000	13862.73	7181.76	4958.64	3849.98	3187.10	2747.09	2434.43
170000	14729.15	7630.62	5268.56	4090.61	3386.29	2918.78	2586.58
180000	15595.57	8079.48	5578.48	4331.23	3585.49	3090.48	2738.73
190000	16461.99	8528.34	5888.39	4571.86	3784.68	3262.17	2890.89
200000	17328.41	8977.20	6198.31	4812.48	3983.87	3433.86	3043.04
210000	18194.83	9426.06	6508.22	5053.10	4183.07	3605.55	3195.19
220000	19061.25	9874.92	6818.14	5293.73	4382.26	3777.25	3347.34
230000	19927.67	10323.78	7128.05	5534.35	4581.45	3948.94	3499.49
240000	20794.09	10772.64	7437.97	5774.98	4780.65	4120.63	3651.64
250000	21660.51	11221.50	7747.88	6015.60	4979.84	4292.33	3803.80
260000	22526.93	11670.36	8057.80	6256.22	5179.03	4464.02	3955.95
270000	23393.35	12119.22	8367.71	6496.85	5378.23	4635.71	4108.10
280000	24259.77	12568.08	8677.63	6737.47	5577.42	4807.41	4260.25
290000	25126.19	13016.94	8987.54	6978.10	5776.61	4979.10	4412.40
300000	25992.61	13465.80	9297.46	7218.72	5975.81	5150.79	4564.56
310000	26859.03	13914.66	9607.37	7459.34	6175.00	5322.48	4716.71
320000	27725.45	14363.52	9917.29	7699.97	6374.20	5494.18	4868.86
330000	28591.87	14812.38	10227.20	7940.59	6573.39	5665.87	5021.01
340000	29458.29	15261.24	10537.12	8181.22	6772.58	5837.56	5173.16
350000	30324.71	15710.10	10847.04	8421.84	6971.78	6009.26	5325.31
400000	34656.82	17954.40	12396.61	9624.96	7967.74	6867.72	6086.07
450000	38988.92	20198.70	13946.19	10828.08	8963.71	7726.19	6846.83
500000	43321.02	22443.00	15495.76	12031.20	9959.68	8584.65	7607.59
550000	47653.12	24687.30	17045.34	13234.32	10955.65	9443.12	8368.35
600000	51985.22	26931.60	18594.92	14437.44	11951.62	10301.58	9129.11

Monthly Payments 7¼%

necessary to amortize a loan

AMOUNT	8 YEARS	9 YEARS	10 YEARS	11 YEARS	12 YEARS	13 YEARS	14 YEARS
100	1.38	1.26	1.17	1.10	1.04	0.99	0.95
200	2.75	2.53	2.35	2.20	2.08	1.98	1.90
500	6.88	6.32	5.87	5.51	5.21	4.96	4.75
1000	13.76	12.63	11.74	11.02	10.42	9.92	9.49
2000	27.52	25.27	23.48	22.03	20.84	19.83	18.98
5000	68.79	63.17	58.70	55.08	52.09	49.58	47.46
6000	82.55	75.80	70.44	66.09	62.51	59.50	56.95
7000	96.31	88.43	82.18	77.11	72.92	69.42	66.45
8000	110.07	101.07	93.92	88.12	83.34	79.33	75.94
9000	123.83	113.70	105.66	99.14	93.76	89.25	85.43
10000	137.58	126.33	117.40	110.16	104.18	99.17	94.92
15000	206.38	189.50	176.10	165.23	156.26	148.75	142.38
20000	275.17	252.67	234.80	220.31	208.35	198.33	189.84
25000	343.96	315.83	293.50	275.39	260.44	247.92	237.30
30000	412.75	379.00	352.20	330.47	312.53	297.50	284.77
35000	481.55	442.16	410.90	385.55	364.61	347.08	332.23
40000	550.34	505.33	469.60	440.62	416.70	396.67	379.69
45000	619.13	568.50	528.30	495.70	468.79	446.25	427.15
50000	687.92	631.66	587.01	550.78	520.88	495.84	474.61
55000	756.72	694.83	645.71	605.86	572.97	545.42	522.07
60000	825.51	758.00	704.41	660.94	625.05	595.00	569.53
65000	894.30	821.16	763.11	716.01	677.14	644.59	616.99
70000	963.09	884.33	821.81	771.09	729.23	694.17	664.45
75000	1031.88	947.50	880.51	826.17	781.32	743.75	711.91
80000	1100.68	1010.66	939.21	881.25	833.40	793.34	759.37
85000	1169.47	1073.83	997.91	936.33	885.49	842.92	806.83
90000	1238.26	1136.99	1056.61	991.40	937.58	892.50	854.30
95000	1307.05	1200.16	1115.31	1046.48	989.67	942.09	901.76
100000	1375.85	1263.33	1174.01	1101.56	1041.76	991.67	949.22
105000	1444.64	1326.49	1232.71	1156.64	1093.84	1041.25	996.68
110000	1513.43	1389.66	1291.41	1211.72	1145.93	1090.84	1044.14
120000	1651.02	1515.99	1408.81	1321.87	1250.11	1190.01	1139.06
130000	1788.60	1642.33	1526.21	1432.03	1354.28	1289.17	1233.98
140000	1926.18	1768.66	1643.61	1542.19	1458.46	1388.34	1328.90
150000	2063.77	1894.99	1761.02	1652.34	1562.63	1487.51	1423.83
160000	2201.35	2021.33	1878.42	1762.50	1666.81	1586.67	1518.75
170000	2338.94	2147.66	1995.82	1872.65	1770.98	1685.84	1613.67
180000	2476.52	2273.99	2113.22	1982.81	1875.16	1785.01	1708.59
190000	2614.11	2400.32	2230.62	2092.97	1979.34	1884.18	1803.51
200000	2751.69	2526.66	2348.02	2203.12	2083.51	1983.34	1898.44
210000	2889.28	2652.99	2465.42	2313.28	2187.69	2082.51	1993.36
220000	3026.86	2779.32	2582.82	2423.43	2291.86	2181.68	2088.28
230000	3164.45	2905.65	2700.22	2533.59	2396.04	2280.84	2183.20
240000	3302.03	3031.99	2817.62	2643.75	2500.21	2380.01	2278.12
250000	3439.62	3158.32	2935.03	2753.90	2604.39	2479.18	2373.04
260000	3577.20	3284.65	3052.43	2864.06	2708.57	2578.34	2467.97
270000	3714.78	3410.98	3169.83	2974.21	2812.74	2677.51	2562.89
280000	3852.37	3537.32	3287.23	3084.37	2916.92	2776.68	2657.81
290000	3989.95	3663.65	3404.63	3194.53	3021.09	2875.85	2752.73
300000	4127.54	3789.98	3522.03	3304.68	3125.27	2975.01	2847.65
310000	4265.12	3916.32	3639.43	3414.84	3229.44	3074.18	2942.57
320000	4402.71	4042.65	3756.83	3524.99	3333.62	3173.35	3037.50
330000	4540.29	4168.98	3874.23	3635.15	3437.79	3272.51	3132.42
340000	4677.88	4295.31	3991.64	3745.31	3541.97	3371.68	3227.34
350000	4815.46	4421.65	4109.04	3855.46	3646.15	3470.85	3322.26
400000	5503.38	5053.31	4696.04	4406.24	4167.02	3966.68	3796.87
450000	6191.31	5684.97	5283.05	4957.02	4687.90	4462.52	4271.48
500000	6879.23	6316.64	5870.05	5507.80	5208.78	4958.36	4746.09
550000	7567.15	6948.30	6457.06	6058.58	5729.66	5454.19	5220.70
600000	8255.08	7579.97	7044.06	6609.37	6250.53	5950.03	5695.31

7¼%

Monthly Payments
necessary to amortize a loan

AMOUNT	15 YEARS	16 YEARS	17 YEARS	18 YEARS	19 YEARS	20 YEARS	21 YEARS
100	0.91	0.88	0.85	0.83	0.81	0.79	0.77
200	1.83	1.76	1.71	1.66	1.62	1.58	1.55
500	4.56	4.41	4.27	4.15	4.05	3.95	3.87
1000	9.13	8.81	8.54	8.30	8.09	7.90	7.74
2000	18.26	17.63	17.08	16.60	16.18	15.81	15.47
5000	45.64	44.07	42.71	41.51	40.45	39.52	38.69
6000	54.77	52.89	51.25	49.81	48.54	47.42	46.42
7000	63.90	61.70	59.79	58.11	56.63	55.33	54.16
8000	73.03	70.52	68.33	66.41	64.73	63.23	61.90
9000	82.16	79.33	76.87	74.72	72.82	71.13	69.64
10000	91.29	88.15	85.41	83.02	80.91	79.04	77.37
15000	136.93	132.22	128.12	124.53	121.36	118.56	116.06
20000	182.57	176.29	170.82	166.03	161.81	158.08	154.75
25000	228.22	220.36	213.53	207.54	202.27	197.59	193.44
30000	273.86	264.44	256.24	249.05	242.72	237.11	232.12
35000	319.50	308.51	298.94	290.56	283.17	276.63	270.81
40000	365.15	352.58	341.65	332.07	323.63	316.15	309.50
45000	410.79	396.66	384.35	373.58	364.08	355.67	348.19
50000	456.43	440.73	427.06	415.09	404.53	395.19	386.87
55000	502.07	484.80	469.77	456.59	444.99	434.71	425.56
60000	547.72	528.87	512.47	498.10	485.44	474.23	464.25
65000	593.36	572.95	555.18	539.61	525.89	513.74	502.94
70000	639.00	617.02	597.89	581.12	566.35	553.26	541.62
75000	684.65	661.09	640.59	622.63	606.80	592.78	580.31
80000	730.29	705.17	683.30	664.14	647.25	632.30	619.00
85000	775.93	749.24	726.00	705.65	687.71	671.82	657.68
90000	821.58	793.31	768.71	747.15	728.16	711.34	696.37
95000	867.22	837.38	811.42	788.66	768.61	750.86	735.06
100000	912.86	881.46	854.12	830.17	809.07	790.38	773.75
105000	958.51	925.53	896.83	871.68	849.52	829.89	812.43
110000	1004.15	969.60	939.53	913.19	889.97	869.41	851.12
120000	1095.44	1057.75	1024.95	996.21	970.88	948.45	928.50
130000	1186.72	1145.89	1110.36	1079.22	1051.79	1027.49	1005.87
140000	1278.01	1234.04	1195.77	1162.24	1132.69	1106.53	1083.25
150000	1369.29	1322.19	1281.18	1245.26	1213.60	1185.56	1160.62
160000	1460.58	1410.33	1366.60	1328.28	1294.51	1264.60	1237.99
170000	1551.87	1498.48	1452.01	1411.29	1375.42	1343.64	1315.37
180000	1643.15	1586.62	1537.42	1494.31	1456.32	1422.68	1392.74
190000	1734.44	1674.77	1622.83	1577.33	1537.23	1501.71	1470.12
200000	1825.73	1762.92	1708.24	1660.34	1618.14	1580.75	1547.49
210000	1917.01	1851.06	1793.66	1743.36	1699.04	1659.79	1624.87
220000	2008.30	1939.21	1879.07	1826.38	1779.95	1738.83	1702.24
230000	2099.58	2027.35	1964.48	1909.40	1860.86	1817.86	1779.62
240000	2190.87	2115.50	2049.89	1992.41	1941.76	1896.90	1856.99
250000	2282.16	2203.64	2135.31	2075.43	2022.67	1975.94	1934.37
260000	2373.44	2291.79	2220.72	2158.45	2103.58	2054.98	2011.74
270000	2464.73	2379.94	2306.13	2241.46	2184.48	2134.02	2089.12
280000	2556.02	2468.08	2391.54	2324.48	2265.39	2213.05	2166.49
290000	2647.30	2556.23	2476.95	2407.50	2346.30	2292.09	2243.87
300000	2738.59	2644.37	2562.37	2490.52	2427.20	2371.13	2321.24
310000	2829.87	2732.52	2647.78	2573.53	2508.11	2450.17	2398.62
320000	2921.16	2820.66	2733.19	2656.55	2589.02	2529.20	2475.99
330000	3012.45	2908.81	2818.60	2739.57	2669.92	2608.24	2553.36
340000	3103.73	2996.96	2904.01	2822.59	2750.83	2687.28	2630.74
350000	3195.02	3085.10	2989.43	2905.60	2831.74	2766.32	2708.11
400000	3651.45	3525.83	3416.49	3320.69	3236.27	3161.50	3094.99
450000	4107.88	3966.56	3843.55	3735.79	3640.80	3556.69	3481.86
500000	4564.31	4407.29	4270.61	4150.86	4045.34	3951.88	3868.73
550000	5020.75	4848.02	4697.67	4565.95	4449.87	4347.07	4255.61
600000	5477.18	5288.75	5124.73	4981.03	4854.41	4742.26	4642.48

Monthly Payments 7¼%

necessary to amortize a loan

AMOUNT	22 YEARS	23 YEARS	24 YEARS	25 YEARS	30 YEARS	35 YEARS	40 YEARS
100	0.76	0.75	0.73	0.72	0.68	0.66	0.64
200	1.52	1.49	1.47	1.45	1.36	1.31	1.28
500	3.79	3.73	3.67	3.61	3.41	3.28	3.20
1000	7.59	7.46	7.34	7.23	6.82	6.56	6.40
2000	15.18	14.91	14.67	14.46	13.64	13.13	12.79
5000	37.94	37.28	36.68	36.14	34.11	32.82	31.98
6000	45.53	44.73	44.02	43.37	40.93	39.39	38.38
7000	53.12	52.19	51.35	50.60	47.75	45.95	44.78
8000	60.71	59.65	58.69	57.82	54.57	52.52	51.17
9000	68.30	67.10	66.02	65.05	61.40	59.08	57.57
10000	75.89	74.56	73.36	72.28	68.22	65.65	63.97
15000	113.83	111.84	110.04	108.42	102.33	98.47	95.95
20000	151.78	149.12	146.72	144.56	136.44	131.29	127.93
25000	189.72	186.39	183.40	180.70	170.54	164.12	159.92
30000	227.67	223.67	220.08	216.84	204.65	196.94	191.90
35000	265.61	260.95	256.76	252.98	238.76	229.76	223.89
40000	303.56	298.23	293.44	289.12	272.87	262.59	255.87
45000	341.50	335.51	330.12	325.26	306.98	295.41	287.85
50000	379.45	372.79	366.80	361.40	341.09	328.23	319.84
55000	417.39	410.07	403.48	397.54	375.20	361.06	351.82
60000	455.34	447.35	440.16	433.68	409.31	393.88	383.80
65000	493.28	484.63	476.84	469.82	443.41	426.70	415.79
70000	531.23	521.91	513.52	505.96	477.52	459.53	447.77
75000	569.17	559.18	550.20	542.11	511.63	492.35	479.75
80000	607.11	596.46	586.88	578.25	545.74	525.17	511.74
85000	645.06	633.74	623.56	614.39	579.85	558.00	543.72
90000	683.00	671.02	660.24	650.53	613.96	590.82	575.70
95000	720.95	708.30	696.92	686.67	648.07	623.64	607.69
100000	758.89	745.58	733.61	722.81	682.18	656.47	639.67
105000	796.84	782.86	770.29	758.95	716.29	689.29	671.66
110000	834.78	820.14	806.97	795.09	750.39	722.11	703.64
120000	910.67	894.69	880.33	867.37	818.61	787.76	767.61
130000	986.56	969.25	953.69	939.65	886.83	853.41	831.57
140000	1062.45	1043.81	1027.05	1011.93	955.05	919.05	895.54
150000	1138.34	1118.37	1100.41	1084.21	1023.26	984.70	959.51
160000	1214.23	1192.93	1173.77	1156.49	1091.48	1050.35	1023.48
170000	1290.12	1267.48	1247.13	1228.77	1159.70	1115.99	1087.44
180000	1366.01	1342.04	1320.49	1301.05	1227.92	1181.64	1151.41
190000	1441.90	1416.60	1393.85	1373.33	1296.13	1247.29	1215.38
200000	1517.79	1491.16	1467.21	1445.61	1364.35	1312.93	1279.34
210000	1593.68	1565.72	1540.57	1517.89	1432.57	1378.58	1343.31
220000	1669.57	1640.27	1613.93	1590.18	1500.79	1444.23	1407.28
230000	1745.45	1714.83	1687.29	1662.46	1569.01	1509.87	1471.25
240000	1821.34	1789.39	1760.65	1734.74	1637.22	1575.52	1535.21
250000	1897.23	1863.95	1834.01	1807.02	1705.44	1641.17	1599.18
260000	1973.12	1938.50	1907.37	1879.30	1773.66	1706.81	1663.15
270000	2049.01	2013.06	1980.73	1951.58	1841.88	1772.46	1727.11
280000	2124.90	2087.62	2054.09	2023.86	1910.09	1838.11	1791.08
290000	2200.79	2162.18	2127.46	2096.14	1978.31	1903.76	1855.05
300000	2276.68	2236.74	2200.82	2168.42	2046.53	1969.40	1919.02
310000	2352.57	2311.29	2274.18	2240.70	2114.75	2035.05	1982.98
320000	2428.46	2385.85	2347.54	2312.98	2182.96	2100.70	2046.95
330000	2504.35	2460.41	2420.90	2385.26	2251.18	2166.34	2110.92
340000	2580.24	2534.97	2494.26	2457.54	2319.40	2231.99	2174.88
350000	2656.13	2609.53	2567.62	2529.82	2387.62	2297.64	2238.85
400000	3035.57	2982.31	2934.47	2891.23	2728.71	2625.87	2558.69
450000	3415.02	3355.10	3301.22	3252.63	3069.79	2954.10	2878.52
500000	3794.47	3727.89	3668.03	3614.03	3410.88	3282.34	3198.36
550000	4173.91	4100.68	4034.83	3975.44	3751.97	3610.57	3518.20
600000	4553.36	4473.47	4401.63	4336.84	4093.06	3938.80	3838.03

7½%

Monthly Payments
necessary to amortize a loan

AMOUNT	1 YEAR	2 YEARS	3 YEARS	4 YEARS	5 YEARS	6 YEARS	7 YEARS
100	8.68	4.50	3.11	2.42	2.00	1.73	1.53
200	17.35	9.00	6.22	4.84	4.01	3.46	3.07
500	43.38	22.50	15.55	12.09	10.02	8.65	7.67
1000	86.76	45.00	31.11	24.18	20.04	17.29	15.34
2000	173.51	90.00	62.21	48.36	40.08	34.58	30.68
5000	433.79	225.00	155.53	120.89	100.19	86.45	76.69
6000	520.54	270.00	186.64	145.07	120.23	103.74	92.03
7000	607.30	315.00	217.74	169.25	140.27	121.03	107.37
8000	694.06	360.00	248.85	193.43	160.30	138.32	122.71
9000	780.82	405.00	279.96	217.61	180.34	155.61	138.04
10000	867.57	450.00	311.06	241.79	200.38	172.90	153.38
15000	1301.36	674.99	466.59	362.68	300.57	259.35	230.07
20000	1735.15	899.99	622.12	483.58	400.76	345.80	306.77
25000	2168.94	1124.99	777.66	604.47	500.95	432.25	383.46
30000	2602.72	1349.99	933.19	725.37	601.14	518.70	460.15
35000	3036.51	1574.99	1088.72	846.26	701.33	605.15	536.84
40000	3470.30	1799.98	1244.25	967.16	801.52	691.60	613.53
45000	3904.08	2024.98	1399.78	1088.05	901.71	778.06	690.22
50000	4337.87	2249.98	1555.31	1208.95	1001.90	864.51	766.91
55000	4771.66	2474.98	1710.84	1329.84	1102.09	950.96	843.61
60000	5205.45	2699.98	1866.37	1450.73	1202.28	1037.41	920.30
65000	5639.23	2924.97	2021.90	1571.63	1302.47	1123.86	996.99
70000	6073.02	3149.97	2177.44	1692.52	1402.66	1210.31	1073.68
75000	6506.81	3374.97	2332.97	1813.42	1502.85	1296.76	1150.37
80000	6940.59	3599.97	2488.50	1934.31	1603.04	1383.21	1227.06
85000	7374.38	3824.97	2644.03	2055.21	1703.23	1469.66	1303.75
90000	7808.17	4049.96	2799.56	2176.10	1803.42	1556.11	1380.44
95000	8241.95	4274.96	2955.09	2297.00	1903.61	1642.56	1457.14
100000	8675.74	4499.96	3110.62	2417.89	2003.79	1729.01	1533.83
105000	9109.53	4724.96	3266.15	2538.78	2103.98	1815.46	1610.52
110000	9543.32	4949.96	3421.68	2659.68	2204.17	1901.91	1687.21
120000	10410.89	5399.95	3732.75	2901.47	2404.55	2074.81	1840.59
130000	11278.46	5849.94	4043.81	3143.26	2604.93	2247.71	1993.98
140000	12146.04	6299.94	4354.87	3385.05	2805.31	2420.62	2147.36
150000	13013.61	6749.94	4665.93	3626.84	3005.69	2593.52	2300.74
160000	13881.19	7199.93	4976.99	3868.62	3206.07	2766.42	2454.12
170000	14748.76	7649.93	5288.06	4110.41	3406.45	2939.32	2607.51
180000	15616.34	8099.93	5599.12	4352.20	3606.83	3112.22	2760.89
190000	16483.91	8549.92	5910.18	4593.99	3807.21	3285.12	2914.27
200000	17351.48	8999.92	6221.24	4835.78	4007.59	3458.02	3067.66
210000	18219.06	9449.91	6532.31	5077.57	4207.97	3630.92	3221.04
220000	19086.63	9899.91	6843.37	5319.36	4408.35	3803.82	3374.42
230000	19954.21	10349.91	7154.43	5561.15	4608.73	3976.73	3527.80
240000	20821.78	10799.90	7465.49	5802.94	4809.11	4149.63	3681.19
250000	21689.35	11249.90	7776.55	6044.73	5009.49	4322.53	3834.57
260000	22556.93	11699.89	8087.62	6286.51	5209.87	4495.43	3987.95
270000	23424.50	12149.89	8398.68	6528.30	5410.25	4668.33	4141.33
280000	24292.08	12599.89	8709.74	6770.09	5610.63	4841.23	4294.72
290000	25159.65	13049.88	9020.80	7011.88	5811.01	5014.13	4448.10
300000	26027.23	13499.88	9331.87	7253.67	6011.38	5187.03	4601.48
310000	26894.80	13949.87	9642.93	7495.46	6211.76	5359.93	4754.87
320000	27762.37	14399.87	9953.99	7737.25	6412.14	5532.84	4908.25
330000	28629.95	14849.87	10265.05	7979.04	6612.52	5705.74	5061.63
340000	29497.52	15299.86	10576.11	8220.83	6812.90	5878.64	5215.01
350000	30365.10	15749.86	10887.18	8462.61	7013.28	6051.54	5368.40
400000	34702.97	17999.84	12442.49	9671.56	8015.18	6916.04	6135.31
450000	39040.84	20249.82	13997.80	10880.51	9017.08	7780.55	6902.22
500000	43378.71	22499.80	15553.11	12089.45	10018.97	8645.06	7669.14
550000	47716.58	24749.78	17108.42	13298.40	11020.87	9509.56	8436.05
600000	52054.45	26999.76	18663.73	14507.34	12022.77	10374.07	9202.97

44

Monthly Payments 7½%
necessary to amortize a loan

AMOUNT	8 YEARS	9 YEARS	10 YEARS	11 YEARS	12 YEARS	13 YEARS	14 YEARS
100	1.39	1.28	1.19	1.11	1.06	1.01	0.96
200	2.78	2.55	2.37	2.23	2.11	2.01	1.93
500	6.94	6.38	5.94	5.57	5.28	5.03	4.82
1000	13.88	12.76	11.87	11.15	10.55	10.05	9.63
2000	27.77	25.52	23.74	22.30	21.10	20.11	19.26
5000	69.42	63.81	59.35	55.74	52.76	50.27	48.16
6000	83.30	76.57	71.22	66.89	63.31	60.32	57.79
7000	97.19	89.33	83.09	78.04	73.87	70.38	67.42
8000	111.07	102.09	94.96	89.18	84.42	80.43	77.05
9000	124.95	114.85	106.83	100.33	94.97	90.48	86.68
10000	138.84	127.61	118.70	111.48	105.52	100.54	96.31
15000	208.26	191.42	178.05	167.22	158.28	150.81	144.47
20000	277.68	255.22	237.40	222.96	211.05	201.07	192.63
25000	347.10	319.03	296.75	278.70	263.81	251.34	240.79
30000	416.52	382.83	356.11	334.44	316.57	301.61	288.94
35000	485.94	446.64	415.46	390.18	369.33	351.88	337.10
40000	555.35	510.44	474.81	445.92	422.09	402.15	385.26
45000	624.77	574.25	534.16	501.66	474.85	452.42	433.41
50000	694.19	638.05	593.51	557.40	527.61	502.69	481.57
55000	763.61	701.86	652.86	613.14	580.37	552.95	529.73
60000	833.03	765.66	712.21	668.88	633.14	603.22	577.89
65000	902.45	829.47	771.56	724.62	685.90	653.49	626.04
70000	971.87	893.27	830.91	780.36	738.66	703.76	674.20
75000	1041.29	957.08	890.26	836.10	791.42	754.03	722.36
80000	1110.71	1020.88	949.61	891.84	844.18	804.30	770.51
85000	1180.13	1084.69	1008.97	947.58	896.94	854.56	818.67
90000	1249.55	1148.49	1068.32	1003.32	949.70	904.83	866.83
95000	1318.97	1212.30	1127.67	1059.06	1002.46	955.10	914.99
100000	1388.93	1276.10	1187.02	1114.80	1055.23	1005.37	963.14
105000	1457.81	1339.91	1246.37	1170.54	1107.99	1055.64	1011.30
110000	1527.23	1403.71	1305.72	1226.28	1160.75	1105.91	1059.46
120000	1666.06	1531.32	1424.42	1337.76	1266.27	1206.44	1155.77
130000	1804.90	1658.93	1543.12	1449.24	1371.79	1306.98	1252.09
140000	1943.74	1786.54	1661.82	1560.72	1477.32	1407.52	1348.40
150000	2082.58	1914.15	1780.53	1672.20	1582.84	1508.06	1444.72
160000	2221.42	2041.76	1899.23	1783.68	1688.36	1608.59	1541.03
170000	2360.26	2169.37	2017.93	1895.16	1793.88	1709.13	1637.34
180000	2499.10	2296.98	2136.63	2006.64	1899.41	1809.67	1733.66
190000	2637.94	2424.59	2255.33	2118.12	2004.93	1910.20	1829.97
200000	2776.77	2552.20	2374.04	2229.60	2110.45	2010.74	1926.29
210000	2915.61	2679.81	2492.74	2341.08	2215.98	2111.28	2022.60
220000	3054.45	2807.42	2611.44	2452.56	2321.50	2211.81	2118.92
230000	3193.29	2935.03	2730.14	2564.04	2427.02	2312.35	2215.23
240000	3332.13	3062.64	2848.84	2675.52	2532.54	2412.89	2311.54
250000	3470.97	3190.25	2967.54	2787.00	2638.07	2513.43	2407.86
260000	3609.81	3317.86	3086.25	2898.48	2743.59	2613.96	2504.17
270000	3748.65	3445.47	3204.95	3009.96	2849.11	2714.50	2600.49
280000	3887.48	3573.08	3323.65	3121.44	2954.63	2815.04	2696.80
290000	4026.32	3700.69	3442.35	3232.92	3060.16	2915.57	2793.12
300000	4165.16	3828.30	3561.05	3344.40	3165.68	3016.11	2889.43
310000	4304.00	3955.92	3679.75	3455.88	3271.20	3116.65	2985.74
320000	4442.84	4083.53	3798.46	3567.36	3376.72	3217.19	3082.06
330000	4581.68	4211.14	3917.16	3678.84	3482.25	3317.72	3178.37
340000	4720.52	4338.75	4035.86	3790.32	3587.77	3418.26	3274.69
350000	4859.35	4466.36	4154.56	3901.80	3693.29	3518.80	3371.00
400000	5553.55	5104.41	4748.07	4459.20	4220.91	4021.48	3852.57
450000	6247.74	5742.46	5341.58	5016.60	4748.52	4524.17	4334.15
500000	6941.94	6380.51	5935.09	5574.00	5276.13	5026.85	4815.72
550000	7636.13	7018.56	6528.60	6131.40	5803.74	5529.54	5297.29
600000	8330.32	7656.61	7122.11	6688.80	6331.36	6032.22	5778.86

7¹/₂%

Monthly Payments
necessary to amortize a loan

AMOUNT	15 YEARS	16 YEARS	17 YEARS	18 YEARS	19 YEARS	20 YEARS	21 YEARS
100	0.93	0.90	0.87	0.84	0.82	0.81	0.79
200	1.85	1.79	1.74	1.69	1.65	1.61	1.58
500	4.64	4.48	4.34	4.22	4.12	4.03	3.95
1000	9.27	8.96	8.69	8.45	8.24	8.06	7.89
2000	18.54	17.92	17.37	16.90	16.48	16.11	15.78
5000	46.35	44.79	43.44	42.25	41.20	40.28	39.46
6000	55.62	53.75	52.12	50.70	49.44	48.34	47.35
7000	64.89	62.71	60.81	59.15	57.69	56.39	55.24
8000	74.16	71.67	69.50	67.60	65.93	64.45	63.13
9000	83.43	80.62	78.18	76.05	74.17	72.50	71.02
10000	92.70	89.58	86.87	84.50	82.41	80.56	78.92
15000	139.05	134.37	130.31	126.75	123.61	120.84	118.37
20000	185.40	179.17	173.74	168.99	164.82	161.12	157.83
25000	231.75	223.96	217.18	211.24	206.02	201.40	197.29
30000	278.10	268.75	260.61	253.49	247.22	241.68	236.75
35000	324.45	313.54	304.05	295.74	288.43	281.96	276.21
40000	370.80	358.33	347.48	337.99	329.63	322.24	315.67
45000	417.16	403.12	390.92	380.24	370.84	362.52	355.12
50000	463.51	447.91	434.35	422.49	412.04	402.80	394.58
55000	509.86	492.71	477.79	464.74	453.24	443.08	434.04
60000	556.21	537.50	521.23	506.98	494.45	483.36	473.50
65000	602.56	582.29	564.66	549.23	535.65	523.64	512.96
70000	648.91	627.08	608.10	591.48	576.86	563.92	552.42
75000	695.26	671.87	651.53	633.73	618.06	604.19	591.87
80000	741.61	716.66	694.97	675.98	659.26	644.47	631.33
85000	787.96	761.45	738.40	718.23	700.47	684.75	670.79
90000	834.31	806.24	781.84	760.48	741.67	725.03	710.25
95000	880.66	851.04	825.27	802.72	782.87	765.31	749.71
100000	927.01	895.83	868.71	844.97	824.08	805.59	789.17
105000	973.36	940.62	912.14	887.22	865.28	845.87	828.62
110000	1019.71	985.41	955.58	929.47	906.49	886.15	868.08
120000	1112.41	1074.99	1042.45	1013.97	988.89	966.71	947.00
130000	1205.12	1164.58	1129.32	1098.47	1071.30	1047.27	1025.92
140000	1297.82	1254.16	1216.19	1182.96	1153.71	1127.83	1104.83
150000	1390.52	1343.74	1303.06	1267.46	1236.12	1208.39	1183.75
160000	1483.22	1433.32	1389.94	1351.96	1318.53	1288.95	1262.67
170000	1575.92	1522.91	1476.81	1436.45	1400.93	1369.51	1341.58
180000	1668.62	1612.49	1563.68	1520.95	1483.34	1450.07	1420.50
190000	1761.32	1702.07	1650.55	1605.45	1565.75	1530.63	1499.42
200000	1854.02	1791.66	1737.42	1689.95	1648.16	1611.19	1578.33
210000	1946.73	1881.24	1824.29	1774.44	1730.57	1691.75	1657.25
220000	2039.43	1970.82	1911.16	1858.94	1812.97	1772.31	1736.17
230000	2132.13	2060.40	1998.03	1943.44	1895.38	1852.86	1815.08
240000	2224.83	2149.99	2084.90	2027.94	1977.79	1933.42	1894.00
250000	2317.53	2239.57	2171.77	2112.43	2060.20	2013.98	1972.92
260000	2410.23	2329.15	2258.64	2196.93	2142.60	2094.54	2051.83
270000	2502.93	2418.73	2345.52	2281.43	2225.01	2175.10	2130.75
280000	2595.63	2508.32	2432.39	2365.93	2307.42	2255.66	2209.66
290000	2688.34	2597.90	2519.26	2450.42	2389.83	2336.22	2288.58
300000	2781.04	2687.48	2606.13	2534.92	2472.24	2416.78	2367.50
310000	2873.74	2777.07	2693.00	2619.42	2554.64	2497.34	2446.41
320000	2966.44	2866.65	2779.87	2703.91	2637.05	2577.90	2525.33
330000	3059.14	2956.23	2866.74	2788.41	2719.46	2658.46	2604.25
340000	3151.84	3045.81	2953.61	2872.91	2801.87	2739.02	2683.16
350000	3244.54	3135.40	3040.48	2957.41	2884.28	2819.58	2762.08
400000	3708.05	3583.31	3474.84	3379.89	3296.32	3222.37	3156.66
450000	4171.56	4031.22	3909.19	3802.38	3708.35	3625.17	3551.25
500000	4635.06	4479.14	4343.55	4224.87	4120.39	4027.97	3945.83
550000	5098.57	4927.05	4777.90	4647.35	4532.43	4430.76	4340.41
600000	5562.07	5374.97	5212.26	5069.84	4944.47	4833.56	4735.00

AMOUNT	22 YEARS	23 YEARS	24 YEARS	25 YEARS	30 YEARS	35 YEARS	40 YEARS
100	0.77	0.76	0.75	0.74	0.70	0.67	0.66
200	1.55	1.52	1.50	1.48	1.40	1.35	1.32
500	3.87	3.81	3.75	3.69	3.50	3.37	3.29
1000	7.75	7.61	7.50	7.39	6.99	6.74	6.58
2000	15.49	15.23	14.99	14.78	13.98	13.48	13.16
5000	38.73	38.07	37.48	36.95	34.96	33.71	32.90
6000	46.47	45.68	44.98	44.34	41.95	40.45	39.48
7000	54.22	53.30	52.47	51.73	48.95	47.20	46.06
8000	61.96	60.91	59.97	59.12	55.94	53.94	52.65
9000	69.71	68.53	67.46	66.51	62.93	60.68	59.23
10000	77.45	76.14	74.96	73.90	69.92	67.42	65.81
15000	116.18	114.21	112.44	110.85	104.88	101.14	98.71
20000	154.90	152.28	149.92	147.80	139.84	134.85	131.61
25000	193.63	190.35	187.40	184.75	174.80	168.56	164.52
30000	232.35	228.42	224.88	221.70	209.76	202.27	197.42
35000	271.08	266.49	262.36	258.65	244.73	235.98	230.32
40000	309.80	304.56	299.84	295.60	279.69	269.70	263.23
45000	348.53	342.63	337.32	332.55	314.65	303.41	296.13
50000	387.26	380.69	374.80	369.50	349.61	337.12	329.04
55000	425.98	418.76	412.28	406.45	384.57	370.83	361.94
60000	464.71	456.83	449.76	443.39	419.53	404.55	394.84
65000	503.43	494.90	487.24	480.34	454.49	438.26	427.75
70000	542.16	532.97	524.72	517.29	489.45	471.97	460.65
75000	580.88	571.04	562.20	554.24	524.41	505.68	493.55
80000	619.61	609.11	599.68	591.19	559.37	539.39	526.46
85000	658.33	647.18	637.16	628.14	594.33	573.11	559.36
90000	697.06	685.25	674.64	665.09	629.29	606.82	592.26
95000	735.78	723.32	712.12	702.04	664.25	640.53	625.17
100000	774.51	761.39	749.60	738.99	699.21	674.24	658.07
105000	813.24	799.46	787.09	775.94	734.18	707.95	690.97
110000	851.96	837.53	824.57	812.89	769.14	741.67	723.88
120000	929.41	913.67	899.53	886.79	839.06	809.09	789.68
130000	1006.86	989.81	974.49	960.69	908.98	876.52	855.49
140000	1084.31	1065.94	1049.45	1034.59	978.90	943.94	921.30
150000	1161.77	1142.08	1124.41	1108.49	1048.82	1011.36	987.11
160000	1239.22	1218.22	1199.37	1182.39	1118.74	1078.79	1052.91
170000	1316.67	1294.36	1274.33	1256.29	1188.66	1146.21	1118.72
180000	1394.12	1370.50	1349.29	1330.18	1258.59	1213.64	1184.53
190000	1471.57	1446.64	1424.25	1404.08	1328.51	1281.06	1250.33
200000	1549.02	1522.78	1499.21	1477.98	1398.43	1348.49	1316.14
210000	1626.47	1598.92	1574.17	1551.88	1468.35	1415.91	1381.95
220000	1703.92	1675.06	1649.13	1625.78	1538.27	1483.33	1447.76
230000	1781.37	1751.20	1724.09	1699.68	1608.19	1550.76	1513.56
240000	1858.82	1827.33	1799.05	1773.58	1678.11	1618.18	1579.37
250000	1936.28	1903.47	1874.01	1847.48	1748.04	1685.61	1645.18
260000	2013.73	1979.61	1948.97	1921.38	1817.96	1753.03	1710.98
270000	2091.18	2055.75	2023.93	1995.28	1887.88	1820.46	1776.79
280000	2168.63	2131.89	2098.89	2069.18	1957.80	1887.88	1842.60
290000	2246.08	2208.03	2173.85	2143.07	2027.72	1955.30	1908.41
300000	2323.53	2284.17	2248.81	2216.97	2097.64	2022.73	1974.21
310000	2400.98	2360.31	2323.78	2290.87	2167.56	2090.15	2040.02
320000	2478.43	2436.45	2398.74	2364.77	2237.49	2157.58	2105.83
330000	2555.88	2512.58	2473.70	2438.67	2307.41	2225.00	2171.63
340000	2633.34	2588.72	2548.66	2512.57	2377.33	2292.42	2237.44
350000	2710.79	2664.86	2623.62	2586.47	2447.25	2359.85	2303.25
400000	3098.04	3045.56	2998.42	2955.96	2796.86	2696.97	2632.28
450000	3485.30	3426.25	3373.22	3325.46	3146.47	3034.09	2961.32
500000	3872.55	3806.95	3748.02	3694.96	3496.07	3371.21	3290.35
550000	4259.81	4187.64	4122.83	4064.45	3845.68	3708.33	3619.39
600000	4647.06	4568.34	4497.63	4433.95	4195.29	4045.46	3948.42

7¾%

Monthly Payments
necessary to amortize a loan

AMOUNT	1 YEAR	2 YEARS	3 YEARS	4 YEARS	5 YEARS	6 YEARS	7 YEARS
100	8.69	4.51	3.12	2.43	2.02	1.74	1.55
200	17.37	9.02	6.24	4.86	4.03	3.48	3.09
500	43.44	22.56	15.61	12.15	10.08	8.71	7.73
1000	86.87	45.11	31.22	24.30	20.16	17.41	15.46
2000	173.75	90.23	62.44	48.59	40.31	34.82	30.92
5000	434.36	225.57	156.11	121.48	100.78	87.06	77.31
6000	521.24	270.68	187.33	145.77	120.94	104.47	92.77
7000	608.11	315.79	218.55	170.07	141.10	121.88	108.23
8000	694.98	360.91	249.77	194.37	161.26	139.29	123.70
9000	781.86	406.02	280.99	218.66	181.41	156.70	139.16
10000	868.73	451.13	312.21	242.96	201.57	174.11	154.62
15000	1303.09	676.70	468.32	364.44	302.35	261.17	231.93
20000	1737.46	902.27	624.42	485.91	403.14	348.23	309.24
25000	2171.82	1127.83	780.53	607.39	503.92	435.29	386.55
30000	2606.19	1353.40	936.63	728.87	604.71	522.34	463.86
35000	3040.55	1578.97	1092.74	850.35	705.49	609.40	541.17
40000	3474.92	1804.53	1248.85	971.83	806.28	696.46	618.48
45000	3909.28	2030.10	1404.95	1093.31	907.06	783.51	695.79
50000	4343.64	2255.67	1561.06	1214.79	1007.85	870.57	773.10
55000	4778.01	2481.23	1717.16	1336.21	1108.63	957.63	850.41
60000	5212.37	2706.80	1873.27	1457.74	1209.42	1044.69	927.72
65000	5646.74	2932.37	2029.38	1579.22	1310.20	1131.74	1005.03
70000	6081.10	3157.93	2185.48	1700.70	1410.99	1218.80	1082.34
75000	6515.47	3383.50	2341.59	1822.18	1511.77	1305.86	1159.65
80000	6949.83	3609.07	2497.69	1943.66	1612.56	1392.91	1236.96
85000	7384.19	3834.64	2653.80	2065.14	1713.34	1479.97	1314.27
90000	7818.56	4060.20	2809.90	2186.62	1814.13	1567.03	1391.58
95000	8252.92	4285.77	2966.01	2308.10	1914.91	1654.09	1468.89
100000	8687.29	4511.34	3122.12	2429.57	2015.70	1741.14	1546.20
105000	9121.65	4736.90	3278.22	2551.05	2116.48	1828.20	1623.51
110000	9556.02	4962.47	3434.33	2672.53	2217.27	1915.26	1700.81
120000	10424.75	5413.60	3746.54	2915.49	2418.84	2089.37	1855.43
130000	11293.47	5864.74	4058.75	3158.45	2620.40	2263.49	2010.05
140000	12162.20	6315.87	4370.96	3401.40	2821.97	2437.60	2164.67
150000	13030.93	6767.00	4683.17	3644.36	3023.54	2611.71	2319.29
160000	13899.66	7218.14	4995.39	3887.32	3225.11	2785.83	2473.91
170000	14768.39	7669.27	5307.60	4130.28	3426.68	2959.94	2628.53
180000	15637.12	8120.40	5619.81	4373.23	3628.25	3134.06	2783.15
190000	16505.85	8571.54	5932.02	4616.19	3829.82	3308.17	2937.77
200000	17374.58	9022.67	6244.23	4859.15	4031.39	3482.28	3092.39
210000	18243.30	9473.80	6556.44	5102.11	4232.96	3656.40	3247.01
220000	19112.03	9924.94	6868.66	5345.06	4434.53	3830.51	3401.63
230000	19980.76	10376.07	7180.87	5588.02	4636.10	4004.63	3556.25
240000	20849.49	10827.21	7493.08	5830.98	4837.67	4178.74	3710.87
250000	21718.22	11278.34	7805.29	6073.94	5039.24	4352.86	3865.49
260000	22586.95	11729.47	8117.50	6316.89	5240.81	4526.97	4020.11
270000	23455.68	12180.61	8429.71	6559.85	5442.38	4701.08	4174.73
280000	24324.41	12631.74	8741.93	6802.81	5643.95	4875.20	4329.35
290000	25193.14	13082.87	9054.14	7045.77	5845.52	5049.31	4483.97
300000	26061.86	13534.01	9366.35	7288.72	6047.09	5223.43	4638.59
310000	26930.59	13985.14	9678.56	7531.68	6248.66	5397.54	4793.21
320000	27799.32	14436.27	9990.77	7774.64	6450.23	5571.66	4947.82
330000	28668.05	14887.41	10302.98	8017.59	6651.80	5745.77	5102.44
340000	29536.78	15338.54	10615.20	8260.55	6853.37	5919.88	5257.06
350000	30405.51	15789.67	10927.41	8503.51	7054.94	6094.00	5411.68
400000	34749.15	18045.34	12488.47	9718.30	8062.78	6964.57	6184.78
450000	39092.80	20301.01	14049.52	10933.08	9070.63	7835.14	6957.88
500000	43436.44	22556.68	15610.58	12147.87	10078.48	8705.71	7730.98
550000	47780.08	24812.35	17171.64	13362.66	11086.33	9576.28	8504.07
600000	52123.73	27068.01	18732.70	14577.45	12094.18	10446.85	9277.17

AMOUNT	8 YEARS	9 YEARS	10 YEARS	11 YEARS	12 YEARS	13 YEARS	14 YEARS
100	1.40	1.29	1.20	1.13	1.07	1.02	0.98
200	2.80	2.58	2.40	2.26	2.14	2.04	1.95
500	7.00	6.44	6.00	5.64	5.34	5.10	4.89
1000	14.01	12.89	12.00	11.28	10.69	10.19	9.77
2000	28.02	25.78	24.00	22.56	21.38	20.38	19.54
5000	70.05	64.45	60.01	56.41	53.44	50.96	48.86
6000	84.06	77.34	72.01	67.69	64.13	61.15	58.63
7000	98.07	90.23	84.01	78.97	74.82	71.34	68.40
8000	112.08	103.12	96.01	90.25	85.50	81.53	78.17
9000	126.09	116.01	108.01	101.53	96.19	91.73	87.95
10000	140.10	128.89	120.01	112.81	106.88	101.92	97.72
15000	210.15	193.34	180.02	169.22	160.32	152.88	146.58
20000	280.20	257.79	240.02	225.63	213.76	203.83	195.44
25000	350.25	322.24	300.03	282.03	267.20	254.79	244.29
30000	420.30	386.68	360.03	338.44	320.64	305.75	293.15
35000	490.35	451.13	420.04	394.85	374.08	356.71	342.01
40000	560.40	515.58	480.04	451.25	427.52	407.67	390.87
45000	630.45	580.03	540.05	507.66	480.96	458.63	439.73
50000	700.50	644.47	600.05	564.06	534.40	509.59	488.59
55000	770.55	708.92	660.06	620.47	587.84	560.54	537.45
60000	840.60	773.37	720.06	676.88	641.28	611.50	586.31
65000	910.65	837.82	780.07	733.28	694.71	662.46	635.17
70000	980.70	902.26	840.07	789.69	748.15	713.42	684.02
75000	1050.75	966.71	900.08	846.10	801.59	764.38	732.88
80000	1120.80	1031.16	960.09	902.50	855.03	815.34	781.74
85000	1190.85	1095.61	1020.09	958.91	908.47	866.30	830.60
90000	1260.89	1160.05	1080.10	1015.32	961.91	917.25	879.46
95000	1330.94	1224.50	1140.10	1071.72	1015.35	968.21	928.32
100000	1400.99	1288.95	1200.11	1128.13	1068.79	1019.17	977.18
105000	1471.04	1353.40	1260.11	1184.54	1122.23	1070.13	1026.04
110000	1541.09	1417.84	1320.12	1240.94	1175.67	1121.09	1074.89
120000	1681.19	1546.74	1440.13	1353.75	1282.55	1223.01	1172.61
130000	1821.29	1675.63	1560.14	1466.57	1389.43	1324.92	1270.33
140000	1961.39	1804.53	1680.15	1579.38	1496.31	1426.84	1368.05
150000	2101.49	1933.42	1800.16	1692.19	1603.19	1528.76	1465.77
160000	2241.59	2062.32	1920.17	1805.01	1710.07	1630.67	1563.48
170000	2381.69	2191.21	2040.18	1917.82	1816.95	1732.59	1661.20
180000	2521.79	2320.11	2160.19	2030.63	1923.83	1834.51	1758.92
190000	2661.89	2449.00	2280.20	2143.44	2030.70	1936.43	1856.64
200000	2801.99	2577.90	2400.21	2256.26	2137.58	2038.34	1954.35
210000	2942.09	2706.79	2520.22	2369.07	2244.46	2140.26	2052.07
220000	3082.19	2835.69	2640.23	2481.88	2351.34	2242.18	2149.79
230000	3222.29	2964.58	2760.24	2594.70	2458.22	2344.09	2247.51
240000	3362.39	3093.48	2880.26	2707.51	2565.10	2446.01	2345.23
250000	3502.49	3222.37	3000.27	2820.32	2671.98	2547.93	2442.94
260000	3642.59	3351.27	3120.28	2933.13	2778.86	2649.85	2540.66
270000	3782.68	3480.16	3240.29	3045.95	2885.74	2751.76	2638.38
280000	3922.78	3609.06	3360.30	3158.76	2992.62	2853.68	2736.10
290000	4062.88	3737.95	3480.31	3271.57	3099.50	2955.60	2833.82
300000	4202.98	3866.85	3600.32	3384.39	3206.38	3057.51	2931.53
310000	4343.08	3995.74	3720.33	3497.20	3313.26	3159.43	3029.25
320000	4483.18	4124.64	3840.34	3610.01	3420.13	3261.35	3126.97
330000	4623.28	4253.53	3960.35	3722.82	3527.01	3363.27	3224.68
340000	4763.38	4382.43	4080.36	3835.64	3633.89	3465.18	3322.40
350000	4903.48	4511.32	4200.37	3948.45	3740.77	3567.10	3420.12
400000	5603.98	5155.80	4800.43	4512.51	4275.17	4076.69	3908.71
450000	6304.47	5800.27	5400.48	5076.58	4809.56	4586.27	4397.30
500000	7004.97	6444.75	6000.53	5640.64	5343.96	5095.86	4885.89
550000	7705.47	7089.22	6600.58	6204.71	5878.36	5605.44	5374.47
600000	8405.97	7733.70	7200.64	6768.77	6412.75	6115.03	5863.06

7¾% Monthly Payments
necessary to amortize a loan

AMOUNT	15 YEARS	16 YEARS	17 YEARS	18 YEARS	19 YEARS	20 YEARS	21 YEARS
100	0.94	0.91	0.88	0.86	0.84	0.82	0.80
200	1.88	1.82	1.77	1.72	1.68	1.64	1.61
500	4.71	4.55	4.42	4.30	4.20	4.10	4.02
1000	9.41	9.10	8.83	8.60	8.39	8.21	8.05
2000	18.83	18.21	17.67	17.20	16.78	16.42	16.09
5000	47.06	45.52	44.17	43.00	41.96	41.05	40.24
6000	56.48	54.62	53.01	51.59	50.35	49.26	48.28
7000	65.89	63.72	61.84	60.19	58.75	57.47	56.33
8000	75.30	72.83	70.67	68.79	67.14	65.68	64.38
9000	84.71	81.93	79.51	77.39	75.53	73.89	72.43
10000	94.13	91.03	88.34	85.99	83.92	82.09	80.47
15000	141.19	136.55	132.51	128.99	125.88	123.14	120.71
20000	188.26	182.06	176.68	171.98	167.84	164.19	160.95
25000	235.32	227.58	220.86	214.98	209.81	205.24	201.18
30000	282.38	273.10	265.03	257.97	251.77	246.28	241.42
35000	329.45	318.61	309.20	300.97	293.73	287.33	281.65
40000	376.51	364.13	353.37	343.96	335.69	328.38	321.89
45000	423.57	409.64	397.54	386.96	377.65	369.43	362.13
50000	470.64	455.16	441.71	429.95	419.61	410.47	402.36
55000	517.70	500.67	485.88	472.95	461.57	451.52	442.60
60000	564.77	546.19	530.05	515.94	503.53	492.57	482.84
65000	611.83	591.71	574.22	558.94	545.50	533.62	523.07
70000	658.89	637.22	618.40	601.93	587.46	574.66	563.31
75000	705.96	682.74	662.57	644.93	629.42	615.71	603.55
80000	753.02	728.25	706.74	687.92	671.38	656.76	643.78
85000	800.08	773.77	750.91	730.92	713.34	697.81	684.02
90000	847.15	819.29	795.08	773.91	755.30	738.85	724.25
95000	894.21	864.80	839.25	816.91	797.26	779.90	764.49
100000	941.28	910.32	883.42	859.90	839.22	820.95	804.73
105000	988.34	955.83	927.59	902.90	881.19	862.00	844.96
110000	1035.40	1001.35	971.76	945.89	923.15	903.04	885.20
120000	1129.53	1092.38	1060.11	1031.88	1007.07	985.14	965.67
130000	1223.66	1183.41	1148.45	1117.88	1090.99	1067.23	1046.15
140000	1317.79	1274.44	1236.79	1203.87	1174.91	1149.33	1126.62
150000	1411.91	1365.48	1325.13	1289.86	1258.84	1231.42	1207.09
160000	1506.04	1456.51	1413.47	1375.85	1342.76	1313.52	1287.56
170000	1600.17	1547.54	1501.82	1461.84	1426.68	1395.61	1368.04
180000	1694.30	1638.57	1590.16	1547.83	1510.60	1477.71	1448.51
190000	1788.42	1729.60	1678.50	1633.82	1594.53	1559.80	1528.98
200000	1882.55	1820.63	1766.84	1719.81	1678.45	1641.90	1609.45
210000	1976.68	1911.67	1855.19	1805.80	1762.37	1723.99	1689.93
220000	2070.81	2002.70	1943.53	1891.79	1846.29	1806.09	1770.40
230000	2164.93	2093.73	2031.87	1977.78	1930.22	1888.18	1850.87
240000	2259.06	2184.76	2120.21	2063.77	2014.14	1970.28	1931.35
250000	2353.19	2275.79	2208.55	2149.76	2098.06	2052.37	2011.82
260000	2447.32	2366.82	2296.90	2235.75	2181.98	2134.47	2092.29
270000	2541.44	2457.86	2385.24	2321.74	2265.90	2216.56	2172.76
280000	2635.57	2548.89	2473.58	2407.73	2349.83	2298.66	2253.24
290000	2729.70	2639.92	2561.92	2493.72	2433.75	2380.75	2333.71
300000	2823.83	2730.95	2650.26	2579.71	2517.67	2462.85	2414.18
310000	2917.95	2821.98	2738.61	2665.70	2601.59	2544.94	2494.65
320000	3012.08	2913.01	2826.95	2751.69	2685.52	2627.04	2575.13
330000	3106.21	3004.05	2915.29	2837.68	2769.44	2709.13	2655.60
340000	3200.34	3095.08	3003.63	2923.67	2853.36	2791.23	2736.07
350000	3294.47	3186.11	3091.98	3009.66	2937.28	2873.32	2816.55
400000	3765.10	3641.27	3533.69	3439.62	3356.90	3283.79	3218.91
450000	4235.74	4096.43	3975.40	3869.57	3776.51	3694.27	3621.27
500000	4706.38	4551.59	4417.11	4299.52	4196.12	4104.74	4023.64
550000	5177.02	5006.74	4858.82	4729.47	4615.73	4515.22	4426.00
600000	5647.65	5461.90	5300.53	5159.42	5035.34	4925.69	4828.36

Monthly Payments 7¾%
necessary to amortize a loan

AMOUNT	22 YEARS	23 YEARS	24 YEARS	25 YEARS	30 YEARS	35 YEARS	40 YEARS
100	0.79	0.78	0.77	0.76	0.72	0.69	0.68
200	1.58	1.55	1.53	1.51	1.43	1.38	1.35
500	3.95	3.89	3.83	3.78	3.58	3.46	3.38
1000	7.90	7.77	7.66	7.56	7.16	6.92	6.77
2000	15.81	15.55	15.32	15.11	14.33	13.84	13.53
5000	39.51	38.87	38.29	37.77	35.82	34.61	33.83
6000	47.42	46.64	45.95	45.32	42.98	41.53	40.60
7000	55.32	54.41	53.60	52.87	50.15	48.45	47.36
8000	63.22	62.19	61.26	60.43	57.31	55.37	54.13
9000	71.12	69.96	68.92	67.98	64.48	62.30	60.90
10000	79.03	77.73	76.58	75.53	71.64	69.22	67.66
15000	118.54	116.60	114.86	113.30	107.46	103.83	101.49
20000	158.05	155.47	153.15	151.07	143.28	138.44	135.32
25000	197.57	194.34	191.44	188.83	179.10	173.04	169.15
30000	237.08	233.20	229.73	226.60	214.92	207.65	202.99
35000	276.60	272.07	268.01	264.37	250.74	242.26	236.82
40000	316.11	310.94	306.30	302.13	286.56	276.87	270.65
45000	355.62	349.81	344.59	339.90	322.39	311.48	304.48
50000	395.14	388.67	382.88	377.66	358.21	346.09	338.31
55000	434.65	427.54	421.17	415.43	394.03	380.70	372.14
60000	474.16	466.41	459.45	453.20	429.85	415.31	405.97
65000	513.68	505.28	497.74	490.96	465.67	449.91	439.80
70000	553.19	544.14	536.03	528.73	501.49	484.52	473.63
75000	592.70	583.01	574.32	566.50	537.31	519.13	507.46
80000	632.22	621.88	612.60	604.26	573.13	553.74	541.30
85000	671.73	660.75	650.89	642.03	608.95	588.35	575.13
90000	711.25	699.61	689.18	679.80	644.77	622.96	608.96
95000	750.76	738.48	727.47	717.56	680.59	657.57	642.79
100000	790.27	777.35	765.76	755.33	716.41	692.18	676.62
105000	829.79	816.22	804.04	793.10	752.23	726.78	710.45
110000	869.30	855.08	842.33	830.86	788.05	761.39	744.28
120000	948.33	932.82	918.91	906.39	859.69	830.61	811.94
130000	1027.35	1010.55	995.48	981.93	931.34	899.83	879.61
140000	1106.38	1088.29	1072.06	1057.46	1002.98	969.05	947.27
150000	1185.41	1166.02	1148.63	1132.99	1074.62	1038.26	1014.93
160000	1264.44	1243.76	1225.21	1208.53	1146.26	1107.48	1082.59
170000	1343.46	1321.49	1301.78	1284.06	1217.90	1176.70	1150.25
180000	1422.49	1399.23	1378.36	1359.59	1289.54	1245.92	1217.92
190000	1501.52	1476.96	1454.94	1435.12	1361.18	1315.13	1285.58
200000	1580.55	1554.70	1531.51	1510.66	1432.82	1384.35	1353.24
210000	1659.57	1632.43	1608.09	1586.19	1504.47	1453.57	1420.90
220000	1738.60	1710.17	1684.66	1661.72	1576.11	1522.79	1488.56
230000	1817.63	1787.90	1761.24	1737.26	1647.75	1592.00	1556.23
240000	1896.65	1865.64	1837.81	1812.79	1719.39	1661.22	1623.89
250000	1975.68	1943.37	1914.39	1888.32	1791.03	1730.44	1691.55
260000	2054.71	2021.11	1990.96	1963.85	1862.67	1799.66	1759.21
270000	2133.74	2098.84	2067.54	2039.39	1934.31	1868.88	1826.87
280000	2212.76	2176.57	2144.12	2114.92	2005.95	1938.09	1894.54
290000	2291.79	2254.31	2220.69	2190.45	2077.60	2007.31	1962.20
300000	2370.82	2332.04	2297.27	2265.99	2149.24	2076.53	2029.86
310000	2449.85	2409.78	2373.84	2341.52	2220.88	2145.75	2097.52
320000	2528.87	2487.51	2450.42	2417.05	2292.52	2214.96	2165.18
330000	2607.90	2565.25	2526.99	2492.58	2364.16	2284.18	2232.85
340000	2686.93	2642.98	2603.57	2568.12	2435.80	2353.40	2300.51
350000	2765.95	2720.72	2680.14	2643.65	2507.44	2422.62	2368.17
400000	3161.09	3109.39	3063.02	3021.32	2865.65	2768.70	2706.48
450000	3556.23	3498.07	3445.90	3398.98	3223.86	3114.79	3044.79
500000	3951.36	3886.74	3828.78	3776.64	3582.06	3460.88	3383.10
550000	4346.50	4275.41	4211.66	4154.31	3940.27	3806.97	3721.41
600000	4741.64	4664.09	4594.53	4531.97	4298.47	4153.06	4059.72

8%   Monthly Payments
necessary to amortize a loan

AMOUNT	1 YEAR	2 YEARS	3 YEARS	4 YEARS	5 YEARS	6 YEARS	7 YEARS
100	8.70	4.52	3.13	2.44	2.03	1.75	1.56
200	17.40	9.05	6.27	4.88	4.06	3.51	3.12
500	43.49	22.61	15.67	12.21	10.14	8.77	7.79
1000	86.99	45.23	31.34	24.41	20.28	17.53	15.59
2000	173.98	90.45	62.67	48.83	40.55	35.07	31.17
5000	434.94	226.14	156.68	122.06	101.38	87.67	77.93
6000	521.93	271.36	188.02	146.48	121.66	105.20	93.52
7000	608.92	316.59	219.35	170.89	141.93	122.73	109.10
8000	695.91	361.82	250.69	195.30	162.21	140.27	124.69
9000	782.90	407.05	282.03	219.72	182.49	157.80	140.28
10000	869.88	452.27	313.36	244.13	202.76	175.33	155.86
15000	1304.83	678.41	470.05	366.19	304.15	263.00	233.79
20000	1739.77	904.55	626.73	488.26	405.53	350.66	311.72
25000	2174.71	1130.68	783.41	610.32	506.91	438.33	389.66
30000	2609.65	1356.82	940.09	732.39	608.29	526.00	467.59
35000	3044.60	1582.96	1096.77	854.45	709.67	613.66	545.52
40000	3479.54	1809.09	1253.45	976.52	811.06	701.33	623.45
45000	3914.48	2035.23	1410.14	1098.58	912.44	789.00	701.38
50000	4349.42	2261.36	1566.82	1220.65	1013.82	876.66	779.31
55000	4784.36	2487.50	1723.50	1342.71	1115.20	964.33	857.24
60000	5219.31	2713.64	1880.18	1464.78	1216.58	1051.99	935.17
65000	5654.25	2939.77	2036.86	1586.84	1317.97	1139.66	1013.10
70000	6089.19	3165.91	2193.55	1708.90	1419.35	1227.33	1091.04
75000	6524.13	3392.05	2350.23	1830.97	1520.73	1314.99	1168.97
80000	6959.07	3618.18	2506.91	1953.03	1622.11	1402.66	1246.90
85000	7394.02	3844.32	2663.59	2075.10	1723.49	1490.33	1324.83
90000	7828.96	4070.46	2820.27	2197.16	1824.88	1577.99	1402.76
95000	8263.90	4296.59	2976.95	2319.23	1926.26	1665.66	1480.69
100000	8698.84	4522.73	3133.64	2441.29	2027.64	1753.32	1558.62
105000	9133.79	4748.87	3290.32	2563.36	2129.02	1840.99	1636.55
110000	9568.73	4975.00	3447.00	2685.42	2230.40	1928.66	1714.48
120000	10438.61	5427.27	3760.36	2929.55	2433.17	2103.99	1870.35
130000	11308.50	5879.55	4073.73	3173.68	2635.93	2279.32	2026.21
140000	12178.38	6331.82	4387.09	3417.81	2838.70	2454.65	2182.07
150000	13048.26	6784.09	4700.45	3661.94	3041.46	2629.99	2337.93
160000	13918.15	7236.37	5013.82	3906.07	3244.22	2805.32	2493.79
170000	14788.03	7688.64	5327.18	4150.20	3446.99	2980.65	2649.66
180000	15657.92	8140.91	5640.55	4394.33	3649.75	3155.98	2805.52
190000	16527.80	8593.19	5953.91	4638.46	3852.51	3331.32	2961.38
200000	17397.69	9045.46	6267.27	4882.58	4055.28	3506.65	3117.24
210000	18267.57	9497.73	6580.64	5126.71	4258.04	3681.98	3273.11
220000	19137.45	9950.00	6894.00	5370.84	4460.81	3857.31	3428.97
230000	20007.34	10402.28	7207.36	5614.97	4663.57	4032.65	3584.83
240000	20877.22	10854.55	7520.73	5859.10	4866.33	4207.98	3740.69
250000	21747.11	11306.82	7834.09	6103.23	5069.10	4383.31	3896.55
260000	22616.99	11759.10	8147.46	6347.36	5271.86	4558.64	4052.42
270000	23486.88	12211.37	8460.82	6591.49	5474.63	4733.97	4208.28
280000	24356.76	12663.64	8774.18	6835.62	5677.39	4909.31	4364.14
290000	25226.64	13115.91	9087.55	7079.75	5880.15	5084.64	4520.00
300000	26096.53	13568.19	9400.91	7323.88	6082.92	5259.97	4675.86
310000	26966.41	14020.46	9714.27	7568.01	6285.68	5435.30	4831.73
320000	27836.30	14472.73	10027.64	7812.14	6488.45	5610.64	4987.59
330000	28706.18	14925.01	10341.00	8056.26	6691.21	5785.97	5143.45
340000	29576.07	15377.28	10654.36	8300.39	6893.97	5961.30	5299.31
350000	30445.95	15829.55	10967.73	8544.52	7096.74	6136.63	5455.18
400000	34795.37	18090.92	12534.55	9765.17	8110.56	7013.30	6234.49
450000	39144.79	20352.28	14101.36	10985.82	9124.38	7889.96	7013.80
500000	43494.21	22613.65	15668.18	12206.46	10138.20	8766.62	7793.11
550000	47843.64	24875.01	17235.00	13427.11	11152.02	9643.28	8572.42
600000	52193.06	27136.37	18801.82	14647.75	12165.84	10519.94	9351.73

Monthly Payments 8%
necessary to amortize a loan

AMOUNT	8 YEARS	9 YEARS	10 YEARS	11 YEARS	12 YEARS	13 YEARS	14 YEARS
100	1.41	1.30	1.21	1.14	1.08	1.03	0.99
200	2.83	2.60	2.43	2.28	2.16	2.07	1.98
500	7.07	6.51	6.07	5.71	5.41	5.17	4.96
1000	14.14	13.02	12.13	11.42	10.82	10.33	9.91
2000	28.27	26.04	24.27	22.83	21.65	20.66	19.83
5000	70.68	65.09	60.66	57.08	54.12	51.65	49.57
6000	84.82	78.11	72.80	68.49	64.95	61.98	59.48
7000	98.96	91.13	84.93	79.91	75.77	72.32	69.39
8000	113.09	104.15	97.06	91.32	86.60	82.65	79.31
9000	127.23	117.17	109.19	102.74	97.42	92.98	89.22
10000	141.37	130.19	121.33	114.15	108.25	103.31	99.13
15000	212.05	195.28	181.99	171.23	162.37	154.96	148.70
20000	282.73	260.37	242.66	228.31	216.49	206.61	198.26
25000	353.42	325.47	303.32	285.39	270.61	258.27	247.83
30000	424.10	390.56	363.98	342.46	324.74	309.92	297.40
35000	494.78	455.66	424.65	399.54	378.86	361.58	346.96
40000	565.47	520.75	485.31	456.62	432.98	413.23	396.53
45000	636.15	585.84	545.97	513.70	487.10	464.88	446.09
50000	706.83	650.94	606.64	570.77	541.23	516.54	495.66
55000	777.52	716.03	667.30	627.85	595.35	568.19	545.23
60000	848.20	781.12	727.97	684.93	649.47	619.84	594.79
65000	918.88	846.22	788.63	742.00	703.59	671.50	644.36
70000	989.57	911.31	849.29	799.08	757.72	723.15	693.92
75000	1060.25	976.40	909.96	856.16	811.84	774.81	743.49
80000	1130.93	1041.50	970.62	913.24	865.96	826.46	793.05
85000	1201.62	1106.59	1031.28	970.31	920.08	878.11	842.62
90000	1272.30	1171.68	1091.95	1027.39	974.21	929.77	892.19
95000	1342.98	1236.78	1152.61	1084.47	1028.33	981.42	941.75
100000	1413.67	1301.87	1213.28	1141.54	1082.45	1033.07	991.32
105000	1484.35	1366.97	1273.94	1198.62	1136.58	1084.73	1040.88
110000	1555.03	1432.06	1334.60	1255.70	1190.70	1136.38	1090.45
120000	1696.40	1562.25	1455.93	1369.85	1298.94	1239.69	1189.58
130000	1837.77	1692.43	1577.26	1484.01	1407.19	1343.00	1288.71
140000	1979.14	1822.62	1698.59	1598.16	1515.43	1446.30	1387.85
150000	2120.50	1952.81	1819.91	1712.32	1623.68	1549.61	1486.98
160000	2261.87	2082.99	1941.24	1826.47	1731.92	1652.92	1586.11
170000	2403.24	2213.18	2062.57	1940.63	1840.17	1756.23	1685.24
180000	2544.60	2343.37	2183.90	2054.78	1948.41	1859.53	1784.37
190000	2685.97	2473.56	2305.22	2168.93	2056.66	1962.84	1883.50
200000	2827.34	2603.74	2426.55	2283.09	2164.91	2066.15	1982.64
210000	2968.70	2733.93	2547.88	2397.24	2273.15	2169.46	2081.77
220000	3110.07	2864.12	2669.21	2511.40	2381.40	2272.76	2180.90
230000	3251.44	2994.30	2790.53	2625.55	2489.64	2376.07	2280.03
240000	3392.80	3124.49	2911.86	2739.71	2597.89	2479.38	2379.16
250000	3534.17	3254.68	3033.19	2853.86	2706.13	2582.68	2478.30
260000	3675.54	3384.87	3154.52	2968.02	2814.38	2685.99	2577.43
270000	3816.90	3515.05	3275.85	3082.17	2922.62	2789.30	2676.56
280000	3958.27	3645.24	3397.17	3196.33	3030.87	2892.61	2775.69
290000	4099.64	3775.43	3518.50	3310.48	3139.11	2995.91	2874.82
300000	4241.00	3905.61	3639.83	3424.63	3247.36	3099.22	2973.95
310000	4382.37	4035.80	3761.16	3538.79	3355.60	3202.53	3073.09
320000	4523.74	4165.99	3882.48	3652.94	3463.85	3305.84	3172.22
330000	4665.10	4296.18	4003.81	3767.10	3572.09	3409.14	3271.35
340000	4806.47	4426.36	4125.14	3881.25	3680.34	3512.45	3370.48
350000	4947.84	4556.55	4246.47	3995.41	3788.58	3615.76	3469.61
400000	5654.67	5207.49	4853.10	4566.18	4329.81	4132.30	3965.27
450000	6361.51	5858.42	5459.74	5136.95	4871.04	4648.83	4460.93
500000	7068.34	6509.36	6066.38	5707.72	5412.26	5165.37	4956.59
550000	7775.17	7160.29	6673.02	6278.50	5953.49	5681.91	5452.25
600000	8482.01	7811.23	7279.66	6849.27	6494.72	6198.44	5947.91

8%

Monthly Payments
necessary to amortize a loan

AMOUNT	15 YEARS	16 YEARS	17 YEARS	18 YEARS	19 YEARS	20 YEARS	21 YEARS
100	0.96	0.92	0.90	0.87	0.85	0.84	0.82
200	1.91	1.85	1.80	1.75	1.71	1.67	1.64
500	4.78	4.62	4.49	4.37	4.27	4.18	4.10
1000	9.56	9.25	8.98	8.75	8.55	8.36	8.20
2000	19.11	18.50	17.97	17.50	17.09	16.73	16.41
5000	47.78	46.25	44.91	43.75	42.73	41.82	41.02
6000	57.34	55.50	53.90	52.50	51.27	50.19	49.23
7000	66.90	64.74	62.88	61.25	59.82	58.55	57.43
8000	76.45	73.99	71.86	70.00	68.36	66.92	65.63
9000	86.01	83.24	80.84	78.75	76.91	75.28	73.84
10000	95.57	92.49	89.83	87.50	85.45	83.64	82.04
15000	143.35	138.74	134.74	131.24	128.18	125.47	123.06
20000	191.13	184.99	179.65	174.99	170.90	167.29	164.09
25000	238.91	231.23	224.56	218.74	213.63	209.11	205.11
30000	286.70	277.48	269.48	262.49	256.35	250.93	246.13
35000	334.48	323.72	314.39	306.24	299.08	292.75	287.15
40000	382.26	369.97	359.30	349.99	341.80	334.58	328.17
45000	430.04	416.22	404.22	393.73	384.53	376.40	369.19
50000	477.83	462.46	449.13	437.48	427.25	418.22	410.21
55000	525.61	508.71	494.04	481.23	469.98	460.04	451.24
60000	573.39	554.96	538.95	524.98	512.70	501.86	492.26
65000	621.17	601.20	583.87	568.73	555.43	543.69	533.28
70000	668.96	647.45	628.78	612.47	598.15	585.51	574.30
75000	716.74	693.69	673.69	656.22	640.88	627.33	615.32
80000	764.52	739.94	718.61	699.97	683.60	669.15	656.34
85000	812.30	786.19	763.52	743.72	726.33	710.97	697.36
90000	860.09	832.43	808.43	787.47	769.05	752.80	738.39
95000	907.87	878.68	853.34	831.21	811.78	794.62	779.41
100000	955.65	924.93	898.26	874.96	854.50	836.44	820.43
105000	1003.43	971.17	943.17	918.71	897.23	878.26	861.45
110000	1051.22	1017.42	988.08	962.46	939.95	920.08	902.47
120000	1146.78	1109.91	1077.91	1049.96	1025.40	1003.73	984.51
130000	1242.35	1202.40	1167.73	1137.45	1110.85	1087.37	1066.56
140000	1337.91	1294.90	1257.56	1224.95	1196.30	1171.02	1148.60
150000	1433.48	1387.39	1347.39	1312.44	1281.75	1254.66	1230.64
160000	1529.04	1479.88	1437.21	1399.94	1367.20	1338.30	1312.68
170000	1624.61	1572.37	1527.04	1487.44	1452.65	1421.95	1394.73
180000	1720.17	1664.87	1616.86	1574.93	1538.10	1505.59	1476.77
190000	1815.74	1757.36	1706.69	1662.43	1623.55	1589.24	1558.81
200000	1911.30	1849.85	1796.51	1749.93	1709.00	1672.88	1640.86
210000	2006.87	1942.34	1886.34	1837.42	1794.45	1756.52	1722.90
220000	2102.43	2034.84	1976.17	1924.92	1879.90	1840.17	1804.94
230000	2198.00	2127.33	2065.99	2012.41	1965.35	1923.81	1886.98
240000	2293.57	2219.82	2155.82	2099.91	2050.80	2007.46	1969.03
250000	2389.13	2312.31	2245.64	2187.41	2136.25	2091.10	2051.07
260000	2484.70	2404.81	2335.47	2274.90	2221.70	2174.74	2133.11
270000	2580.26	2497.30	2425.29	2362.40	2307.15	2258.39	2215.16
280000	2675.83	2589.79	2515.12	2449.90	2392.60	2342.03	2297.20
290000	2771.39	2682.28	2604.94	2537.39	2478.05	2425.68	2379.24
300000	2866.96	2774.78	2694.77	2624.89	2563.50	2509.32	2461.28
310000	2962.52	2867.27	2784.60	2712.38	2648.95	2592.96	2543.33
320000	3058.09	2959.76	2874.42	2799.88	2734.40	2676.61	2625.37
330000	3153.65	3052.25	2964.25	2887.38	2819.85	2760.25	2707.41
340000	3249.22	3144.75	3054.07	2974.87	2905.30	2843.90	2789.46
350000	3344.78	3237.24	3143.90	3062.37	2990.75	2927.54	2871.50
400000	3822.61	3699.70	3593.03	3499.85	3418.01	3345.76	3281.71
450000	4300.43	4162.16	4042.16	3937.33	3845.26	3763.98	3691.93
500000	4778.26	4624.63	4491.28	4374.81	4272.51	4182.20	4102.14
550000	5256.09	5087.09	4940.41	4812.29	4699.76	4600.42	4512.35
600000	5733.91	5549.55	5389.54	5249.78	5127.01	5018.64	4922.57

Monthly Payments 8%
necessary to amortize a loan

AMOUNT	22 YEARS	23 YEARS	24 YEARS	25 YEARS	30 YEARS	35 YEARS	40 YEARS
100	0.81	0.79	0.78	0.77	0.73	0.71	0.70
200	1.61	1.59	1.56	1.54	1.47	1.42	1.39
500	4.03	3.97	3.91	3.86	3.67	3.55	3.48
1000	8.06	7.93	7.82	7.72	7.34	7.10	6.95
2000	16.12	15.87	15.64	15.44	14.68	14.21	13.91
5000	40.31	39.67	39.10	38.59	36.69	35.51	34.77
6000	48.37	47.61	46.92	46.31	44.03	42.62	41.72
7000	56.43	55.54	54.74	54.03	51.36	49.72	48.67
8000	64.49	63.48	62.56	61.75	58.70	56.82	55.62
9000	72.56	71.41	70.38	69.46	66.04	63.92	62.58
10000	80.62	79.35	78.21	77.18	73.38	71.03	69.53
15000	120.93	119.02	117.31	115.77	110.06	106.54	104.30
20000	161.24	158.69	156.41	154.36	146.75	142.05	139.06
25000	201.54	198.36	195.51	192.95	183.44	177.57	173.83
30000	241.85	238.04	234.62	231.54	220.13	213.08	208.59
35000	282.16	277.71	273.72	270.14	256.82	248.59	243.36
40000	322.47	317.38	312.82	308.73	293.51	284.10	278.12
45000	362.78	357.05	351.92	347.32	330.19	319.62	312.89
50000	403.09	396.73	391.03	385.91	366.88	355.13	347.66
55000	443.40	436.40	430.13	424.50	403.57	390.64	382.42
60000	483.71	476.07	469.23	463.09	440.26	426.16	417.19
65000	524.02	515.74	508.34	501.68	476.95	461.67	451.95
70000	564.32	555.42	547.44	540.27	513.64	497.18	486.72
75000	604.63	595.09	586.54	578.86	550.32	532.70	521.48
80000	644.94	634.76	625.64	617.45	587.01	568.21	556.25
85000	685.25	674.43	664.75	656.04	623.70	603.72	591.01
90000	725.56	714.11	703.85	694.63	660.39	639.23	625.78
95000	765.87	753.78	742.95	733.23	697.08	674.75	660.55
100000	806.18	793.45	782.05	771.82	733.76	710.26	695.31
105000	846.49	833.13	821.16	810.41	770.45	745.77	730.08
110000	886.80	872.80	860.26	849.00	807.14	781.29	764.84
120000	967.41	952.14	938.46	926.18	880.52	852.31	834.37
130000	1048.03	1031.49	1016.67	1003.36	953.89	923.34	903.91
140000	1128.65	1110.83	1094.88	1080.54	1027.27	994.37	973.44
150000	1209.27	1190.18	1173.08	1157.72	1100.65	1065.39	1042.97
160000	1289.88	1269.52	1251.29	1234.91	1174.02	1136.42	1112.50
170000	1370.50	1348.87	1329.49	1312.09	1247.40	1207.44	1182.03
180000	1451.12	1428.21	1407.70	1389.27	1320.78	1278.47	1251.56
190000	1531.74	1507.56	1485.90	1466.45	1394.15	1349.50	1321.09
200000	1612.36	1586.91	1564.11	1543.63	1467.53	1420.52	1390.62
210000	1692.97	1666.25	1642.31	1620.81	1540.91	1491.55	1460.15
220000	1773.59	1745.60	1720.52	1698.00	1614.28	1562.57	1529.69
230000	1854.21	1824.94	1798.72	1775.18	1687.66	1633.60	1599.22
240000	1934.83	1904.29	1876.93	1852.36	1761.03	1704.63	1668.75
250000	2015.44	1983.63	1955.14	1929.54	1834.41	1775.65	1738.28
260000	2096.06	2062.98	2033.34	2006.72	1907.79	1846.68	1807.81
270000	2176.68	2142.32	2111.55	2083.90	1981.16	1917.70	1877.34
280000	2257.30	2221.67	2189.75	2161.09	2054.54	1988.73	1946.87
290000	2337.92	2301.01	2267.96	2238.27	2127.92	2059.76	2016.40
300000	2418.53	2380.36	2346.16	2315.45	2201.29	2130.78	2085.94
310000	2499.15	2459.70	2424.37	2392.63	2274.67	2201.81	2155.47
320000	2579.77	2539.05	2502.57	2469.81	2348.05	2272.83	2225.00
330000	2660.39	2618.39	2580.78	2546.99	2421.42	2343.86	2294.53
340000	2741.00	2697.74	2658.98	2624.18	2494.80	2414.89	2364.06
350000	2821.62	2777.08	2737.19	2701.36	2568.18	2485.91	2433.59
400000	3224.71	3173.81	3128.22	3087.26	2935.06	2841.04	2781.25
450000	3627.80	3570.54	3519.24	3473.17	3301.94	3196.17	3128.90
500000	4030.89	3967.26	3910.27	3859.08	3668.82	3551.30	3476.56
550000	4433.98	4363.99	4301.30	4244.99	4035.71	3906.43	3824.21
600000	4837.07	4760.72	4692.32	4630.90	4402.59	4261.57	4171.87

8¼%   **Monthly Payments**
necessary to amortize a loan

AMOUNT	1 YEAR	2 YEARS	3 YEARS	4 YEARS	5 YEARS	6 YEARS	7 YEARS
100	8.71	4.53	3.15	2.45	2.04	1.77	1.57
200	17.42	9.07	6.29	4.91	4.08	3.53	3.14
500	43.55	22.67	15.73	12.27	10.20	8.83	7.86
1000	87.10	45.34	31.45	24.53	20.40	17.66	15.71
2000	174.21	90.68	62.90	49.06	40.79	35.31	31.42
5000	435.52	226.71	157.26	122.65	101.98	88.28	78.56
6000	522.62	272.05	188.71	147.18	122.38	105.93	94.27
7000	609.73	317.39	220.16	171.71	142.77	123.59	109.98
8000	696.83	362.73	251.61	196.24	163.17	141.24	125.69
9000	783.94	408.07	283.07	220.77	183.57	158.90	141.40
10000	871.04	453.41	314.52	245.30	203.96	176.56	157.11
15000	1306.56	680.12	471.78	367.96	305.94	264.83	235.67
20000	1742.08	906.83	629.04	490.61	407.93	353.11	314.22
25000	2177.60	1133.53	786.30	613.26	509.91	441.39	392.78
30000	2613.12	1360.24	943.55	735.91	611.89	529.67	471.33
35000	3048.64	1586.95	1100.81	858.57	713.87	617.94	549.89
40000	3484.16	1813.66	1258.07	981.22	815.85	706.22	628.44
45000	3919.68	2040.36	1415.33	1103.87	917.83	794.50	707.00
50000	4355.20	2267.07	1572.59	1226.52	1019.81	882.78	785.55
55000	4790.72	2493.78	1729.85	1349.17	1121.79	971.06	864.11
60000	5226.24	2720.48	1887.11	1471.83	1223.78	1059.33	942.66
65000	5661.76	2947.19	2044.37	1594.48	1325.76	1147.61	1021.22
70000	6097.28	3173.90	2201.63	1717.13	1427.74	1235.89	1099.77
75000	6532.80	3400.60	2358.89	1839.78	1529.72	1324.17	1178.33
80000	6968.33	3627.31	2516.15	1962.44	1631.70	1412.44	1256.88
85000	7403.85	3854.02	2673.40	2085.09	1733.68	1500.72	1335.44
90000	7839.37	4080.73	2830.66	2207.74	1835.66	1589.00	1414.00
95000	8274.89	4307.43	2987.92	2330.39	1937.64	1677.28	1492.55
100000	8710.41	4534.14	3145.18	2453.04	2039.63	1765.56	1571.11
105000	9145.93	4760.85	3302.44	2575.70	2141.61	1853.83	1649.66
110000	9581.45	4987.55	3459.70	2698.35	2243.59	1942.11	1728.22
120000	10452.49	5440.97	3774.22	2943.65	2447.55	2118.67	1885.33
130000	11323.53	5894.38	4088.74	3188.96	2651.51	2295.22	2042.44
140000	12194.57	6347.80	4403.26	3434.26	2855.48	2471.78	2199.55
150000	13065.61	6801.21	4717.77	3679.57	3059.44	2648.33	2356.66
160000	13936.65	7254.62	5032.29	3924.87	3263.40	2824.89	2513.77
170000	14807.69	7708.04	5346.81	4170.18	3467.36	3001.45	2670.88
180000	15678.73	8161.45	5661.33	4415.48	3671.33	3178.00	2827.99
190000	16549.77	8614.87	5975.85	4660.78	3875.29	3354.56	2985.10
200000	17420.81	9068.28	6290.36	4906.09	4079.25	3531.11	3142.21
210000	18291.85	9521.69	6604.88	5151.39	4283.21	3707.67	3299.32
220000	19162.89	9975.11	6919.40	5396.70	4487.18	3884.22	3456.43
230000	20033.93	10428.52	7233.92	5642.00	4691.14	4060.78	3613.54
240000	20904.98	10881.94	7548.44	5887.31	4895.10	4237.33	3770.65
250000	21776.02	11335.35	7862.96	6132.61	5099.06	4413.89	3927.76
260000	22647.06	11788.76	8177.47	6377.92	5303.03	4590.45	4084.88
270000	23518.10	12242.18	8491.99	6623.22	5506.99	4767.00	4241.99
280000	24389.14	12695.59	8806.51	6868.52	5710.95	4943.56	4399.10
290000	25260.18	13149.01	9121.03	7113.83	5914.91	5120.11	4556.21
300000	26131.22	13602.42	9435.55	7359.13	6118.88	5296.67	4713.32
310000	27002.26	14055.83	9750.07	7604.44	6322.84	5473.22	4870.43
320000	27873.30	14509.25	10064.58	7849.74	6526.80	5649.78	5027.54
330000	28744.34	14962.66	10379.10	8095.05	6730.76	5826.34	5184.65
340000	29615.38	15416.08	10693.62	8340.35	6934.73	6002.89	5341.76
350000	30486.42	15869.49	11008.14	8585.66	7138.69	6179.45	5498.87
400000	34841.63	18136.56	12580.73	9812.18	8158.50	7062.22	6284.42
450000	39196.83	20403.63	14153.32	11038.70	9178.31	7945.00	7069.98
500000	43552.03	22670.70	15725.91	12265.22	10198.13	8827.78	7855.53
550000	47907.23	24937.77	17298.50	13491.74	11217.94	9710.56	8641.08
600000	52262.44	27204.84	18871.09	14718.27	12237.75	10593.34	9426.64

Monthly Payments 8¼%
necessary to amortize a loan

AMOUNT	8 YEARS	9 YEARS	10 YEARS	11 YEARS	12 YEARS	13 YEARS	14 YEARS
100	1.43	1.31	1.23	1.16	1.10	1.05	1.01
200	2.85	2.63	2.45	2.31	2.19	2.09	2.01
500	7.13	6.57	6.13	5.78	5.48	5.24	5.03
1000	14.26	13.15	12.27	11.55	10.96	10.47	10.06
2000	28.53	26.30	24.53	23.10	21.92	20.94	20.11
5000	71.32	65.74	61.33	57.75	54.81	52.35	50.28
6000	85.58	78.89	73.59	69.30	65.77	62.82	60.33
7000	99.85	92.04	85.86	80.85	76.73	73.30	70.39
8000	114.11	105.19	98.12	92.40	87.70	83.77	80.45
9000	128.38	118.34	110.39	103.95	98.66	94.24	90.50
10000	142.64	131.49	122.65	115.50	109.62	104.71	100.56
15000	213.96	197.23	183.98	173.26	164.43	157.06	150.83
20000	285.28	262.97	245.31	231.01	219.24	209.42	201.11
25000	356.60	328.72	306.63	288.76	274.05	261.77	251.39
30000	427.92	394.46	367.96	346.51	328.86	314.12	301.67
35000	499.24	460.20	429.28	404.27	383.67	366.48	351.95
40000	570.56	525.95	490.61	462.02	438.48	418.83	402.23
45000	641.88	591.69	551.94	519.77	493.29	471.18	452.50
50000	713.20	657.43	613.26	577.52	548.10	523.54	502.78
55000	784.52	723.18	674.59	635.28	602.91	575.89	553.06
60000	855.84	788.92	735.92	693.03	657.72	628.25	603.34
65000	927.16	854.66	797.24	750.78	712.53	680.60	653.62
70000	998.49	920.41	858.57	808.53	767.35	732.95	703.90
75000	1069.81	986.15	919.89	866.29	822.16	785.31	754.17
80000	1141.13	1051.89	981.22	924.04	876.97	837.66	804.45
85000	1212.45	1117.64	1042.55	981.79	931.78	890.02	854.73
90000	1283.77	1183.38	1103.87	1039.54	986.59	942.37	905.01
95000	1355.09	1249.12	1165.20	1097.30	1041.40	994.72	955.29
100000	1426.41	1314.87	1226.53	1155.05	1096.21	1047.08	1005.57
105000	1497.73	1380.61	1287.85	1212.80	1151.02	1099.43	1055.84
110000	1569.05	1446.35	1349.18	1270.55	1205.83	1151.78	1106.12
120000	1711.69	1577.84	1471.83	1386.06	1315.45	1256.49	1206.68
130000	1854.33	1709.33	1594.48	1501.56	1425.07	1361.20	1307.24
140000	1996.97	1840.81	1717.14	1617.07	1534.69	1465.91	1407.79
150000	2139.61	1972.30	1839.79	1732.57	1644.31	1570.61	1508.35
160000	2282.25	2103.79	1962.44	1848.08	1753.93	1675.32	1608.90
170000	2424.89	2235.27	2085.09	1963.58	1863.55	1780.03	1709.46
180000	2567.53	2366.76	2207.75	2079.09	1973.17	1884.74	1810.02
190000	2710.17	2498.25	2330.40	2194.59	2082.79	1989.45	1910.57
200000	2852.81	2629.73	2453.05	2310.10	2192.41	2094.15	2011.13
210000	2995.46	2761.22	2575.71	2425.60	2302.04	2198.86	2111.69
220000	3138.10	2892.71	2698.36	2541.11	2411.66	2303.57	2212.24
230000	3280.74	3024.19	2821.01	2656.61	2521.28	2408.28	2312.80
240000	3423.38	3155.68	2943.66	2772.12	2630.90	2512.98	2413.36
250000	3566.02	3287.17	3066.32	2887.62	2740.52	2617.69	2513.91
260000	3708.66	3418.65	3188.97	3003.13	2850.14	2722.40	2614.47
270000	3851.30	3550.14	3311.62	3118.63	2959.76	2827.11	2715.03
280000	3993.94	3681.63	3434.27	3234.14	3069.38	2931.81	2815.58
290000	4136.58	3813.11	3556.93	3349.64	3179.00	3036.52	2916.14
300000	4279.22	3944.60	3679.58	3465.15	3288.62	3141.23	3016.70
310000	4421.86	4076.09	3802.23	3580.65	3398.24	3245.94	3117.25
320000	4564.50	4207.57	3924.88	3696.15	3507.86	3350.65	3217.81
330000	4707.14	4339.06	4047.54	3811.66	3617.48	3455.35	3318.37
340000	4849.79	4470.55	4170.19	3927.16	3727.10	3560.06	3418.92
350000	4992.43	4602.03	4292.84	4042.67	3836.73	3664.77	3519.48
400000	5705.63	5259.47	4906.11	4620.19	4384.83	4188.31	4022.26
450000	6418.83	5916.90	5519.37	5197.72	4932.93	4711.84	4525.05
500000	7132.04	6574.33	6132.63	5775.24	5481.04	5235.38	5027.83
550000	7845.24	7231.77	6745.89	6352.77	6029.14	5758.92	5530.61
600000	8558.44	7889.20	7359.16	6930.29	6577.24	6282.46	6033.39

57

8¼%

Monthly Payments
necessary to amortize a loan

AMOUNT	15 YEARS	16 YEARS	17 YEARS	18 YEARS	19 YEARS	20 YEARS	21 YEARS
100	0.97	0.94	0.91	0.89	0.87	0.85	0.84
200	1.94	1.88	1.83	1.78	1.74	1.70	1.67
500	4.85	4.70	4.57	4.45	4.35	4.26	4.18
1000	9.70	9.40	9.13	8.90	8.70	8.52	8.36
2000	19.40	18.79	18.26	17.80	17.40	17.04	16.73
5000	48.51	46.98	45.66	44.51	43.50	42.60	41.81
6000	58.21	56.38	54.79	53.41	52.19	51.12	50.18
7000	67.91	65.78	63.92	62.31	60.89	59.64	58.54
8000	77.61	75.17	73.06	71.21	69.59	68.17	66.90
9000	87.31	84.57	82.19	80.11	78.29	76.69	75.26
10000	97.01	93.97	91.32	89.01	86.99	85.21	83.63
15000	145.52	140.95	136.98	133.52	130.49	127.81	125.44
20000	194.03	187.93	182.64	178.03	173.98	170.41	167.25
25000	242.54	234.91	228.30	222.54	217.48	213.02	209.07
30000	291.04	281.90	273.96	267.04	260.97	255.62	250.88
35000	339.55	328.88	319.62	311.55	304.47	298.22	292.69
40000	388.06	375.86	365.29	356.06	347.96	340.83	334.51
45000	436.56	422.84	410.95	400.57	391.46	383.43	376.32
50000	485.07	469.83	456.61	445.07	434.95	426.03	418.13
55000	533.58	516.81	502.27	489.58	478.45	468.64	459.95
60000	582.08	563.79	547.93	534.09	521.95	511.24	501.76
65000	630.59	610.77	593.59	578.60	565.44	553.84	543.57
70000	679.10	657.76	639.25	623.10	608.94	596.45	585.39
75000	727.61	704.74	684.91	667.61	652.43	639.05	627.20
80000	776.11	751.72	730.57	712.12	695.93	681.65	669.01
85000	824.62	798.70	776.23	756.63	739.42	724.26	710.83
90000	873.13	845.69	821.89	801.13	782.92	766.86	752.64
95000	921.63	892.67	867.55	845.64	826.41	809.46	794.45
100000	970.14	939.65	913.21	890.15	869.91	852.07	836.27
105000	1018.65	986.63	958.87	934.66	913.40	894.67	878.08
110000	1067.15	1033.62	1004.54	979.16	956.90	937.27	919.89
120000	1164.17	1127.58	1095.86	1068.18	1043.89	1022.48	1003.52
130000	1261.18	1221.55	1187.18	1157.19	1130.88	1107.69	1087.15
140000	1358.20	1315.51	1278.50	1246.21	1217.87	1192.89	1170.77
150000	1455.21	1409.48	1369.82	1335.22	1304.86	1278.10	1254.40
160000	1552.22	1503.44	1461.14	1424.24	1391.85	1363.31	1338.03
170000	1649.24	1597.41	1552.46	1513.25	1478.85	1448.51	1421.65
180000	1746.25	1691.37	1643.79	1602.27	1565.84	1533.72	1505.28
190000	1843.27	1785.34	1735.11	1691.28	1652.83	1618.92	1588.91
200000	1940.28	1879.30	1826.43	1780.30	1739.82	1704.13	1672.53
210000	2037.29	1973.27	1917.75	1869.31	1826.81	1789.34	1756.16
220000	2134.31	2067.23	2009.07	1958.32	1913.80	1874.54	1839.79
230000	2231.32	2161.20	2100.39	2047.34	2000.79	1959.75	1923.41
240000	2328.34	2255.16	2191.71	2136.35	2087.78	2044.96	2007.04
250000	2425.35	2349.13	2283.04	2225.37	2174.77	2130.16	2090.67
260000	2522.36	2443.09	2374.36	2314.38	2261.76	2215.37	2174.29
270000	2619.38	2537.06	2465.68	2403.40	2348.75	2300.58	2257.92
280000	2716.39	2631.02	2557.00	2492.41	2435.75	2385.78	2341.55
290000	2813.41	2724.99	2648.32	2581.43	2522.74	2470.99	2425.17
300000	2910.42	2818.95	2739.64	2670.44	2609.73	2556.20	2508.80
310000	3007.44	2912.92	2830.96	2759.46	2696.72	2641.40	2592.42
320000	3104.45	3006.88	2922.29	2848.47	2783.71	2726.61	2676.05
330000	3201.46	3100.85	3013.61	2937.49	2870.70	2811.82	2759.68
340000	3298.48	3194.81	3104.93	3026.50	2957.69	2897.02	2843.30
350000	3395.49	3288.78	3196.25	3115.52	3044.68	2982.23	2926.93
400000	3880.56	3758.60	3652.86	3560.59	3479.64	3408.26	3345.06
450000	4365.63	4228.43	4109.46	4005.66	3914.59	3834.30	3763.20
500000	4850.70	4698.25	4566.07	4450.74	4349.55	4260.33	4181.33
550000	5335.77	5168.08	5022.68	4895.81	4784.50	4686.36	4599.46
600000	5820.84	5637.90	5479.29	5340.89	5219.46	5112.39	5017.60

Monthly Payments 8¼%

necessary to amortize a loan

AMOUNT	22 YEARS	23 YEARS	24 YEARS	25 YEARS	30 YEARS	35 YEARS	40 YEARS
100	0.82	0.81	0.80	0.79	0.75	0.73	0.71
200	1.64	1.62	1.60	1.58	1.50	1.46	1.43
500	4.11	4.05	3.99	3.94	3.76	3.64	3.57
1000	8.22	8.10	7.98	7.88	7.51	7.28	7.14
2000	16.44	16.19	15.97	15.77	15.03	14.57	14.28
5000	41.11	40.48	39.92	39.42	37.56	36.42	35.71
6000	49.33	48.58	47.91	47.31	45.08	43.71	42.85
7000	57.56	56.68	55.89	55.19	52.59	50.99	49.99
8000	65.78	64.78	63.88	63.08	60.10	58.28	57.13
9000	74.00	72.87	71.86	70.96	67.61	65.56	64.27
10000	82.22	80.97	79.85	78.85	75.13	72.85	71.41
15000	123.33	121.45	119.77	118.27	112.69	109.27	107.12
20000	164.44	161.94	159.70	157.69	150.25	145.70	142.83
25000	205.56	202.42	199.62	197.11	187.82	182.12	178.53
30000	246.67	242.91	239.55	236.54	225.38	218.55	214.24
35000	287.78	283.39	279.47	275.96	262.94	254.97	249.95
40000	328.89	323.88	319.40	315.38	300.51	291.40	285.66
45000	370.00	364.36	359.32	354.80	338.07	327.82	321.36
50000	411.11	404.85	399.25	394.23	375.63	364.25	357.07
55000	452.22	445.33	439.17	433.65	413.20	400.67	392.78
60000	493.33	485.82	479.10	473.07	450.76	437.09	428.48
65000	534.45	526.30	519.02	512.49	488.32	473.52	464.19
70000	575.56	566.79	558.95	551.92	525.89	509.94	499.90
75000	616.67	607.27	598.87	591.34	563.45	546.37	535.60
80000	657.78	647.76	638.80	630.76	601.01	582.79	571.31
85000	698.89	688.24	678.72	670.18	638.58	619.22	607.02
90000	740.00	728.73	718.65	709.61	676.14	655.64	642.72
95000	781.11	769.21	758.57	749.03	713.70	692.07	678.43
100000	822.22	809.70	798.50	788.45	751.27	728.49	714.14
105000	863.33	850.18	838.42	827.87	788.83	764.92	749.85
110000	904.45	890.67	878.35	867.30	826.39	801.34	785.55
120000	986.67	971.64	958.20	946.14	901.52	874.19	856.97
130000	1068.89	1052.61	1038.05	1024.99	976.65	947.04	928.38
140000	1151.11	1133.58	1117.90	1103.83	1051.77	1019.89	999.79
150000	1233.33	1214.55	1197.75	1182.68	1126.90	1092.74	1071.21
160000	1315.56	1295.52	1277.60	1261.52	1202.03	1165.59	1142.62
170000	1397.78	1376.49	1357.45	1340.37	1277.15	1238.43	1214.04
180000	1480.00	1457.46	1437.30	1419.21	1352.28	1311.28	1285.45
190000	1562.22	1538.43	1517.15	1498.06	1427.41	1384.13	1356.86
200000	1644.45	1619.40	1596.99	1576.90	1502.53	1456.98	1428.28
210000	1726.67	1700.37	1676.84	1655.75	1577.66	1529.83	1499.69
220000	1808.89	1781.34	1756.69	1734.59	1652.79	1602.68	1571.11
230000	1891.11	1862.31	1836.54	1813.44	1727.91	1675.53	1642.52
240000	1973.34	1943.28	1916.39	1892.28	1803.04	1748.38	1713.93
250000	2055.56	2024.25	1996.24	1971.13	1878.17	1821.23	1785.35
260000	2137.78	2105.22	2076.09	2049.97	1953.29	1894.08	1856.76
270000	2220.00	2186.19	2155.94	2128.82	2028.42	1966.93	1928.17
280000	2302.23	2267.16	2235.79	2207.66	2103.55	2039.78	1999.59
290000	2384.45	2348.13	2315.64	2286.51	2178.67	2112.62	2071.00
300000	2466.67	2429.10	2395.49	2365.35	2253.80	2185.47	2142.42
310000	2548.89	2510.07	2475.34	2444.20	2328.93	2258.32	2213.83
320000	2631.11	2591.04	2555.19	2523.04	2404.05	2331.17	2285.24
330000	2713.34	2672.01	2635.04	2601.89	2479.18	2404.02	2356.66
340000	2795.56	2752.98	2714.89	2680.73	2554.31	2476.87	2428.07
350000	2877.78	2833.95	2794.74	2759.58	2629.43	2549.72	2499.49
400000	3288.89	3238.80	3193.99	3153.80	3005.07	2913.96	2856.56
450000	3700.00	3643.65	3593.24	3548.03	3380.70	3278.21	3213.62
500000	4111.12	4048.50	3992.49	3942.25	3756.33	3642.46	3570.69
550000	4522.23	4453.35	4391.74	4336.48	4131.97	4006.70	3927.76
600000	4933.34	4858.20	4790.98	4730.70	4507.60	4370.95	4284.83

8 1/2%

Monthly Payments
necessary to amortize a loan

AMOUNT	1 YEAR	2 YEARS	3 YEARS	4 YEARS	5 YEARS	6 YEARS	7 YEARS
100	8.72	4.55	3.16	2.46	2.05	1.78	1.58
200	17.44	9.09	6.31	4.93	4.10	3.56	3.17
500	43.61	22.73	15.78	12.32	10.26	8.89	7.92
1000	87.22	45.46	31.57	24.65	20.52	17.78	15.84
2000	174.44	90.91	63.14	49.30	41.03	35.56	31.67
5000	436.10	227.28	157.84	123.24	102.58	88.89	79.18
6000	523.32	272.73	189.41	147.89	123.10	106.67	95.02
7000	610.54	318.19	220.97	172.54	143.62	124.45	110.86
8000	697.76	363.65	252.54	197.19	164.13	142.23	126.69
9000	784.98	409.10	284.11	221.83	184.65	160.01	142.53
10000	872.20	454.56	315.68	246.48	205.17	177.78	158.36
15000	1308.30	681.84	473.51	369.72	307.75	266.68	237.55
20000	1744.40	909.11	631.35	492.97	410.33	355.57	316.73
25000	2180.49	1136.39	789.19	616.21	512.91	444.46	395.91
30000	2616.59	1363.67	947.03	739.45	615.50	533.35	475.09
35000	3052.69	1590.95	1104.86	862.69	718.08	622.24	554.28
40000	3488.79	1818.23	1262.70	985.93	820.66	711.14	633.46
45000	3924.89	2045.51	1420.54	1109.17	923.24	800.03	712.64
50000	4360.99	2272.78	1578.38	1232.42	1025.83	888.92	791.82
55000	4797.09	2500.06	1736.21	1355.66	1128.41	977.81	871.01
60000	5233.19	2727.34	1894.05	1478.90	1230.99	1066.70	950.19
65000	5669.29	2954.62	2051.89	1602.14	1333.57	1155.59	1029.37
70000	6105.38	3181.90	2209.73	1725.38	1436.16	1244.49	1108.55
75000	6541.48	3409.18	2367.57	1848.62	1538.74	1333.38	1187.74
80000	6977.58	3636.45	2525.40	1971.86	1641.32	1422.27	1266.92
85000	7413.68	3863.73	2683.24	2095.11	1743.91	1511.16	1346.10
90000	7849.78	4091.01	2841.08	2218.35	1846.49	1600.05	1425.28
95000	8285.88	4318.29	2998.92	2341.59	1949.07	1688.95	1504.47
100000	8721.98	4545.57	3156.75	2464.83	2051.65	1777.84	1583.65
105000	9158.08	4772.85	3314.59	2588.07	2154.24	1866.73	1662.83
110000	9594.18	5000.12	3472.43	2711.31	2256.82	1955.62	1742.01
120000	10466.37	5454.68	3788.10	2957.80	2461.98	2133.41	1900.38
130000	11338.57	5909.24	4103.78	3204.28	2667.15	2311.19	2058.74
140000	12210.77	6363.79	4419.46	3450.76	2872.31	2488.97	2217.11
150000	13082.97	6818.35	4735.13	3697.25	3077.48	2666.76	2375.47
160000	13955.17	7272.91	5050.81	3943.73	3282.65	2844.54	2533.84
170000	14827.36	7727.46	5366.48	4190.21	3487.81	3022.33	2692.20
180000	15699.56	8182.02	5682.16	4436.69	3692.98	3200.11	2850.57
190000	16571.76	8636.58	5997.83	4683.18	3898.14	3377.89	3008.93
200000	17443.96	9091.13	6313.51	4929.66	4103.31	3555.68	3167.30
210000	18316.15	9545.69	6629.18	5176.14	4308.47	3733.46	3325.66
220000	19188.35	10000.25	6944.86	5422.63	4513.64	3911.24	3484.03
230000	20060.55	10454.81	7260.53	5669.11	4718.80	4089.03	3642.39
240000	20932.75	10909.36	7576.21	5915.59	4923.97	4266.81	3800.76
250000	21804.95	11363.92	7891.88	6162.08	5129.13	4444.60	3959.12
260000	22677.14	11818.48	8207.56	6408.56	5334.30	4622.38	4117.49
270000	23549.34	12273.03	8523.24	6655.04	5539.46	4800.16	4275.85
280000	24421.54	12727.59	8838.91	6901.52	5744.63	4977.95	4434.22
290000	25293.74	13182.15	9154.59	7148.01	5949.79	5155.73	4592.58
300000	26165.93	13636.70	9470.26	7394.49	6154.96	5333.52	4750.95
310000	27038.13	14091.26	9785.94	7640.97	6360.12	5511.30	4909.31
320000	27910.33	14545.82	10101.61	7887.46	6565.29	5689.08	5067.68
330000	28782.53	15000.37	10417.29	8133.94	6770.46	5866.87	5226.04
340000	29654.73	15454.93	10732.96	8380.42	6975.62	6044.65	5384.41
350000	30526.92	15909.49	11048.64	8626.91	7180.79	6222.43	5542.77
400000	34887.91	18182.27	12627.01	9859.32	8206.61	7111.35	6334.59
450000	39248.90	20455.05	14205.39	11091.74	9232.44	8000.27	7126.42
500000	43609.89	22727.84	15783.77	12324.15	10258.27	8889.19	7918.24
550000	47970.88	25000.62	17362.15	13556.57	11284.09	9778.11	8710.07
600000	52331.87	27273.40	18940.52	14788.98	12309.92	10667.03	9501.89

Monthly Payments 8½%
necessary to amortize a loan

AMOUNT	8 YEARS	9 YEARS	10 YEARS	11 YEARS	12 YEARS	13 YEARS	14 YEARS
100	1.44	1.33	1.24	1.17	1.11	1.06	1.02
200	2.88	2.66	2.48	2.34	2.22	2.12	2.04
500	7.20	6.64	6.20	5.84	5.55	5.31	5.10
1000	14.39	13.28	12.40	11.69	11.10	10.61	10.20
2000	28.78	26.56	24.80	23.37	22.20	21.22	20.40
5000	71.96	66.40	61.99	58.43	55.50	53.06	51.00
6000	86.35	79.68	74.39	70.12	66.60	63.67	61.20
7000	100.74	92.96	86.79	81.80	77.70	74.28	71.39
8000	115.14	106.23	99.19	93.49	88.80	84.89	81.59
9000	129.53	119.51	111.59	105.18	99.91	95.51	91.79
10000	143.92	132.79	123.99	116.86	111.01	106.12	101.99
15000	215.88	199.19	185.98	175.30	166.51	159.18	152.99
20000	287.84	265.59	247.97	233.73	222.01	212.24	203.98
25000	359.80	331.98	309.96	292.16	277.51	265.29	254.98
30000	431.76	398.38	371.96	350.59	333.02	318.35	305.98
35000	503.72	464.78	433.95	409.02	388.52	371.41	356.97
40000	575.69	531.17	495.94	467.46	444.02	424.47	407.97
45000	647.65	597.57	557.94	525.89	499.53	477.53	458.96
50000	719.61	663.97	619.93	584.32	555.03	530.59	509.96
55000	791.57	730.36	681.92	642.75	610.53	583.65	560.96
60000	863.53	796.76	743.91	701.18	666.03	636.71	611.95
65000	935.49	863.16	805.91	759.62	721.54	689.77	662.95
70000	1007.45	929.55	867.90	818.05	777.04	742.83	713.94
75000	1079.41	995.95	929.89	876.48	832.54	795.88	764.94
80000	1151.37	1062.35	991.89	934.91	888.04	848.94	815.93
85000	1223.33	1128.74	1053.88	993.34	943.55	902.00	866.93
90000	1295.29	1195.14	1115.87	1051.78	999.05	955.06	917.93
95000	1367.25	1261.54	1177.86	1110.21	1054.55	1008.12	968.92
100000	1439.21	1327.94	1239.86	1168.64	1110.06	1061.18	1019.92
105000	1511.17	1394.33	1301.85	1227.07	1165.56	1114.24	1070.91
110000	1583.13	1460.73	1363.84	1285.50	1221.06	1167.30	1121.91
120000	1727.06	1593.52	1487.83	1402.37	1332.07	1273.41	1223.90
130000	1870.98	1726.32	1611.81	1519.23	1443.07	1379.53	1325.89
140000	2014.90	1859.11	1735.80	1636.09	1554.08	1485.65	1427.89
150000	2158.82	1991.90	1859.79	1752.96	1665.08	1591.77	1529.88
160000	2302.74	2124.70	1983.77	1869.82	1776.09	1697.89	1631.87
170000	2446.66	2257.49	2107.76	1986.69	1887.09	1804.00	1733.86
180000	2590.58	2390.28	2231.74	2103.55	1998.10	1910.12	1835.85
190000	2734.50	2523.08	2355.73	2220.41	2109.11	2016.24	1937.85
200000	2878.43	2655.87	2479.71	2337.28	2220.11	2122.36	2039.84
210000	3022.35	2788.66	2603.70	2454.14	2331.12	2228.48	2141.83
220000	3166.27	2921.46	2727.69	2571.01	2442.12	2334.59	2243.82
230000	3310.19	3054.25	2851.67	2687.87	2553.13	2440.71	2345.81
240000	3454.11	3187.04	2975.66	2804.73	2664.13	2546.83	2447.80
250000	3598.03	3319.84	3099.64	2921.60	2775.14	2652.95	2549.80
260000	3741.95	3452.63	3223.63	3038.46	2886.14	2759.07	2651.79
270000	3885.87	3585.43	3347.61	3155.33	2997.15	2865.18	2753.78
280000	4029.80	3718.22	3471.60	3272.19	3108.16	2971.30	2855.77
290000	4173.72	3851.01	3595.58	3389.05	3219.16	3077.42	2957.76
300000	4317.64	3983.81	3719.57	3505.92	3330.17	3183.54	3059.76
310000	4461.56	4116.60	3843.56	3622.78	3441.17	3289.66	3161.75
320000	4605.48	4249.39	3967.54	3739.65	3552.18	3395.77	3263.74
330000	4749.40	4382.19	4091.53	3856.51	3663.18	3501.89	3365.73
340000	4893.32	4514.98	4215.51	3973.37	3774.19	3608.01	3467.72
350000	5037.25	4647.77	4339.50	4090.24	3885.19	3714.13	3569.71
400000	5756.85	5311.74	4959.43	4674.56	4440.22	4244.72	4079.67
450000	6476.46	5975.71	5579.36	5258.88	4995.25	4775.31	4589.63
500000	7196.06	6639.68	6199.28	5843.20	5550.28	5305.90	5099.59
550000	7915.67	7303.64	6819.21	6427.52	6105.31	5836.49	5609.55
600000	8635.28	7967.61	7439.14	7011.84	6660.33	6367.07	6119.51

8¹/₂%

Monthly Payments
necessary to amortize a loan

AMOUNT	15 YEARS	16 YEARS	17 YEARS	18 YEARS	19 YEARS	20 YEARS	21 YEARS
100	0.98	0.95	0.93	0.91	0.89	0.87	0.85
200	1.97	1.91	1.86	1.81	1.77	1.74	1.70
500	4.92	4.77	4.64	4.53	4.43	4.34	4.26
1000	9.85	9.54	9.28	9.05	8.85	8.68	8.52
2000	19.69	19.09	18.57	18.11	17.71	17.36	17.04
5000	49.24	47.72	46.41	45.27	44.27	43.39	42.61
6000	59.08	57.27	55.70	54.33	53.13	52.07	51.13
7000	68.93	66.81	64.98	63.38	61.98	60.75	59.66
8000	78.78	76.36	74.26	72.44	70.84	69.43	68.18
9000	88.63	85.90	83.55	81.49	79.69	78.10	76.70
10000	98.47	95.45	92.83	90.55	88.54	86.78	85.22
15000	147.71	143.17	139.24	135.82	132.82	130.17	127.84
20000	196.95	190.90	185.66	181.09	177.09	173.56	170.45
25000	246.18	238.62	232.07	226.36	221.36	216.96	213.06
30000	295.42	286.35	278.49	271.64	265.63	260.35	255.67
35000	344.66	334.07	324.90	316.91	309.91	303.74	298.28
40000	393.90	381.80	371.32	362.18	354.18	347.13	340.90
45000	443.13	429.52	417.73	407.46	398.45	390.52	383.51
50000	492.37	477.25	464.15	452.73	442.72	433.91	426.12
55000	541.61	524.97	510.56	498.00	487.00	477.30	468.73
60000	590.84	572.69	556.98	543.27	531.27	520.69	511.34
65000	640.08	620.42	603.39	588.55	575.54	564.09	553.96
70000	689.32	668.14	649.80	633.82	619.81	607.48	596.57
75000	738.55	715.87	696.22	679.09	664.08	650.87	639.18
80000	787.79	763.59	742.63	724.37	708.36	694.26	681.79
85000	837.03	811.32	789.05	769.64	752.63	737.65	724.40
90000	886.27	859.04	835.46	814.91	796.90	781.04	767.02
95000	935.50	906.77	881.88	860.18	841.17	824.43	809.63
100000	984.74	954.49	928.29	905.46	885.45	867.82	852.24
105000	1033.98	1002.22	974.71	950.73	929.72	911.21	894.85
110000	1083.21	1049.94	1021.12	996.00	973.99	954.61	937.46
120000	1181.69	1145.39	1113.95	1086.55	1062.53	1041.39	1022.69
130000	1280.16	1240.84	1206.78	1177.09	1151.08	1128.17	1107.91
140000	1378.64	1336.29	1299.61	1267.64	1239.62	1214.95	1193.13
150000	1477.11	1431.74	1392.44	1358.19	1328.17	1301.73	1278.36
160000	1575.58	1527.19	1485.27	1448.73	1416.71	1388.52	1363.58
170000	1674.06	1622.63	1578.10	1539.28	1505.26	1475.30	1448.81
180000	1772.53	1718.08	1670.93	1629.82	1593.80	1562.08	1534.03
190000	1871.01	1813.53	1763.75	1720.37	1682.35	1648.86	1619.25
200000	1969.48	1908.98	1856.58	1810.91	1770.89	1735.65	1704.48
210000	2067.95	2004.43	1949.41	1901.46	1859.44	1822.43	1789.70
220000	2166.43	2099.88	2042.24	1992.01	1947.98	1909.21	1874.93
230000	2264.90	2195.33	2135.07	2082.55	2036.52	1995.99	1960.15
240000	2363.37	2290.78	2227.90	2173.10	2125.07	2082.78	2045.37
250000	2461.85	2386.23	2320.73	2263.64	2213.61	2169.56	2130.60
260000	2560.32	2481.68	2413.56	2354.19	2302.16	2256.34	2215.82
270000	2658.80	2577.13	2506.39	2444.74	2390.70	2343.12	2301.05
280000	2757.27	2672.57	2599.22	2535.28	2479.25	2429.91	2386.27
290000	2855.74	2768.02	2692.05	2625.83	2567.79	2516.69	2471.49
300000	2954.22	2863.47	2784.88	2716.37	2656.34	2603.47	2556.72
310000	3052.69	2958.92	2877.71	2806.92	2744.88	2690.25	2641.94
320000	3151.17	3054.37	2970.53	2897.46	2833.43	2777.03	2727.17
330000	3249.64	3149.82	3063.36	2988.01	2921.97	2863.82	2812.39
340000	3348.11	3245.27	3156.19	3078.56	3010.52	2950.60	2897.61
350000	3446.59	3340.72	3249.02	3169.10	3099.06	3037.38	2982.84
400000	3938.96	3817.96	3713.17	3621.83	3541.78	3471.29	3408.96
450000	4431.33	4295.21	4177.31	4074.56	3984.51	3905.20	3835.08
500000	4923.70	4772.46	4641.46	4527.29	4427.23	4339.12	4261.20
550000	5416.07	5249.70	5105.61	4980.02	4869.95	4773.03	4687.32
600000	5908.44	5726.95	5569.75	5432.74	5312.67	5206.94	5113.44

Monthly Payments 8½%

necessary to amortize a loan

AMOUNT	22 YEARS	23 YEARS	24 YEARS	25 YEARS	30 YEARS	35 YEARS	40 YEARS
100	0.84	0.83	0.82	0.81	0.77	0.75	0.73
200	1.68	1.65	1.63	1.61	1.54	1.49	1.47
500	4.19	4.13	4.08	4.03	3.84	3.73	3.67
1000	8.38	8.26	8.15	8.05	7.69	7.47	7.33
2000	16.77	16.52	16.30	16.10	15.38	14.94	14.66
5000	41.92	41.30	40.75	40.26	38.45	37.34	36.65
6000	50.30	49.57	48.90	48.31	46.13	44.81	43.99
7000	58.69	57.83	57.06	56.37	53.82	52.28	51.32
8000	67.07	66.09	65.21	64.42	61.51	59.75	58.65
9000	75.46	74.35	73.36	72.47	69.20	67.22	65.98
10000	83.84	82.61	81.51	80.52	76.89	74.69	73.31
15000	125.76	123.91	122.26	120.78	115.34	112.03	109.96
20000	167.68	165.22	163.02	161.05	153.78	149.37	146.62
25000	209.60	206.52	203.77	201.31	192.23	186.72	183.27
30000	251.52	247.83	244.52	241.57	230.67	224.06	219.93
35000	293.44	289.13	285.28	281.83	269.12	261.40	256.58
40000	335.36	330.43	326.03	322.09	307.57	298.74	293.24
45000	377.28	371.74	366.79	362.35	346.01	336.09	329.89
50000	419.20	413.04	407.54	402.61	384.46	373.43	366.55
55000	461.12	454.35	448.30	442.87	422.90	410.77	403.20
60000	503.04	495.65	489.05	483.14	461.35	448.12	439.86
65000	544.96	536.96	529.80	523.40	499.79	485.46	476.51
70000	586.88	578.26	570.56	563.66	538.24	522.80	513.17
75000	628.80	619.56	611.31	603.92	576.69	560.15	549.82
80000	670.72	660.87	652.07	644.18	615.13	597.49	586.48
85000	712.65	702.17	692.82	684.44	653.58	634.83	623.13
90000	754.57	743.48	733.57	724.70	692.02	672.17	659.78
95000	796.49	784.78	774.33	764.97	730.47	709.52	696.44
100000	838.41	826.05	815.08	805.23	768.91	746.86	733.09
105000	880.33	867.39	855.84	845.49	807.36	784.20	769.75
110000	922.25	908.70	896.59	885.75	845.80	821.55	806.40
120000	1006.09	991.30	978.10	966.27	922.70	896.23	879.71
130000	1089.93	1073.91	1059.61	1046.80	999.59	970.92	953.02
140000	1173.77	1156.52	1141.12	1127.32	1076.48	1045.60	1026.33
150000	1257.61	1239.13	1222.62	1207.84	1153.37	1120.29	1099.64
160000	1341.45	1321.74	1304.13	1288.36	1230.26	1194.98	1172.95
170000	1425.29	1404.35	1385.64	1368.89	1307.15	1269.66	1246.26
180000	1509.13	1486.96	1467.15	1449.41	1384.04	1344.35	1319.57
190000	1592.97	1569.56	1548.66	1529.93	1460.94	1419.04	1392.88
200000	1676.81	1652.17	1630.16	1610.45	1537.83	1493.72	1466.19
210000	1760.65	1734.78	1711.67	1690.98	1614.72	1568.41	1539.50
220000	1844.49	1817.39	1793.18	1771.50	1691.61	1643.09	1612.81
230000	1928.33	1900.00	1874.69	1852.02	1768.50	1717.78	1686.12
240000	2012.17	1982.61	1956.20	1932.55	1845.39	1792.47	1759.43
250000	2096.02	2065.22	2037.71	2013.07	1922.28	1867.15	1832.74
260000	2179.86	2147.83	2119.21	2093.59	1999.18	1941.84	1906.04
270000	2263.70	2230.43	2200.72	2174.11	2076.07	2016.52	1979.35
280000	2347.54	2313.04	2282.23	2254.64	2152.96	2091.21	2052.66
290000	2431.38	2395.65	2363.74	2335.16	2229.85	2165.90	2125.97
300000	2515.22	2478.26	2445.25	2415.68	2306.74	2240.58	2199.28
310000	2599.06	2560.87	2526.76	2496.20	2383.63	2315.27	2272.59
320000	2682.90	2643.48	2608.26	2576.73	2460.52	2389.95	2345.90
330000	2766.74	2726.09	2689.77	2657.25	2537.41	2464.64	2419.21
340000	2850.58	2808.69	2771.28	2737.77	2614.31	2539.33	2492.52
350000	2934.42	2891.30	2852.79	2818.29	2691.20	2614.01	2565.83
400000	3353.62	3304.35	3260.33	3220.91	3075.65	2987.44	2932.38
450000	3772.83	3717.39	3667.87	3623.52	3460.11	3360.87	3298.92
500000	4192.03	4130.43	4075.41	4026.14	3844.57	3734.30	3665.47
550000	4611.23	4543.48	4482.95	4428.75	4229.02	4107.73	4032.02
600000	5030.44	4956.52	4890.49	4831.36	4613.48	4481.16	4398.56

8¾%

Monthly Payments
necessary to amortize a loan

AMOUNT	1 YEAR	2 YEARS	3 YEARS	4 YEARS	5 YEARS	6 YEARS	7 YEARS
100	8.73	4.56	3.17	2.48	2.06	1.79	1.60
200	17.47	9.11	6.34	4.95	4.13	3.58	3.19
500	43.67	22.79	15.84	12.38	10.32	8.95	7.98
1000	87.34	45.57	31.68	24.77	20.64	17.90	15.96
2000	174.67	91.14	63.37	49.53	41.27	35.80	31.92
5000	436.68	227.85	158.42	123.83	103.19	89.51	79.81
6000	524.01	273.42	190.10	148.60	123.82	107.41	95.77
7000	611.35	318.99	221.78	173.37	144.46	125.31	111.74
8000	698.68	364.56	253.47	198.13	165.10	143.21	127.70
9000	786.02	410.13	285.15	222.90	185.74	161.12	143.66
10000	873.36	455.70	316.84	247.67	206.37	179.02	159.62
15000	1310.03	683.55	475.25	371.50	309.56	268.53	239.44
20000	1746.71	911.40	633.67	495.33	412.74	358.03	319.25
25000	2183.39	1139.25	792.09	619.16	515.93	447.54	399.06
30000	2620.07	1367.10	950.51	743.00	619.12	537.05	478.87
35000	3056.75	1594.95	1108.92	866.83	722.30	626.56	558.69
40000	3493.42	1822.80	1267.34	990.66	825.49	716.07	638.50
45000	3930.10	2050.66	1425.76	1114.49	928.68	805.58	718.31
50000	4366.78	2278.51	1584.18	1238.33	1031.86	895.09	798.12
55000	4803.46	2506.36	1742.59	1362.16	1135.05	984.59	877.94
60000	5240.14	2734.21	1901.01	1485.99	1238.23	1074.10	957.75
65000	5676.81	2962.06	2059.43	1609.82	1341.42	1163.61	1037.56
70000	6113.49	3189.91	2217.85	1733.66	1444.61	1253.12	1117.37
75000	6550.17	3417.76	2376.26	1857.49	1547.79	1342.63	1197.19
80000	6986.85	3645.61	2534.68	1981.32	1650.98	1432.14	1277.00
85000	7423.52	3873.46	2693.10	2105.15	1754.16	1521.65	1356.81
90000	7860.20	4101.31	2851.52	2228.99	1857.35	1611.15	1436.62
95000	8296.88	4329.16	3009.93	2352.82	1960.54	1700.66	1516.44
100000	8733.56	4557.01	3168.35	2476.65	2063.72	1790.17	1596.25
105000	9170.24	4784.86	3326.77	2600.48	2166.91	1879.68	1676.06
110000	9606.91	5012.71	3485.19	2724.32	2270.10	1969.19	1755.87
120000	10480.27	5468.41	3802.02	2971.98	2476.47	2148.21	1915.50
130000	11353.63	5924.12	4118.86	3219.65	2682.84	2327.22	2075.12
140000	12226.98	6379.82	4435.69	3467.31	2889.21	2506.24	2234.75
150000	13100.34	6835.52	4752.53	3714.98	3095.58	2685.26	2394.37
160000	13973.69	7291.22	5069.36	3962.64	3301.96	2864.27	2554.00
170000	14847.05	7746.92	5386.20	4210.31	3508.33	3043.29	2713.62
180000	15720.41	8202.62	5703.03	4457.97	3714.70	3222.31	2873.25
190000	16593.76	8658.32	6019.87	4705.64	3921.07	3401.32	3032.87
200000	17467.12	9114.02	6336.70	4953.30	4127.45	3580.34	3192.50
210000	18340.47	9569.73	6653.54	5200.97	4333.82	3759.36	3352.12
220000	19213.83	10025.43	6970.37	5448.63	4540.19	3938.38	3511.75
230000	20087.19	10481.13	7287.21	5696.30	4746.56	4117.39	3671.37
240000	20960.54	10936.83	7604.04	5943.96	4952.94	4296.41	3831.00
250000	21833.90	11392.53	7920.88	6191.63	5159.31	4475.43	3990.62
260000	22707.25	11848.23	8237.71	6439.29	5365.68	4654.44	4150.25
270000	23580.61	12303.93	8554.55	6686.96	5572.05	4833.46	4309.87
280000	24453.96	12759.63	8871.38	6934.62	5778.43	5012.48	4469.50
290000	25327.32	13215.34	9188.22	7182.29	5984.80	5191.50	4629.12
300000	26200.68	13671.04	9505.05	7429.95	6191.17	5370.51	4788.75
310000	27074.03	14126.74	9821.89	7677.62	6397.54	5549.53	4948.37
320000	27947.39	14582.44	10138.72	7925.28	6603.91	5728.55	5108.00
330000	28820.74	15038.14	10455.56	8172.95	6810.29	5907.56	5267.62
340000	29694.10	15493.84	10772.39	8420.61	7016.66	6086.58	5427.25
350000	30567.46	15949.54	11089.23	8668.28	7223.03	6265.60	5586.87
400000	34934.23	18228.05	12673.40	9906.60	8254.89	7160.68	6385.00
450000	39301.01	20506.56	14257.58	11144.93	9286.75	8055.77	7183.12
500000	43667.79	22785.06	15841.75	12383.25	10318.62	8950.86	7981.25
550000	48034.57	25063.57	17425.93	13621.58	11350.48	9845.94	8779.37
600000	52401.35	27342.07	19010.10	14859.90	12382.34	10741.03	9577.50

Monthly Payments 8³/₄%
necessary to amortize a loan

AMOUNT	8 YEARS	9 YEARS	10 YEARS	11 YEARS	12 YEARS	13 YEARS	14 YEARS
100	1.45	1.34	1.25	1.18	1.12	1.08	1.03
200	2.90	2.68	2.51	2.36	2.25	2.15	2.07
500	7.26	6.71	6.27	5.91	5.62	5.38	5.17
1000	14.52	13.41	12.53	11.82	11.24	10.75	10.34
2000	29.04	26.82	25.07	23.65	22.48	21.51	20.69
5000	72.60	67.05	62.66	59.12	56.20	53.77	51.72
6000	87.13	80.46	75.20	70.94	67.44	64.52	62.06
7000	101.65	93.88	87.73	82.76	78.68	75.28	72.41
8000	116.17	107.29	100.26	94.59	89.92	86.03	82.75
9000	130.69	120.70	112.79	106.41	101.16	96.78	93.09
10000	145.21	134.11	125.33	118.23	112.40	107.54	103.44
15000	217.81	201.16	187.99	177.35	168.60	161.31	155.16
20000	290.42	268.22	250.65	236.46	224.80	215.08	206.88
25000	363.02	335.27	313.32	295.58	281.00	268.85	258.59
30000	435.63	402.32	375.98	354.70	337.20	322.61	310.31
35000	508.23	469.38	438.64	413.81	393.40	376.38	362.03
40000	580.83	536.43	501.31	472.93	449.60	430.15	413.75
45000	653.44	603.48	563.97	532.04	505.80	483.92	465.47
50000	726.04	670.54	626.63	591.16	562.00	537.69	517.19
55000	798.65	737.59	689.30	650.27	618.20	591.46	568.91
60000	871.25	804.65	751.96	709.39	674.40	645.23	620.62
65000	943.85	871.70	814.62	768.51	730.60	699.00	672.34
70000	1016.46	938.75	877.29	827.62	786.80	752.77	724.06
75000	1089.06	1005.81	939.95	886.74	843.00	806.54	775.78
80000	1161.67	1072.86	1002.61	945.85	899.20	860.30	827.50
85000	1234.27	1139.92	1065.28	1004.97	955.40	914.07	879.22
90000	1306.88	1206.97	1127.94	1064.09	1011.60	967.84	930.94
95000	1379.48	1274.02	1190.60	1123.20	1067.80	1021.61	982.66
100000	1452.08	1341.08	1253.27	1182.32	1124.00	1075.38	1034.38
105000	1524.69	1408.13	1315.93	1241.43	1180.20	1129.15	1086.09
110000	1597.29	1475.18	1378.59	1300.55	1236.40	1182.92	1137.81
120000	1742.50	1609.29	1503.92	1418.78	1348.80	1290.46	1241.25
130000	1887.71	1743.40	1629.25	1537.01	1461.20	1397.99	1344.69
140000	2032.92	1877.51	1754.57	1655.24	1573.60	1505.53	1448.13
150000	2178.13	2011.62	1879.90	1773.48	1686.00	1613.07	1551.56
160000	2323.33	2145.72	2005.23	1891.71	1798.40	1720.61	1655.00
170000	2468.54	2279.83	2130.55	2009.94	1910.79	1828.15	1758.44
180000	2613.75	2413.94	2255.88	2128.17	2023.19	1935.69	1861.88
190000	2758.96	2548.05	2381.21	2246.40	2135.59	2043.22	1965.31
200000	2904.17	2682.15	2506.54	2364.63	2247.99	2150.76	2068.75
210000	3049.38	2816.26	2631.86	2482.87	2360.39	2258.30	2172.19
220000	3194.58	2950.37	2757.19	2601.10	2472.79	2365.84	2275.63
230000	3339.79	3084.48	2882.52	2719.33	2585.19	2473.38	2379.07
240000	3485.00	3218.58	3007.84	2837.56	2697.59	2580.91	2482.50
250000	3630.21	3352.69	3133.17	2955.79	2809.99	2688.45	2585.94
260000	3775.42	3486.80	3258.50	3074.02	2922.39	2795.99	2689.38
270000	3920.63	3620.91	3383.82	3192.26	3034.79	2903.53	2792.82
280000	4065.83	3755.01	3509.15	3310.49	3147.19	3011.07	2896.25
290000	4211.04	3889.12	3634.48	3428.72	3259.59	3118.60	2999.69
300000	4356.25	4023.23	3759.80	3546.95	3371.99	3226.14	3103.13
310000	4501.46	4157.34	3885.13	3665.18	3484.39	3333.68	3206.57
320000	4646.67	4291.45	4010.46	3783.41	3596.79	3441.22	3310.00
330000	4791.88	4425.55	4135.78	3901.65	3709.19	3548.76	3413.44
340000	4937.09	4559.66	4261.11	4019.88	3821.59	3656.29	3516.88
350000	5082.29	4693.77	4386.44	4138.11	3933.99	3763.83	3620.32
400000	5808.34	5364.31	5013.07	4729.27	4495.99	4301.52	4137.50
450000	6534.38	6034.85	5639.70	5320.43	5057.99	4839.21	4654.69
500000	7260.42	6705.38	6266.34	5911.58	5619.98	5376.90	5171.88
550000	7986.46	7375.92	6892.97	6502.74	6181.98	5914.59	5689.07
600000	8712.50	8046.46	7519.61	7093.90	6743.98	6452.28	6206.26

8³/₄%   Monthly Payments
necessary to amortize a loan

AMOUNT	15 YEARS	16 YEARS	17 YEARS	18 YEARS	19 YEARS	20 YEARS	21 YEARS
100	1.00	0.97	0.94	0.92	0.90	0.88	0.87
200	2.00	1.94	1.89	1.84	1.80	1.77	1.74
500	5.00	4.85	4.72	4.60	4.51	4.42	4.34
1000	9.99	9.69	9.43	9.21	9.01	8.84	8.68
2000	19.99	19.39	18.87	18.42	18.02	17.67	17.37
5000	49.97	48.47	47.17	46.04	45.06	44.19	43.42
6000	59.97	58.17	56.61	55.25	54.07	53.02	52.10
7000	69.96	67.86	66.04	64.46	63.08	61.86	60.78
8000	79.96	77.56	75.48	73.67	72.09	70.70	69.47
9000	89.95	87.25	84.91	82.88	81.10	79.53	78.15
10000	99.94	96.94	94.35	92.09	90.11	88.37	86.83
15000	149.92	145.42	141.52	138.13	135.17	132.56	130.25
20000	199.89	193.89	188.70	184.18	180.22	176.74	173.67
25000	249.86	242.36	235.87	230.22	225.28	220.93	217.09
30000	299.83	290.83	283.05	276.27	270.33	265.11	260.50
35000	349.81	339.31	330.22	322.31	315.39	309.30	303.92
40000	399.78	387.78	377.40	368.36	360.44	353.48	347.34
45000	449.75	436.25	424.57	414.40	405.50	397.67	390.76
50000	499.72	484.72	471.75	460.45	450.55	441.86	434.17
55000	549.70	533.20	518.92	506.49	495.61	486.04	477.59
60000	599.67	581.67	566.09	552.53	540.67	530.23	521.01
65000	649.64	630.14	613.27	598.58	585.72	574.41	564.42
70000	699.61	678.61	660.44	644.62	630.78	618.60	607.84
75000	749.59	727.09	707.62	690.67	675.83	662.78	651.26
80000	799.56	775.56	754.79	736.71	720.89	706.97	694.68
85000	849.53	824.03	801.97	782.76	765.94	751.15	738.09
90000	899.50	872.50	849.14	828.80	811.00	795.34	781.51
95000	949.48	920.97	896.31	874.85	856.05	839.53	824.93
100000	999.45	969.45	943.49	920.89	901.11	883.71	868.34
105000	1049.42	1017.92	990.66	966.93	946.16	927.90	911.76
110000	1099.39	1066.39	1037.84	1012.98	991.22	972.08	955.18
120000	1199.34	1163.34	1132.19	1105.07	1081.33	1060.45	1042.01
130000	1299.28	1260.28	1226.54	1197.16	1171.44	1148.82	1128.85
140000	1399.23	1357.23	1320.88	1289.25	1261.55	1237.19	1215.68
150000	1499.17	1454.17	1415.23	1381.34	1351.66	1325.57	1302.52
160000	1599.12	1551.11	1509.58	1473.43	1441.77	1413.94	1389.35
170000	1699.06	1648.06	1603.93	1565.51	1531.88	1502.31	1476.19
180000	1799.01	1745.00	1698.28	1657.60	1622.00	1590.68	1563.02
190000	1898.95	1841.95	1792.63	1749.69	1712.11	1679.05	1649.86
200000	1998.90	1938.89	1886.98	1841.78	1802.22	1767.42	1736.69
210000	2098.84	2035.84	1981.33	1933.87	1892.33	1855.79	1823.52
220000	2198.79	2132.78	2075.68	2025.96	1982.44	1944.16	1910.36
230000	2298.73	2229.73	2170.03	2118.05	2072.55	2032.53	1997.19
240000	2398.68	2326.67	2264.37	2210.14	2162.66	2120.91	2084.03
250000	2498.62	2423.62	2358.72	2302.23	2252.77	2209.28	2170.86
260000	2598.57	2520.56	2453.07	2394.32	2342.88	2297.65	2257.70
270000	2698.51	2617.51	2547.42	2486.40	2432.99	2386.02	2344.53
280000	2798.46	2714.45	2641.77	2578.49	2523.10	2474.39	2431.37
290000	2898.40	2811.40	2736.12	2670.58	2613.22	2562.76	2518.20
300000	2998.35	2908.34	2830.47	2762.67	2703.33	2651.13	2605.03
310000	3098.29	3005.28	2924.82	2854.76	2793.44	2739.50	2691.87
320000	3198.24	3102.23	3019.17	2946.85	2883.55	2827.87	2778.70
330000	3298.18	3199.17	3113.51	3038.94	2973.66	2916.25	2865.54
340000	3398.13	3296.12	3207.86	3131.03	3063.77	3004.62	2952.37
350000	3498.07	3393.06	3302.21	3223.12	3153.88	3092.99	3039.21
400000	3997.79	3877.79	3773.96	3683.56	3604.44	3534.84	3473.38
450000	4497.52	4362.51	4245.70	4144.01	4054.99	3976.70	3907.55
500000	4997.24	4847.23	4717.45	4604.45	4505.54	4418.55	4341.72
550000	5496.97	5331.96	5189.19	5064.90	4956.10	4860.41	4775.90
600000	5996.69	5816.68	5660.93	5525.34	5406.65	5302.26	5210.07

Monthly Payments 8¾%

necessary to amortize a loan

AMOUNT	22 YEARS	23 YEARS	24 YEARS	25 YEARS	30 YEARS	35 YEARS	40 YEARS
100	0.85	0.84	0.83	0.82	0.79	0.77	0.75
200	1.71	1.69	1.66	1.64	1.57	1.53	1.50
500	4.27	4.21	4.16	4.11	3.93	3.83	3.76
1000	8.55	8.43	8.32	8.22	7.87	7.65	7.52
2000	17.09	16.85	16.64	16.44	15.73	15.31	15.04
5000	42.74	42.13	41.59	41.11	39.34	38.27	37.61
6000	51.28	50.56	49.91	49.33	47.20	45.92	45.13
7000	59.83	58.98	58.23	57.55	55.07	53.58	52.65
8000	68.38	67.41	66.54	65.77	62.94	61.23	60.17
9000	76.93	75.83	74.86	73.99	70.80	68.88	67.70
10000	85.47	84.26	83.18	82.21	78.67	76.54	75.22
15000	128.21	126.39	124.77	123.32	118.01	114.80	112.83
20000	170.94	168.52	166.36	164.43	157.34	153.07	150.43
25000	213.68	210.65	207.95	205.54	196.68	191.34	188.04
30000	256.42	252.78	249.54	246.64	236.01	229.61	225.65
35000	299.15	294.91	291.13	287.75	275.35	267.88	263.26
40000	341.89	337.04	332.72	328.86	314.68	306.15	300.87
45000	384.63	379.17	374.31	369.96	354.02	344.41	338.48
50000	427.36	421.31	415.90	411.07	393.35	382.68	376.09
55000	470.10	463.44	457.49	452.18	432.69	420.95	413.69
60000	512.83	505.57	499.08	493.29	472.02	459.22	451.30
65000	555.57	547.70	540.67	534.39	511.36	497.49	488.91
70000	598.31	589.83	582.26	575.50	550.69	535.75	526.52
75000	641.04	631.96	623.85	616.61	590.03	574.02	564.13
80000	683.78	674.09	665.44	657.71	629.36	612.29	601.74
85000	726.52	716.22	707.03	698.82	668.70	650.56	639.34
90000	769.25	758.35	748.63	739.93	708.03	688.83	676.95
95000	811.99	800.48	790.22	781.04	747.37	727.09	714.56
100000	854.72	842.61	831.81	822.14	786.70	765.36	752.17
105000	897.46	884.74	873.40	863.25	826.04	803.63	789.78
110000	940.20	926.87	914.99	904.36	865.37	841.90	827.39
120000	1025.67	1011.13	998.17	986.57	944.04	918.44	902.60
130000	1111.14	1095.39	1081.35	1068.79	1022.71	994.97	977.82
140000	1196.61	1179.65	1164.53	1151.00	1101.38	1071.51	1053.04
150000	1282.09	1263.92	1247.71	1233.22	1180.05	1148.04	1128.26
160000	1367.56	1348.18	1330.89	1315.43	1258.72	1224.58	1203.47
170000	1453.03	1432.44	1414.07	1397.64	1337.39	1301.12	1278.69
180000	1538.50	1516.70	1497.25	1479.86	1416.06	1377.65	1353.91
190000	1623.98	1600.96	1580.43	1562.07	1494.73	1454.19	1429.12
200000	1709.45	1685.22	1663.61	1644.29	1573.40	1530.73	1504.34
210000	1794.92	1769.48	1746.79	1726.50	1652.07	1607.26	1579.56
220000	1880.39	1853.74	1829.97	1808.72	1730.74	1683.80	1654.78
230000	1965.87	1938.00	1913.15	1890.93	1809.41	1760.34	1729.99
240000	2051.34	2022.26	1996.33	1973.14	1888.08	1836.87	1805.21
250000	2136.81	2106.53	2079.51	2055.36	1966.75	1913.41	1880.43
260000	2222.28	2190.79	2162.69	2137.57	2045.42	1989.94	1955.64
270000	2307.75	2275.05	2245.88	2219.79	2124.09	2066.48	2030.86
280000	2393.23	2359.31	2329.06	2302.00	2202.76	2143.02	2106.08
290000	2478.70	2443.57	2412.24	2384.22	2281.43	2219.55	2181.29
300000	2564.17	2527.83	2495.42	2466.43	2360.10	2296.09	2256.51
310000	2649.64	2612.09	2578.60	2548.65	2438.77	2372.63	2331.73
320000	2735.12	2696.35	2661.78	2630.86	2517.44	2449.16	2406.95
330000	2820.59	2780.61	2744.96	2713.07	2596.11	2525.70	2482.16
340000	2906.06	2864.88	2828.14	2795.29	2674.78	2602.23	2557.38
350000	2991.53	2949.14	2911.32	2877.50	2753.45	2678.77	2632.60
400000	3418.90	3370.44	3327.22	3288.57	3146.80	3061.45	3008.68
450000	3846.26	3791.75	3743.13	3699.65	3540.15	3444.13	3384.77
500000	4273.62	4213.05	4159.03	4110.72	3933.50	3826.82	3760.85
550000	4700.98	4634.36	4574.93	4521.79	4326.85	4209.50	4136.94
600000	5128.34	5055.66	4990.83	4932.86	4720.20	4592.18	4513.02

9%   Monthly Payments
necessary to amortize a loan

AMOUNT	1 YEAR	2 YEARS	3 YEARS	4 YEARS	5 YEARS	6 YEARS	7 YEARS
100	8.75	4.57	3.18	2.49	2.08	1.80	1.61
200	17.49	9.14	6.36	4.98	4.15	3.61	3.22
500	43.73	22.84	15.90	12.44	10.38	9.01	8.04
1000	87.45	45.68	31.80	24.89	20.76	18.03	16.09
2000	174.90	91.37	63.60	49.77	41.52	36.05	32.18
5000	437.26	228.42	159.00	124.43	103.79	90.13	80.45
6000	524.71	274.11	190.80	149.31	124.55	108.15	96.53
7000	612.16	319.79	222.60	174.20	145.31	126.18	112.62
8000	699.61	365.48	254.40	199.08	166.07	144.20	128.71
9000	787.06	411.16	286.20	223.97	186.83	162.23	144.80
10000	874.51	456.85	318.00	248.85	207.58	180.26	160.89
15000	1311.77	685.27	477.00	373.28	311.38	270.38	241.34
20000	1749.03	913.69	635.99	497.70	415.17	360.51	321.78
25000	2186.29	1142.12	794.99	622.13	518.96	450.64	402.23
30000	2623.54	1370.54	953.99	746.55	622.75	540.77	482.67
35000	3060.80	1598.97	1112.99	870.98	726.54	630.89	563.12
40000	3498.06	1827.39	1271.99	995.40	830.33	721.02	643.56
45000	3935.32	2055.81	1430.99	1119.83	934.13	811.15	724.01
50000	4372.57	2284.24	1589.99	1244.25	1037.92	901.28	804.45
55000	4809.83	2512.66	1748.99	1368.68	1141.71	991.40	884.90
60000	5247.09	2741.08	1907.98	1493.10	1245.50	1081.53	965.34
65000	5684.35	2969.51	2066.98	1617.53	1349.29	1171.66	1045.79
70000	6121.60	3197.93	2225.98	1741.95	1453.08	1261.79	1126.24
75000	6558.86	3426.36	2384.98	1866.38	1556.88	1351.92	1206.68
80000	6996.12	3654.78	2543.98	1990.80	1660.67	1442.04	1287.13
85000	7433.38	3883.20	2702.98	2115.23	1764.46	1532.17	1367.57
90000	7870.63	4111.63	2861.98	2239.65	1868.25	1622.30	1448.02
95000	8307.89	4340.05	3020.97	2364.08	1972.04	1712.43	1528.46
100000	8745.15	4568.47	3179.97	2488.50	2075.84	1802.55	1608.91
105000	9182.41	4796.90	3338.97	2612.93	2179.63	1892.68	1689.35
110000	9619.66	5025.32	3497.97	2737.35	2283.42	1982.81	1769.80
120000	10494.18	5482.17	3815.97	2986.21	2491.00	2163.06	1930.69
130000	11368.69	5939.02	4133.97	3235.06	2698.59	2343.32	2091.58
140000	12243.21	6395.86	4451.96	3483.91	2906.17	2523.58	2252.47
150000	13117.72	6852.71	4769.96	3732.76	3113.75	2703.83	2413.36
160000	13992.24	7309.56	5087.96	3981.61	3321.34	2884.09	2574.25
170000	14866.75	7766.41	5405.95	4230.46	3528.92	3064.34	2735.14
180000	15741.27	8223.25	5723.95	4479.31	3736.50	3244.60	2896.03
190000	16615.78	8680.10	6041.95	4728.16	3944.09	3424.85	3056.92
200000	17490.30	9136.95	6359.95	4977.01	4151.67	3605.11	3217.82
210000	18364.81	9593.80	6677.94	5225.86	4359.25	3785.36	3378.71
220000	19239.32	10050.64	6995.94	5474.71	4566.84	3965.62	3539.60
230000	20113.84	10507.49	7313.94	5723.56	4774.42	4145.87	3700.49
240000	20988.35	10964.34	7631.94	5972.41	4982.01	4326.13	3861.38
250000	21862.87	11421.19	7949.93	6221.26	5189.59	4506.38	4022.27
260000	22737.38	11878.03	8267.93	6470.11	5397.17	4686.64	4183.16
270000	23611.90	12334.88	8585.93	6718.96	5604.76	4866.90	4344.05
280000	24486.41	12791.73	8903.93	6967.81	5812.34	5047.15	4504.94
290000	25360.93	13248.58	9221.92	7216.66	6019.92	5227.41	4665.83
300000	26235.44	13705.42	9539.92	7465.51	6227.51	5407.66	4826.72
310000	27109.96	14162.27	9857.92	7714.36	6435.09	5587.92	4987.61
320000	27984.47	14619.12	10175.91	7963.21	6642.67	5768.17	5148.51
330000	28858.99	15075.96	10493.91	8212.06	6850.26	5948.43	5309.40
340000	29733.50	15532.81	10811.91	8460.91	7057.84	6128.68	5470.29
350000	30608.02	15989.66	11129.91	8709.76	7265.42	6308.94	5631.18
400000	34980.59	18273.90	12719.89	9954.02	8303.34	7210.21	6435.63
450000	39353.16	20558.13	14309.88	11198.27	9341.26	8111.49	7240.09
500000	43725.74	22842.37	15899.87	12442.52	10379.18	9012.77	8044.54
550000	48098.31	25126.61	17489.85	13686.77	11417.10	9914.05	8848.99
600000	52470.89	27410.85	19079.84	14931.03	12455.01	10815.32	9653.45

Monthly Payments 9%
necessary to amortize a loan

AMOUNT	8 YEARS	9 YEARS	10 YEARS	11 YEARS	12 YEARS	13 YEARS	14 YEARS
100	1.47	1.35	1.27	1.20	1.14	1.09	1.05
200	2.93	2.71	2.53	2.39	2.28	2.18	2.10
500	7.33	6.77	6.33	5.98	5.69	5.45	5.24
1000	14.65	13.54	12.67	11.96	11.38	10.90	10.49
2000	29.30	27.09	25.34	23.92	22.76	21.79	20.98
5000	73.25	67.71	63.34	59.80	56.90	54.48	52.45
6000	87.90	81.26	76.01	71.76	68.28	65.38	62.94
7000	102.55	94.80	88.67	83.73	79.66	76.28	73.43
8000	117.20	108.34	101.34	95.69	91.04	87.17	83.92
9000	131.85	121.89	114.01	107.65	102.42	98.07	94.40
10000	146.50	135.43	126.68	119.61	113.80	108.97	104.89
15000	219.75	203.14	190.01	179.41	170.70	163.45	157.34
20000	293.00	270.86	253.35	239.22	227.61	217.94	209.79
25000	366.26	338.57	316.69	299.02	284.51	272.42	262.23
30000	439.51	406.29	380.03	358.82	341.41	326.90	314.68
35000	512.76	474.00	443.37	418.63	398.31	381.39	367.13
40000	586.01	541.72	506.70	478.43	455.21	435.87	419.58
45000	659.26	609.43	570.04	538.24	512.11	490.36	472.02
50000	732.51	677.15	633.38	598.04	569.02	544.84	524.47
55000	805.76	744.86	696.72	657.84	625.92	599.32	576.92
60000	879.01	812.57	760.05	717.65	682.82	653.81	629.36
65000	952.26	880.29	823.39	777.45	739.72	708.29	681.81
70000	1025.51	948.00	886.73	837.26	796.62	762.78	734.26
75000	1098.77	1015.72	950.07	897.06	853.52	817.26	786.70
80000	1172.02	1083.43	1013.41	956.86	910.42	871.74	839.15
85000	1245.27	1151.15	1076.74	1016.67	967.33	926.23	891.60
90000	1318.52	1218.86	1140.08	1076.47	1024.23	980.71	944.04
95000	1391.77	1286.58	1203.42	1136.28	1081.13	1035.20	996.49
100000	1465.02	1354.29	1266.76	1196.08	1138.03	1089.68	1048.94
105000	1538.27	1422.01	1330.10	1255.88	1194.93	1144.16	1101.38
110000	1611.52	1489.72	1393.43	1315.69	1251.83	1198.65	1153.83
120000	1758.02	1625.15	1520.11	1435.30	1365.64	1307.62	1258.73
130000	1904.53	1760.58	1646.79	1554.90	1479.44	1416.58	1363.62
140000	2051.03	1896.01	1773.46	1674.51	1593.24	1525.55	1468.51
150000	2197.53	2031.44	1900.14	1794.12	1707.05	1634.52	1573.41
160000	2344.03	2166.87	2026.81	1913.73	1820.85	1743.49	1678.30
170000	2490.53	2302.29	2153.49	2033.34	1934.65	1852.46	1783.19
180000	2637.04	2437.72	2280.16	2152.94	2048.46	1961.42	1888.09
190000	2783.54	2573.15	2406.84	2272.55	2162.26	2070.39	1992.98
200000	2930.04	2708.58	2533.52	2392.16	2276.06	2179.36	2097.88
210000	3076.54	2844.01	2660.19	2511.77	2389.86	2288.33	2202.77
220000	3223.04	2979.44	2786.87	2631.38	2503.67	2397.30	2307.66
230000	3369.55	3114.87	2913.54	2750.98	2617.47	2506.27	2412.56
240000	3516.05	3250.30	3040.22	2870.59	2731.27	2615.23	2517.45
250000	3662.55	3385.73	3166.89	2990.20	2845.08	2724.20	2622.34
260000	3809.05	3521.16	3293.57	3109.81	2958.88	2833.17	2727.24
270000	3955.55	3656.59	3420.25	3229.42	3072.68	2942.14	2832.13
280000	4102.06	3792.01	3546.92	3349.03	3186.49	3051.11	2937.03
290000	4248.56	3927.44	3673.60	3468.63	3300.29	3160.07	3041.92
300000	4395.06	4062.87	3800.27	3588.24	3414.09	3269.04	3146.81
310000	4541.56	4198.30	3926.95	3707.85	3527.90	3378.01	3251.71
320000	4688.07	4333.73	4053.62	3827.46	3641.70	3486.98	3356.60
330000	4834.57	4469.16	4180.30	3947.07	3755.50	3595.95	3461.49
340000	4981.07	4604.59	4306.98	4066.67	3869.30	3704.91	3566.39
350000	5127.57	4740.02	4433.65	4186.28	3983.11	3813.88	3671.28
400000	5860.08	5417.16	5067.03	4784.32	4552.12	4358.72	4195.75
450000	6592.59	6094.31	5700.41	5382.36	5121.14	4903.56	4720.22
500000	7325.10	6771.45	6333.79	5980.40	5690.15	5448.40	5244.69
550000	8057.61	7448.60	6967.17	6578.44	6259.17	5993.24	5769.16
600000	8790.12	8125.75	7600.55	7176.48	6828.18	6538.08	6293.63

AMOUNT	15 YEARS	16 YEARS	17 YEARS	18 YEARS	19 YEARS	20 YEARS	21 YEARS
100	1.01	0.98	0.96	0.94	0.92	0.90	0.88
200	2.03	1.97	1.92	1.87	1.83	1.80	1.77
500	5.07	4.92	4.79	4.68	4.58	4.50	4.42
1000	10.14	9.85	9.59	9.36	9.17	9.00	8.85
2000	20.29	19.69	19.18	18.73	18.34	17.99	17.69
5000	50.71	49.23	47.94	46.82	45.84	44.99	44.23
6000	60.86	59.07	57.53	56.19	55.01	53.98	53.07
7000	71.00	68.92	67.12	65.55	64.18	62.98	61.92
8000	81.14	78.76	76.70	74.92	73.35	71.98	70.77
9000	91.28	88.61	86.29	84.28	82.52	80.98	79.61
10000	101.43	98.45	95.88	93.64	91.69	89.97	88.46
15000	152.14	147.68	143.82	140.47	137.53	134.96	132.69
20000	202.85	196.90	191.76	187.29	183.38	179.95	176.92
25000	253.57	246.13	239.70	234.11	229.22	224.93	221.15
30000	304.28	295.35	287.64	280.93	275.07	269.92	265.37
35000	354.99	344.58	335.58	327.76	320.91	314.90	309.60
40000	405.71	393.81	383.52	374.58	366.76	359.89	353.83
45000	456.42	443.03	431.46	421.40	412.60	404.88	398.06
50000	507.13	492.26	479.40	468.22	458.45	449.86	442.29
55000	557.85	541.48	527.34	515.04	504.29	494.85	486.52
60000	608.56	590.71	575.28	561.87	550.14	539.84	530.75
65000	659.27	639.94	623.22	608.69	595.98	584.82	574.98
70000	709.99	689.16	671.16	655.51	641.83	629.81	619.21
75000	760.70	738.39	719.10	702.33	687.67	674.79	663.44
80000	811.41	787.61	767.04	749.16	733.52	719.78	707.66
85000	862.13	836.84	814.98	795.98	779.36	764.77	751.89
90000	912.84	886.06	862.92	842.80	825.21	809.75	796.12
95000	963.55	935.29	910.86	889.62	871.05	854.74	840.35
100000	1014.27	984.52	958.80	936.44	916.90	899.73	884.58
105000	1064.98	1033.74	1006.74	983.27	962.74	944.71	928.81
110000	1115.69	1082.97	1054.68	1030.09	1008.59	989.70	973.04
120000	1217.12	1181.42	1150.56	1123.73	1100.28	1079.67	1061.50
130000	1318.55	1279.87	1246.45	1217.38	1191.97	1169.64	1149.96
140000	1419.97	1378.32	1342.33	1311.02	1283.66	1259.62	1238.41
150000	1521.40	1476.77	1438.21	1404.67	1375.35	1349.59	1326.87
160000	1622.83	1575.23	1534.09	1498.31	1467.03	1439.56	1415.33
170000	1724.25	1673.68	1629.97	1591.96	1558.72	1529.53	1503.79
180000	1825.68	1772.13	1725.85	1685.60	1650.41	1619.51	1592.25
190000	1927.11	1870.58	1821.73	1779.25	1742.10	1709.48	1680.70
200000	2028.53	1969.03	1917.61	1872.89	1833.79	1799.45	1769.16
210000	2129.96	2067.48	2013.49	1966.53	1925.48	1889.42	1857.62
220000	2231.39	2165.93	2109.37	2060.18	2017.17	1979.40	1946.08
230000	2332.81	2264.39	2205.25	2153.82	2108.86	2069.37	2034.54
240000	2434.24	2362.84	2301.13	2247.47	2200.55	2159.34	2122.99
250000	2535.67	2461.29	2397.01	2341.11	2292.24	2249.31	2211.45
260000	2637.09	2559.74	2492.89	2434.76	2383.93	2339.29	2299.91
270000	2738.52	2658.19	2588.77	2528.40	2475.62	2429.26	2388.37
280000	2839.95	2756.64	2684.65	2622.05	2567.31	2519.23	2476.83
290000	2941.37	2855.10	2780.53	2715.69	2659.00	2609.21	2565.28
300000	3042.80	2953.55	2876.41	2809.33	2750.69	2699.18	2653.74
310000	3144.23	3052.00	2972.29	2902.98	2842.38	2789.15	2742.20
320000	3245.65	3150.45	3068.17	2996.62	2934.07	2879.12	2830.66
330000	3347.08	3248.90	3164.05	3090.27	3025.76	2969.10	2919.12
340000	3448.51	3347.35	3259.93	3183.91	3117.45	3059.07	3007.58
350000	3549.93	3445.81	3355.81	3277.56	3209.14	3149.04	3096.03
400000	4057.07	3938.06	3835.22	3745.78	3667.59	3598.90	3538.32
450000	4564.20	4430.32	4314.62	4214.00	4126.04	4048.77	3980.61
500000	5071.33	4922.58	4794.02	4682.22	4584.48	4498.63	4422.91
550000	5578.47	5414.84	5273.42	5150.45	5042.93	4948.49	4865.20
600000	6085.60	5907.10	5752.82	5618.67	5501.38	5398.36	5307.49

AMOUNT	22 YEARS	23 YEARS	24 YEARS	25 YEARS	30 YEARS	35 YEARS	40 YEARS
100	0.87	0.86	0.85	0.84	0.80	0.78	0.77
200	1.74	1.72	1.70	1.68	1.61	1.57	1.54
500	4.36	4.30	4.24	4.20	4.02	3.92	3.86
1000	8.71	8.59	8.49	8.39	8.05	7.84	7.71
2000	17.42	17.19	16.97	16.78	16.09	15.68	15.43
5000	43.56	42.96	42.43	41.96	40.23	39.20	38.57
6000	52.27	51.56	50.92	50.35	48.28	47.04	46.28
7000	60.98	60.15	59.41	58.74	56.32	54.88	54.00
8000	69.69	68.74	67.89	67.14	64.37	62.72	61.71
9000	78.41	77.33	76.38	75.53	72.42	70.56	69.42
10000	87.12	85.93	84.87	83.92	80.46	78.40	77.14
15000	130.68	128.89	127.30	125.88	120.69	117.60	115.70
20000	174.23	171.85	169.73	167.84	160.92	156.80	154.27
25000	217.79	214.82	212.17	209.80	201.16	196.00	192.84
30000	261.35	257.78	254.60	251.76	241.39	235.20	231.41
35000	304.91	300.74	297.03	293.72	281.62	274.40	269.98
40000	348.47	343.71	339.47	335.68	321.85	313.60	308.54
45000	392.03	386.67	381.90	377.64	362.08	352.80	347.11
50000	435.59	429.63	424.33	419.60	402.31	392.00	385.68
55000	479.15	472.60	466.77	461.56	442.54	431.20	424.25
60000	522.70	515.56	509.20	503.52	482.77	470.40	462.82
65000	566.26	558.52	551.63	545.48	523.00	509.60	501.38
70000	609.82	601.49	594.07	587.44	563.24	548.80	539.95
75000	653.38	644.45	636.50	629.40	603.47	587.99	578.52
80000	696.94	687.41	678.93	671.36	643.70	627.19	617.09
85000	740.50	730.38	721.36	713.32	683.93	666.39	655.66
90000	784.06	773.34	763.80	755.28	724.16	705.59	694.23
95000	827.62	816.30	806.23	797.24	764.39	744.79	732.79
100000	871.17	859.27	848.66	839.20	804.62	783.99	771.36
105000	914.73	902.23	891.10	881.16	844.85	823.19	809.93
110000	958.29	945.19	933.53	923.12	885.08	862.39	848.50
120000	1045.41	1031.12	1018.40	1007.04	965.55	940.79	925.63
130000	1132.53	1117.05	1103.26	1090.96	1046.01	1019.19	1002.77
140000	1219.64	1202.98	1188.13	1174.87	1126.47	1097.59	1079.91
150000	1306.76	1288.90	1273.00	1258.79	1206.93	1175.99	1157.04
160000	1393.88	1374.83	1357.86	1342.71	1287.40	1254.39	1234.18
170000	1481.00	1460.76	1442.73	1426.63	1367.86	1332.79	1311.31
180000	1568.11	1546.68	1527.60	1510.55	1448.32	1411.19	1388.45
190000	1655.23	1632.61	1612.46	1594.47	1528.78	1489.59	1465.59
200000	1742.35	1718.54	1697.33	1678.39	1609.25	1567.99	1542.72
210000	1829.47	1804.46	1782.20	1762.31	1689.71	1646.39	1619.86
220000	1916.58	1890.39	1867.06	1846.23	1770.17	1724.78	1697.00
230000	2003.70	1976.32	1951.93	1930.15	1850.63	1803.18	1774.13
240000	2090.82	2062.24	2036.79	2014.07	1931.09	1881.58	1851.27
250000	2177.94	2148.17	2121.66	2097.99	2011.56	1959.98	1928.40
260000	2265.05	2234.10	2206.53	2181.91	2092.02	2038.38	2005.54
270000	2352.17	2320.02	2291.39	2265.83	2172.48	2116.78	2082.68
280000	2439.29	2405.95	2376.26	2349.75	2252.94	2195.18	2159.81
290000	2526.41	2491.88	2461.13	2433.67	2333.41	2273.58	2236.95
300000	2613.52	2577.80	2545.99	2517.59	2413.87	2351.98	2314.08
310000	2700.64	2663.73	2630.86	2601.51	2494.33	2430.38	2391.22
320000	2787.76	2749.66	2715.73	2685.43	2574.79	2508.78	2468.36
330000	2874.88	2835.58	2800.59	2769.35	2655.25	2587.18	2545.49
340000	2961.99	2921.51	2885.46	2853.27	2735.72	2665.58	2622.63
350000	3049.11	3007.44	2970.33	2937.19	2816.18	2743.98	2699.77
400000	3484.70	3437.07	3394.66	3356.79	3218.49	3135.97	3085.45
450000	3920.28	3866.71	3818.99	3776.38	3620.80	3527.97	3471.13
500000	4355.87	4296.34	4243.32	4195.98	4023.11	3919.96	3856.81
550000	4791.46	4725.97	4667.65	4615.58	4425.42	4311.96	4242.49
600000	5227.05	5155.61	5091.99	5035.18	4827.74	4703.96	4628.17

9¼%   Monthly Payments
necessary to amortize a loan

AMOUNT	1 YEAR	2 YEARS	3 YEARS	4 YEARS	5 YEARS	6 YEARS	7 YEARS
100	8.76	4.58	3.19	2.50	2.09	1.81	1.62
200	17.51	9.16	6.38	5.00	4.18	3.63	3.24
500	43.78	22.90	15.96	12.50	10.44	9.07	8.11
1000	87.57	45.80	31.92	25.00	20.88	18.15	16.22
2000	175.13	91.60	63.83	50.01	41.76	36.30	32.43
5000	437.84	229.00	159.58	125.02	104.40	90.75	81.08
6000	525.40	274.80	191.50	150.02	125.28	108.90	97.30
7000	612.97	320.60	223.41	175.03	146.16	127.05	113.51
8000	700.54	366.40	255.33	200.03	167.04	145.20	129.73
9000	788.11	412.20	287.25	225.04	187.92	163.35	145.95
10000	875.67	458.00	319.16	250.04	208.80	181.50	162.16
15000	1313.51	686.99	478.74	375.05	313.20	272.25	243.24
20000	1751.35	915.99	638.32	500.08	417.60	363.00	324.32
25000	2189.19	1144.99	797.91	625.10	522.00	453.75	405.41
30000	2627.02	1373.99	957.49	750.12	626.40	544.50	486.49
35000	3064.86	1602.98	1117.07	875.14	730.80	635.25	567.57
40000	3502.70	1831.98	1276.65	1000.16	835.20	725.99	648.65
45000	3940.54	2060.98	1436.23	1125.18	939.60	816.74	729.73
50000	4378.37	2289.98	1595.81	1250.20	1043.99	907.49	810.81
55000	4816.21	2518.97	1755.39	1375.22	1148.39	998.24	891.89
60000	5254.05	2747.97	1914.97	1500.24	1252.79	1088.99	972.97
65000	5691.88	2976.97	2074.55	1625.25	1357.19	1179.74	1054.06
70000	6129.72	3205.97	2234.13	1750.27	1461.59	1270.49	1135.14
75000	6567.56	3434.96	2393.72	1875.29	1565.99	1361.24	1216.22
80000	7005.40	3663.96	2553.30	2000.31	1670.39	1451.99	1297.30
85000	7443.23	3892.96	2712.88	2125.33	1774.79	1542.74	1378.38
90000	7881.07	4121.96	2872.46	2250.35	1879.19	1633.49	1459.46
95000	8318.91	4350.96	3032.04	2375.37	1983.59	1724.24	1540.54
100000	8756.75	4579.95	3191.62	2500.39	2087.99	1814.99	1621.62
105000	9194.58	4808.95	3351.20	2625.41	2192.39	1905.74	1702.71
110000	9632.42	5037.95	3510.78	2750.43	2296.79	1996.49	1783.79
120000	10508.09	5495.94	3829.95	3000.47	2505.59	2177.98	1945.95
130000	11383.77	5953.94	4149.11	3250.51	2714.39	2359.48	2108.11
140000	12259.44	6411.93	4468.27	3500.55	2923.19	2540.98	2270.27
150000	13135.12	6869.93	4787.43	3750.59	3131.98	2722.48	2432.44
160000	14010.79	7327.93	5106.59	4000.63	3340.78	2903.98	2594.60
170000	14886.47	7785.92	5425.76	4250.67	3549.58	3085.48	2756.76
180000	15762.14	8243.92	5744.92	4500.71	3758.38	3266.98	2918.92
190000	16637.82	8701.91	6064.08	4750.74	3967.18	3448.47	3081.09
200000	17513.49	9159.91	6383.24	5000.78	4175.98	3629.97	3243.25
210000	18389.16	9617.90	6702.40	5250.82	4384.78	3811.47	3405.41
220000	19264.84	10075.90	7021.57	5500.86	4593.58	3992.97	3567.57
230000	20140.51	10533.89	7340.73	5750.90	4802.38	4174.47	3729.74
240000	21016.19	10991.89	7659.89	6000.94	5011.18	4355.97	3891.90
250000	21891.86	11449.88	7979.05	6250.98	5219.97	4537.47	4054.06
260000	22767.54	11907.88	8298.22	6501.02	5428.77	4718.96	4216.22
270000	23643.21	12365.87	8617.38	6751.06	5637.57	4900.46	4378.39
280000	24518.89	12823.87	8936.54	7001.10	5846.37	5081.96	4540.55
290000	25394.56	13281.86	9255.70	7251.14	6055.17	5263.46	4702.71
300000	26270.24	13739.86	9574.86	7501.18	6263.97	5444.96	4864.87
310000	27145.91	14197.86	9894.03	7751.22	6472.77	5626.46	5027.03
320000	28021.58	14655.85	10213.19	8001.25	6681.57	5807.96	5189.20
330000	28897.26	15113.85	10532.35	8251.29	6890.37	5989.46	5351.36
340000	29772.93	15571.84	10851.51	8501.33	7099.17	6170.95	5513.52
350000	30648.61	16029.84	11170.67	8751.37	7307.96	6352.45	5675.68
400000	35026.98	18319.81	12766.49	10001.57	8351.96	7259.95	6486.50
450000	39405.35	20609.79	14362.30	11251.76	9395.95	8167.44	7297.31
500000	43783.73	22899.77	15958.11	12501.96	10439.95	9074.93	8108.12
550000	48162.10	25189.74	17553.92	13752.16	11483.94	9982.43	8918.93
600000	52540.47	27479.72	19149.73	15002.35	12527.94	10889.92	9729.75

Monthly Payments 9¼%
necessary to amortize a loan

AMOUNT	8 YEARS	9 YEARS	10 YEARS	11 YEARS	12 YEARS	13 YEARS	14 YEARS
100	1.48	1.37	1.28	1.21	1.15	1.10	1.06
200	2.96	2.74	2.56	2.42	2.30	2.21	2.13
500	7.39	6.84	6.40	6.05	5.76	5.52	5.32
1000	14.78	13.68	12.80	12.10	11.52	11.04	10.64
2000	29.56	27.35	25.61	24.20	23.04	22.08	21.27
5000	73.90	68.38	64.02	60.50	57.61	55.20	53.18
6000	88.68	82.05	76.82	72.60	69.13	66.24	63.82
7000	103.46	95.73	89.62	84.70	80.65	77.29	74.45
8000	118.24	109.41	102.43	96.79	92.17	88.33	85.09
9000	133.02	123.08	115.23	108.89	103.69	99.37	95.72
10000	147.80	136.76	128.03	120.99	115.23	110.41	106.36
15000	221.70	205.14	192.05	181.49	172.82	165.61	159.54
20000	295.60	273.52	256.07	241.99	230.43	220.82	212.72
25000	369.51	341.89	320.08	302.48	288.04	276.02	265.90
30000	443.41	410.27	384.10	362.98	345.65	331.22	319.08
35000	517.31	478.65	448.11	423.48	403.25	386.43	372.26
40000	591.21	547.03	512.13	483.97	460.86	441.63	425.44
45000	665.11	615.41	576.15	544.47	518.47	496.84	478.62
50000	739.01	683.79	640.16	604.96	576.08	552.04	531.80
55000	812.91	752.17	704.18	665.46	633.69	607.24	584.98
60000	886.81	820.55	768.20	725.96	691.29	662.45	638.16
65000	960.71	888.93	832.21	786.45	748.90	717.65	691.34
70000	1034.62	957.30	896.23	846.95	806.51	772.85	744.52
75000	1108.52	1025.68	960.25	907.45	864.12	828.06	797.70
80000	1182.42	1094.06	1024.26	967.94	921.73	883.26	850.88
85000	1256.32	1162.44	1088.28	1028.44	979.33	938.47	904.06
90000	1330.22	1230.82	1152.29	1088.94	1036.94	993.67	957.24
95000	1404.12	1299.20	1216.31	1149.43	1094.55	1048.87	1010.42
100000	1478.02	1367.58	1280.33	1209.93	1152.16	1104.08	1063.60
105000	1551.92	1435.96	1344.34	1270.43	1209.76	1159.28	1116.78
110000	1625.82	1504.34	1408.36	1330.92	1267.37	1214.49	1169.96
120000	1773.62	1641.09	1536.39	1451.92	1382.59	1324.89	1276.32
130000	1921.43	1777.85	1664.43	1572.91	1497.80	1435.30	1382.68
140000	2069.23	1914.61	1792.46	1693.90	1613.02	1545.71	1489.04
150000	2217.03	2051.37	1920.49	1814.89	1728.23	1656.12	1595.40
160000	2364.84	2188.12	2048.52	1935.89	1843.45	1766.52	1701.76
170000	2512.64	2324.88	2176.56	2056.88	1958.67	1876.93	1808.12
180000	2660.44	2461.64	2304.59	2177.87	2073.88	1987.34	1914.48
190000	2808.24	2598.40	2432.62	2298.87	2189.10	2097.75	2020.84
200000	2956.04	2735.15	2560.65	2419.86	2304.31	2208.16	2127.20
210000	3103.85	2871.91	2688.69	2540.85	2419.53	2318.56	2233.56
220000	3251.65	3008.67	2816.72	2661.85	2534.74	2428.97	2339.92
230000	3399.45	3145.43	2944.75	2782.84	2649.96	2539.38	2446.28
240000	3547.25	3282.19	3072.79	2903.83	2765.18	2649.79	2552.64
250000	3695.06	3418.94	3200.82	3024.82	2880.39	2760.19	2659.00
260000	3842.86	3555.70	3328.85	3145.82	2995.61	2870.60	2765.36
270000	3990.66	3692.46	3456.88	3266.81	3110.82	2981.01	2871.72
280000	4138.46	3829.22	3584.92	3387.80	3226.04	3091.42	2978.08
290000	4286.26	3965.97	3712.95	3508.80	3341.25	3201.83	3084.45
300000	4434.07	4102.73	3840.98	3629.79	3456.47	3312.23	3190.81
310000	4581.87	4239.49	3969.01	3750.78	3571.68	3422.64	3297.17
320000	4729.67	4376.25	4097.05	3871.78	3686.90	3533.05	3403.53
330000	4877.47	4513.01	4225.08	3992.77	3802.12	3643.46	3509.89
340000	5025.27	4649.76	4353.11	4113.76	3917.33	3753.87	3616.25
350000	5173.08	4786.52	4481.15	4234.75	4032.55	3864.27	3722.61
400000	5912.09	5470.31	5121.31	4839.72	4608.63	4416.31	4254.41
450000	6651.10	6154.10	5761.47	5444.68	5184.70	4968.35	4786.21
500000	7390.11	6837.89	6401.64	6049.65	5760.78	5520.39	5318.01
550000	8129.12	7521.68	7041.80	6654.61	6336.86	6072.43	5849.81
600000	8868.13	8205.46	7681.96	7259.58	6912.94	6624.47	6381.61

9¼%

Monthly Payments
necessary to amortize a loan

AMOUNT	15 YEARS	16 YEARS	17 YEARS	18 YEARS	19 YEARS	20 YEARS	21 YEARS
100	1.03	1.00	0.97	0.95	0.93	0.92	0.90
200	2.06	2.00	1.95	1.90	1.87	1.83	1.80
500	5.15	5.00	4.87	4.76	4.66	4.58	4.50
1000	10.29	10.00	9.74	9.52	9.33	9.16	9.01
2000	20.58	19.99	19.48	19.04	18.66	18.32	18.02
5000	51.46	49.98	48.71	47.61	46.64	45.79	45.05
6000	61.75	59.98	58.45	57.13	55.97	54.95	54.06
7000	72.04	69.98	68.20	66.65	65.30	64.11	63.07
8000	82.34	79.98	77.94	76.17	74.62	73.27	72.08
9000	92.63	89.97	87.68	85.69	83.95	82.43	81.09
10000	102.92	99.97	97.42	95.21	93.28	91.59	90.09
15000	154.38	149.95	146.14	142.82	139.92	137.38	135.14
20000	205.84	199.94	194.85	190.42	186.56	183.17	180.19
25000	257.30	249.92	243.56	238.03	233.20	228.97	225.24
30000	308.76	299.91	292.27	285.64	279.84	274.76	270.28
35000	360.22	349.89	340.98	333.24	326.48	320.55	315.33
40000	411.68	399.88	389.69	380.85	373.12	366.35	360.38
45000	463.14	449.86	438.41	428.45	419.76	412.14	405.43
50000	514.60	499.85	487.12	476.06	466.40	457.93	450.47
55000	566.06	549.83	535.83	523.67	513.04	503.73	495.52
60000	617.52	599.82	584.54	571.27	559.68	549.52	540.57
65000	668.97	649.80	633.25	618.88	606.33	595.31	585.61
70000	720.43	699.79	681.96	666.48	652.97	641.11	630.66
75000	771.89	749.77	730.68	714.09	699.61	686.90	675.71
80000	823.35	799.76	779.39	761.70	746.25	732.69	720.76
85000	874.81	849.74	828.10	809.30	792.89	778.49	765.80
90000	926.27	899.73	876.81	856.91	839.53	824.28	810.85
95000	977.73	949.71	925.52	904.51	886.17	870.07	855.90
100000	1029.19	999.70	974.23	952.12	932.81	915.87	900.94
105000	1080.65	1049.68	1022.95	999.73	979.45	961.66	945.99
110000	1132.11	1099.67	1071.66	1047.33	1026.09	1007.45	991.04
120000	1235.03	1199.64	1169.08	1142.54	1119.37	1099.04	1081.13
130000	1337.95	1299.61	1266.51	1237.75	1212.65	1190.63	1171.23
140000	1440.87	1399.58	1363.93	1332.97	1305.93	1282.21	1261.32
150000	1543.79	1499.55	1461.35	1428.18	1399.21	1373.80	1351.42
160000	1646.71	1599.52	1558.78	1523.39	1492.49	1465.39	1441.51
170000	1749.63	1699.49	1656.20	1618.60	1585.77	1556.97	1531.61
180000	1852.55	1799.46	1753.62	1713.81	1679.05	1648.56	1621.70
190000	1955.47	1899.42	1851.05	1809.03	1772.33	1740.15	1711.80
200000	2058.38	1999.39	1948.47	1904.24	1865.62	1831.73	1801.89
210000	2161.30	2099.36	2045.89	1999.45	1958.90	1923.32	1891.98
220000	2264.22	2199.33	2143.32	2094.66	2052.18	2014.91	1982.08
230000	2367.14	2299.30	2240.74	2189.87	2145.46	2106.49	2072.17
240000	2470.06	2399.27	2338.16	2285.09	2238.74	2198.08	2162.27
250000	2572.98	2499.24	2435.59	2380.30	2332.02	2289.67	2252.36
260000	2675.90	2599.21	2533.01	2475.51	2425.30	2381.25	2342.46
270000	2778.82	2699.18	2630.43	2570.72	2518.58	2472.84	2432.55
280000	2881.74	2799.15	2727.86	2665.93	2611.86	2564.43	2522.65
290000	2984.66	2899.12	2825.28	2761.15	2705.14	2656.01	2612.74
300000	3087.58	2999.09	2922.70	2856.36	2798.42	2747.60	2702.83
310000	3190.50	3099.06	3020.13	2951.57	2891.70	2839.19	2792.93
320000	3293.42	3199.03	3117.55	3046.78	2984.98	2930.77	2883.02
330000	3396.33	3299.00	3214.98	3141.99	3078.27	3022.36	2973.12
340000	3499.25	3398.97	3312.40	3237.20	3171.55	3113.95	3063.21
350000	3602.17	3498.94	3409.82	3332.42	3264.83	3205.53	3153.31
400000	4116.77	3998.79	3896.94	3808.48	3731.23	3663.47	3603.78
450000	4631.37	4498.64	4384.06	4284.54	4197.63	4121.40	4054.25
500000	5145.96	4998.49	4871.17	4760.60	4664.04	4579.33	4504.72
550000	5660.56	5498.33	5358.29	5236.65	5130.44	5037.27	4955.20
600000	6175.15	5998.18	5845.41	5712.71	5596.85	5495.20	5405.67

74

Monthly Payments 9¹/₄%
necessary to amortize a loan

AMOUNT	22 YEARS	23 YEARS	24 YEARS	25 YEARS	30 YEARS	35 YEARS	40 YEARS
100	0.89	0.88	0.87	0.86	0.82	0.80	0.79
200	1.78	1.75	1.73	1.71	1.65	1.61	1.58
500	4.44	4.38	4.33	4.28	4.11	4.01	3.95
1000	8.88	8.76	8.66	8.56	8.23	8.03	7.91
2000	17.76	17.52	17.31	17.13	16.45	16.05	15.81
5000	44.39	43.80	43.28	42.82	41.13	40.14	39.53
6000	53.27	52.56	51.94	51.38	49.36	48.16	47.44
7000	62.14	61.32	60.60	59.95	57.59	56.19	55.35
8000	71.02	70.08	69.25	68.51	65.81	64.22	63.25
9000	79.90	78.85	77.91	77.07	74.04	72.25	71.16
10000	88.78	87.61	86.57	85.64	82.27	80.27	79.07
15000	133.16	131.41	129.85	128.46	123.40	120.41	118.60
20000	177.55	175.21	173.13	171.28	164.54	160.55	158.13
25000	221.94	219.01	216.41	214.10	205.67	200.69	197.67
30000	266.33	262.82	259.70	256.91	246.80	240.82	237.20
35000	310.71	306.62	302.98	299.73	287.94	280.96	276.73
40000	355.10	350.42	346.26	342.55	329.07	321.10	316.26
45000	399.49	394.23	389.54	385.37	370.20	361.23	355.80
50000	443.88	438.03	432.83	428.19	411.34	401.37	395.33
55000	488.26	481.83	476.11	471.01	452.47	441.51	434.86
60000	532.65	525.63	519.39	513.83	493.61	481.65	474.40
65000	577.04	569.44	562.68	556.65	534.74	521.78	513.93
70000	621.43	613.24	605.96	599.47	575.87	561.92	553.46
75000	665.82	657.04	649.24	642.29	617.01	602.06	593.00
80000	710.20	700.85	692.52	685.11	658.14	642.20	632.53
85000	754.59	744.65	735.81	727.92	699.27	682.33	672.06
90000	798.98	788.45	779.09	770.74	740.41	722.47	711.59
95000	843.37	832.25	822.37	813.56	781.54	762.61	751.13
100000	887.75	876.06	865.66	856.38	822.68	802.74	790.66
105000	932.14	919.86	908.94	899.20	863.81	842.88	830.19
110000	976.53	963.66	952.22	942.02	904.94	883.02	869.73
120000	1065.31	1051.27	1038.79	1027.66	987.21	963.29	948.79
130000	1154.08	1138.87	1125.35	1113.30	1069.48	1043.57	1027.86
140000	1242.86	1226.48	1211.92	1198.93	1151.75	1123.84	1106.92
150000	1331.63	1314.09	1298.48	1284.57	1234.01	1204.12	1185.99
160000	1420.41	1401.69	1385.05	1370.21	1316.28	1284.39	1265.05
170000	1509.18	1489.30	1471.61	1455.85	1398.55	1364.67	1344.12
180000	1597.96	1576.90	1558.18	1541.49	1480.82	1444.94	1423.19
190000	1686.73	1664.51	1644.74	1627.13	1563.08	1525.21	1502.26
200000	1775.51	1752.11	1731.31	1712.76	1645.35	1605.49	1581.32
210000	1864.28	1839.72	1817.88	1798.40	1727.62	1685.76	1660.39
220000	1953.06	1927.33	1904.44	1884.04	1809.89	1766.04	1739.45
230000	2041.83	2014.93	1991.01	1969.68	1892.15	1846.31	1818.52
240000	2130.61	2102.54	2077.57	2055.32	1974.42	1926.59	1897.59
250000	2219.39	2190.14	2164.14	2140.95	2056.69	2006.86	1976.65
260000	2308.16	2277.75	2250.70	2226.59	2138.96	2087.14	2055.72
270000	2396.94	2365.35	2337.27	2312.23	2221.22	2167.41	2134.78
280000	2485.71	2452.96	2423.83	2397.87	2303.49	2247.68	2213.85
290000	2574.49	2540.57	2510.40	2483.51	2385.76	2327.96	2292.92
300000	2663.26	2628.17	2596.97	2569.15	2468.03	2408.23	2371.98
310000	2752.04	2715.78	2683.53	2654.78	2550.29	2488.51	2451.05
320000	2840.81	2803.38	2770.10	2740.42	2632.56	2568.78	2530.11
330000	2929.59	2890.99	2856.66	2826.06	2714.83	2649.06	2609.18
340000	3018.36	2978.59	2943.23	2911.70	2797.10	2729.33	2688.25
350000	3107.14	3066.20	3029.79	2997.34	2879.36	2809.61	2767.31
400000	3551.02	3504.23	3462.62	3425.53	3290.70	3210.98	3162.64
450000	3994.89	3942.26	3895.45	3853.72	3702.04	3612.35	3557.97
500000	4438.77	4380.29	4328.28	4281.91	4113.38	4013.72	3953.30
550000	4882.65	4818.31	4761.10	4710.10	4524.71	4415.09	4348.63
600000	5326.53	5256.34	5193.93	5138.29	4936.05	4816.47	4743.96

Monthly Payments
necessary to amortize a loan

AMOUNT	1 YEAR	2 YEARS	3 YEARS	4 YEARS	5 YEARS	6 YEARS	7 YEARS
100	8.77	4.59	3.20	2.51	2.10	1.83	1.63
200	17.54	9.18	6.41	5.02	4.20	3.65	3.27
500	43.84	22.96	16.02	12.56	10.50	9.14	8.17
1000	87.68	45.91	32.03	25.12	21.00	18.27	16.34
2000	175.37	91.83	64.07	50.25	42.00	36.55	32.69
5000	438.42	229.57	160.16	125.62	105.01	91.37	81.72
6000	526.10	275.49	192.20	150.74	126.01	109.65	98.06
7000	613.78	321.40	224.23	175.86	147.01	127.92	114.41
8000	701.47	367.32	256.26	200.99	168.01	146.20	130.75
9000	789.15	413.23	288.30	226.11	189.02	164.47	147.10
10000	876.84	459.14	320.33	251.23	210.02	182.75	163.44
15000	1315.25	688.72	480.49	376.85	315.03	274.12	245.16
20000	1753.67	918.29	640.66	502.46	420.04	365.49	326.88
25000	2192.09	1147.86	800.82	628.08	525.05	456.87	408.60
30000	2630.51	1377.43	960.99	753.69	630.06	548.24	490.32
35000	3068.92	1607.01	1121.15	879.31	735.07	639.61	572.04
40000	3507.34	1836.58	1281.32	1004.93	840.07	730.99	653.76
45000	3945.76	2066.15	1441.48	1130.54	945.08	822.36	735.48
50000	4384.18	2295.72	1601.65	1256.16	1050.09	913.73	817.20
55000	4822.59	2525.30	1761.81	1381.77	1155.10	1005.11	898.92
60000	5261.01	2754.87	1921.98	1507.39	1260.11	1096.48	980.64
65000	5699.43	2984.44	2082.14	1633.00	1365.12	1187.85	1062.36
70000	6137.85	3214.01	2242.31	1758.62	1470.13	1279.23	1144.08
75000	6576.26	3443.59	2402.47	1884.24	1575.14	1370.60	1225.80
80000	7014.68	3673.16	2562.64	2009.85	1680.15	1461.98	1307.52
85000	7453.10	3902.73	2722.80	2135.47	1785.16	1553.35	1389.24
90000	7891.52	4132.30	2882.97	2261.08	1890.17	1644.72	1470.96
95000	8329.93	4361.88	3043.13	2386.70	1995.18	1736.10	1552.68
100000	8768.35	4591.45	3203.29	2512.31	2100.19	1827.47	1634.40
105000	9206.77	4821.02	3363.46	2637.93	2205.20	1918.84	1716.12
110000	9645.19	5050.59	3523.62	2763.55	2310.20	2010.22	1797.84
120000	10522.02	5509.74	3843.95	3014.78	2520.22	2192.96	1961.28
130000	11398.86	5968.88	4164.28	3266.01	2730.24	2375.71	2124.72
140000	12275.69	6428.03	4484.61	3517.24	2940.26	2558.46	2288.16
150000	13152.53	6887.17	4804.94	3768.47	3150.28	2741.20	2451.60
160000	14029.36	7346.32	5125.27	4019.70	3360.30	2923.95	2615.04
170000	14906.20	7805.46	5445.60	4270.93	3570.32	3106.70	2778.48
180000	15783.03	8264.61	5765.93	4522.16	3780.34	3289.44	2941.92
190000	16659.87	8723.75	6086.26	4773.40	3990.35	3472.19	3105.36
200000	17536.70	9182.90	6406.59	5024.63	4200.37	3654.94	3268.80
210000	18413.54	9642.04	6726.92	5275.86	4410.39	3837.69	3432.24
220000	19290.37	10101.19	7047.25	5527.09	4620.41	4020.43	3595.68
230000	20167.21	10560.33	7367.58	5778.32	4830.43	4203.18	3759.12
240000	21044.04	11019.48	7687.91	6029.55	5040.45	4385.93	3922.56
250000	21920.88	11478.62	8008.24	6280.78	5250.47	4568.67	4086.00
260000	22797.71	11937.77	8328.57	6532.02	5460.48	4751.42	4249.44
270000	23674.55	12396.91	8648.90	6783.25	5670.50	4934.17	4412.88
280000	24551.38	12856.06	8969.23	7034.48	5880.52	5116.91	4576.31
290000	25428.22	13315.20	9289.56	7285.71	6090.54	5299.66	4739.75
300000	26305.05	13774.35	9609.88	7536.94	6300.56	5482.41	4903.19
310000	27181.89	14233.49	9930.21	7788.17	6510.58	5665.15	5066.63
320000	28058.72	14692.64	10250.54	8039.40	6720.60	5847.90	5230.07
330000	28935.56	15151.78	10570.87	8290.64	6930.61	6030.65	5393.51
340000	29812.39	15610.93	10891.20	8541.87	7140.63	6213.39	5556.95
350000	30689.23	16070.07	11211.53	8793.10	7350.65	6396.14	5720.39
400000	35073.40	18365.80	12813.18	10049.25	8400.74	7309.88	6537.59
450000	39457.58	20661.52	14414.83	11305.41	9450.84	8223.61	7354.79
500000	43841.76	22957.25	16016.47	12561.57	10500.93	9137.35	8171.99
550000	48225.93	25252.97	17618.12	13817.73	11551.02	10051.08	8989.19
600000	52610.11	27548.70	19219.77	15073.88	12601.12	10964.81	9806.39

Monthly Payments 9½%

necessary to amortize a loan

AMOUNT	8 YEARS	9 YEARS	10 YEARS	11 YEARS	12 YEARS	13 YEARS	14 YEARS
100	1.49	1.38	1.29	1.22	1.17	1.12	1.08
200	2.98	2.76	2.59	2.45	2.33	2.24	2.16
500	7.46	6.90	6.47	6.12	5.83	5.59	5.39
1000	14.91	13.81	12.94	12.24	11.66	11.19	10.78
2000	29.82	27.62	25.88	24.48	23.33	22.37	21.57
5000	74.55	69.05	64.70	61.19	58.32	55.93	53.92
6000	89.47	82.86	77.64	73.43	69.98	67.11	64.70
7000	104.38	96.67	90.58	85.67	81.65	78.30	75.49
8000	119.29	110.47	103.52	97.91	93.31	89.49	86.27
9000	134.20	124.28	116.46	110.15	104.97	100.67	97.05
10000	149.11	138.09	129.40	122.39	116.64	111.86	107.84
15000	223.66	207.14	194.10	183.58	174.96	167.79	161.76
20000	298.22	276.19	258.80	244.77	233.27	223.71	215.67
25000	372.77	345.23	323.49	305.97	291.59	279.64	269.59
30000	447.33	414.28	388.19	367.16	349.91	335.57	323.51
35000	521.88	483.33	452.89	428.35	408.23	391.50	377.43
40000	596.44	552.37	517.59	489.55	466.55	447.43	431.35
45000	670.99	621.42	582.29	550.74	524.87	503.36	485.27
50000	745.54	690.47	646.99	611.93	583.19	559.29	539.18
55000	820.10	759.51	711.69	673.13	641.51	615.21	593.10
60000	894.65	828.56	776.39	734.32	699.82	671.14	647.02
65000	969.21	897.61	841.08	795.51	758.14	727.07	700.94
70000	1043.76	966.66	905.78	856.71	816.46	783.00	754.86
75000	1118.32	1035.70	970.48	917.90	874.78	838.93	808.78
80000	1192.87	1104.75	1035.18	979.09	933.10	894.86	862.69
85000	1267.43	1173.80	1099.88	1040.28	991.42	950.79	916.61
90000	1341.98	1242.84	1164.58	1101.48	1049.74	1006.71	970.53
95000	1416.53	1311.89	1229.28	1162.67	1108.05	1062.64	1024.45
100000	1491.09	1380.94	1293.98	1223.86	1166.37	1118.57	1078.37
105000	1565.64	1449.98	1358.67	1285.06	1224.69	1174.50	1132.29
110000	1640.20	1519.03	1423.37	1346.25	1283.01	1230.43	1186.20
120000	1789.31	1657.12	1552.77	1468.64	1399.65	1342.29	1294.04
130000	1938.42	1795.22	1682.17	1591.02	1516.29	1454.14	1401.88
140000	2087.52	1933.31	1811.57	1713.41	1632.92	1566.00	1509.72
150000	2236.63	2071.40	1940.96	1835.80	1749.56	1677.86	1617.55
160000	2385.74	2209.50	2070.36	1958.18	1866.20	1789.72	1725.39
170000	2534.85	2347.59	2199.76	2080.57	1982.83	1901.57	1833.23
180000	2683.96	2485.68	2329.16	2202.96	2099.47	2013.43	1941.06
190000	2833.07	2623.78	2458.55	2325.34	2216.11	2125.29	2048.90
200000	2982.18	2761.87	2587.95	2447.73	2332.75	2237.14	2156.74
210000	3131.29	2899.97	2717.35	2570.12	2449.38	2349.00	2264.57
220000	3280.40	3038.06	2846.75	2692.50	2566.02	2460.86	2372.41
230000	3429.50	3176.15	2976.14	2814.89	2682.66	2572.72	2480.25
240000	3578.61	3314.25	3105.54	2937.27	2799.30	2684.57	2588.08
250000	3727.72	3452.34	3234.94	3059.66	2915.93	2796.43	2695.92
260000	3876.83	3590.43	3364.34	3182.05	3032.57	2908.29	2803.76
270000	4025.94	3728.53	3493.73	3304.43	3149.21	3020.14	2911.59
280000	4175.05	3866.62	3623.13	3426.82	3265.85	3132.00	3019.43
290000	4324.16	4004.71	3752.53	3549.21	3382.48	3243.86	3127.27
300000	4473.27	4142.81	3881.93	3671.59	3499.12	3355.72	3235.10
310000	4622.38	4280.90	4011.32	3793.98	3615.76	3467.57	3342.94
320000	4771.48	4419.00	4140.72	3916.37	3732.39	3579.43	3450.78
330000	4920.59	4557.09	4270.12	4038.75	3849.03	3691.29	3558.61
340000	5069.70	4695.18	4399.52	4161.14	3965.67	3803.15	3666.45
350000	5218.81	4833.28	4528.91	4283.53	4082.31	3915.00	3774.29
400000	5964.35	5523.74	5175.90	4895.46	4665.49	4474.29	4313.47
450000	6709.90	6214.21	5822.89	5507.39	5248.68	5033.57	4852.66
500000	7455.44	6904.68	6469.88	6119.32	5831.87	5592.86	5391.84
550000	8200.99	7595.15	7116.87	6731.26	6415.05	6152.15	5931.02
600000	8946.53	8285.62	7763.85	7343.19	6998.24	6711.43	6470.21

9¹/₂% Monthly Payments
necessary to amortize a loan

AMOUNT	15 YEARS	16 YEARS	17 YEARS	18 YEARS	19 YEARS	20 YEARS	21 YEARS
100	1.04	1.01	0.99	0.97	0.95	0.93	0.92
200	2.09	2.03	1.98	1.94	1.90	1.86	1.83
500	5.22	5.07	4.95	4.84	4.74	4.66	4.59
1000	10.44	10.15	9.90	9.68	9.49	9.32	9.17
2000	20.88	20.30	19.80	19.36	18.98	18.64	18.35
5000	52.21	50.75	49.49	48.40	47.44	46.61	45.87
6000	62.65	60.90	59.39	58.07	56.93	55.93	55.05
7000	73.10	71.05	69.28	67.75	66.42	65.25	64.22
8000	83.54	81.20	79.18	77.43	75.91	74.57	73.39
9000	93.98	91.35	89.08	87.11	85.40	83.89	82.57
10000	104.42	101.50	98.98	96.79	94.88	93.21	91.74
15000	156.63	152.25	148.47	145.19	142.33	139.82	137.62
20000	208.84	203.00	197.96	193.58	189.77	186.43	183.49
25000	261.06	253.75	247.45	241.98	237.21	233.03	229.36
30000	313.27	304.50	296.93	290.37	284.65	279.64	275.23
35000	365.48	355.25	346.42	338.77	332.09	326.25	321.10
40000	417.69	406.00	395.91	387.16	379.54	372.85	366.97
45000	469.90	456.75	445.40	435.56	426.98	419.46	412.85
50000	522.11	507.49	494.89	483.96	474.42	466.07	458.72
55000	574.32	558.24	544.38	532.35	521.86	512.67	504.59
60000	626.53	608.99	593.87	580.75	569.30	559.28	550.46
65000	678.75	659.74	643.36	629.14	616.75	605.89	596.33
70000	730.96	710.49	692.85	677.54	664.19	652.49	642.20
75000	783.17	761.24	742.34	725.93	711.63	699.10	688.08
80000	835.38	811.99	791.82	774.33	759.07	745.70	733.95
85000	887.59	862.74	841.31	822.72	806.51	792.31	779.82
90000	939.80	913.49	890.80	871.12	853.96	838.92	825.69
95000	992.01	964.24	940.29	919.52	901.40	885.52	871.56
100000	1044.22	1014.99	989.78	967.91	948.84	932.13	917.43
105000	1096.44	1065.74	1039.27	1016.31	996.28	978.74	963.31
110000	1148.65	1116.49	1088.76	1064.70	1043.72	1025.34	1009.18
120000	1253.07	1217.99	1187.74	1161.49	1138.61	1118.56	1100.92
130000	1357.49	1319.49	1286.71	1258.28	1233.49	1211.77	1192.66
140000	1461.91	1420.99	1385.69	1355.08	1328.38	1304.98	1284.41
150000	1566.34	1522.48	1484.67	1451.87	1423.26	1398.20	1376.15
160000	1670.76	1623.98	1583.65	1548.66	1518.14	1491.41	1467.89
170000	1775.18	1725.48	1682.63	1645.45	1613.03	1584.62	1559.64
180000	1879.60	1826.98	1781.61	1742.24	1707.91	1677.84	1651.38
190000	1984.03	1928.48	1880.58	1839.03	1802.80	1771.05	1743.13
200000	2088.45	2029.98	1979.56	1935.82	1897.68	1864.26	1834.87
210000	2192.87	2131.48	2078.54	2032.61	1992.56	1957.48	1926.61
220000	2297.29	2232.98	2177.52	2129.41	2087.45	2050.69	2018.36
230000	2401.72	2334.48	2276.50	2226.20	2182.33	2143.90	2110.10
240000	2506.14	2435.98	2375.47	2322.99	2277.22	2237.11	2201.84
250000	2610.56	2537.47	2474.45	2419.78	2372.10	2330.33	2293.59
260000	2714.98	2638.97	2573.43	2516.57	2466.98	2423.54	2385.33
270000	2819.41	2740.47	2672.41	2613.36	2561.87	2516.75	2477.07
280000	2923.83	2841.97	2771.39	2710.15	2656.75	2609.97	2568.82
290000	3028.25	2943.47	2870.36	2806.94	2751.64	2703.18	2660.56
300000	3132.67	3044.97	2969.34	2903.73	2846.52	2796.39	2752.30
310000	3237.10	3146.47	3068.32	3000.53	2941.40	2889.61	2844.05
320000	3341.52	3247.97	3167.30	3097.32	3036.29	2982.82	2935.79
330000	3445.94	3349.47	3266.28	3194.11	3131.17	3076.03	3027.53
340000	3550.36	3450.96	3365.25	3290.90	3226.05	3169.25	3119.28
350000	3654.79	3552.46	3464.23	3387.69	3320.94	3262.46	3211.02
400000	4176.90	4059.96	3959.12	3871.65	3795.36	3728.52	3669.74
450000	4699.01	4567.45	4454.01	4355.60	4269.78	4194.59	4128.45
500000	5221.12	5074.95	4948.90	4839.56	4744.20	4660.66	4587.17
550000	5743.24	5582.44	5443.79	5323.51	5218.62	5126.72	5045.89
600000	6265.35	6089.94	5938.68	5807.47	5693.04	5592.79	5504.61

Monthly Payments 9¹/₂%
necessary to amortize a loan

AMOUNT	22 YEARS	23 YEARS	24 YEARS	25 YEARS	30 YEARS	35 YEARS	40 YEARS
100	0.90	0.89	0.88	0.87	0.84	0.82	0.81
200	1.81	1.79	1.77	1.75	1.68	1.64	1.62
500	4.52	4.46	4.41	4.37	4.20	4.11	4.05
1000	9.04	8.93	8.83	8.74	8.41	8.22	8.10
2000	18.09	17.86	17.66	17.47	16.82	16.43	16.20
5000	45.22	44.65	44.14	43.68	42.04	41.08	40.50
6000	54.27	53.58	52.97	52.42	50.45	49.30	48.60
7000	63.31	62.51	61.79	61.16	58.86	57.51	56.70
8000	72.36	71.44	70.62	69.90	67.27	65.73	64.80
9000	81.40	80.37	79.45	78.63	75.68	73.95	72.91
10000	90.45	89.30	88.28	87.37	84.09	82.16	81.01
15000	135.67	133.95	132.42	131.05	126.13	123.24	121.51
20000	180.89	178.59	176.55	174.74	168.17	164.32	162.01
25000	226.12	223.24	220.69	218.42	210.21	205.40	202.52
30000	271.34	267.89	264.83	262.11	252.26	246.48	243.02
35000	316.56	312.54	308.97	305.79	294.30	287.56	283.52
40000	361.78	357.19	353.11	349.48	336.34	328.64	324.02
45000	407.01	401.84	397.25	393.16	378.38	369.73	364.53
50000	452.23	446.49	441.39	436.85	420.43	410.81	405.03
55000	497.45	491.14	485.53	480.53	462.47	451.89	445.53
60000	542.68	535.78	529.66	524.22	504.51	492.97	486.04
65000	587.90	580.43	573.80	567.90	546.56	534.05	526.54
70000	633.12	625.08	617.94	611.59	588.60	575.13	567.04
75000	678.35	669.73	662.08	655.27	630.64	616.21	607.55
80000	723.57	714.38	706.22	698.96	672.68	657.29	648.05
85000	768.79	759.03	750.36	742.64	714.73	698.37	688.55
90000	814.02	803.68	794.50	786.33	756.77	739.45	729.06
95000	859.24	848.33	838.64	830.01	798.81	780.53	769.56
100000	904.46	892.97	882.77	873.70	840.85	821.61	810.06
105000	949.68	937.62	926.91	917.38	882.90	862.69	850.56
110000	994.91	982.27	971.05	961.07	924.94	903.77	891.07
120000	1085.35	1071.57	1059.33	1048.44	1009.03	985.93	972.07
130000	1175.80	1160.87	1147.61	1135.81	1093.11	1068.10	1053.08
140000	1266.25	1250.16	1235.88	1223.18	1177.20	1150.26	1134.09
150000	1356.69	1339.46	1324.16	1310.54	1261.28	1232.42	1215.09
160000	1447.14	1428.76	1412.44	1397.91	1345.37	1314.58	1296.10
170000	1537.58	1518.06	1500.72	1485.28	1429.45	1396.74	1377.10
180000	1628.03	1607.35	1588.99	1572.65	1513.54	1478.90	1458.11
190000	1718.48	1696.65	1677.27	1660.02	1597.62	1561.06	1539.12
200000	1808.92	1785.95	1765.55	1747.39	1681.71	1643.22	1620.12
210000	1899.37	1875.25	1853.83	1834.76	1765.79	1725.38	1701.13
220000	1989.81	1964.54	1942.10	1922.13	1849.88	1807.55	1782.14
230000	2080.26	2053.84	2030.38	2009.50	1933.96	1889.71	1863.14
240000	2170.71	2143.14	2118.66	2096.87	2018.05	1971.87	1944.15
250000	2261.15	2232.44	2206.94	2184.24	2102.14	2054.03	2025.15
260000	2351.60	2321.73	2295.21	2271.61	2186.22	2136.19	2106.16
270000	2442.05	2411.03	2383.49	2358.98	2270.31	2218.35	2187.17
280000	2532.49	2500.33	2471.77	2446.35	2354.39	2300.51	2268.17
290000	2622.94	2589.63	2560.05	2533.72	2438.48	2382.67	2349.18
300000	2713.38	2678.92	2648.32	2621.09	2522.56	2464.83	2430.18
310000	2803.83	2768.22	2736.60	2708.46	2606.65	2547.00	2511.19
320000	2894.28	2857.52	2824.88	2795.83	2690.73	2629.16	2592.20
330000	2984.72	2946.82	2913.16	2883.20	2774.82	2711.32	2673.20
340000	3075.17	3036.11	3001.43	2970.57	2858.90	2793.48	2754.21
350000	3165.61	3125.41	3089.71	3057.94	2942.99	2875.64	2835.22
400000	3617.85	3571.90	3531.10	3494.79	3363.42	3286.45	3240.25
450000	4070.08	4018.38	3972.49	3931.63	3783.84	3697.25	3645.28
500000	4522.31	4464.87	4413.87	4368.48	4204.27	4108.06	4050.31
550000	4974.54	4911.36	4855.26	4805.33	4624.70	4518.86	4455.34
600000	5426.77	5357.85	5296.65	5242.18	5045.13	4929.67	4860.37

9¾%

Monthly Payments
necessary to amortize a loan

AMOUNT	1 YEAR	2 YEARS	3 YEARS	4 YEARS	5 YEARS	6 YEARS	7 YEARS
100	8.78	4.60	3.21	2.52	2.11	1.84	1.65
200	17.56	9.21	6.43	5.05	4.22	3.68	3.29
500	43.90	23.01	16.07	12.62	10.56	9.20	8.24
1000	87.80	46.03	32.15	25.24	21.12	18.40	16.47
2000	175.60	92.06	64.30	50.49	42.25	36.80	32.94
5000	439.00	230.15	160.75	126.21	105.62	92.00	82.36
6000	526.80	276.18	192.90	151.46	126.75	110.40	98.83
7000	614.60	322.21	225.05	176.70	147.87	128.80	115.31
8000	702.60	368.24	257.20	201.94	168.99	147.20	131.78
9000	790.20	414.27	289.35	227.18	190.12	165.60	148.25
10000	878.00	460.30	321.50	252.43	211.24	184.00	164.72
15000	1316.99	690.44	482.25	378.64	316.86	276.00	247.08
20000	1755.99	920.59	643.00	504.85	422.48	368.00	329.45
25000	2194.99	1150.74	803.75	631.07	528.11	460.00	411.81
30000	2633.99	1380.89	964.50	757.28	633.73	552.00	494.17
35000	3072.99	1611.04	1125.25	883.49	739.35	644.00	576.53
40000	3511.99	1841.18	1286.00	1009.71	844.97	736.00	658.89
45000	3950.98	2071.33	1446.75	1135.92	950.59	828.00	741.25
50000	4389.98	2301.48	1607.50	1262.13	1056.21	920.00	823.61
55000	4828.98	2531.63	1768.25	1388.35	1161.83	1012.00	905.98
60000	5267.98	2761.78	1929.00	1514.56	1267.45	1104.00	988.34
65000	5706.98	2991.93	2089.75	1640.77	1373.08	1196.00	1070.70
70000	6145.98	3222.07	2250.50	1766.99	1478.70	1288.00	1153.06
75000	6584.97	3452.22	2411.25	1893.20	1584.32	1380.00	1235.42
80000	7023.97	3682.37	2572.00	2019.42	1689.94	1472.00	1317.78
85000	7462.97	3912.52	2732.74	2145.63	1795.56	1564.00	1400.15
90000	7901.97	4142.67	2893.49	2271.84	1901.18	1656.00	1482.51
95000	8340.97	4372.81	3054.24	2398.06	2006.80	1748.00	1564.87
100000	8779.97	4602.96	3214.99	2524.27	2112.42	1840.00	1647.23
105000	9218.96	4833.11	3375.74	2650.48	2218.05	1932.00	1729.59
110000	9657.96	5063.26	3536.49	2776.70	2323.67	2024.00	1811.95
120000	10535.96	5523.55	3857.99	3029.12	2534.91	2208.00	1976.68
130000	11413.96	5983.85	4179.49	3281.55	2746.15	2392.00	2141.40
140000	12291.95	6444.15	4500.99	3533.98	2957.39	2576.00	2306.12
150000	13169.95	6904.44	4822.49	3786.40	3168.64	2760.00	2470.84
160000	14047.95	7364.74	5143.99	4038.83	3379.88	2944.00	2635.57
170000	14925.94	7825.04	5465.49	4291.26	3591.12	3128.00	2800.29
180000	15803.94	8285.33	5786.99	4543.68	3802.36	3312.00	2965.01
190000	16681.93	8745.63	6108.49	4796.11	4013.61	3496.00	3129.74
200000	17559.93	9205.92	6429.99	5048.54	4224.85	3680.00	3294.46
210000	18437.93	9666.22	6751.49	5300.97	4436.09	3864.00	3459.18
220000	19315.92	10126.52	7072.99	5553.39	4647.33	4048.00	3623.91
230000	20193.92	10586.81	7394.49	5805.82	4858.58	4232.00	3788.63
240000	21071.92	11047.11	7715.99	6058.25	5069.82	4416.00	3953.35
250000	21949.91	11507.41	8037.49	6310.67	5281.06	4600.00	4118.07
260000	22827.91	11967.70	8358.98	6563.10	5492.30	4784.00	4282.80
270000	23705.91	12428.00	8680.48	6815.53	5703.55	4968.00	4447.52
280000	24583.90	12888.29	9001.98	7067.95	5914.79	5152.00	4612.24
290000	25461.90	13348.59	9323.48	7320.38	6126.03	5336.00	4776.97
300000	26339.90	13808.89	9644.98	7572.81	6337.27	5520.00	4941.69
310000	27217.89	14269.18	9966.48	7825.23	6548.52	5704.00	5106.41
320000	28095.89	14729.48	10287.98	8077.66	6759.76	5888.00	5271.13
330000	28973.89	15189.78	10609.48	8330.09	6971.00	6072.01	5435.86
340000	29851.88	15650.07	10930.98	8582.51	7182.24	6256.01	5600.58
350000	30729.88	16110.37	11252.48	8834.94	7393.49	6440.01	5765.30
400000	35119.86	18411.85	12859.98	10097.08	8449.70	7360.01	6588.92
450000	39509.85	20713.33	14467.47	11359.21	9505.91	8280.01	7412.53
500000	43899.83	23014.81	16074.97	12621.35	10562.12	9200.01	8236.15
550000	48289.81	25316.29	17682.47	13883.48	11618.33	10120.01	9059.76
600000	52679.79	27617.77	19289.96	15145.61	12674.55	11040.01	9883.38

Monthly Payments 9¾%
necessary to amortize a loan

AMOUNT	8 YEARS	9 YEARS	10 YEARS	11 YEARS	12 YEARS	13 YEARS	14 YEARS
100	1.50	1.39	1.31	1.24	1.18	1.13	1.09
200	3.01	2.79	2.62	2.48	2.36	2.27	2.19
500	7.52	6.97	6.54	6.19	5.90	5.67	5.47
1000	15.04	13.94	13.08	12.38	11.81	11.33	10.93
2000	30.08	27.89	26.15	24.76	23.61	22.66	21.86
5000	75.21	69.72	65.39	61.89	59.03	56.66	54.66
6000	90.25	83.66	78.46	74.27	70.84	67.99	65.59
7000	105.30	97.61	91.54	86.65	82.65	79.32	76.53
8000	120.34	111.55	104.62	99.03	94.45	90.65	87.46
9000	135.38	125.49	117.69	111.41	106.26	101.98	98.39
10000	150.42	139.44	130.77	123.79	118.07	113.32	109.32
15000	225.63	209.15	196.16	185.68	177.10	169.97	163.99
20000	300.84	278.87	261.54	247.58	236.14	226.63	218.65
25000	376.06	348.59	326.93	309.47	295.17	283.29	273.31
30000	451.27	418.31	392.31	371.37	354.20	339.95	327.97
35000	526.48	488.03	457.70	433.26	413.24	396.61	382.63
40000	601.69	557.75	523.08	495.15	472.27	453.27	437.29
45000	676.90	627.46	588.47	557.05	531.31	509.92	491.96
50000	752.11	697.18	653.85	618.94	590.34	566.58	546.62
55000	827.32	766.90	719.24	680.84	649.37	623.24	601.28
60000	902.53	836.62	784.62	742.73	708.41	679.90	655.94
65000	977.74	906.34	850.01	804.62	767.44	736.56	710.60
70000	1052.95	976.06	915.39	866.52	826.48	793.21	765.26
75000	1128.17	1045.77	980.78	928.41	885.51	849.87	819.93
80000	1203.38	1115.49	1046.16	990.31	944.54	906.53	874.59
85000	1278.59	1185.21	1111.55	1052.20	1003.58	963.19	929.25
90000	1353.80	1254.93	1176.93	1114.10	1062.61	1019.85	983.91
95000	1429.01	1324.65	1242.32	1175.99	1121.65	1076.50	1038.57
100000	1504.22	1394.37	1307.70	1237.88	1180.68	1133.16	1093.24
105000	1579.43	1464.08	1373.09	1299.78	1239.71	1189.82	1147.90
110000	1654.64	1533.80	1438.47	1361.67	1298.75	1246.48	1202.56
120000	1805.06	1673.24	1569.24	1485.46	1416.82	1359.80	1311.88
130000	1955.49	1812.68	1700.01	1609.25	1534.88	1473.11	1421.21
140000	2105.91	1952.11	1830.78	1733.04	1652.95	1586.43	1530.53
150000	2256.33	2091.55	1961.55	1856.83	1771.02	1699.74	1639.85
160000	2406.75	2230.99	2092.32	1980.61	1889.09	1813.06	1749.18
170000	2557.17	2370.42	2223.09	2104.40	2007.16	1926.38	1858.50
180000	2707.60	2509.86	2353.86	2228.19	2125.23	2039.69	1967.82
190000	2858.02	2649.30	2484.63	2351.98	2243.29	2153.01	2077.15
200000	3008.44	2788.73	2615.40	2475.77	2361.36	2266.33	2186.47
210000	3158.86	2928.17	2746.18	2599.56	2479.43	2379.64	2295.79
220000	3309.28	3067.61	2876.95	2723.34	2597.50	2492.96	2405.12
230000	3459.71	3207.04	3007.72	2847.13	2715.57	2606.27	2514.44
240000	3610.13	3346.48	3138.49	2970.92	2833.63	2719.59	2623.76
250000	3760.55	3485.92	3269.26	3094.71	2951.70	2832.91	2733.09
260000	3910.97	3625.35	3400.03	3218.50	3069.77	2946.22	2842.41
270000	4061.39	3764.79	3530.80	3342.29	3187.84	3059.54	2951.74
280000	4211.82	3904.23	3661.57	3466.08	3305.91	3172.86	3061.06
290000	4362.24	4043.66	3792.34	3589.86	3423.97	3286.17	3170.38
300000	4512.66	4183.10	3923.11	3713.65	3542.04	3399.49	3279.71
310000	4663.08	4322.54	4053.88	3837.44	3660.11	3512.80	3389.03
320000	4813.50	4461.97	4184.65	3961.23	3778.18	3626.12	3498.35
330000	4963.93	4601.41	4315.42	4085.02	3896.25	3739.44	3607.68
340000	5114.35	4740.85	4446.19	4208.81	4014.31	3852.75	3717.00
350000	5264.77	4880.28	4576.96	4332.59	4132.38	3966.07	3826.32
400000	6016.88	5577.47	5230.81	4951.54	4722.72	4532.65	4372.94
450000	6768.99	6274.65	5884.66	5570.48	5313.06	5099.23	4919.56
500000	7521.10	6971.83	6538.51	6189.42	5903.40	5665.81	5466.18
550000	8273.21	7669.02	7192.36	6808.36	6493.74	6232.39	6012.79
600000	9025.32	8366.20	7846.21	7427.30	7084.08	6798.98	6559.41

9¾%   Monthly Payments
necessary to amortize a loan

AMOUNT	15 YEARS	16 YEARS	17 YEARS	18 YEARS	19 YEARS	20 YEARS	21 YEARS
100	1.06	1.03	1.01	0.98	0.96	0.95	0.93
200	2.12	2.06	2.01	1.97	1.93	1.90	1.87
500	5.30	5.15	5.03	4.92	4.82	4.74	4.67
1000	10.59	10.30	10.05	9.84	9.65	9.49	9.34
2000	21.19	20.61	20.11	19.68	19.30	18.97	18.68
5000	52.97	51.52	50.27	49.19	48.25	47.43	46.70
6000	63.56	61.82	60.33	59.03	57.90	56.91	56.04
7000	74.16	72.13	70.38	68.87	67.55	66.40	65.38
8000	84.75	82.43	80.44	78.71	77.20	75.88	74.72
9000	95.34	92.74	90.49	88.54	86.85	85.37	84.06
10000	105.94	103.04	100.54	98.38	96.50	94.85	93.40
15000	158.90	154.56	150.82	147.57	144.75	142.28	140.11
20000	211.87	206.08	201.09	196.76	193.00	189.70	186.81
25000	264.84	257.60	251.36	245.96	241.25	237.13	233.51
30000	317.81	309.12	301.63	295.15	289.50	284.56	280.21
35000	370.78	360.64	351.90	344.34	337.75	331.98	326.92
40000	423.75	412.16	402.18	393.53	386.00	379.41	373.62
45000	476.71	463.68	452.45	442.72	434.25	426.83	420.32
50000	529.68	515.20	502.72	491.91	482.50	474.26	467.02
55000	582.65	566.72	552.99	541.10	530.74	521.68	513.73
60000	635.62	618.23	603.26	590.29	578.99	569.11	560.43
65000	688.59	669.75	653.54	639.48	627.24	616.54	607.13
70000	741.55	721.27	703.81	688.67	675.49	663.96	653.83
75000	794.52	772.79	754.08	737.87	723.74	711.39	700.54
80000	847.49	824.31	804.35	787.06	771.99	758.81	747.24
85000	900.46	875.83	854.62	836.25	820.24	806.24	793.94
90000	953.43	927.35	904.90	885.44	868.49	853.67	840.64
95000	1006.39	978.87	955.17	934.63	916.74	901.09	887.34
100000	1059.36	1030.39	1005.44	983.82	964.99	948.52	934.05
105000	1112.33	1081.91	1055.71	1033.01	1013.24	995.94	980.75
110000	1165.30	1133.43	1105.98	1082.20	1061.49	1043.37	1027.45
120000	1271.24	1236.47	1206.53	1180.58	1157.99	1138.22	1120.86
130000	1377.17	1339.51	1307.07	1278.97	1254.49	1233.07	1214.26
140000	1483.11	1442.55	1407.62	1377.35	1350.99	1327.92	1307.67
150000	1589.04	1545.59	1508.16	1475.73	1447.49	1422.78	1401.07
160000	1694.98	1648.63	1608.70	1574.11	1543.99	1517.63	1494.47
170000	1800.92	1751.67	1709.25	1672.49	1640.48	1612.48	1587.88
180000	1906.85	1854.70	1809.79	1770.88	1736.98	1707.33	1681.28
190000	2012.79	1957.74	1910.34	1869.26	1833.48	1802.18	1774.69
200000	2118.73	2060.78	2010.88	1967.64	1929.98	1897.03	1868.09
210000	2224.66	2163.82	2111.42	2066.02	2026.48	1991.89	1961.50
220000	2330.60	2266.86	2211.97	2164.40	2122.98	2086.74	2054.90
230000	2436.53	2369.90	2312.51	2262.79	2219.48	2181.59	2148.31
240000	2542.47	2472.94	2413.06	2361.17	2315.98	2276.44	2241.71
250000	2648.41	2575.98	2513.60	2459.55	2412.48	2371.29	2335.12
260000	2754.34	2679.02	2614.14	2557.93	2508.98	2466.14	2428.52
270000	2860.28	2782.06	2714.69	2656.31	2605.47	2561.00	2521.93
280000	2966.22	2885.10	2815.23	2754.70	2701.97	2655.85	2615.33
290000	3072.15	2988.14	2915.78	2853.08	2798.42	2750.70	2708.74
300000	3178.09	3091.17	3016.32	2951.46	2894.97	2845.55	2802.14
310000	3284.02	3194.21	3116.86	3049.84	2991.47	2940.40	2895.55
320000	3389.96	3297.25	3217.41	3148.22	3087.97	3035.25	2988.95
330000	3495.90	3400.29	3317.95	3246.61	3184.47	3130.11	3082.35
340000	3601.83	3503.33	3418.49	3344.99	3280.97	3224.96	3175.76
350000	3707.77	3606.37	3519.04	3443.37	3377.47	3319.81	3269.16
400000	4237.45	4121.57	4021.76	3935.28	3859.96	3794.07	3736.19
450000	4767.13	4636.76	4524.48	4427.19	4342.46	4268.33	4203.21
500000	5296.81	5151.96	5027.20	4919.10	4824.95	4742.58	4670.23
550000	5826.49	5667.15	5529.92	5411.01	5307.45	5216.84	5137.26
600000	6356.18	6182.35	6032.64	5902.92	5789.94	5691.10	5604.28

Monthly Payments 9¾%
necessary to amortize a loan

AMOUNT	22 YEARS	23 YEARS	24 YEARS	25 YEARS	30 YEARS	35 YEARS	40 YEARS
100	0.92	0.91	0.90	0.89	0.86	0.84	0.83
200	1.84	1.82	1.80	1.78	1.72	1.68	1.66
500	4.61	4.55	4.50	4.46	4.30	4.20	4.15
1000	9.21	9.10	9.00	8.91	8.59	8.41	8.30
2000	18.43	18.20	18.00	17.82	17.18	16.81	16.59
5000	46.06	45.50	45.00	44.56	42.96	42.03	41.48
6000	55.28	54.60	54.00	53.47	51.55	50.44	49.77
7000	64.49	63.70	63.00	62.38	60.14	58.84	58.07
8000	73.70	72.80	72.00	71.29	68.73	67.25	66.36
9000	82.92	81.90	81.00	80.20	77.32	75.65	74.66
10000	92.13	91.00	90.00	89.11	85.92	84.06	82.96
15000	138.19	136.50	135.00	133.67	128.87	126.09	124.43
20000	184.26	182.00	180.00	178.23	171.83	168.12	165.91
25000	230.32	227.50	225.01	222.78	214.79	210.15	207.39
30000	276.39	273.00	270.00	267.34	257.75	252.18	248.87
35000	322.45	318.51	315.00	311.90	300.70	294.21	290.35
40000	368.52	364.01	360.00	356.45	343.66	336.24	331.82
45000	414.58	409.51	405.01	401.01	386.62	378.27	373.30
50000	460.65	455.01	450.01	445.57	429.58	420.29	414.78
55000	506.71	500.51	495.01	490.13	472.53	462.32	456.26
60000	552.78	546.01	540.01	534.68	515.49	504.35	497.74
65000	598.84	591.51	585.01	579.24	558.45	546.38	539.21
70000	644.90	637.01	630.01	623.80	601.41	588.41	580.69
75000	690.97	682.51	675.01	668.35	644.37	630.44	622.17
80000	737.03	728.01	720.02	712.91	687.32	672.47	663.65
85000	783.10	773.51	765.02	757.47	730.28	714.50	705.12
90000	829.16	819.02	810.02	802.02	773.24	756.53	746.60
95000	875.23	864.52	855.02	846.58	816.20	798.56	788.08
100000	921.29	910.02	900.02	891.14	859.15	840.59	829.56
105000	967.36	955.52	945.02	935.69	902.11	882.62	871.04
110000	1013.42	1001.02	990.02	980.25	945.07	924.65	912.51
120000	1105.55	1092.02	1080.02	1069.36	1030.99	1008.71	995.47
130000	1197.68	1183.02	1170.03	1158.48	1116.90	1092.77	1078.43
140000	1289.81	1274.03	1260.03	1247.59	1202.82	1176.83	1161.38
150000	1381.94	1365.03	1350.03	1336.71	1288.73	1260.88	1244.34
160000	1474.07	1456.03	1440.03	1425.82	1374.65	1344.94	1327.29
170000	1566.20	1547.03	1530.03	1514.93	1460.56	1429.00	1410.25
180000	1658.33	1638.03	1620.04	1604.05	1546.48	1513.06	1493.21
190000	1750.46	1729.03	1710.04	1693.16	1632.39	1597.12	1576.16
200000	1842.59	1820.03	1800.04	1782.27	1718.31	1681.18	1659.12
210000	1934.71	1911.04	1890.04	1871.39	1804.22	1765.24	1742.07
220000	2026.84	2002.04	1980.05	1960.50	1890.14	1849.30	1825.03
230000	2118.97	2093.04	2070.05	2049.62	1976.06	1933.36	1907.98
240000	2211.10	2184.04	2160.05	2138.73	2061.97	2017.41	1990.94
250000	2303.23	2275.04	2250.05	2227.84	2147.89	2101.47	2073.90
260000	2395.36	2366.04	2340.05	2316.96	2233.80	2185.53	2156.85
270000	2487.49	2457.05	2430.06	2406.07	2319.72	2269.59	2239.81
280000	2579.62	2548.05	2520.06	2495.18	2405.63	2353.65	2322.76
290000	2671.75	2639.05	2610.06	2584.30	2491.55	2437.71	2405.72
300000	2763.88	2730.05	2700.06	2673.41	2577.46	2521.77	2488.68
310000	2856.01	2821.05	2790.06	2762.53	2663.38	2605.83	2571.63
320000	2948.14	2912.05	2880.07	2851.64	2749.29	2689.89	2654.59
330000	3040.27	3003.06	2970.07	2940.75	2835.21	2773.94	2737.54
340000	3132.40	3094.06	3060.07	3029.87	2921.13	2858.00	2820.50
350000	3224.52	3185.06	3150.07	3118.98	3007.04	2942.06	2903.45
400000	3685.17	3640.07	3600.08	3564.55	3436.62	3362.36	3318.23
450000	4145.83	4095.08	4050.09	4010.12	3866.19	3782.65	3733.01
500000	4606.46	4550.08	4500.10	4455.69	4295.77	4202.95	4147.79
550000	5067.11	5005.09	4950.11	4901.26	4725.35	4623.24	4562.57
600000	5527.76	5460.10	5400.12	5346.82	5154.93	5043.54	4977.35

10%

Monthly Payments
necessary to amortize a loan

AMOUNT	1 YEAR	2 YEARS	3 YEARS	4 YEARS	5 YEARS	6 YEARS	7 YEARS
100	8.79	4.61	3.23	2.54	2.12	1.85	1.66
200	17.58	9.23	6.45	5.07	4.25	3.71	3.32
500	43.96	23.07	16.13	12.68	10.62	9.26	8.30
1000	87.92	46.14	32.27	25.36	21.25	18.53	16.60
2000	175.83	92.29	64.53	50.73	42.49	37.05	33.20
5000	439.58	230.72	161.34	126.81	106.24	92.63	83.01
6000	527.50	276.87	193.60	152.18	127.48	111.16	99.61
7000	615.41	323.01	225.87	177.54	148.73	129.68	116.21
8000	703.33	369.16	258.14	202.90	169.98	148.21	132.81
9000	791.24	415.30	290.40	228.26	191.22	166.73	149.41
10000	879.16	461.45	322.67	253.63	212.47	185.26	166.01
15000	1318.74	692.17	484.01	380.44	318.71	277.89	249.02
20000	1758.32	922.90	645.34	507.25	424.94	370.52	332.02
25000	2197.90	1153.62	806.68	634.06	531.18	463.15	415.03
30000	2637.48	1384.35	968.02	760.88	637.41	555.78	498.04
35000	3077.06	1615.07	1129.35	887.69	743.65	648.40	581.04
40000	3516.63	1845.80	1290.69	1014.50	849.88	741.03	664.05
45000	3956.21	2076.52	1452.02	1141.32	956.12	833.66	747.05
50000	4395.79	2307.25	1613.36	1268.13	1062.35	926.29	830.06
55000	4835.37	2537.97	1774.70	1394.94	1168.59	1018.92	913.07
60000	5274.95	2768.70	1936.03	1521.76	1274.82	1111.55	996.07
65000	5714.53	2999.42	2097.37	1648.57	1381.06	1204.18	1079.08
70000	6154.11	3230.14	2258.70	1775.38	1487.29	1296.81	1162.08
75000	6593.69	3460.87	2420.04	1902.19	1593.53	1389.44	1245.09
80000	7033.27	3691.59	2581.37	2029.01	1699.76	1482.07	1328.09
85000	7472.85	3922.32	2742.71	2155.82	1806.00	1574.70	1411.10
90000	7912.43	4153.04	2904.05	2282.63	1912.23	1667.33	1494.11
95000	8352.01	4383.77	3065.38	2409.45	2018.47	1759.95	1577.11
100000	8791.59	4614.49	3226.72	2536.26	2124.70	1852.58	1660.12
105000	9231.17	4845.22	3388.05	2663.07	2230.94	1945.21	1743.12
110000	9670.75	5075.94	3549.39	2789.88	2337.17	2037.84	1826.13
120000	10549.91	5537.39	3872.06	3043.51	2549.65	2223.10	1992.14
130000	11429.07	5998.84	4194.73	3297.14	2762.12	2408.36	2158.15
140000	12308.22	6460.29	4517.41	3550.76	2974.59	2593.62	2324.17
150000	13187.38	6921.74	4840.08	3804.39	3187.06	2778.88	2490.18
160000	14066.54	7383.19	5162.75	4058.01	3399.53	2964.13	2656.19
170000	14945.70	7844.64	5485.42	4311.64	3612.00	3149.39	2822.20
180000	15824.86	8306.09	5808.09	4565.27	3824.47	3334.65	2988.21
190000	16704.02	8767.54	6130.77	4818.89	4036.94	3519.91	3154.23
200000	17583.18	9228.99	6453.44	5072.52	4249.41	3705.17	3320.24
210000	18462.34	9690.43	6776.11	5326.14	4461.88	3890.43	3486.25
220000	19341.50	10151.88	7098.78	5579.77	4674.35	4075.68	3652.26
230000	20220.65	10613.33	7421.45	5833.39	4886.82	4260.94	3818.27
240000	21099.81	11074.78	7744.12	6087.02	5099.29	4446.20	3984.28
250000	21978.97	11536.23	8066.80	6340.65	5311.76	4631.46	4150.30
260000	22858.13	11997.68	8389.47	6594.27	5524.23	4816.72	4316.31
270000	23737.29	12459.13	8712.14	6847.90	5736.70	5001.98	4482.32
280000	24616.45	12920.58	9034.81	7101.52	5949.17	5187.23	4648.33
290000	25495.61	13382.03	9357.48	7355.15	6161.64	5372.49	4814.34
300000	26374.77	13843.48	9680.16	7608.78	6374.11	5557.75	4980.36
310000	27253.93	14304.93	10002.83	7862.40	6586.58	5743.01	5146.37
320000	28133.08	14766.38	10325.50	8116.03	6799.05	5928.27	5312.38
330000	29012.24	15227.83	10648.17	8369.65	7011.52	6113.53	5478.39
340000	29891.40	15689.27	10970.84	8623.28	7224.00	6298.78	5644.40
350000	30770.56	16150.72	11293.52	8876.90	7436.47	6484.04	5810.41
400000	35166.35	18457.97	12906.87	10145.03	8498.82	7410.34	6640.47
450000	39562.15	20765.22	14520.23	11413.16	9561.17	8336.63	7470.53
500000	43957.94	23072.46	16133.59	12681.29	10623.52	9262.92	8300.59
550000	48353.74	25379.71	17746.95	13949.42	11685.87	10189.21	9130.65
600000	52749.53	27686.96	19360.31	15217.55	12748.23	11115.50	9960.71

Monthly Payments 10%

necessary to amortize a loan

AMOUNT	8 YEARS	9 YEARS	10 YEARS	11 YEARS	12 YEARS	13 YEARS	14 YEARS
100	1.52	1.41	1.32	1.25	1.20	1.15	1.11
200	3.03	2.82	2.64	2.50	2.39	2.30	2.22
500	7.59	7.04	6.61	6.26	5.98	5.74	5.54
1000	15.17	14.08	13.22	12.52	11.95	11.48	11.08
2000	30.35	28.16	26.43	25.04	23.90	22.96	22.16
5000	75.87	70.39	66.08	62.60	59.75	57.39	55.41
6000	91.04	84.47	79.29	75.12	71.70	68.87	66.49
7000	106.22	98.55	92.51	87.64	83.66	80.35	77.57
8000	121.39	112.63	105.72	100.16	95.61	91.83	88.66
9000	136.57	126.71	118.94	112.68	107.56	103.31	99.74
10000	151.74	140.79	132.15	125.20	119.51	114.78	110.82
15000	227.61	211.18	198.23	187.80	179.26	172.18	166.23
20000	303.48	281.57	264.30	250.40	239.02	229.57	221.64
25000	379.35	351.97	330.38	313.00	298.77	286.96	277.05
30000	455.22	422.36	396.45	375.60	358.52	344.35	332.46
35000	531.10	492.75	462.53	438.20	418.28	401.75	387.87
40000	606.97	563.15	528.60	500.80	478.03	459.14	443.28
45000	682.84	633.54	594.68	563.39	537.79	516.53	498.69
50000	758.71	703.93	660.75	625.99	597.54	573.92	554.10
55000	834.58	774.33	726.83	688.59	657.29	631.32	609.51
60000	910.45	844.72	792.90	751.19	717.05	688.71	664.92
65000	986.32	915.11	858.98	813.79	776.80	746.10	720.33
70000	1062.19	985.51	925.06	876.39	836.55	803.49	775.74
75000	1138.06	1055.90	991.13	938.99	896.31	860.89	831.15
80000	1213.93	1126.29	1057.21	1001.59	956.06	918.28	886.56
85000	1289.80	1196.69	1123.28	1064.19	1015.82	975.67	941.97
90000	1365.67	1267.08	1189.36	1126.79	1075.57	1033.06	997.38
95000	1441.55	1337.48	1255.43	1189.39	1135.32	1090.46	1052.79
100000	1517.42	1407.87	1321.51	1251.99	1195.08	1147.85	1108.20
105000	1593.29	1478.26	1387.58	1314.59	1254.83	1205.24	1163.61
110000	1669.16	1548.66	1453.66	1377.19	1314.59	1262.63	1219.02
120000	1820.90	1689.44	1585.81	1502.39	1434.09	1377.42	1329.84
130000	1972.64	1830.23	1717.96	1627.58	1553.60	1492.20	1440.66
140000	2124.38	1971.02	1850.11	1752.78	1673.11	1606.99	1551.48
150000	2276.12	2111.80	1982.26	1877.98	1792.62	1721.77	1662.30
160000	2427.87	2252.59	2114.41	2003.18	1912.13	1836.56	1773.12
170000	2579.61	2393.38	2246.56	2128.38	2031.63	1951.34	1883.94
180000	2731.35	2534.16	2378.71	2253.58	2151.14	2066.13	1994.76
190000	2883.09	2674.95	2510.86	2378.78	2270.65	2180.91	2105.59
200000	3034.83	2815.74	2643.01	2503.98	2390.16	2295.70	2216.41
210000	3186.57	2956.52	2775.17	2629.17	2509.66	2410.48	2327.23
220000	3338.32	3097.31	2907.32	2754.37	2629.17	2525.27	2438.05
230000	3490.06	3238.10	3039.47	2879.57	2748.68	2640.05	2548.87
240000	3641.80	3378.88	3171.62	3004.77	2868.19	2754.84	2659.69
250000	3793.54	3519.67	3303.77	3129.97	2987.70	2869.62	2770.51
260000	3945.28	3660.46	3435.92	3255.17	3107.20	2984.41	2881.33
270000	4097.02	3801.25	3568.07	3380.37	3226.71	3099.19	2992.15
280000	4248.77	3942.03	3700.22	3505.57	3346.22	3213.97	3102.97
290000	4400.51	4082.82	3832.37	3630.76	3465.73	3328.76	3213.79
300000	4552.25	4223.61	3964.52	3755.96	3585.23	3443.54	3324.61
310000	4703.99	4364.39	4096.67	3881.16	3704.74	3558.33	3435.43
320000	4855.73	4505.18	4228.82	4006.36	3824.25	3673.11	3546.25
330000	5007.47	4645.97	4360.97	4131.56	3943.76	3787.90	3657.07
340000	5159.22	4786.75	4493.13	4256.76	4063.27	3902.68	3767.89
350000	5310.96	4927.54	4625.28	4381.96	4182.77	4017.47	3878.71
400000	6069.67	5631.47	5286.03	5007.95	4780.31	4591.39	4432.81
450000	6828.37	6335.41	5946.78	5633.94	5377.85	5165.32	4986.91
500000	7587.08	7039.34	6607.54	6259.94	5975.39	5739.24	5541.01
550000	8345.79	7743.28	7268.29	6885.93	6572.93	6313.16	6095.11
600000	9104.50	8447.21	7929.04	7511.93	7170.47	6887.09	6649.22

10%

Monthly Payments
necessary to amortize a loan

AMOUNT	15 YEARS	16 YEARS	17 YEARS	18 YEARS	19 YEARS	20 YEARS	21 YEARS
100	1.07	1.05	1.02	1.00	0.98	0.97	0.95
200	2.15	2.09	2.04	2.00	1.96	1.93	1.90
500	5.37	5.23	5.11	5.00	4.91	4.83	4.75
1000	10.75	10.46	10.21	10.00	9.81	9.65	9.51
2000	21.49	20.92	20.42	20.00	19.63	19.30	19.02
5000	53.73	52.30	51.06	49.99	49.06	48.25	47.54
6000	64.48	62.75	61.27	59.99	58.88	57.90	57.05
7000	75.22	73.21	71.48	69.99	68.69	67.55	66.55
8000	85.97	83.67	81.70	79.99	78.50	77.20	76.06
9000	96.71	94.13	91.91	89.99	88.31	86.85	85.57
10000	107.46	104.59	102.12	99.98	98.13	96.50	95.08
15000	161.19	156.89	153.18	149.98	147.19	144.75	142.62
20000	214.92	209.18	204.24	199.97	196.25	193.00	190.16
25000	268.65	261.48	255.30	249.96	245.31	241.26	237.70
30000	322.38	313.77	306.36	299.95	294.38	289.51	285.23
35000	376.11	366.07	357.42	349.95	343.44	337.76	332.77
40000	429.84	418.36	408.48	399.94	392.50	386.01	380.31
45000	483.57	470.66	459.54	449.93	441.57	434.26	427.85
50000	537.30	522.95	510.61	499.92	490.63	482.51	475.39
55000	591.03	575.25	561.67	549.91	539.69	530.76	522.93
60000	644.76	627.54	612.73	599.91	588.76	579.01	570.47
65000	698.49	679.84	663.79	649.90	637.82	627.26	618.01
70000	752.22	732.13	714.85	699.89	686.88	675.52	665.55
75000	805.95	784.43	765.91	749.88	735.94	723.77	713.09
80000	859.68	836.72	816.97	799.87	785.01	772.02	760.62
85000	913.41	889.02	868.03	849.87	834.07	820.27	808.16
90000	967.14	941.31	919.09	899.86	883.13	868.52	855.70
95000	1020.87	993.61	970.15	949.85	932.20	916.77	903.24
100000	1074.61	1045.90	1021.21	999.84	981.26	965.02	950.78
105000	1128.34	1098.20	1072.27	1049.84	1030.32	1013.27	998.32
110000	1182.07	1150.49	1123.33	1099.83	1079.38	1061.52	1045.86
120000	1289.53	1255.08	1225.45	1199.81	1177.51	1158.03	1140.94
130000	1396.99	1359.67	1327.57	1299.80	1275.64	1254.53	1236.01
140000	1504.45	1464.26	1429.69	1399.78	1373.76	1351.03	1331.09
150000	1611.91	1568.85	1531.82	1499.77	1471.89	1447.53	1426.17
160000	1719.37	1673.44	1633.94	1599.75	1570.01	1544.03	1521.25
170000	1826.83	1778.03	1736.06	1699.73	1668.14	1640.54	1616.33
180000	1934.29	1882.62	1838.18	1799.72	1766.27	1737.04	1711.40
190000	2041.75	1987.21	1940.30	1899.70	1864.39	1833.54	1806.48
200000	2149.21	2091.80	2042.42	1999.69	1962.52	1930.04	1901.56
210000	2256.67	2196.39	2144.54	2099.67	2060.64	2026.55	1996.64
220000	2364.13	2300.98	2246.66	2199.66	2158.77	2123.05	2091.72
230000	2471.59	2405.57	2348.78	2299.64	2256.90	2219.55	2186.79
240000	2579.05	2510.16	2450.91	2399.62	2355.02	2316.05	2281.87
250000	2686.51	2614.75	2553.03	2499.61	2453.15	2412.55	2376.95
260000	2793.97	2719.35	2655.15	2599.59	2551.27	2509.06	2472.03
270000	2901.43	2823.94	2757.27	2699.58	2649.40	2605.56	2567.11
280000	3008.89	2928.53	2859.39	2799.56	2747.52	2702.06	2662.18
290000	3116.35	3033.12	2961.51	2899.55	2845.65	2798.56	2757.26
300000	3223.82	3137.71	3063.63	2999.53	2943.78	2895.06	2852.34
310000	3331.28	3242.30	3165.75	3099.52	3041.90	2991.57	2947.42
320000	3438.74	3346.89	3267.87	3199.50	3140.03	3088.07	3042.50
330000	3546.20	3451.48	3369.99	3299.48	3238.15	3184.57	3137.57
340000	3653.66	3556.07	3472.12	3399.47	3336.28	3281.07	3232.65
350000	3761.12	3660.66	3574.24	3499.45	3434.41	3377.58	3327.73
400000	4298.42	4183.61	4084.84	3999.37	3925.04	3860.09	3803.12
450000	4835.72	4706.56	4595.45	4499.30	4415.67	4342.60	4278.51
500000	5373.02	5229.51	5106.05	4999.22	4906.29	4825.11	4753.90
550000	5910.33	5752.46	5616.66	5499.14	5396.92	5307.62	5229.29
600000	6447.63	6275.41	6127.26	5999.06	5887.55	5790.13	5704.68

Monthly Payments 10%

necessary to amortize a loan

AMOUNT	22 YEARS	23 YEARS	24 YEARS	25 YEARS	30 YEARS	35 YEARS	40 YEARS
100	0.94	0.93	0.92	0.91	0.88	0.86	0.85
200	1.88	1.85	1.83	1.82	1.76	1.72	1.70
500	4.69	4.64	4.59	4.54	4.39	4.30	4.25
1000	9.38	9.27	9.17	9.09	8.78	8.60	8.49
2000	18.76	18.54	18.35	18.17	17.55	17.19	16.98
5000	46.91	46.36	45.87	45.44	43.88	42.98	42.46
6000	56.29	55.63	55.04	54.52	52.65	51.58	50.95
7000	65.68	64.90	64.22	63.61	61.43	60.18	59.44
8000	75.06	74.17	73.39	72.70	70.21	68.77	67.93
9000	84.44	83.45	82.56	81.78	78.98	77.37	76.42
10000	93.82	92.72	91.74	90.87	87.76	85.97	84.91
15000	140.74	139.08	137.61	136.31	131.64	128.95	127.37
20000	187.65	185.44	183.48	181.74	175.51	171.93	169.83
25000	234.56	231.80	229.35	227.18	219.39	214.92	212.29
30000	281.47	278.15	275.22	272.61	263.27	257.90	254.74
35000	328.39	324.51	321.09	318.05	307.15	300.89	297.20
40000	375.30	370.87	366.96	363.48	351.03	343.87	339.66
45000	422.21	417.23	412.82	408.92	394.91	386.85	382.12
50000	469.12	463.59	458.69	454.35	438.79	429.84	424.57
55000	516.04	509.95	504.56	499.79	482.66	472.82	467.03
60000	562.95	556.31	550.43	545.22	526.54	515.80	509.49
65000	609.86	602.67	596.30	590.66	570.42	558.79	551.94
70000	656.77	649.03	642.17	636.09	614.30	601.77	594.40
75000	703.68	695.39	688.04	681.53	658.18	644.75	636.86
80000	750.60	741.75	733.91	726.96	702.06	687.74	679.32
85000	797.51	788.10	779.78	772.40	745.94	730.72	721.77
90000	844.42	834.46	825.65	817.83	789.81	773.71	764.23
95000	891.33	880.82	871.52	863.27	833.69	816.69	806.69
100000	938.25	927.18	917.39	908.70	877.57	859.67	849.15
105000	985.16	973.54	963.26	954.14	921.45	902.66	891.60
110000	1032.07	1019.90	1009.13	999.57	965.33	945.64	934.06
120000	1125.90	1112.62	1100.87	1090.44	1053.09	1031.61	1018.98
130000	1219.72	1205.34	1192.61	1181.31	1140.84	1117.57	1103.89
140000	1313.54	1298.05	1284.34	1272.18	1228.60	1203.54	1188.80
150000	1407.37	1390.77	1376.08	1363.05	1316.36	1289.51	1273.72
160000	1501.19	1483.49	1467.82	1453.92	1404.11	1375.48	1358.63
170000	1595.02	1576.21	1559.56	1544.79	1491.87	1461.44	1443.55
180000	1688.84	1668.93	1651.30	1635.66	1579.63	1547.41	1528.46
190000	1782.67	1761.65	1743.04	1726.53	1667.39	1633.38	1613.38
200000	1876.49	1854.36	1834.78	1817.40	1755.14	1719.34	1698.29
210000	1970.32	1947.08	1926.52	1908.27	1842.90	1805.31	1783.21
220000	2064.14	2039.80	2018.26	1999.14	1930.66	1891.28	1868.12
230000	2157.97	2132.52	2109.99	2090.01	2018.41	1977.25	1953.04
240000	2251.79	2225.24	2201.73	2180.88	2106.17	2063.21	2037.95
250000	2345.61	2317.95	2293.47	2271.75	2193.93	2149.18	2122.86
260000	2439.44	2410.67	2385.21	2362.62	2281.69	2235.15	2207.78
270000	2533.26	2503.39	2476.95	2453.49	2369.44	2321.12	2292.69
280000	2627.09	2596.11	2568.69	2544.36	2457.20	2407.08	2377.61
290000	2720.91	2688.83	2660.43	2635.23	2544.96	2493.05	2462.52
300000	2814.74	2781.54	2752.17	2726.10	2632.71	2579.02	2547.44
310000	2908.56	2874.26	2843.91	2816.97	2720.47	2664.98	2632.35
320000	3002.39	2966.98	2935.64	2907.84	2808.23	2750.95	2717.27
330000	3096.21	3059.70	3027.38	2998.71	2895.99	2836.92	2802.18
340000	3190.04	3152.42	3119.12	3089.58	2983.74	2922.89	2887.10
350000	3283.86	3245.14	3210.86	3180.45	3071.50	3008.85	2972.01
400000	3752.98	3708.73	3669.55	3634.80	3510.29	3438.69	3396.58
450000	4222.11	4172.32	4128.25	4089.15	3949.07	3868.53	3821.16
500000	4691.23	4635.91	4586.94	4543.50	4387.86	4298.36	4245.73
550000	5160.35	5099.50	5045.64	4997.85	4826.64	4728.20	4670.30
600000	5629.48	5563.09	5504.33	5452.20	5265.43	5158.03	5094.88

10¼%

Monthly Payments
necessary to amortize a loan

AMOUNT	1 YEAR	2 YEARS	3 YEARS	4 YEARS	5 YEARS	6 YEARS	7 YEARS
100	8.80	4.63	3.24	2.55	2.14	1.87	1.67
200	17.61	9.25	6.48	5.10	4.27	3.73	3.35
500	44.02	23.13	16.19	12.74	10.69	9.33	8.37
1000	88.03	46.26	32.38	25.48	21.37	18.65	16.73
2000	176.06	92.52	64.77	50.97	42.74	37.30	33.46
5000	440.16	231.30	161.92	127.41	106.85	93.26	83.65
6000	528.19	277.56	194.31	152.90	128.22	111.91	100.38
7000	616.23	323.82	226.69	178.38	149.59	130.57	117.11
8000	704.26	370.08	259.08	203.86	170.96	149.22	133.85
9000	792.29	416.34	291.46	229.35	192.33	167.87	150.58
10000	880.32	462.60	323.85	254.83	213.70	186.52	167.31
15000	1320.48	693.91	485.77	382.24	320.55	279.78	250.96
20000	1760.64	925.21	647.69	509.66	427.41	373.04	334.61
25000	2200.81	1156.51	809.62	637.07	534.26	466.30	418.27
30000	2640.97	1387.81	971.54	764.48	641.11	559.56	501.92
35000	3081.13	1619.11	1133.46	891.90	747.96	652.83	585.57
40000	3521.29	1850.42	1295.39	1019.31	854.81	746.09	669.23
45000	3961.45	2081.72	1457.31	1146.73	961.66	839.35	752.88
50000	4401.61	2313.02	1619.23	1274.14	1068.51	932.61	836.53
55000	4841.77	2544.32	1781.16	1401.55	1175.36	1025.87	920.19
60000	5281.93	2775.62	1943.08	1528.97	1282.22	1119.13	1003.84
65000	5722.09	3006.93	2105.00	1656.38	1389.07	1212.39	1087.49
70000	6162.25	3238.23	2266.93	1783.80	1495.92	1305.65	1171.15
75000	6602.42	3469.53	2428.85	1911.21	1602.77	1398.91	1254.80
80000	7042.58	3700.83	2590.78	2038.63	1709.62	1492.17	1338.45
85000	7482.74	3932.13	2752.70	2166.04	1816.47	1585.43	1422.10
90000	7922.90	4163.44	2914.62	2293.45	1923.32	1678.69	1505.76
95000	8363.06	4394.74	3076.55	2420.87	2030.18	1771.95	1589.41
100000	8803.22	4626.04	3238.47	2548.28	2137.03	1865.22	1673.06
105000	9243.38	4857.34	3400.39	2675.70	2243.88	1958.48	1756.72
110000	9683.54	5088.64	3562.32	2803.11	2350.73	2051.74	1840.37
120000	10563.86	5551.25	3886.16	3057.94	2564.43	2238.26	2007.68
130000	11444.19	6013.85	4210.01	3312.77	2778.13	2424.78	2174.98
140000	12324.51	6476.46	4533.86	3567.59	2991.84	2611.30	2342.29
150000	13204.83	6939.06	4857.70	3822.42	3205.54	2797.82	2509.60
160000	14085.15	7401.66	5181.55	4077.25	3419.24	2984.34	2676.90
170000	14965.47	7864.27	5505.40	4332.08	3632.94	3170.87	2844.21
180000	15845.80	8326.87	5829.24	4586.91	3846.65	3357.39	3011.52
190000	16726.12	8789.48	6153.09	4841.73	4060.35	3543.91	3178.82
200000	17606.44	9252.08	6476.94	5096.56	4274.05	3730.43	3346.13
210000	18486.76	9714.68	6800.78	5351.39	4487.76	3916.95	3513.44
220000	19367.08	10177.29	7124.63	5606.22	4701.46	4103.47	3680.74
230000	20247.41	10639.89	7448.48	5861.05	4915.16	4290.00	3848.05
240000	21127.73	11102.50	7772.33	6115.88	5128.86	4476.52	4015.35
250000	22008.05	11565.10	8096.17	6370.70	5342.57	4663.04	4182.66
260000	22888.37	12027.70	8420.02	6625.53	5556.27	4849.56	4349.97
270000	23768.69	12490.31	8743.87	6880.36	5769.97	5036.08	4517.27
280000	24649.02	12952.91	9067.71	7135.19	5983.67	5222.60	4684.58
290000	25529.34	13415.52	9391.56	7390.02	6197.38	5409.13	4851.89
300000	26409.66	13878.12	9715.41	7644.84	6411.08	5595.65	5019.19
310000	27289.98	14340.72	10039.25	7899.67	6624.78	5782.17	5186.50
320000	28170.30	14803.33	10363.10	8154.50	6838.48	5968.69	5353.81
330000	29050.63	15265.93	10686.95	8409.33	7052.19	6155.21	5521.11
340000	29930.95	15728.54	11010.79	8664.16	7265.89	6341.73	5688.42
350000	30811.27	16191.14	11334.64	8918.98	7479.59	6528.25	5855.73
400000	35212.88	18504.16	12953.88	10193.13	8548.11	7460.86	6692.26
450000	39614.49	20817.18	14573.11	11467.27	9616.62	8393.47	7528.79
500000	44016.10	23130.20	16192.34	12741.41	10685.13	9326.08	8365.32
550000	48417.71	25443.22	17811.58	14015.55	11753.65	10258.69	9201.85
600000	52819.32	27756.24	19430.81	15289.69	12822.16	11191.29	10038.39

Monthly Payments 10¼%
necessary to amortize a loan

AMOUNT	8 YEARS	9 YEARS	10 YEARS	11 YEARS	12 YEARS	13 YEARS	14 YEARS
100	1.53	1.42	1.34	1.27	1.21	1.16	1.12
200	3.06	2.84	2.67	2.53	2.42	2.33	2.25
500	7.65	7.11	6.68	6.33	6.05	5.81	5.62
1000	15.31	14.21	13.35	12.66	12.10	11.63	11.23
2000	30.61	28.43	26.71	25.32	24.19	23.25	22.47
5000	76.53	71.07	66.77	63.31	60.48	58.13	56.16
6000	91.84	85.29	80.12	75.97	72.57	69.76	67.40
7000	107.15	99.50	93.48	88.63	84.67	81.38	78.63
8000	122.45	113.72	106.83	101.29	96.77	93.01	89.86
9000	137.76	127.93	120.19	113.96	108.86	104.64	101.09
10000	153.07	142.14	133.54	126.62	120.96	116.26	112.33
15000	229.60	213.22	200.31	189.93	181.43	174.39	168.49
20000	306.14	284.29	267.08	253.24	241.91	232.53	224.65
25000	382.67	355.36	333.85	316.54	302.39	290.66	280.82
30000	459.20	426.43	400.62	379.85	362.87	348.79	336.98
35000	535.74	497.50	467.39	443.16	423.35	406.92	393.14
40000	612.27	568.58	534.16	506.47	483.83	465.05	449.31
45000	688.80	639.65	600.93	569.78	544.30	523.18	505.47
50000	765.34	710.72	667.70	633.09	604.78	581.31	561.63
55000	841.87	781.79	734.46	696.40	665.26	639.45	617.80
60000	918.41	852.87	801.23	759.71	725.74	697.58	673.96
65000	994.94	923.94	868.00	823.01	786.22	755.71	730.13
70000	1071.47	995.01	934.77	886.32	846.70	813.84	786.29
75000	1148.01	1066.08	1001.54	949.63	907.17	871.97	842.45
80000	1224.54	1137.15	1068.31	1012.94	967.65	930.10	898.62
85000	1301.08	1208.23	1135.08	1076.25	1028.13	988.23	954.78
90000	1377.61	1279.30	1201.85	1139.56	1088.61	1046.37	1010.94
95000	1454.14	1350.37	1268.62	1202.87	1149.09	1104.50	1067.11
100000	1530.68	1421.44	1335.39	1266.18	1209.57	1162.63	1123.27
105000	1607.21	1492.51	1402.16	1329.48	1270.04	1220.76	1179.43
110000	1683.74	1563.59	1468.93	1392.79	1330.52	1278.89	1235.60
120000	1836.81	1705.73	1602.47	1519.41	1451.48	1395.15	1347.92
130000	1989.88	1847.87	1736.01	1646.03	1572.43	1511.42	1460.25
140000	2142.95	1990.02	1869.55	1772.65	1693.39	1627.68	1572.58
150000	2296.02	2132.16	2003.09	1899.26	1814.35	1743.94	1684.90
160000	2449.08	2274.31	2136.62	2025.88	1935.30	1860.21	1797.23
170000	2602.15	2416.45	2270.16	2152.50	2056.26	1976.47	1909.56
180000	2755.22	2558.60	2403.70	2279.12	2177.22	2092.73	2021.88
190000	2908.29	2700.74	2537.24	2405.73	2298.17	2208.99	2134.21
200000	3061.35	2842.88	2670.78	2532.35	2419.13	2325.26	2246.54
210000	3214.42	2985.03	2804.32	2658.97	2540.09	2441.52	2358.87
220000	3367.49	3127.17	2937.86	2785.59	2661.04	2557.78	2471.19
230000	3520.56	3269.32	3071.40	2912.20	2782.00	2674.04	2583.52
240000	3673.62	3411.46	3204.94	3038.82	2902.96	2790.31	2695.85
250000	3826.69	3553.60	3338.48	3165.44	3023.91	2906.57	2808.17
260000	3979.76	3695.75	3472.01	3292.06	3144.87	3022.83	2920.50
270000	4132.83	3837.89	3605.55	3418.67	3265.83	3139.10	3032.83
280000	4285.90	3980.04	3739.09	3545.29	3386.78	3255.36	3145.15
290000	4438.96	4122.18	3872.63	3671.91	3507.74	3371.62	3257.48
300000	4592.03	4264.33	4006.17	3798.53	3628.70	3487.88	3369.81
310000	4745.10	4406.47	4139.71	3925.14	3749.65	3604.15	3482.13
320000	4898.17	4548.61	4273.25	4051.76	3870.61	3720.41	3594.46
330000	5051.23	4690.76	4406.79	4178.38	3991.56	3836.67	3706.79
340000	5204.30	4832.90	4540.33	4305.00	4112.52	3952.94	3819.12
350000	5357.37	4975.05	4673.87	4431.61	4233.48	4069.20	3931.44
400000	6122.71	5685.77	5341.56	5064.70	4838.26	4650.51	4493.08
450000	6888.05	6396.49	6009.26	5697.79	5443.04	5231.83	5054.71
500000	7653.38	7107.21	6676.95	6330.88	6047.83	5813.14	5616.35
550000	8418.72	7817.93	7344.65	6963.96	6652.61	6394.45	6177.98
600000	9184.06	8528.65	8012.34	7597.05	7257.39	6975.77	6739.62

10¼%

Monthly Payments
necessary to amortize a loan

AMOUNT	15 YEARS	16 YEARS	17 YEARS	18 YEARS	19 YEARS	20 YEARS	21 YEARS
100	1.09	1.06	1.04	1.02	1.00	0.98	0.97
200	2.18	2.12	2.07	2.03	2.00	1.96	1.94
500	5.45	5.31	5.19	5.08	4.99	4.91	4.84
1000	10.90	10.62	10.37	10.16	9.98	9.82	9.68
2000	21.80	21.23	20.74	20.32	19.95	19.63	19.35
5000	54.50	53.08	51.85	50.80	49.88	49.08	48.38
6000	65.40	63.69	62.23	60.96	59.86	58.90	58.06
7000	76.30	74.31	72.60	71.12	69.83	68.72	67.73
8000	87.20	84.92	82.97	81.28	79.81	78.53	77.41
9000	98.10	95.54	93.34	91.44	89.79	88.35	87.09
10000	109.00	106.15	103.71	101.60	99.76	98.16	96.76
15000	163.49	159.23	155.56	152.40	149.65	147.25	145.14
20000	217.99	212.30	207.42	203.20	199.53	196.33	193.53
25000	272.49	265.38	259.27	254.00	249.41	245.41	241.91
30000	326.99	318.46	311.13	304.79	299.29	294.49	290.29
35000	381.48	371.53	362.98	355.59	349.17	343.58	338.67
40000	435.98	424.61	414.84	406.39	399.06	392.66	387.05
45000	490.48	477.68	466.69	457.19	448.94	441.74	435.43
50000	544.98	530.76	518.55	507.99	498.82	490.82	483.82
55000	599.47	583.84	570.40	558.79	548.70	539.90	532.20
60000	653.97	636.91	622.25	609.59	598.59	588.99	580.58
65000	708.47	689.99	674.11	660.39	648.47	638.07	628.96
70000	762.97	743.06	725.96	711.19	698.35	687.15	677.34
75000	817.46	796.14	777.82	761.99	748.23	736.23	725.72
80000	871.96	849.22	829.67	812.78	798.11	785.31	774.11
85000	926.46	902.29	881.53	863.58	848.00	834.40	822.49
90000	980.96	955.37	933.38	914.38	897.88	883.48	870.87
95000	1035.45	1008.44	985.24	965.18	947.76	932.56	919.25
100000	1089.95	1061.52	1037.09	1015.98	997.64	981.64	967.63
105000	1144.45	1114.60	1088.95	1066.78	1047.52	1030.73	1016.01
110000	1198.95	1167.67	1140.80	1117.58	1097.41	1079.81	1064.39
120000	1307.94	1273.82	1244.51	1219.18	1197.17	1177.97	1161.16
130000	1416.94	1379.98	1348.22	1320.77	1296.93	1276.14	1257.92
140000	1525.93	1486.13	1451.93	1422.37	1396.70	1374.30	1354.68
150000	1634.93	1592.28	1555.64	1523.97	1496.46	1472.47	1451.45
160000	1743.92	1698.43	1659.35	1625.57	1596.23	1570.63	1548.21
170000	1852.92	1804.58	1763.06	1727.17	1695.99	1668.79	1644.97
180000	1961.91	1910.73	1866.76	1828.76	1795.76	1766.96	1741.74
190000	2070.91	2016.89	1970.47	1930.36	1895.52	1865.12	1838.50
200000	2179.90	2123.04	2074.18	2031.96	1995.28	1963.29	1935.26
210000	2288.90	2229.19	2177.89	2133.56	2095.05	2061.45	2032.03
220000	2397.89	2335.34	2281.60	2235.16	2194.81	2159.62	2128.79
230000	2506.89	2441.49	2385.31	2336.75	2294.58	2257.78	2225.55
240000	2615.88	2547.65	2489.02	2438.35	2394.34	2355.94	2322.32
250000	2724.88	2653.80	2592.73	2539.95	2494.11	2454.11	2419.08
260000	2833.87	2759.95	2696.44	2641.55	2593.87	2552.27	2515.84
270000	2942.87	2866.10	2800.15	2743.15	2693.63	2650.44	2612.60
280000	3051.86	2972.25	2903.86	2844.74	2793.40	2748.60	2709.37
290000	3160.86	3078.41	3007.57	2946.34	2893.16	2846.77	2806.13
300000	3269.85	3184.56	3111.27	3047.94	2992.93	2944.93	2902.89
310000	3378.85	3290.71	3214.98	3149.54	3092.69	3043.09	2999.66
320000	3487.84	3396.86	3318.69	3251.14	3192.46	3141.26	3096.42
330000	3596.84	3503.01	3422.40	3352.73	3292.22	3239.42	3193.18
340000	3705.83	3609.17	3526.11	3454.33	3391.98	3337.59	3289.95
350000	3814.83	3715.32	3629.82	3555.93	3491.75	3435.75	3386.71
400000	4359.80	4246.08	4148.37	4063.92	3990.57	3926.57	3870.53
450000	4904.78	4776.84	4666.91	4571.91	4489.39	4417.04	4354.34
500000	5449.75	5307.60	5185.46	5079.90	4988.21	4908.22	4838.16
550000	5994.73	5838.36	5704.00	5587.89	5487.03	5399.04	5321.97
600000	6539.71	6369.12	6222.55	6095.88	5985.85	5889.86	5805.79

Monthly Payments 10¼%
necessary to amortize a loan

AMOUNT	22 YEARS	23 YEARS	24 YEARS	25 YEARS	30 YEARS	35 YEARS	40 YEARS
100	0.96	0.94	0.93	0.93	0.90	0.88	0.87
200	1.91	1.89	1.87	1.85	1.79	1.76	1.74
500	4.78	4.72	4.67	4.63	4.48	4.39	4.34
1000	9.55	9.44	9.35	9.26	8.96	8.79	8.69
2000	19.11	18.89	18.70	18.53	17.92	17.58	17.38
5000	47.77	47.22	46.74	46.32	44.81	43.94	43.44
6000	57.32	56.67	56.09	55.58	53.77	52.73	52.13
7000	66.87	66.11	65.44	64.85	62.73	61.52	60.82
8000	76.43	75.56	74.79	74.11	71.69	70.31	69.51
9000	85.98	85.00	84.14	83.37	80.65	79.10	78.19
10000	95.53	94.45	93.49	92.64	89.61	87.89	86.88
15000	143.30	141.67	140.23	138.96	134.42	131.83	130.32
20000	191.06	188.89	186.98	185.28	179.22	175.77	173.76
25000	238.83	236.12	233.72	231.60	224.03	219.71	217.20
30000	286.60	283.34	280.46	277.91	268.83	263.66	260.65
35000	334.36	330.56	327.21	324.23	313.64	307.60	304.09
40000	382.13	377.79	373.95	370.55	358.44	351.54	347.53
45000	429.89	425.01	420.69	416.87	403.25	395.49	390.97
50000	477.66	472.23	467.44	463.19	448.05	439.43	434.41
55000	525.43	519.46	514.18	509.51	492.86	483.37	477.85
60000	573.19	566.68	560.93	555.83	537.66	527.31	521.29
65000	620.96	613.90	607.67	602.15	582.47	571.26	564.73
70000	668.72	661.13	654.41	648.47	627.27	615.20	608.17
75000	716.49	708.35	701.16	694.79	672.08	659.14	651.61
80000	764.25	755.57	747.90	741.11	716.88	703.08	695.05
85000	812.02	802.80	794.65	787.43	761.69	747.03	738.50
90000	859.79	850.02	841.39	833.74	806.49	790.97	781.94
95000	907.55	897.24	888.13	880.06	851.30	834.91	825.38
100000	955.32	944.47	934.88	926.38	896.10	878.86	868.82
105000	1003.08	991.69	981.62	972.70	940.91	922.80	912.26
110000	1050.85	1038.91	1028.36	1019.02	985.71	966.74	955.70
120000	1146.38	1133.36	1121.85	1111.66	1075.32	1054.63	1042.58
130000	1241.91	1227.81	1215.34	1204.30	1164.93	1142.51	1129.46
140000	1337.45	1322.25	1308.83	1296.94	1254.54	1230.40	1216.35
150000	1432.98	1416.70	1402.31	1389.57	1344.15	1318.28	1303.23
160000	1528.51	1511.15	1495.80	1482.21	1433.76	1406.17	1390.11
170000	1624.04	1605.59	1589.29	1574.85	1523.37	1494.05	1476.99
180000	1719.57	1700.04	1682.78	1667.49	1612.98	1581.94	1563.87
190000	1815.10	1794.49	1776.27	1760.13	1702.59	1669.83	1650.75
200000	1910.64	1888.93	1869.75	1852.77	1792.20	1757.71	1737.64
210000	2006.17	1983.38	1963.24	1945.40	1881.81	1845.60	1824.52
220000	2101.70	2077.83	2056.73	2038.04	1971.42	1933.48	1911.40
230000	2197.23	2172.27	2150.22	2130.68	2061.03	2021.37	1998.28
240000	2292.76	2266.72	2243.70	2223.32	2150.64	2109.25	2085.16
250000	2388.30	2361.17	2337.19	2315.96	2240.25	2197.14	2172.05
260000	2483.83	2455.61	2430.68	2408.60	2329.86	2285.02	2258.93
270000	2579.36	2550.06	2524.17	2501.23	2419.47	2372.91	2345.81
280000	2674.89	2644.51	2617.65	2593.87	2509.08	2460.80	2432.69
290000	2770.42	2738.95	2711.14	2686.51	2598.69	2548.68	2519.57
300000	2865.95	2833.40	2804.63	2779.15	2688.30	2636.57	2606.45
310000	2961.49	2927.85	2898.12	2871.79	2777.91	2724.45	2693.34
320000	3057.02	3022.29	2991.61	2964.43	2867.52	2812.34	2780.22
330000	3152.55	3116.74	3085.09	3057.06	2957.13	2900.22	2867.10
340000	3248.08	3211.18	3178.58	3149.70	3046.74	2988.11	2953.98
350000	3343.61	3305.63	3272.07	3242.34	3136.35	3075.99	3040.86
400000	3821.27	3777.86	3739.51	3705.53	3584.41	3515.42	3475.27
450000	4298.93	4250.10	4206.94	4168.72	4032.46	3954.85	3909.68
500000	4776.59	4722.33	4674.38	4631.92	4480.51	4394.28	4344.09
550000	5254.25	5194.56	5141.82	5095.11	4928.56	4833.71	4778.50
600000	5731.91	5666.80	5609.26	5558.30	5376.61	5273.13	5212.91

10½%

Monthly Payments
necessary to amortize a loan

AMOUNT	1 YEAR	2 YEARS	3 YEARS	4 YEARS	5 YEARS	6 YEARS	7 YEARS
100	8.81	4.64	3.25	2.56	2.15	1.88	1.69
200	17.63	9.28	6.50	5.12	4.30	3.76	3.37
500	44.07	23.19	16.25	12.80	10.75	9.39	8.43
1000	88.15	46.38	32.50	25.60	21.49	18.78	16.86
2000	176.30	92.75	65.00	51.21	42.99	37.56	33.72
5000	440.74	231.88	162.51	128.02	107.47	93.89	84.30
6000	528.89	278.26	195.01	153.62	128.96	112.67	101.16
7000	617.04	324.63	227.52	179.22	150.46	131.45	118.02
8000	705.19	371.01	260.02	204.83	171.95	150.23	134.89
9000	793.34	417.38	292.52	230.43	193.45	169.01	151.75
10000	881.49	463.76	325.02	256.03	214.94	187.79	168.61
15000	1322.23	695.64	487.54	384.05	322.41	281.68	252.91
20000	1762.97	927.52	650.05	512.07	429.88	375.58	337.21
25000	2203.72	1159.40	812.56	640.08	537.35	469.47	421.52
30000	2644.46	1391.28	975.07	768.10	644.82	563.37	505.82
35000	3085.20	1623.16	1137.59	896.12	752.29	657.26	590.12
40000	3525.94	1855.04	1300.10	1024.14	859.76	751.16	674.43
45000	3966.69	2086.92	1462.61	1152.15	967.23	845.05	758.73
50000	4407.43	2318.80	1625.12	1280.17	1074.70	938.95	843.03
55000	4848.17	2550.68	1787.63	1408.19	1182.16	1032.84	927.34
60000	5288.92	2782.56	1950.15	1536.20	1289.63	1126.74	1011.64
65000	5729.66	3014.44	2112.66	1664.22	1397.10	1220.63	1095.94
70000	6170.40	3246.32	2275.17	1792.24	1504.57	1314.53	1180.25
75000	6611.15	3478.20	2437.68	1920.25	1612.04	1408.42	1264.55
80000	7051.89	3710.08	2600.20	2048.27	1719.51	1502.32	1348.85
85000	7492.63	3941.96	2762.71	2176.29	1826.98	1596.21	1433.16
90000	7933.37	4173.84	2925.22	2304.30	1934.45	1690.11	1517.46
95000	8374.12	4405.72	3087.73	2432.32	2041.92	1784.00	1601.76
100000	8814.86	4637.60	3250.24	2560.34	2149.39	1877.90	1686.07
105000	9255.60	4869.48	3412.76	2688.35	2256.86	1971.79	1770.37
110000	9696.35	5101.36	3575.27	2816.37	2364.33	2065.69	1854.67
120000	10577.83	5565.12	3900.29	3072.41	2579.27	2253.48	2023.28
130000	11459.32	6028.89	4225.32	3328.44	2794.21	2441.27	2191.89
140000	12340.80	6492.65	4550.34	3584.47	3009.15	2629.06	2360.49
150000	13222.29	6956.41	4875.37	3840.51	3224.09	2816.85	2529.10
160000	14103.78	7420.17	5200.39	4096.54	3439.02	3004.64	2697.71
170000	14985.26	7883.93	5525.42	4352.57	3653.96	3192.42	2866.31
180000	15866.75	8347.69	5850.44	4608.61	3868.90	3380.21	3034.92
190000	16748.23	8811.45	6175.46	4864.64	4083.84	3568.00	3203.53
200000	17629.72	9275.21	6500.49	5120.68	4298.78	3755.79	3372.13
210000	18511.21	9738.97	6825.51	5376.71	4513.72	3943.58	3540.74
220000	19392.69	10202.73	7150.54	5632.74	4728.66	4131.37	3709.35
230000	20274.18	10666.49	7475.56	5888.78	4943.60	4319.16	3877.95
240000	21155.66	11130.25	7800.59	6144.81	5158.54	4506.95	4046.56
250000	22037.15	11594.01	8125.61	6400.84	5373.48	4694.74	4215.17
260000	22918.64	12057.77	8450.64	6656.88	5588.41	4882.53	4383.78
270000	23800.12	12521.53	8775.66	6912.91	5803.35	5070.32	4552.38
280000	24681.61	12985.29	9100.68	7168.95	6018.29	5258.11	4720.99
290000	25563.09	13449.05	9425.71	7424.98	6233.23	5445.90	4889.60
300000	26444.58	13912.81	9750.73	7681.01	6448.17	5633.69	5058.20
310000	27326.07	14376.57	10075.76	7937.05	6663.11	5821.48	5226.81
320000	28207.55	14840.33	10400.78	8193.08	6878.05	6009.27	5395.42
330000	29089.04	15304.09	10725.81	8449.12	7092.99	6197.06	5564.02
340000	29970.52	15767.85	11050.83	8705.15	7307.93	6384.85	5732.63
350000	30852.01	16231.61	11375.86	8961.18	7522.87	6572.64	5901.24
400000	35259.44	18550.42	13000.98	10241.35	8597.56	7511.59	6744.27
450000	39666.87	20869.22	14626.10	11521.52	9672.26	8450.54	7587.30
500000	44074.30	23188.02	16251.22	12801.69	10746.95	9389.48	8430.34
550000	48481.73	25506.82	17876.34	14081.86	11821.65	10328.43	9273.37
600000	52889.16	27825.62	19501.47	15362.03	12896.34	11267.38	10116.40

Monthly Payments 10½%
necessary to amortize a loan

AMOUNT	8 YEARS	9 YEARS	10 YEARS	11 YEARS	12 YEARS	13 YEARS	14 YEARS
100	1.54	1.44	1.35	1.28	1.22	1.18	1.14
200	3.09	2.87	2.70	2.56	2.45	2.36	2.28
500	7.72	7.18	6.75	6.40	6.12	5.89	5.69
1000	15.44	14.35	13.49	12.80	12.24	11.78	11.38
2000	30.88	28.70	26.99	25.61	24.48	23.55	22.77
5000	77.20	71.75	67.47	64.02	61.21	58.88	56.92
6000	92.64	86.11	80.96	76.83	73.45	70.65	68.31
7000	108.08	100.46	94.45	89.63	85.69	82.43	79.69
8000	123.52	114.81	107.95	102.44	97.93	94.20	91.07
9000	138.96	129.16	121.44	115.24	110.17	105.98	102.46
10000	154.40	143.51	134.93	128.04	122.41	117.75	113.84
15000	231.60	215.26	202.40	192.07	183.62	176.63	170.77
20000	308.80	287.02	269.87	256.09	244.83	235.50	227.69
25000	386.00	358.77	337.34	320.11	306.04	294.38	284.61
30000	463.20	430.53	404.80	384.13	367.24	353.25	341.53
35000	540.40	502.28	472.27	448.16	428.45	412.13	398.45
40000	617.60	574.03	539.74	512.18	489.66	471.00	455.37
45000	694.80	645.79	607.21	576.20	550.86	529.88	512.30
50000	772.00	717.54	674.67	640.22	612.07	588.75	569.22
55000	849.20	789.30	742.14	704.25	673.28	647.63	626.14
60000	926.40	861.05	809.61	768.27	734.48	706.50	683.06
65000	1003.60	932.81	877.08	832.29	795.69	765.38	739.98
70000	1080.80	1004.56	944.54	896.31	856.90	824.25	796.90
75000	1158.00	1076.31	1012.01	960.33	918.11	883.13	853.83
80000	1235.20	1148.07	1079.48	1024.36	979.31	942.00	910.75
85000	1312.40	1219.82	1146.95	1088.38	1040.52	1000.88	967.67
90000	1389.60	1291.58	1214.41	1152.40	1101.73	1059.75	1024.59
95000	1466.80	1363.33	1281.88	1216.42	1162.93	1118.63	1081.51
100000	1544.00	1435.09	1349.35	1280.45	1224.14	1177.50	1138.43
105000	1621.20	1506.84	1416.82	1344.47	1285.35	1236.38	1195.36
110000	1698.40	1578.59	1484.28	1408.49	1346.55	1295.25	1252.28
120000	1852.80	1722.10	1619.22	1536.54	1468.97	1413.00	1366.12
130000	2007.20	1865.61	1754.15	1664.58	1591.38	1530.75	1479.96
140000	2161.60	2009.12	1889.09	1792.62	1713.80	1648.50	1593.81
150000	2316.00	2152.63	2024.02	1920.67	1836.21	1766.25	1707.65
160000	2470.40	2296.14	2158.96	2048.71	1958.63	1884.00	1821.49
170000	2624.80	2439.65	2293.89	2176.76	2081.04	2001.75	1935.34
180000	2779.20	2583.16	2428.83	2304.80	2203.45	2119.50	2049.18
190000	2933.60	2726.66	2563.76	2432.85	2325.87	2237.25	2163.02
200000	3088.00	2870.17	2698.70	2560.89	2448.28	2355.00	2276.87
210000	3242.40	3013.68	2833.63	2688.94	2570.70	2472.75	2390.71
220000	3396.80	3157.19	2968.57	2816.98	2693.11	2590.50	2504.55
230000	3551.20	3300.70	3103.50	2945.03	2815.52	2708.25	2618.40
240000	3705.60	3444.21	3238.44	3073.07	2937.94	2826.00	2732.24
250000	3860.00	3587.72	3373.37	3201.11	3060.35	2943.75	2846.09
260000	4014.40	3731.22	3508.31	3329.16	3182.77	3061.51	2959.93
270000	4168.80	3874.73	3643.24	3457.20	3305.18	3179.26	3073.77
280000	4323.20	4018.24	3778.18	3585.25	3427.59	3297.01	3187.62
290000	4477.60	4161.75	3913.11	3713.29	3550.01	3414.76	3301.46
300000	4632.00	4305.26	4048.05	3841.34	3672.42	3532.51	3415.30
310000	4786.41	4448.77	4182.98	3969.38	3794.84	3650.26	3529.15
320000	4940.81	4592.28	4317.92	4097.43	3917.25	3768.01	3642.99
330000	5095.21	4735.78	4452.85	4225.47	4039.66	3885.76	3756.83
340000	5249.61	4879.29	4587.79	4353.52	4162.08	4003.51	3870.68
350000	5404.01	5022.80	4722.72	4481.56	4284.49	4121.26	3984.52
400000	6176.01	5740.34	5397.40	5121.78	4896.56	4710.01	4553.74
450000	6948.01	6457.89	6072.07	5762.01	5508.63	5298.76	5122.95
500000	7720.01	7175.43	6746.75	6402.23	6120.70	5887.51	5692.17
550000	8492.01	7892.97	7421.42	7042.45	6732.77	6476.26	6261.39
600000	9264.01	8610.52	8096.10	7682.68	7344.84	7065.01	6830.60

Monthly Payments
necessary to amortize a loan

AMOUNT	15 YEARS	16 YEARS	17 YEARS	18 YEARS	19 YEARS	20 YEARS	21 YEARS
100	1.11	1.08	1.05	1.03	1.01	1.00	0.98
200	2.21	2.15	2.11	2.06	2.03	2.00	1.97
500	5.53	5.39	5.27	5.16	5.07	4.99	4.92
1000	11.05	10.77	10.53	10.32	10.14	9.98	9.85
2000	22.11	21.54	21.06	20.64	20.28	19.97	19.69
5000	55.27	53.86	52.65	51.61	50.71	49.92	49.23
6000	66.32	64.63	63.18	61.93	60.85	59.90	59.08
7000	77.38	75.41	73.72	72.26	70.99	69.89	68.92
8000	88.43	86.18	84.25	82.58	81.13	79.87	78.77
9000	99.49	96.95	94.78	92.90	91.27	89.85	88.61
10000	110.54	107.72	105.31	103.22	101.41	99.84	98.46
15000	165.81	161.59	157.96	154.83	152.12	149.76	147.69
20000	221.08	215.45	210.62	206.45	202.83	199.68	196.92
25000	276.35	269.31	263.27	258.06	253.53	249.59	246.15
30000	331.62	323.17	315.92	309.67	304.24	299.51	295.38
35000	386.89	377.03	368.58	361.28	354.95	349.43	344.61
40000	442.16	430.90	421.23	412.89	405.66	399.35	393.84
45000	497.43	484.76	473.89	464.50	456.36	449.27	443.07
50000	552.70	538.62	526.54	516.11	507.07	499.19	492.30
55000	607.97	592.48	579.19	567.73	557.78	549.11	541.53
60000	663.24	646.35	631.85	619.34	608.48	599.03	590.76
65000	718.51	700.21	684.50	670.95	659.19	648.95	639.99
70000	773.78	754.07	737.16	722.56	709.90	698.87	689.22
75000	829.05	807.93	789.81	774.17	760.60	748.78	738.45
80000	884.32	861.79	842.46	825.78	811.31	798.70	787.68
85000	939.59	915.66	895.12	877.39	862.02	848.62	836.91
90000	994.86	969.52	947.77	929.00	912.73	898.54	886.14
95000	1050.13	1023.38	1000.43	980.62	963.43	948.46	935.37
100000	1105.40	1077.24	1053.08	1032.23	1014.14	998.38	984.60
105000	1160.67	1131.10	1105.74	1083.84	1064.85	1048.30	1033.83
110000	1215.94	1184.97	1158.39	1135.45	1115.55	1098.22	1083.06
120000	1326.48	1292.69	1263.70	1238.67	1216.97	1198.06	1181.52
130000	1437.02	1400.42	1369.01	1341.90	1318.38	1297.89	1279.98
140000	1547.56	1508.14	1474.31	1445.12	1419.79	1397.73	1378.44
150000	1658.10	1615.86	1579.62	1548.34	1521.21	1497.57	1476.90
160000	1768.64	1723.59	1684.93	1651.56	1622.62	1597.41	1575.36
170000	1879.18	1831.31	1790.24	1754.79	1724.04	1697.25	1673.82
180000	1989.72	1939.04	1895.55	1858.01	1825.45	1797.08	1772.28
190000	2100.26	2046.76	2000.85	1961.23	1926.86	1896.92	1870.74
200000	2210.80	2154.48	2106.16	2064.46	2028.28	1996.76	1969.20
210000	2321.34	2262.21	2211.47	2167.68	2129.69	2096.60	2067.66
220000	2431.88	2369.93	2316.78	2270.90	2231.11	2196.44	2166.12
230000	2542.42	2477.66	2422.09	2374.12	2332.52	2296.27	2264.58
240000	2652.96	2585.38	2527.39	2477.35	2433.93	2396.11	2363.04
250000	2763.50	2693.11	2632.70	2580.57	2535.35	2495.95	2461.50
260000	2874.04	2800.83	2738.01	2683.79	2636.76	2595.79	2559.96
270000	2984.58	2908.55	2843.32	2787.01	2738.18	2695.63	2658.42
280000	3095.12	3016.28	2948.63	2890.24	2839.59	2795.46	2756.88
290000	3205.66	3124.00	3053.94	2993.46	2941.00	2895.30	2855.34
300000	3316.20	3231.73	3159.24	3096.68	3042.42	2995.14	2953.80
310000	3426.74	3339.45	3264.55	3199.91	3143.83	3094.98	3052.26
320000	3537.28	3447.18	3369.86	3303.13	3245.24	3194.82	3150.72
330000	3647.82	3554.90	3475.17	3406.35	3346.66	3294.65	3249.18
340000	3758.36	3662.62	3580.48	3509.57	3448.07	3394.49	3347.64
350000	3868.90	3770.35	3685.78	3612.80	3549.49	3494.33	3446.10
400000	4421.60	4308.97	4212.32	4128.91	4056.56	3993.52	3938.39
450000	4974.30	4847.59	4738.87	4645.02	4563.63	4492.71	4430.69
500000	5526.99	5386.21	5265.41	5161.14	5070.69	4991.90	4922.99
550000	6079.69	5924.83	5791.95	5677.25	5577.76	5491.09	5415.29
600000	6632.39	6463.45	6318.49	6193.37	6084.83	5990.28	5907.59

Monthly Payments 10½%

necessary to amortize a loan

AMOUNT	22 YEARS	23 YEARS	24 YEARS	25 YEARS	30 YEARS	35 YEARS	40 YEARS
100	0.97	0.96	0.95	0.94	0.91	0.90	0.89
200	1.95	1.92	1.90	1.89	1.83	1.80	1.78
500	4.86	4.81	4.76	4.72	4.57	4.49	4.44
1000	9.73	9.62	9.52	9.44	9.15	8.98	8.89
2000	19.45	19.24	19.05	18.88	18.29	17.96	17.77
5000	48.63	48.09	47.62	47.21	45.74	44.91	44.43
6000	58.35	57.71	57.15	56.65	54.88	53.89	53.31
7000	68.08	67.33	66.67	66.09	64.03	62.87	62.20
8000	77.80	76.95	76.20	75.53	73.18	71.85	71.09
9000	87.53	86.57	85.72	84.98	82.33	80.83	79.97
10000	97.25	96.19	95.25	94.42	91.47	89.81	88.86
15000	145.88	144.28	142.87	141.63	137.21	134.72	133.29
20000	194.50	192.37	190.50	188.84	182.95	179.63	177.71
25000	243.13	240.47	238.12	236.05	228.68	224.53	222.14
30000	291.75	288.56	285.74	283.25	274.42	269.44	266.57
35000	340.38	336.65	333.37	330.46	320.16	314.35	311.00
40000	389.00	384.75	380.99	377.67	365.90	359.25	355.43
45000	437.63	432.84	428.62	424.88	411.63	404.16	399.86
50000	486.25	480.93	476.24	472.09	457.37	449.07	444.29
55000	534.88	529.03	523.86	519.30	503.11	493.97	488.71
60000	583.50	577.12	571.49	566.51	548.84	538.88	533.14
65000	632.13	625.21	619.11	613.72	594.58	583.79	577.57
70000	680.75	673.31	666.74	660.93	640.32	628.69	622.00
75000	729.38	721.40	714.36	708.14	686.05	673.60	666.43
80000	778.01	769.49	761.98	755.35	731.79	718.51	710.86
85000	826.63	817.59	809.61	802.55	777.53	763.41	755.28
90000	875.26	865.68	857.23	849.76	823.27	808.32	799.71
95000	923.88	913.77	904.86	896.97	869.00	853.23	844.14
100000	972.51	961.87	952.48	944.18	914.74	898.13	888.57
105000	1021.13	1009.96	1000.10	991.39	960.48	943.04	933.00
110000	1069.76	1058.05	1047.73	1038.60	1006.21	987.95	977.43
120000	1167.01	1154.24	1142.98	1133.02	1097.69	1077.76	1066.28
130000	1264.26	1250.43	1238.23	1227.44	1189.16	1167.57	1155.14
140000	1361.51	1346.61	1333.47	1321.85	1280.64	1257.39	1244.00
150000	1458.76	1442.80	1428.72	1416.27	1372.11	1347.20	1332.86
160000	1556.01	1538.99	1523.97	1510.69	1463.58	1437.01	1421.71
170000	1653.26	1635.17	1619.22	1605.11	1555.06	1526.83	1510.57
180000	1750.51	1731.36	1714.47	1699.53	1646.53	1616.64	1599.43
190000	1847.76	1827.55	1809.71	1793.95	1738.00	1706.45	1688.28
200000	1945.01	1923.73	1904.96	1888.36	1829.48	1796.27	1777.14
210000	2042.26	2019.92	2000.21	1982.78	1920.95	1886.08	1866.00
220000	2139.52	2116.11	2095.46	2077.20	2012.43	1975.89	1954.85
230000	2236.77	2212.29	2190.71	2171.62	2103.90	2065.71	2043.71
240000	2334.02	2308.48	2285.95	2266.04	2195.37	2155.52	2132.57
250000	2431.27	2404.67	2381.20	2360.45	2286.85	2245.34	2221.43
260000	2528.52	2500.85	2476.45	2454.87	2378.32	2335.15	2310.28
270000	2625.77	2597.04	2571.70	2549.29	2469.80	2424.96	2399.14
280000	2723.02	2693.23	2666.95	2643.71	2561.27	2514.78	2488.00
290000	2820.27	2789.41	2762.19	2738.13	2652.74	2604.59	2576.85
300000	2917.52	2885.60	2857.44	2832.55	2744.22	2694.40	2665.71
310000	3014.77	2981.79	2952.69	2926.96	2835.69	2784.22	2754.57
320000	3112.02	3077.98	3047.94	3021.38	2927.17	2874.03	2843.42
330000	3209.27	3174.16	3143.19	3115.80	3018.64	2963.84	2932.28
340000	3306.52	3270.35	3238.43	3210.22	3110.11	3053.66	3021.14
350000	3403.77	3366.54	3333.68	3304.64	3201.59	3143.47	3110.00
400000	3890.03	3847.47	3809.92	3776.73	3658.96	3592.54	3554.28
450000	4376.28	4328.40	4286.16	4248.82	4116.33	4041.60	3998.57
500000	4862.54	4809.34	4762.40	4720.91	4573.70	4490.67	4442.85
550000	5348.79	5290.27	5238.64	5193.00	5031.07	4939.74	4887.14
600000	5835.04	5771.20	5714.89	5665.09	5488.44	5388.80	5331.42

10¾%

Monthly Payments
necessary to amortize a loan

AMOUNT	1 YEAR	2 YEARS	3 YEARS	4 YEARS	5 YEARS	6 YEARS	7 YEARS
100	8.83	4.65	3.26	2.57	2.16	1.89	1.70
200	17.65	9.30	6.52	5.14	4.32	3.78	3.40
500	44.13	23.25	16.31	12.86	10.81	9.45	8.50
1000	88.27	46.49	32.62	25.72	21.62	18.91	16.99
2000	176.53	92.98	65.24	51.45	43.24	37.81	33.98
5000	441.33	232.46	163.10	128.62	108.09	94.53	84.96
6000	529.59	278.95	195.72	154.35	129.71	113.44	101.95
7000	617.86	325.44	228.34	180.07	151.33	132.34	118.94
8000	706.12	371.93	260.96	205.79	172.94	151.25	135.93
9000	794.39	418.43	293.58	231.52	194.56	170.16	152.92
10000	882.65	464.92	326.20	257.24	216.18	189.06	169.91
15000	1323.98	697.38	489.31	385.86	324.27	283.59	254.87
20000	1765.30	929.84	652.41	514.49	432.36	378.13	339.83
25000	2206.63	1162.30	815.51	643.11	540.45	472.66	424.78
30000	2647.95	1394.76	978.61	771.73	648.54	567.19	509.74
35000	3089.28	1627.21	1141.72	900.35	756.63	661.72	594.69
40000	3530.60	1859.67	1304.82	1028.97	864.72	756.25	679.65
45000	3971.93	2092.13	1467.92	1157.59	972.81	850.78	764.61
50000	4413.26	2324.59	1631.02	1286.21	1080.90	945.31	849.56
55000	4854.58	2557.05	1794.12	1414.84	1188.99	1039.85	934.52
60000	5295.91	2789.51	1957.23	1543.46	1297.08	1134.38	1019.46
65000	5737.23	3021.97	2120.33	1672.08	1405.17	1228.91	1104.43
70000	6178.56	3254.43	2283.43	1800.70	1513.26	1323.44	1189.39
75000	6619.88	3486.89	2446.53	1929.32	1621.35	1417.97	1274.35
80000	7061.21	3719.35	2609.64	2057.94	1729.44	1512.50	1359.30
85000	7502.53	3951.81	2772.74	2186.56	1837.53	1607.03	1444.26
90000	7943.86	4184.27	2935.84	2315.19	1945.62	1701.57	1529.21
95000	8385.18	4416.73	3098.94	2443.81	2053.71	1796.10	1614.17
100000	8826.51	4649.19	3262.05	2572.43	2161.80	1890.63	1699.13
105000	9267.83	4881.64	3425.15	2701.05	2269.89	1985.16	1784.08
110000	9709.16	5114.10	3588.25	2829.67	2377.97	2079.69	1869.04
120000	10591.81	5579.02	3914.45	3086.91	2594.15	2268.75	2038.95
130000	11474.46	6043.94	4240.66	3344.16	2810.33	2457.82	2208.87
140000	12357.11	6508.86	4566.86	3601.40	3026.51	2646.88	2378.78
150000	13239.76	6973.78	4893.07	3858.64	3242.69	2835.94	2548.69
160000	14122.41	7438.70	5219.27	4115.89	3458.87	3025.00	2718.60
170000	15005.06	7903.62	5545.48	4373.13	3675.05	3214.07	2888.52
180000	15887.72	8368.53	5871.68	4630.37	3891.23	3403.13	3058.43
190000	16770.37	8833.45	6197.89	4887.61	4107.41	3592.19	3228.34
200000	17653.02	9298.37	6524.09	5144.86	4323.59	3781.26	3398.25
210000	18535.67	9763.29	6850.30	5402.10	4539.77	3970.32	3568.17
220000	19418.32	10228.21	7176.50	5659.34	4755.95	4159.38	3738.08
230000	20300.97	10693.13	7502.70	5916.59	4972.13	4348.44	3907.99
240000	21183.62	11158.05	7828.91	6173.83	5188.31	4537.51	4077.91
250000	22066.27	11622.96	8155.11	6431.07	5404.49	4726.57	4247.82
260000	22948.92	12087.88	8481.32	6688.31	5620.67	4915.63	4417.73
270000	23831.57	12552.80	8807.52	6945.56	5836.85	5104.70	4587.64
280000	24714.22	13017.72	9133.73	7202.80	6053.03	5293.76	4757.56
290000	25596.88	13482.64	9459.93	7460.04	6269.21	5482.82	4927.47
300000	26479.53	13947.56	9786.14	7717.28	6485.39	5671.88	5097.38
310000	27362.18	14412.47	10112.34	7974.53	6701.57	5860.95	5267.29
320000	28244.83	14877.39	10438.55	8231.77	6917.75	6050.01	5437.21
330000	29127.48	15342.31	10764.75	8489.01	7133.92	6239.07	5607.12
340000	30010.13	15807.23	11090.95	8746.26	7350.10	6428.13	5777.03
350000	30892.78	16272.15	11417.16	9003.50	7566.28	6617.20	5946.94
400000	35306.04	18596.74	13048.18	10289.71	8647.18	7562.51	6796.51
450000	39719.29	20921.33	14679.20	11575.93	9728.08	8507.83	7646.07
500000	44132.54	23245.93	16310.23	12862.14	10808.98	9453.14	8495.64
550000	48545.80	25570.52	17941.25	14148.36	11889.87	10398.45	9345.20
600000	52959.05	27895.11	19572.27	15434.57	12970.77	11343.77	10194.76

Monthly Payments $10^3/_4\%$
necessary to amortize a loan

AMOUNT	8 YEARS	9 YEARS	10 YEARS	11 YEARS	12 YEARS	13 YEARS	14 YEARS
100	1.56	1.45	1.36	1.29	1.24	1.19	1.15
200	3.11	2.90	2.73	2.59	2.48	2.38	2.31
500	7.79	7.24	6.82	6.47	6.19	5.96	5.77
1000	15.57	14.49	13.63	12.95	12.39	11.92	11.54
2000	31.15	28.98	27.27	25.90	24.78	23.85	23.07
5000	77.87	72.44	68.17	64.74	61.94	59.62	57.68
6000	93.44	86.93	81.80	77.69	74.33	71.55	69.22
7000	109.02	101.42	95.44	90.64	86.72	83.47	80.76
8000	124.59	115.90	109.07	103.58	99.10	95.40	92.30
9000	140.17	130.39	122.70	116.53	111.49	107.32	103.83
10000	155.74	144.88	136.34	129.48	123.88	119.25	115.37
15000	233.61	217.32	204.50	194.22	185.82	178.87	173.05
20000	311.48	289.76	272.68	258.96	247.76	238.49	230.74
25000	389.35	362.20	340.85	323.70	309.70	298.12	288.42
30000	467.22	434.64	409.02	388.44	371.64	357.74	346.11
35000	545.09	507.08	477.19	453.18	433.58	417.36	403.79
40000	622.96	579.52	545.35	517.92	495.52	476.99	461.48
45000	700.83	651.96	613.52	582.66	557.46	536.61	519.16
50000	778.70	724.40	681.69	647.40	619.40	596.23	576.85
55000	856.56	796.84	749.86	712.14	681.34	655.86	634.53
60000	934.43	869.28	818.03	776.88	743.28	715.48	692.22
65000	1012.30	941.72	886.20	841.62	805.22	775.10	749.90
70000	1090.17	1014.16	954.37	906.36	867.16	834.73	807.59
75000	1168.04	1086.60	1022.54	971.10	929.10	894.35	865.27
80000	1245.91	1159.04	1090.71	1035.84	991.04	953.97	922.96
85000	1323.78	1231.48	1158.88	1100.58	1052.98	1013.60	980.64
90000	1401.65	1303.92	1227.05	1165.32	1114.92	1073.22	1038.33
95000	1479.52	1376.36	1295.22	1230.06	1176.86	1132.85	1096.01
100000	1557.39	1448.80	1363.39	1294.80	1238.80	1192.47	1153.70
105000	1635.26	1521.24	1431.56	1359.54	1300.74	1252.09	1211.38
110000	1713.13	1593.68	1499.73	1424.28	1362.68	1311.72	1269.07
120000	1868.87	1738.56	1636.06	1553.76	1486.57	1430.96	1384.44
130000	2024.61	1883.44	1772.40	1683.24	1610.45	1550.21	1499.80
140000	2180.35	2028.32	1908.74	1812.72	1734.33	1669.46	1615.17
150000	2336.09	2173.20	2045.08	1942.20	1858.21	1788.70	1730.54
160000	2491.82	2318.08	2181.42	2071.68	1982.09	1907.95	1845.91
170000	2647.56	2462.96	2317.76	2201.16	2105.97	2027.20	1961.28
180000	2803.30	2607.84	2454.10	2330.64	2229.85	2146.44	2076.65
190000	2959.04	2752.72	2590.43	2460.12	2353.73	2265.69	2192.02
200000	3114.78	2897.60	2726.77	2589.60	2477.61	2384.94	2307.39
210000	3270.52	3042.48	2863.11	2719.08	2601.49	2504.18	2422.76
220000	3426.26	3187.36	2999.45	2848.56	2725.37	2623.43	2538.13
230000	3582.00	3332.24	3135.79	2978.04	2849.25	2742.68	2653.50
240000	3737.74	3477.12	3272.13	3107.52	2973.13	2861.92	2768.87
250000	3893.48	3622.00	3408.47	3237.00	3097.01	2981.17	2884.24
260000	4049.21	3766.88	3544.81	3366.48	3220.89	3100.42	2999.61
270000	4204.95	3911.76	3681.14	3495.96	3344.77	3219.67	3114.98
280000	4360.69	4056.64	3817.48	3625.44	3468.65	3338.91	3230.35
290000	4516.43	4201.52	3953.82	3754.92	3592.53	3458.16	3345.72
300000	4672.17	4346.40	4090.16	3884.40	3716.41	3577.41	3461.09
310000	4827.91	4491.28	4226.50	4013.88	3840.29	3696.65	3576.46
320000	4983.65	4636.16	4362.84	4143.36	3964.17	3815.90	3691.83
330000	5139.39	4781.04	4499.18	4272.84	4088.05	3935.15	3807.20
340000	5295.13	4925.92	4635.52	4402.32	4211.93	4054.39	3922.57
350000	5450.87	5070.80	4771.85	4531.80	4335.81	4173.64	4037.94
400000	6229.56	5795.20	5453.55	5179.20	4955.22	4769.87	4614.78
450000	7008.26	6519.60	6135.24	5826.60	5574.62	5366.11	5191.63
500000	7786.95	7244.00	6816.93	6474.00	6194.02	5962.34	5768.48
550000	8565.65	7968.41	7498.63	7121.40	6813.42	6558.58	6345.33
600000	9344.34	8692.81	8180.32	7768.80	7432.83	7154.81	6922.18

10¾%

Monthly Payments
necessary to amortize a loan

AMOUNT	15 YEARS	16 YEARS	17 YEARS	18 YEARS	19 YEARS	20 YEARS	21 YEARS
100	1.12	1.09	1.07	1.05	1.03	1.02	1.00
200	2.24	2.19	2.14	2.10	2.06	2.03	2.00
500	5.60	5.47	5.35	5.24	5.15	5.08	5.01
1000	11.21	10.93	10.69	10.49	10.31	10.15	10.02
2000	22.42	21.86	21.38	20.97	20.61	20.30	20.03
5000	56.05	54.65	53.46	52.43	51.54	50.76	50.08
6000	67.26	65.58	64.15	62.92	61.84	60.91	60.10
7000	78.47	76.51	74.84	73.40	72.15	71.07	70.12
8000	89.68	87.45	85.53	83.89	82.46	81.22	80.13
9000	100.89	98.38	96.23	94.37	92.77	91.37	90.15
10000	112.09	109.31	106.92	104.86	103.07	101.52	100.17
15000	168.14	163.96	160.38	157.29	154.61	152.28	150.25
20000	224.19	218.61	213.84	209.72	206.15	203.05	200.34
25000	280.24	273.27	267.29	262.15	257.69	253.81	250.42
30000	336.28	327.92	320.75	314.58	309.22	304.57	300.50
35000	392.33	382.57	374.21	367.00	360.76	355.33	350.59
40000	448.38	437.23	427.67	419.43	412.30	406.09	400.67
45000	504.43	491.88	481.13	471.86	463.84	456.85	450.76
50000	560.47	546.53	534.59	524.29	515.37	507.61	500.84
55000	616.52	601.19	588.05	576.72	566.91	558.38	550.92
60000	672.57	655.84	641.51	629.15	618.45	609.14	601.01
65000	728.62	710.50	694.97	681.58	669.99	659.90	651.09
70000	784.66	765.15	748.42	734.01	721.52	710.66	701.18
75000	840.71	819.80	801.88	786.44	773.06	761.42	751.26
80000	896.76	874.46	855.34	838.87	824.60	812.18	801.34
85000	952.81	929.11	908.80	891.30	876.13	862.94	851.43
90000	1008.85	983.76	962.26	943.73	927.67	913.71	901.51
95000	1064.90	1038.42	1015.72	996.16	979.21	964.47	951.60
100000	1120.95	1093.07	1069.18	1048.58	1030.75	1015.23	1001.68
105000	1177.00	1147.72	1122.64	1101.01	1082.28	1065.99	1051.76
110000	1233.04	1202.38	1176.10	1153.44	1133.82	1116.75	1101.85
120000	1345.14	1311.68	1283.01	1258.30	1236.90	1218.27	1202.02
130000	1457.23	1420.99	1389.93	1363.16	1339.97	1319.80	1302.18
140000	1569.33	1530.30	1496.85	1468.02	1443.05	1421.32	1402.35
150000	1681.42	1639.60	1603.77	1572.88	1546.12	1522.84	1502.52
160000	1793.52	1748.91	1710.69	1677.74	1649.19	1624.37	1602.69
170000	1905.61	1858.22	1817.60	1782.59	1752.27	1725.89	1702.85
180000	2017.71	1967.53	1924.52	1887.45	1855.34	1827.41	1803.02
190000	2129.80	2076.83	2031.44	1992.31	1958.42	1928.94	1903.19
200000	2241.90	2186.14	2138.36	2097.17	2061.49	2030.46	2003.36
210000	2353.99	2295.45	2245.27	2202.03	2164.57	2131.98	2103.53
220000	2466.09	2404.75	2352.19	2306.89	2267.64	2233.50	2203.69
230000	2578.18	2514.06	2459.11	2411.75	2370.72	2335.03	2303.86
240000	2690.28	2623.37	2566.03	2516.60	2473.79	2436.55	2404.03
250000	2802.37	2732.67	2672.95	2621.46	2576.87	2538.07	2504.20
260000	2914.46	2841.98	2779.86	2726.32	2679.94	2639.60	2604.37
270000	3026.56	2951.29	2886.78	2831.18	2783.02	2741.12	2704.53
280000	3138.65	3060.60	2993.70	2936.04	2886.09	2842.64	2804.70
290000	3250.75	3169.90	3100.62	3040.90	2989.17	2944.16	2904.87
300000	3362.84	3279.21	3207.53	3145.75	3092.24	3045.69	3005.04
310000	3474.94	3388.52	3314.45	3250.61	3195.31	3147.21	3105.21
320000	3587.03	3497.82	3421.37	3355.47	3298.39	3248.73	3205.37
330000	3699.13	3607.13	3528.29	3460.33	3401.46	3350.26	3305.54
340000	3811.22	3716.44	3635.21	3565.19	3504.54	3451.78	3405.71
350000	3923.32	3825.74	3742.12	3670.05	3607.61	3553.30	3505.88
400000	4483.79	4372.28	4276.71	4194.34	4122.99	4060.92	4006.72
450000	5044.27	4918.81	4811.30	4718.63	4638.36	4568.53	4507.56
500000	5604.74	5465.35	5345.89	5242.92	5153.73	5076.14	5008.40
550000	6165.21	6011.88	5880.48	5767.22	5669.11	5583.76	5509.24
600000	6725.69	6558.42	6415.07	6291.51	6184.48	6091.37	6010.08

Monthly Payments 10¾%

necessary to amortize a loan

AMOUNT	22 YEARS	23 YEARS	24 YEARS	25 YEARS	30 YEARS	35 YEARS	40 YEARS
100	0.99	0.98	0.97	0.96	0.93	0.92	0.91
200	1.98	1.96	1.94	1.92	1.87	1.84	1.82
500	4.95	4.90	4.85	4.81	4.67	4.59	4.54
1000	9.90	9.79	9.70	9.62	9.33	9.18	9.08
2000	19.80	19.59	19.40	19.24	18.67	18.35	18.17
5000	49.49	48.97	48.51	48.10	46.67	45.88	45.42
6000	59.39	58.76	58.21	57.73	56.01	55.05	54.50
7000	69.29	68.56	67.91	67.35	65.34	64.23	63.59
8000	79.18	78.35	77.62	76.97	74.68	73.40	72.67
9000	89.08	88.14	87.32	86.59	84.01	82.58	81.76
10000	98.98	97.94	97.02	96.21	93.35	91.75	90.84
15000	148.47	146.91	145.53	144.31	140.02	137.63	136.26
20000	197.96	195.88	194.04	192.42	186.70	183.50	181.68
25000	247.45	244.85	242.55	240.52	233.37	229.38	227.10
30000	296.94	293.81	291.06	288.63	280.04	275.25	272.52
35000	346.43	342.78	339.57	336.73	326.72	321.13	317.94
40000	395.92	391.75	388.08	384.84	373.39	367.00	363.36
45000	445.41	440.72	436.59	432.94	420.07	412.88	408.78
50000	494.90	489.69	485.10	481.05	466.74	458.75	454.20
55000	544.40	538.66	533.61	529.15	513.41	504.63	499.62
60000	593.89	587.63	582.12	577.26	560.09	550.50	545.04
65000	643.38	636.60	630.63	625.36	606.76	596.38	590.46
70000	692.87	685.57	679.14	673.46	653.44	642.25	635.88
75000	742.36	734.54	727.65	721.57	700.11	688.13	681.30
80000	791.85	783.51	776.16	769.67	746.79	734.00	726.72
85000	841.34	832.47	824.67	817.78	793.46	779.88	772.14
90000	890.83	881.44	873.18	865.88	840.13	825.75	817.56
95000	940.32	930.41	921.69	913.99	886.81	871.63	862.98
100000	989.81	979.38	970.20	962.09	933.48	917.50	908.40
105000	1039.30	1028.35	1018.71	1010.20	980.16	963.38	953.82
110000	1088.79	1077.32	1067.22	1058.30	1026.83	1009.25	999.24
120000	1187.77	1175.26	1164.24	1154.51	1120.18	1101.00	1090.08
130000	1286.75	1273.20	1261.26	1250.72	1213.53	1192.75	1180.92
140000	1385.73	1371.13	1358.28	1346.93	1306.87	1284.50	1271.76
150000	1484.71	1469.07	1455.30	1443.14	1400.22	1376.25	1362.60
160000	1583.70	1567.01	1552.32	1539.35	1493.57	1468.00	1453.44
170000	1682.68	1664.95	1649.34	1635.56	1586.92	1559.75	1544.28
180000	1781.66	1762.89	1746.36	1731.77	1680.27	1651.51	1635.12
190000	1880.64	1860.83	1843.38	1827.98	1773.61	1743.26	1725.95
200000	1979.62	1958.76	1940.40	1924.19	1866.96	1835.01	1816.79
210000	2078.60	2056.70	2037.42	2020.39	1960.31	1926.76	1907.63
220000	2177.58	2154.64	2134.44	2116.60	2053.66	2018.51	1998.47
230000	2276.56	2252.58	2231.46	2212.81	2147.01	2110.26	2089.31
240000	2375.54	2350.52	2328.48	2309.02	2240.36	2202.01	2180.15
250000	2474.52	2448.46	2425.50	2405.23	2333.70	2293.76	2270.99
260000	2573.51	2546.39	2522.52	2501.44	2427.05	2385.51	2361.83
270000	2672.49	2644.33	2619.54	2597.65	2520.40	2477.26	2452.67
280000	2771.47	2742.27	2716.56	2693.86	2613.75	2569.01	2543.51
290000	2870.45	2840.21	2813.58	2790.07	2707.10	2660.76	2634.35
300000	2969.43	2938.15	2910.60	2886.28	2800.44	2752.51	2725.19
310000	3068.41	3036.08	3007.62	2982.49	2893.79	2844.26	2816.03
320000	3167.39	3134.02	3104.64	3078.70	2987.14	2936.01	2906.87
330000	3266.37	3231.96	3201.66	3174.91	3080.49	3027.76	2997.71
340000	3365.35	3329.90	3298.68	3271.12	3173.84	3119.51	3088.55
350000	3464.33	3427.84	3395.69	3367.32	3267.18	3211.26	3179.39
400000	3959.24	3917.53	3880.79	3848.37	3733.93	3670.01	3633.59
450000	4454.14	4407.22	4365.89	4329.42	4200.67	4128.76	4087.79
500000	4949.05	4896.91	4850.99	4810.46	4667.41	4587.51	4541.99
550000	5443.95	5386.60	5336.09	5291.51	5134.15	5046.27	4996.18
600000	5938.86	5876.29	5821.19	5772.56	5600.89	5505.02	5450.38

11%

Monthly Payments
necessary to amortize a loan

AMOUNT	1 YEAR	2 YEARS	3 YEARS	4 YEARS	5 YEARS	6 YEARS	7 YEARS
100	8.84	4.66	3.27	2.58	2.17	1.90	1.71
200	17.68	9.32	6.55	5.17	4.35	3.81	3.42
500	44.19	23.30	16.37	12.92	10.87	9.52	8.56
1000	88.38	46.61	32.74	25.85	21.74	19.03	17.12
2000	176.76	93.22	65.48	51.69	43.48	38.07	34.24
5000	441.91	233.04	163.69	129.23	108.71	95.17	85.61
6000	530.29	279.65	196.43	155.07	130.45	114.20	102.73
7000	618.67	326.25	229.17	180.92	152.20	133.24	119.86
8000	707.05	372.86	261.91	206.76	173.94	152.27	136.98
9000	795.43	419.47	294.65	232.61	195.68	171.31	154.10
10000	883.82	466.08	327.39	258.46	217.42	190.34	171.22
15000	1325.72	699.12	491.08	387.68	326.14	285.51	256.84
20000	1767.63	932.16	654.77	516.91	434.85	380.68	342.45
25000	2209.54	1165.20	818.47	646.14	543.56	475.85	428.06
30000	2651.45	1398.24	982.16	775.37	652.27	571.02	513.67
35000	3093.36	1631.27	1145.86	904.59	760.98	666.19	599.29
40000	3535.27	1864.31	1309.55	1033.82	869.70	761.36	684.90
45000	3977.17	2097.35	1473.24	1163.05	978.41	856.53	770.51
50000	4419.08	2330.39	1636.94	1292.28	1087.12	951.70	856.12
55000	4860.99	2563.43	1800.63	1421.50	1195.83	1046.87	941.73
60000	5302.90	2796.47	1964.32	1550.73	1304.55	1142.04	1027.35
65000	5744.81	3029.51	2128.02	1679.96	1413.26	1237.22	1112.96
70000	6186.72	3262.55	2291.71	1809.19	1521.97	1332.39	1198.57
75000	6628.62	3495.59	2455.40	1938.41	1630.68	1427.56	1284.18
80000	7070.53	3728.63	2619.10	2067.64	1739.39	1522.73	1369.79
85000	7512.44	3961.67	2782.79	2196.87	1848.11	1617.90	1455.41
90000	7954.35	4194.71	2946.48	2326.10	1956.82	1713.07	1541.02
95000	8396.26	4427.74	3110.18	2455.32	2065.53	1808.24	1626.63
100000	8838.17	4660.78	3273.87	2584.55	2174.24	1903.41	1712.24
105000	9280.07	4893.82	3437.57	2713.78	2282.95	1998.58	1797.86
110000	9721.98	5126.86	3601.26	2843.01	2391.67	2093.75	1883.47
120000	10605.80	5592.94	3928.65	3101.46	2609.09	2284.09	2054.69
130000	11489.62	6059.02	4256.03	3359.92	2826.51	2474.43	2225.92
140000	12373.43	6525.10	4583.42	3618.37	3043.94	2664.77	2397.14
150000	13257.25	6991.18	4910.81	3876.83	3261.36	2855.11	2568.37
160000	14141.07	7457.25	5238.19	4135.28	3478.79	3045.45	2739.59
170000	15024.88	7923.33	5565.58	4393.74	3696.21	3235.79	2910.81
180000	15908.70	8389.41	5892.97	4652.19	3913.64	3426.13	3082.04
190000	16792.52	8855.49	6220.36	4910.65	4131.06	3616.48	3253.26
200000	17676.33	9321.57	6547.74	5169.10	4348.48	3806.82	3424.49
210000	18560.15	9787.65	6875.13	5427.56	4565.91	3997.16	3595.71
220000	19443.96	10253.72	7202.52	5686.01	4783.33	4187.50	3766.94
230000	20327.78	10719.80	7529.90	5944.47	5000.76	4377.84	3938.16
240000	21211.60	11185.88	7857.29	6202.93	5218.18	4568.18	4109.38
250000	22095.41	11651.96	8184.68	6461.38	5435.61	4758.52	4280.61
260000	22979.23	12118.04	8512.07	6719.84	5653.03	4948.86	4451.83
270000	23863.05	12584.12	8839.45	6978.29	5870.45	5139.20	4623.06
280000	24746.86	13050.19	9166.84	7236.75	6087.88	5329.54	4794.28
290000	25630.68	13516.27	9494.23	7495.20	6305.30	5519.88	4965.51
300000	26514.50	13982.35	9821.62	7753.66	6522.73	5710.22	5136.73
310000	27398.31	14448.43	10149.00	8012.11	6740.15	5900.56	5307.96
320000	28282.13	14914.51	10476.39	8270.57	6957.58	6090.91	5479.18
330000	29165.95	15380.59	10803.78	8529.02	7175.00	6281.25	5650.40
340000	30049.76	15846.66	11131.16	8787.48	7392.42	6471.59	5821.63
350000	30933.58	16312.74	11458.55	9045.93	7609.85	6661.93	5992.85
400000	35352.66	18643.14	13095.49	10338.21	8696.97	7613.63	6848.97
450000	39771.75	20973.53	14732.42	11630.49	9784.09	8565.34	7705.10
500000	44190.83	23303.92	16369.36	12922.76	10871.21	9517.04	8561.22
550000	48609.91	25634.31	18006.29	14215.04	11958.33	10468.74	9417.34
600000	53029.00	27964.70	19643.23	15507.31	13045.45	11420.45	10273.46

Monthly Payments 11%
necessary to amortize a loan

AMOUNT	8 YEARS	9 YEARS	10 YEARS	11 YEARS	12 YEARS	13 YEARS	14 YEARS
100	1.57	1.46	1.38	1.31	1.25	1.21	1.17
200	3.14	2.93	2.76	2.62	2.51	2.42	2.34
500	7.85	7.31	6.89	6.55	6.27	6.04	5.85
1000	15.71	14.63	13.78	13.09	12.54	12.08	11.69
2000	31.42	29.25	27.55	26.18	25.07	24.15	23.38
5000	78.54	73.13	68.88	65.46	62.68	60.38	58.45
6000	94.25	87.76	82.65	78.55	75.21	72.45	70.14
7000	109.96	102.38	96.43	91.65	87.75	84.53	81.83
8000	125.67	117.01	110.20	104.74	100.28	96.60	93.52
9000	141.38	131.63	123.98	117.83	112.82	108.68	105.21
10000	157.08	146.26	137.75	130.92	125.36	120.75	116.91
15000	235.63	219.39	206.63	196.39	188.03	181.13	175.36
20000	314.17	292.52	275.50	261.85	250.71	241.51	233.81
25000	392.71	365.65	344.38	327.31	313.39	301.88	292.26
30000	471.25	438.78	413.25	392.77	376.07	362.26	350.72
35000	549.79	511.91	482.13	458.23	438.74	422.63	409.17
40000	628.34	585.03	551.00	523.69	501.42	483.01	467.62
45000	706.88	658.16	619.88	589.16	564.10	543.39	526.07
50000	785.42	731.29	688.75	654.62	626.78	603.76	584.53
55000	863.96	804.42	757.63	720.08	689.46	664.14	642.98
60000	942.51	877.55	826.50	785.54	752.13	724.52	701.43
65000	1021.05	950.68	895.38	851.00	814.81	784.89	759.89
70000	1099.59	1023.81	964.25	916.46	877.49	845.27	818.34
75000	1178.13	1096.94	1033.13	981.93	940.17	905.65	876.79
80000	1256.67	1170.07	1102.00	1047.39	1002.84	966.02	935.24
85000	1335.22	1243.20	1170.88	1112.85	1065.52	1026.40	993.70
90000	1413.76	1316.33	1239.75	1178.31	1128.20	1086.77	1052.15
95000	1492.30	1389.46	1308.63	1243.77	1190.88	1147.15	1110.60
100000	1570.84	1462.59	1377.50	1309.23	1253.56	1207.53	1169.05
105000	1649.38	1535.72	1446.38	1374.70	1316.23	1267.90	1227.51
110000	1727.93	1608.84	1515.25	1440.16	1378.91	1328.28	1285.96
120000	1885.01	1755.10	1653.00	1571.08	1504.27	1449.03	1402.87
130000	2042.10	1901.36	1790.75	1702.01	1629.62	1569.79	1519.77
140000	2199.18	2047.62	1928.50	1832.93	1754.98	1690.54	1636.68
150000	2356.26	2193.88	2066.25	1963.85	1880.33	1811.29	1753.58
160000	2513.35	2340.14	2204.00	2094.78	2005.69	1932.04	1870.49
170000	2670.43	2486.40	2341.75	2225.70	2131.04	2052.80	1987.39
180000	2827.52	2632.65	2479.50	2356.62	2256.40	2173.55	2104.30
190000	2984.60	2778.91	2617.25	2487.55	2381.75	2294.30	2221.20
200000	3141.69	2925.17	2755.00	2618.47	2507.11	2415.05	2338.11
210000	3298.77	3071.43	2892.75	2749.39	2632.47	2535.81	2455.01
220000	3455.85	3217.69	3030.50	2880.32	2757.82	2656.56	2571.92
230000	3612.94	3363.95	3168.25	3011.24	2883.18	2777.31	2688.82
240000	3770.02	3510.21	3306.00	3142.16	3008.53	2898.07	2805.73
250000	3927.11	3656.47	3443.75	3273.09	3133.89	3018.82	2922.64
260000	4084.19	3802.72	3581.50	3404.01	3259.24	3139.57	3039.54
270000	4241.27	3948.98	3719.25	3534.93	3384.60	3260.32	3156.45
280000	4398.36	4095.24	3857.00	3665.86	3509.95	3381.08	3273.35
290000	4555.44	4241.50	3994.75	3796.78	3635.31	3501.83	3390.26
300000	4712.53	4387.76	4132.50	3927.70	3760.67	3622.58	3507.16
310000	4869.61	4534.02	4270.25	4058.63	3886.02	3743.33	3624.07
320000	5026.70	4680.28	4408.00	4189.55	4011.38	3864.09	3740.97
330000	5183.78	4826.53	4545.75	4320.48	4136.73	3984.84	3857.88
340000	5340.86	4972.79	4683.50	4451.40	4262.09	4105.59	3974.78
350000	5497.95	5119.05	4821.25	4582.32	4387.44	4226.35	4091.69
400000	6283.37	5850.34	5510.00	5236.94	5014.22	4830.11	4676.22
450000	7068.79	6581.64	6198.75	5891.56	5641.00	5433.87	5260.74
500000	7854.21	7312.93	6887.50	6546.17	6267.78	6037.64	5845.27
550000	8639.63	8044.22	7576.25	7200.79	6894.55	6641.40	6429.80
600000	9425.06	8775.52	8265.00	7855.41	7521.33	7245.16	7014.33

11%

Monthly Payments
necessary to amortize a loan

AMOUNT	15 YEARS	16 YEARS	17 YEARS	18 YEARS	19 YEARS	20 YEARS	21 YEARS
100	1.14	1.11	1.09	1.07	1.05	1.03	1.02
200	2.27	2.22	2.17	2.13	2.09	2.06	2.04
500	5.68	5.55	5.43	5.33	5.24	5.16	5.09
1000	11.37	11.09	10.85	10.65	10.47	10.32	10.19
2000	22.73	22.18	21.71	21.30	20.95	20.64	20.38
5000	56.83	55.45	54.27	53.25	52.37	51.61	50.94
6000	68.20	66.54	65.12	63.90	62.85	61.93	61.13
7000	79.56	77.63	75.98	74.55	73.32	72.25	71.32
8000	90.93	88.72	86.83	85.20	83.80	82.58	81.51
9000	102.29	99.81	97.68	95.85	94.27	92.90	91.70
10000	113.66	110.90	108.54	106.50	104.75	103.22	101.89
15000	170.49	166.35	162.81	159.76	157.12	154.83	152.83
20000	227.32	221.80	217.08	213.01	209.49	206.44	203.77
25000	284.15	277.25	271.35	266.26	261.87	258.05	254.72
30000	340.98	332.70	325.61	319.51	314.24	309.66	305.66
35000	397.81	388.15	379.88	372.77	366.61	361.27	356.60
40000	454.64	443.60	434.15	426.02	418.99	412.88	407.55
45000	511.47	499.05	488.42	479.27	471.36	464.48	458.49
50000	568.30	554.50	542.69	532.52	523.73	516.09	509.44
55000	625.13	609.95	596.96	585.78	576.11	567.70	560.38
60000	681.96	665.40	651.23	639.03	628.48	619.31	611.32
65000	738.79	720.85	705.50	692.28	680.85	670.92	662.27
70000	795.62	776.30	759.77	745.53	733.22	722.53	713.21
75000	852.45	831.75	814.04	798.79	785.60	774.14	764.15
80000	909.28	887.20	868.30	852.04	837.97	825.75	815.10
85000	966.11	942.65	922.57	905.29	890.34	877.36	866.04
90000	1022.94	998.10	976.84	958.54	942.72	928.97	916.98
95000	1079.77	1053.55	1031.11	1011.80	995.09	980.58	967.93
100000	1136.60	1109.00	1085.38	1065.05	1047.46	1032.19	1018.87
105000	1193.43	1164.45	1139.65	1118.30	1099.84	1083.80	1069.81
110000	1250.26	1219.90	1193.92	1171.55	1152.21	1135.41	1120.76
120000	1363.92	1330.80	1302.46	1278.06	1256.96	1238.63	1222.65
130000	1477.58	1441.70	1410.99	1384.56	1361.70	1341.84	1324.53
140000	1591.24	1552.60	1519.53	1491.07	1466.45	1445.06	1426.42
150000	1704.90	1663.50	1628.07	1597.57	1571.20	1548.28	1528.31
160000	1818.56	1774.40	1736.61	1704.08	1675.94	1651.50	1630.19
170000	1932.21	1885.30	1845.15	1810.58	1780.69	1754.72	1732.08
180000	2045.87	1996.20	1953.69	1917.09	1885.44	1857.94	1833.97
190000	2159.53	2107.10	2062.22	2023.59	1990.18	1961.16	1935.85
200000	2273.19	2218.00	2170.76	2130.10	2094.93	2064.38	2037.74
210000	2386.85	2328.90	2279.30	2236.60	2199.67	2167.60	2139.63
220000	2500.51	2439.80	2387.84	2343.11	2304.42	2270.81	2241.52
230000	2614.17	2550.70	2496.38	2449.61	2409.17	2374.03	2343.40
240000	2727.83	2661.60	2604.91	2556.12	2513.91	2477.25	2445.29
250000	2841.49	2772.50	2713.45	2662.62	2618.66	2580.47	2547.18
260000	2955.15	2883.40	2821.99	2769.13	2723.41	2683.69	2649.06
270000	3068.81	2994.30	2930.53	2875.63	2828.15	2786.91	2750.95
280000	3182.47	3105.20	3039.07	2982.14	2932.90	2890.13	2852.84
290000	3296.13	3216.10	3147.60	3088.64	3037.65	2993.35	2954.73
300000	3409.79	3327.00	3256.14	3195.15	3142.39	3096.61	3056.61
310000	3523.45	3437.90	3364.68	3301.65	3247.14	3199.78	3158.50
320000	3637.11	3548.80	3473.22	3408.16	3351.88	3303.00	3260.39
330000	3750.77	3659.70	3581.76	3514.66	3456.63	3406.22	3362.27
340000	3864.43	3770.60	3690.29	3621.17	3561.38	3509.44	3464.16
350000	3978.09	3881.50	3798.83	3727.67	3666.12	3612.66	3566.05
400000	4546.39	4436.00	4341.52	4260.20	4189.86	4128.75	4075.48
450000	5114.69	4990.50	4884.21	4792.72	4713.59	4644.85	4584.92
500000	5682.98	5545.00	5426.90	5325.25	5237.32	5160.94	5094.35
550000	6251.28	6099.50	5969.59	5857.77	5761.05	5677.04	5603.79
600000	6819.58	6654.00	6512.28	6390.30	6284.78	6193.13	6113.23

Monthly Payments 11%

necessary to amortize a loan

AMOUNT	22 YEARS	23 YEARS	24 YEARS	25 YEARS	30 YEARS	35 YEARS	40 YEARS
100	1.01	1.00	0.99	0.98	0.95	0.94	0.93
200	2.01	1.99	1.98	1.96	1.90	1.87	1.86
500	5.04	4.99	4.94	4.90	4.76	4.68	4.64
1000	10.07	9.97	9.88	9.80	9.52	9.37	9.28
2000	20.14	19.94	19.76	19.60	19.05	18.74	18.57
5000	50.36	49.85	49.40	49.01	47.62	46.85	46.41
6000	60.43	59.82	59.28	58.81	57.14	56.22	55.70
7000	70.51	69.79	69.16	68.61	66.66	65.59	64.98
8000	80.58	79.76	79.04	78.41	76.19	74.96	74.26
9000	90.65	89.73	88.92	88.21	85.71	84.33	83.55
10000	100.72	99.70	98.80	98.01	95.23	93.70	92.83
15000	151.08	149.55	148.20	147.02	142.85	140.54	139.24
20000	201.44	199.40	197.61	196.02	190.46	187.39	185.66
25000	251.81	249.25	247.01	245.03	238.08	234.24	232.07
30000	302.17	299.10	296.41	294.03	285.70	281.09	278.49
35000	352.53	348.95	345.81	343.04	333.31	327.94	324.90
40000	402.89	398.80	395.21	392.05	380.93	374.78	371.32
45000	453.25	448.65	444.61	441.05	428.55	421.63	417.73
50000	503.61	498.50	494.01	490.06	476.16	468.48	464.15
55000	553.97	548.35	543.41	539.06	523.78	515.33	510.56
60000	604.33	598.20	592.82	588.07	571.39	562.17	556.98
65000	654.70	648.06	642.22	637.07	619.01	609.02	603.39
70000	705.06	697.91	691.62	686.08	666.63	655.87	649.81
75000	755.42	747.76	741.02	735.08	714.24	702.72	696.22
80000	805.78	797.61	790.42	784.09	761.86	749.57	742.64
85000	856.14	847.46	839.82	833.10	809.47	796.41	789.05
90000	906.50	897.31	889.22	882.10	857.09	843.26	835.46
95000	956.86	947.16	938.63	931.11	904.71	890.11	881.88
100000	1007.22	997.01	988.03	980.11	952.32	936.96	928.29
105000	1057.58	1046.86	1037.43	1029.12	999.94	983.81	974.71
110000	1107.95	1096.71	1086.83	1078.12	1047.56	1030.65	1021.12
120000	1208.67	1196.41	1185.63	1176.14	1142.79	1124.35	1113.95
130000	1309.39	1296.11	1284.43	1274.15	1238.02	1218.04	1206.78
140000	1410.11	1395.81	1383.24	1372.16	1333.25	1311.74	1299.61
150000	1510.84	1495.51	1482.04	1470.17	1428.49	1405.44	1392.44
160000	1611.56	1595.21	1580.84	1568.18	1523.72	1499.13	1485.27
170000	1712.28	1694.91	1679.65	1666.19	1618.95	1592.83	1578.10
180000	1813.00	1794.61	1778.45	1764.20	1714.18	1686.52	1670.93
190000	1913.72	1894.32	1877.25	1862.21	1809.41	1780.22	1763.76
200000	2014.45	1994.02	1976.05	1960.23	1904.65	1873.92	1856.59
210000	2115.17	2093.72	2074.86	2058.24	1999.88	1967.61	1949.42
220000	2215.89	2193.42	2173.66	2156.25	2095.11	2061.31	2042.25
230000	2316.61	2293.12	2272.46	2254.26	2190.34	2155.00	2135.08
240000	2417.34	2392.82	2371.26	2352.27	2285.58	2248.70	2227.91
250000	2518.06	2492.52	2470.07	2450.28	2380.81	2342.39	2320.74
260000	2618.78	2592.22	2568.87	2548.29	2476.04	2436.09	2413.57
270000	2719.50	2691.92	2667.67	2646.31	2571.27	2529.79	2506.39
280000	2820.23	2791.62	2766.47	2744.32	2666.51	2623.48	2599.22
290000	2920.95	2891.32	2865.28	2842.33	2761.74	2717.18	2692.05
300000	3021.67	2991.02	2964.08	2940.34	2856.97	2810.87	2784.88
310000	3122.39	3090.72	3062.88	3038.35	2952.20	2904.57	2877.71
320000	3223.12	3190.43	3161.69	3136.36	3047.43	2998.26	2970.54
330000	3323.84	3290.13	3260.49	3234.37	3142.67	3091.96	3063.37
340000	3424.56	3389.83	3359.29	3332.38	3237.90	3185.66	3156.20
350000	3525.28	3489.53	3458.09	3430.40	3333.13	3279.35	3249.03
400000	4028.89	3988.03	3952.11	3920.45	3809.29	3747.83	3713.18
450000	4532.51	4486.54	4446.12	4410.51	4285.46	4216.31	4177.32
500000	5036.12	4985.04	4940.13	4900.57	4761.62	4684.79	4641.47
550000	5539.73	5483.54	5434.15	5390.62	5237.78	5153.27	5105.62
600000	6043.34	5982.05	5928.16	5880.68	5713.94	5621.75	5569.77

11¼%

Monthly Payments
necessary to amortize a loan

AMOUNT	1 YEAR	2 YEARS	3 YEARS	4 YEARS	5 YEARS	6 YEARS	7 YEARS
100	8.85	4.67	3.29	2.60	2.19	1.92	1.73
200	17.70	9.34	6.57	5.19	4.37	3.83	3.45
500	44.25	23.36	16.43	12.98	10.93	9.58	8.63
1000	88.50	46.72	32.86	25.97	21.87	19.16	17.25
2000	177.00	93.45	65.71	51.93	43.73	38.32	34.51
5000	442.49	233.62	164.29	129.84	109.34	95.81	86.27
6000	530.99	280.34	197.14	155.80	131.20	114.97	103.53
7000	619.49	327.07	230.00	181.77	153.07	134.14	120.78
8000	707.99	373.79	262.86	207.74	174.94	153.30	138.03
9000	796.48	420.52	295.72	233.70	196.81	172.46	155.29
10000	884.98	467.24	328.57	259.67	218.67	191.62	172.54
15000	1327.47	700.86	492.86	389.51	328.01	287.44	258.81
20000	1769.92	934.48	657.14	519.34	437.35	383.25	345.08
25000	2212.46	1168.10	821.43	649.18	546.68	479.06	431.35
30000	2654.95	1401.72	985.72	779.01	656.02	574.87	517.63
35000	3097.44	1635.34	1150.00	908.85	765.36	670.68	603.90
40000	3539.93	1868.96	1314.29	1038.68	874.69	766.49	690.17
45000	3982.42	2102.58	1478.58	1168.52	984.03	862.31	776.44
50000	4424.92	2336.20	1642.86	1298.35	1093.37	958.12	862.71
55000	4867.41	2569.82	1807.15	1428.19	1202.70	1053.93	948.98
60000	5309.90	2803.44	1971.43	1558.03	1312.04	1149.74	1035.25
65000	5752.39	3037.06	2135.72	1687.86	1421.38	1245.55	1121.52
70000	6194.88	3270.68	2300.01	1817.70	1530.71	1341.37	1207.79
75000	6637.37	3504.30	2464.29	1947.53	1640.05	1437.18	1294.06
80000	7079.87	3737.92	2628.58	2077.37	1749.38	1532.99	1380.33
85000	7522.36	3971.54	2792.86	2207.20	1858.72	1628.80	1466.60
90000	7964.85	4205.16	2957.15	2337.04	1968.06	1724.61	1552.88
95000	8407.34	4438.78	3121.44	2466.87	2077.39	1820.43	1639.15
100000	8849.83	4672.40	3285.72	2596.71	2186.73	1916.24	1725.42
105000	9292.32	4906.02	3450.01	2726.55	2296.07	2012.05	1811.69
110000	9734.81	5139.64	3614.30	2856.38	2405.40	2107.86	1897.96
120000	10619.80	5606.88	3942.87	3116.05	2624.08	2299.48	2070.50
130000	11504.78	6074.12	4271.44	3375.72	2842.75	2491.11	2243.04
140000	12389.76	6541.36	4600.01	3635.39	3061.42	2682.73	2415.58
150000	13274.75	7008.60	4928.59	3895.06	3280.10	2874.36	2588.13
160000	14159.73	7475.84	5257.16	4154.74	3498.77	3065.98	2760.67
170000	15044.71	7943.08	5585.73	4414.41	3717.44	3257.60	2933.21
180000	15929.70	8410.32	5914.30	4674.08	3936.12	3449.23	3105.75
190000	16814.68	8877.56	6242.87	4933.75	4154.79	3640.85	3278.29
200000	17699.66	9344.80	6571.45	5193.42	4373.46	3832.47	3450.83
210000	18584.65	9812.04	6900.02	5453.09	4592.13	4024.10	3623.38
220000	19469.63	10279.28	7228.59	5712.76	4810.81	4215.72	3795.92
230000	20354.61	10746.52	7557.16	5972.43	5029.48	4407.35	3968.46
240000	21239.60	11213.76	7885.74	6232.10	5248.15	4598.97	4141.00
250000	22124.58	11681.00	8214.31	6491.77	5466.83	4790.59	4313.54
260000	23009.56	12148.24	8542.88	6751.45	5685.50	4982.22	4486.08
270000	23894.54	12615.48	8871.45	7011.12	5904.17	5173.84	4658.63
280000	24779.53	13082.72	9200.03	7270.79	6122.85	5365.46	4831.17
290000	25664.51	13549.96	9528.60	7530.46	6341.52	5557.09	5003.71
300000	26549.49	14017.20	9857.17	7790.13	6560.19	5748.71	5176.25
310000	27434.48	14484.44	10185.74	8049.80	6778.87	5940.34	5348.79
320000	28319.46	14951.68	10514.32	8309.47	6997.54	6131.96	5521.33
330000	29204.44	15418.92	10842.89	8569.14	7216.21	6323.58	5693.88
340000	30089.43	15886.16	11171.46	8828.81	7434.88	6515.21	5866.42
350000	30974.41	16353.40	11500.03	9088.48	7653.56	6706.83	6038.96
400000	35399.33	18689.60	13142.89	10386.84	8746.92	7664.95	6901.67
450000	39824.24	21025.80	14785.76	11685.19	9840.29	8623.07	7764.38
500000	44249.16	23362.00	16428.62	12983.55	10933.65	9581.19	8627.08
550000	48674.07	25698.20	18071.48	14281.90	12027.02	10539.30	9489.79
600000	53098.99	28034.40	19714.34	15580.26	13120.38	11497.42	10352.50

Monthly Payments 11¼%
necessary to amortize a loan

AMOUNT	8 YEARS	9 YEARS	10 YEARS	11 YEARS	12 YEARS	13 YEARS	14 YEARS
100	1.58	1.48	1.39	1.32	1.27	1.22	1.18
200	3.17	2.95	2.78	2.65	2.54	2.45	2.37
500	7.92	7.38	6.96	6.62	6.34	6.11	5.92
1000	15.84	14.76	13.92	13.24	12.68	12.23	11.85
2000	31.69	29.53	27.83	26.48	25.37	24.45	23.69
5000	79.22	73.82	69.58	66.19	63.42	61.13	59.23
6000	95.06	88.59	83.50	79.43	76.10	73.36	71.07
7000	110.91	103.35	97.42	92.66	88.79	85.59	82.92
8000	126.75	118.12	111.34	105.90	101.47	97.81	94.76
9000	142.59	132.88	125.25	119.14	114.16	110.04	106.61
10000	158.44	147.64	139.17	132.38	126.84	122.27	118.45
15000	237.65	221.47	208.75	198.56	190.26	183.40	177.68
20000	316.87	295.29	278.34	264.75	253.68	244.54	236.90
25000	396.09	369.11	347.92	330.93	317.10	305.67	296.13
30000	475.31	442.93	417.51	397.13	380.52	366.80	355.35
35000	554.53	516.75	487.09	463.31	443.94	427.94	414.58
40000	633.74	590.58	556.68	529.50	507.36	489.07	473.80
45000	712.96	664.40	626.26	595.69	570.78	550.20	533.03
50000	792.18	738.22	695.84	661.88	634.20	611.34	592.25
55000	871.40	812.04	765.43	728.06	697.62	672.47	651.48
60000	950.62	885.86	835.01	794.25	761.04	733.61	710.70
65000	1029.83	959.69	904.60	860.44	824.46	794.74	769.93
70000	1109.05	1033.51	974.18	926.63	887.88	855.87	829.16
75000	1188.27	1107.33	1043.77	992.81	951.29	917.01	888.38
80000	1267.49	1181.15	1113.35	1059.00	1014.71	978.14	947.61
85000	1346.70	1254.98	1182.94	1125.19	1078.13	1039.28	1006.83
90000	1425.92	1328.80	1252.52	1191.38	1141.55	1100.41	1066.06
95000	1505.14	1402.62	1322.10	1257.56	1204.97	1161.54	1125.28
100000	1584.36	1476.44	1391.69	1323.75	1268.39	1222.68	1184.51
105000	1663.58	1550.26	1461.27	1389.94	1331.81	1283.81	1243.73
110000	1742.79	1624.09	1530.86	1456.13	1395.23	1344.95	1302.96
120000	1901.23	1771.73	1670.03	1588.50	1522.07	1467.21	1421.41
130000	2059.67	1919.37	1809.20	1720.88	1648.91	1589.48	1539.86
140000	2218.10	2067.02	1948.37	1853.25	1775.75	1711.75	1658.31
150000	2376.54	2214.66	2087.53	1985.63	1902.59	1834.02	1776.76
160000	2534.97	2362.31	2226.70	2118.00	2029.43	1956.28	1895.21
170000	2693.41	2509.95	2365.87	2250.38	2156.27	2078.55	2013.66
180000	2851.85	2657.59	2505.04	2382.75	2283.11	2200.82	2132.11
190000	3010.28	2805.24	2644.21	2515.13	2409.95	2323.09	2250.56
200000	3168.72	2952.88	2783.38	2647.50	2536.79	2445.35	2369.02
210000	3327.15	3100.53	2922.55	2779.88	2663.63	2567.62	2487.47
220000	3485.59	3248.17	3061.72	2912.25	2790.46	2689.89	2605.92
230000	3644.02	3395.81	3200.89	3044.63	2917.30	2812.16	2724.37
240000	3802.46	3543.46	3340.05	3177.01	3044.14	2934.43	2842.82
250000	3960.90	3691.10	3479.22	3309.38	3170.98	3056.69	2961.27
260000	4119.33	3838.75	3618.39	3441.76	3297.82	3178.96	3079.72
270000	4277.77	3986.39	3757.56	3574.13	3424.66	3301.23	3198.17
280000	4436.20	4134.04	3896.73	3706.51	3551.50	3423.50	3316.62
290000	4594.64	4281.68	4035.90	3838.88	3678.34	3545.76	3435.07
300000	4753.08	4429.32	4175.07	3971.26	3805.18	3668.03	3553.52
310000	4911.51	4576.97	4314.24	4103.63	3932.02	3790.30	3671.97
320000	5069.95	4724.61	4453.41	4236.01	4058.86	3912.57	3790.42
330000	5228.38	4872.26	4592.58	4368.38	4185.70	4034.84	3908.88
340000	5386.82	5019.90	4731.74	4500.76	4312.54	4157.10	4027.33
350000	5545.25	5167.54	4870.91	4633.13	4439.38	4279.37	4145.78
400000	6337.43	5905.76	5566.76	5295.01	5073.57	4890.71	4738.03
450000	7129.61	6643.99	6262.60	5956.88	5707.77	5502.05	5330.28
500000	7921.79	7382.21	6958.45	6618.76	6341.96	6113.39	5922.54
550000	8713.97	8120.43	7654.29	7280.64	6976.16	6724.73	6514.79
600000	9506.15	8858.65	8350.14	7942.51	7610.36	7336.06	7107.05

11¼%

Monthly Payments
necessary to amortize a loan

AMOUNT	15 YEARS	16 YEARS	17 YEARS	18 YEARS	19 YEARS	20 YEARS	21 YEARS
100	1.15	1.13	1.10	1.08	1.06	1.05	1.04
200	2.30	2.25	2.20	2.16	2.13	2.10	2.07
500	5.76	5.63	5.51	5.41	5.32	5.25	5.18
1000	11.52	11.25	11.02	10.82	10.64	10.49	10.36
2000	23.05	22.50	22.03	21.63	21.29	20.99	20.72
5000	57.62	56.25	55.08	54.08	53.21	52.46	51.81
6000	69.14	67.50	66.10	64.90	63.86	62.96	62.17
7000	80.66	78.75	77.12	75.71	74.50	73.45	72.53
8000	92.19	90.00	88.13	86.53	85.14	83.94	82.89
9000	103.71	101.25	99.15	97.35	95.79	94.43	93.26
10000	115.23	112.50	110.17	108.16	106.43	104.93	103.62
15000	172.85	168.75	165.25	162.24	159.64	157.39	155.43
20000	230.47	225.01	220.34	216.32	212.86	209.85	207.23
25000	288.09	281.26	275.42	270.41	266.07	262.31	259.04
30000	345.70	337.51	330.51	324.49	319.29	314.78	310.85
35000	403.32	393.76	385.59	378.57	372.50	367.24	362.66
40000	460.94	450.01	440.67	432.65	425.72	419.70	414.47
45000	518.56	506.26	495.76	486.73	478.93	472.17	466.28
50000	576.17	562.52	550.84	540.81	532.14	524.63	518.09
55000	633.79	618.77	605.93	594.89	585.36	577.09	569.89
60000	691.41	675.02	661.01	648.97	638.57	629.55	621.70
65000	749.02	731.27	716.10	703.05	691.79	682.02	673.51
70000	806.64	787.52	771.18	757.13	745.00	734.48	725.32
75000	864.26	843.77	826.27	811.22	798.22	786.94	777.13
80000	921.88	900.03	881.35	865.30	851.43	839.40	828.94
85000	979.49	956.28	936.43	919.38	904.65	891.87	880.75
90000	1037.11	1012.53	991.52	973.46	957.86	944.33	932.55
95000	1094.73	1068.78	1046.60	1027.54	1011.07	996.79	984.36
100000	1152.34	1125.03	1101.69	1081.62	1064.29	1049.26	1036.17
105000	1209.96	1181.28	1156.77	1135.70	1117.50	1101.72	1087.98
110000	1267.58	1237.54	1211.86	1189.78	1170.72	1154.18	1139.79
120000	1382.81	1350.04	1322.02	1297.94	1277.15	1259.11	1243.41
130000	1498.05	1462.54	1432.19	1406.11	1383.57	1364.03	1347.02
140000	1613.28	1575.05	1542.36	1514.27	1490.00	1468.96	1450.64
150000	1728.52	1687.55	1652.53	1622.43	1596.43	1573.88	1554.26
160000	1843.75	1800.05	1762.70	1730.59	1702.86	1678.81	1657.87
170000	1958.99	1912.56	1872.87	1838.75	1809.29	1783.74	1761.49
180000	2074.22	2025.06	1983.04	1946.92	1915.72	1888.66	1865.11
190000	2189.45	2137.56	2093.21	2055.08	2022.15	1993.59	1968.73
200000	2304.69	2250.07	2203.37	2163.24	2128.58	2098.51	2072.34
210000	2419.92	2362.57	2313.54	2271.40	2235.01	2203.44	2175.96
220000	2535.16	2475.07	2423.71	2379.56	2341.43	2308.36	2279.58
230000	2650.39	2587.57	2533.88	2487.73	2447.86	2413.29	2383.19
240000	2765.63	2700.08	2644.05	2595.89	2554.29	2518.21	2486.81
250000	2880.86	2812.58	2754.22	2704.05	2660.72	2623.14	2590.43
260000	2996.10	2925.08	2864.39	2812.21	2767.15	2728.07	2694.05
270000	3111.33	3037.59	2974.56	2920.37	2873.58	2832.99	2797.66
280000	3226.56	3150.09	3084.72	3028.54	2980.01	2937.92	2901.28
290000	3341.80	3262.59	3194.89	3136.70	3086.44	3042.84	3004.90
300000	3457.03	3375.10	3305.06	3244.86	3192.86	3147.77	3108.51
310000	3572.27	3487.60	3415.23	3353.02	3299.29	3252.69	3212.13
320000	3687.50	3600.10	3525.40	3461.19	3405.72	3357.62	3315.75
330000	3802.74	3712.61	3635.57	3569.35	3512.15	3462.54	3419.36
340000	3917.97	3825.11	3745.74	3677.51	3618.58	3567.47	3522.98
350000	4033.21	3937.61	3855.91	3785.67	3725.01	3672.40	3626.60
400000	4609.38	4500.13	4406.75	4326.48	4257.15	4197.02	4144.68
450000	5185.55	5062.65	4957.59	4867.29	4789.30	4721.65	4662.77
500000	5761.72	5625.16	5508.44	5408.10	5321.44	5246.28	5180.86
550000	6337.90	6187.68	6059.28	5948.91	5853.59	5770.91	5698.94
600000	6914.07	6750.20	6610.12	6489.72	6385.73	6295.54	6217.03

Monthly Payments 11 1/4%

necessary to amortize a loan

AMOUNT	22 YEARS	23 YEARS	24 YEARS	25 YEARS	30 YEARS	35 YEARS	40 YEARS
100	1.02	1.01	1.01	1.00	0.97	0.96	0.95
200	2.05	2.03	2.01	2.00	1.94	1.91	1.90
500	5.12	5.07	5.03	4.99	4.86	4.78	4.74
1000	10.25	10.15	10.06	9.98	9.71	9.56	9.48
2000	20.49	20.29	20.12	19.96	19.43	19.13	18.97
5000	51.24	50.74	50.30	49.91	48.56	47.82	47.41
6000	61.48	60.88	60.36	59.89	58.28	57.39	56.90
7000	71.73	71.03	70.42	69.88	67.99	66.95	66.38
8000	81.98	81.18	80.48	79.86	77.70	76.52	75.86
9000	92.23	91.33	90.54	89.84	87.41	86.08	85.34
10000	102.47	101.47	100.60	99.82	97.13	95.65	94.83
15000	153.71	152.21	150.89	149.74	145.69	143.47	142.24
20000	204.95	202.95	201.19	199.65	194.25	191.30	189.65
25000	256.19	253.69	251.49	249.56	242.82	239.12	237.06
30000	307.42	304.42	301.79	299.47	291.38	286.95	284.48
35000	358.66	355.16	352.09	349.38	339.94	334.77	331.89
40000	409.90	405.90	402.38	399.30	388.50	382.60	379.30
45000	461.14	456.63	452.68	449.21	437.07	430.42	426.72
50000	512.37	507.37	502.98	499.12	485.63	478.25	474.13
55000	563.61	558.11	553.28	549.03	534.19	526.07	521.54
60000	614.85	608.85	603.58	598.94	582.76	573.90	568.95
65000	666.08	659.58	653.88	648.86	631.32	621.72	616.37
70000	717.32	710.32	704.17	698.77	679.88	669.55	663.78
75000	768.56	761.06	754.47	748.68	728.45	717.37	711.19
80000	819.80	811.79	804.77	798.59	777.01	765.20	758.61
85000	871.03	862.53	855.07	848.50	825.57	813.02	806.02
90000	922.27	913.27	905.37	898.42	874.14	860.84	853.43
95000	973.51	964.00	955.66	948.33	922.70	908.67	900.84
100000	1024.75	1014.74	1005.96	998.24	971.26	956.49	948.26
105000	1075.98	1065.48	1056.26	1048.15	1019.82	1004.32	995.67
110000	1127.22	1116.22	1106.56	1098.06	1068.39	1052.14	1043.08
120000	1229.69	1217.69	1207.15	1197.89	1165.51	1147.79	1137.91
130000	1332.17	1319.16	1307.75	1297.71	1262.64	1243.44	1232.73
140000	1434.64	1420.64	1408.35	1397.54	1359.77	1339.09	1327.56
150000	1537.12	1522.11	1508.94	1497.36	1456.89	1434.74	1422.39
160000	1639.59	1623.59	1609.54	1597.18	1554.02	1530.39	1517.21
170000	1742.07	1725.06	1710.14	1697.01	1651.14	1626.04	1612.04
180000	1844.54	1826.54	1810.73	1796.83	1748.27	1721.69	1706.86
190000	1947.02	1928.01	1911.33	1896.66	1845.40	1817.34	1801.69
200000	2049.49	2029.48	2011.92	1996.48	1942.52	1912.99	1896.51
210000	2151.97	2130.96	2112.52	2096.30	2039.65	2008.64	1991.34
220000	2254.44	2232.43	2213.12	2196.13	2136.78	2104.29	2086.17
230000	2356.92	2333.91	2313.71	2295.95	2233.90	2199.94	2180.99
240000	2459.39	2435.38	2414.31	2395.77	2331.03	2295.59	2275.82
250000	2561.86	2536.85	2514.90	2495.60	2428.15	2391.23	2370.64
260000	2664.34	2638.33	2615.50	2595.42	2525.28	2486.88	2465.47
270000	2766.81	2739.80	2716.10	2695.25	2622.41	2582.53	2560.29
280000	2869.29	2841.28	2816.69	2795.07	2719.53	2678.18	2655.12
290000	2971.76	2942.75	2917.29	2894.89	2816.66	2773.83	2749.95
300000	3074.24	3044.23	3017.89	2994.72	2913.78	2869.48	2844.77
310000	3176.71	3145.70	3118.48	3094.54	3010.91	2965.13	2939.60
320000	3279.19	3247.17	3219.08	3194.37	3108.04	3060.78	3034.42
330000	3381.66	3348.65	3319.67	3294.19	3205.16	3156.43	3129.25
340000	3484.14	3450.12	3420.27	3394.01	3302.29	3252.08	3224.07
350000	3586.61	3551.60	3520.87	3493.84	3399.41	3347.73	3318.90
400000	4098.98	4058.97	4023.85	3992.96	3885.05	3825.98	3793.03
450000	4611.36	4566.34	4526.83	4492.08	4370.68	4304.22	4267.16
500000	5123.73	5073.71	5029.81	4991.20	4856.31	4782.47	4741.29
550000	5636.10	5581.08	5532.79	5490.32	5341.94	5260.72	5215.42
600000	6148.47	6088.45	6035.77	5989.44	5827.57	5738.96	5689.54

11½%

Monthly Payments
necessary to amortize a loan

AMOUNT	1 YEAR	2 YEARS	3 YEARS	4 YEARS	5 YEARS	6 YEARS	7 YEARS
100	8.86	4.68	3.30	2.61	2.20	1.93	1.74
200	17.72	9.37	6.60	5.22	4.40	3.86	3.48
500	44.31	23.42	16.49	13.04	11.00	9.65	8.69
1000	88.62	46.84	32.98	26.09	21.99	19.29	17.39
2000	177.23	93.68	65.95	52.18	43.99	38.58	34.77
5000	443.08	234.20	164.88	130.45	109.96	96.46	86.93
6000	531.69	281.04	197.86	156.53	131.96	115.75	104.32
7000	620.31	327.88	230.83	182.62	153.95	135.04	121.71
8000	708.92	374.72	263.81	208.71	175.94	154.33	139.09
9000	797.54	421.56	296.78	234.80	197.93	173.62	156.48
10000	886.15	468.40	329.76	260.89	219.93	192.91	173.86
15000	1329.23	702.60	494.64	391.34	329.89	289.37	260.80
20000	1772.30	936.81	659.52	521.78	439.85	385.82	347.73
25000	2215.38	1171.01	824.40	652.23	549.82	482.28	434.66
30000	2658.45	1405.21	989.28	782.67	659.78	578.73	521.59
35000	3101.53	1639.41	1154.16	913.12	769.74	675.19	608.53
40000	3544.60	1873.61	1319.04	1043.56	879.70	771.65	695.46
45000	3987.68	2107.81	1483.92	1174.01	989.67	868.10	782.39
50000	4430.75	2342.02	1648.80	1304.45	1099.63	964.56	869.32
55000	4873.83	2576.22	1813.68	1434.90	1209.59	1061.01	956.26
60000	5316.90	2810.42	1978.56	1565.34	1319.56	1157.47	1043.19
65000	5759.98	3044.62	2143.44	1695.79	1429.52	1253.93	1130.12
70000	6203.05	3278.82	2308.32	1826.23	1539.48	1350.38	1217.05
75000	6646.13	3513.02	2473.20	1956.68	1649.45	1446.84	1303.98
80000	7089.20	3747.23	2638.08	2087.12	1759.41	1543.29	1390.92
85000	7532.28	3981.43	2802.96	2217.57	1869.37	1639.75	1477.85
90000	7975.35	4215.63	2967.84	2348.01	1979.33	1736.20	1564.78
95000	8418.43	4449.83	3132.72	2478.46	2089.30	1832.66	1651.71
100000	8861.51	4684.03	3297.60	2608.90	2199.26	1929.12	1738.65
105000	9304.58	4918.23	3462.48	2739.35	2309.22	2025.57	1825.58
110000	9747.66	5152.43	3627.36	2869.79	2419.19	2122.03	1912.51
120000	10633.81	5620.84	3957.12	3130.68	2639.11	2314.94	2086.38
130000	11519.96	6089.24	4286.88	3391.57	2859.04	2507.85	2260.24
140000	12406.11	6557.64	4616.64	3652.46	3078.97	2700.76	2434.10
150000	13292.26	7026.05	4946.40	3913.35	3298.89	2893.67	2607.97
160000	14178.41	7494.45	5276.16	4174.24	3518.82	3086.58	2781.83
170000	15064.56	7962.85	5605.92	4435.13	3738.74	3279.50	2955.70
180000	15950.71	8431.26	5935.68	4696.02	3958.67	3472.41	3129.56
190000	16836.86	8899.66	6265.44	4956.91	4178.60	3665.32	3303.43
200000	17723.01	9368.06	6595.20	5217.80	4398.52	3858.23	3477.29
210000	18609.16	9836.47	6924.96	5478.69	4618.45	4051.14	3651.16
220000	19495.31	10304.87	7254.72	5739.58	4838.37	4244.05	3825.02
230000	20381.46	10773.27	7584.48	6000.47	5058.30	4436.97	3998.89
240000	21267.61	11241.68	7914.24	6261.36	5278.23	4629.88	4172.75
250000	22153.76	11710.08	8244.00	6522.25	5498.15	4822.79	4346.62
260000	23039.91	12178.48	8573.76	6783.14	5718.08	5015.70	4520.48
270000	23926.06	12646.89	8903.52	7044.03	5938.00	5208.61	4694.34
280000	24812.22	13115.29	9233.28	7304.92	6157.93	5401.52	4868.21
290000	25698.37	13583.69	9563.05	7565.81	6377.86	5594.44	5042.07
300000	26584.52	14052.09	9892.80	7826.70	6597.78	5787.35	5215.94
310000	27470.67	14520.50	10222.56	8087.59	6817.71	5980.26	5389.80
320000	28356.82	14988.90	10552.32	8348.48	7037.63	6173.17	5563.67
330000	29242.97	15457.30	10882.08	8609.37	7257.56	6366.08	5737.53
340000	30129.12	15925.71	11211.84	8870.26	7477.49	6558.99	5911.40
350000	31015.27	16394.11	11541.60	9131.15	7697.41	6751.90	6085.26
400000	35446.02	18736.13	13190.40	10435.60	8797.04	7716.46	6954.58
450000	39876.77	21078.14	14839.20	11740.05	9896.67	8681.02	7823.91
500000	44307.53	23420.16	16488.00	13044.50	10996.30	9645.58	8693.23
550000	48738.28	25762.17	18136.80	14348.95	12095.93	10610.14	9562.55
600000	53169.03	28104.19	19785.60	15653.41	13195.56	11574.69	10431.88

Monthly Payments 11½%

necessary to amortize a loan

AMOUNT	8 YEARS	9 YEARS	10 YEARS	11 YEARS	12 YEARS	13 YEARS	14 YEARS
100	1.60	1.49	1.41	1.34	1.28	1.24	1.20
200	3.20	2.98	2.81	2.68	2.57	2.48	2.40
500	7.99	7.45	7.03	6.69	6.42	6.19	6.00
1000	15.98	14.90	14.06	13.38	12.83	12.38	12.00
2000	31.96	29.81	28.12	26.77	25.67	24.76	24.00
5000	79.90	74.52	70.30	66.92	64.17	61.90	60.00
6000	95.88	89.42	84.36	80.30	77.00	74.28	72.00
7000	111.86	104.33	98.42	93.68	89.83	86.65	84.00
8000	127.83	119.23	112.48	107.07	102.67	99.03	96.00
9000	143.81	134.13	126.54	120.45	115.50	111.41	108.00
10000	159.79	149.04	140.60	133.84	128.33	123.79	120.01
15000	239.69	223.55	210.89	200.75	192.50	185.69	180.01
20000	319.59	298.07	281.19	267.67	256.66	247.58	240.01
25000	399.48	372.59	351.49	334.59	320.83	309.48	300.01
30000	479.38	447.11	421.79	401.51	384.99	371.38	360.02
35000	559.28	521.63	492.08	468.42	449.16	433.27	420.02
40000	639.17	596.15	562.38	535.34	513.33	495.17	480.02
45000	719.07	670.66	632.68	602.26	577.49	557.06	540.02
50000	798.97	745.18	702.98	669.18	641.66	618.96	600.03
55000	878.87	819.70	773.27	736.09	705.82	680.85	660.03
60000	958.76	894.22	843.57	803.01	769.99	742.75	720.03
65000	1038.66	968.74	913.87	869.93	834.16	804.65	780.04
70000	1118.56	1043.26	984.17	936.85	898.32	866.54	840.04
75000	1198.45	1117.77	1054.47	1003.76	962.49	928.44	900.04
80000	1278.35	1192.29	1124.76	1070.68	1026.65	990.33	960.04
85000	1358.25	1266.81	1195.06	1137.60	1090.82	1052.23	1020.05
90000	1438.14	1341.33	1265.36	1204.52	1154.98	1114.13	1080.05
95000	1518.04	1415.85	1335.66	1271.43	1219.15	1176.02	1140.05
100000	1597.94	1490.37	1405.95	1338.35	1283.32	1237.92	1200.06
105000	1677.83	1564.88	1476.25	1405.27	1347.48	1299.81	1260.06
110000	1757.73	1639.40	1546.55	1472.19	1411.65	1361.71	1320.06
120000	1917.52	1788.44	1687.15	1606.02	1539.98	1485.50	1440.07
130000	2077.32	1937.48	1827.74	1739.86	1668.31	1609.29	1560.07
140000	2237.11	2086.51	1968.34	1873.69	1796.64	1733.08	1680.08
150000	2396.91	2235.55	2108.93	2007.53	1924.97	1856.88	1800.08
160000	2556.70	2384.59	2249.53	2141.36	2053.31	1980.67	1920.09
170000	2716.49	2533.62	2390.12	2275.20	2181.64	2104.46	2040.09
180000	2876.29	2682.66	2530.72	2409.03	2309.97	2228.25	2160.10
190000	3036.08	2831.70	2671.31	2542.87	2438.30	2352.04	2280.11
200000	3195.87	2980.73	2811.91	2676.70	2566.63	2475.84	2400.11
210000	3355.67	3129.77	2952.50	2810.54	2694.96	2599.63	2520.12
220000	3515.46	3278.81	3093.10	2944.37	2823.30	2723.42	2640.12
230000	3675.26	3427.84	3233.70	3078.21	2951.63	2847.21	2760.13
240000	3835.05	3576.88	3374.29	3212.04	3079.96	2971.00	2880.13
250000	3994.84	3725.92	3514.89	3345.88	3208.29	3094.79	3000.14
260000	4154.64	3874.95	3655.48	3479.71	3336.62	3218.59	3120.14
270000	4314.43	4023.99	3796.08	3613.55	3464.95	3342.38	3240.15
280000	4474.22	4173.02	3936.67	3747.38	3593.29	3466.17	3360.16
290000	4634.02	4322.06	4077.27	3881.22	3721.62	3589.96	3480.16
300000	4793.81	4471.10	4217.86	4015.05	3849.95	3713.75	3600.17
310000	4953.61	4620.13	4358.46	4148.89	3978.28	3837.54	3720.17
320000	5113.40	4769.17	4499.05	4282.72	4106.61	3961.34	3840.18
330000	5273.19	4918.21	4639.65	4416.56	4234.94	4085.13	3960.18
340000	5432.99	5067.24	4780.25	4550.39	4363.28	4208.92	4080.19
350000	5592.78	5216.28	4920.84	4684.23	4491.61	4332.71	4200.19
400000	6391.75	5961.46	5623.82	5353.40	5133.27	4951.67	4800.22
450000	7190.72	6706.65	6326.79	6022.58	5774.92	5570.63	5400.25
500000	7989.69	7451.83	7029.77	6691.75	6416.58	6189.59	6000.28
550000	8788.66	8197.01	7732.75	7360.93	7058.24	6808.55	6600.30
600000	9587.62	8942.20	8435.73	8030.10	7699.90	7427.51	7200.33

11½%

Monthly Payments
necessary to amortize a loan

AMOUNT	15 YEARS	16 YEARS	17 YEARS	18 YEARS	19 YEARS	20 YEARS	21 YEARS
100	1.17	1.14	1.12	1.10	1.08	1.07	1.05
200	2.34	2.28	2.24	2.20	2.16	2.13	2.11
500	5.84	5.71	5.59	5.49	5.41	5.33	5.27
1000	11.68	11.41	11.18	10.98	10.81	10.66	10.54
2000	23.36	22.82	22.36	21.97	21.62	21.33	21.07
5000	58.41	57.06	55.90	54.91	54.06	53.32	52.68
6000	70.09	68.47	67.09	65.90	64.87	63.99	63.21
7000	81.77	79.88	78.27	76.88	75.69	74.65	73.75
8000	93.46	91.29	89.45	87.86	86.50	85.31	84.29
9000	105.14	102.70	100.63	98.85	97.31	95.98	94.82
10000	116.82	114.12	111.81	109.83	108.12	106.64	105.36
15000	175.23	171.17	167.71	164.74	162.18	159.96	158.04
20000	233.64	228.23	223.62	219.66	216.24	213.29	210.72
25000	292.05	285.29	279.52	274.57	270.30	266.61	263.39
30000	350.46	342.35	335.43	329.49	324.37	319.93	316.07
35000	408.87	399.41	391.33	384.40	378.43	373.25	368.75
40000	467.28	456.47	447.24	439.32	432.49	426.57	421.43
45000	525.69	513.52	503.14	494.23	486.55	479.89	474.11
50000	584.09	570.58	559.05	549.15	540.61	533.21	526.79
55000	642.50	627.64	614.95	604.06	594.67	586.54	579.47
60000	700.91	684.70	670.86	658.98	648.73	639.86	632.15
65000	759.32	741.76	726.76	713.89	702.79	693.18	684.83
70000	817.73	798.82	782.67	768.81	756.85	746.50	737.50
75000	876.14	855.87	838.57	823.72	810.91	799.82	790.18
80000	934.55	912.93	894.48	878.64	864.97	853.14	842.86
85000	992.96	969.99	950.38	933.55	919.04	906.47	895.54
90000	1051.37	1027.05	1006.29	988.47	973.10	959.79	948.22
95000	1109.78	1084.11	1062.19	1043.38	1027.16	1013.11	1000.90
100000	1168.19	1141.16	1118.10	1098.30	1081.22	1066.43	1053.58
105000	1226.60	1198.22	1174.00	1153.21	1135.28	1119.75	1106.26
110000	1285.01	1255.28	1229.91	1208.12	1189.34	1173.07	1158.94
120000	1401.83	1369.40	1341.72	1317.95	1297.46	1279.72	1264.29
130000	1518.65	1483.51	1453.53	1427.78	1405.58	1386.36	1369.65
140000	1635.47	1597.63	1565.33	1537.61	1513.71	1493.00	1475.01
150000	1752.28	1711.75	1677.14	1647.44	1621.83	1599.64	1580.37
160000	1869.10	1825.86	1788.95	1757.27	1729.95	1706.29	1685.72
170000	1985.92	1939.98	1900.76	1867.10	1838.07	1812.93	1791.08
180000	2102.74	2054.10	2012.57	1976.93	1946.19	1919.57	1896.44
190000	2219.56	2168.21	2124.38	2086.76	2054.31	2026.22	2001.80
200000	2336.38	2282.33	2236.19	2196.59	2162.44	2132.86	2107.16
210000	2453.20	2396.45	2348.00	2306.42	2270.56	2239.50	2212.51
220000	2570.02	2510.56	2459.81	2416.25	2378.68	2346.15	2317.87
230000	2686.84	2624.68	2571.62	2526.08	2486.80	2452.79	2423.23
240000	2803.66	2738.80	2683.43	2635.91	2594.92	2559.43	2528.59
250000	2920.47	2852.91	2795.24	2745.74	2703.05	2666.07	2633.94
260000	3037.29	2967.03	2907.05	2855.57	2811.17	2772.72	2739.30
270000	3154.11	3081.15	3018.86	2965.40	2919.29	2879.36	2844.66
280000	3270.93	3195.26	3130.67	3075.23	3027.41	2986.00	2950.02
290000	3387.75	3309.38	3242.48	3185.06	3135.53	3092.65	3055.38
300000	3504.57	3423.49	3354.29	3294.89	3243.65	3199.29	3160.73
310000	3621.39	3537.61	3466.10	3404.72	3351.78	3305.93	3266.09
320000	3738.21	3651.73	3577.91	3514.54	3459.90	3412.57	3371.45
330000	3855.03	3765.84	3689.72	3624.37	3568.02	3519.22	3476.81
340000	3971.85	3879.96	3801.53	3734.20	3676.14	3625.86	3582.16
350000	4088.66	3994.08	3913.34	3844.03	3784.26	3732.50	3687.52
400000	4672.76	4564.66	4472.39	4393.18	4324.87	4265.72	4214.31
450000	5256.85	5135.24	5031.43	4942.33	4865.48	4798.93	4741.10
500000	5840.95	5705.82	5590.48	5491.48	5406.09	5332.15	5267.89
550000	6425.04	6276.41	6149.53	6040.62	5946.70	5865.36	5794.68
600000	7009.14	6846.99	6708.58	6589.77	6487.31	6398.58	6321.47

Monthly Payments 11½%
necessary to amortize a loan

AMOUNT	22 YEARS	23 YEARS	24 YEARS	25 YEARS	30 YEARS	35 YEARS	40 YEARS
100	1.04	1.03	1.02	1.02	0.99	0.98	0.97
200	2.08	2.07	2.05	2.03	1.98	1.95	1.94
500	5.21	5.16	5.12	5.08	4.95	4.88	4.84
1000	10.42	10.33	10.24	10.16	9.90	9.76	9.68
2000	20.85	20.65	20.48	20.33	19.81	19.52	19.37
5000	52.12	51.63	51.20	50.82	49.51	48.81	48.41
6000	62.54	61.95	61.44	60.99	59.42	58.57	58.10
7000	72.97	72.28	71.68	71.15	69.32	68.33	67.78
8000	83.39	82.61	81.92	81.32	79.22	78.09	77.46
9000	93.81	92.93	92.16	91.48	89.13	87.85	87.15
10000	104.24	103.26	102.40	101.65	99.03	97.61	96.83
15000	156.36	154.89	153.60	152.47	148.54	146.42	145.24
20000	208.47	206.52	204.80	203.29	198.06	195.22	193.66
25000	260.59	258.15	256.00	254.12	247.57	244.03	242.07
30000	312.71	309.77	307.20	304.94	297.09	292.83	290.48
35000	364.83	361.40	358.40	355.76	346.60	341.64	338.90
40000	416.95	413.03	409.60	406.59	396.12	390.44	387.31
45000	469.07	464.66	460.80	457.41	445.63	439.25	435.73
50000	521.19	516.29	512.00	508.23	495.15	488.05	484.14
55000	573.31	567.92	563.20	559.06	544.66	536.86	532.56
60000	625.42	619.55	614.40	609.88	594.17	585.66	580.97
65000	677.54	671.18	665.60	660.70	643.69	634.47	629.38
70000	729.66	722.81	716.80	711.53	693.20	683.28	677.80
75000	781.78	774.44	768.00	762.35	742.72	732.08	726.21
80000	833.90	826.07	819.20	813.18	792.23	780.89	774.63
85000	886.02	877.69	870.40	864.00	841.75	829.69	823.04
90000	938.14	929.32	921.60	914.82	891.26	878.50	871.45
95000	990.26	980.95	972.80	965.65	940.78	927.30	919.87
100000	1042.37	1032.58	1024.00	1016.47	990.29	976.11	968.28
105000	1094.49	1084.21	1075.20	1067.29	1039.81	1024.91	1016.70
110000	1146.61	1135.84	1126.40	1118.12	1089.32	1073.72	1065.11
120000	1250.85	1239.10	1228.80	1219.76	1188.35	1171.33	1161.94
130000	1355.09	1342.36	1331.20	1321.41	1287.38	1268.94	1258.77
140000	1459.32	1445.61	1433.60	1423.06	1386.41	1366.55	1355.59
150000	1563.56	1548.87	1536.00	1524.70	1485.44	1464.16	1452.42
160000	1667.80	1652.13	1638.40	1626.35	1584.47	1561.77	1549.25
170000	1772.04	1755.39	1740.80	1728.00	1683.50	1659.38	1646.08
180000	1876.27	1858.65	1843.20	1829.64	1782.52	1756.99	1742.91
190000	1980.51	1961.90	1945.60	1931.29	1881.55	1854.60	1839.74
200000	2084.75	2065.16	2048.00	2032.94	1980.58	1952.21	1936.56
210000	2188.99	2168.42	2150.40	2134.58	2079.61	2049.83	2033.39
220000	2293.22	2271.68	2252.80	2236.23	2178.64	2147.44	2130.22
230000	2397.46	2374.94	2355.20	2337.88	2277.67	2245.05	2227.05
240000	2501.70	2478.20	2457.60	2439.53	2376.70	2342.66	2323.88
250000	2605.94	2581.45	2560.00	2541.17	2475.73	2440.27	2420.70
260000	2710.17	2684.71	2662.40	2642.82	2574.76	2537.88	2517.53
270000	2814.41	2787.97	2764.80	2744.47	2673.79	2635.49	2614.36
280000	2918.65	2891.23	2867.20	2846.11	2772.82	2733.10	2711.19
290000	3022.88	2994.49	2969.60	2947.76	2871.85	2830.71	2808.02
300000	3127.12	3097.74	3072.00	3049.41	2970.87	2928.32	2904.85
310000	3231.36	3201.00	3174.40	3151.05	3069.90	3025.93	3001.67
320000	3335.60	3304.26	3276.80	3252.70	3168.93	3123.54	3098.50
330000	3439.83	3407.52	3379.20	3354.35	3267.96	3221.15	3195.33
340000	3544.07	3510.78	3481.61	3455.99	3366.99	3318.76	3292.16
350000	3648.31	3614.03	3584.01	3557.64	3466.02	3416.38	3388.99
400000	4169.50	4130.33	4096.01	4065.88	3961.17	3904.43	3873.13
450000	4690.68	4646.62	4608.01	4574.11	4456.31	4392.48	4357.27
500000	5211.87	5162.91	5120.01	5082.34	4951.46	4880.54	4841.41
550000	5733.06	5679.20	5632.01	5590.58	5446.60	5368.59	5325.55
600000	6254.24	6195.49	6144.01	6098.81	5941.75	5856.64	5809.69

11¾%

Monthly Payments
necessary to amortize a loan

AMOUNT	1 YEAR	2 YEARS	3 YEARS	4 YEARS	5 YEARS	6 YEARS	7 YEARS
100	8.87	4.70	3.31	2.62	2.21	1.94	1.75
200	17.75	9.39	6.62	5.24	4.42	3.88	3.50
500	44.37	23.48	16.55	13.11	11.06	9.71	8.76
1000	88.73	46.96	33.10	26.21	22.12	19.42	17.52
2000	177.46	93.91	66.19	52.42	44.24	38.84	35.04
5000	443.66	234.78	165.48	131.06	110.59	97.10	87.60
6000	532.39	281.74	198.57	157.27	132.71	116.52	105.12
7000	621.12	328.70	231.67	183.48	154.83	135.94	122.64
8000	709.86	375.65	264.76	209.69	176.95	155.36	140.15
9000	798.59	422.61	297.86	235.90	199.06	174.78	157.67
10000	887.32	469.57	330.95	262.11	221.18	194.20	175.19
15000	1330.98	704.35	496.43	393.17	331.77	291.31	262.79
20000	1774.64	939.14	661.90	524.23	442.37	388.41	350.39
25000	2218.30	1173.92	827.38	655.28	552.96	485.51	437.98
30000	2661.96	1408.70	992.85	786.34	663.55	582.61	525.58
35000	3105.62	1643.49	1158.33	917.39	774.14	679.72	613.18
40000	3549.28	1878.27	1323.80	1048.45	884.73	776.82	700.77
45000	3992.93	2113.06	1489.28	1179.51	995.32	873.92	788.37
50000	4436.59	2347.84	1654.75	1310.56	1105.92	971.02	875.97
55000	4880.25	2582.62	1820.23	1441.62	1216.51	1068.12	963.56
60000	5323.91	2817.41	1985.70	1572.68	1327.10	1165.23	1051.16
65000	5767.57	3052.19	2151.18	1703.73	1437.69	1262.33	1138.76
70000	6211.23	3286.98	2316.65	1834.79	1548.28	1359.43	1226.35
75000	6654.89	3521.76	2482.13	1965.84	1658.87	1456.53	1313.95
80000	7098.55	3756.54	2647.60	2096.90	1769.47	1553.63	1401.55
85000	7542.21	3991.33	2813.08	2227.96	1880.06	1650.74	1489.14
90000	7985.87	4226.11	2978.55	2359.01	1990.65	1747.84	1576.74
95000	8429.53	4460.90	3144.03	2490.07	2101.24	1844.94	1664.34
100000	8873.19	4695.68	3309.50	2621.13	2211.83	1942.04	1751.93
105000	9316.85	4930.46	3474.98	2752.18	2322.42	2039.15	1839.53
110000	9760.51	5165.25	3640.45	2883.24	2433.02	2136.25	1927.12
120000	10647.83	5634.82	3971.40	3145.35	2654.20	2330.45	2102.32
130000	11535.14	6104.39	4302.35	3407.46	2875.38	2524.66	2277.51
140000	12422.46	6573.95	4633.30	3669.58	3096.56	2718.86	2452.70
150000	13309.78	7043.52	4964.25	3931.69	3317.75	2913.06	2627.90
160000	14197.10	7513.09	5295.21	4193.80	3538.93	3107.27	2803.09
170000	15084.42	7982.66	5626.16	4455.91	3760.11	3301.47	2978.28
180000	15971.74	8452.23	5957.11	4718.03	3981.30	3495.68	3153.48
190000	16859.06	8921.79	6288.06	4980.14	4202.48	3689.88	3328.67
200000	17746.38	9391.36	6619.01	5242.25	4423.66	3884.09	3503.86
210000	18633.69	9860.93	6949.96	5504.36	4644.85	4078.29	3679.06
220000	19521.01	10330.50	7280.91	5766.48	4866.03	4272.49	3854.25
230000	20408.33	10800.07	7611.86	6028.59	5087.21	4466.70	4029.44
240000	21295.65	11269.63	7942.81	6290.70	5308.40	4660.90	4204.64
250000	22182.97	11739.20	8273.76	6552.81	5529.58	4855.11	4379.83
260000	23070.29	12208.77	8604.71	6814.93	5750.76	5049.31	4555.02
270000	23957.61	12678.34	8935.66	7077.04	5971.95	5243.52	4730.22
280000	24844.93	13147.91	9266.61	7339.15	6193.13	5437.72	4905.41
290000	25732.24	13617.47	9597.56	7601.26	6414.31	5631.92	5080.60
300000	26619.56	14087.04	9928.51	7863.38	6635.50	5826.13	5255.80
310000	27506.88	14556.61	10259.46	8125.49	6856.68	6020.33	5430.99
320000	28394.20	15026.18	10590.41	8387.60	7077.86	6214.54	5606.18
330000	29281.52	15495.75	10921.36	8649.71	7299.05	6408.74	5781.37
340000	30168.84	15965.32	11252.31	8911.83	7520.23	6602.95	5956.57
350000	31056.16	16434.88	11583.26	9173.94	7741.41	6797.15	6131.76
400000	35492.75	18782.72	13238.01	10484.50	8847.33	7768.17	7007.73
450000	39929.35	21130.56	14892.76	11795.06	9953.24	8739.19	7883.69
500000	44365.94	23478.40	16547.52	13105.63	11059.16	9710.22	8759.66
550000	48802.53	25826.24	18202.27	14416.19	12165.08	10681.24	9635.62
600000	53239.13	28174.09	19857.02	15726.75	13270.99	11652.26	10511.59

Monthly Payments 11¾%
necessary to amortize a loan

AMOUNT	8 YEARS	9 YEARS	10 YEARS	11 YEARS	12 YEARS	13 YEARS	14 YEARS
100	1.61	1.50	1.42	1.35	1.30	1.25	1.22
200	3.22	3.01	2.84	2.71	2.60	2.51	2.43
500	8.06	7.52	7.10	6.77	6.49	6.27	6.08
1000	16.12	15.04	14.20	13.53	12.98	12.53	12.16
2000	32.23	30.09	28.41	27.06	25.97	25.06	24.31
5000	80.58	75.22	71.01	67.65	64.92	62.66	60.78
6000	96.69	90.26	85.22	81.18	77.90	75.19	72.94
7000	112.81	105.31	99.42	94.71	90.88	87.73	85.10
8000	128.93	120.35	113.62	108.24	103.87	100.26	97.26
9000	145.04	135.39	127.83	121.77	116.85	112.79	109.41
10000	161.16	150.44	142.03	135.30	129.83	125.26	121.57
15000	241.74	225.65	213.04	202.95	194.75	187.99	182.35
20000	322.32	300.87	284.06	270.61	259.67	250.65	243.14
25000	402.89	376.09	355.07	338.26	324.58	313.31	303.92
30000	483.47	451.31	426.09	405.91	389.50	375.97	364.71
35000	564.05	526.53	497.10	473.56	454.41	438.64	425.49
40000	644.63	601.74	568.12	541.21	519.33	501.30	486.28
45000	725.21	676.96	639.13	608.86	584.25	563.96	547.06
50000	805.79	752.18	710.15	676.51	649.16	626.62	607.85
55000	886.37	827.40	781.16	744.17	714.08	689.29	668.63
60000	966.95	902.62	852.18	811.82	779.00	751.95	729.42
65000	1047.53	977.83	923.19	879.47	843.91	814.61	790.20
70000	1128.11	1053.05	994.21	947.12	908.83	877.27	850.99
75000	1208.68	1128.27	1065.22	1014.77	973.74	939.94	911.77
80000	1289.26	1203.49	1136.24	1082.42	1038.66	1002.60	972.56
85000	1369.84	1278.71	1207.25	1150.07	1103.58	1065.26	1033.34
90000	1450.42	1353.92	1278.27	1217.73	1168.49	1127.92	1094.13
95000	1531.00	1429.14	1349.28	1285.38	1233.41	1190.59	1154.91
100000	1611.58	1504.36	1420.29	1353.03	1298.33	1253.25	1215.70
105000	1692.16	1579.58	1491.31	1420.68	1363.24	1315.91	1276.48
110000	1772.74	1654.80	1562.32	1488.33	1428.16	1378.57	1337.27
120000	1933.90	1805.23	1704.35	1623.63	1557.99	1503.90	1458.84
130000	2095.05	1955.67	1846.38	1758.94	1687.82	1629.22	1580.41
140000	2256.21	2106.10	1988.41	1894.24	1817.66	1754.55	1701.97
150000	2417.37	2256.54	2130.44	2029.54	1947.49	1879.87	1823.54
160000	2578.53	2406.98	2272.47	2164.85	2077.32	2005.20	1945.11
170000	2739.68	2557.41	2414.50	2300.15	2207.15	2130.52	2066.68
180000	2900.84	2707.85	2556.53	2435.45	2336.99	2255.85	2188.25
190000	3062.00	2858.28	2698.56	2570.76	2466.82	2381.17	2309.82
200000	3223.16	3008.72	2840.59	2706.06	2596.65	2506.50	2431.39
210000	3384.32	3159.16	2982.62	2841.36	2726.48	2631.82	2552.96
220000	3545.47	3309.59	3124.65	2976.66	2856.32	2757.14	2674.53
230000	3706.63	3460.03	3266.68	3111.97	2986.15	2882.47	2796.10
240000	3867.79	3610.46	3408.71	3247.27	3115.98	3007.79	2917.67
250000	4028.95	3760.90	3550.74	3382.57	3245.81	3133.12	3039.24
260000	4190.11	3911.34	3692.77	3517.88	3375.65	3258.44	3160.81
270000	4351.26	4061.77	3834.80	3653.18	3505.48	3383.77	3282.38
280000	4512.42	4212.21	3976.82	3788.48	3635.31	3509.09	3403.95
290000	4673.58	4362.64	4118.85	3923.78	3765.14	3634.42	3525.52
300000	4834.74	4513.08	4260.88	4059.09	3894.98	3759.74	3647.09
310000	4995.90	4663.52	4402.91	4194.39	4024.81	3885.07	3768.66
320000	5157.05	4813.95	4544.94	4329.69	4154.64	4010.39	3890.23
330000	5318.21	4964.39	4686.97	4465.00	4284.47	4135.72	4011.80
340000	5479.37	5114.82	4829.00	4600.30	4414.31	4261.04	4133.37
350000	5640.53	5265.26	4971.03	4735.60	4544.14	4386.37	4254.94
400000	6446.32	6017.44	5681.18	5412.12	5193.30	5012.99	4862.79
450000	7252.11	6769.62	6391.33	6088.63	5842.47	5639.61	5470.63
500000	8057.90	7521.80	7101.47	6765.15	6491.63	6266.24	6078.48
550000	8863.69	8273.98	7811.62	7441.66	7140.79	6892.86	6686.33
600000	9669.48	9026.16	8521.77	8118.17	7789.95	7519.49	7294.18

113

11¾%

Monthly Payments
necessary to amortize a loan

AMOUNT	15 YEARS	16 YEARS	17 YEARS	18 YEARS	19 YEARS	20 YEARS	21 YEARS
100	1.18	1.16	1.13	1.12	1.10	1.08	1.07
200	2.37	2.31	2.27	2.23	2.20	2.17	2.14
500	5.92	5.79	5.67	5.58	5.49	5.42	5.36
1000	11.84	11.57	11.35	11.15	10.98	10.84	10.71
2000	23.68	23.15	22.69	22.30	21.97	21.67	21.42
5000	59.21	57.87	56.73	55.75	54.91	54.19	53.55
6000	71.05	69.44	68.08	66.90	65.90	65.02	64.27
7000	82.89	81.02	79.42	78.06	76.88	75.86	74.98
8000	94.73	92.59	90.77	89.21	87.86	86.70	85.69
9000	106.57	104.17	102.11	100.36	98.84	97.53	96.40
10000	118.41	115.74	113.46	111.51	109.83	108.37	107.11
15000	177.62	173.61	170.19	167.26	164.74	162.56	160.66
20000	236.83	231.48	226.92	223.01	219.65	216.74	214.22
25000	296.03	289.35	283.65	278.77	274.56	270.93	267.77
30000	355.24	347.22	340.38	334.52	329.48	325.11	321.33
35000	414.45	405.09	397.11	390.28	384.39	379.30	374.88
40000	473.65	462.96	453.84	446.03	439.30	433.48	428.44
45000	532.86	520.83	510.57	501.78	494.21	487.67	481.99
50000	592.07	578.70	567.30	557.54	549.13	541.85	535.54
55000	651.27	636.57	624.03	613.29	604.04	596.04	589.10
60000	710.48	694.44	680.76	669.04	658.95	650.22	642.65
65000	769.69	752.31	737.49	724.80	713.86	704.41	696.21
70000	828.89	810.18	794.22	780.55	768.78	758.59	749.76
75000	888.10	868.05	850.95	836.30	823.69	812.78	803.32
80000	947.31	925.92	907.68	892.06	878.60	866.97	856.87
85000	1006.51	983.79	964.42	947.81	933.51	921.15	910.42
90000	1065.72	1041.66	1021.15	1003.57	988.43	975.34	963.98
95000	1124.92	1099.53	1077.88	1059.32	1043.34	1029.52	1017.53
100000	1184.13	1157.40	1134.61	1115.07	1098.25	1083.71	1071.09
105000	1243.34	1215.27	1191.34	1170.83	1153.16	1137.89	1124.64
110000	1302.54	1273.14	1248.07	1226.58	1208.08	1192.08	1178.20
120000	1420.96	1388.88	1361.53	1338.09	1317.90	1300.45	1285.31
130000	1539.37	1504.62	1474.99	1449.59	1427.73	1408.82	1392.41
140000	1657.78	1620.35	1588.45	1561.10	1537.55	1517.19	1499.52
150000	1776.20	1736.09	1701.91	1672.61	1647.38	1625.56	1606.63
160000	1894.61	1851.83	1815.37	1784.12	1757.20	1733.93	1713.74
170000	2013.02	1967.57	1928.83	1895.62	1867.03	1842.30	1820.85
180000	2131.44	2083.31	2042.29	2007.13	1976.85	1950.67	1927.96
190000	2249.85	2199.05	2155.75	2118.64	2086.68	2059.04	2035.07
200000	2368.26	2314.79	2269.21	2230.15	2196.50	2167.41	2142.18
210000	2486.68	2430.53	2382.67	2341.65	2306.33	2275.78	2249.28
220000	2605.09	2546.27	2496.13	2453.16	2416.15	2384.16	2356.39
230000	2723.50	2662.01	2609.59	2564.67	2525.98	2492.53	2463.50
240000	2841.92	2777.75	2723.05	2676.17	2635.80	2600.90	2570.61
250000	2960.33	2893.49	2836.52	2787.68	2745.63	2709.27	2677.72
260000	3078.74	3009.23	2949.98	2899.19	2855.45	2817.64	2784.83
270000	3197.15	3124.97	3063.44	3010.70	2965.28	2926.01	2891.94
280000	3315.57	3240.71	3176.90	3122.20	3075.10	3034.38	2999.05
290000	3433.98	3356.45	3290.36	3233.71	3184.93	3142.75	3106.15
300000	3552.39	3472.19	3403.82	3345.22	3294.75	3251.12	3213.26
310000	3670.81	3587.93	3517.28	3456.72	3404.58	3359.49	3320.37
320000	3789.22	3703.67	3630.74	3568.23	3514.40	3467.86	3427.48
330000	3907.63	3819.40	3744.20	3679.74	3624.23	3576.23	3534.59
340000	4026.05	3935.15	3857.66	3791.25	3734.05	3684.60	3641.70
350000	4144.46	4050.89	3971.12	3902.75	3843.88	3792.97	3748.81
400000	4736.53	4629.59	4538.42	4460.29	4393.00	4334.83	4284.35
450000	5328.59	5208.28	5105.73	5017.83	4942.13	4876.68	4819.90
500000	5920.66	5786.98	5673.03	5575.36	5491.26	5418.54	5355.44
550000	6512.72	6365.68	6240.33	6132.90	6040.38	5960.39	5890.98
600000	7104.79	6944.38	6807.64	6690.44	6589.51	6502.24	6426.53

Monthly Payments 11¾%
necessary to amortize a loan

AMOUNT	22 YEARS	23 YEARS	24 YEARS	25 YEARS	30 YEARS	35 YEARS	40 YEARS
100	1.06	1.05	1.04	1.03	1.01	1.00	0.99
200	2.12	2.10	2.08	2.07	2.02	1.99	1.98
500	5.30	5.25	5.21	5.17	5.05	4.98	4.94
1000	10.60	10.51	10.42	10.35	10.09	9.96	9.88
2000	21.20	21.01	20.84	20.70	20.19	19.92	19.77
5000	53.01	52.53	52.11	51.74	50.47	49.79	49.42
6000	63.61	63.03	62.53	62.09	60.56	59.75	59.30
7000	74.21	73.54	72.95	72.44	70.66	69.71	69.19
8000	84.81	84.04	83.37	82.78	80.75	79.66	79.07
9000	95.41	94.55	93.79	93.13	90.85	89.62	88.95
10000	106.01	105.05	104.21	103.48	100.94	99.58	98.84
15000	159.02	157.58	156.32	155.22	151.41	149.37	148.25
20000	212.02	210.10	208.43	206.96	201.88	199.16	197.67
25000	265.03	262.63	260.54	258.70	252.35	248.95	247.09
30000	318.03	315.16	312.64	310.44	302.82	298.74	296.51
35000	371.04	367.68	364.75	362.18	353.29	348.53	345.93
40000	424.04	420.21	416.86	413.92	403.76	398.32	395.35
45000	477.05	472.74	468.96	465.66	454.23	448.11	444.76
50000	530.05	525.26	521.07	517.40	504.70	497.90	494.18
55000	583.06	577.79	573.18	569.14	555.18	547.69	543.60
60000	636.06	630.31	625.29	620.88	605.65	597.48	593.02
65000	689.07	682.84	677.39	672.62	656.12	647.27	642.44
70000	742.07	735.37	729.50	724.36	706.59	697.06	691.85
75000	795.08	787.89	781.61	776.10	757.06	746.85	741.27
80000	848.08	840.42	833.71	827.84	807.53	796.64	790.69
85000	901.09	892.94	885.82	879.58	858.00	846.42	840.11
90000	954.10	945.47	937.93	931.32	908.47	896.21	889.53
95000	1007.10	998.00	990.04	983.06	958.94	946.00	938.95
100000	1060.11	1050.52	1042.14	1034.80	1009.41	995.79	988.36
105000	1113.11	1103.05	1094.25	1086.54	1059.88	1045.58	1037.78
110000	1166.12	1155.58	1146.36	1138.28	1110.35	1095.37	1087.20
120000	1272.13	1260.63	1250.57	1241.76	1211.29	1194.95	1186.04
130000	1378.14	1365.68	1354.79	1345.24	1312.23	1294.53	1284.87
140000	1484.15	1470.73	1459.00	1448.72	1413.17	1394.11	1383.71
150000	1590.16	1575.78	1563.21	1552.05	1514.11	1493.69	1482.55
160000	1696.17	1680.84	1667.43	1655.68	1615.06	1593.27	1581.38
170000	1802.18	1785.89	1771.64	1759.16	1716.00	1692.85	1680.22
180000	1908.19	1890.94	1875.86	1862.64	1816.94	1792.43	1779.06
190000	2014.20	1995.99	1980.07	1966.12	1917.88	1892.01	1877.89
200000	2120.21	2101.05	2084.28	2069.60	2018.82	1991.59	1976.73
210000	2226.22	2206.10	2188.50	2173.08	2119.76	2091.17	2075.56
220000	2332.23	2311.15	2292.71	2276.56	2220.70	2190.75	2174.40
230000	2438.24	2416.20	2396.93	2380.04	2321.64	2290.33	2273.24
240000	2544.25	2521.26	2501.14	2483.52	2422.58	2389.91	2372.07
250000	2650.26	2626.31	2605.36	2587.00	2523.52	2489.48	2470.91
260000	2756.28	2731.36	2709.57	2690.48	2624.47	2589.06	2569.75
270000	2862.29	2836.41	2813.78	2793.96	2725.41	2688.64	2668.58
280000	2968.30	2941.46	2918.00	2897.43	2826.35	2788.22	2767.42
290000	3074.31	3046.52	3022.21	3000.91	2927.29	2887.80	2866.26
300000	3180.32	3151.57	3126.43	3104.39	3028.23	2987.38	2965.09
310000	3286.33	3256.62	3230.64	3207.87	3129.17	3086.96	3063.93
320000	3392.34	3361.67	3334.86	3311.35	3230.11	3186.54	3162.76
330000	3498.35	3466.73	3439.07	3414.83	3331.05	3286.12	3261.60
340000	3604.36	3571.78	3543.28	3518.31	3431.99	3385.70	3360.44
350000	3710.37	3676.83	3647.50	3621.79	3532.93	3485.28	3459.27
400000	4240.42	4202.09	4168.57	4139.19	4037.64	3983.18	3953.46
450000	4770.48	4727.35	4689.64	4656.59	4542.34	4481.07	4447.64
500000	5300.53	5252.62	5210.71	5173.99	5047.05	4978.97	4941.82
550000	5830.58	5777.88	5731.78	5691.39	5551.75	5476.87	5436.00
600000	6360.63	6303.14	6252.85	6208.79	6056.46	5974.76	5930.18

12%

Monthly Payments
necessary to amortize a loan

AMOUNT	1 YEAR	2 YEARS	3 YEARS	4 YEARS	5 YEARS	6 YEARS	7 YEARS
100	8.88	4.71	3.32	2.63	2.22	1.96	1.77
200	17.77	9.41	6.64	5.27	4.45	3.91	3.53
500	44.42	23.54	16.61	13.17	11.12	9.78	8.83
1000	88.85	47.07	33.21	26.33	22.24	19.55	17.65
2000	177.70	94.15	66.43	52.67	44.49	39.10	35.31
5000	444.24	235.37	166.07	131.67	111.22	97.75	88.26
6000	533.09	282.44	199.29	158.00	133.47	117.30	105.92
7000	621.94	329.51	232.50	184.34	155.71	136.85	123.57
8000	710.79	376.59	265.71	210.67	177.96	156.40	141.22
9000	799.64	423.66	298.93	237.00	200.20	175.95	158.87
10000	888.49	470.73	332.14	263.34	222.44	195.50	176.53
15000	1332.73	706.10	498.21	395.01	333.67	293.25	264.79
20000	1776.98	941.47	664.29	526.68	444.89	391.00	353.05
25000	2221.22	1176.84	830.36	658.35	556.11	488.75	441.32
30000	2665.46	1412.20	996.43	790.02	667.33	586.51	529.58
35000	3109.71	1647.57	1162.50	921.68	778.56	684.26	617.85
40000	3553.95	1882.94	1328.57	1053.35	889.78	782.01	706.11
45000	3998.20	2118.31	1494.64	1185.02	1001.00	879.76	794.37
50000	4442.44	2353.67	1660.72	1316.69	1112.22	977.51	882.64
55000	4886.68	2589.04	1826.79	1448.36	1223.44	1075.26	970.90
60000	5330.93	2824.41	1992.86	1580.03	1334.67	1173.01	1059.16
65000	5775.17	3059.78	2158.93	1711.70	1445.89	1270.76	1147.43
70000	6219.42	3295.14	2325.00	1843.37	1557.11	1368.51	1235.69
75000	6663.66	3530.51	2491.07	1975.04	1668.33	1466.26	1323.95
80000	7107.90	3765.88	2657.14	2106.71	1779.56	1564.02	1412.22
85000	7552.15	4001.25	2823.22	2238.38	1890.78	1661.77	1500.48
90000	7996.39	4236.61	2989.29	2370.05	2002.00	1759.52	1588.75
95000	8440.63	4471.98	3155.36	2501.71	2113.22	1857.27	1677.01
100000	8884.88	4707.35	3321.43	2633.38	2224.44	1955.02	1765.27
105000	9329.12	4942.71	3487.50	2765.05	2335.67	2052.77	1853.54
110000	9773.37	5178.08	3653.57	2896.72	2446.89	2150.52	1941.80
120000	10661.85	5648.82	3985.72	3160.06	2669.33	2346.02	2118.33
130000	11550.34	6119.55	4317.86	3423.40	2891.78	2541.53	2294.86
140000	12438.83	6590.29	4650.00	3686.74	3114.22	2737.03	2471.38
150000	13327.32	7061.02	4982.15	3950.08	3336.67	2932.53	2647.91
160000	14215.81	7531.76	5314.29	4213.41	3559.11	3128.03	2824.44
170000	15104.29	8002.49	5646.43	4476.75	3781.56	3323.53	3000.96
180000	15992.78	8473.23	5978.58	4740.09	4004.00	3519.03	3177.49
190000	16881.27	8943.96	6310.72	5003.43	4226.45	3714.54	3354.02
200000	17769.76	9414.69	6642.86	5266.77	4448.89	3910.04	3530.55
210000	18658.25	9885.43	6975.01	5530.11	4671.33	4105.54	3707.07
220000	19546.73	10356.16	7307.15	5793.44	4893.78	4301.04	3883.60
230000	20435.22	10826.90	7639.29	6056.78	5116.22	4496.54	4060.13
240000	21323.71	11297.63	7971.43	6320.12	5338.67	4692.05	4236.66
250000	22212.20	11768.37	8303.58	6583.46	5561.11	4887.55	4413.18
260000	23100.69	12239.10	8635.72	6846.80	5783.56	5083.05	4589.71
270000	23989.17	12709.84	8967.86	7110.14	6006.00	5278.55	4766.24
280000	24877.66	13180.57	9300.01	7373.47	6228.45	5474.05	4942.77
290000	25766.15	13651.31	9632.15	7636.81	6450.89	5669.56	5119.29
300000	26654.64	14122.04	9964.29	7900.15	6673.33	5865.06	5295.82
310000	27543.12	14592.78	10296.44	8163.49	6895.78	6060.56	5472.35
320000	28431.61	15063.51	10628.58	8426.83	7118.22	6256.06	5648.87
330000	29320.10	15534.25	10960.72	8690.17	7340.67	6451.56	5825.40
340000	30208.59	16004.98	11292.87	8953.50	7563.11	6647.07	6001.93
350000	31097.08	16475.72	11625.01	9216.84	7785.56	6842.57	6178.46
400000	35539.52	18829.39	13285.72	10533.68	8897.78	7820.08	7061.09
450000	39981.95	21183.06	14946.44	11850.23	10010.00	8797.59	7943.73
500000	44424.39	23536.74	16607.15	13166.92	11122.22	9775.10	8826.37
550000	48866.83	25890.41	18267.87	14483.61	12234.45	10752.61	9709.00
600000	53309.27	28244.08	19928.59	15800.30	13346.67	11730.12	10591.64

Monthly Payments 12%
necessary to amortize a loan

AMOUNT	8 YEARS	9 YEARS	10 YEARS	11 YEARS	12 YEARS	13 YEARS	14 YEARS
100	1.63	1.52	1.43	1.37	1.31	1.27	1.23
200	3.25	3.04	2.87	2.74	2.63	2.54	2.46
500	8.13	7.59	7.17	6.84	6.57	6.34	6.16
1000	16.25	15.18	14.35	13.68	13.13	12.69	12.31
2000	32.51	30.37	28.69	27.36	26.27	25.37	24.63
5000	81.26	75.92	71.74	68.39	65.67	63.43	61.57
6000	97.52	91.11	86.08	82.07	78.81	76.12	73.89
7000	113.77	106.29	100.43	95.75	91.94	88.81	86.20
8000	130.02	121.47	114.78	109.42	105.07	101.49	98.51
9000	146.28	136.66	129.12	123.10	118.21	114.18	110.83
10000	162.53	151.84	143.47	136.78	131.34	126.87	123.14
15000	243.79	227.76	215.21	205.17	197.01	190.30	184.71
20000	325.06	303.68	286.94	273.56	262.68	253.73	246.29
25000	406.32	379.61	358.68	341.95	328.35	317.17	307.86
30000	487.59	455.53	430.41	410.34	394.03	380.60	369.43
35000	568.85	531.45	502.15	478.73	459.70	444.03	431.00
40000	650.11	607.37	573.88	547.12	525.37	507.47	492.57
45000	731.38	683.29	645.62	615.50	591.04	570.90	554.14
50000	812.64	759.21	717.35	683.89	656.71	634.33	615.71
55000	893.91	835.13	789.09	752.28	722.38	697.77	677.29
60000	975.17	911.05	860.83	820.67	788.05	761.20	738.86
65000	1056.43	986.98	932.56	889.06	853.72	824.63	800.43
70000	1137.70	1062.90	1004.30	957.45	919.39	888.07	862.00
75000	1218.96	1138.82	1076.03	1025.84	985.06	951.50	923.57
80000	1300.23	1214.74	1147.77	1094.23	1050.74	1014.93	985.14
85000	1381.49	1290.66	1219.50	1162.62	1116.41	1078.37	1046.72
90000	1462.76	1366.58	1291.24	1231.01	1182.08	1141.80	1108.29
95000	1544.02	1442.50	1362.97	1299.40	1247.75	1205.23	1169.86
100000	1625.28	1518.42	1434.71	1367.79	1313.42	1268.67	1231.43
105000	1706.55	1594.34	1506.44	1436.18	1379.09	1332.10	1293.00
110000	1787.81	1670.27	1578.18	1504.57	1444.76	1395.53	1354.57
120000	1950.34	1822.11	1721.65	1641.35	1576.10	1522.40	1477.72
130000	2112.87	1973.95	1865.12	1778.12	1707.44	1649.27	1600.86
140000	2275.40	2125.79	2008.59	1914.90	1838.79	1776.13	1724.00
150000	2437.93	2277.63	2152.06	2051.68	1970.13	1903.00	1847.14
160000	2600.45	2429.48	2295.54	2188.46	2101.47	2029.87	1970.29
170000	2762.98	2581.32	2439.01	2325.24	2232.81	2156.73	2093.43
180000	2925.51	2733.16	2582.48	2462.02	2364.15	2283.60	2216.57
190000	3088.04	2885.00	2725.95	2598.80	2495.50	2410.47	2339.72
200000	3250.57	3036.85	2869.42	2735.58	2626.84	2537.33	2462.86
210000	3413.10	3188.69	3012.89	2872.35	2758.18	2664.20	2586.00
220000	3575.63	3340.53	3156.36	3009.13	2889.52	2791.07	2709.14
230000	3738.15	3492.37	3299.83	3145.91	3020.86	2917.93	2832.29
240000	3900.68	3644.22	3443.30	3282.69	3152.21	3044.80	2955.43
250000	4063.21	3796.06	3586.77	3419.47	3283.55	3171.67	3078.57
260000	4225.74	3947.90	3730.24	3556.25	3414.89	3298.53	3201.72
270000	4388.27	4099.74	3873.72	3693.03	3546.23	3425.40	3324.86
280000	4550.80	4251.59	4017.19	3829.81	3677.57	3552.27	3448.00
290000	4713.32	4403.43	4160.66	3966.58	3808.92	3679.13	3571.15
300000	4875.85	4555.27	4304.13	4103.36	3940.26	3806.00	3694.29
310000	5038.38	4707.11	4447.60	4240.14	4071.60	3932.87	3817.43
320000	5200.91	4858.95	4591.07	4376.92	4202.94	4059.73	3940.57
330000	5363.44	5010.80	4734.54	4513.70	4334.28	4186.60	4063.72
340000	5525.97	5162.64	4878.01	4650.48	4465.63	4313.47	4186.86
350000	5688.49	5314.48	5021.48	4787.26	4596.97	4440.33	4310.00
400000	6501.14	6073.69	5738.84	5471.15	5253.68	5074.66	4925.72
450000	7313.78	6832.90	6456.19	6155.05	5910.39	5709.00	5541.43
500000	8126.42	7592.12	7173.55	6838.94	6567.10	6343.33	6157.15
550000	8939.06	8351.33	7890.90	7522.83	7223.81	6977.66	6772.86
600000	9751.70	9110.54	8608.26	8206.73	7880.51	7612.00	7388.58

Monthly Payments
necessary to amortize a loan

AMOUNT	15 YEARS	16 YEARS	17 YEARS	18 YEARS	19 YEARS	20 YEARS	21 YEARS
100	1.20	1.17	1.15	1.13	1.12	1.10	1.09
200	2.40	2.35	2.30	2.26	2.23	2.20	2.18
500	6.00	5.87	5.76	5.66	5.58	5.51	5.44
1000	12.00	11.74	11.51	11.32	11.15	11.01	10.89
2000	24.00	23.47	23.02	22.64	22.31	22.02	21.77
5000	60.01	58.69	57.56	56.60	55.77	55.05	54.43
6000	72.01	70.42	69.07	67.92	66.92	66.07	65.32
7000	84.01	82.16	80.59	79.24	78.08	77.08	76.21
8000	96.01	93.90	92.10	90.56	89.23	88.09	87.10
9000	108.02	105.64	103.61	101.88	100.38	99.10	97.98
10000	120.02	117.37	115.12	113.20	111.54	110.11	108.87
15000	180.03	176.06	172.68	169.79	167.31	165.16	163.30
20000	240.03	234.75	230.24	226.39	223.08	220.22	217.74
25000	300.04	293.43	287.80	282.99	278.85	275.27	272.17
30000	360.05	352.12	345.36	339.59	334.62	330.33	326.61
35000	420.06	410.80	402.93	396.18	390.38	385.38	381.04
40000	480.07	469.49	460.49	452.78	446.15	440.43	435.48
45000	540.08	528.18	518.05	509.38	501.92	495.49	489.91
50000	600.08	586.86	575.61	565.98	557.69	550.54	544.35
55000	660.09	645.55	633.17	622.57	613.46	605.60	598.78
60000	720.10	704.24	690.73	679.17	669.23	660.65	653.22
65000	780.11	762.92	748.29	735.77	725.00	715.71	707.65
70000	840.12	821.61	805.85	792.37	780.77	770.76	762.09
75000	900.13	880.29	863.41	848.96	836.54	825.81	816.52
80000	960.13	938.98	920.97	905.56	892.31	880.87	870.96
85000	1020.14	997.67	978.53	962.16	948.08	935.92	925.39
90000	1080.15	1056.35	1036.09	1018.76	1003.85	990.98	979.83
95000	1140.16	1115.04	1093.65	1075.35	1059.62	1046.03	1034.26
100000	1200.17	1173.73	1151.22	1131.95	1115.39	1101.09	1088.70
105000	1260.18	1232.41	1208.78	1188.55	1171.15	1156.14	1143.13
110000	1320.18	1291.10	1266.34	1245.15	1226.92	1211.19	1197.57
120000	1440.20	1408.47	1381.46	1358.34	1338.46	1321.30	1306.44
130000	1560.22	1525.84	1496.58	1471.54	1450.00	1431.41	1415.31
140000	1680.24	1643.22	1611.70	1584.73	1561.54	1541.52	1524.18
150000	1800.25	1760.59	1726.82	1697.93	1673.08	1651.63	1633.05
160000	1920.27	1877.96	1841.94	1811.12	1784.62	1761.74	1741.92
170000	2040.29	1995.33	1957.07	1924.32	1896.16	1871.85	1850.79
180000	2160.30	2112.71	2072.19	2037.51	2007.69	1981.96	1959.66
190000	2280.32	2230.08	2187.31	2150.71	2119.23	2092.06	2068.53
200000	2400.34	2347.45	2302.43	2263.90	2230.77	2202.17	2177.40
210000	2520.35	2464.82	2417.55	2377.10	2342.31	2312.28	2286.27
220000	2640.37	2582.20	2532.67	2490.29	2453.85	2422.39	2395.14
230000	2760.39	2699.57	2647.80	2603.49	2565.39	2532.50	2504.01
240000	2880.40	2816.94	2762.92	2716.68	2676.93	2642.61	2612.88
250000	3000.42	2934.31	2878.04	2829.88	2788.46	2752.72	2721.75
260000	3120.44	3051.69	2993.16	2943.07	2900.00	2862.82	2830.62
270000	3240.45	3169.06	3108.28	3056.27	3011.54	2972.93	2939.49
280000	3360.47	3286.43	3223.40	3169.46	3123.08	3083.04	3048.36
290000	3480.49	3403.80	3338.53	3282.66	3234.62	3193.15	3157.23
300000	3600.50	3521.18	3453.65	3395.85	3346.16	3303.26	3266.10
310000	3720.52	3638.55	3568.77	3509.05	3457.70	3413.37	3374.97
320000	3840.54	3755.92	3683.89	3622.24	3569.23	3523.48	3483.84
330000	3960.55	3873.29	3799.01	3735.44	3680.77	3633.58	3592.71
340000	4080.57	3990.67	3914.13	3848.63	3792.31	3743.69	3701.58
350000	4200.58	4108.04	4029.25	3961.83	3903.85	3853.80	3810.45
400000	4800.67	4694.90	4604.86	4527.80	4461.54	4404.34	4354.80
450000	5400.76	5281.76	5180.47	5093.78	5019.24	4954.89	4899.15
500000	6000.84	5868.63	5756.08	5659.75	5576.93	5505.43	5443.50
550000	6600.92	6455.49	6331.69	6225.73	6134.62	6055.97	5987.85
600000	7201.01	7042.35	6907.29	6791.70	6692.31	6606.52	6532.20

Monthly Payments **12%**
necessary to amortize a loan

AMOUNT	22 YEARS	23 YEARS	24 YEARS	25 YEARS	30 YEARS	35 YEARS	40 YEARS
100	1.08	1.07	1.06	1.05	1.03	1.02	1.01
200	2.16	2.14	2.12	2.11	2.06	2.03	2.02
500	5.39	5.34	5.30	5.27	5.14	5.08	5.04
1000	10.78	10.69	10.60	10.53	10.29	10.16	10.08
2000	21.56	21.37	21.21	21.06	20.57	20.31	20.17
5000	53.90	53.43	53.02	52.66	51.43	50.78	50.42
6000	64.68	64.11	63.62	63.19	61.72	60.93	60.51
7000	75.46	74.80	74.23	73.73	72.00	71.09	70.59
8000	86.24	85.49	84.83	84.26	82.29	81.24	80.68
9000	97.01	96.17	95.43	94.79	92.58	91.40	90.76
10000	107.79	106.86	106.04	105.32	102.86	101.55	100.85
15000	161.69	160.28	159.06	157.98	154.29	152.33	151.27
20000	215.59	213.71	212.08	210.64	205.72	203.11	201.70
25000	269.48	267.14	265.10	263.31	257.15	253.89	252.12
30000	323.38	320.57	318.11	315.97	308.58	304.66	302.55
35000	377.28	374.00	371.13	368.63	360.01	355.44	352.97
40000	431.18	427.43	424.15	421.29	411.45	406.22	403.40
45000	485.07	480.85	477.17	473.95	462.88	457.00	453.82
50000	538.97	534.28	530.19	526.61	514.31	507.77	504.25
55000	592.87	587.71	583.21	579.27	565.74	558.55	554.67
60000	646.76	641.14	636.23	631.93	617.17	609.33	605.10
65000	700.66	694.57	689.25	684.60	668.60	660.11	655.52
70000	754.56	748.00	742.27	737.26	720.03	710.88	705.95
75000	808.45	801.42	795.29	789.92	771.46	761.66	756.37
80000	862.35	854.85	848.31	842.58	822.89	812.44	806.80
85000	916.25	908.28	901.32	895.24	874.32	863.22	857.22
90000	970.14	961.71	954.34	947.90	925.75	913.99	907.65
95000	1024.04	1015.14	1007.36	1000.56	977.18	964.77	958.07
100000	1077.94	1068.56	1060.38	1053.22	1028.61	1015.55	1008.50
105000	1131.84	1121.99	1113.40	1105.89	1080.04	1066.33	1058.92
110000	1185.73	1175.42	1166.42	1158.55	1131.47	1117.10	1109.35
120000	1293.53	1282.28	1272.46	1263.87	1234.34	1218.66	1210.20
130000	1401.32	1389.13	1378.50	1369.19	1337.20	1320.21	1311.05
140000	1509.11	1495.99	1484.53	1474.51	1440.06	1421.77	1411.90
150000	1616.91	1602.85	1590.57	1579.84	1542.92	1523.32	1512.75
160000	1724.70	1709.70	1696.61	1685.16	1645.78	1624.88	1613.60
170000	1832.50	1816.56	1802.65	1790.48	1748.64	1726.43	1714.45
180000	1940.29	1923.42	1908.69	1895.80	1851.50	1827.99	1815.30
190000	2048.08	2030.27	2014.73	2001.13	1954.36	1929.54	1916.15
200000	2155.88	2137.13	2120.76	2106.45	2057.23	2031.10	2017.00
210000	2263.67	2243.99	2226.80	2211.77	2160.09	2132.65	2117.85
220000	2371.46	2350.84	2332.84	2317.09	2262.95	2234.21	2218.70
230000	2479.26	2457.70	2438.88	2422.42	2365.81	2335.76	2319.55
240000	2587.05	2564.56	2544.92	2527.74	2468.67	2437.32	2420.40
250000	2694.85	2671.41	2650.95	2633.06	2571.53	2538.87	2521.25
260000	2802.64	2778.27	2756.99	2738.38	2674.39	2640.43	2622.10
270000	2910.43	2885.13	2863.03	2843.71	2777.25	2741.98	2722.95
280000	3018.23	2991.98	2969.07	2949.03	2880.12	2843.54	2823.80
290000	3126.02	3098.84	3075.11	3054.35	2982.98	2945.09	2924.65
300000	3233.82	3205.69	3181.15	3159.67	3085.84	3046.65	3025.50
310000	3341.61	3312.55	3287.18	3264.99	3188.70	3148.20	3126.35
320000	3449.40	3419.41	3393.22	3370.32	3291.56	3249.76	3227.20
330000	3557.20	3526.26	3499.26	3475.64	3394.42	3351.31	3328.05
340000	3664.99	3633.12	3605.30	3580.96	3497.28	3452.87	3428.90
350000	3772.78	3739.98	3711.34	3686.28	3600.14	3554.42	3529.75
400000	4311.75	4274.26	4241.53	4212.90	4114.45	4062.20	4034.00
450000	4850.72	4808.54	4771.72	4739.51	4628.76	4569.97	4538.25
500000	5389.69	5342.82	5301.91	5266.12	5143.06	5077.75	5042.50
550000	5928.66	5877.11	5832.10	5792.73	5657.37	5585.52	5546.75
600000	6467.63	6411.39	6362.29	6319.34	6171.68	6093.30	6051.00

12¼%   Monthly Payments
necessary to amortize a loan

AMOUNT	1 YEAR	2 YEARS	3 YEARS	4 YEARS	5 YEARS	6 YEARS	7 YEARS
100	8.90	4.72	3.33	2.65	2.24	1.97	1.78
200	17.79	9.44	6.67	5.29	4.47	3.94	3.56
500	44.48	23.60	16.67	13.23	11.19	9.84	8.89
1000	88.97	47.19	33.33	26.46	22.37	19.68	17.79
2000	177.93	94.38	66.67	52.91	44.74	39.36	35.57
5000	444.83	235.95	166.67	132.28	111.85	98.40	88.93
6000	533.79	283.14	200.00	158.74	134.23	118.08	106.72
7000	622.76	330.33	233.34	185.20	156.60	137.76	124.51
8000	711.73	377.52	266.67	211.65	178.97	157.44	142.29
9000	800.69	424.71	300.00	238.11	201.34	177.12	160.08
10000	889.66	471.90	333.34	264.57	223.71	196.80	177.87
15000	1334.49	707.85	500.01	396.85	335.56	295.21	266.80
20000	1779.32	943.81	666.68	529.14	447.42	393.61	355.73
25000	2224.14	1179.76	833.35	661.42	559.27	492.01	444.67
30000	2668.97	1415.71	1000.02	793.70	671.13	590.41	533.60
35000	3113.80	1651.66	1166.68	925.99	782.98	688.82	622.53
40000	3558.63	1887.61	1333.35	1058.27	894.84	787.22	711.47
45000	4003.46	2123.56	1500.02	1190.55	1006.69	885.62	800.40
50000	4448.29	2359.52	1666.69	1322.84	1118.55	984.02	889.34
55000	4893.12	2595.47	1833.36	1455.12	1230.40	1082.42	978.27
60000	5337.95	2831.42	2000.03	1587.41	1342.26	1180.83	1067.20
65000	5782.78	3067.37	2166.70	1719.69	1454.11	1279.23	1156.14
70000	6227.60	3303.32	2333.37	1851.97	1565.97	1377.63	1245.07
75000	6672.43	3539.27	2500.04	1984.26	1677.82	1476.03	1334.00
80000	7117.26	3775.22	2666.71	2116.54	1789.68	1574.44	1422.94
85000	7562.09	4011.18	2833.38	2248.82	1901.53	1672.84	1511.87
90000	8006.92	4247.13	3000.05	2381.11	2013.39	1771.24	1600.80
95000	8451.75	4483.08	3166.71	2513.39	2125.24	1869.64	1689.74
100000	8896.58	4719.03	3333.38	2645.68	2237.10	1968.04	1778.67
105000	9341.41	4954.98	3500.05	2777.96	2348.95	2066.45	1867.60
110000	9786.24	5190.93	3666.72	2910.24	2460.81	2164.85	1956.54
120000	10675.89	5662.84	4000.06	3174.81	2684.52	2361.65	2134.40
130000	11565.55	6134.74	4333.40	3439.38	2908.23	2558.46	2312.27
140000	12455.21	6606.64	4666.74	3703.95	3131.94	2755.26	2490.14
150000	13344.87	7078.55	5000.08	3968.51	3355.65	2952.07	2668.01
160000	14234.53	7550.45	5333.41	4233.08	3579.36	3148.87	2845.87
170000	15124.18	8022.35	5666.75	4497.65	3803.07	3345.68	3023.74
180000	16013.84	8494.25	6000.09	4762.22	4026.78	3542.48	3201.61
190000	16903.50	8966.16	6333.43	5026.78	4250.49	3739.28	3379.47
200000	17793.16	9438.06	6666.77	5291.35	4474.20	3936.09	3557.34
210000	18682.81	9909.96	7000.11	5555.92	4697.91	4132.89	3735.21
220000	19572.47	10381.87	7333.45	5820.49	4921.62	4329.70	3913.08
230000	20462.13	10853.77	7666.78	6085.05	5145.33	4526.50	4090.94
240000	21351.79	11325.67	8000.12	6349.62	5369.04	4723.31	4268.81
250000	22241.45	11797.58	8333.46	6614.19	5592.75	4920.11	4446.68
260000	23131.10	12269.48	8666.80	6878.76	5816.46	5116.92	4624.54
270000	24020.76	12741.38	9000.14	7143.32	6040.17	5313.72	4802.41
280000	24910.42	13213.29	9333.48	7407.89	6263.88	5510.52	4980.28
290000	25800.08	13685.19	9666.81	7672.46	6487.59	5707.33	5158.15
300000	26689.73	14157.09	10000.15	7937.03	6711.30	5904.13	5336.01
310000	27579.39	14628.99	10333.49	8201.59	6935.01	6100.94	5513.88
320000	28469.05	15100.90	10666.83	8466.16	7158.72	6297.74	5691.75
330000	29358.71	15572.80	11000.17	8730.73	7382.43	6494.55	5869.61
340000	30248.37	16044.70	11333.51	8995.30	7606.14	6691.35	6047.48
350000	31138.02	16516.61	11666.84	9259.86	7829.85	6888.15	6225.35
400000	35586.31	18876.12	13333.54	10582.70	8948.39	7872.18	7114.68
450000	40034.60	21235.64	15000.23	11905.54	10066.94	8856.20	8004.02
500000	44482.89	23595.15	16666.92	13228.38	11185.49	9840.22	8893.35
550000	48931.18	25954.67	18333.61	14551.21	12304.04	10824.24	9782.69
600000	53379.47	28314.18	20000.30	15874.05	13422.59	11808.27	10672.02

Monthly Payments 12¼%
necessary to amortize a loan

AMOUNT	8 YEARS	9 YEARS	10 YEARS	11 YEARS	12 YEARS	13 YEARS	14 YEARS
100	1.64	1.53	1.45	1.38	1.33	1.28	1.25
200	3.28	3.07	2.90	2.77	2.66	2.57	2.49
500	8.20	7.66	7.25	6.91	6.64	6.42	6.24
1000	16.39	15.33	14.49	13.83	13.29	12.84	12.47
2000	32.78	30.65	28.98	27.65	26.57	25.68	24.95
5000	81.95	76.63	72.46	69.13	66.43	64.21	62.36
6000	98.34	91.95	86.95	82.96	79.72	77.05	74.84
7000	114.73	107.28	101.44	96.78	93.00	89.89	87.31
8000	131.12	122.60	115.94	110.61	106.29	102.73	99.78
9000	147.51	137.93	130.43	124.44	119.57	115.58	112.25
10000	163.91	153.26	144.92	138.26	132.86	128.42	124.73
15000	245.86	229.88	217.38	207.39	199.29	192.63	187.09
20000	327.81	306.51	289.84	276.53	265.72	256.83	249.45
25000	409.76	383.14	362.30	345.66	332.15	321.04	311.81
30000	491.72	459.77	434.76	414.79	398.58	385.25	374.18
35000	573.67	536.39	507.22	483.92	465.01	449.46	436.54
40000	655.62	613.02	579.68	553.05	531.44	513.67	498.90
45000	737.57	689.65	652.14	622.18	597.87	577.88	561.26
50000	819.53	766.28	724.60	691.31	664.30	642.09	623.63
55000	901.48	842.91	797.06	760.44	730.73	706.29	685.99
60000	983.43	919.53	869.52	829.58	797.16	770.50	748.35
65000	1065.38	996.16	941.98	898.71	863.59	834.71	810.72
70000	1147.34	1072.79	1014.44	967.84	930.02	898.92	873.08
75000	1229.29	1149.42	1086.90	1036.97	996.45	963.13	935.44
80000	1311.24	1226.04	1159.36	1106.10	1062.88	1027.34	997.80
85000	1393.19	1302.67	1231.82	1175.23	1129.31	1091.55	1060.17
90000	1475.15	1379.30	1304.28	1244.36	1195.74	1155.76	1122.53
95000	1557.10	1455.93	1376.74	1313.49	1262.17	1219.96	1184.89
100000	1639.05	1532.56	1449.20	1382.63	1328.60	1284.17	1247.25
105000	1721.00	1609.18	1521.66	1451.76	1395.03	1348.38	1309.62
110000	1802.96	1685.81	1594.12	1520.89	1461.46	1412.59	1371.98
120000	1966.86	1839.07	1739.04	1659.15	1594.32	1541.01	1496.70
130000	2130.77	1992.32	1883.96	1797.41	1727.18	1669.42	1621.43
140000	2294.67	2145.58	2028.88	1935.68	1860.04	1797.84	1746.16
150000	2458.58	2298.83	2173.80	2073.94	1992.89	1926.26	1870.88
160000	2622.48	2452.09	2318.72	2212.20	2125.75	2054.68	1995.61
170000	2786.39	2605.34	2463.64	2350.46	2258.61	2183.09	2120.33
180000	2950.29	2758.60	2608.56	2488.73	2391.47	2311.51	2245.06
190000	3114.20	2911.85	2753.48	2626.99	2524.33	2439.93	2369.78
200000	3278.10	3065.11	2898.40	2765.25	2657.19	2568.35	2494.51
210000	3442.01	3218.37	3043.32	2903.51	2790.05	2696.76	2619.23
220000	3605.91	3371.62	3188.24	3041.78	2922.91	2825.18	2743.96
230000	3769.82	3524.88	3333.16	3180.04	3055.77	2953.60	2868.68
240000	3933.72	3678.13	3478.08	3318.30	3188.63	3082.01	2993.41
250000	4097.63	3831.39	3623.00	3456.56	3321.49	3210.43	3118.13
260000	4261.53	3984.64	3767.92	3594.83	3454.35	3338.85	3242.86
270000	4425.44	4137.90	3912.84	3733.09	3587.21	3467.27	3367.59
280000	4589.34	4291.15	4057.76	3871.35	3720.07	3595.68	3492.31
290000	4753.25	4444.41	4202.68	4009.62	3852.93	3724.10	3617.04
300000	4917.15	4597.67	4347.60	4147.88	3985.79	3852.52	3741.76
310000	5081.06	4750.92	4492.52	4286.14	4118.65	3980.94	3866.49
320000	5244.96	4904.18	4637.44	4424.40	4251.51	4109.35	3991.21
330000	5408.87	5057.43	4782.36	4562.67	4384.37	4237.77	4115.94
340000	5572.77	5210.69	4927.28	4700.93	4517.23	4366.19	4240.66
350000	5736.68	5363.94	5072.20	4839.19	4650.09	4494.60	4365.39
400000	6556.21	6130.22	5796.79	5530.50	5314.39	5136.69	4989.02
450000	7375.73	6896.50	6521.39	6221.82	5978.68	5778.78	5612.64
500000	8195.26	7662.78	7245.99	6913.13	6642.98	6420.86	6236.27
550000	9014.78	8429.05	7970.59	7604.44	7307.28	7062.95	6859.90
600000	9834.31	9195.33	8695.19	8295.76	7971.58	7705.04	7483.52

12¼%

Monthly Payments
necessary to amortize a loan

AMOUNT	15 YEARS	16 YEARS	17 YEARS	18 YEARS	19 YEARS	20 YEARS	21 YEARS
100	1.22	1.19	1.17	1.15	1.13	1.12	1.11
200	2.43	2.38	2.34	2.30	2.27	2.24	2.21
500	6.08	5.95	5.84	5.74	5.66	5.59	5.53
1000	12.16	11.90	11.68	11.49	11.33	11.19	11.06
2000	24.33	23.80	23.36	22.98	22.65	22.37	22.13
5000	60.81	59.51	58.40	57.45	56.63	55.93	55.32
6000	72.98	71.41	70.08	68.94	67.96	67.11	66.38
7000	85.14	83.31	81.75	80.42	79.28	78.30	77.45
8000	97.30	95.21	93.43	91.91	90.61	89.49	88.51
9000	109.47	107.11	105.11	103.40	101.94	100.67	99.58
10000	121.63	119.02	116.79	114.89	113.26	111.86	110.64
15000	182.44	178.52	175.19	172.34	169.89	167.78	165.96
20000	243.26	238.03	233.58	229.79	226.52	223.71	221.28
25000	304.07	297.54	291.98	287.23	283.15	279.64	276.60
30000	364.89	357.05	350.38	344.68	339.79	335.57	331.92
35000	425.70	416.55	408.77	402.12	396.42	391.50	387.24
40000	486.52	476.06	467.17	459.57	453.05	447.43	442.56
45000	547.33	535.57	525.57	517.02	509.68	503.35	497.88
50000	608.15	595.08	583.96	574.46	566.31	559.28	553.21
55000	668.96	654.58	642.36	631.91	622.94	615.21	608.53
60000	729.78	714.09	700.75	689.36	679.57	671.14	663.85
65000	790.59	773.60	759.15	746.80	736.20	727.07	719.17
70000	851.41	833.11	817.55	804.25	792.83	783.00	774.49
75000	912.22	892.61	875.94	861.70	849.46	838.92	829.81
80000	973.04	952.12	934.34	919.14	906.10	894.85	885.13
85000	1033.85	1011.63	992.73	976.59	962.73	950.78	940.45
90000	1094.67	1071.14	1051.13	1034.03	1019.36	1006.71	995.77
95000	1155.48	1130.64	1109.53	1091.48	1075.99	1062.64	1051.09
100000	1216.30	1190.15	1167.92	1148.93	1132.62	1118.56	1106.41
105000	1277.11	1249.66	1226.32	1206.37	1189.25	1174.49	1161.73
110000	1337.93	1309.17	1284.71	1263.82	1245.88	1230.42	1217.05
120000	1459.56	1428.18	1401.51	1378.71	1359.14	1342.28	1327.69
130000	1581.19	1547.20	1518.30	1493.61	1472.41	1454.13	1438.33
140000	1702.82	1666.21	1635.09	1608.50	1585.67	1565.99	1548.97
150000	1824.45	1785.23	1751.89	1723.39	1698.93	1677.85	1659.62
160000	1946.08	1904.24	1868.68	1838.28	1812.19	1789.70	1770.26
170000	2067.71	2023.26	1985.47	1953.18	1925.45	1901.56	1880.90
180000	2189.34	2142.27	2102.26	2068.07	2038.72	2013.42	1991.54
190000	2310.97	2261.29	2219.05	2182.96	2151.98	2125.27	2102.18
200000	2432.60	2380.30	2335.85	2297.85	2265.24	2237.13	2212.82
210000	2554.23	2499.32	2452.64	2412.75	2378.50	2348.99	2323.46
220000	2675.86	2618.33	2569.43	2527.64	2491.76	2460.84	2434.10
230000	2797.49	2737.35	2686.22	2642.53	2605.02	2572.70	2544.74
240000	2919.12	2856.36	2803.01	2757.43	2718.29	2684.56	2655.39
250000	3040.75	2975.38	2919.80	2872.32	2831.55	2796.41	2766.03
260000	3162.38	3094.39	3036.60	2987.21	2944.81	2908.27	2876.67
270000	3284.01	3213.41	3153.39	3102.10	3058.07	3020.12	2987.31
280000	3405.64	3332.42	3270.18	3217.00	3171.33	3131.98	3097.95
290000	3527.27	3451.44	3386.98	3331.89	3284.60	3243.84	3208.59
300000	3648.90	3570.45	3503.77	3446.78	3397.86	3355.69	3319.23
310000	3770.53	3689.47	3620.56	3561.67	3511.12	3467.55	3429.87
320000	3892.16	3808.48	3737.35	3676.57	3624.38	3579.41	3540.51
330000	4013.79	3927.50	3854.14	3791.46	3737.64	3691.26	3651.15
340000	4135.42	4046.51	3970.94	3906.35	3850.91	3803.12	3761.80
350000	4257.05	4165.53	4087.73	4021.24	3964.17	3914.98	3872.44
400000	4865.19	4760.60	4671.69	4595.71	4530.48	4474.26	4425.64
450000	5473.34	5355.68	5255.65	5170.17	5096.79	5033.54	4978.85
500000	6081.49	5950.75	5839.61	5744.64	5663.10	5592.82	5532.05
550000	6689.64	6545.83	6423.57	6319.10	6229.41	6152.11	6085.26
600000	7297.79	7140.90	7007.54	6893.56	6795.72	6711.39	6638.46

Monthly Payments 12¹/₄%

necessary to amortize a loan

AMOUNT	22 YEARS	23 YEARS	24 YEARS	25 YEARS	30 YEARS	35 YEARS	40 YEARS
100	1.10	1.09	1.08	1.07	1.05	1.04	1.03
200	2.19	2.17	2.16	2.14	2.10	2.07	2.06
500	5.48	5.43	5.39	5.36	5.24	5.18	5.14
1000	10.96	10.87	10.79	10.72	10.48	10.35	10.29
2000	21.92	21.73	21.57	21.43	20.96	20.71	20.57
5000	54.79	54.34	53.94	53.59	52.39	51.77	51.43
6000	65.75	65.20	64.72	64.30	62.87	62.12	61.72
7000	76.71	76.07	75.51	75.02	73.35	72.48	72.01
8000	87.67	86.94	86.30	85.74	83.83	82.83	82.29
9000	98.63	97.80	97.08	96.46	94.31	93.18	92.58
10000	109.59	108.67	107.87	107.17	104.79	103.54	102.87
15000	164.38	163.01	161.81	160.76	157.18	155.31	154.30
20000	219.17	217.34	215.74	214.35	209.58	207.07	205.74
25000	273.97	271.68	269.68	267.94	261.97	258.84	257.17
30000	328.76	326.01	323.62	321.52	314.37	310.61	308.61
35000	383.55	380.35	377.55	375.11	366.76	362.38	360.04
40000	438.35	434.68	431.49	428.70	419.16	414.15	411.47
45000	493.14	489.02	485.42	482.28	471.55	465.92	462.91
50000	547.93	543.35	539.36	535.87	523.95	517.69	514.34
55000	602.73	597.69	593.29	589.46	576.34	569.45	565.78
60000	657.52	652.02	647.23	643.05	628.74	621.22	617.21
65000	712.31	706.36	701.17	696.63	681.13	672.99	668.65
70000	767.11	760.69	755.10	750.22	733.53	724.76	720.08
75000	821.90	815.03	809.04	803.81	785.92	776.53	771.51
80000	876.70	869.36	862.97	857.40	838.32	828.30	822.95
85000	931.49	923.70	916.91	910.98	890.71	880.07	874.38
90000	986.28	978.03	970.85	964.57	943.11	931.83	925.82
95000	1041.08	1032.37	1024.78	1018.16	995.50	983.60	977.25
100000	1095.87	1086.70	1078.72	1071.74	1047.90	1035.37	1028.69
105000	1150.66	1141.04	1132.65	1125.33	1100.29	1087.14	1080.12
110000	1205.46	1195.37	1186.59	1178.92	1152.69	1138.91	1131.55
120000	1315.04	1304.04	1294.46	1286.09	1257.48	1242.45	1234.42
130000	1424.63	1412.71	1402.33	1393.27	1362.27	1345.98	1337.29
140000	1534.22	1521.39	1510.20	1500.44	1467.06	1449.52	1440.16
150000	1643.80	1630.06	1618.08	1607.62	1571.84	1553.06	1543.03
160000	1753.39	1738.73	1725.95	1714.79	1676.63	1656.59	1645.90
170000	1862.98	1847.40	1833.82	1821.96	1781.42	1760.13	1748.77
180000	1972.56	1956.07	1941.69	1929.14	1886.21	1863.67	1851.64
190000	2082.15	2064.74	2049.56	2036.31	1991.00	1967.21	1954.50
200000	2191.74	2173.41	2157.43	2143.49	2095.79	2070.74	2057.37
210000	2301.33	2282.08	2265.31	2250.66	2200.58	2174.28	2160.24
220000	2410.91	2390.75	2373.18	2357.84	2305.37	2277.82	2263.11
230000	2520.50	2499.42	2481.05	2465.01	2410.16	2381.35	2365.98
240000	2630.09	2608.09	2588.92	2572.19	2514.95	2484.89	2468.85
250000	2739.67	2716.76	2696.79	2679.36	2619.74	2588.43	2571.72
260000	2849.26	2825.43	2804.66	2786.53	2724.53	2691.96	2674.58
270000	2958.85	2934.10	2912.54	2893.71	2829.32	2795.50	2777.45
280000	3068.43	3042.77	3020.41	3000.88	2934.11	2899.04	2880.32
290000	3178.02	3151.44	3128.28	3108.06	3038.90	3002.58	2983.19
300000	3287.61	3260.11	3236.15	3215.23	3143.69	3106.11	3086.06
310000	3397.19	3368.78	3344.02	3322.41	3248.48	3209.65	3188.93
320000	3506.78	3477.45	3451.89	3429.58	3353.27	3313.19	3291.80
330000	3616.37	3586.12	3559.77	3536.75	3458.06	3416.72	3394.66
340000	3725.96	3694.79	3667.64	3643.93	3562.85	3520.26	3497.53
350000	3835.54	3803.46	3775.51	3751.10	3667.64	3623.80	3600.40
400000	4383.48	4346.81	4314.87	4286.98	4191.59	4141.48	4114.74
450000	4931.41	4890.17	4854.23	4822.85	4715.53	4659.17	4629.09
500000	5479.35	5433.52	5393.58	5358.72	5239.48	5176.86	5143.43
550000	6027.28	5976.87	5932.94	5894.59	5763.43	5694.54	5657.77
600000	6575.22	6520.22	6472.30	6430.46	6287.38	6212.23	6172.12

12½%

Monthly Payments
necessary to amortize a loan

AMOUNT	1 YEAR	2 YEARS	3 YEARS	4 YEARS	5 YEARS	6 YEARS	7 YEARS
100	8.91	4.73	3.35	2.66	2.25	1.98	1.79
200	17.82	9.46	6.69	5.32	4.50	3.96	3.58
500	44.54	23.65	16.73	13.29	11.25	9.91	8.96
1000	89.08	47.31	33.45	26.58	22.50	19.81	17.92
2000	178.17	94.61	66.91	53.16	45.00	39.62	35.84
5000	445.41	236.54	167.27	132.90	112.49	99.06	89.61
6000	534.50	283.84	200.72	159.48	134.99	118.87	107.53
7000	623.58	331.15	234.18	186.06	157.49	138.68	125.45
8000	712.66	378.46	267.63	212.64	179.98	158.49	143.37
9000	801.75	425.77	301.08	239.22	202.48	178.30	161.29
10000	890.83	473.07	334.54	265.80	224.98	198.11	179.21
15000	1336.24	709.61	501.80	398.70	337.47	297.17	268.82
20000	1781.66	946.15	669.07	531.60	449.96	396.22	358.42
25000	2227.07	1182.68	836.34	664.50	562.45	495.28	448.03
30000	2672.49	1419.22	1003.61	797.40	674.94	594.34	537.64
35000	3117.90	1655.76	1170.88	930.30	787.43	693.39	627.24
40000	3563.31	1892.29	1338.15	1063.20	899.92	792.45	716.85
45000	4008.73	2128.83	1505.41	1196.10	1012.41	891.50	806.46
50000	4454.14	2365.37	1672.68	1329.00	1124.90	990.56	896.06
55000	4899.56	2601.90	1839.95	1461.90	1237.39	1089.61	985.67
60000	5344.97	2838.44	2007.22	1594.80	1349.88	1188.67	1075.27
65000	5790.39	3074.98	2174.49	1727.70	1462.37	1287.73	1164.88
70000	6235.80	3311.51	2341.75	1860.60	1574.86	1386.78	1254.49
75000	6681.21	3548.05	2509.02	1993.50	1687.35	1485.84	1344.09
80000	7126.63	3784.58	2676.29	2126.40	1799.84	1584.89	1433.70
85000	7572.04	4021.12	2843.56	2259.30	1912.32	1683.95	1523.31
90000	8017.46	4257.66	3010.83	2392.20	2024.81	1783.01	1612.91
95000	8462.87	4494.19	3178.09	2525.10	2137.30	1882.06	1702.52
100000	8908.29	4730.73	3345.36	2658.00	2249.79	1981.12	1792.12
105000	9353.70	4967.27	3512.63	2790.90	2362.28	2080.17	1881.73
110000	9799.11	5203.80	3679.90	2923.80	2474.77	2179.23	1971.34
120000	10689.94	5676.88	4014.44	3189.60	2699.75	2377.34	2150.55
130000	11580.77	6149.95	4348.97	3455.40	2924.73	2575.45	2329.76
140000	12471.60	6623.02	4683.51	3721.20	3149.71	2773.57	2508.97
150000	13362.43	7096.10	5018.04	3987.00	3374.69	2971.68	2688.19
160000	14253.26	7569.17	5352.58	4252.80	3599.67	3169.79	2867.40
170000	15144.09	8042.24	5687.12	4518.60	3824.65	3367.90	3046.61
180000	16034.92	8515.32	6021.65	4784.40	4049.63	3566.01	3225.82
190000	16925.74	8988.39	6356.19	5050.20	4274.61	3764.12	3405.04
200000	17816.57	9461.46	6690.73	5316.00	4499.59	3962.24	3584.25
210000	18707.40	9934.53	7025.26	5581.80	4724.57	4160.35	3763.46
220000	19598.23	10407.61	7359.80	5847.60	4949.55	4358.46	3942.67
230000	20489.06	10880.68	7694.33	6113.40	5174.53	4556.57	4121.88
240000	21379.89	11353.75	8028.87	6379.20	5399.51	4754.68	4301.10
250000	22270.72	11826.83	8363.41	6645.00	5624.48	4952.79	4480.31
260000	23161.54	12299.90	8697.94	6910.80	5849.46	5150.91	4659.52
270000	24052.37	12772.97	9032.48	7176.60	6074.44	5349.02	4838.73
280000	24943.20	13246.05	9367.02	7442.40	6299.42	5547.13	5017.95
290000	25834.03	13719.12	9701.55	7708.20	6524.40	5745.24	5197.16
300000	26724.86	14192.19	10036.09	7974.00	6749.38	5943.35	5376.37
310000	27615.69	14665.27	10370.62	8239.80	6974.36	6141.47	5555.58
320000	28506.52	15138.34	10705.16	8505.60	7199.34	6339.58	5734.80
330000	29397.34	15611.41	11039.70	8771.40	7424.32	6537.69	5914.01
340000	30288.17	16084.48	11374.23	9037.20	7649.30	6735.80	6093.22
350000	31179.00	16557.56	11708.77	9303.00	7874.28	6933.91	6272.43
400000	35633.15	18922.92	13381.45	10632.00	8999.18	7924.47	7168.50
450000	40087.29	21288.29	15054.13	11961.00	10124.07	8915.03	8064.56
500000	44541.43	23653.65	16726.81	13290.00	11248.97	9905.59	8960.62
550000	48995.57	26019.02	18399.49	14619.00	12373.87	10896.15	9856.68
600000	53449.72	28384.38	20072.18	15948.00	13498.76	11886.71	10752.74

Monthly Payments 12½%
necessary to amortize a loan

AMOUNT	8 YEARS	9 YEARS	10 YEARS	11 YEARS	12 YEARS	13 YEARS	14 YEARS
100	1.65	1.55	1.46	1.40	1.34	1.30	1.26
200	3.31	3.09	2.93	2.80	2.69	2.60	2.53
500	8.26	7.73	7.32	6.99	6.72	6.50	6.32
1000	16.53	15.47	14.64	13.98	13.44	13.00	12.63
2000	33.06	30.94	29.28	27.95	26.88	26.00	25.26
5000	82.64	77.34	73.19	69.88	67.19	64.99	63.16
6000	99.17	92.81	87.83	83.85	80.63	77.99	75.79
7000	115.70	108.27	102.46	97.83	94.07	90.98	88.42
8000	132.23	123.74	117.10	111.80	107.51	103.98	101.05
9000	148.76	139.21	131.74	125.78	120.95	116.98	113.69
10000	165.29	154.68	146.38	139.75	134.39	129.98	126.32
15000	247.93	232.01	219.56	209.63	201.58	194.96	189.48
20000	330.58	309.35	292.75	279.51	268.77	259.95	252.63
25000	413.22	386.69	365.94	349.39	335.96	324.94	315.79
30000	495.86	464.03	439.13	419.26	403.16	389.93	378.95
35000	578.51	541.36	512.32	489.14	470.35	454.92	442.11
40000	661.15	618.70	585.50	559.02	537.54	519.91	505.27
45000	743.80	696.04	658.69	628.89	604.74	584.89	568.43
50000	826.44	773.38	731.88	698.77	671.93	649.88	631.58
55000	909.08	850.72	805.07	768.65	739.12	714.87	694.74
60000	991.73	928.05	878.26	838.53	806.31	779.86	757.90
65000	1074.37	1005.39	951.45	908.40	873.51	844.85	821.06
70000	1157.02	1082.73	1024.63	978.28	940.70	909.84	884.22
75000	1239.66	1160.07	1097.82	1048.16	1007.89	974.82	947.38
80000	1322.30	1237.40	1171.01	1118.03	1075.08	1039.81	1010.53
85000	1404.95	1314.74	1244.20	1187.91	1142.28	1104.80	1073.69
90000	1487.59	1392.08	1317.39	1257.79	1209.47	1169.79	1136.85
95000	1570.24	1469.42	1390.57	1327.67	1276.66	1234.78	1200.01
100000	1652.88	1546.76	1463.76	1397.54	1343.86	1299.77	1263.17
105000	1735.52	1624.09	1536.95	1467.42	1411.05	1364.75	1326.33
110000	1818.17	1701.43	1610.14	1537.30	1478.24	1429.74	1389.49
120000	1983.46	1856.11	1756.51	1677.05	1612.63	1559.72	1515.80
130000	2148.75	2010.78	1902.89	1816.81	1747.01	1689.70	1642.12
140000	2314.03	2165.46	2049.27	1956.56	1881.40	1819.67	1768.44
150000	2479.32	2320.13	2195.64	2096.31	2015.79	1949.65	1894.75
160000	2644.61	2474.81	2342.02	2236.07	2150.17	2079.63	2021.07
170000	2809.90	2629.48	2488.39	2375.82	2284.56	2209.60	2147.39
180000	2975.19	2784.16	2634.77	2515.58	2418.94	2339.58	2273.70
190000	3140.47	2938.83	2781.15	2655.33	2553.33	2469.56	2400.02
200000	3305.76	3093.51	2927.52	2795.09	2687.71	2599.53	2526.34
210000	3471.05	3248.19	3073.90	2934.84	2822.10	2729.51	2652.65
220000	3636.34	3402.86	3220.28	3074.59	2956.49	2859.49	2778.97
230000	3801.63	3557.54	3366.65	3214.35	3090.87	2989.46	2905.29
240000	3966.91	3712.21	3513.03	3354.10	3225.26	3119.44	3031.60
250000	4132.20	3866.89	3659.40	3493.86	3359.64	3249.42	3157.92
260000	4297.49	4021.56	3805.78	3633.61	3494.03	3379.39	3284.24
270000	4462.78	4176.24	3952.16	3773.37	3628.41	3509.37	3410.55
280000	4628.07	4330.91	4098.53	3913.12	3762.80	3639.35	3536.87
290000	4793.35	4485.59	4244.91	4052.87	3897.19	3769.32	3663.19
300000	4958.64	4640.27	4391.29	4192.63	4031.57	3899.30	3789.51
310000	5123.93	4794.94	4537.66	4332.38	4165.96	4029.27	3915.82
320000	5289.22	4949.62	4684.04	4472.14	4300.34	4159.25	4042.14
330000	5454.51	5104.29	4830.41	4611.89	4434.73	4289.23	4168.46
340000	5619.79	5258.97	4976.79	4751.65	4569.11	4419.20	4294.77
350000	5785.08	5413.64	5123.17	4891.40	4703.50	4549.18	4421.09
400000	6611.52	6187.02	5855.05	5590.17	5375.43	5199.06	5052.67
450000	7437.96	6960.40	6586.93	6288.94	6047.36	5848.95	5684.26
500000	8264.40	7733.78	7318.81	6987.71	6719.29	6498.83	6315.84
550000	9090.84	8507.15	8050.69	7686.49	7391.22	7148.71	6947.43
600000	9917.29	9280.53	8782.57	8385.26	8063.14	7798.60	7579.01

12¹/₂% Monthly Payments
necessary to amortize a loan

AMOUNT	15 YEARS	16 YEARS	17 YEARS	18 YEARS	19 YEARS	20 YEARS	21 YEARS
100	1.23	1.21	1.18	1.17	1.15	1.14	1.12
200	2.47	2.41	2.37	2.33	2.30	2.27	2.25
500	6.16	6.03	5.92	5.83	5.75	5.68	5.62
1000	12.33	12.07	11.85	11.66	11.50	11.36	11.24
2000	24.65	24.13	23.69	23.32	23.00	22.72	22.48
5000	61.63	60.33	59.24	58.30	57.50	56.81	56.21
6000	73.95	72.40	71.08	69.96	69.00	68.17	67.45
7000	86.28	84.47	82.93	81.62	80.50	79.53	78.70
8000	98.60	96.53	94.78	93.28	92.00	90.89	89.94
9000	110.93	108.60	106.63	104.94	103.50	102.25	101.18
10000	123.25	120.67	118.47	116.60	115.00	113.61	112.42
15000	184.88	181.00	177.71	174.90	172.49	170.42	168.63
20000	246.50	241.33	236.95	233.20	229.99	227.23	224.84
25000	308.13	301.67	296.18	291.50	287.49	284.04	281.05
30000	369.76	362.00	355.42	349.80	344.99	340.84	337.27
35000	431.38	422.33	414.65	408.10	402.48	397.65	393.48
40000	493.01	482.67	473.89	466.40	459.98	454.46	449.69
45000	554.63	543.00	533.13	524.70	517.48	511.26	505.90
50000	616.26	603.33	592.36	583.00	574.98	568.07	562.11
55000	677.89	663.67	651.60	641.30	632.47	624.88	618.32
60000	739.51	724.00	710.84	699.60	689.97	681.68	674.53
65000	801.14	784.34	770.07	757.90	747.47	738.49	730.74
70000	862.77	844.67	829.31	816.20	804.97	795.30	786.95
75000	924.39	905.00	888.54	874.50	862.46	852.11	843.16
80000	986.02	965.34	947.78	932.80	919.96	908.91	899.37
85000	1047.64	1025.67	1007.02	991.10	977.46	965.72	955.59
90000	1109.27	1086.00	1066.25	1049.40	1034.96	1022.53	1011.80
95000	1170.90	1146.34	1125.49	1107.70	1092.45	1079.33	1068.01
100000	1232.52	1206.67	1184.73	1166.00	1149.95	1136.14	1124.22
105000	1294.15	1267.00	1243.96	1224.30	1207.45	1192.95	1180.43
110000	1355.77	1327.34	1303.20	1282.60	1264.95	1249.75	1236.64
120000	1479.03	1448.00	1421.67	1399.20	1379.94	1363.37	1349.06
130000	1602.28	1568.67	1540.14	1515.80	1494.94	1476.98	1461.48
140000	1725.53	1689.34	1658.62	1632.40	1609.93	1590.60	1573.91
150000	1848.78	1810.00	1777.09	1749.00	1724.93	1704.21	1686.33
160000	1972.04	1930.67	1895.56	1865.60	1839.92	1817.82	1798.75
170000	2095.29	2051.34	2014.03	1982.20	1954.92	1931.44	1911.17
180000	2218.54	2172.01	2132.51	2098.80	2069.91	2045.05	2023.59
190000	2341.79	2292.67	2250.98	2215.40	2184.91	2158.67	2136.01
200000	2465.04	2413.34	2369.45	2332.00	2299.90	2272.28	2248.44
210000	2588.30	2534.01	2487.92	2448.60	2414.90	2385.90	2360.86
220000	2711.55	2654.67	2606.40	2565.20	2529.89	2499.51	2473.28
230000	2834.80	2775.34	2724.87	2681.80	2644.89	2613.12	2585.70
240000	2958.05	2896.01	2843.34	2798.40	2759.88	2726.74	2698.12
250000	3081.31	3016.67	2961.81	2915.00	2874.88	2840.35	2810.55
260000	3204.56	3137.34	3080.29	3031.60	2989.87	2953.97	2922.97
270000	3327.81	3258.01	3198.76	3148.20	3104.87	3067.58	3035.39
280000	3451.06	3378.68	3317.23	3264.80	3219.86	3181.19	3147.81
290000	3574.31	3499.34	3435.70	3381.40	3334.86	3294.81	3260.23
300000	3697.57	3620.01	3554.18	3498.00	3449.85	3408.42	3372.65
310000	3820.82	3740.68	3672.65	3614.60	3564.85	3522.04	3485.08
320000	3944.07	3861.34	3791.12	3731.20	3679.84	3635.65	3597.50
330000	4067.32	3982.01	3909.60	3847.80	3794.84	3749.26	3709.92
340000	4190.58	4102.68	4028.07	3964.40	3909.83	3862.88	3822.34
350000	4313.83	4223.34	4146.54	4081.00	4024.83	3976.49	3934.76
400000	4930.09	4826.68	4738.90	4664.00	4599.80	4544.56	4496.87
450000	5546.35	5430.01	5331.27	5247.00	5174.78	5112.63	5058.98
500000	6162.61	6033.35	5923.63	5830.00	5749.75	5680.70	5621.09
550000	6778.87	6636.68	6515.99	6413.00	6324.73	6248.77	6183.20
600000	7395.13	7240.02	7108.35	6996.01	6899.71	6816.84	6745.31

Monthly Payments   12¹/₂%
necessary to amortize a loan

AMOUNT	22 YEARS	23 YEARS	24 YEARS	25 YEARS	30 YEARS	35 YEARS	40 YEARS
100	1.11	1.10	1.10	1.09	1.07	1.06	1.05
200	2.23	2.21	2.19	2.18	2.13	2.11	2.10
500	5.57	5.52	5.49	5.45	5.34	5.28	5.24
1000	11.14	11.05	10.97	10.90	10.67	10.55	10.49
2000	22.28	22.10	21.94	21.81	21.35	21.11	20.98
5000	55.69	55.25	54.86	54.52	53.36	52.76	52.45
6000	66.83	66.30	65.83	65.42	64.04	63.32	62.94
7000	77.97	77.35	76.80	76.32	74.71	73.87	73.42
8000	89.11	88.39	87.77	87.23	85.38	84.42	83.91
9000	100.25	99.44	98.74	98.13	96.05	94.97	94.40
10000	111.39	110.49	109.71	109.04	106.73	105.53	104.89
15000	167.08	165.74	164.57	163.55	160.09	158.29	157.34
20000	222.78	220.99	219.43	218.07	213.45	211.05	209.78
25000	278.47	276.23	274.29	272.59	266.81	263.81	262.23
30000	334.17	331.48	329.14	327.11	320.18	316.58	314.68
35000	389.86	386.73	384.00	381.62	373.54	369.34	367.12
40000	445.56	441.97	438.86	436.14	426.90	422.10	419.57
45000	501.25	497.22	493.72	490.66	480.27	474.86	472.01
50000	556.95	552.47	548.57	545.18	533.63	527.63	524.46
55000	612.64	607.72	603.43	599.69	586.99	580.39	576.91
60000	668.34	662.96	658.29	654.21	640.35	633.15	629.35
65000	724.03	718.21	713.14	708.73	693.72	685.92	681.80
70000	779.73	773.46	768.00	763.25	747.08	738.68	734.24
75000	835.42	828.70	822.86	817.77	800.44	791.44	786.69
80000	891.12	883.95	877.72	872.28	853.81	844.20	839.14
85000	946.81	939.20	932.57	926.80	907.17	896.97	891.58
90000	1002.51	994.44	987.43	981.32	960.53	949.73	944.03
95000	1058.20	1049.69	1042.29	1035.84	1013.89	1002.49	996.47
100000	1113.90	1104.94	1097.14	1090.35	1067.26	1055.25	1048.92
105000	1169.59	1160.18	1152.00	1144.87	1120.62	1108.02	1101.37
110000	1225.29	1215.43	1206.86	1199.39	1173.98	1160.78	1153.81
120000	1336.67	1325.92	1316.57	1308.42	1280.71	1266.31	1258.70
130000	1448.06	1436.42	1426.29	1417.46	1387.44	1371.83	1363.60
140000	1559.45	1546.91	1536.00	1526.50	1494.16	1477.36	1468.49
150000	1670.84	1657.41	1645.72	1635.53	1600.89	1582.88	1573.38
160000	1782.23	1767.90	1755.43	1744.57	1707.61	1688.41	1678.27
170000	1893.62	1878.39	1865.15	1853.60	1814.34	1793.93	1783.16
180000	2005.01	1988.89	1974.86	1962.64	1921.06	1899.46	1888.05
190000	2116.40	2099.38	2084.57	2071.67	2027.79	2004.98	1992.95
200000	2227.79	2209.87	2194.29	2180.71	2134.52	2110.51	2097.84
210000	2339.18	2320.37	2304.00	2289.74	2241.24	2216.03	2202.73
220000	2450.57	2430.86	2413.72	2398.78	2347.97	2321.56	2307.62
230000	2561.96	2541.35	2523.43	2507.81	2454.69	2427.09	2412.51
240000	2673.35	2651.85	2633.15	2616.85	2561.42	2532.61	2517.41
250000	2784.74	2762.34	2742.86	2725.89	2668.14	2638.14	2622.30
260000	2896.13	2872.84	2852.58	2834.92	2774.87	2743.66	2727.19
270000	3007.52	2983.33	2962.29	2943.96	2881.60	2849.19	2832.08
280000	3118.91	3093.82	3072.00	3052.99	2988.32	2954.71	2936.97
290000	3230.30	3204.32	3181.72	3162.03	3095.05	3060.24	3041.87
300000	3341.69	3314.81	3291.43	3271.06	3201.77	3165.76	3146.76
310000	3453.08	3425.30	3401.15	3380.10	3308.50	3271.29	3251.65
320000	3564.47	3535.80	3510.86	3489.13	3415.22	3376.81	3356.54
330000	3675.86	3646.29	3620.58	3598.17	3521.95	3482.34	3461.43
340000	3787.25	3756.79	3730.29	3707.20	3628.68	3587.86	3566.33
350000	3898.64	3867.28	3840.01	3816.24	3735.40	3693.39	3671.22
400000	4455.58	4419.75	4388.58	4361.42	4269.03	4221.02	4195.68
450000	5012.53	4972.22	4937.15	4906.59	4802.66	4748.64	4720.14
500000	5569.48	5524.68	5485.72	5451.77	5336.29	5276.27	5244.60
550000	6126.43	6077.15	6034.29	5996.95	5869.92	5803.90	5769.06
600000	6683.37	6629.62	6582.87	6542.12	6403.55	6331.53	6293.52

12³/₄%   **Monthly Payments**
necessary to amortize a loan

AMOUNT	1 YEAR	2 YEARS	3 YEARS	4 YEARS	5 YEARS	6 YEARS	7 YEARS
100	8.92	4.74	3.36	2.67	2.26	1.99	1.81
200	17.84	9.48	6.71	5.34	4.53	3.99	3.61
500	44.60	23.71	16.79	13.35	11.31	9.97	9.03
1000	89.20	47.42	33.57	26.70	22.63	19.94	18.06
2000	178.40	94.85	67.15	53.41	45.25	39.88	36.11
5000	446.00	237.12	167.87	133.52	113.13	99.71	90.28
6000	535.20	284.55	201.44	160.22	135.75	119.65	108.34
7000	624.40	331.97	235.02	186.93	158.38	139.60	126.39
8000	713.60	379.40	268.59	213.63	181.00	159.54	144.45
9000	802.80	426.82	302.16	240.33	203.63	179.48	162.51
10000	892.00	474.24	335.74	267.04	226.25	199.42	180.56
15000	1338.00	711.37	503.60	400.55	339.38	299.14	270.84
20000	1784.00	948.49	671.47	534.07	452.51	398.85	361.13
25000	2230.00	1185.61	839.34	667.59	565.63	498.56	451.41
30000	2676.00	1422.73	1007.21	801.11	678.76	598.27	541.69
35000	3122.00	1659.86	1175.08	934.63	791.89	697.98	631.97
40000	3568.00	1896.98	1342.95	1068.14	905.01	797.70	722.25
45000	4014.00	2134.10	1510.81	1201.66	1018.14	897.41	812.53
50000	4460.00	2371.22	1678.68	1335.18	1131.27	997.12	902.82
55000	4906.00	2608.35	1846.55	1468.70	1244.39	1096.83	993.10
60000	5352.00	2845.47	2014.42	1602.21	1357.52	1196.54	1083.38
65000	5798.00	3082.59	2182.29	1735.73	1470.64	1296.26	1173.66
70000	6244.00	3319.71	2350.16	1869.25	1583.77	1395.97	1263.94
75000	6690.00	3556.84	2518.02	2002.77	1696.90	1495.68	1354.22
80000	7136.00	3793.96	2685.89	2136.29	1810.02	1595.39	1444.51
85000	7582.00	4031.08	2853.76	2269.80	1923.15	1695.10	1534.79
90000	8028.00	4268.20	3021.63	2403.32	2036.28	1794.82	1625.07
95000	8474.00	4505.33	3189.50	2536.84	2149.40	1894.53	1715.35
100000	8920.00	4742.45	3357.37	2670.36	2262.53	1994.24	1805.63
105000	9366.00	4979.57	3525.23	2803.88	2375.66	2093.95	1895.91
110000	9812.00	5216.69	3693.10	2937.39	2488.78	2193.66	1986.20
120000	10704.00	5690.94	4028.84	3204.43	2715.04	2393.09	2166.76
130000	11596.00	6165.18	4364.58	3471.47	2941.29	2592.51	2347.32
140000	12488.00	6639.43	4700.31	3738.50	3167.54	2791.94	2527.89
150000	13380.00	7113.67	5036.05	4005.54	3393.80	2991.36	2708.45
160000	14272.00	7587.92	5371.79	4272.57	3620.05	3190.78	2889.01
170000	15164.00	8062.16	5707.52	4539.61	3846.30	3390.21	3069.58
180000	16056.00	8536.41	6043.26	4806.64	4072.55	3589.63	3250.14
190000	16948.01	9010.65	6379.00	5073.68	4298.81	3789.06	3430.70
200000	17840.01	9484.90	6714.73	5340.72	4525.06	3988.48	3611.26
210000	18732.01	9959.14	7050.47	5607.75	4751.31	4187.90	3791.83
220000	19624.01	10433.39	7386.21	5874.79	4977.57	4387.33	3972.39
230000	20516.01	10907.63	7721.94	6141.82	5203.82	4586.75	4152.95
240000	21408.01	11381.88	8057.68	6408.86	5430.07	4786.18	4333.52
250000	22300.01	11856.12	8393.42	6675.90	5656.33	4985.60	4514.08
260000	23192.01	12330.36	8729.15	6942.93	5882.58	5185.02	4694.64
270000	24084.01	12804.61	9064.89	7209.97	6108.83	5384.45	4875.21
280000	24976.00	13278.85	9400.63	7477.00	6335.08	5583.87	5055.77
290000	25868.01	13753.10	9736.36	7744.04	6561.34	5783.30	5236.33
300000	26760.01	14227.34	10072.10	8011.07	6787.59	5982.72	5416.90
310000	27652.01	14701.59	10407.84	8278.11	7013.84	6182.14	5597.46
320000	28544.01	15175.83	10743.57	8545.15	7240.10	6381.57	5778.02
330000	29436.01	15650.08	11079.31	8812.18	7466.35	6580.99	5958.59
340000	30328.01	16124.32	11415.05	9079.22	7692.60	6780.42	6139.15
350000	31220.01	16598.57	11750.78	9346.25	7918.86	6979.84	6319.71
400000	35680.01	18969.79	13429.47	10681.43	9050.12	7976.96	7222.53
450000	40140.01	21341.02	15108.15	12016.61	10181.39	8974.08	8125.35
500000	44600.01	23712.24	16786.83	13351.79	11312.65	9971.20	9028.16
550000	49060.01	26083.46	18465.51	14686.97	12443.92	10968.32	9930.98
600000	53520.02	28454.69	20144.20	16022.15	13575.18	11965.44	10833.79

128

Monthly Payments 12¾%
necessary to amortize a loan

AMOUNT	8 YEARS	9 YEARS	10 YEARS	11 YEARS	12 YEARS	13 YEARS	14 YEARS
100	1.67	1.56	1.48	1.41	1.36	1.32	1.28
200	3.33	3.12	2.96	2.83	2.72	2.63	2.56
500	8.33	7.81	7.39	7.06	6.80	6.58	6.40
1000	16.67	15.61	14.78	14.13	13.59	13.15	12.79
2000	33.34	31.22	29.57	28.25	27.18	26.31	25.58
5000	83.34	78.05	73.92	70.63	67.96	65.77	63.96
6000	100.01	93.66	88.70	84.75	81.55	78.93	76.75
7000	116.67	109.27	103.49	98.88	95.14	92.08	89.54
8000	133.34	124.88	118.27	113.00	108.74	105.24	102.33
9000	150.01	140.49	133.06	127.13	122.33	118.39	115.13
10000	166.68	156.10	147.84	141.25	135.92	131.54	127.92
15000	250.02	234.13	221.76	211.88	203.88	197.32	191.88
20000	333.35	312.20	295.68	282.51	271.84	263.09	255.83
25000	416.69	390.26	369.60	353.13	339.80	328.86	319.79
30000	500.03	468.31	443.52	423.76	407.76	394.63	383.75
35000	583.37	546.36	517.44	494.39	475.72	460.41	447.71
40000	666.71	624.41	591.36	565.02	543.68	526.18	511.67
45000	750.05	702.46	665.28	635.64	611.64	591.95	575.63
50000	833.39	780.51	739.20	706.27	679.60	657.72	639.59
55000	916.72	858.56	813.12	776.90	747.56	723.50	703.54
60000	1000.06	936.61	887.04	847.52	815.52	789.27	767.50
65000	1083.40	1014.67	960.96	918.15	883.48	855.04	831.46
70000	1166.74	1092.72	1034.88	988.78	951.44	920.81	895.42
75000	1250.08	1170.77	1108.80	1059.40	1019.40	986.58	959.38
80000	1333.42	1248.82	1182.72	1130.03	1087.36	1052.36	1023.34
85000	1416.76	1326.87	1256.64	1200.66	1155.32	1118.13	1087.30
90000	1500.10	1404.92	1330.56	1271.28	1223.28	1183.90	1151.25
95000	1583.43	1482.97	1404.48	1341.91	1291.24	1249.67	1215.21
100000	1666.77	1561.02	1478.40	1412.54	1359.20	1315.45	1279.17
105000	1750.11	1639.07	1552.32	1483.16	1427.16	1381.22	1343.13
110000	1833.45	1717.13	1626.24	1553.79	1495.12	1446.99	1407.09
120000	2000.13	1873.23	1774.08	1695.05	1631.04	1578.53	1535.01
130000	2166.80	2029.33	1921.92	1836.30	1766.96	1710.08	1662.92
140000	2333.48	2185.43	2069.76	1977.55	1902.88	1841.62	1790.84
150000	2500.16	2341.53	2217.60	2118.81	2038.80	1973.17	1918.76
160000	2666.84	2497.64	2365.44	2260.06	2174.72	2104.71	2046.68
170000	2833.51	2653.74	2513.28	2401.31	2310.64	2236.26	2174.59
180000	3000.19	2809.84	2661.12	2542.57	2446.56	2367.80	2302.51
190000	3166.87	2965.94	2808.98	2683.82	2582.48	2499.35	2430.43
200000	3333.54	3122.05	2956.80	2825.08	2718.40	2630.89	2558.34
210000	3500.22	3278.15	3104.64	2966.33	2854.32	2762.44	2686.26
220000	3666.90	3434.25	3252.48	3107.58	2990.24	2893.98	2814.18
230000	3833.58	3590.35	3400.32	3248.84	3126.16	3025.52	2942.10
240000	4000.25	3746.46	3548.16	3390.09	3262.08	3157.07	3070.01
250000	4166.93	3902.56	3696.00	3531.35	3398.00	3288.61	3197.93
260000	4333.61	4058.66	3843.84	3672.60	3533.92	3420.16	3325.85
270000	4500.29	4214.76	3991.67	3813.85	3669.84	3551.70	3453.76
280000	4666.96	4370.86	4139.51	3955.11	3805.76	3683.25	3581.68
290000	4833.64	4526.97	4287.35	4096.36	3941.68	3814.79	3709.60
300000	5000.32	4683.07	4435.19	4237.61	4077.60	3946.34	3837.52
310000	5166.99	4839.17	4583.03	4378.87	4213.52	4077.88	3965.43
320000	5333.67	4995.27	4730.87	4520.12	4349.44	4209.43	4093.35
330000	5500.35	5151.38	4878.71	4661.38	4485.36	4340.97	4221.27
340000	5667.03	5307.48	5026.55	4802.63	4621.28	4472.51	4349.18
350000	5833.70	5463.58	5174.39	4943.88	4757.20	4604.06	4477.10
400000	6667.09	6244.09	5913.59	5650.15	5436.80	5261.78	5116.69
450000	7500.48	7024.60	6652.79	6356.42	6116.40	5919.51	5756.27
500000	8333.86	7805.12	7391.99	7062.69	6796.00	6577.23	6395.86
550000	9167.25	8585.63	8131.19	7768.96	7475.60	7234.95	7035.45
600000	10000.63	9366.14	8870.39	8475.23	8155.20	7892.67	7675.03

129

12³/₄%

Monthly Payments
necessary to amortize a loan

AMOUNT	15 YEARS	16 YEARS	17 YEARS	18 YEARS	19 YEARS	20 YEARS	21 YEARS
100	1.25	1.22	1.20	1.18	1.17	1.15	1.14
200	2.50	2.45	2.40	2.37	2.33	2.31	2.28
500	6.24	6.12	6.01	5.92	5.84	5.77	5.71
1000	12.49	12.23	12.02	11.83	11.67	11.54	11.42
2000	24.98	24.47	24.03	23.66	23.35	23.08	22.84
5000	62.44	61.16	60.08	59.16	58.37	57.69	57.11
6000	74.93	73.40	72.10	70.99	70.04	69.23	68.53
7000	87.42	85.63	84.11	82.82	81.72	80.77	79.95
8000	99.91	97.86	96.13	94.65	93.39	92.30	91.37
9000	112.40	110.10	108.15	106.49	105.06	103.84	102.79
10000	124.88	122.33	120.16	118.32	116.74	115.38	114.21
15000	187.33	183.49	180.24	177.48	175.11	173.07	171.32
20000	249.77	244.66	240.32	236.63	233.48	230.76	228.42
25000	312.21	305.82	300.41	295.79	291.84	288.45	285.53
30000	374.65	366.98	360.49	354.95	350.21	346.14	342.64
35000	437.09	428.15	420.57	414.11	408.58	403.83	399.74
40000	499.53	489.31	480.65	473.27	466.95	461.52	456.85
45000	561.98	550.48	540.73	532.43	525.32	519.22	513.95
50000	624.42	611.64	600.81	591.58	583.69	576.91	571.06
55000	686.86	672.81	660.89	650.74	642.06	634.60	628.17
60000	749.30	733.97	720.97	709.90	700.43	692.29	685.27
65000	811.74	795.13	781.06	769.06	758.80	749.98	742.38
70000	874.19	856.30	841.14	828.22	817.16	807.67	799.48
75000	936.63	917.46	901.22	887.38	875.53	865.36	856.59
80000	999.07	978.63	961.30	946.54	933.90	923.05	913.70
85000	1061.51	1039.79	1021.38	1005.69	992.27	980.74	970.80
90000	1123.95	1100.95	1081.46	1064.85	1050.64	1038.43	1027.91
95000	1186.40	1162.12	1141.54	1124.01	1109.01	1096.12	1085.01
100000	1248.84	1223.28	1201.62	1183.17	1167.38	1153.81	1142.12
105000	1311.28	1284.45	1261.70	1242.33	1225.75	1211.50	1199.23
110000	1373.72	1345.61	1321.79	1301.49	1284.12	1269.19	1256.33
120000	1498.60	1467.94	1441.95	1419.80	1400.85	1384.57	1370.54
130000	1623.49	1590.27	1562.11	1538.12	1517.59	1499.96	1484.76
140000	1748.37	1712.60	1682.27	1656.44	1634.33	1615.34	1598.97
150000	1873.26	1834.92	1802.44	1774.75	1751.07	1730.72	1713.18
160000	1998.14	1957.25	1922.60	1893.07	1867.80	1846.10	1827.39
170000	2123.02	2079.58	2042.76	2011.39	1984.54	1961.48	1941.60
180000	2247.91	2201.91	2162.92	2129.71	2101.28	2076.86	2055.82
190000	2372.79	2324.24	2283.08	2248.02	2218.02	2192.24	2170.03
200000	2497.67	2446.57	2403.25	2366.34	2334.76	2307.62	2284.24
210000	2622.56	2568.89	2523.41	2484.66	2451.49	2423.00	2398.45
220000	2747.44	2691.22	2643.57	2602.97	2568.23	2538.39	2512.66
230000	2872.33	2813.55	2763.73	2721.29	2684.97	2653.77	2626.88
240000	2997.21	2935.88	2883.90	2839.61	2801.71	2769.15	2741.09
250000	3122.09	3058.21	3004.06	2957.92	2918.44	2884.53	2855.30
260000	3246.98	3180.54	3124.22	3076.24	3035.18	2999.91	2969.51
270000	3371.86	3302.86	3244.38	3194.56	3151.92	3115.29	3083.72
280000	3496.74	3425.19	3364.55	3312.88	3268.66	3230.67	3197.94
290000	3621.63	3547.52	3484.71	3431.19	3385.40	3346.05	3312.15
300000	3746.51	3669.85	3604.87	3549.51	3502.13	3461.43	3426.36
310000	3871.39	3792.18	3725.03	3667.83	3618.87	3576.82	3540.57
320000	3996.28	3914.51	3845.20	3786.14	3735.61	3692.20	3654.78
330000	4121.16	4036.83	3965.36	3904.46	3852.35	3807.58	3769.00
340000	4246.05	4159.16	4085.52	4022.78	3969.08	3922.96	3883.21
350000	4370.93	4281.49	4205.68	4141.09	4085.82	4038.34	3997.42
400000	4995.35	4893.13	4806.49	4732.68	4669.51	4615.25	4568.48
450000	5619.77	5504.77	5407.31	5324.26	5253.20	5192.15	5139.54
500000	6244.18	6116.41	6008.12	5915.85	5836.89	5769.06	5710.60
550000	6868.60	6728.06	6608.93	6507.43	6420.58	6345.96	6281.66
600000	7493.02	7339.70	7209.74	7099.02	7004.27	6922.87	6852.72

Monthly Payments 12³/₄%
necessary to amortize a loan

AMOUNT	22 YEARS	23 YEARS	24 YEARS	25 YEARS	30 YEARS	35 YEARS	40 YEARS
100	1.13	1.12	1.12	1.11	1.09	1.08	1.07
200	2.26	2.25	2.23	2.22	2.17	2.15	2.14
500	5.66	5.62	5.58	5.55	5.43	5.38	5.35
1000	11.32	11.23	11.16	11.09	10.87	10.75	10.69
2000	22.64	22.47	22.31	22.18	21.73	21.50	21.38
5000	56.60	56.16	55.78	55.45	54.33	53.76	53.46
6000	67.92	67.40	66.94	66.54	65.20	64.51	64.15
7000	79.24	78.63	78.10	77.63	76.07	75.26	74.84
8000	90.56	89.86	89.25	88.72	86.94	86.02	85.54
9000	101.88	101.09	100.41	99.81	97.80	96.77	96.23
10000	113.20	112.33	111.57	110.91	108.67	107.52	106.92
15000	169.80	168.49	167.35	166.36	163.00	161.28	160.38
20000	226.40	224.65	223.13	221.81	217.34	215.04	213.84
25000	283.00	280.82	278.92	277.26	271.67	268.80	267.30
30000	339.60	336.98	334.70	332.72	326.01	322.56	320.76
35000	396.21	393.14	390.48	388.17	380.34	376.32	374.22
40000	452.81	449.30	446.26	443.62	434.68	430.08	427.68
45000	509.41	505.47	502.05	499.07	489.01	483.84	481.14
50000	566.01	561.63	557.83	554.53	543.35	537.60	534.60
55000	622.61	617.79	613.61	609.98	597.68	591.36	588.06
60000	679.21	673.96	669.40	665.43	652.02	645.12	641.52
65000	735.81	730.12	725.18	720.88	706.35	698.88	694.98
70000	792.41	786.28	780.96	776.34	760.69	752.64	748.44
75000	849.01	842.45	836.75	831.79	815.02	806.40	801.90
80000	905.61	898.61	892.53	887.24	869.35	860.16	855.36
85000	962.21	954.77	948.31	942.69	923.69	913.92	908.82
90000	1018.81	1010.94	1004.10	998.15	978.02	967.68	962.28
95000	1075.41	1067.10	1059.88	1053.60	1032.36	1021.44	1015.74
100000	1132.02	1123.26	1115.66	1109.05	1086.69	1075.20	1069.20
105000	1188.62	1179.42	1171.45	1164.50	1141.03	1128.96	1122.66
110000	1245.22	1235.59	1227.23	1219.96	1195.36	1182.72	1176.12
120000	1358.42	1347.91	1338.79	1330.86	1304.03	1290.24	1283.04
130000	1471.62	1460.24	1450.36	1441.77	1412.70	1397.75	1389.96
140000	1584.82	1572.57	1561.93	1552.67	1521.37	1505.27	1496.87
150000	1698.02	1684.89	1673.49	1663.58	1630.04	1612.79	1603.79
160000	1811.23	1797.22	1785.06	1774.48	1738.71	1720.31	1710.71
170000	1924.43	1909.55	1896.63	1885.39	1847.38	1827.83	1817.63
180000	2037.63	2021.87	2008.19	1996.29	1956.05	1935.35	1924.55
190000	2150.83	2134.20	2119.76	2107.20	2064.72	2042.87	2031.47
200000	2264.03	2246.52	2231.32	2218.10	2173.39	2150.39	2138.39
210000	2377.23	2358.85	2342.89	2329.01	2282.06	2257.91	2245.31
220000	2490.43	2471.18	2454.46	2439.91	2390.73	2365.43	2352.23
230000	2603.64	2583.50	2566.02	2550.82	2499.39	2472.95	2459.15
240000	2716.84	2695.83	2677.59	2661.73	2608.06	2580.47	2566.07
250000	2830.04	2808.15	2789.16	2772.63	2716.73	2687.99	2672.99
260000	2943.24	2920.48	2900.72	2883.54	2825.40	2795.51	2779.91
270000	3056.44	3032.81	3012.29	2994.44	2934.07	2903.03	2886.83
280000	3169.64	3145.13	3123.85	3105.35	3042.74	3010.55	2993.75
290000	3282.85	3257.46	3235.42	3216.25	3151.41	3118.07	3100.67
300000	3396.05	3369.79	3346.99	3327.16	3260.08	3225.59	3207.59
310000	3509.25	3482.11	3458.55	3438.06	3368.75	3333.11	3314.51
320000	3622.45	3594.44	3570.12	3548.97	3477.42	3440.63	3421.43
330000	3735.65	3706.76	3681.68	3659.87	3586.09	3548.15	3528.35
340000	3848.85	3819.09	3793.25	3770.78	3694.76	3655.67	3635.27
350000	3962.05	3931.42	3904.82	3881.68	3803.43	3763.19	3742.19
400000	4528.06	4493.05	4462.65	4436.21	4346.77	4300.78	4276.79
450000	5094.07	5054.68	5020.48	4990.74	4890.12	4838.38	4811.38
500000	5660.07	5616.31	5578.31	5545.26	5433.47	5375.98	5345.98
550000	6226.09	6177.94	6136.14	6099.79	5976.81	5913.58	5880.58
600000	6792.09	6739.57	6693.97	6654.31	6520.16	6451.18	6415.18

Monthly Payments
necessary to amortize a loan

AMOUNT	1 YEAR	2 YEARS	3 YEARS	4 YEARS	5 YEARS	6 YEARS	7 YEARS
100	8.93	4.75	3.37	2.68	2.28	2.01	1.82
200	17.86	9.51	6.74	5.37	4.55	4.01	3.64
500	44.66	23.77	16.85	13.41	11.38	10.04	9.10
1000	89.32	47.54	33.69	26.83	22.75	20.07	18.19
2000	178.63	95.08	67.39	53.65	45.51	40.15	36.38
5000	446.59	237.71	168.47	134.14	113.77	100.37	90.96
6000	535.90	285.25	202.16	160.96	136.52	120.44	109.15
7000	625.22	332.79	235.86	187.79	159.27	140.52	127.34
8000	714.54	380.33	269.55	214.62	182.02	160.59	145.54
9000	803.86	427.88	303.25	241.45	204.78	180.67	163.73
10000	893.17	475.42	336.94	268.27	227.53	200.74	181.92
15000	1339.76	713.13	505.41	402.41	341.30	301.11	272.88
20000	1786.35	950.84	673.88	536.55	455.06	401.48	363.84
25000	2232.93	1188.55	842.35	670.69	568.83	501.85	454.80
30000	2679.52	1426.25	1010.82	804.82	682.59	602.22	545.76
35000	3126.10	1663.96	1179.29	938.96	796.36	702.59	636.72
40000	3572.69	1901.67	1347.76	1073.10	910.12	802.96	727.68
45000	4019.28	2139.38	1516.23	1207.24	1023.89	903.33	818.64
50000	4465.86	2377.09	1684.70	1341.37	1137.65	1003.71	909.60
55000	4912.45	2614.80	1853.17	1475.51	1251.42	1104.08	1000.56
60000	5359.04	2852.51	2021.64	1609.65	1365.18	1204.45	1091.52
65000	5805.62	3090.22	2190.11	1743.79	1478.95	1304.82	1182.48
70000	6252.21	3327.93	2358.58	1877.92	1592.72	1405.19	1273.44
75000	6698.80	3565.64	2527.05	2012.06	1706.48	1505.56	1364.40
80000	7145.38	3803.35	2695.52	2146.20	1820.25	1605.93	1455.36
85000	7591.97	4041.05	2863.99	2280.34	1934.01	1706.30	1546.32
90000	8038.55	4278.76	3032.46	2414.47	2047.78	1806.67	1637.28
95000	8485.14	4516.47	3200.93	2548.61	2161.54	1907.04	1728.24
100000	8931.73	4754.18	3369.40	2682.75	2275.31	2007.41	1819.20
105000	9378.31	4991.89	3537.86	2816.89	2389.07	2107.78	1910.16
110000	9824.90	5229.60	3706.33	2951.02	2502.84	2208.15	2001.12
120000	10718.07	5705.02	4043.27	3219.30	2730.37	2408.89	2183.04
130000	11611.25	6180.44	4380.21	3487.57	2957.90	2609.63	2364.96
140000	12504.42	6655.86	4717.15	3755.85	3185.43	2810.37	2546.87
150000	13397.59	7131.27	5054.09	4024.12	3412.96	3011.12	2728.79
160000	14290.76	7606.69	5391.03	4292.40	3640.49	3211.86	2910.71
170000	15183.94	8082.11	5727.97	4560.67	3868.02	3412.60	3092.63
180000	16077.11	8557.53	6064.91	4828.95	4095.55	3613.34	3274.55
190000	16970.28	9032.95	6401.85	5097.22	4323.08	3814.08	3456.47
200000	17863.46	9508.36	6738.79	5365.50	4550.61	4014.82	3638.39
210000	18756.63	9983.78	7075.73	5633.77	4778.15	4215.56	3820.31
220000	19649.80	10459.20	7412.67	5902.05	5005.68	4416.30	4002.23
230000	20542.97	10934.62	7749.61	6170.32	5233.21	4617.04	4184.15
240000	21436.15	11410.04	8086.55	6438.60	5460.74	4817.79	4366.07
250000	22329.32	11885.46	8423.49	6706.87	5688.27	5018.53	4547.95
260000	23222.49	12360.87	8760.43	6975.15	5915.80	5219.27	4729.91
270000	24115.66	12836.29	9097.37	7243.42	6143.33	5420.01	4911.83
280000	25008.84	13311.71	9434.31	7511.70	6370.86	5620.75	5093.75
290000	25902.01	13787.13	9771.25	7779.97	6598.39	5821.49	5275.67
300000	26795.18	14262.55	10108.19	8048.25	6825.92	6022.23	5457.59
310000	27688.36	14737.97	10445.13	8316.52	7053.45	6222.97	5639.51
320000	28581.53	15213.38	10782.06	8584.80	7280.98	6423.71	5821.43
330000	29474.70	15688.80	11119.00	8853.07	7508.51	6624.45	6003.35
340000	30367.87	16164.22	11455.94	9121.35	7736.04	6825.20	6185.27
350000	31261.05	16639.64	11792.88	9389.62	7963.58	7025.94	6367.19
400000	35726.91	19016.73	13477.58	10731.00	9101.23	8029.64	7276.79
450000	40192.77	21393.82	15162.28	12072.37	10238.88	9033.35	8186.38
500000	44658.64	23770.91	16846.98	13413.75	11376.54	10037.05	9095.98
550000	49124.50	26148.00	18531.67	14755.12	12514.19	11040.76	10005.58
600000	53590.37	28525.09	20216.37	16096.50	13651.84	12044.46	10915.18

Monthly Payments 13%

necessary to amortize a loan

AMOUNT	8 YEARS	9 YEARS	10 YEARS	11 YEARS	12 YEARS	13 YEARS	14 YEARS
100	1.68	1.58	1.49	1.43	1.37	1.33	1.30
200	3.36	3.15	2.99	2.86	2.75	2.66	2.59
500	8.40	7.88	7.47	7.14	6.87	6.66	6.48
1000	16.81	15.75	14.93	14.28	13.75	13.31	12.95
2000	33.61	31.51	29.86	28.55	27.49	26.62	25.91
5000	84.04	78.77	74.66	71.38	68.73	66.56	64.76
6000	100.84	94.52	89.59	85.66	82.48	79.87	77.72
7000	117.65	110.28	104.52	99.93	96.22	93.18	90.67
8000	134.46	126.03	119.45	114.21	109.97	106.50	103.62
9000	151.27	141.78	134.38	128.48	123.72	119.81	116.57
10000	168.07	157.54	149.31	142.76	137.46	133.12	129.53
15000	252.11	236.30	223.97	214.14	206.19	199.68	194.29
20000	336.15	315.07	298.62	285.52	274.93	266.24	259.05
25000	420.18	393.84	373.28	356.90	343.66	332.80	323.82
30000	504.22	472.61	447.93	428.28	412.39	399.36	388.58
35000	588.25	551.38	522.59	499.66	481.12	465.92	453.34
40000	672.29	630.14	597.24	571.04	549.85	532.48	518.11
45000	756.33	708.91	671.90	642.42	618.58	599.04	582.87
50000	840.36	787.68	746.55	713.81	687.31	665.61	647.63
55000	924.40	866.45	821.21	785.19	756.04	732.17	712.39
60000	1008.44	945.22	895.86	856.57	824.78	798.73	777.16
65000	1092.47	1023.98	970.52	927.95	893.51	865.29	841.92
70000	1176.51	1102.75	1045.18	999.33	962.24	931.85	906.68
75000	1260.54	1181.52	1119.83	1070.71	1030.97	998.41	971.45
80000	1344.58	1260.29	1194.49	1142.09	1099.70	1064.97	1036.21
85000	1428.62	1339.05	1269.14	1213.47	1168.43	1131.53	1100.97
90000	1512.65	1417.82	1343.80	1284.85	1237.16	1198.09	1165.74
95000	1596.69	1496.59	1418.45	1356.23	1305.89	1264.65	1230.50
100000	1680.73	1575.36	1493.11	1427.61	1374.63	1331.21	1295.26
105000	1764.76	1654.13	1567.76	1498.99	1443.36	1397.77	1360.03
110000	1848.80	1732.89	1642.42	1570.37	1512.09	1464.33	1424.79
120000	2016.87	1890.43	1791.73	1713.13	1649.55	1597.45	1554.32
130000	2184.94	2047.97	1941.04	1855.89	1787.01	1730.57	1683.84
140000	2353.02	2205.50	2090.35	1998.66	1924.48	1863.69	1813.37
150000	2521.09	2363.04	2239.66	2141.42	2061.94	1996.82	1942.90
160000	2689.16	2520.57	2388.97	2284.18	2199.40	2129.94	2072.42
170000	2857.23	2678.11	2538.28	2426.94	2336.86	2263.06	2201.95
180000	3025.31	2835.65	2687.59	2569.70	2474.33	2396.18	2331.47
190000	3193.38	2993.18	2836.90	2712.46	2611.79	2529.30	2461.00
200000	3361.45	3150.72	2986.21	2855.22	2749.25	2662.42	2590.53
210000	3529.52	3308.25	3135.53	2997.98	2886.71	2795.54	2720.05
220000	3697.60	3465.79	3284.84	3140.74	3024.18	2928.66	2849.58
230000	3865.67	3623.33	3434.15	3283.50	3161.64	3061.78	2979.11
240000	4033.74	3780.86	3583.46	3426.27	3299.10	3194.90	3108.63
250000	4201.81	3938.40	3732.77	3569.03	3436.56	3328.03	3238.16
260000	4369.89	4095.93	3882.08	3711.79	3574.03	3461.15	3367.69
270000	4537.96	4253.47	4031.39	3854.55	3711.49	3594.27	3497.21
280000	4706.03	4411.00	4180.70	3997.31	3848.95	3727.39	3626.74
290000	4874.10	4568.54	4330.01	4140.07	3986.41	3860.51	3756.26
300000	5042.18	4726.08	4479.32	4282.83	4123.88	3993.63	3885.79
310000	5210.25	4883.61	4628.63	4425.59	4261.34	4126.75	4015.32
320000	5378.32	5041.15	4777.94	4568.35	4398.80	4259.87	4144.84
330000	5546.39	5198.68	4927.25	4711.12	4536.26	4392.99	4274.37
340000	5714.47	5356.22	5076.57	4853.88	4673.73	4526.11	4403.90
350000	5882.54	5513.76	5225.88	4996.64	4811.19	4659.24	4533.42
400000	6722.90	6301.44	5972.43	5710.44	5498.50	5324.84	5181.05
450000	7563.26	7089.11	6718.98	6424.25	6185.81	5990.45	5828.69
500000	8403.63	7876.79	7465.54	7138.05	6873.13	6656.05	6476.32
550000	9243.99	8664.47	8212.09	7851.86	7560.44	7321.66	7123.95
600000	10084.35	9452.15	8958.64	8565.66	8247.75	7987.26	7771.58

Monthly Payments
necessary to amortize a loan

AMOUNT	15 YEARS	16 YEARS	17 YEARS	18 YEARS	19 YEARS	20 YEARS	21 YEARS
100	1.27	1.24	1.22	1.20	1.18	1.17	1.16
200	2.53	2.48	2.44	2.40	2.37	2.34	2.32
500	6.33	6.20	6.09	6.00	5.92	5.86	5.80
1000	12.65	12.40	12.19	12.00	11.85	11.72	11.60
2000	25.30	24.80	24.37	24.01	23.70	23.43	23.20
5000	63.26	62.00	60.93	60.02	59.24	58.58	58.01
6000	75.91	74.40	73.12	72.03	71.09	70.29	69.61
7000	88.57	86.80	85.30	84.03	82.94	82.01	81.21
8000	101.22	99.20	97.49	96.03	94.79	93.73	92.81
9000	113.87	111.60	109.68	108.04	106.64	105.44	104.41
10000	126.52	124.00	121.86	120.04	118.49	117.16	116.01
15000	189.79	186.00	182.79	180.06	177.73	175.74	174.02
20000	253.05	248.00	243.72	240.09	236.98	234.32	232.02
25000	316.31	310.00	304.65	300.11	296.22	292.89	290.03
30000	379.57	372.00	365.58	360.13	355.47	351.47	348.03
35000	442.83	434.00	426.52	420.15	414.71	410.05	406.04
40000	506.10	496.00	487.45	480.17	473.96	468.63	464.05
45000	569.36	557.99	548.38	540.19	533.20	527.21	522.05
50000	632.62	619.99	609.31	600.22	592.45	585.79	580.06
55000	695.88	681.99	670.24	660.24	651.69	644.37	638.06
60000	759.15	743.99	731.17	720.26	710.94	702.95	696.07
65000	822.41	805.99	792.10	780.28	770.18	761.52	754.07
70000	885.67	867.99	853.04	840.30	829.43	820.10	812.08
75000	948.93	929.99	913.96	900.32	888.67	878.68	870.09
80000	1012.19	991.99	974.89	960.35	947.92	937.26	928.09
85000	1075.46	1053.99	1035.82	1020.37	1007.16	995.84	986.10
90000	1138.72	1115.99	1096.75	1080.39	1066.41	1054.42	1044.10
95000	1201.98	1177.99	1157.68	1140.41	1125.65	1113.00	1102.11
100000	1265.24	1239.99	1218.61	1200.43	1184.90	1171.58	1160.11
105000	1328.50	1301.99	1279.55	1260.45	1244.14	1230.15	1218.12
110000	1391.77	1363.99	1340.48	1320.48	1303.39	1288.73	1276.13
120000	1518.29	1487.99	1462.34	1440.52	1421.88	1405.89	1392.14
130000	1644.81	1611.98	1584.20	1560.56	1540.37	1523.05	1508.15
140000	1771.34	1735.98	1706.06	1680.61	1658.86	1640.21	1624.16
150000	1897.86	1859.98	1827.92	1800.65	1777.35	1757.36	1740.17
160000	2024.39	1983.98	1949.78	1920.69	1895.84	1874.52	1856.18
170000	2150.91	2107.98	2071.64	2040.74	2014.33	1991.68	1972.19
180000	2277.44	2231.98	2193.51	2160.78	2132.82	2108.84	2088.21
190000	2403.96	2355.98	2315.37	2280.82	2251.31	2225.99	2204.22
200000	2530.48	2479.98	2437.23	2400.87	2369.80	2343.15	2320.23
210000	2657.01	2603.97	2559.09	2520.91	2488.29	2460.31	2436.24
220000	2783.53	2727.97	2680.95	2640.95	2606.78	2577.47	2552.25
230000	2910.06	2851.97	2802.81	2760.99	2725.27	2694.62	2668.26
240000	3036.58	2975.97	2924.67	2881.04	2843.76	2811.78	2784.27
250000	3163.11	3099.97	3046.54	3001.08	2962.24	2928.94	2900.29
260000	3289.63	3223.97	3168.40	3121.12	3080.73	3046.10	3016.30
270000	3416.15	3347.97	3290.26	3241.17	3199.22	3163.25	3132.31
280000	3542.68	3471.97	3412.12	3361.21	3317.71	3280.41	3248.32
290000	3669.20	3595.96	3533.98	3481.25	3436.20	3397.57	3364.33
300000	3795.73	3719.96	3655.84	3601.30	3554.69	3514.73	3480.34
310000	3922.25	3843.96	3777.70	3721.34	3673.18	3631.88	3596.35
320000	4048.77	3967.96	3899.57	3841.38	3791.67	3749.04	3712.37
330000	4175.30	4091.96	4021.43	3961.43	3910.16	3866.20	3828.38
340000	4301.82	4215.96	4143.29	4081.47	4028.65	3983.36	3944.39
350000	4428.35	4339.96	4265.15	4201.51	4147.14	4100.51	4060.40
400000	5060.97	4959.95	4874.46	4801.73	4739.59	4686.30	4640.46
450000	5693.59	5579.95	5483.76	5401.95	5332.04	5272.09	5220.51
500000	6326.21	6199.94	6093.07	6002.16	5924.49	5857.88	5800.57
550000	6958.83	6819.93	6702.38	6602.38	6516.94	6443.67	6380.63
600000	7591.45	7439.93	7311.69	7202.60	7109.39	7029.45	6960.69

Monthly Payments 13%

necessary to amortize a loan

AMOUNT	22 YEARS	23 YEARS	24 YEARS	25 YEARS	30 YEARS	35 YEARS	40 YEARS
100	1.15	1.14	1.13	1.13	1.11	1.10	1.09
200	2.30	2.28	2.27	2.26	2.21	2.19	2.18
500	5.75	5.71	5.67	5.64	5.53	5.48	5.45
1000	11.50	11.42	11.34	11.28	11.06	10.95	10.90
2000	23.00	22.83	22.69	22.56	22.12	21.90	21.79
5000	57.51	57.08	56.71	56.39	55.31	54.76	54.48
6000	69.01	68.50	68.06	67.67	66.37	65.71	65.37
7000	80.52	79.92	79.40	78.95	77.43	76.66	76.27
8000	92.02	91.33	90.74	90.23	88.50	87.62	87.16
9000	103.52	102.75	102.08	101.51	99.56	98.57	98.06
10000	115.02	114.17	113.43	112.78	110.62	109.52	108.95
15000	172.53	171.25	170.14	169.18	165.93	164.28	163.43
20000	230.05	228.34	226.85	225.57	221.24	219.04	217.90
25000	287.56	285.42	283.57	281.96	276.55	273.80	272.38
30000	345.07	342.50	340.28	338.35	331.86	328.56	326.85
35000	402.58	399.59	396.99	394.74	387.17	383.32	381.33
40000	460.09	456.67	453.71	451.13	442.48	438.08	435.81
45000	517.60	513.75	510.42	507.53	497.79	492.84	490.28
50000	575.11	570.84	567.13	563.92	553.10	547.60	544.76
55000	632.62	627.92	623.85	620.31	608.41	602.36	599.23
60000	690.14	685.01	680.56	676.70	663.72	657.12	653.71
65000	747.65	742.09	737.27	733.09	719.03	711.88	708.18
70000	805.16	799.17	793.99	789.48	774.34	766.64	762.66
75000	862.67	856.26	850.70	845.88	829.65	821.39	817.14
80000	920.18	913.34	907.41	902.27	884.96	876.15	871.61
85000	977.69	970.42	964.13	958.66	940.27	930.91	926.09
90000	1035.20	1027.51	1020.84	1015.05	995.58	985.67	980.56
95000	1092.72	1084.59	1077.55	1071.44	1050.89	1040.43	1035.04
100000	1150.23	1141.68	1134.27	1127.84	1106.20	1095.19	1089.51
105000	1207.74	1198.76	1190.98	1184.23	1161.51	1149.95	1143.99
110000	1265.25	1255.84	1247.69	1240.62	1216.82	1204.71	1198.47
120000	1380.27	1370.01	1361.12	1353.40	1327.44	1314.23	1307.42
130000	1495.29	1484.18	1474.55	1466.19	1438.06	1423.75	1416.37
140000	1610.32	1598.35	1587.97	1578.97	1548.68	1533.27	1525.32
150000	1725.34	1712.51	1701.40	1691.75	1659.30	1642.79	1634.27
160000	1840.36	1826.68	1814.83	1804.54	1769.92	1752.31	1743.22
170000	1955.38	1940.85	1928.25	1917.32	1880.54	1861.83	1852.17
180000	2070.41	2055.02	2041.68	2030.10	1991.16	1971.35	1961.13
190000	2185.43	2169.18	2155.11	2142.89	2101.78	2080.87	2070.08
200000	2300.45	2283.35	2268.53	2255.67	2212.40	2190.39	2179.03
210000	2415.48	2397.52	2381.96	2368.45	2323.02	2299.91	2287.98
220000	2530.50	2511.69	2495.39	2481.24	2433.64	2409.42	2396.93
230000	2645.52	2625.85	2608.81	2594.02	2544.26	2518.94	2505.88
240000	2760.54	2740.02	2722.24	2706.80	2654.88	2628.46	2614.83
250000	2875.57	2854.19	2835.67	2819.59	2765.50	2737.98	2723.79
260000	2990.59	2968.36	2949.09	2932.37	2876.12	2847.50	2832.74
270000	3105.61	3082.52	3062.52	3045.16	2986.74	2957.02	2941.69
280000	3220.63	3196.69	3175.95	3157.94	3097.36	3066.54	3050.64
290000	3335.66	3310.86	3289.37	3270.72	3207.98	3176.06	3159.59
300000	3450.68	3425.03	3402.80	3383.51	3318.60	3285.58	3268.54
310000	3565.70	3539.20	3516.23	3496.29	3429.22	3395.10	3377.49
320000	3680.72	3653.36	3629.65	3609.07	3539.84	3504.62	3486.45
330000	3795.75	3767.53	3743.08	3721.86	3650.46	3614.14	3595.40
340000	3910.77	3881.70	3856.51	3834.64	3761.08	3723.66	3704.35
350000	4025.79	3995.87	3969.93	3947.42	3871.70	3833.18	3813.30
400000	4600.91	4566.70	4537.07	4511.34	4424.80	4380.77	4358.06
450000	5176.02	5137.54	5104.20	5075.26	4977.90	4928.37	4902.81
500000	5751.13	5708.38	5671.33	5639.18	5531.00	5475.97	5447.57
550000	6326.24	6279.22	6238.47	6203.09	6084.10	6023.56	5992.33
600000	6901.36	6850.06	6805.60	6767.01	6637.20	6571.16	6537.08

13¼%

Monthly Payments
necessary to amortize a loan

AMOUNT	1 YEAR	2 YEARS	3 YEARS	4 YEARS	5 YEARS	6 YEARS	7 YEARS
100	8.94	4.77	3.38	2.70	2.29	2.02	1.83
200	17.89	9.53	6.76	5.39	4.58	4.04	3.67
500	44.72	23.83	16.91	13.48	11.44	10.10	9.16
1000	89.43	47.66	33.81	26.95	22.88	20.21	18.33
2000	178.87	95.32	67.63	53.90	45.76	40.41	36.66
5000	447.17	238.30	169.07	134.76	114.41	101.03	91.64
6000	536.61	285.96	202.89	161.71	137.29	121.24	109.97
7000	626.04	333.62	236.70	188.66	160.17	141.44	128.30
8000	715.48	381.27	270.52	215.61	183.05	161.65	146.63
9000	804.91	428.93	304.33	242.57	205.93	181.86	164.95
10000	894.35	476.59	338.14	269.52	228.81	202.06	183.28
15000	1341.52	714.89	507.22	404.28	343.22	303.09	274.92
20000	1788.69	953.19	676.29	539.03	457.63	404.13	366.56
25000	2235.87	1191.48	845.36	673.79	572.03	505.16	458.20
30000	2683.04	1429.78	1014.43	808.55	686.44	606.19	549.84
35000	3130.21	1668.08	1183.51	943.31	800.84	707.22	641.49
40000	3577.38	1906.37	1352.58	1078.07	915.25	808.25	733.13
45000	4024.56	2144.67	1521.65	1212.83	1029.66	909.28	824.77
50000	4471.73	2382.97	1690.72	1347.59	1144.06	1010.31	916.41
55000	4918.90	2621.26	1859.80	1482.34	1258.47	1111.35	1008.05
60000	5366.08	2859.56	2028.87	1617.10	1372.88	1212.38	1099.69
65000	5813.25	3097.86	2197.94	1751.86	1487.28	1313.41	1191.33
70000	6260.42	3336.15	2367.01	1886.62	1601.69	1414.44	1282.97
75000	6707.60	3574.45	2536.09	2021.38	1716.09	1515.47	1374.61
80000	7154.77	3812.75	2705.16	2156.14	1830.50	1616.50	1466.25
85000	7601.94	4051.04	2874.23	2290.89	1944.91	1717.53	1557.89
90000	8049.11	4289.34	3043.30	2425.66	2059.31	1818.57	1649.53
95000	8496.29	4527.64	3212.38	2560.42	2173.72	1919.60	1741.17
100000	8943.46	4765.93	3381.45	2695.17	2288.13	2020.63	1832.82
105000	9390.63	5004.23	3550.52	2829.93	2402.53	2121.66	1924.46
110000	9837.81	5242.53	3719.59	2964.69	2516.94	2222.69	2016.10
120000	10732.15	5719.12	4057.74	3234.21	2745.75	2424.76	2199.38
130000	11626.50	6195.71	4395.88	3503.73	2974.56	2626.82	2382.66
140000	12520.85	6672.31	4734.03	3773.24	3203.38	2828.88	2565.94
150000	13415.19	7148.90	5072.17	4042.76	3432.19	3030.94	2749.22
160000	14309.54	7625.49	5410.32	4312.28	3661.00	3233.01	2932.50
170000	15203.88	8102.09	5748.46	4581.80	3889.81	3435.07	3115.79
180000	16098.23	8578.68	6086.61	4851.31	4118.63	3637.13	3299.07
190000	16992.58	9055.27	6424.75	5120.83	4347.44	3839.20	3482.35
200000	17886.92	9531.87	6762.90	5390.35	4576.25	4041.26	3665.63
210000	18781.27	10008.46	7101.04	5659.87	4805.06	4243.32	3848.91
220000	19675.61	10485.05	7439.19	5929.38	5033.88	4445.38	4032.19
230000	20569.96	10961.65	7777.33	6198.90	5262.69	4647.45	4215.48
240000	21464.31	11438.24	8115.48	6468.42	5491.50	4849.51	4398.76
250000	22358.65	11914.83	8453.62	6737.94	5720.31	5051.57	4582.04
260000	23253.00	12391.43	8791.77	7007.45	5949.13	5253.64	4765.32
270000	24147.34	12868.02	9129.91	7276.97	6177.94	5455.70	4948.60
280000	25041.69	13344.61	9468.06	7546.49	6406.75	5657.76	5131.88
290000	25936.04	13821.21	9806.20	7816.01	6635.56	5859.82	5315.16
300000	26830.38	14297.80	10144.35	8085.52	6864.38	6061.89	5498.45
310000	27724.73	14774.39	10482.49	8355.04	7093.19	6263.95	5681.73
320000	28619.07	15250.99	10820.64	8624.56	7322.00	6466.01	5865.01
330000	29513.42	15727.58	11158.78	8894.08	7550.81	6668.08	6048.29
340000	30407.77	16204.17	11496.93	9163.59	7779.63	6870.14	6231.57
350000	31302.11	16680.77	11835.07	9433.11	8008.44	7072.20	6414.85
400000	35773.84	19063.73	13525.80	10780.70	9152.50	8082.52	7331.26
450000	40245.57	21446.70	15216.52	12128.28	10296.56	9092.83	8247.67
500000	44717.30	23829.67	16907.25	13475.87	11440.63	10103.15	9164.08
550000	49189.04	26212.63	18597.97	14823.46	12584.69	11113.46	10080.48
600000	53660.77	28595.60	20288.70	16171.05	13728.75	12123.78	10996.89

Monthly Payments 13¼%
necessary to amortize a loan

AMOUNT	8 YEARS	9 YEARS	10 YEARS	11 YEARS	12 YEARS	13 YEARS	14 YEARS
100	1.69	1.59	1.51	1.44	1.39	1.35	1.31
200	3.39	3.18	3.02	2.89	2.78	2.69	2.62
500	8.47	7.95	7.54	7.21	6.95	6.74	6.56
1000	16.95	15.90	15.08	14.43	13.90	13.47	13.11
2000	33.89	31.80	30.16	28.86	27.80	26.94	26.23
5000	84.74	79.49	75.39	72.14	69.51	67.35	65.57
6000	101.68	95.39	90.47	86.57	83.41	80.82	78.69
7000	118.63	111.28	105.55	100.99	97.31	94.29	91.80
8000	135.58	127.18	120.63	115.42	111.21	107.76	104.92
9000	152.53	143.08	135.71	129.85	125.11	121.24	118.03
10000	169.47	158.98	150.79	144.28	139.01	134.71	131.14
15000	254.21	238.46	226.18	216.41	208.52	202.06	196.72
20000	338.95	317.95	301.58	288.55	278.03	269.41	262.29
25000	423.69	397.44	376.97	360.69	347.53	336.76	327.86
30000	508.42	476.93	452.37	432.83	417.04	404.12	393.43
35000	593.16	556.42	527.76	504.97	486.55	471.47	459.00
40000	677.90	635.90	603.16	577.10	556.05	538.82	524.58
45000	762.63	715.39	678.55	649.24	625.56	606.18	590.15
50000	847.37	794.88	753.94	721.38	695.07	673.53	655.72
55000	932.11	874.37	829.34	793.52	764.57	740.88	721.29
60000	1016.84	953.86	904.73	865.66	834.08	808.24	786.87
65000	1101.58	1033.35	980.13	937.79	903.59	875.59	852.44
70000	1186.32	1112.83	1055.52	1009.93	973.09	942.94	918.01
75000	1271.06	1192.32	1130.92	1082.07	1042.60	1010.29	983.58
80000	1355.79	1271.81	1206.31	1154.21	1112.10	1077.65	1049.15
85000	1440.53	1351.30	1281.71	1226.35	1181.61	1145.00	1114.73
90000	1525.27	1430.79	1357.10	1298.48	1251.12	1212.35	1180.30
95000	1610.00	1510.27	1432.49	1370.62	1320.62	1279.71	1245.87
100000	1694.74	1589.76	1507.89	1442.76	1390.13	1347.06	1311.44
105000	1779.48	1669.25	1583.28	1514.90	1459.64	1414.41	1377.01
110000	1864.21	1748.74	1658.68	1587.04	1529.14	1481.77	1442.59
120000	2033.69	1907.71	1809.47	1731.31	1668.16	1616.47	1573.73
130000	2203.16	2066.69	1960.26	1875.59	1807.17	1751.18	1704.87
140000	2372.64	2225.67	2111.04	2019.86	1946.18	1885.88	1836.02
150000	2542.11	2384.64	2261.83	2164.14	2085.20	2020.59	1967.16
160000	2711.58	2543.62	2412.62	2308.42	2224.21	2155.29	2098.31
170000	2881.06	2702.59	2563.41	2452.69	2363.22	2290.00	2229.45
180000	3050.53	2861.57	2714.20	2596.97	2502.24	2424.71	2360.60
190000	3220.01	3020.55	2864.99	2741.25	2641.25	2559.41	2491.74
200000	3389.48	3179.52	3015.78	2885.52	2780.26	2694.12	2622.88
210000	3558.95	3338.50	3166.57	3029.80	2919.28	2828.82	2754.03
220000	3728.43	3497.48	3317.36	3174.07	3058.29	2963.53	2885.17
230000	3897.90	3656.45	3468.15	3318.35	3197.30	3098.24	3016.32
240000	4067.38	3815.43	3618.93	3462.63	3336.31	3232.94	3147.46
250000	4236.85	3974.40	3769.72	3606.90	3475.33	3367.65	3278.61
260000	4406.32	4133.38	3920.51	3751.18	3614.34	3502.35	3409.75
270000	4575.80	4292.36	4071.30	3895.45	3753.35	3637.06	3540.89
280000	4745.27	4451.33	4222.09	4039.73	3892.37	3771.77	3672.04
290000	4914.75	4610.31	4372.88	4184.01	4031.38	3906.47	3803.18
300000	5084.22	4769.28	4523.67	4328.28	4170.39	4041.18	3934.33
310000	5253.69	4928.26	4674.46	4472.56	4309.41	4175.88	4065.47
320000	5423.17	5087.24	4825.25	4616.83	4448.42	4310.59	4196.62
330000	5592.64	5246.21	4976.03	4761.11	4587.43	4445.30	4327.76
340000	5762.12	5405.19	5126.82	4905.39	4726.45	4580.00	4458.90
350000	5931.59	5564.17	5277.61	5049.66	4865.46	4714.71	4590.05
400000	6778.96	6359.05	6031.56	5771.14	5560.52	5388.24	5245.75
450000	7626.33	7153.93	6785.50	6492.42	6255.59	6061.77	5901.49
500000	8473.70	7948.81	7539.45	7213.80	6950.66	6735.30	6557.21
550000	9321.07	8743.69	8293.39	7935.18	7645.72	7408.83	7212.93
600000	10168.44	9538.57	9047.33	8656.56	8340.79	8082.36	7868.65

13¼%

Monthly Payments
necessary to amortize a loan

AMOUNT	15 YEARS	16 YEARS	17 YEARS	18 YEARS	19 YEARS	20 YEARS	21 YEARS
100	1.28	1.26	1.24	1.22	1.20	1.19	1.18
200	2.56	2.51	2.47	2.44	2.41	2.38	2.36
500	6.41	6.28	6.18	6.09	6.01	5.95	5.89
1000	12.82	12.57	12.36	12.18	12.03	11.89	11.78
2000	25.63	25.14	24.71	24.36	24.05	23.79	23.56
5000	64.09	62.84	61.78	60.89	60.13	59.47	58.91
6000	76.90	75.41	74.14	73.07	72.15	71.37	70.69
7000	89.72	87.97	86.50	85.25	84.18	83.26	82.47
8000	102.54	100.54	98.86	97.42	96.20	95.15	94.26
9000	115.36	113.11	111.21	109.60	108.23	107.05	106.04
10000	128.17	125.68	123.57	121.78	120.25	118.94	117.82
15000	192.26	188.52	185.35	182.67	180.38	178.41	176.73
20000	256.35	251.36	247.14	243.56	240.50	237.89	235.64
25000	320.43	314.20	308.92	304.45	300.63	297.36	294.55
30000	384.52	377.04	370.71	365.34	360.75	356.83	353.46
35000	448.61	439.87	432.49	426.23	420.88	416.30	412.37
40000	512.69	502.71	494.28	487.11	481.00	475.77	471.28
45000	576.78	565.55	556.06	548.00	541.13	535.24	530.19
50000	640.87	628.39	617.85	608.89	601.25	594.72	589.10
55000	704.96	691.23	679.63	669.78	661.38	654.19	648.01
60000	769.04	754.07	741.42	730.67	721.51	713.66	706.92
65000	833.13	816.91	803.20	791.56	781.63	773.13	765.83
70000	897.22	879.75	864.99	852.45	841.76	832.60	824.74
75000	961.30	942.59	926.77	913.34	901.88	892.07	883.65
80000	1025.39	1005.43	988.56	974.23	962.01	951.54	942.56
85000	1089.48	1068.27	1050.34	1035.12	1022.13	1011.02	1001.47
90000	1153.56	1131.11	1112.13	1096.01	1082.26	1070.49	1060.38
95000	1217.65	1193.94	1173.91	1156.90	1142.38	1129.96	1119.29
100000	1281.74	1256.78	1235.70	1217.79	1202.51	1189.43	1178.20
105000	1345.82	1319.62	1297.48	1278.68	1262.64	1248.90	1237.11
110000	1409.91	1382.46	1359.27	1339.57	1322.76	1308.37	1296.02
120000	1538.08	1508.14	1482.84	1461.34	1443.01	1427.32	1413.84
130000	1666.26	1633.82	1606.41	1583.12	1563.26	1546.26	1531.66
140000	1794.43	1759.50	1729.98	1704.90	1683.51	1665.20	1649.48
150000	1922.60	1885.18	1853.55	1826.68	1803.76	1784.15	1767.30
160000	2050.78	2010.85	1977.11	1948.46	1924.02	1903.09	1885.12
170000	2178.95	2136.53	2100.68	2070.24	2044.27	2022.03	2002.94
180000	2307.13	2262.21	2224.25	2192.02	2164.52	2140.98	2120.76
190000	2435.30	2387.89	2347.82	2313.80	2284.77	2259.92	2238.58
200000	2563.47	2513.57	2471.39	2435.57	2405.02	2378.86	2356.40
210000	2691.65	2639.25	2594.96	2557.35	2525.27	2497.80	2474.22
220000	2819.82	2764.92	2718.53	2679.13	2645.52	2616.75	2592.04
230000	2947.99	2890.60	2842.10	2800.91	2765.77	2735.69	2709.86
240000	3076.17	3016.28	2965.67	2922.69	2886.02	2854.63	2827.68
250000	3204.34	3141.96	3089.24	3044.47	3006.27	2973.58	2945.50
260000	3332.51	3267.64	3212.81	3166.25	3126.53	3092.52	3063.32
270000	3460.69	3393.32	3336.38	3288.02	3246.78	3211.46	3181.14
280000	3588.86	3518.99	3459.95	3409.80	3367.03	3330.41	3298.95
290000	3717.04	3644.67	3583.52	3531.58	3487.28	3449.35	3416.77
300000	3845.21	3770.35	3707.09	3653.36	3607.53	3568.29	3534.59
310000	3973.38	3896.03	3830.66	3775.14	3727.78	3687.24	3652.41
320000	4101.56	4021.71	3954.23	3896.92	3848.03	3806.18	3770.23
330000	4229.73	4147.39	4077.80	4018.70	3968.28	3925.12	3888.05
340000	4357.90	4273.06	4201.37	4140.48	4088.53	4044.06	4005.87
350000	4486.08	4398.74	4324.94	4262.25	4208.78	4163.01	4123.69
400000	5126.95	5027.13	4942.79	4871.15	4810.04	4757.72	4712.79
450000	5767.81	5655.53	5560.64	5480.04	5411.29	5352.44	5301.89
500000	6408.68	6283.92	6178.48	6088.93	6012.55	5947.15	5890.99
550000	7049.55	6912.31	6796.33	6697.83	6613.80	6541.87	6480.09
600000	7690.42	7540.70	7414.18	7306.72	7215.06	7136.58	7069.19

Monthly Payments 13¼%

necessary to amortize a loan

AMOUNT	22 YEARS	23 YEARS	24 YEARS	25 YEARS	30 YEARS	35 YEARS	40 YEARS
100	1.17	1.16	1.15	1.15	1.13	1.12	1.11
200	2.34	2.32	2.31	2.29	2.25	2.23	2.22
500	5.84	5.80	5.76	5.73	5.63	5.58	5.55
1000	11.69	11.60	11.53	11.47	11.26	11.15	11.10
2000	23.37	23.20	23.06	22.93	22.52	22.30	22.20
5000	58.43	58.01	57.65	57.34	56.29	55.76	55.49
6000	70.11	69.61	69.18	68.80	67.55	66.91	66.59
7000	81.80	81.21	80.71	80.27	78.80	78.07	77.69
8000	93.48	92.81	92.24	91.74	90.06	89.22	88.79
9000	105.17	104.42	103.77	103.20	101.32	100.37	99.89
10000	116.85	116.02	115.30	114.67	112.58	111.52	110.99
15000	175.28	174.03	172.94	172.01	168.87	167.29	166.48
20000	233.71	232.04	230.59	229.34	225.15	223.05	221.97
25000	292.13	290.04	288.24	286.68	281.44	278.81	277.47
30000	350.56	348.05	345.89	344.01	337.73	334.57	332.96
35000	408.98	406.06	403.53	401.35	394.02	390.33	388.45
40000	467.41	464.07	461.18	458.68	450.31	446.10	443.95
45000	525.84	522.08	518.83	516.02	506.60	501.86	499.44
50000	584.26	580.09	576.48	573.35	562.89	557.62	554.93
55000	642.69	638.10	634.13	630.69	619.18	613.38	610.43
60000	701.12	696.11	691.77	688.02	675.46	669.15	665.92
65000	759.54	754.11	749.42	745.36	731.75	724.91	721.42
70000	817.97	812.12	807.07	802.69	788.04	780.67	776.91
75000	876.39	870.13	864.72	860.03	844.33	836.43	832.40
80000	934.82	928.14	922.36	917.36	900.62	892.19	887.90
85000	993.25	986.15	980.01	974.70	956.91	947.96	943.39
90000	1051.67	1044.16	1037.66	1032.03	1013.20	1003.72	998.88
95000	1110.10	1102.17	1095.31	1089.37	1069.48	1059.48	1054.38
100000	1168.53	1160.18	1152.96	1146.70	1125.77	1115.24	1109.87
105000	1226.95	1218.19	1210.60	1204.04	1182.06	1171.00	1165.36
110000	1285.38	1276.19	1268.25	1261.37	1238.35	1226.77	1220.86
120000	1402.23	1392.21	1383.55	1376.04	1350.93	1338.29	1331.84
130000	1519.08	1508.23	1498.84	1490.71	1463.51	1449.81	1442.83
140000	1635.94	1624.25	1614.14	1605.38	1576.08	1561.34	1553.82
150000	1752.79	1740.26	1729.43	1720.05	1688.66	1672.86	1664.80
160000	1869.64	1856.28	1844.73	1834.72	1801.24	1784.39	1775.79
170000	1986.49	1972.30	1960.03	1949.39	1913.81	1895.91	1886.78
180000	2103.35	2088.32	2075.32	2064.06	2026.39	2007.44	1997.77
190000	2220.20	2204.34	2190.62	2178.73	2138.97	2118.96	2108.75
200000	2337.05	2320.35	2305.91	2293.40	2251.55	2230.48	2219.74
210000	2453.90	2436.37	2421.21	2408.07	2364.12	2342.01	2330.73
220000	2570.76	2552.39	2536.50	2522.74	2476.70	2453.53	2441.71
230000	2687.61	2668.41	2651.80	2637.41	2589.28	2565.06	2552.70
240000	2804.46	2784.42	2767.09	2752.08	2701.86	2676.58	2663.69
250000	2921.31	2900.44	2882.39	2866.75	2814.43	2788.11	2774.67
260000	3038.17	3016.46	2997.69	2981.42	2927.01	2899.63	2885.66
270000	3155.02	3132.48	3112.98	3096.09	3039.59	3011.15	2996.65
280000	3271.87	3248.49	3228.28	3210.76	3152.17	3122.68	3107.64
290000	3388.72	3364.51	3343.57	3325.43	3264.74	3234.20	3218.62
300000	3505.58	3480.53	3458.87	3440.10	3377.32	3345.73	3329.61
310000	3622.43	3596.55	3574.16	3554.77	3489.90	3457.25	3440.60
320000	3739.28	3712.57	3689.46	3669.44	3602.48	3568.78	3551.58
330000	3856.13	3828.58	3804.75	3784.11	3715.05	3680.30	3662.57
340000	3972.99	3944.60	3920.05	3898.78	3827.63	3791.82	3773.56
350000	4089.84	4060.62	4035.35	4013.45	3940.21	3903.35	3884.54
400000	4674.10	4640.71	4611.82	4586.80	4503.09	4460.97	4439.48
450000	5258.36	5220.79	5188.30	5160.15	5065.98	5018.59	4994.41
500000	5842.63	5800.88	5764.78	5733.50	5628.87	5576.21	5549.35
550000	6426.89	6380.97	6341.26	6306.85	6191.75	6133.83	6104.28
600000	7011.15	6961.06	6917.74	6880.20	6754.64	6691.45	6659.22

13¹/₂%

Monthly Payments
necessary to amortize a loan

AMOUNT	1 YEAR	2 YEARS	3 YEARS	4 YEARS	5 YEARS	6 YEARS	7 YEARS
100	8.96	4.78	3.39	2.71	2.30	2.03	1.85
200	17.91	9.56	6.79	5.42	4.60	4.07	3.69
500	44.78	23.89	16.97	13.54	11.50	10.17	9.23
1000	89.55	47.78	33.94	27.08	23.01	20.34	18.46
2000	179.10	95.55	67.87	54.15	46.02	40.68	36.93
5000	447.76	238.89	169.68	135.38	115.05	101.69	92.32
6000	537.31	286.66	203.61	162.46	138.06	122.03	110.79
7000	626.86	334.44	237.55	189.53	161.07	142.37	129.25
8000	716.42	382.22	271.48	216.61	184.08	162.71	147.72
9000	805.97	429.99	305.42	243.69	207.09	183.05	166.18
10000	895.52	477.77	339.35	270.76	230.10	203.39	184.65
15000	1343.28	716.66	509.03	406.14	345.15	305.08	276.97
20000	1791.04	955.54	678.71	541.53	460.20	406.78	369.30
25000	2238.80	1194.43	848.38	676.91	575.25	508.47	461.62
30000	2686.56	1433.31	1018.06	812.29	690.30	610.17	553.95
35000	3134.32	1672.20	1187.74	947.67	805.34	711.86	646.27
40000	3582.08	1911.08	1357.41	1083.05	920.39	813.56	738.60
45000	4029.84	2149.97	1527.09	1218.43	1035.44	915.25	830.92
50000	4477.60	2388.85	1696.76	1353.82	1150.49	1016.95	923.24
55000	4925.36	2627.74	1866.44	1489.20	1265.54	1118.64	1015.57
60000	5373.12	2866.62	2036.12	1624.58	1380.59	1220.34	1107.89
65000	5820.68	3105.51	2205.79	1759.96	1495.64	1322.03	1200.22
70000	6268.64	3344.39	2375.47	1895.34	1610.69	1423.73	1292.54
75000	6716.40	3583.28	2545.15	2030.72	1725.74	1525.42	1384.87
80000	7164.16	3822.16	2714.82	2166.11	1840.79	1627.12	1477.19
85000	7611.92	4061.05	2884.50	2301.49	1955.84	1728.81	1569.52
90000	8059.68	4299.93	3054.18	2436.87	2070.89	1830.51	1661.84
95000	8507.44	4538.82	3223.85	2572.25	2185.94	1932.20	1754.16
100000	8955.20	4777.70	3393.53	2707.63	2300.98	2033.90	1846.49
105000	9402.96	5016.59	3563.21	2843.01	2416.03	2135.59	1938.81
110000	9850.72	5255.47	3732.88	2978.40	2531.08	2237.29	2031.14
120000	10746.24	5733.24	4072.23	3249.16	2761.18	2440.68	2215.79
130000	11641.76	6211.01	4411.59	3519.92	2991.28	2644.07	2400.44
140000	12537.28	6688.78	4750.94	3790.69	3221.38	2847.45	2585.08
150000	13432.80	7166.55	5090.29	4061.45	3451.48	3050.84	2769.73
160000	14328.32	7644.32	5429.65	4332.21	3681.58	3254.23	2954.38
170000	15223.84	8122.09	5769.00	4602.97	3911.67	3457.62	3139.03
180000	16119.36	8599.86	6108.35	4873.74	4141.77	3661.01	3323.68
190000	17014.89	9077.63	6447.70	5144.50	4371.87	3864.40	3508.33
200000	17910.41	9555.40	6787.06	5415.26	4601.97	4067.79	3692.98
210000	18805.93	10033.17	7126.41	5686.03	4832.07	4271.18	3877.63
220000	19701.45	10510.94	7465.76	5956.79	5062.17	4474.57	4062.28
230000	20596.97	10988.71	7805.12	6227.55	5292.26	4677.96	4246.93
240000	21492.49	11466.48	8144.47	6498.32	5522.36	4881.35	4431.57
250000	22388.01	11944.25	8483.82	6769.08	5752.46	5084.74	4616.22
260000	23283.53	12422.02	8823.17	7039.84	5982.56	5288.13	4800.87
270000	24179.05	12899.79	9162.53	7310.61	6212.66	5491.52	4985.52
280000	25074.57	13377.56	9501.88	7581.37	6442.76	5694.91	5170.17
290000	25970.09	13855.33	9841.23	7852.13	6672.86	5898.30	5354.82
300000	26865.61	14333.10	10180.59	8122.90	6902.95	6101.69	5539.47
310000	27761.13	14810.87	10519.94	8393.66	7133.05	6305.08	5724.12
320000	28656.65	15288.64	10859.29	8664.42	7363.15	6508.47	5908.77
330000	29552.17	15766.41	11198.64	8935.19	7593.25	6711.86	6093.41
340000	30447.69	16244.18	11538.00	9205.95	7823.35	6915.25	6278.06
350000	31343.21	16721.96	11877.35	9476.71	8053.45	7118.64	6462.71
400000	35820.81	19110.81	13574.11	10830.53	9203.94	8135.58	7385.96
450000	40298.41	21499.66	15270.88	12184.35	10354.43	9152.53	8309.20
500000	44776.01	23888.51	16967.64	13538.16	11504.92	10169.48	9232.45
550000	49253.62	26277.36	18664.41	14891.98	12655.42	11186.43	10155.69
600000	53731.22	28666.21	20361.17	16245.79	13805.91	12203.38	11078.94

Monthly Payments 13½%
necessary to amortize a loan

AMOUNT	8 YEARS	9 YEARS	10 YEARS	11 YEARS	12 YEARS	13 YEARS	14 YEARS
100	1.71	1.60	1.52	1.46	1.41	1.36	1.33
200	3.42	3.21	3.05	2.92	2.81	2.73	2.66
500	8.54	8.02	7.61	7.29	7.03	6.81	6.64
1000	17.09	16.04	15.23	14.58	14.06	13.63	13.28
2000	34.18	32.08	30.45	29.16	28.11	27.26	26.55
5000	85.44	80.21	76.14	72.90	70.29	68.15	66.39
6000	102.53	96.25	91.36	87.48	84.34	81.78	79.66
7000	119.62	112.30	106.59	102.06	98.40	95.41	92.94
8000	136.71	128.34	121.82	116.64	112.46	109.04	106.22
9000	153.79	144.38	137.05	131.22	126.51	122.67	119.49
10000	170.88	160.42	152.27	145.80	140.57	136.30	132.77
15000	256.32	240.63	228.41	218.70	210.86	204.45	199.16
20000	341.76	320.85	304.55	291.60	281.14	272.60	265.54
25000	427.20	401.06	380.69	364.50	351.43	340.75	331.93
30000	512.64	481.27	456.82	437.40	421.72	408.90	398.31
35000	598.09	561.48	532.96	510.30	492.00	477.05	464.70
40000	683.53	641.69	609.10	583.19	562.29	545.20	531.08
45000	768.97	721.90	685.23	656.09	632.57	613.35	597.47
50000	854.41	802.12	761.37	728.99	702.86	681.50	663.85
55000	939.85	882.33	837.51	801.89	773.14	749.65	730.24
60000	1025.29	962.54	913.65	874.79	843.43	817.80	796.62
65000	1110.73	1042.75	989.78	947.69	913.72	885.94	863.01
70000	1196.17	1122.96	1065.92	1020.59	984.00	954.09	929.39
75000	1281.61	1203.17	1142.06	1093.49	1054.29	1022.24	995.78
80000	1367.05	1283.39	1218.19	1166.39	1124.57	1090.39	1062.17
85000	1452.49	1363.60	1294.33	1239.29	1194.86	1158.54	1128.55
90000	1537.93	1443.81	1370.47	1312.19	1265.15	1226.69	1194.94
95000	1623.38	1524.02	1446.61	1385.09	1335.43	1294.84	1261.32
100000	1708.82	1604.23	1522.74	1457.99	1405.72	1362.99	1327.71
105000	1794.26	1684.44	1598.88	1530.89	1476.00	1431.14	1394.09
110000	1879.70	1764.65	1675.02	1603.79	1546.29	1499.29	1460.48
120000	2050.58	1925.08	1827.29	1749.58	1686.86	1635.59	1593.25
130000	2221.46	2085.50	1979.57	1895.38	1827.43	1771.89	1726.02
140000	2392.34	2245.92	2131.84	2041.18	1968.00	1908.19	1858.79
150000	2563.22	2406.35	2284.11	2186.98	2108.58	2044.49	1991.56
160000	2734.11	2566.77	2436.39	2332.77	2249.15	2180.79	2124.33
170000	2904.99	2727.19	2588.66	2478.58	2389.72	2317.09	2257.10
180000	3075.87	2887.62	2740.94	2624.38	2530.29	2453.39	2389.87
190000	3246.75	3048.04	2893.21	2770.17	2670.86	2589.68	2522.64
200000	3417.63	3208.46	3045.49	2915.97	2811.43	2725.98	2655.41
210000	3588.51	3368.89	3197.76	3061.77	2952.01	2862.28	2788.18
220000	3759.40	3529.31	3350.03	3207.57	3092.58	2998.58	2920.96
230000	3930.28	3689.73	3502.31	3353.37	3233.15	3134.88	3053.73
240000	4101.16	3850.16	3654.58	3499.17	3373.72	3271.18	3186.50
250000	4272.04	4010.58	3806.86	3644.97	3514.29	3407.48	3319.27
260000	4442.92	4171.00	3959.13	3790.77	3654.86	3543.78	3452.04
270000	4613.80	4331.42	4111.41	3936.56	3795.44	3680.08	3584.81
280000	4784.68	4491.85	4263.68	4082.36	3936.01	3816.38	3717.58
290000	4955.57	4652.27	4415.95	4228.16	4076.58	3952.68	3850.35
300000	5126.45	4812.69	4568.23	4373.96	4217.15	4088.98	3983.12
310000	5297.33	4973.12	4720.50	4519.76	4357.72	4225.27	4115.89
320000	5468.21	5133.54	4872.78	4665.56	4498.29	4361.57	4248.66
330000	5639.09	5293.96	5025.05	4811.36	4638.87	4497.87	4381.43
340000	5809.97	5454.39	5177.33	4957.16	4779.44	4634.17	4514.20
350000	5980.86	5614.81	5329.60	5102.95	4920.01	4770.47	4646.97
400000	6835.26	6416.93	6090.97	5831.95	5622.87	5451.97	5310.83
450000	7689.67	7219.04	6852.34	6560.94	6325.73	6133.46	5974.68
500000	8544.08	8021.16	7613.71	7289.93	7028.59	6814.96	6638.53
550000	9398.49	8823.27	8375.09	8018.93	7731.44	7496.45	7302.39
600000	10252.90	9625.39	9136.46	8747.92	8434.30	8177.95	7966.24

13¹/₂%

Monthly Payments
necessary to amortize a loan

AMOUNT	15 YEARS	16 YEARS	17 YEARS	18 YEARS	19 YEARS	20 YEARS	21 YEARS
100	1.30	1.27	1.25	1.24	1.22	1.21	1.20
200	2.60	2.55	2.51	2.47	2.44	2.41	2.39
500	6.49	6.37	6.26	6.18	6.10	6.04	5.98
1000	12.98	12.74	12.53	12.35	12.20	12.07	11.96
2000	25.97	25.47	25.06	24.70	24.40	24.15	23.93
5000	64.92	63.68	62.64	61.76	61.01	60.37	59.82
6000	77.90	76.42	75.17	74.11	73.21	72.44	71.78
7000	90.88	89.16	87.70	86.47	85.41	84.52	83.75
8000	103.87	101.89	100.23	98.82	97.62	96.59	95.71
9000	116.85	114.63	112.76	111.17	109.82	108.66	107.67
10000	129.83	127.37	125.29	123.52	122.02	120.74	119.64
15000	194.75	191.05	187.93	185.28	183.03	181.11	179.46
20000	259.66	254.73	250.57	247.05	244.04	241.47	239.27
25000	324.58	318.42	313.22	308.81	305.05	301.84	299.09
30000	389.50	382.10	375.86	370.57	366.06	362.21	358.91
35000	454.41	445.78	438.50	432.33	427.07	422.58	418.73
40000	519.33	509.47	501.15	494.09	488.08	482.95	478.55
45000	584.24	573.15	563.79	555.85	549.10	543.32	538.37
50000	649.16	636.83	626.43	617.62	610.11	603.69	598.18
55000	714.08	700.52	689.08	679.38	671.12	664.06	658.00
60000	778.99	764.20	751.72	741.14	732.13	724.42	717.82
65000	843.91	827.88	814.36	802.90	793.14	784.79	777.64
70000	908.82	891.57	877.01	864.66	854.15	845.16	837.46
75000	973.74	955.25	939.65	926.42	915.16	905.53	897.28
80000	1038.65	1018.93	1002.30	988.19	976.17	965.90	957.10
85000	1103.57	1082.62	1064.94	1049.95	1037.18	1026.27	1016.91
90000	1168.49	1146.30	1127.58	1111.71	1098.19	1086.64	1076.73
95000	1233.40	1209.98	1190.23	1173.47	1159.20	1147.01	1136.55
100000	1298.32	1273.67	1252.87	1235.23	1220.21	1207.37	1196.37
105000	1363.23	1337.35	1315.51	1296.99	1281.22	1267.74	1256.19
110000	1428.15	1401.03	1378.16	1358.75	1342.23	1328.11	1316.01
120000	1557.98	1528.40	1503.44	1482.28	1464.25	1448.85	1435.64
130000	1687.81	1655.77	1628.73	1605.80	1586.27	1569.59	1555.28
140000	1817.65	1783.14	1754.02	1729.32	1708.30	1690.32	1674.92
150000	1947.48	1910.50	1879.30	1852.85	1830.32	1811.06	1794.55
160000	2077.31	2037.87	2004.59	1976.37	1952.34	1931.80	1914.19
170000	2207.14	2165.24	2129.88	2099.89	2074.36	2052.54	2033.83
180000	2336.97	2292.60	2255.16	2223.42	2196.38	2173.27	2153.47
190000	2466.81	2419.97	2380.45	2346.94	2318.40	2294.01	2273.10
200000	2596.64	2547.34	2505.74	2470.46	2440.42	2414.75	2392.74
210000	2726.47	2674.70	2631.02	2593.99	2562.44	2535.49	2512.38
220000	2856.30	2802.07	2756.31	2717.51	2684.47	2656.22	2632.01
230000	2986.13	2929.44	2881.60	2841.03	2806.49	2776.96	2751.65
240000	3115.96	3056.80	3006.89	2964.56	2928.51	2897.70	2871.29
250000	3245.80	3184.17	3132.17	3088.08	3050.53	3018.44	2990.92
260000	3375.63	3311.54	3257.46	3211.60	3172.55	3139.17	3110.56
270000	3505.46	3438.90	3382.75	3335.12	3294.57	3259.91	3230.20
280000	3635.29	3566.27	3508.03	3458.65	3416.59	3380.65	3349.84
290000	3765.12	3693.64	3633.32	3582.17	3538.61	3501.39	3469.47
300000	3894.96	3821.00	3758.61	3705.69	3660.63	3622.12	3589.11
310000	4024.79	3948.37	3883.89	3829.22	3782.66	3742.86	3708.75
320000	4154.62	4075.74	4009.18	3952.74	3904.68	3863.60	3828.38
330000	4284.45	4203.10	4134.47	4076.26	4026.70	3984.34	3948.02
340000	4414.28	4330.47	4259.75	4199.79	4148.72	4105.07	4067.66
350000	4544.11	4457.84	4385.04	4323.31	4270.74	4225.81	4187.29
400000	5193.27	5094.67	5011.48	4940.93	4880.85	4829.50	4785.48
450000	5842.43	5731.51	5637.91	5558.54	5490.95	5433.19	5383.66
500000	6491.59	6368.34	6264.34	6176.16	6101.06	6036.87	5981.85
550000	7140.75	7005.17	6890.78	6793.77	6711.16	6640.56	6580.03
600000	7789.91	7642.01	7517.21	7411.39	7321.27	7244.25	7178.22

Monthly Payments 13½%
necessary to amortize a loan

AMOUNT	22 YEARS	23 YEARS	24 YEARS	25 YEARS	30 YEARS	35 YEARS	40 YEARS
100	1.19	1.18	1.17	1.17	1.15	1.14	1.13
200	2.37	2.36	2.34	2.33	2.29	2.27	2.26
500	5.93	5.89	5.86	5.83	5.73	5.68	5.65
1000	11.87	11.79	11.72	11.66	11.45	11.35	11.30
2000	23.74	23.58	23.43	23.31	22.91	22.71	22.61
5000	59.35	58.94	58.59	58.28	57.27	56.77	56.51
6000	71.21	70.73	70.30	69.94	68.72	68.12	67.82
7000	83.08	82.51	82.02	81.60	80.18	79.47	79.12
8000	94.95	94.30	93.74	93.25	91.63	90.83	90.42
9000	106.82	106.09	105.46	104.91	103.09	102.18	101.72
10000	118.69	117.88	117.17	116.56	114.54	113.53	113.03
15000	178.04	176.81	175.76	174.85	171.81	170.30	169.54
20000	237.38	235.75	234.35	233.13	229.08	227.07	226.05
25000	296.73	294.69	292.93	291.41	286.35	283.84	282.57
30000	356.07	353.63	351.52	349.69	343.62	340.60	339.08
35000	415.42	412.57	410.10	407.98	400.89	397.37	395.59
40000	474.76	471.50	468.69	466.26	458.16	454.14	452.10
45000	534.11	530.44	527.28	524.54	515.44	510.90	508.62
50000	593.46	589.38	585.86	582.82	572.71	567.67	565.13
55000	652.80	648.32	644.45	641.10	629.98	624.44	621.64
60000	712.15	707.26	703.04	699.39	687.25	681.20	678.16
65000	771.49	766.19	761.62	757.67	744.52	737.97	734.67
70000	830.84	825.13	820.21	815.95	801.79	794.74	791.18
75000	890.18	884.07	878.80	874.23	859.06	851.51	847.70
80000	949.53	943.01	937.38	932.52	916.33	908.27	904.21
85000	1008.87	1001.95	995.97	990.80	973.60	965.04	960.72
90000	1068.22	1060.89	1054.55	1049.08	1030.87	1021.81	1017.24
95000	1127.57	1119.82	1113.14	1107.36	1088.14	1078.57	1073.75
100000	1186.91	1178.76	1171.73	1165.64	1145.41	1135.34	1130.26
105000	1246.26	1237.70	1230.31	1223.93	1202.68	1192.11	1186.77
110000	1305.60	1296.64	1288.90	1282.21	1259.95	1248.87	1243.29
120000	1424.29	1414.51	1406.07	1398.77	1374.49	1362.41	1356.31
130000	1542.98	1532.39	1523.25	1515.34	1489.04	1475.94	1469.34
140000	1661.67	1650.27	1640.42	1631.90	1603.58	1589.48	1582.37
150000	1780.37	1768.14	1757.59	1748.47	1718.12	1703.01	1695.39
160000	1899.06	1886.02	1874.78	1865.03	1832.66	1816.54	1808.42
170000	2017.75	2003.89	1991.94	1981.60	1947.20	1930.08	1921.44
180000	2136.44	2121.77	2109.11	2098.16	2061.74	2043.61	2034.47
190000	2255.13	2239.65	2226.28	2214.73	2176.28	2157.15	2147.50
200000	2373.82	2357.52	2343.45	2331.29	2290.82	2270.68	2260.52
210000	2492.51	2475.40	2460.63	2447.85	2405.37	2384.22	2373.55
220000	2611.20	2593.28	2577.80	2564.42	2519.91	2497.75	2486.57
230000	2729.89	2711.15	2694.97	2680.98	2634.45	2611.28	2599.60
240000	2848.59	2829.03	2812.14	2797.55	2748.99	2724.82	2712.63
250000	2967.28	2946.90	2929.32	2914.11	2863.53	2838.35	2825.65
260000	3085.97	3064.78	3046.49	3030.68	2978.07	2951.89	2938.68
270000	3204.66	3182.66	3163.66	3147.24	3092.61	3065.42	3051.71
280000	3323.35	3300.53	3280.84	3263.81	3207.15	3178.95	3164.73
290000	3442.04	3418.41	3398.01	3380.37	3321.70	3292.49	3277.76
300000	3560.73	3536.28	3515.18	3496.93	3436.24	3406.02	3390.78
310000	3679.42	3654.16	3632.35	3613.50	3550.78	3519.56	3503.81
320000	3798.11	3772.04	3749.53	3730.06	3665.32	3633.09	3616.84
330000	3916.80	3889.91	3866.70	3846.63	3779.86	3746.62	3729.86
340000	4035.50	4007.79	3983.87	3963.19	3894.40	3860.16	3842.89
350000	4154.19	4125.66	4101.04	4079.76	4008.94	3973.69	3955.91
400000	4747.64	4715.05	4686.91	4662.58	4581.65	4541.36	4521.04
450000	5341.10	5304.43	5272.77	5245.40	5154.35	5109.03	5086.18
500000	5934.55	5893.81	5858.64	5828.22	5727.06	5676.70	5651.31
550000	6528.01	6483.19	6444.50	6411.05	6299.77	6244.37	6216.44
600000	7121.46	7072.57	7030.36	6993.87	6872.47	6812.04	6781.57

13³/₄%

Monthly Payments
necessary to amortize a loan

AMOUNT	1 YEAR	2 YEARS	3 YEARS	4 YEARS	5 YEARS	6 YEARS	7 YEARS
100	8.97	4.79	3.41	2.72	2.31	2.05	1.86
200	17.93	9.58	6.81	5.44	4.63	4.09	3.72
500	44.83	23.95	17.03	13.60	11.57	10.24	9.30
1000	89.67	47.89	34.06	27.20	23.14	20.47	18.60
2000	179.34	95.79	68.11	54.40	46.28	40.94	37.20
5000	448.35	239.47	170.28	136.01	115.69	102.36	93.01
6000	538.02	287.37	204.34	163.21	138.83	122.83	111.61
7000	627.69	335.26	238.39	190.41	161.97	143.30	130.22
8000	717.36	383.16	272.45	217.61	185.11	163.78	148.82
9000	807.03	431.05	306.51	244.81	208.25	184.25	167.42
10000	896.70	478.95	340.56	272.01	231.39	204.72	186.02
15000	1345.04	718.42	510.84	408.02	347.08	307.08	279.03
20000	1793.39	957.90	681.13	544.02	462.78	409.44	372.04
25000	2241.74	1197.37	851.41	680.03	578.47	511.80	465.05
30000	2690.09	1436.85	1021.69	816.04	694.17	614.16	558.07
35000	3138.43	1676.32	1191.97	952.04	809.86	716.52	651.08
40000	3586.78	1915.79	1362.25	1088.05	925.55	818.88	744.09
45000	4035.13	2155.27	1532.53	1224.06	1041.25	921.25	837.10
50000	4483.48	2394.74	1702.82	1360.06	1156.94	1023.61	930.11
55000	4931.82	2634.22	1873.10	1496.07	1272.64	1125.97	1023.12
60000	5380.17	2873.69	2043.38	1632.07	1388.33	1228.33	1116.13
65000	5828.52	3113.17	2213.66	1768.08	1504.02	1330.69	1209.14
70000	6276.87	3352.64	2383.94	1904.09	1619.72	1433.05	1302.15
75000	6725.21	3592.11	2554.22	2040.09	1735.41	1535.41	1395.16
80000	7173.56	3831.59	2724.51	2176.10	1851.11	1637.77	1488.17
85000	7621.91	4071.06	2894.79	2312.10	1966.80	1740.13	1581.19
90000	8070.26	4310.54	3065.07	2448.11	2082.50	1842.49	1674.20
95000	8518.61	4550.01	3235.35	2584.12	2198.19	1944.85	1767.21
100000	8966.95	4789.49	3405.63	2720.12	2313.88	2047.21	1860.22
105000	9415.30	5028.96	3575.91	2856.13	2429.58	2149.57	1953.23
110000	9863.65	5268.44	3746.20	2992.14	2545.27	2251.93	2046.24
120000	10760.34	5747.38	4086.76	3264.15	2776.66	2456.65	2232.26
130000	11657.04	6226.33	4427.32	3536.16	3008.05	2661.37	2418.28
140000	12553.73	6705.28	4767.89	3808.17	3239.44	2866.10	2604.31
150000	13450.43	7184.23	5108.45	4080.19	3470.83	3070.82	2790.33
160000	14347.12	7663.18	5449.01	4352.20	3702.22	3275.54	2976.35
170000	15243.82	8142.13	5789.58	4624.21	3933.60	3480.26	3162.37
180000	16140.52	8621.08	6130.14	4896.22	4164.99	3684.98	3348.39
190000	17037.21	9100.02	6470.70	5168.23	4396.38	3889.70	3534.41
200000	17933.90	9578.97	6811.27	5440.25	4627.77	4094.42	3720.44
210000	18830.60	10057.92	7151.83	5712.26	4859.16	4299.14	3906.46
220000	19727.30	10536.87	7492.39	5984.27	5090.55	4503.86	4092.48
230000	20623.99	11015.82	7832.96	6256.28	5321.93	4708.59	4278.50
240000	21520.69	11494.77	8173.52	6528.30	5553.32	4913.31	4464.52
250000	22417.38	11973.72	8514.08	6800.31	5784.71	5118.03	4650.54
260000	23314.08	12452.66	8854.65	7072.32	6016.10	5322.75	4836.57
270000	24210.77	12931.61	9195.21	7344.33	6247.49	5527.47	5022.59
280000	25107.47	13410.56	9535.77	7616.35	6478.88	5732.19	5208.61
290000	26004.16	13889.51	9876.34	7888.36	6710.27	5936.91	5394.63
300000	26900.86	14368.46	10216.90	8160.37	6941.65	6141.63	5580.65
310000	27797.55	14847.41	10557.46	8432.38	7173.04	6346.35	5766.68
320000	28694.25	15326.36	10898.03	8704.39	7404.43	6551.08	5952.70
330000	29590.94	15805.31	11238.59	8976.41	7635.82	6755.80	6138.72
340000	30487.64	16284.25	11579.15	9248.42	7867.21	6960.52	6324.74
350000	31384.34	16763.20	11919.72	9520.43	8098.60	7165.24	6510.76
400000	35867.81	19157.95	13622.53	10880.49	9255.54	8188.84	7440.87
450000	40351.29	21552.69	15325.35	12240.56	10412.48	9212.45	8370.98
500000	44834.77	23947.43	17028.17	13600.62	11569.42	10236.06	9301.09
550000	49318.24	26342.18	18730.98	14960.68	12726.36	11259.66	10231.20
600000	53801.72	28736.92	20433.80	16320.74	13883.31	12283.27	11161.31

Monthly Payments 13¾%
necessary to amortize a loan

AMOUNT	8 YEARS	9 YEARS	10 YEARS	11 YEARS	12 YEARS	13 YEARS	14 YEARS
100	1.72	1.62	1.54	1.47	1.42	1.38	1.34
200	3.45	3.24	3.08	2.95	2.84	2.76	2.69
500	8.61	8.09	7.69	7.37	7.11	6.90	6.72
1000	17.23	16.19	15.38	14.73	14.21	13.79	13.44
2000	34.46	32.38	30.75	29.47	28.43	27.58	26.88
5000	86.15	80.94	76.88	73.66	71.07	68.95	67.20
6000	103.38	97.13	92.26	88.40	85.28	82.74	80.64
7000	120.61	113.31	107.64	103.13	99.50	96.53	94.08
8000	137.84	129.50	123.01	117.86	113.71	110.32	107.52
9000	155.07	145.69	138.39	132.60	127.92	124.11	120.97
10000	172.30	161.88	153.77	147.33	142.14	137.90	134.41
15000	258.44	242.82	230.65	220.99	213.21	206.85	201.61
20000	344.59	323.75	307.53	294.66	284.28	275.80	268.81
25000	430.74	404.69	384.42	368.32	355.35	344.75	336.01
30000	516.89	485.63	461.30	441.99	426.41	413.70	403.22
35000	603.03	566.57	538.18	515.65	497.48	482.65	470.42
40000	689.18	647.51	615.07	589.32	568.55	551.60	537.62
45000	775.33	728.45	691.95	662.98	639.62	620.55	604.83
50000	861.48	809.38	768.83	736.64	710.69	689.50	672.03
55000	947.62	890.32	845.72	810.31	781.76	758.45	739.23
60000	1033.77	971.26	922.60	883.97	852.83	827.40	806.43
65000	1119.92	1052.20	999.48	957.64	923.90	896.35	873.64
70000	1206.07	1133.14	1076.37	1031.30	994.97	965.30	940.84
75000	1292.21	1214.08	1153.25	1104.97	1066.04	1034.25	1008.04
80000	1378.36	1295.01	1230.13	1178.63	1137.11	1103.21	1075.25
85000	1464.51	1375.95	1307.02	1252.30	1208.18	1172.16	1142.45
90000	1550.66	1456.89	1383.90	1325.96	1279.24	1241.11	1209.65
95000	1636.81	1537.83	1460.78	1399.62	1350.31	1310.06	1276.85
100000	1722.95	1618.77	1537.67	1473.29	1421.38	1379.01	1344.06
105000	1809.10	1699.71	1614.55	1546.95	1492.45	1447.96	1411.26
110000	1895.25	1780.64	1691.43	1620.62	1563.52	1516.91	1478.46
120000	2067.54	1942.52	1845.20	1767.95	1705.66	1654.81	1612.87
130000	2239.84	2104.40	1998.97	1915.28	1847.80	1792.71	1747.27
140000	2412.13	2266.27	2152.74	2062.60	1989.94	1930.61	1881.68
150000	2584.43	2428.15	2306.50	2209.93	2132.07	2068.51	2016.08
160000	2756.72	2590.03	2460.27	2357.26	2274.21	2206.41	2150.49
170000	2929.02	2751.91	2614.04	2504.59	2416.35	2344.31	2284.90
180000	3101.31	2913.78	2767.80	2651.92	2558.49	2482.21	2419.30
190000	3273.61	3075.66	2921.57	2799.25	2700.63	2620.11	2553.71
200000	3445.91	3237.54	3075.34	2946.58	2842.77	2758.01	2688.11
210000	3618.20	3399.41	3229.10	3093.91	2984.90	2895.91	2822.52
220000	3790.50	3561.29	3382.87	3241.24	3127.04	3033.81	2956.92
230000	3962.79	3723.17	3536.64	3388.56	3269.18	3171.72	3091.33
240000	4135.09	3885.04	3690.40	3535.89	3411.32	3309.62	3225.74
250000	4307.38	4046.92	3844.17	3683.22	3553.46	3447.52	3360.14
260000	4479.68	4208.80	3997.94	3830.55	3695.60	3585.42	3494.55
270000	4651.97	4370.67	4151.70	3977.88	3837.73	3723.32	3628.95
280000	4824.27	4532.55	4305.47	4125.21	3979.87	3861.22	3763.36
290000	4996.56	4694.43	4459.24	4272.54	4122.01	3999.12	3897.76
300000	5168.86	4856.30	4613.00	4419.87	4264.15	4137.02	4032.17
310000	5341.15	5018.18	4766.77	4567.20	4406.29	4274.92	4166.57
320000	5513.45	5180.06	4920.54	4714.52	4548.42	4412.82	4300.98
330000	5685.74	5341.93	5074.30	4861.85	4690.56	4550.72	4435.39
340000	5858.04	5503.81	5228.07	5009.18	4832.70	4688.62	4569.79
350000	6030.33	5665.69	5381.84	5156.51	4974.84	4826.52	4704.20
400000	6891.81	6475.07	6150.67	5893.16	5685.53	5516.03	5376.23
450000	7753.29	7284.45	6919.51	6629.80	6396.22	6205.53	6048.25
500000	8614.76	8093.84	7688.34	7366.44	7106.91	6895.03	6720.28
550000	9476.24	8903.22	8457.17	8103.09	7817.61	7584.54	7392.31
600000	10337.72	9712.61	9226.01	8839.73	8528.30	8274.04	8064.34

AMOUNT	15 YEARS	16 YEARS	17 YEARS	18 YEARS	19 YEARS	20 YEARS	21 YEARS
100	1.31	1.29	1.27	1.25	1.24	1.23	1.21
200	2.63	2.58	2.54	2.51	2.48	2.45	2.43
500	6.57	6.45	6.35	6.26	6.19	6.13	6.07
1000	13.15	12.91	12.70	12.53	12.38	12.25	12.15
2000	26.30	25.81	25.40	25.06	24.76	24.51	24.29
5000	65.75	64.53	63.51	62.64	61.90	61.27	60.73
6000	78.90	77.44	76.21	75.17	74.28	73.52	72.88
7000	92.05	90.34	88.91	87.69	86.66	85.78	85.02
8000	105.20	103.25	101.61	100.22	99.04	98.03	97.17
9000	118.35	116.16	114.31	112.75	111.42	110.29	109.32
10000	131.50	129.06	127.01	125.28	123.80	122.54	121.46
15000	197.25	193.60	190.52	187.91	185.70	183.81	182.19
20000	263.00	258.13	254.03	250.55	247.60	245.08	242.93
25000	328.75	322.66	317.53	313.19	309.50	306.35	303.66
30000	394.50	387.19	381.04	375.83	371.40	367.62	364.39
35000	460.25	451.72	444.55	438.47	433.30	428.89	425.12
40000	525.99	516.26	508.05	501.11	495.20	490.16	485.85
45000	591.74	580.79	571.56	563.74	557.10	551.43	546.58
50000	657.49	645.32	635.06	626.38	619.00	612.70	607.31
55000	723.24	709.85	698.57	689.02	680.90	673.97	668.04
60000	788.99	774.38	762.08	751.66	742.80	735.24	728.78
65000	854.74	838.92	825.58	814.30	804.70	796.51	789.51
70000	920.49	903.45	889.09	876.93	866.60	857.78	850.24
75000	986.24	967.98	952.60	939.57	928.50	919.05	910.97
80000	1051.99	1032.51	1016.10	1002.21	990.40	980.32	971.70
85000	1117.74	1097.04	1079.61	1064.85	1052.30	1041.59	1032.43
90000	1183.49	1161.58	1143.12	1127.49	1114.20	1102.86	1093.16
95000	1249.24	1226.11	1206.62	1190.13	1176.10	1164.14	1153.90
100000	1314.99	1290.64	1270.13	1252.76	1238.00	1225.41	1214.63
105000	1380.74	1355.17	1333.64	1315.40	1299.90	1286.68	1275.36
110000	1446.49	1419.70	1397.14	1378.04	1361.80	1347.95	1336.09
120000	1577.98	1548.77	1524.15	1503.32	1485.60	1470.49	1457.55
130000	1709.48	1677.83	1651.17	1628.59	1609.40	1593.03	1579.01
140000	1840.98	1806.90	1778.18	1753.87	1733.20	1715.57	1700.46
150000	1972.48	1935.96	1905.19	1879.15	1857.00	1838.11	1821.94
160000	2103.98	2065.02	2032.21	2004.42	1980.80	1960.65	1943.40
170000	2235.48	2194.09	2159.22	2129.70	2104.60	2083.19	2064.87
180000	2366.98	2323.15	2286.23	2254.98	2228.40	2205.73	2186.33
190000	2498.48	2452.22	2413.25	2380.25	2352.20	2328.27	2307.79
200000	2629.97	2581.28	2540.26	2505.53	2476.00	2450.81	2429.25
210000	2761.47	2710.34	2667.27	2630.80	2599.80	2573.35	2550.72
220000	2892.97	2839.41	2794.28	2756.08	2723.60	2695.89	2672.18
230000	3024.47	2968.47	2921.30	2881.36	2847.40	2818.43	2793.64
240000	3155.97	3097.54	3048.31	3006.63	2971.20	2940.97	2915.10
250000	3287.47	3226.60	3175.32	3131.91	3095.00	3063.51	3036.57
260000	3418.97	3355.67	3302.34	3257.19	3218.80	3186.05	3158.03
270000	3550.47	3484.73	3429.35	3382.46	3342.60	3308.59	3279.49
280000	3681.96	3613.79	3556.36	3507.74	3466.40	3431.14	3400.96
290000	3813.46	3742.86	3683.37	3633.02	3590.20	3553.68	3522.42
300000	3944.96	3871.92	3810.39	3758.29	3714.00	3676.22	3643.88
310000	4076.46	4000.99	3937.40	3883.57	3837.80	3798.76	3765.34
320000	4207.96	4130.05	4064.41	4008.84	3961.60	3921.30	3886.81
330000	4339.46	4259.11	4191.43	4134.12	4085.40	4043.84	4008.27
340000	4470.96	4388.18	4318.44	4259.40	4209.20	4166.38	4129.73
350000	4602.46	4517.24	4445.45	4384.67	4333.00	4288.92	4251.19
400000	5259.95	5162.56	5080.52	5011.06	4952.00	4901.62	4858.51
450000	5917.44	5807.88	5715.58	5637.44	5571.00	5514.32	5465.82
500000	6574.94	6453.20	6350.65	6263.82	6190.00	6127.03	6073.13
550000	7232.43	7098.52	6985.71	6890.20	6809.00	6739.73	6680.45
600000	7889.92	7743.84	7620.77	7516.58	7428.00	7352.43	7287.76

Monthly Payments 13¾%

necessary to amortize a loan

AMOUNT	22 YEARS	23 YEARS	24 YEARS	25 YEARS	30 YEARS	35 YEARS	40 YEARS
100	1.21	1.20	1.19	1.18	1.17	1.16	1.15
200	2.41	2.39	2.38	2.37	2.33	2.31	2.30
500	6.03	5.99	5.95	5.92	5.83	5.78	5.75
1000	12.05	11.97	11.91	11.85	11.65	11.55	11.51
2000	24.11	23.95	23.81	23.69	23.30	23.11	23.01
5000	60.27	59.87	59.53	59.23	58.26	57.77	57.53
6000	72.32	71.85	71.43	71.08	69.91	69.33	69.04
7000	84.38	83.82	83.34	82.93	81.56	80.88	80.55
8000	96.43	95.79	95.25	94.77	93.21	92.44	92.05
9000	108.48	107.77	107.15	106.62	104.86	103.99	103.56
10000	120.54	119.74	119.06	118.47	116.51	115.55	115.07
15000	180.81	179.61	178.59	177.70	174.77	173.32	172.60
20000	241.08	239.49	238.12	236.93	233.02	231.10	230.14
25000	301.34	299.36	297.64	296.17	291.28	288.87	287.67
30000	361.61	359.23	357.17	355.40	349.53	346.65	345.21
35000	421.88	419.10	416.70	414.63	407.79	404.42	402.74
40000	482.15	478.97	476.23	473.87	466.05	462.19	460.27
45000	542.42	538.84	535.76	533.10	524.30	519.97	517.81
50000	602.69	598.71	595.29	592.33	582.56	577.74	575.34
55000	662.96	658.59	654.82	651.57	640.81	635.52	632.88
60000	723.23	718.46	714.35	710.80	699.07	693.29	690.41
65000	783.50	778.33	773.88	770.03	757.32	751.07	747.95
70000	843.77	838.20	833.40	829.27	815.58	808.84	805.48
75000	904.03	898.07	892.93	888.50	873.83	866.61	863.01
80000	964.30	957.94	952.46	947.73	932.09	924.39	920.55
85000	1024.57	1017.81	1011.99	1006.97	990.35	982.16	978.08
90000	1084.84	1077.68	1071.52	1066.20	1048.60	1039.94	1035.62
95000	1145.11	1137.56	1131.05	1125.43	1106.86	1097.71	1093.15
100000	1205.38	1197.43	1190.58	1184.67	1165.11	1155.49	1150.69
105000	1265.65	1257.30	1250.11	1243.90	1223.37	1213.26	1208.22
110000	1325.92	1317.17	1309.64	1303.13	1281.62	1271.03	1265.75
120000	1446.46	1436.91	1428.69	1421.60	1398.14	1386.58	1380.82
130000	1566.99	1556.66	1547.75	1540.07	1514.65	1502.13	1495.89
140000	1687.53	1676.40	1666.81	1658.53	1631.16	1617.68	1610.96
150000	1808.07	1796.14	1785.87	1777.00	1747.67	1733.23	1726.03
160000	1928.61	1915.88	1904.92	1895.47	1864.18	1848.78	1841.10
170000	2049.14	2035.63	2023.98	2013.93	1980.69	1964.32	1956.17
180000	2169.68	2155.37	2143.04	2132.40	2097.20	2079.87	2071.23
190000	2290.22	2275.11	2262.10	2250.87	2213.71	2195.42	2186.30
200000	2410.76	2394.86	2381.15	2369.33	2330.23	2310.97	2301.37
210000	2531.30	2514.60	2500.21	2487.80	2446.74	2426.52	2416.44
220000	2651.83	2634.34	2619.27	2606.27	2563.25	2542.07	2531.51
230000	2772.37	2754.08	2738.33	2724.73	2679.76	2657.62	2646.58
240000	2892.91	2873.83	2857.39	2843.20	2796.27	2773.16	2761.64
250000	3013.45	2993.57	2976.44	2961.66	2912.78	2888.71	2876.71
260000	3133.99	3113.31	3095.50	3080.13	3029.29	3004.26	2991.78
270000	3254.52	3233.05	3214.56	3198.60	3145.80	3119.81	3106.85
280000	3375.06	3352.80	3333.62	3317.06	3262.32	3235.36	3221.92
290000	3495.60	3472.54	3452.67	3435.53	3378.83	3350.91	3336.99
300000	3616.14	3592.28	3571.73	3554.00	3495.34	3466.46	3452.06
310000	3736.68	3712.03	3690.79	3672.46	3611.85	3582.00	3567.12
320000	3857.21	3831.77	3809.85	3790.93	3728.36	3697.55	3682.19
330000	3977.75	3951.51	3928.91	3909.40	3844.87	3813.10	3797.26
340000	4098.29	4071.25	4047.96	4027.86	3961.38	3928.65	3912.33
350000	4218.83	4191.00	4167.02	4146.33	4077.89	4044.20	4027.40
400000	4821.52	4789.71	4762.31	4738.66	4660.45	4621.94	4602.74
450000	5424.21	5388.42	5357.60	5331.00	5243.01	5199.68	5178.08
500000	6026.90	5987.14	5952.89	5923.33	5825.56	5777.43	5753.43
550000	6629.59	6585.85	6548.18	6515.66	6408.12	6355.17	6328.77
600000	7232.28	7184.57	7143.46	7108.00	6990.68	6932.91	6904.11

14%

Monthly Payments
necessary to amortize a loan

AMOUNT	1 YEAR	2 YEARS	3 YEARS	4 YEARS	5 YEARS	6 YEARS	7 YEARS
100	8.98	4.80	3.42	2.73	2.33	2.06	1.87
200	17.96	9.60	6.84	5.47	4.65	4.12	3.75
500	44.89	24.01	17.09	13.66	11.63	10.30	9.37
1000	89.79	48.01	34.18	27.33	23.27	20.61	18.74
2000	179.57	96.03	68.36	54.65	46.54	41.21	37.48
5000	448.94	240.06	170.89	136.63	116.34	103.03	93.70
6000	538.72	288.08	205.07	163.96	139.61	123.63	112.44
7000	628.51	336.09	239.24	191.29	162.88	144.24	131.18
8000	718.30	384.10	273.42	218.61	186.15	164.85	149.92
9000	808.08	432.12	307.60	245.94	209.41	185.45	168.66
10000	897.87	480.13	341.78	273.26	232.68	206.06	187.40
15000	1346.81	720.19	512.66	409.90	349.02	309.09	281.10
20000	1795.74	960.26	683.55	546.53	465.37	412.11	374.80
25000	2244.68	1200.32	854.44	683.16	581.71	515.14	468.50
30000	2693.61	1440.39	1025.33	819.79	698.05	618.17	562.20
35000	3142.55	1680.45	1196.22	956.43	814.39	721.20	655.90
40000	3591.48	1920.52	1367.11	1093.06	930.73	824.23	749.60
45000	4040.42	2160.58	1537.99	1229.69	1047.07	927.26	843.30
50000	4489.36	2400.64	1708.88	1366.32	1163.41	1030.29	937.00
55000	4938.29	2640.71	1879.77	1502.96	1279.75	1133.32	1030.70
60000	5387.23	2880.77	2050.66	1639.59	1396.10	1236.34	1124.40
65000	5836.16	3120.84	2221.55	1776.22	1512.44	1339.37	1218.10
70000	6285.10	3360.90	2392.43	1912.85	1628.78	1442.40	1311.80
75000	6734.03	3600.97	2563.32	2049.49	1745.12	1545.43	1405.50
80000	7182.97	3841.03	2734.21	2186.12	1861.46	1648.46	1499.20
85000	7631.90	4081.10	2905.10	2322.75	1977.80	1751.49	1592.90
90000	8080.84	4321.16	3075.99	2459.38	2094.14	1854.52	1686.60
95000	8529.78	4561.22	3246.87	2596.02	2210.48	1957.55	1780.30
100000	8978.71	4801.29	3417.76	2732.65	2326.83	2060.57	1874.00
105000	9427.65	5041.35	3588.65	2869.28	2443.17	2163.60	1967.70
110000	9876.58	5281.42	3759.54	3005.91	2559.51	2266.63	2061.40
120000	10774.45	5761.55	4101.32	3279.18	2792.19	2472.69	2248.80
130000	11672.33	6241.68	4443.09	3552.44	3024.87	2678.75	2436.20
140000	12570.20	6721.80	4784.87	3825.71	3257.56	2884.80	2623.60
150000	13468.07	7201.93	5126.64	4098.97	3490.24	3090.86	2811.00
160000	14365.94	7682.06	5468.42	4372.24	3722.92	3296.92	2998.40
170000	15263.81	8162.19	5810.20	4645.50	3955.60	3502.98	3185.80
180000	16161.68	8642.32	6151.97	4918.77	4188.29	3709.03	3373.20
190000	17059.55	9122.45	6493.75	5192.03	4420.97	3915.09	3560.60
200000	17957.42	9602.58	6835.53	5465.30	4653.65	4121.15	3748.00
210000	18855.29	10082.71	7177.30	5738.56	4886.33	4327.21	3935.40
220000	19753.17	10562.83	7519.08	6011.82	5119.02	4533.26	4122.80
230000	20651.04	11042.96	7860.85	6285.09	5351.70	4739.32	4310.20
240000	21548.91	11523.09	8202.63	6558.35	5584.38	4945.38	4497.60
250000	22446.78	12003.22	8544.41	6831.62	5817.06	5151.43	4685.00
260000	23344.65	12483.35	8886.18	7104.88	6049.75	5357.49	4872.40
270000	24242.52	12963.48	9227.96	7378.15	6282.43	5563.55	5059.80
280000	25140.39	13443.61	9569.74	7651.41	6515.11	5769.61	5247.20
290000	26038.26	13923.74	9911.51	7924.68	6747.79	5975.66	5434.60
300000	26936.14	14403.86	10253.29	8197.94	6980.48	6181.72	5622.00
310000	27834.01	14883.99	10595.07	8471.21	7213.16	6387.78	5809.40
320000	28731.88	15364.12	10936.84	8744.47	7445.84	6593.84	5996.80
330000	29629.75	15844.25	11278.62	9017.74	7678.52	6799.89	6184.20
340000	30527.62	16324.38	11620.39	9291.00	7911.21	7005.95	6371.60
350000	31425.49	16804.51	11962.17	9564.27	8143.89	7212.01	6559.00
400000	35914.85	19205.15	13671.05	10930.59	9307.30	8242.30	7496.00
450000	40404.20	21605.80	15379.93	12296.91	10470.71	9272.58	8433.01
500000	44893.56	24006.44	17088.81	13663.24	11634.13	10302.87	9370.01
550000	49382.91	26407.09	18797.70	15029.56	12797.54	11333.16	10307.01
600000	53872.27	28807.73	20506.58	16395.89	13960.95	12363.44	11244.01

Monthly Payments 14%
necessary to amortize a loan

AMOUNT	8 YEARS	9 YEARS	10 YEARS	11 YEARS	12 YEARS	13 YEARS	14 YEARS
100	1.74	1.63	1.55	1.49	1.44	1.40	1.36
200	3.47	3.27	3.11	2.98	2.87	2.79	2.72
500	8.69	8.17	7.76	7.44	7.19	6.98	6.80
1000	17.37	16.33	15.53	14.89	14.37	13.95	13.60
2000	34.74	32.67	31.05	29.77	28.74	27.90	27.21
5000	86.86	81.67	77.63	74.43	71.86	69.76	68.02
6000	104.23	98.00	93.16	89.32	86.23	83.71	81.63
7000	121.60	114.34	108.69	104.21	100.60	97.66	95.23
8000	138.97	130.67	124.21	119.10	114.97	111.61	108.84
9000	156.34	147.00	139.74	133.98	129.34	125.56	122.44
10000	173.72	163.34	155.27	148.87	143.71	139.51	136.05
15000	260.57	245.01	232.90	223.30	215.57	209.27	204.07
20000	347.43	326.67	310.53	297.73	287.43	279.02	272.10
25000	434.29	408.34	388.17	372.17	359.28	348.78	340.12
30000	521.15	490.01	465.80	446.60	431.14	418.53	408.15
35000	608.00	571.68	543.43	521.03	502.99	488.29	476.17
40000	694.86	653.35	621.07	595.47	574.85	558.04	544.20
45000	781.72	735.02	698.70	669.90	646.71	627.80	612.22
50000	868.58	816.69	776.33	744.33	718.56	697.55	680.24
55000	955.43	898.35	853.97	818.77	790.42	767.31	748.27
60000	1042.29	980.02	931.60	893.20	862.28	837.06	816.29
65000	1129.15	1061.69	1009.23	967.63	934.13	906.82	884.32
70000	1216.01	1143.36	1086.87	1042.07	1005.99	976.57	952.34
75000	1302.86	1225.03	1164.50	1116.50	1077.85	1046.33	1020.37
80000	1389.72	1306.70	1242.13	1190.93	1149.70	1116.08	1088.39
85000	1476.58	1388.36	1319.76	1265.37	1221.56	1185.84	1156.42
90000	1563.44	1470.03	1397.40	1339.80	1293.41	1255.59	1224.44
95000	1650.29	1551.70	1475.03	1414.23	1365.27	1325.35	1292.47
100000	1737.15	1633.37	1552.66	1488.67	1437.13	1395.10	1360.49
105000	1824.01	1715.04	1630.30	1563.10	1508.98	1464.86	1428.51
110000	1910.87	1796.71	1707.93	1637.53	1580.84	1534.61	1496.54
120000	2084.58	1960.04	1863.20	1786.40	1724.55	1674.12	1632.59
130000	2258.30	2123.38	2018.46	1935.27	1868.27	1813.63	1768.64
140000	2432.01	2286.72	2173.73	2084.13	2011.98	1953.14	1904.69
150000	2605.73	2450.06	2329.00	2233.00	2155.69	2092.65	2040.73
160000	2779.44	2613.39	2484.26	2381.87	2299.40	2232.17	2176.78
170000	2953.16	2776.73	2639.53	2530.73	2443.12	2371.68	2312.83
180000	3126.87	2940.07	2794.80	2679.60	2586.83	2511.19	2448.88
190000	3300.59	3103.40	2950.06	2828.47	2730.54	2650.70	2584.93
200000	3474.30	3266.74	3105.33	2977.33	2874.25	2790.21	2720.98
210000	3648.02	3430.08	3260.60	3126.20	3017.97	2929.72	2857.03
220000	3821.73	3593.41	3415.86	3275.07	3161.68	3069.23	2993.08
230000	3995.45	3756.75	3571.13	3423.93	3305.39	3208.74	3129.13
240000	4169.16	3920.09	3726.39	3572.80	3449.11	3348.25	3265.18
250000	4342.88	4083.43	3881.66	3721.67	3592.82	3487.76	3401.22
260000	4516.59	4246.76	4036.93	3870.53	3736.53	3627.27	3537.27
270000	4690.31	4410.10	4192.19	4019.40	3880.24	3766.78	3673.32
280000	4864.02	4573.44	4347.46	4168.27	4023.96	3906.29	3809.37
290000	5037.74	4736.77	4502.73	4317.13	4167.67	4045.80	3945.42
300000	5211.45	4900.11	4657.99	4466.00	4311.38	4185.31	4081.47
310000	5385.17	5063.45	4813.26	4614.86	4455.09	4324.82	4217.52
320000	5558.88	5226.78	4968.53	4763.73	4598.81	4464.33	4353.57
330000	5732.60	5390.12	5123.79	4912.60	4742.52	4603.84	4489.62
340000	5906.31	5553.46	5279.06	5061.46	4886.23	4743.35	4625.66
350000	6080.03	5716.80	5434.33	5210.33	5029.94	4882.86	4761.71
400000	6948.60	6533.48	6210.66	5954.66	5748.51	5580.41	5441.96
450000	7817.18	7350.17	6986.99	6699.00	6467.07	6277.96	6122.20
500000	8685.75	8166.85	7763.32	7443.33	7185.64	6975.51	6802.45
550000	9554.33	8983.54	8539.65	8187.66	7904.20	7673.07	7482.69
600000	10422.90	9800.22	9315.99	8932.00	8622.76	8370.62	8162.94

Monthly Payments
necessary to amortize a loan

AMOUNT	15 YEARS	16 YEARS	17 YEARS	18 YEARS	19 YEARS	20 YEARS	21 YEARS
100	1.33	1.31	1.29	1.27	1.26	1.24	1.23
200	2.66	2.62	2.57	2.54	2.51	2.49	2.47
500	6.66	6.54	6.44	6.35	6.28	6.22	6.16
1000	13.32	13.08	12.87	12.70	12.56	12.44	12.33
2000	26.63	26.15	25.75	25.41	25.12	24.87	24.66
5000	66.59	65.38	64.37	63.52	62.79	62.18	61.65
6000	79.90	78.46	77.25	76.22	75.35	74.61	73.98
7000	93.22	91.54	90.12	88.93	87.91	87.05	86.31
8000	106.54	104.62	103.00	101.63	100.47	99.48	98.64
9000	119.86	117.69	115.87	114.33	113.03	111.92	110.97
10000	133.17	130.77	128.75	127.04	125.59	124.35	123.30
15000	199.76	196.15	193.12	190.56	188.38	186.53	184.95
20000	266.35	261.54	257.50	254.08	251.18	248.70	246.59
25000	332.94	326.92	321.87	317.60	313.97	310.88	308.24
30000	399.52	392.31	386.24	381.11	376.76	373.06	369.89
35000	466.11	457.69	450.62	444.63	439.56	435.23	431.54
40000	532.70	523.08	514.99	508.15	502.35	497.41	493.19
45000	599.28	588.46	579.36	571.67	565.14	559.58	554.84
50000	665.87	653.85	643.74	635.19	627.94	621.76	616.48
55000	732.46	719.23	708.11	698.71	690.73	683.94	678.13
60000	799.04	784.62	772.49	762.23	753.53	746.11	739.78
65000	865.63	850.00	836.86	825.75	816.32	808.29	801.43
70000	932.22	915.39	901.23	889.27	879.11	870.46	863.08
75000	998.81	980.77	965.61	952.79	941.91	932.64	924.73
80000	1065.39	1046.16	1029.98	1016.31	1004.70	994.82	986.37
85000	1131.98	1111.54	1094.35	1079.83	1067.49	1056.99	1048.02
90000	1198.57	1176.93	1158.73	1143.34	1130.29	1119.17	1109.67
95000	1265.15	1242.31	1223.10	1206.86	1193.08	1181.34	1171.32
100000	1331.74	1307.70	1287.48	1270.38	1255.88	1243.52	1232.97
105000	1398.33	1373.08	1351.85	1333.90	1318.67	1305.70	1294.62
110000	1464.92	1438.47	1416.22	1397.42	1381.46	1367.87	1356.26
120000	1598.09	1569.24	1544.97	1524.46	1507.05	1492.22	1479.56
130000	1731.26	1700.01	1673.72	1651.50	1632.64	1616.58	1602.86
140000	1864.43	1830.78	1802.47	1778.54	1758.23	1740.93	1726.15
150000	1997.61	1961.55	1931.21	1905.57	1883.81	1865.28	1849.45
160000	2130.79	2092.32	2059.96	2032.61	2009.40	1989.63	1972.75
170000	2263.96	2223.09	2188.71	2159.65	2134.99	2113.99	2096.04
180000	2397.13	2353.86	2317.46	2286.69	2260.58	2238.34	2219.34
190000	2530.31	2484.63	2446.20	2413.73	2386.16	2362.69	2342.64
200000	2663.48	2615.40	2574.95	2540.77	2511.75	2487.04	2465.93
210000	2796.66	2746.17	2703.70	2667.80	2637.34	2611.39	2589.23
220000	2929.83	2876.94	2832.45	2794.84	2762.93	2735.75	2712.53
230000	3063.01	3007.71	2961.20	2921.88	2888.51	2860.10	2835.82
240000	3196.18	3138.48	3089.94	3048.92	3014.10	2984.45	2959.12
250000	3329.35	3269.25	3218.69	3175.96	3139.69	3108.80	3082.42
260000	3462.53	3400.02	3347.44	3303.00	3265.28	3233.15	3205.71
270000	3595.70	3530.79	3476.19	3430.03	3390.87	3357.51	3329.01
280000	3728.88	3661.56	3604.93	3557.07	3516.45	3481.86	3452.31
290000	3862.05	3792.33	3733.68	3684.11	3642.04	3606.21	3575.60
300000	3995.22	3923.10	3862.43	3811.15	3767.63	3730.56	3698.90
310000	4128.40	4053.87	3991.18	3938.19	3893.22	3854.91	3822.20
320000	4261.57	4184.64	4119.92	4065.23	4018.80	3979.27	3945.49
330000	4394.75	4315.41	4248.67	4192.26	4144.39	4103.62	4068.79
340000	4527.92	4446.18	4377.42	4319.30	4269.98	4227.97	4192.09
350000	4661.09	4576.95	4506.17	4446.34	4395.57	4352.32	4315.38
400000	5326.97	5230.80	5149.90	5081.53	5023.50	4974.08	4931.87
450000	5992.84	5884.65	5793.64	5716.72	5651.44	5595.84	5548.35
500000	6658.71	6538.50	6437.38	6351.92	6279.38	6217.60	6164.84
550000	7324.58	7192.35	7081.12	6987.11	6907.32	6839.36	6781.32
600000	7990.45	7846.20	7724.86	7622.30	7535.26	7461.12	7397.80

Monthly Payments 14%
necessary to amortize a loan

AMOUNT	22 YEARS	23 YEARS	24 YEARS	25 YEARS	30 YEARS	35 YEARS	40 YEARS
100	1.22	1.22	1.21	1.20	1.18	1.18	1.17
200	2.45	2.43	2.42	2.41	2.37	2.35	2.34
500	6.12	6.08	6.05	6.02	5.92	5.88	5.86
1000	12.24	12.16	12.10	12.04	11.85	11.76	11.71
2000	24.48	24.32	24.19	24.08	23.70	23.51	23.42
5000	61.20	60.81	60.48	60.19	59.24	58.78	58.56
6000	73.44	72.97	72.57	72.23	71.09	70.54	70.27
7000	85.68	85.13	84.67	84.26	82.94	82.30	81.98
8000	97.91	97.29	96.76	96.30	94.79	94.05	93.69
9000	110.15	109.46	108.86	108.34	106.64	105.81	105.40
10000	122.39	121.62	120.95	120.38	118.49	117.57	117.11
15000	183.59	182.43	181.43	180.56	177.73	176.35	175.67
20000	244.79	243.23	241.90	240.75	236.97	235.13	234.23
25000	305.98	304.04	302.38	300.94	296.22	293.92	292.79
30000	367.18	364.85	362.85	361.13	355.46	352.70	351.34
35000	428.38	425.66	423.33	421.32	414.71	411.49	409.90
40000	489.57	486.47	483.80	481.50	473.95	470.27	468.46
45000	550.77	547.28	544.28	541.69	533.19	529.05	527.01
50000	611.96	608.09	604.75	601.88	592.44	587.84	585.57
55000	673.16	668.90	665.23	662.07	651.68	646.62	644.13
60000	734.36	729.70	725.70	722.26	710.92	705.40	702.68
65000	795.55	790.51	786.18	782.44	770.17	764.19	761.24
70000	856.75	851.32	846.65	842.63	829.41	822.97	819.80
75000	917.95	912.13	907.13	902.82	888.65	881.75	878.36
80000	979.14	972.94	967.60	963.01	947.90	940.54	936.91
85000	1040.34	1033.75	1028.07	1023.20	1007.14	999.32	995.47
90000	1101.54	1094.56	1088.55	1083.38	1066.38	1058.11	1054.03
95000	1162.73	1155.36	1149.03	1143.57	1125.63	1116.89	1112.58
100000	1223.93	1216.17	1209.50	1203.76	1184.87	1175.67	1171.14
105000	1285.13	1276.98	1269.98	1263.95	1244.12	1234.46	1229.70
110000	1346.32	1337.79	1330.45	1324.14	1303.36	1293.24	1288.25
120000	1468.72	1459.41	1451.41	1444.51	1421.85	1410.81	1405.37
130000	1591.11	1581.03	1572.36	1564.89	1540.33	1528.38	1522.48
140000	1713.50	1702.64	1693.31	1685.27	1658.82	1645.94	1639.60
150000	1835.89	1824.26	1814.26	1805.64	1777.31	1763.51	1756.71
160000	1958.29	1945.88	1935.21	1926.02	1895.79	1881.08	1873.82
170000	2080.68	2067.49	2056.16	2046.39	2014.28	1998.64	1990.94
180000	2203.07	2189.11	2177.11	2166.77	2132.77	2116.21	2108.05
190000	2325.47	2310.73	2298.06	2287.15	2251.26	2233.78	2225.17
200000	2447.86	2432.35	2419.01	2407.52	2369.74	2351.35	2342.28
210000	2570.25	2553.96	2539.96	2527.90	2488.23	2468.91	2459.39
220000	2692.64	2675.58	2660.91	2648.27	2606.72	2586.48	2576.51
230000	2815.04	2797.20	2781.86	2768.65	2725.21	2704.05	2693.62
240000	2937.43	2918.82	2902.81	2889.03	2843.69	2821.62	2810.74
250000	3059.82	3040.43	3023.76	3009.40	2962.18	2939.18	2927.85
260000	3182.22	3162.05	3144.71	3129.78	3080.67	3056.75	3044.96
270000	3304.61	3283.67	3265.66	3250.15	3199.15	3174.32	3162.08
280000	3427.00	3405.28	3386.61	3370.53	3317.64	3291.89	3279.19
290000	3549.40	3526.90	3507.56	3490.91	3436.13	3409.45	3396.31
300000	3671.79	3648.52	3628.51	3611.28	3554.62	3527.02	3513.42
310000	3794.18	3770.14	3749.46	3731.66	3673.10	3644.59	3630.53
320000	3916.57	3891.75	3870.41	3852.04	3791.59	3762.15	3747.65
330000	4038.97	4013.37	3991.36	3972.41	3910.08	3879.72	3864.76
340000	4161.36	4134.99	4112.31	4092.79	4028.56	3997.29	3981.88
350000	4283.75	4256.61	4233.26	4213.16	4147.05	4114.86	4098.99
400000	4895.72	4864.69	4838.02	4815.04	4739.49	4702.69	4684.56
450000	5507.68	5472.78	5442.77	5416.92	5331.92	5290.53	5270.13
500000	6119.65	6080.87	6047.52	6018.81	5924.36	5878.37	5855.70
550000	6731.61	6688.95	6652.27	6620.69	6516.79	6466.20	6441.27
600000	7343.58	7297.04	7257.03	7222.57	7109.23	7054.04	7026.84

14¼%

Monthly Payments
necessary to amortize a loan

AMOUNT	1 YEAR	2 YEARS	3 YEARS	4 YEARS	5 YEARS	6 YEARS	7 YEARS
100	8.99	4.81	3.43	2.75	2.34	2.07	1.89
200	17.98	9.63	6.86	5.49	4.68	4.15	3.78
500	44.95	24.07	17.15	13.73	11.70	10.37	9.44
1000	89.90	48.13	34.30	27.45	23.40	20.74	18.88
2000	179.81	96.26	68.60	54.90	46.80	41.48	37.76
5000	449.52	240.66	171.50	137.26	116.99	103.70	94.39
6000	539.43	288.79	205.80	164.71	140.39	124.44	113.27
7000	629.33	336.92	240.09	192.16	163.79	145.18	132.15
8000	719.24	385.05	274.39	219.62	187.18	165.92	151.03
9000	809.14	433.18	308.69	247.07	210.58	186.66	169.91
10000	899.05	481.31	342.99	274.52	233.98	207.40	188.78
15000	1348.57	721.97	514.49	411.78	350.97	311.10	283.18
20000	1798.10	962.62	685.98	549.04	467.96	414.80	377.57
25000	2247.62	1203.28	857.48	686.30	584.95	518.50	471.96
30000	2697.14	1443.93	1028.98	823.56	701.94	622.20	566.35
35000	3146.67	1684.59	1200.47	960.82	818.93	725.89	660.74
40000	3596.19	1925.24	1371.97	1098.08	935.92	829.59	755.14
45000	4045.72	2165.90	1543.46	1235.34	1052.91	933.29	849.53
50000	4495.24	2406.55	1714.96	1372.60	1169.90	1036.99	943.92
55000	4944.76	2647.21	1886.45	1509.86	1286.89	1140.69	1038.31
60000	5394.29	2887.86	2057.95	1647.12	1403.88	1244.39	1132.70
65000	5843.81	3128.52	2229.45	1784.38	1520.87	1348.09	1227.10
70000	6293.34	3369.17	2400.94	1921.64	1637.86	1451.79	1321.49
75000	6742.86	3609.83	2572.44	2058.90	1754.85	1555.49	1415.88
80000	7192.38	3850.49	2743.93	2196.16	1871.85	1659.19	1510.27
85000	7641.91	4091.14	2915.43	2333.42	1988.84	1762.89	1604.66
90000	8091.43	4331.80	3086.93	2470.68	2105.83	1866.59	1699.05
95000	8540.96	4572.45	3258.42	2607.94	2222.82	1970.29	1793.45
100000	8990.48	4813.11	3429.92	2745.20	2339.81	2073.98	1887.84
105000	9440.00	5053.76	3601.41	2882.47	2456.80	2177.68	1982.23
110000	9889.53	5294.42	3772.91	3019.73	2573.79	2281.38	2076.62
120000	10788.57	5775.73	4115.90	3294.25	2807.77	2488.78	2265.41
130000	11687.62	6257.04	4458.89	3568.77	3041.75	2696.18	2454.19
140000	12586.67	6738.35	4801.88	3843.29	3275.73	2903.58	2642.97
150000	13485.72	7219.66	5144.88	4117.81	3509.71	3110.98	2831.76
160000	14384.77	7700.97	5487.87	4392.33	3743.69	3318.39	3020.54
170000	15283.81	8182.28	5830.86	4666.85	3977.67	3525.77	3209.33
180000	16182.86	8663.59	6173.85	4941.37	4211.65	3733.17	3398.11
190000	17081.91	9144.90	6516.84	5215.89	4445.63	3940.57	3586.89
200000	17980.96	9626.21	6859.84	5490.41	4679.61	4147.97	3775.68
210000	18880.01	10107.52	7202.83	5764.93	4913.59	4355.37	3964.46
220000	19779.05	10588.84	7545.82	6039.45	5147.57	4562.77	4153.25
230000	20678.10	11070.15	7888.81	6313.97	5381.55	4770.16	4342.03
240000	21577.15	11551.46	8231.80	6588.49	5615.54	4977.56	4530.81
250000	22476.20	12032.77	8574.79	6863.01	5849.52	5184.96	4719.60
260000	23375.25	12514.08	8917.79	7137.53	6083.50	5392.36	4908.38
270000	24274.29	12995.39	9260.78	7412.05	6317.48	5599.76	5097.16
280000	25173.34	13476.70	9603.77	7686.57	6551.46	5807.16	5285.95
290000	26072.39	13958.01	9946.76	7961.09	6785.44	6014.56	5474.73
300000	26971.44	14439.32	10289.75	8235.61	7019.42	6221.95	5663.52
310000	27870.48	14920.63	10632.75	8510.14	7253.40	6429.35	5852.30
320000	28769.53	15401.94	10975.74	8784.66	7487.38	6636.75	6041.08
330000	29668.58	15883.25	11318.73	9059.18	7721.36	6844.15	6229.87
340000	30567.63	16364.56	11661.72	9333.70	7955.34	7051.55	6418.65
350000	31466.68	16845.87	12004.71	9608.22	8189.32	7258.95	6607.44
400000	35961.92	19252.43	13719.67	10980.82	9359.23	8295.94	7551.35
450000	40457.16	21658.98	15434.63	12353.42	10529.13	9332.93	8495.27
500000	44952.39	24065.54	17149.59	13726.02	11699.03	10369.92	9439.19
550000	49447.63	26472.09	18864.55	15098.63	12868.93	11406.91	10383.11
600000	53942.87	28878.64	20579.51	16471.23	14038.84	12443.91	11327.03

Monthly Payments 14¼%
necessary to amortize a loan

AMOUNT	8 YEARS	9 YEARS	10 YEARS	11 YEARS	12 YEARS	13 YEARS	14 YEARS
100	1.75	1.65	1.57	1.50	1.45	1.41	1.38
200	3.50	3.30	3.14	3.01	2.91	2.82	2.75
500	8.76	8.24	7.84	7.52	7.26	7.06	6.89
1000	17.51	16.48	15.68	15.04	14.53	14.11	13.77
2000	35.03	32.96	31.35	30.08	29.06	28.23	27.54
5000	87.57	82.40	78.39	75.21	72.65	70.56	68.85
6000	105.08	98.88	94.06	90.25	87.18	84.68	82.62
7000	122.60	115.36	109.74	105.29	101.71	98.79	96.39
8000	140.11	131.84	125.42	120.33	116.24	112.90	110.16
9000	157.63	148.32	141.10	135.37	130.77	127.02	123.93
10000	175.14	164.80	156.77	150.41	145.29	141.13	137.70
15000	262.71	247.21	235.16	225.62	217.94	211.69	206.55
20000	350.28	329.61	313.55	300.82	290.59	282.26	275.40
25000	437.85	412.01	391.93	376.03	363.24	352.82	344.25
30000	525.42	494.41	470.32	451.24	435.88	423.38	413.10
35000	612.99	576.81	548.71	526.44	508.53	493.95	481.95
40000	700.56	659.22	627.09	601.65	581.18	564.51	550.80
45000	788.13	741.62	705.48	676.85	653.83	635.08	619.65
50000	875.70	824.02	783.87	752.06	726.47	705.64	688.50
55000	963.27	906.42	862.25	827.26	799.12	776.20	757.35
60000	1050.84	988.82	940.64	902.47	871.77	846.77	826.20
65000	1138.42	1071.22	1019.03	977.68	944.42	917.33	895.05
70000	1225.99	1153.63	1097.41	1052.88	1017.06	987.90	963.90
75000	1313.56	1236.03	1175.80	1128.09	1089.71	1058.46	1032.75
80000	1401.13	1318.43	1254.18	1203.29	1162.36	1129.02	1101.60
85000	1488.70	1400.83	1332.57	1278.50	1235.01	1199.59	1170.45
90000	1576.27	1483.23	1410.96	1353.71	1307.65	1270.15	1239.31
95000	1663.84	1565.64	1489.34	1428.91	1380.30	1340.72	1308.16
100000	1751.41	1648.04	1567.73	1504.12	1452.95	1411.28	1377.01
105000	1838.98	1730.44	1646.12	1579.32	1525.60	1481.84	1445.86
110000	1926.55	1812.84	1724.50	1654.53	1598.24	1552.41	1514.71
120000	2101.69	1977.65	1881.28	1804.94	1743.54	1693.54	1652.41
130000	2276.83	2142.45	2038.05	1955.35	1888.83	1834.66	1790.11
140000	2451.97	2307.25	2194.82	2105.77	2034.13	1975.79	1927.81
150000	2627.11	2472.06	2351.60	2256.18	2179.42	2116.92	2065.51
160000	2802.25	2636.86	2508.37	2406.59	2324.72	2258.05	2203.21
170000	2977.39	2801.67	2665.14	2557.00	2470.01	2399.18	2340.91
180000	3152.53	2966.47	2821.92	2707.41	2615.31	2540.30	2478.61
190000	3327.67	3131.27	2978.69	2857.82	2760.60	2681.43	2616.31
200000	3502.82	3296.08	3135.46	3008.24	2905.90	2822.56	2754.01
210000	3677.96	3460.88	3292.24	3158.65	3051.19	2963.69	2891.71
220000	3853.10	3625.68	3449.01	3309.06	3196.49	3104.82	3029.41
230000	4028.24	3790.49	3605.78	3459.47	3341.78	3245.95	3167.11
240000	4203.38	3955.29	3762.55	3609.88	3487.08	3387.07	3304.81
250000	4378.52	4120.10	3919.33	3760.29	3632.37	3528.20	3442.51
260000	4553.66	4284.90	4076.10	3910.71	3777.67	3669.33	3580.21
270000	4728.80	4449.70	4232.87	4061.12	3922.96	3810.46	3717.92
280000	4903.94	4614.51	4389.65	4211.53	4068.26	3951.59	3855.62
290000	5079.08	4779.31	4546.42	4361.94	4213.55	4092.71	3993.32
300000	5254.22	4944.11	4703.19	4512.35	4358.85	4233.84	4131.02
310000	5429.36	5108.92	4859.97	4662.77	4504.14	4374.97	4268.72
320000	5604.51	5273.72	5016.74	4813.18	4649.44	4516.10	4406.42
330000	5779.65	5438.53	5173.51	4963.59	4794.73	4657.23	4544.12
340000	5954.79	5603.33	5330.29	5114.00	4940.03	4798.35	4681.82
350000	6129.93	5768.13	5487.06	5264.41	5085.32	4939.48	4819.52
400000	7005.63	6592.15	6270.92	6016.47	5811.80	5645.12	5508.02
450000	7881.34	7416.17	7054.79	6768.53	6538.27	6350.76	6196.53
500000	8757.04	8240.19	7838.66	7520.59	7264.75	7056.40	6885.03
550000	9632.74	9064.21	8622.52	8272.65	7991.22	7762.04	7573.53
600000	10508.45	9888.23	9406.39	9024.71	8717.70	8467.68	8262.03

14¼%

Monthly Payments
necessary to amortize a loan

AMOUNT	15 YEARS	16 YEARS	17 YEARS	18 YEARS	19 YEARS	20 YEARS	21 YEARS
100	1.35	1.32	1.30	1.29	1.27	1.26	1.25
200	2.70	2.65	2.61	2.58	2.55	2.52	2.50
500	6.74	6.62	6.52	6.44	6.37	6.31	6.26
1000	13.49	13.25	13.05	12.88	12.74	12.62	12.51
2000	26.97	26.50	26.10	25.76	25.48	25.23	25.03
5000	67.43	66.24	65.25	64.40	63.69	63.09	62.57
6000	80.91	79.49	78.29	77.29	76.43	75.70	75.08
7000	94.40	92.74	91.34	90.17	89.17	88.32	87.60
8000	107.89	105.99	104.39	103.05	101.91	100.94	100.11
9000	121.37	119.24	117.44	115.93	114.65	113.55	112.62
10000	134.86	132.48	130.49	128.81	127.38	126.17	125.14
15000	202.29	198.73	195.74	193.21	191.08	189.26	187.71
20000	269.72	264.97	260.98	257.62	254.77	252.34	250.28
25000	337.14	331.21	326.23	322.02	318.46	315.43	312.85
30000	404.57	397.45	391.47	386.43	382.15	378.52	375.42
35000	472.00	463.70	456.72	450.83	445.84	441.60	437.99
40000	539.43	529.94	521.96	515.23	509.53	504.69	500.56
45000	606.86	596.18	587.21	579.64	573.23	567.77	563.12
50000	674.29	662.42	652.45	644.04	636.92	630.86	625.69
55000	741.72	728.66	717.70	708.45	700.61	693.95	688.26
60000	809.15	794.91	782.95	772.85	764.30	757.03	750.83
65000	876.58	861.15	848.19	837.26	827.99	820.12	813.40
70000	944.01	927.39	913.44	901.66	891.68	883.20	875.97
75000	1011.43	993.63	978.68	966.07	955.38	946.29	938.54
80000	1078.86	1059.87	1043.93	1030.47	1019.07	1009.38	1001.11
85000	1146.29	1126.12	1109.17	1094.87	1082.76	1072.46	1063.68
90000	1213.72	1192.36	1174.42	1159.28	1146.45	1135.55	1126.25
95000	1281.15	1258.60	1239.66	1223.68	1210.14	1198.63	1188.82
100000	1348.58	1324.84	1304.91	1288.09	1273.84	1261.72	1251.39
105000	1416.01	1391.08	1370.15	1352.49	1337.53	1324.80	1313.96
110000	1483.44	1457.33	1435.40	1416.90	1401.22	1387.89	1376.53
120000	1618.30	1589.81	1565.89	1545.70	1528.60	1514.06	1501.67
130000	1753.15	1722.30	1696.38	1674.51	1655.99	1640.23	1626.80
140000	1888.01	1854.78	1826.87	1803.32	1783.37	1766.41	1751.94
150000	2022.87	1987.26	1957.36	1932.13	1910.75	1892.58	1877.08
160000	2157.73	2119.75	2087.85	2060.94	2038.14	2018.75	2002.22
170000	2292.59	2252.23	2218.34	2189.75	2165.52	2144.92	2127.36
180000	2427.44	2384.72	2348.84	2318.56	2292.90	2271.09	2252.50
190000	2562.30	2517.20	2479.33	2447.37	2420.29	2397.27	2377.64
200000	2697.16	2649.69	2609.82	2576.17	2547.67	2523.44	2502.78
210000	2832.02	2782.17	2740.31	2704.98	2675.05	2649.61	2627.92
220000	2966.88	2914.65	2870.80	2833.79	2802.44	2775.78	2753.05
230000	3101.73	3047.14	3001.29	2962.60	2929.82	2901.95	2878.19
240000	3236.59	3179.62	3131.78	3091.41	3057.20	3028.13	3003.33
250000	3371.45	3312.11	3262.27	3220.22	3184.59	3154.30	3128.47
260000	3506.31	3444.59	3392.76	3349.03	3311.97	3280.47	3253.61
270000	3641.17	3577.08	3523.25	3477.84	3439.35	3406.64	3378.75
280000	3776.02	3709.56	3653.74	3606.64	3566.74	3532.81	3503.89
290000	3910.88	3842.04	3784.23	3735.45	3694.12	3658.98	3629.03
300000	4045.74	3974.53	3914.73	3864.26	3821.51	3785.16	3754.17
310000	4180.60	4107.01	4045.22	3993.07	3948.89	3911.33	3879.30
320000	4315.45	4239.50	4175.71	4121.88	4076.27	4037.50	4004.44
330000	4450.31	4371.98	4306.20	4250.69	4203.66	4163.67	4129.58
340000	4585.17	4504.47	4436.69	4379.50	4331.04	4289.84	4254.72
350000	4720.03	4636.95	4567.18	4508.30	4458.42	4416.02	4379.86
400000	5394.32	5299.37	5219.63	5152.35	5095.34	5046.88	5005.55
450000	6068.61	5961.70	5872.09	5796.39	5732.26	5677.74	5631.25
500000	6742.90	6624.21	6524.54	6440.44	6369.18	6308.59	6256.94
550000	7417.19	7286.64	7177.00	7084.48	7006.09	6939.45	6882.64
600000	8091.48	7949.06	7829.45	7728.52	7643.01	7570.31	7508.33

Monthly Payments 14¼%

necessary to amortize a loan

AMOUNT	22 YEARS	23 YEARS	24 YEARS	25 YEARS	30 YEARS	35 YEARS	40 YEARS
100	1.24	1.23	1.23	1.22	1.20	1.20	1.19
200	2.49	2.47	2.46	2.45	2.41	2.39	2.38
500	6.21	6.17	6.14	6.11	6.02	5.98	5.96
1000	12.43	12.35	12.29	12.23	12.05	11.96	11.92
2000	24.85	24.70	24.57	24.46	24.09	23.92	23.83
5000	62.13	61.75	61.43	61.15	60.23	59.80	59.58
6000	74.55	74.10	73.71	73.38	72.28	71.75	71.50
7000	86.98	86.45	86.00	85.60	84.33	83.71	83.41
8000	99.40	98.80	98.28	97.83	96.37	95.67	95.33
9000	111.83	111.15	110.57	110.06	108.42	107.63	107.25
10000	124.26	123.50	122.85	122.29	120.47	119.59	119.16
15000	186.38	185.25	184.28	183.44	180.70	179.39	178.74
20000	248.51	247.00	245.70	244.59	240.94	239.18	238.32
25000	310.64	308.75	307.13	305.73	301.17	298.98	297.91
30000	372.77	370.50	368.55	366.88	361.41	358.77	357.49
35000	434.90	432.25	429.98	428.02	421.64	418.57	417.07
40000	497.02	494.00	491.40	489.17	481.87	478.36	476.65
45000	559.15	555.75	552.83	550.32	542.11	538.16	536.23
50000	621.28	617.50	614.25	611.46	602.34	597.95	595.81
55000	683.41	679.25	675.68	672.61	662.58	657.75	655.39
60000	745.54	741.00	737.10	733.76	722.81	717.54	714.97
65000	807.66	802.75	798.53	794.90	783.05	777.34	774.56
70000	869.79	864.50	859.95	856.05	843.28	837.13	834.14
75000	931.92	926.25	921.38	917.20	903.52	896.93	893.72
80000	994.05	988.00	982.80	978.34	963.75	956.72	953.30
85000	1056.17	1049.75	1044.23	1039.49	1023.98	1016.52	1012.88
90000	1118.30	1111.50	1105.65	1100.63	1084.22	1076.31	1072.46
95000	1180.43	1173.25	1167.08	1161.78	1144.45	1136.11	1132.04
100000	1242.56	1235.00	1228.51	1222.93	1204.69	1195.90	1191.62
105000	1304.69	1296.75	1289.93	1284.07	1264.92	1255.70	1251.20
110000	1366.81	1358.49	1351.36	1345.22	1325.16	1315.49	1310.79
120000	1491.07	1481.99	1474.21	1467.51	1445.62	1435.08	1429.95
130000	1615.33	1605.49	1597.06	1589.81	1566.09	1554.67	1549.11
140000	1739.58	1728.99	1719.91	1712.10	1686.56	1674.26	1668.27
150000	1863.84	1852.49	1842.76	1834.39	1807.03	1793.85	1787.43
160000	1988.09	1975.99	1965.61	1956.68	1927.50	1913.44	1906.60
170000	2112.35	2099.49	2088.46	2078.98	2047.97	2033.03	2025.76
180000	2236.61	2222.99	2211.31	2201.27	2168.44	2152.62	2144.92
190000	2360.86	2346.49	2334.16	2323.56	2288.91	2272.21	2264.08
200000	2485.12	2469.99	2457.01	2445.86	2409.37	2391.81	2383.25
210000	2609.37	2593.49	2579.86	2568.15	2529.84	2511.40	2502.41
220000	2733.63	2716.99	2702.71	2690.44	2650.31	2630.99	2621.57
230000	2857.88	2840.49	2825.56	2812.73	2770.78	2750.58	2740.73
240000	2982.14	2963.99	2948.41	2935.03	2891.25	2870.17	2859.90
250000	3106.40	3087.49	3071.26	3057.32	3011.72	2989.76	2979.06
260000	3230.65	3210.99	3194.11	3179.61	3132.19	3109.35	3098.22
270000	3354.91	3334.49	3316.96	3301.90	3252.66	3228.94	3217.38
280000	3479.16	3457.99	3439.81	3424.20	3373.12	3348.53	3336.55
290000	3603.42	3581.49	3562.67	3546.49	3493.59	3468.12	3455.71
300000	3727.68	3704.99	3685.52	3668.78	3614.06	3587.71	3574.87
310000	3851.93	3828.49	3808.37	3791.08	3734.53	3707.30	3694.03
320000	3976.19	3951.98	3931.22	3913.37	3855.00	3826.89	3813.19
330000	4100.44	4075.48	4054.07	4035.66	3975.47	3946.48	3932.36
340000	4224.70	4198.98	4176.92	4157.95	4095.94	4066.07	4051.52
350000	4348.95	4322.48	4299.77	4280.25	4216.40	4185.66	4170.68
400000	4970.23	4939.98	4914.02	4891.71	4818.75	4783.61	4766.49
450000	5591.51	5557.48	5528.27	5503.17	5421.09	5381.56	5362.30
500000	6212.79	6174.98	6142.53	6114.64	6023.44	5979.51	5958.12
550000	6834.07	6792.47	6756.78	6726.10	6625.78	6577.46	6553.93
600000	7455.35	7409.97	7371.03	7337.57	7228.12	7175.42	7149.74

14¹/₂%

Monthly Payments
necessary to amortize a loan

AMOUNT	1 YEAR	2 YEARS	3 YEARS	4 YEARS	5 YEARS	6 YEARS	7 YEARS
100	9.00	4.82	3.44	2.76	2.35	2.09	1.90
200	18.00	9.65	6.88	5.52	4.71	4.17	3.80
500	45.01	24.12	17.21	13.79	11.76	10.44	9.51
1000	90.02	48.25	34.42	27.58	23.53	20.87	19.02
2000	180.05	96.50	68.84	55.16	47.06	41.75	38.03
5000	450.11	241.25	172.10	137.89	117.64	104.37	95.09
6000	540.14	289.50	206.53	165.47	141.17	125.25	114.10
7000	630.16	337.75	240.95	193.05	164.70	146.12	133.12
8000	720.18	386.00	275.37	220.62	188.23	167.00	152.14
9000	810.20	434.24	309.79	248.20	211.75	187.87	171.16
10000	900.23	482.49	344.21	275.78	235.28	208.74	190.17
15000	1350.34	723.74	516.31	413.67	352.92	313.12	285.26
20000	1800.45	964.99	688.42	551.56	470.57	417.49	380.35
25000	2250.56	1206.24	860.52	689.45	588.21	521.86	475.43
30000	2700.68	1447.48	1032.63	827.34	705.85	626.23	570.52
35000	3150.79	1688.73	1204.73	965.23	823.49	730.60	665.61
40000	3600.90	1929.98	1376.84	1103.12	941.13	834.98	760.69
45000	4051.01	2171.22	1548.94	1241.01	1058.77	939.35	855.78
50000	4501.13	2412.47	1721.05	1378.90	1176.41	1043.72	950.87
55000	4951.24	2653.72	1893.15	1516.79	1294.06	1148.09	1045.95
60000	5401.35	2894.97	2065.26	1654.68	1411.70	1252.47	1141.04
65000	5851.47	3136.21	2237.36	1792.57	1529.34	1356.84	1236.12
70000	6301.58	3377.46	2409.47	1930.46	1646.98	1461.21	1331.21
75000	6751.69	3618.71	2581.57	2068.35	1764.62	1565.58	1426.30
80000	7201.80	3859.95	2753.68	2206.24	1882.26	1669.95	1521.38
85000	7651.92	4101.20	2925.78	2344.13	1999.90	1774.33	1616.47
90000	8102.03	4342.45	3097.89	2482.02	2117.55	1878.70	1711.56
95000	8552.14	4583.70	3269.99	2619.91	2235.19	1983.07	1806.64
100000	9002.25	4824.94	3442.10	2757.80	2352.83	2087.44	1901.73
105000	9452.37	5066.19	3614.20	2895.69	2470.47	2191.81	1996.82
110000	9902.48	5307.44	3786.31	3033.57	2588.11	2296.19	2091.90
120000	10802.71	5789.93	4130.52	3309.35	2823.39	2504.93	2282.08
130000	11702.93	6272.43	4474.73	3585.13	3058.68	2713.68	2472.25
140000	12603.16	6754.92	4818.94	3860.91	3293.96	2922.42	2662.42
150000	13503.38	7237.41	5163.15	4136.69	3529.24	3131.16	2852.60
160000	14403.61	7719.91	5507.36	4412.47	3764.52	3339.91	3042.77
170000	15303.83	8202.40	5851.57	4688.25	3999.81	3548.65	3232.94
180000	16204.06	8684.90	6195.78	4964.03	4235.09	3757.40	3423.11
190000	17104.28	9167.39	6539.99	5239.81	4470.37	3966.14	3613.29
200000	18004.51	9649.89	6884.20	5515.59	4705.66	4174.89	3803.46
210000	18904.73	10132.38	7228.41	5791.37	4940.94	4383.63	3993.63
220000	19804.96	10614.87	7572.62	6067.15	5176.22	4592.37	4183.81
230000	20705.19	11097.37	7916.82	6342.93	5411.50	4801.12	4373.98
240000	21605.41	11579.86	8261.03	6618.71	5646.79	5009.86	4564.15
250000	22505.64	12062.36	8605.24	6894.49	5882.07	5218.61	4754.33
260000	23405.86	12544.85	8949.45	7170.27	6117.35	5427.35	4944.50
270000	24306.09	13027.35	9293.66	7446.05	6352.64	5636.10	5134.67
280000	25206.31	13509.84	9637.87	7721.83	6587.92	5844.84	5324.85
290000	26106.54	13992.33	9982.08	7997.61	6823.20	6053.58	5515.02
300000	27006.76	14474.83	10326.29	8273.39	7058.48	6262.33	5705.19
310000	27906.99	14957.32	10670.50	8549.17	7293.77	6471.07	5895.36
320000	28807.21	15439.82	11014.71	8824.94	7529.05	6679.82	6085.54
330000	29707.44	15922.31	11358.92	9100.72	7764.33	6888.56	6275.71
340000	30607.67	16404.81	11703.13	9376.50	7999.62	7097.31	6465.88
350000	31507.89	16887.30	12047.34	9652.28	8234.90	7306.05	6656.06
400000	36009.02	19299.77	13768.39	11031.18	9411.31	8349.77	7606.92
450000	40510.15	21712.24	15489.44	12410.08	10587.73	9393.49	8557.79
500000	45011.27	24124.71	17210.49	13788.98	11764.14	10437.21	9508.65
550000	49512.40	26537.19	18931.54	15167.87	12940.55	11480.93	10459.52
600000	54013.53	28949.66	20652.59	16546.77	14116.97	12524.66	11410.38

Monthly Payments 14½%

necessary to amortize a loan

AMOUNT	8 YEARS	9 YEARS	10 YEARS	11 YEARS	12 YEARS	13 YEARS	14 YEARS
100	1.77	1.66	1.58	1.52	1.47	1.43	1.39
200	3.53	3.33	3.17	3.04	2.94	2.86	2.79
500	8.83	8.31	7.91	7.60	7.34	7.14	6.97
1000	17.66	16.63	15.83	15.20	14.69	14.28	13.94
2000	35.31	33.26	31.66	30.39	29.38	28.55	27.87
5000	88.29	83.14	79.14	75.98	73.44	71.38	69.68
6000	105.94	99.77	94.97	91.18	88.13	85.65	83.62
7000	123.60	116.39	110.80	106.38	102.82	99.93	97.55
8000	141.26	133.02	126.63	121.57	117.51	114.20	111.49
9000	158.92	149.65	142.46	136.77	132.20	128.48	125.42
10000	176.57	166.28	158.29	151.96	146.88	142.75	139.36
15000	264.86	249.42	237.43	227.95	220.33	214.13	209.04
20000	353.15	332.55	316.57	303.93	293.77	285.51	278.72
25000	441.43	415.69	395.72	379.91	367.21	356.88	348.40
30000	529.72	498.83	474.86	455.89	440.65	428.26	418.08
35000	618.00	581.97	554.00	531.88	514.10	499.64	487.76
40000	706.29	665.11	633.15	607.86	587.54	571.02	557.44
45000	794.58	748.25	712.29	683.84	660.98	642.39	627.12
50000	882.86	831.39	791.43	759.82	734.42	713.77	696.80
55000	971.15	914.52	870.58	835.80	807.87	785.15	766.48
60000	1059.44	997.66	949.72	911.79	881.31	856.52	836.16
65000	1147.72	1080.80	1028.86	987.77	954.75	927.90	905.84
70000	1236.01	1163.94	1108.01	1063.75	1028.19	999.28	975.52
75000	1324.29	1247.08	1187.15	1139.73	1101.64	1070.65	1045.20
80000	1412.58	1330.22	1266.29	1215.72	1175.08	1142.03	1114.88
85000	1500.87	1413.36	1345.44	1291.70	1248.52	1213.41	1184.56
90000	1589.15	1496.49	1424.58	1367.68	1321.96	1284.78	1254.24
95000	1677.44	1579.63	1503.72	1443.66	1395.41	1356.16	1323.92
100000	1765.73	1662.77	1582.87	1519.64	1468.85	1427.54	1393.60
105000	1854.01	1745.91	1662.01	1595.63	1542.29	1498.91	1463.28
110000	1942.30	1829.05	1741.15	1671.61	1615.73	1570.29	1532.96
120000	2118.87	1995.33	1899.44	1823.57	1762.62	1713.05	1672.32
130000	2295.44	2161.60	2057.73	1975.54	1909.50	1855.80	1811.68
140000	2472.02	2327.88	2216.02	2127.50	2056.39	1998.55	1951.04
150000	2648.59	2494.16	2374.30	2279.47	2175.08	2141.31	2090.41
160000	2825.16	2660.44	2532.59	2431.43	2350.16	2284.06	2229.77
170000	3001.73	2826.71	2690.88	2583.39	2497.04	2426.81	2369.13
180000	3178.31	2992.99	2849.16	2735.36	2643.93	2569.57	2508.49
190000	3354.88	3159.27	3007.45	2887.32	2790.81	2712.32	2647.85
200000	3531.45	3325.54	3165.74	3039.29	2937.70	2855.08	2787.21
210000	3708.02	3491.82	3324.02	3191.25	3084.58	2997.83	2926.57
220000	3884.60	3658.10	3482.31	3343.22	3231.47	3140.58	3065.93
230000	4061.17	3824.38	3640.60	3495.18	3378.35	3283.34	3205.29
240000	4237.74	3990.65	3798.88	3647.15	3525.24	3426.09	3344.65
250000	4414.31	4156.93	3957.17	3799.11	3672.12	3568.84	3484.01
260000	4590.89	4323.21	4115.46	3951.07	3819.01	3711.60	3623.37
270000	4767.46	4489.48	4273.74	4103.04	3965.89	3854.35	3762.73
280000	4944.03	4655.76	4432.03	4255.00	4112.78	3997.11	3902.09
290000	5120.60	4822.04	4590.32	4406.97	4259.66	4139.86	4041.45
300000	5297.18	4988.32	4748.60	4558.93	4406.55	4282.61	4180.81
310000	5473.75	5154.59	4906.89	4710.90	4553.43	4425.37	4320.17
320000	5650.32	5320.87	5065.18	4862.86	4700.32	4568.12	4459.53
330000	5826.89	5487.15	5223.46	5014.82	4847.20	4710.87	4598.89
340000	6003.47	5653.42	5381.75	5166.79	4994.09	4853.63	4738.25
350000	6180.04	5819.70	5540.04	5318.75	5140.97	4996.38	4877.61
400000	7062.90	6651.09	6331.47	6078.58	5875.40	5710.15	5574.41
450000	7945.77	7482.47	7122.91	6838.40	6609.82	6423.92	6271.22
500000	8828.63	8313.86	7914.34	7598.22	7344.24	7137.69	6968.02
550000	9711.49	9145.25	8705.77	8358.04	8078.67	7851.46	7664.82
600000	10594.35	9976.63	9497.21	9117.86	8813.09	8565.23	8361.62

14¹/₂%

Monthly Payments
necessary to amortize a loan

AMOUNT	15 YEARS	16 YEARS	17 YEARS	18 YEARS	19 YEARS	20 YEARS	21 YEARS
100	1.37	1.34	1.32	1.31	1.29	1.28	1.27
200	2.73	2.68	2.64	2.61	2.58	2.56	2.54
500	6.83	6.71	6.61	6.53	6.46	6.40	6.35
1000	13.66	13.42	13.22	13.06	12.92	12.80	12.70
2000	27.31	26.84	26.45	26.12	25.84	25.60	25.40
5000	68.28	67.10	66.12	65.29	64.59	64.00	63.49
6000	81.93	80.52	79.35	78.35	77.51	76.80	76.19
7000	95.59	93.94	92.57	91.41	90.43	89.60	88.89
8000	109.24	107.37	105.79	104.47	103.35	102.40	101.59
9000	122.90	120.79	119.02	117.53	116.27	115.20	114.29
10000	136.55	134.21	132.24	130.59	129.19	128.00	126.99
15000	204.83	201.31	198.36	195.88	193.78	192.00	190.48
20000	273.10	268.41	264.48	261.17	258.38	256.00	253.98
25000	341.38	335.52	330.61	326.47	322.97	320.00	317.47
30000	409.65	402.62	396.73	391.76	387.56	384.00	380.97
35000	477.93	469.72	462.85	457.06	452.16	448.00	444.46
40000	546.20	536.83	528.97	522.35	516.75	512.00	507.96
45000	614.48	603.93	595.09	587.64	581.34	576.00	571.45
50000	682.75	671.04	661.21	652.94	645.94	640.00	634.94
55000	751.03	738.14	727.33	718.23	710.53	704.00	698.44
60000	819.30	805.24	793.45	783.52	775.13	768.00	761.93
65000	887.58	872.35	859.58	848.82	839.72	832.00	825.43
70000	955.85	939.45	925.70	914.11	904.31	896.00	888.92
75000	1024.13	1006.55	991.82	979.41	968.91	960.00	952.42
80000	1092.40	1073.66	1057.94	1044.70	1033.50	1024.00	1015.91
85000	1160.68	1140.76	1124.06	1109.99	1098.09	1088.00	1079.41
90000	1228.95	1207.86	1190.18	1175.29	1162.69	1152.00	1142.90
95000	1297.23	1274.97	1256.30	1240.58	1227.28	1216.00	1206.39
100000	1365.50	1342.07	1322.42	1305.87	1291.88	1280.00	1269.89
105000	1433.78	1409.17	1388.55	1371.17	1356.47	1344.00	1333.38
110000	1502.05	1476.28	1454.67	1436.46	1421.06	1408.00	1396.88
120000	1638.60	1610.48	1586.91	1567.05	1550.25	1536.00	1523.87
130000	1775.15	1744.69	1719.15	1697.64	1679.44	1664.00	1650.86
140000	1911.70	1878.90	1851.39	1828.22	1808.63	1792.00	1777.84
150000	2048.25	2013.11	1983.64	1958.81	1937.81	1920.00	1904.83
160000	2184.80	2147.31	2115.88	2089.40	2067.00	2048.00	2031.82
170000	2321.35	2281.52	2248.12	2219.99	2196.19	2176.00	2158.81
180000	2457.90	2415.73	2380.36	2350.57	2325.38	2304.00	2285.80
190000	2594.45	2549.93	2512.61	2481.16	2454.57	2432.00	2412.79
200000	2731.00	2684.14	2644.85	2611.75	2583.75	2560.00	2539.78
210000	2867.55	2818.35	2777.09	2742.34	2712.94	2688.00	2666.77
220000	3004.10	2952.55	2909.33	2872.92	2842.13	2816.00	2793.75
230000	3140.65	3086.76	3041.58	3003.51	2971.32	2943.99	2920.74
240000	3277.20	3220.97	3173.82	3134.10	3100.50	3071.99	3047.73
250000	3413.75	3355.18	3306.06	3264.69	3229.69	3199.99	3174.72
260000	3550.30	3489.38	3438.30	3395.27	3358.88	3327.99	3301.71
270000	3686.85	3623.59	3570.55	3525.86	3488.07	3455.99	3428.70
280000	3823.40	3757.80	3702.79	3656.45	3617.25	3583.99	3555.69
290000	3959.95	3892.00	3835.03	3787.03	3746.44	3711.99	3682.68
300000	4096.50	4026.21	3967.27	3917.62	3875.63	3839.99	3809.67
310000	4233.05	4160.42	4099.52	4048.21	4004.82	3967.99	3936.65
320000	4369.60	4294.62	4231.76	4178.80	4134.00	4095.99	4063.64
330000	4506.15	4428.83	4364.00	4309.38	4263.19	4223.99	4190.63
340000	4642.70	4563.04	4496.24	4439.97	4392.38	4351.99	4317.62
350000	4779.25	4697.25	4628.48	4570.56	4521.57	4479.99	4444.61
400000	5462.00	5368.28	5289.70	5223.50	5167.51	5119.99	5079.55
450000	6144.75	6039.32	5950.91	5876.43	5813.44	5759.99	5714.50
500000	6827.50	6710.35	6612.12	6529.37	6459.38	6399.99	6349.44
550000	7510.25	7381.39	7273.33	7182.31	7105.32	7039.99	6984.39
600000	8193.01	8052.42	7934.55	7835.24	7751.26	7679.99	7619.33

Monthly Payments 14½%
necessary to amortize a loan

AMOUNT	22 YEARS	23 YEARS	24 YEARS	25 YEARS	30 YEARS	35 YEARS	40 YEARS
100	1.26	1.25	1.25	1.24	1.22	1.22	1.21
200	2.52	2.51	2.50	2.48	2.45	2.43	2.42
500	6.31	6.27	6.24	6.21	6.12	6.08	6.06
1000	12.61	12.54	12.48	12.42	12.25	12.16	12.12
2000	25.23	25.08	24.95	24.84	24.49	24.32	24.24
5000	63.06	62.69	62.38	62.11	61.23	60.81	60.61
6000	75.68	75.23	74.85	74.53	73.47	72.97	72.73
7000	88.29	87.77	87.33	86.95	85.72	85.13	84.85
8000	100.90	100.31	99.81	99.37	97.96	97.29	96.97
9000	113.51	112.85	112.28	111.79	110.21	109.46	109.09
10000	126.13	125.39	124.76	124.22	122.46	121.62	121.21
15000	189.19	188.08	187.14	186.32	183.68	182.43	181.82
20000	252.25	250.78	249.52	248.43	244.91	243.23	242.42
25000	315.32	313.47	311.89	310.54	306.14	304.04	303.03
30000	378.38	376.17	374.27	372.65	367.37	364.85	363.64
35000	441.44	438.86	436.65	434.76	428.59	425.66	424.25
40000	504.51	501.56	499.03	496.87	489.82	486.47	484.85
45000	567.57	564.25	561.41	558.97	551.05	547.28	545.46
50000	630.63	626.95	623.79	621.08	612.28	608.09	606.07
55000	693.70	689.64	686.17	683.19	673.51	668.89	666.67
60000	756.76	752.34	748.55	745.30	734.73	729.70	727.28
65000	819.82	815.03	810.93	807.41	795.96	790.51	787.89
70000	882.89	877.72	873.30	869.51	857.19	851.32	848.49
75000	945.95	940.42	935.68	931.62	918.42	912.13	909.10
80000	1009.01	1003.11	998.06	993.73	979.64	972.94	969.71
85000	1072.07	1065.81	1060.44	1055.84	1040.87	1033.74	1030.31
90000	1135.14	1128.50	1122.82	1117.95	1102.10	1094.55	1090.92
95000	1198.20	1191.20	1185.20	1180.05	1163.33	1155.36	1151.53
100000	1261.26	1253.89	1247.58	1242.16	1224.56	1216.17	1212.13
105000	1324.33	1316.59	1309.96	1304.27	1285.78	1276.98	1272.74
110000	1387.39	1379.28	1372.34	1366.38	1347.01	1337.79	1333.35
120000	1513.52	1504.67	1497.09	1490.60	1469.47	1459.40	1454.56
130000	1639.64	1630.06	1621.85	1614.81	1591.92	1581.02	1575.77
140000	1765.77	1755.45	1746.61	1739.03	1714.38	1702.64	1696.99
150000	1891.90	1880.84	1871.37	1863.24	1836.83	1824.26	1818.20
160000	2018.02	2006.23	1996.12	1987.46	1959.29	1945.87	1939.41
170000	2144.15	2131.62	2120.88	2111.68	2081.75	2067.49	2060.63
180000	2270.28	2257.01	2245.64	2235.89	2204.20	2189.11	2181.84
190000	2396.40	2382.39	2370.40	2360.11	2326.66	2310.72	2303.05
200000	2522.53	2507.78	2495.16	2484.33	2449.11	2432.34	2424.27
210000	2648.66	2633.17	2619.91	2608.54	2571.57	2553.96	2545.48
220000	2774.78	2758.56	2744.67	2732.76	2694.02	2675.58	2666.69
230000	2900.91	2883.95	2869.43	2856.97	2816.48	2797.19	2787.90
240000	3027.03	3009.34	2994.19	2981.19	2938.93	2918.81	2909.12
250000	3153.16	3134.83	3118.95	3105.41	3061.39	3040.43	3030.33
260000	3279.29	3260.12	3243.70	3229.62	3183.85	3162.04	3151.55
270000	3405.41	3385.51	3368.46	3353.84	3306.30	3283.66	3272.76
280000	3531.54	3510.90	3493.22	3478.06	3428.76	3405.28	3393.97
290000	3657.67	3636.29	3617.98	3602.27	3551.21	3526.89	3515.19
300000	3783.79	3761.68	3742.73	3726.49	3673.67	3648.51	3636.40
310000	3909.92	3887.06	3867.49	3850.71	3796.12	3770.13	3757.61
320000	4036.05	4012.45	3992.25	3974.92	3918.58	3891.75	3878.83
330000	4162.17	4137.84	4117.01	4099.14	4041.03	4013.36	4000.04
340000	4288.30	4263.23	4241.77	4223.35	4163.49	4134.98	4121.25
350000	4414.43	4388.62	4366.52	4347.57	4285.95	4256.60	4242.47
400000	5045.06	5015.57	4990.31	4968.65	4898.22	4864.68	4848.53
450000	5675.69	5642.51	5614.10	5589.73	5510.50	5472.77	5454.60
500000	6306.32	6269.46	6237.89	6210.81	6122.78	6080.85	6060.66
550000	6936.95	6896.40	6861.68	6831.90	6735.06	6688.94	6666.73
600000	7567.59	7523.35	7485.47	7452.98	7347.34	7297.02	7272.80

14³/₄%

Monthly Payments
necessary to amortize a loan

AMOUNT	1 YEAR	2 YEARS	3 YEARS	4 YEARS	5 YEARS	6 YEARS	7 YEARS
100	9.01	4.84	3.45	2.77	2.37	2.10	1.92
200	18.03	9.67	6.91	5.54	4.73	4.20	3.83
500	45.07	24.18	17.27	13.85	11.83	10.50	9.58
1000	90.14	48.37	34.54	27.70	23.66	21.01	19.16
2000	180.28	96.74	69.09	55.41	47.32	42.02	38.31
5000	450.70	241.84	172.72	138.52	118.29	105.05	95.78
6000	540.84	290.21	207.26	166.23	141.95	126.06	114.94
7000	630.98	338.58	241.80	193.93	165.61	147.07	134.10
8000	721.12	386.94	276.34	221.63	189.27	168.08	153.25
9000	811.26	435.31	310.89	249.34	212.93	189.09	172.41
10000	901.40	483.68	345.43	277.04	236.59	210.09	191.57
15000	1352.11	725.52	518.15	415.56	354.88	315.14	287.35
20000	1802.81	967.36	690.86	554.08	473.18	420.19	383.14
25000	2253.51	1209.20	863.58	692.60	591.47	525.24	478.92
30000	2704.21	1451.04	1036.29	831.13	709.77	630.28	574.70
35000	3154.91	1692.88	1209.01	969.65	828.06	735.33	670.49
40000	3605.62	1934.72	1381.72	1108.17	946.36	840.38	766.27
45000	4056.32	2176.56	1554.44	1246.69	1064.65	945.43	862.05
50000	4507.02	2418.40	1727.15	1385.21	1182.95	1050.47	957.84
55000	4957.72	2660.24	1899.87	1523.73	1301.24	1155.52	1053.62
60000	5408.42	2902.08	2072.58	1662.25	1419.53	1260.57	1149.41
65000	5859.13	3143.92	2245.30	1800.77	1537.83	1365.62	1245.19
70000	6309.83	3385.76	2418.01	1939.29	1656.12	1470.66	1340.97
75000	6760.53	3627.60	2590.73	2077.81	1774.42	1575.71	1436.76
80000	7211.23	3869.44	2763.44	2216.33	1892.71	1680.76	1532.54
85000	7661.93	4111.28	2936.16	2354.86	2011.01	1785.81	1628.32
90000	8112.63	4353.12	3108.87	2493.38	2129.30	1890.85	1724.11
95000	8563.34	4594.96	3281.59	2631.90	2247.60	1995.90	1819.89
100000	9014.04	4836.80	3454.30	2770.42	2365.89	2100.95	1915.68
105000	9464.74	5078.64	3627.02	2908.94	2484.18	2206.00	2011.46
110000	9915.44	5320.47	3799.73	3047.46	2602.48	2311.04	2107.24
120000	10816.85	5804.15	4145.16	3324.50	2839.07	2521.14	2298.81
130000	11718.26	6287.83	4490.59	3601.54	3075.66	2731.23	2490.38
140000	12619.65	6771.51	4836.02	3878.59	3312.25	2941.33	2681.95
150000	13521.06	7255.19	5181.45	4155.63	3548.84	3151.42	2873.51
160000	14422.46	7738.87	5526.88	4432.67	3785.42	3361.52	3065.08
170000	15323.87	8222.55	5872.31	4709.71	4022.01	3571.61	3256.65
180000	16225.27	8706.23	6217.74	4986.75	4258.60	3781.71	3448.22
190000	17126.67	9189.91	6563.18	5263.80	4495.19	3991.80	3639.78
200000	18028.08	9673.59	6908.61	5540.84	4731.78	4201.90	3831.35
210000	18929.48	10157.27	7254.04	5817.88	4968.37	4411.99	4022.92
220000	19830.89	10640.95	7599.47	6094.92	5204.96	4622.09	4214.49
230000	20732.29	11124.63	7944.90	6371.96	5441.55	4832.18	4406.05
240000	21633.69	11608.31	8290.33	6649.00	5678.14	5042.28	4597.62
250000	22535.10	12091.99	8635.76	6926.05	5914.73	5252.37	4789.19
260000	23436.50	12575.67	8981.19	7203.09	6151.31	5462.47	4980.76
270000	24337.90	13059.35	9326.62	7480.13	6387.90	5672.56	5172.33
280000	25239.31	13543.03	9672.05	7757.17	6624.49	5882.66	5363.89
290000	26140.71	14026.71	10017.48	8034.21	6861.08	6092.75	5555.46
300000	27042.12	14510.39	10362.91	8311.26	7097.67	6302.84	5747.03
310000	27943.52	14994.07	10708.34	8588.30	7334.26	6512.94	5938.60
320000	28844.92	15477.75	11053.77	8865.34	7570.85	6723.03	6130.16
330000	29746.33	15961.42	11399.20	9142.38	7807.44	6933.13	6321.73
340000	30647.73	16445.10	11744.63	9419.42	8044.03	7143.22	6513.30
350000	31549.14	16928.78	12090.06	9696.47	8280.62	7353.32	6704.87
400000	36056.15	19347.18	13817.21	11081.67	9463.56	8403.79	7662.70
450000	40563.17	21765.58	15544.36	12466.88	10646.51	9454.27	8620.54
500000	45070.19	24183.98	17271.51	13852.09	11829.45	10504.74	9578.38
550000	49577.21	26602.37	18998.67	15237.30	13012.40	11555.22	10536.22
600000	54084.23	29020.77	20725.82	16622.51	14195.34	12605.69	11494.06

Monthly Payments 14¾%
necessary to amortize a loan

AMOUNT	8 YEARS	9 YEARS	10 YEARS	11 YEARS	12 YEARS	13 YEARS	14 YEARS
100	1.78	1.68	1.60	1.54	1.48	1.44	1.41
200	3.56	3.36	3.20	3.07	2.97	2.89	2.82
500	8.90	8.39	7.99	7.68	7.42	7.22	7.05
1000	17.80	16.78	15.98	15.35	14.85	14.44	14.10
2000	35.60	33.55	31.96	30.70	29.70	28.88	28.21
5000	89.01	83.88	79.90	76.76	74.24	72.19	70.51
6000	106.81	100.65	95.88	92.11	89.09	86.63	84.62
7000	124.61	117.43	111.87	107.47	103.94	101.07	98.72
8000	142.41	134.21	127.85	122.82	118.79	115.51	112.82
9000	160.21	150.98	143.83	138.17	133.63	129.95	126.93
10000	178.01	167.76	159.81	153.52	148.48	144.39	141.03
15000	267.02	251.64	239.71	230.29	222.72	216.58	211.54
20000	356.02	335.51	319.61	307.05	296.97	288.77	282.06
25000	445.03	419.39	399.52	383.81	371.21	360.97	352.57
30000	534.03	503.27	479.42	460.57	445.45	433.16	423.08
35000	623.04	587.15	559.33	537.34	519.69	505.36	493.60
40000	712.04	671.03	639.23	614.10	593.93	577.55	564.11
45000	801.05	754.91	719.13	690.86	668.17	649.74	634.63
50000	890.05	838.79	799.04	767.62	742.41	721.94	705.14
55000	979.06	922.66	878.94	844.38	816.65	794.13	775.65
60000	1068.06	1006.54	958.84	921.15	890.90	866.32	846.17
65000	1157.07	1090.42	1038.75	997.91	965.14	938.52	916.68
70000	1246.07	1174.30	1118.65	1074.67	1039.38	1010.71	987.20
75000	1335.08	1258.18	1198.56	1151.43	1113.62	1082.91	1057.71
80000	1424.08	1342.06	1278.46	1228.19	1187.86	1155.10	1128.23
85000	1513.09	1425.93	1358.36	1304.96	1262.10	1227.29	1198.74
90000	1602.09	1509.81	1438.27	1381.72	1336.34	1299.49	1269.25
95000	1691.10	1593.69	1518.17	1458.48	1410.58	1371.68	1339.77
100000	1780.10	1677.57	1598.07	1535.24	1484.83	1443.87	1410.28
105000	1869.11	1761.45	1677.98	1612.01	1559.07	1516.07	1480.80
110000	1958.11	1845.33	1757.88	1688.77	1633.31	1588.26	1551.31
120000	2136.12	2013.08	1917.69	1842.29	1781.79	1732.65	1692.34
130000	2314.13	2180.84	2077.50	1995.82	1930.27	1877.04	1833.37
140000	2492.14	2348.60	2237.30	2149.34	2078.76	2021.42	1974.39
150000	2670.16	2516.36	2397.11	2302.86	2227.24	2165.81	2115.42
160000	2848.17	2684.11	2556.92	2456.39	2375.72	2310.20	2256.45
170000	3026.18	2851.87	2716.73	2609.91	2524.20	2454.59	2397.48
180000	3204.19	3019.63	2876.53	2763.44	2672.69	2598.97	2538.51
190000	3382.20	3187.38	3036.34	2916.96	2821.17	2743.36	2679.54
200000	3560.21	3355.14	3196.15	3070.49	2969.65	2887.75	2820.56
210000	3738.22	3522.90	3355.96	3224.01	3118.13	3032.13	2961.59
220000	3916.23	3690.66	3515.76	3377.53	3266.62	3176.52	3102.62
230000	4094.24	3858.41	3675.57	3531.06	3415.10	3320.91	3243.65
240000	4272.25	4026.17	3835.38	3684.58	3563.58	3465.30	3384.68
250000	4450.26	4193.93	3995.19	3838.11	3712.06	3609.68	3525.70
260000	4628.27	4361.68	4154.99	3991.63	3860.55	3754.07	3666.73
270000	4806.28	4529.44	4314.80	4145.16	4009.03	3898.46	3807.76
280000	4984.29	4697.20	4474.61	4298.68	4157.51	4042.85	3948.79
290000	5162.30	4864.95	4634.42	4452.20	4305.99	4187.23	4089.82
300000	5340.31	5032.71	4794.22	4605.73	4454.48	4331.62	4230.85
310000	5518.32	5200.47	4954.03	4759.25	4602.96	4476.01	4371.87
320000	5696.33	5368.23	5113.84	4912.78	4751.44	4620.40	4512.90
330000	5874.34	5535.98	5273.64	5066.30	4899.92	4764.78	4653.93
340000	6052.35	5703.74	5433.45	5219.83	5048.41	4909.17	4794.96
350000	6230.36	5871.50	5593.26	5373.35	5196.89	5053.56	4935.99
400000	7120.41	6710.28	6392.30	6140.97	5939.30	5775.49	5641.13
450000	8010.47	7549.07	7191.33	6908.59	6681.71	6497.43	6346.27
500000	8900.52	8387.85	7990.37	7676.22	7424.13	7219.37	7051.41
550000	9790.57	9226.64	8789.41	8443.84	8166.54	7941.30	7756.55
600000	10680.62	10065.42	9588.45	9211.46	8908.95	8663.24	8461.69

14³/4%

Monthly Payments
necessary to amortize a loan

AMOUNT	15 YEARS	16 YEARS	17 YEARS	18 YEARS	19 YEARS	20 YEARS	21 YEARS
100	1.38	1.36	1.34	1.32	1.31	1.30	1.29
200	2.77	2.72	2.68	2.65	2.62	2.60	2.58
500	6.91	6.80	6.70	6.62	6.55	6.49	6.44
1000	13.83	13.59	13.40	13.24	13.10	12.98	12.88
2000	27.65	27.19	26.80	26.47	26.20	25.97	25.77
5000	69.13	67.97	67.00	66.19	65.50	64.92	64.42
6000	82.95	81.56	80.40	79.42	78.60	77.90	77.31
7000	96.78	95.16	93.80	92.66	91.70	90.88	90.19
8000	110.60	108.75	107.20	105.90	104.80	103.87	103.08
9000	124.43	122.34	120.60	119.14	117.90	116.85	115.96
10000	138.25	135.94	134.00	132.37	131.00	129.84	128.85
15000	207.38	203.91	201.00	198.56	196.50	194.75	193.27
20000	276.50	271.88	268.00	264.75	262.00	259.67	257.69
25000	345.63	339.84	335.01	330.94	327.50	324.59	322.12
30000	414.75	407.81	402.01	397.12	393.00	389.51	386.54
35000	483.88	475.78	469.01	463.31	458.50	454.42	450.96
40000	553.00	543.75	536.01	529.50	524.00	519.34	515.39
45000	622.13	611.72	603.01	595.68	589.50	584.26	579.81
50000	691.25	679.69	670.01	661.87	655.00	649.18	644.23
55000	760.38	747.66	737.01	728.06	720.52	714.10	708.66
60000	829.50	815.63	804.01	794.25	786.00	779.01	773.08
65000	898.63	883.60	871.01	860.43	851.50	843.93	837.50
70000	967.75	951.57	938.02	926.62	917.00	908.85	901.93
75000	1036.88	1019.53	1005.02	992.81	982.50	973.77	966.35
80000	1106.00	1087.50	1072.02	1058.99	1048.00	1038.68	1030.77
85000	1175.13	1155.47	1139.02	1125.18	1113.50	1103.60	1095.20
90000	1244.25	1223.44	1206.02	1191.37	1179.00	1168.52	1159.62
95000	1313.38	1291.41	1273.02	1257.56	1244.50	1233.44	1224.04
100000	1382.50	1359.38	1340.02	1323.74	1310.00	1298.36	1288.47
105000	1451.63	1427.35	1407.02	1389.93	1375.50	1363.27	1352.89
110000	1520.75	1495.32	1474.02	1456.12	1441.00	1428.19	1417.31
120000	1659.00	1631.26	1608.03	1588.49	1572.00	1558.03	1546.16
130000	1797.25	1767.19	1742.03	1720.87	1703.00	1687.86	1675.01
140000	1935.51	1903.13	1876.03	1853.24	1834.00	1817.70	1803.85
150000	2073.76	2039.07	2010.03	1985.61	1965.00	1947.53	1932.70
160000	2212.01	2175.04	2144.04	2117.99	2096.00	2077.37	2061.54
170000	2350.26	2310.95	2278.04	2250.36	2227.00	2207.20	2190.39
180000	2488.51	2446.88	2412.04	2382.74	2358.00	2337.04	2319.24
190000	2626.76	2582.82	2546.04	2515.11	2489.00	2466.88	2448.08
200000	2765.01	2718.76	2680.04	2647.49	2620.00	2596.71	2576.93
210000	2903.26	2854.70	2814.05	2779.86	2751.00	2726.55	2705.78
220000	3041.51	2990.63	2948.05	2912.23	2882.00	2856.38	2834.62
230000	3179.76	3126.57	3082.05	3044.61	3013.00	2986.22	2963.47
240000	3318.01	3262.51	3216.05	3176.98	3144.00	3116.05	3092.32
250000	3456.26	3398.45	3350.06	3309.36	3275.00	3245.89	3221.16
260000	3594.51	3534.39	3484.06	3441.73	3405.99	3375.72	3350.01
270000	3732.76	3670.32	3618.06	3574.11	3536.99	3505.56	3478.86
280000	3871.01	3806.26	3752.06	3706.48	3667.99	3635.39	3607.70
290000	4009.26	3942.20	3886.06	3838.85	3798.99	3765.23	3736.55
300000	4147.51	4078.14	4020.07	3971.23	3929.99	3895.07	3865.40
310000	4285.76	4214.08	4154.07	4103.60	4060.99	4024.90	3994.24
320000	4424.01	4350.01	4288.07	4235.98	4191.99	4154.74	4123.09
330000	4562.26	4485.95	4422.07	4368.35	4322.99	4284.57	4251.94
340000	4700.51	4621.89	4556.08	4500.72	4453.99	4414.41	4380.78
350000	4838.76	4757.83	4690.08	4633.10	4584.99	4544.24	4509.63
400000	5530.02	5437.52	5360.09	5294.97	5239.99	5193.42	5153.86
450000	6221.27	6117.21	6030.10	5956.84	5894.99	5842.60	5798.09
500000	6912.52	6796.90	6700.11	6618.71	6549.99	6491.78	6442.33
550000	7603.77	7476.59	7370.12	7280.58	7204.99	7140.95	7086.56
600000	8295.02	8156.28	8040.13	7942.46	7859.99	7790.13	7730.79

Monthly Payments 14¾%

necessary to amortize a loan

AMOUNT	22 YEARS	23 YEARS	24 YEARS	25 YEARS	30 YEARS	35 YEARS	40 YEARS
100	1.28	1.27	1.27	1.26	1.24	1.24	1.23
200	2.56	2.55	2.53	2.52	2.49	2.47	2.47
500	6.40	6.36	6.33	6.31	6.22	6.18	6.16
1000	12.80	12.73	12.67	12.61	12.44	12.36	12.33
2000	25.60	25.46	25.33	25.23	24.89	24.73	24.65
5000	64.00	63.64	63.34	63.07	62.22	61.82	61.63
6000	76.80	76.37	76.00	75.69	74.67	74.19	73.96
7000	89.60	89.10	88.67	88.30	87.11	86.55	86.29
8000	102.40	101.83	101.34	100.92	99.56	98.92	98.61
9000	115.20	114.56	114.00	113.53	112.00	111.28	110.94
10000	128.00	127.29	126.67	126.15	124.45	123.65	123.27
15000	192.01	190.93	190.01	189.22	186.67	185.47	184.90
20000	256.01	254.57	253.34	252.29	248.90	247.29	246.53
25000	320.01	318.22	316.68	315.37	311.12	309.12	308.17
30000	384.01	381.86	380.02	378.44	373.34	370.94	369.80
35000	448.02	445.50	443.35	441.51	435.57	432.77	431.43
40000	512.02	509.14	506.69	504.59	497.79	494.59	493.07
45000	576.02	572.79	570.02	567.66	560.01	556.41	554.70
50000	640.02	636.43	633.36	630.73	622.24	618.24	616.33
55000	704.02	700.07	696.70	693.81	684.46	680.06	677.97
60000	768.03	763.72	760.03	756.88	746.69	741.88	739.60
65000	832.03	827.36	823.37	819.95	808.91	803.71	801.23
70000	896.03	891.00	886.70	883.03	871.13	865.53	862.87
75000	960.03	954.65	950.04	946.10	933.36	927.36	924.50
80000	1024.04	1018.29	1013.38	1009.17	995.58	989.18	986.13
85000	1088.04	1081.93	1076.71	1072.25	1057.80	1051.00	1047.77
90000	1152.04	1145.57	1140.05	1135.32	1120.03	1112.83	1109.40
95000	1216.04	1209.22	1203.38	1198.39	1182.25	1174.65	1171.03
100000	1280.04	1272.86	1266.72	1261.46	1244.48	1236.47	1232.67
105000	1344.05	1336.50	1330.06	1324.54	1306.70	1298.30	1294.30
110000	1408.05	1400.15	1393.39	1387.61	1368.92	1360.12	1355.93
120000	1536.05	1527.43	1520.06	1513.76	1493.37	1483.77	1479.20
130000	1664.06	1654.72	1646.74	1639.90	1617.82	1607.42	1602.47
140000	1792.06	1782.00	1773.41	1766.05	1742.27	1731.06	1725.73
150000	1920.07	1909.29	1900.08	1892.20	1866.71	1854.71	1849.00
160000	2048.07	2036.58	2026.75	2018.34	1991.16	1978.36	1972.27
170000	2176.08	2163.86	2153.42	2144.49	2115.61	2102.01	2095.53
180000	2304.08	2291.15	2280.10	2270.64	2240.06	2225.65	2218.80
190000	2432.08	2418.43	2406.77	2396.78	2364.50	2349.30	2342.07
200000	2560.09	2545.72	2533.44	2522.93	2488.95	2472.95	2465.33
210000	2688.09	2673.01	2660.11	2649.08	2613.40	2596.60	2588.60
220000	2816.09	2800.29	2786.78	2775.22	2737.85	2720.24	2711.87
230000	2944.10	2927.58	2913.46	2901.37	2862.29	2843.89	2835.13
240000	3072.11	3054.86	3040.13	3027.52	2986.74	2967.54	2958.40
250000	3200.11	3182.15	3166.80	3153.66	3111.19	3091.19	3081.67
260000	3328.12	3309.44	3293.47	3279.81	3235.64	3214.83	3204.93
270000	3456.12	3436.72	3420.14	3405.95	3360.08	3338.48	3328.20
280000	3584.13	3564.01	3546.82	3532.10	3484.53	3462.13	3451.47
290000	3712.13	3691.29	3673.49	3658.25	3608.98	3585.78	3574.73
300000	3840.13	3818.58	3800.16	3784.39	3733.43	3709.42	3698.00
310000	3968.14	3945.87	3926.83	3910.54	3857.87	3833.07	3821.27
320000	4096.14	4073.15	4053.50	4036.69	3982.32	3956.72	3944.53
330000	4224.15	4200.44	4180.18	4162.83	4106.77	4080.37	4067.80
340000	4352.15	4327.73	4306.85	4288.98	4231.22	4204.01	4191.07
350000	4480.16	4455.01	4433.52	4415.13	4355.67	4327.66	4314.34
400000	5120.18	5091.44	5066.88	5045.86	4977.90	4945.90	4930.67
450000	5760.20	5727.87	5700.24	5676.59	5600.14	5564.14	5547.00
500000	6400.22	6364.30	6333.60	6307.32	6222.38	6182.37	6163.34
550000	7040.25	7000.73	6966.96	6938.06	6844.62	6800.61	6779.67
600000	7680.27	7637.16	7600.32	7568.79	7466.85	7418.85	7396.00

15%

Monthly Payments
necessary to amortize a loan

AMOUNT	1 YEAR	2 YEARS	3 YEARS	4 YEARS	5 YEARS	6 YEARS	7 YEARS
100	9.03	4.85	3.47	2.78	2.38	2.11	1.93
200	18.05	9.70	6.93	5.57	4.76	4.23	3.86
500	45.13	24.24	17.33	13.92	11.89	10.57	9.65
1000	90.26	48.49	34.67	27.83	23.79	21.15	19.30
2000	180.52	96.97	69.33	55.66	47.58	42.29	38.59
5000	451.29	242.43	173.33	139.15	118.95	105.73	96.48
6000	541.55	290.92	207.99	166.98	142.74	126.87	115.78
7000	631.81	339.41	242.66	194.82	166.53	148.02	135.08
8000	722.07	387.89	277.32	222.65	190.32	169.16	154.37
9000	812.32	436.38	311.99	250.48	214.11	190.31	173.67
10000	902.58	484.87	346.65	278.31	237.90	211.45	192.97
15000	1353.87	727.30	519.98	417.46	356.85	317.18	289.45
20000	1805.17	969.73	693.31	556.61	475.80	422.90	385.94
25000	2256.46	1212.17	866.63	695.77	594.75	528.63	482.42
30000	2707.75	1454.60	1039.96	834.92	713.70	634.35	578.90
35000	3159.04	1697.03	1213.29	974.08	832.65	740.08	675.39
40000	3610.33	1939.47	1386.61	1113.23	951.60	845.80	771.87
45000	4061.62	2181.90	1559.94	1252.38	1070.55	951.53	868.35
50000	4512.92	2424.33	1733.27	1391.54	1189.50	1057.25	964.84
55000	4964.21	2666.77	1906.59	1530.69	1308.45	1162.98	1061.32
60000	5415.50	2909.20	2079.92	1669.84	1427.40	1268.70	1157.81
65000	5866.79	3151.63	2253.25	1809.00	1546.35	1374.43	1254.29
70000	6318.08	3394.07	2426.57	1948.15	1665.30	1480.15	1350.77
75000	6769.37	3636.50	2599.90	2087.31	1784.24	1585.88	1447.26
80000	7220.66	3878.93	2773.23	2226.46	1903.19	1691.60	1543.74
85000	7671.96	4121.37	2946.55	2365.61	2022.14	1797.33	1640.22
90000	8123.25	4363.80	3119.88	2504.77	2141.09	1903.05	1736.71
95000	8574.54	4606.23	3293.21	2643.92	2260.04	2008.78	1833.19
100000	9025.83	4848.66	3466.53	2783.07	2378.99	2114.50	1929.68
105000	9477.12	5091.10	3639.86	2922.23	2497.94	2220.23	2026.16
110000	9928.41	5333.53	3813.19	3061.38	2616.89	2325.95	2122.64
120000	10831.00	5818.40	4159.84	3339.69	2854.79	2537.40	2315.61
130000	11733.58	6303.26	4506.49	3618.00	3092.69	2748.85	2508.58
140000	12636.16	6788.13	4853.15	3896.30	3330.59	2960.30	2701.55
150000	13538.75	7273.00	5199.80	4174.61	3568.49	3171.75	2894.51
160000	14441.33	7757.86	5546.45	4452.92	3806.39	3383.20	3087.48
170000	15343.91	8242.73	5893.11	4731.23	4044.29	3594.65	3280.45
180000	16246.50	8727.60	6239.76	5009.53	4282.19	3806.10	3473.42
190000	17149.08	9212.46	6586.41	5287.84	4520.09	4017.55	3666.38
200000	18051.66	9697.33	6933.07	5566.15	4757.99	4229.00	3859.35
210000	18954.25	10182.20	7279.72	5844.46	4995.89	4440.45	4052.32
220000	19856.83	10667.06	7626.37	6122.76	5233.78	4651.90	4245.29
230000	20759.41	11151.93	7973.03	6401.07	5471.68	4863.35	4438.25
240000	21661.99	11636.80	8319.68	6679.38	5709.58	5074.80	4631.22
250000	22564.58	12121.66	8666.33	6957.69	5947.48	5286.25	4824.19
260000	23467.16	12606.53	9012.99	7235.99	6185.38	5497.70	5017.16
270000	24369.74	13091.39	9359.64	7514.30	6423.28	5709.15	5210.12
280000	25272.33	13576.26	9706.29	7792.61	6661.18	5920.60	5403.09
290000	26174.91	14061.13	10052.95	8070.92	6899.08	6132.05	5596.06
300000	27077.49	14545.99	10399.60	8349.22	7136.98	6343.50	5789.03
310000	27980.08	15030.86	10746.25	8627.53	7374.88	6554.95	5981.99
320000	28882.66	15515.73	11092.91	8905.84	7612.78	6766.40	6174.96
330000	29785.24	16000.59	11439.56	9184.15	7850.68	6977.85	6367.93
340000	30687.83	16485.46	11786.21	9462.45	8088.58	7189.30	6560.90
350000	31590.41	16970.33	12132.86	9740.76	8326.48	7400.75	6753.86
400000	36103.32	19394.66	13866.13	11132.30	9515.97	8458.01	7718.70
450000	40616.24	21818.99	15599.40	12523.84	10705.47	9515.26	8683.54
500000	45129.16	24243.32	17332.66	13915.37	11894.97	10572.51	9648.38
550000	49642.07	26667.66	19065.93	15306.91	13084.46	11629.76	10613.22
600000	54154.99	29091.99	20799.20	16698.45	14273.96	12687.01	11578.05

Monthly Payments **15%**
necessary to amortize a loan

AMOUNT	8 YEARS	9 YEARS	10 YEARS	11 YEARS	12 YEARS	13 YEARS	14 YEARS
100	1.79	1.69	1.61	1.55	1.50	1.46	1.43
200	3.59	3.38	3.23	3.10	3.00	2.92	2.85
500	8.97	8.46	8.07	7.75	7.50	7.30	7.14
1000	17.95	16.92	16.13	15.51	15.01	14.60	14.27
2000	35.89	33.85	32.27	31.02	30.02	29.21	28.54
5000	89.73	84.62	80.67	77.55	75.04	73.01	71.35
6000	107.67	101.55	96.80	93.05	90.05	87.62	85.62
7000	125.62	118.47	112.93	108.56	105.06	102.22	99.89
8000	143.56	135.39	129.07	124.07	120.07	116.82	114.16
9000	161.51	152.32	145.20	139.58	135.08	131.43	128.43
10000	179.45	169.24	161.33	155.09	150.09	146.03	142.70
15000	269.18	253.87	242.00	232.64	225.13	219.04	214.06
20000	358.91	338.49	322.67	310.18	300.18	292.06	285.41
25000	448.64	423.11	403.34	387.73	375.22	365.07	356.76
30000	538.36	507.73	484.00	465.27	450.26	438.09	428.11
35000	628.09	592.35	564.67	542.82	525.31	511.10	499.46
40000	717.82	676.97	645.34	620.37	600.35	584.11	570.82
45000	807.54	761.60	726.01	697.91	675.39	657.13	642.17
50000	897.27	846.22	806.67	775.46	750.44	730.14	713.52
55000	987.00	930.84	887.34	853.00	825.48	803.16	784.87
60000	1076.72	1015.46	968.01	930.55	900.53	876.17	856.22
65000	1166.45	1100.08	1048.68	1008.09	975.57	949.19	927.58
70000	1256.18	1184.70	1129.34	1085.64	1050.61	1022.20	998.93
75000	1345.91	1269.33	1210.01	1163.19	1125.66	1095.22	1070.28
80000	1435.63	1353.95	1290.68	1240.73	1200.70	1168.23	1141.63
85000	1525.36	1438.57	1371.35	1318.28	1275.75	1241.24	1212.98
90000	1615.09	1523.19	1452.01	1395.82	1350.79	1314.26	1284.34
95000	1704.81	1607.81	1532.68	1473.37	1425.83	1387.27	1355.69
100000	1794.54	1692.43	1613.35	1550.91	1500.88	1460.29	1427.04
105000	1884.27	1777.06	1694.02	1628.46	1575.92	1533.30	1498.39
110000	1973.99	1861.68	1774.68	1706.01	1650.96	1606.32	1569.74
120000	2153.45	2030.92	1936.02	1861.10	1801.05	1752.34	1712.45
130000	2332.90	2200.16	2097.35	2016.19	1951.14	1898.37	1855.15
140000	2512.36	2369.41	2258.69	2171.28	2101.23	2044.40	1997.86
150000	2691.81	2538.65	2420.02	2326.37	2251.32	2190.43	2140.56
160000	2871.26	2707.89	2581.36	2481.46	2401.40	2336.46	2283.26
170000	3050.72	2877.14	2742.69	2636.56	2551.49	2482.49	2425.97
180000	3230.17	3046.38	2904.03	2791.65	2701.58	2628.52	2568.67
190000	3409.63	3215.62	3065.36	2946.74	2851.67	2774.55	2711.38
200000	3589.08	3384.87	3226.70	3101.83	3001.75	2920.57	2854.08
210000	3768.54	3554.11	3388.03	3256.92	3151.84	3066.60	2996.78
220000	3947.99	3723.35	3549.37	3412.01	3301.93	3212.63	3139.49
230000	4127.44	3892.60	3710.70	3567.10	3452.02	3358.66	3282.19
240000	4306.90	4061.84	3872.04	3722.20	3602.10	3504.69	3424.90
250000	4486.35	4231.08	4033.37	3877.29	3752.19	3650.72	3567.60
260000	4665.81	4400.33	4194.71	4032.38	3902.28	3796.75	3710.30
270000	4845.26	4569.57	4356.04	4187.47	4052.37	3942.78	3853.01
280000	5024.71	4738.81	4517.38	4342.56	4202.45	4088.80	3995.71
290000	5204.17	4908.06	4678.71	4497.65	4352.54	4234.83	4138.42
300000	5383.62	5077.30	4840.05	4652.74	4502.63	4380.86	4281.12
310000	5563.08	5246.54	5001.38	4807.84	4652.72	4526.89	4423.82
320000	5742.53	5415.79	5162.72	4962.93	4802.81	4672.92	4566.53
330000	5921.98	5585.03	5324.05	5118.02	4952.89	4818.95	4709.23
340000	6101.44	5754.27	5485.39	5273.11	5102.98	4964.98	4851.94
350000	6280.89	5923.52	5646.72	5428.20	5253.07	5111.01	4994.64
400000	7178.16	6769.73	6453.40	6203.66	6003.51	5841.15	5708.16
450000	8075.43	7615.95	7260.07	6979.12	6753.95	6571.29	6421.68
500000	8972.70	8462.17	8066.75	7754.57	7504.38	7301.44	7135.20
550000	9869.97	9308.39	8873.42	8530.03	8254.82	8031.58	7848.72
600000	10767.24	10154.60	9680.10	9305.49	9005.26	8761.72	8562.24

15%

Monthly Payments
necessary to amortize a loan

AMOUNT	15 YEARS	16 YEARS	17 YEARS	18 YEARS	19 YEARS	20 YEARS	21 YEARS
100	1.40	1.38	1.36	1.34	1.33	1.32	1.31
200	2.80	2.75	2.72	2.68	2.66	2.63	2.61
500	7.00	6.88	6.79	6.71	6.64	6.58	6.54
1000	14.00	13.77	13.58	13.42	13.28	13.17	13.07
2000	27.99	27.54	27.15	26.83	26.56	26.34	26.14
5000	69.98	68.84	67.89	67.08	66.41	65.84	65.36
6000	83.98	82.61	81.46	80.50	79.69	79.01	78.43
7000	97.97	96.37	95.04	93.92	92.97	92.18	91.50
8000	111.97	110.14	108.62	107.34	106.26	105.34	104.57
9000	125.96	123.91	122.19	120.75	119.54	118.51	117.64
10000	139.96	137.68	135.77	134.17	132.82	131.68	130.71
15000	209.94	206.52	203.66	201.25	199.23	197.52	196.07
20000	279.92	275.35	271.54	268.34	265.64	263.36	261.42
25000	349.90	344.19	339.43	335.42	332.05	329.20	326.78
30000	419.88	413.03	407.31	402.51	398.46	395.04	392.14
35000	489.86	481.87	475.20	469.59	464.87	460.88	457.49
40000	559.83	550.71	543.08	536.68	531.28	526.72	522.85
45000	629.81	619.55	610.97	603.76	597.69	592.56	588.20
50000	699.79	688.38	678.85	670.85	664.10	658.39	653.56
55000	769.77	757.22	746.74	737.93	730.51	724.23	718.91
60000	839.75	826.06	814.62	805.01	796.92	790.07	784.27
65000	909.73	894.90	882.51	872.10	863.33	855.91	849.63
70000	979.71	963.74	950.39	939.18	929.74	921.75	914.98
75000	1049.69	1032.58	1018.28	1006.27	996.15	987.59	980.34
80000	1119.67	1101.42	1086.16	1073.35	1062.56	1053.43	1045.69
85000	1189.65	1170.25	1154.05	1140.44	1128.97	1119.27	1111.05
90000	1259.63	1239.09	1221.93	1207.52	1195.38	1185.11	1176.41
95000	1329.61	1307.93	1289.82	1274.61	1261.79	1250.95	1241.76
100000	1399.59	1376.77	1357.70	1341.69	1328.20	1316.79	1307.12
105000	1469.57	1445.61	1425.59	1408.78	1394.61	1382.63	1372.47
110000	1539.55	1514.45	1493.47	1475.86	1461.02	1448.47	1437.83
120000	1679.50	1652.12	1629.24	1610.03	1593.84	1580.15	1568.54
130000	1819.46	1789.80	1765.01	1744.20	1726.66	1711.83	1699.25
140000	1959.42	1927.48	1900.78	1878.37	1859.48	1843.51	1829.96
150000	2099.38	2065.15	2036.55	2012.54	1992.30	1975.18	1960.68
160000	2239.34	2202.83	2172.32	2146.71	2125.12	2106.86	2091.39
170000	2379.30	2340.51	2308.09	2280.87	2257.94	2238.54	2222.10
180000	2519.26	2478.19	2443.86	2415.04	2390.76	2370.22	2352.81
190000	2659.22	2615.86	2579.63	2549.21	2523.58	2501.90	2483.52
200000	2799.17	2753.54	2715.40	2683.38	2656.40	2633.58	2614.23
210000	2939.13	2891.22	2851.17	2817.55	2789.22	2765.26	2744.95
220000	3079.09	3028.89	2986.94	2951.72	2922.04	2896.94	2875.66
230000	3219.05	3166.57	3122.71	3085.89	3054.86	3028.62	3006.37
240000	3359.01	3304.25	3258.48	3220.06	3187.68	3160.29	3137.08
250000	3498.97	3441.92	3394.25	3354.23	3320.49	3291.97	3267.79
260000	3638.93	3579.60	3530.02	3488.40	3453.31	3423.65	3398.50
270000	3778.89	3717.28	3665.79	3622.57	3586.13	3555.33	3529.22
280000	3918.84	3854.95	3801.56	3756.73	3718.95	3687.01	3659.93
290000	4058.80	3992.63	3937.33	3890.90	3851.77	3818.69	3790.64
300000	4198.76	4130.31	4073.10	4025.07	3984.59	3950.37	3921.35
310000	4338.72	4267.99	4208.87	4159.24	4117.41	4082.05	4052.06
320000	4478.68	4405.66	4344.64	4293.41	4250.23	4213.73	4182.77
330000	4618.64	4543.34	4480.41	4427.58	4383.05	4345.41	4313.49
340000	4758.60	4681.02	4616.18	4561.75	4515.87	4477.08	4444.20
350000	4898.55	4818.69	4751.95	4695.92	4648.69	4608.76	4574.91
400000	5598.35	5507.08	5430.80	5366.76	5312.79	5267.16	5228.47
450000	6298.14	6195.46	6109.65	6037.61	5976.89	5925.55	5882.03
500000	6997.94	6883.85	6788.50	6708.45	6640.99	6583.95	6535.59
550000	7697.73	7572.23	7467.35	7379.30	7305.09	7242.34	7189.14
600000	8397.52	8260.62	8146.20	8050.14	7969.19	7900.74	7842.70

Monthly Payments
necessary to amortize a loan

15%

AMOUNT	22 YEARS	23 YEARS	24 YEARS	25 YEARS	30 YEARS	35 YEARS	40 YEARS
100	1.30	1.29	1.29	1.28	1.26	1.26	1.25
200	2.60	2.58	2.57	2.56	2.53	2.51	2.51
500	6.49	6.46	6.43	6.40	6.32	6.28	6.27
1000	12.99	12.92	12.86	12.81	12.64	12.57	12.53
2000	25.98	25.84	25.72	25.62	25.29	25.14	25.06
5000	64.94	64.59	64.30	64.04	63.22	62.84	62.66
6000	77.93	77.51	77.16	76.85	75.87	75.41	75.19
7000	90.92	90.43	90.02	89.66	88.51	87.98	87.73
8000	103.91	103.35	102.87	102.47	101.16	100.55	100.26
9000	116.90	116.27	115.73	115.27	113.80	113.11	112.79
10000	129.89	129.19	128.59	128.08	126.44	125.68	125.32
15000	194.83	193.78	192.89	192.12	189.67	188.52	187.98
20000	259.78	258.38	257.19	256.17	252.89	251.36	250.64
25000	324.72	322.97	321.48	320.21	316.11	314.20	313.31
30000	389.67	387.57	385.78	384.25	379.33	377.04	375.97
35000	454.61	452.16	450.08	448.29	442.56	439.88	438.63
40000	519.56	516.76	514.37	512.33	505.78	502.73	501.29
45000	584.50	581.35	578.67	576.37	569.00	565.57	563.95
50000	649.45	645.95	642.96	640.42	632.22	628.41	626.61
55000	714.39	710.54	707.26	704.46	695.44	691.25	689.27
60000	779.34	775.14	771.56	768.50	758.67	754.09	751.93
65000	844.28	839.73	835.85	832.54	821.89	816.93	814.60
70000	909.23	904.33	900.15	896.58	885.11	879.77	877.26
75000	974.17	968.92	964.45	960.62	948.33	942.61	939.92
80000	1039.12	1033.52	1028.74	1024.66	1011.56	1005.45	1002.58
85000	1104.06	1098.11	1093.04	1088.71	1074.78	1068.29	1065.24
90000	1169.01	1162.71	1157.34	1152.75	1138.00	1131.13	1127.90
95000	1233.95	1227.30	1221.63	1216.79	1201.22	1193.97	1190.56
100000	1298.90	1291.90	1285.93	1280.83	1264.44	1256.81	1253.22
105000	1363.84	1356.49	1350.23	1344.87	1327.67	1319.65	1315.89
110000	1428.79	1421.09	1414.52	1408.91	1390.89	1382.49	1378.55
120000	1558.68	1550.28	1543.12	1537.00	1517.33	1508.18	1503.87
130000	1688.57	1679.47	1671.71	1665.08	1643.78	1633.86	1629.19
140000	1818.46	1808.66	1800.30	1793.16	1770.22	1759.54	1754.51
150000	1948.35	1937.85	1928.89	1921.25	1896.67	1885.22	1879.84
160000	2078.24	2067.04	2057.49	2049.33	2023.11	2010.90	2005.16
170000	2208.13	2196.23	2186.08	2177.41	2149.55	2136.58	2130.48
180000	2338.02	2325.42	2314.67	2305.50	2276.00	2262.26	2255.80
190000	2467.91	2454.61	2443.27	2433.58	2402.44	2387.95	2381.13
200000	2597.79	2583.80	2571.86	2561.66	2528.89	2513.63	2506.45
210000	2727.68	2712.99	2700.45	2689.74	2655.33	2639.31	2631.77
220000	2857.57	2842.18	2829.04	2817.83	2781.78	2764.99	2757.09
230000	2987.46	2971.37	2957.64	2945.91	2908.22	2890.67	2882.42
240000	3117.35	3100.56	3086.23	3073.99	3034.67	3016.35	3007.74
250000	3247.24	3229.75	3214.82	3202.08	3161.11	3142.03	3133.06
260000	3377.13	3358.94	3343.42	3330.16	3287.55	3267.71	3258.38
270000	3507.02	3488.13	3472.01	3458.24	3414.00	3393.40	3383.71
280000	3636.91	3617.32	3600.60	3586.33	3540.44	3519.08	3509.03
290000	3766.80	3746.51	3729.19	3714.41	3666.89	3644.76	3634.35
300000	3896.69	3875.70	3857.79	3842.49	3793.33	3770.44	3759.67
310000	4026.58	4004.89	3986.38	3970.57	3919.78	3896.12	3884.99
320000	4156.47	4134.08	4114.97	4098.66	4046.22	4021.80	4010.32
330000	4286.36	4263.27	4243.57	4226.74	4172.67	4147.48	4135.64
340000	4416.25	4392.46	4372.16	4354.82	4299.11	4273.17	4260.96
350000	4546.14	4521.65	4500.75	4482.91	4425.55	4398.85	4386.28
400000	5195.59	5167.59	5143.72	5123.32	5057.78	5027.25	5012.90
450000	5845.04	5813.54	5786.68	5763.74	5690.00	5655.66	5639.51
500000	6494.49	6459.49	6429.65	6404.15	6322.22	6284.07	6266.12
550000	7143.94	7105.44	7072.61	7044.57	6954.44	6912.47	6892.73
600000	7793.38	7751.39	7715.58	7684.98	7586.66	7540.88	7519.34

15¼%

Monthly Payments
necessary to amortize a loan

AMOUNT	1 YEAR	2 YEARS	3 YEARS	4 YEARS	5 YEARS	6 YEARS	7 YEARS
100	9.04	4.86	3.48	2.80	2.39	2.13	1.94
200	18.08	9.72	6.96	5.59	4.78	4.26	3.89
500	45.19	24.30	17.39	13.98	11.96	10.64	9.72
1000	90.38	48.61	34.79	27.96	23.92	21.28	19.44
2000	180.75	97.21	69.58	55.92	47.84	42.56	38.87
5000	451.88	243.03	173.94	139.79	119.61	106.41	97.19
6000	542.26	291.63	208.73	167.75	143.53	127.69	116.62
7000	632.63	340.24	243.52	195.70	167.45	148.97	136.06
8000	723.01	388.84	278.30	223.66	191.37	170.25	155.50
9000	813.39	437.45	313.09	251.62	215.29	191.53	174.94
10000	903.76	486.06	347.88	279.58	239.21	212.81	194.37
15000	1355.64	729.08	521.82	419.36	358.82	319.22	291.56
20000	1807.53	972.11	695.76	559.15	478.43	425.62	388.75
25000	2259.41	1215.14	869.70	698.94	598.03	532.03	485.93
30000	2711.29	1458.17	1043.64	838.73	717.64	638.43	583.12
35000	3163.17	1701.19	1217.58	978.52	837.25	744.84	680.30
40000	3615.05	1944.22	1391.52	1118.31	956.85	851.24	777.49
45000	4066.93	2187.25	1565.46	1258.09	1076.46	957.65	874.68
50000	4518.82	2430.28	1739.39	1397.88	1196.07	1064.05	971.86
55000	4970.70	2673.30	1913.33	1537.67	1315.67	1170.46	1069.05
60000	5422.58	2916.33	2087.27	1677.46	1435.28	1276.86	1166.24
65000	5874.46	3159.36	2261.21	1817.25	1554.89	1383.27	1263.42
70000	6326.34	3402.39	2435.15	1957.03	1674.50	1489.67	1360.61
75000	6778.22	3645.41	2609.09	2096.82	1794.10	1596.08	1457.80
80000	7230.11	3888.44	2783.03	2236.61	1913.71	1702.48	1554.98
85000	7681.99	4131.47	2956.97	2376.40	2033.32	1808.89	1652.17
90000	8133.87	4374.50	3130.91	2516.19	2152.92	1915.29	1749.36
95000	8585.75	4617.52	3304.85	2655.98	2272.53	2021.70	1846.54
100000	9037.63	4860.55	3478.79	2795.76	2392.14	2128.10	1943.73
105000	9489.51	5103.58	3652.73	2935.55	2511.74	2234.51	2040.91
110000	9941.40	5346.61	3826.67	3075.34	2631.35	2340.91	2138.10
120000	10845.16	5832.66	4174.55	3354.92	2870.56	2553.72	2332.47
130000	11748.92	6318.72	4522.42	3634.49	3109.78	2766.53	2526.85
140000	12652.69	6804.77	4870.30	3914.07	3348.99	2979.34	2721.22
150000	13556.45	7290.83	5218.18	4193.65	3588.20	3192.15	2915.59
160000	14460.21	7776.88	5566.06	4473.22	3827.42	3404.96	3109.97
170000	15363.97	8262.94	5913.94	4752.80	4066.63	3617.77	3304.34
180000	16267.74	8748.99	6261.82	5032.38	4305.84	3830.58	3498.71
190000	17171.50	9235.05	6609.70	5311.95	4545.06	4043.39	3693.08
200000	18075.26	9721.10	6957.58	5591.53	4784.27	4256.20	3887.46
210000	18979.03	10207.16	7305.45	5871.10	5023.49	4469.01	4081.83
220000	19882.79	10693.21	7653.33	6150.68	5262.70	4681.82	4276.20
230000	20786.55	11179.27	8001.21	6430.26	5501.91	4894.63	4470.58
240000	21690.32	11665.32	8349.09	6709.83	5741.13	5107.44	4664.95
250000	22594.08	12151.38	8696.97	6989.41	5980.34	5320.25	4859.32
260000	23497.84	12637.43	9044.85	7268.99	6219.55	5533.06	5053.69
270000	24401.61	13123.49	9392.73	7548.56	6458.77	5745.87	5248.07
280000	25305.37	13609.54	9740.61	7828.14	6697.98	5958.68	5442.44
290000	26209.13	14095.60	10088.49	8107.72	6937.19	6171.49	5636.81
300000	27112.90	14581.65	10436.36	8387.29	7176.41	6384.30	5831.19
310000	28016.66	15067.71	10784.24	8666.87	7415.62	6597.11	6025.56
320000	28920.42	15553.76	11132.12	8946.44	7654.84	6809.92	6219.93
330000	29824.19	16039.82	11480.00	9226.02	7894.05	7022.74	6414.30
340000	30727.95	16525.87	11827.88	9505.60	8133.26	7235.55	6608.68
350000	31631.71	17011.93	12175.76	9785.17	8372.48	7448.36	6803.05
400000	36150.53	19442.20	13915.15	11183.06	9568.54	8512.41	7774.91
450000	40669.34	21872.48	15654.55	12580.94	10764.61	9576.46	8746.78
500000	45188.16	24302.76	17393.94	13978.82	11960.68	10640.51	9718.64
550000	49706.98	26733.03	19133.33	15376.70	13156.75	11704.56	10690.51
600000	54225.79	29163.31	20872.73	16774.58	14352.82	12768.61	11662.37

Monthly Payments 15¼%
necessary to amortize a loan

AMOUNT	8 YEARS	9 YEARS	10 YEARS	11 YEARS	12 YEARS	13 YEARS	14 YEARS
100	1.81	1.71	1.63	1.57	1.52	1.48	1.44
200	3.62	3.41	3.26	3.13	3.03	2.95	2.89
500	9.05	8.54	8.14	7.83	7.59	7.38	7.22
1000	18.09	17.07	16.29	15.67	15.17	14.77	14.44
2000	36.18	34.15	32.57	31.33	30.34	29.54	28.88
5000	90.45	85.37	81.43	78.33	75.85	73.84	72.19
6000	108.54	102.44	97.72	94.00	91.02	88.61	86.63
7000	126.63	119.52	114.01	109.67	106.19	103.37	101.07
8000	144.72	136.59	130.30	125.33	121.36	118.14	115.51
9000	162.81	153.66	146.58	141.00	136.53	132.91	129.95
10000	180.90	170.74	162.87	156.67	151.70	147.68	144.39
15000	271.36	256.10	244.30	235.00	227.55	221.52	216.58
20000	361.81	341.47	325.74	313.33	303.40	295.36	288.78
25000	452.26	426.84	407.17	391.66	379.25	369.19	360.97
30000	542.71	512.21	488.61	470.00	455.10	443.03	433.16
35000	633.16	597.58	570.04	548.33	530.95	516.87	505.36
40000	723.62	682.94	651.48	626.66	606.80	590.71	577.55
45000	814.07	768.31	732.91	705.00	682.65	664.55	649.74
50000	904.52	853.68	814.35	783.33	758.50	738.39	721.94
55000	994.97	939.05	895.78	861.66	834.35	812.23	794.13
60000	1085.42	1024.42	977.22	940.00	910.20	886.07	866.33
65000	1175.87	1109.78	1058.65	1018.33	986.05	959.91	938.52
70000	1266.33	1195.15	1140.09	1096.66	1061.90	1033.74	1010.71
75000	1356.78	1280.52	1221.52	1174.99	1137.75	1107.58	1082.91
80000	1447.23	1365.89	1302.95	1253.33	1213.60	1181.42	1155.10
85000	1537.68	1451.26	1384.39	1331.66	1289.45	1255.26	1227.29
90000	1628.13	1536.63	1465.82	1409.99	1365.30	1329.10	1299.49
95000	1718.59	1621.99	1547.26	1488.33	1441.15	1402.94	1371.68
100000	1809.04	1707.36	1628.69	1566.66	1517.00	1476.78	1443.88
105000	1899.49	1792.73	1710.13	1644.99	1592.85	1550.62	1516.07
110000	1989.94	1878.10	1791.56	1723.32	1668.70	1624.46	1588.26
120000	2170.84	2048.83	1954.43	1879.99	1820.40	1772.13	1732.65
130000	2351.75	2219.57	2117.30	2036.66	1972.10	1919.81	1877.04
140000	2532.65	2390.31	2280.17	2193.32	2123.80	2067.49	2021.43
150000	2713.56	2561.04	2443.04	2349.99	2275.51	2215.17	2165.81
160000	2894.46	2731.78	2605.91	2506.65	2427.21	2362.85	2310.20
170000	3075.36	2902.51	2768.78	2663.32	2578.91	2510.52	2454.59
180000	3256.27	3073.25	2931.65	2819.99	2730.61	2658.20	2598.98
190000	3437.17	3243.99	3094.52	2976.65	2882.31	2805.88	2743.36
200000	3618.07	3414.72	3257.39	3133.32	3034.01	2953.56	2887.75
210000	3798.98	3585.46	3420.26	3289.98	3185.71	3101.23	3032.14
220000	3979.88	3756.19	3583.13	3446.65	3337.41	3248.91	3176.53
230000	4160.78	3926.93	3745.99	3603.32	3489.11	3396.59	3320.92
240000	4341.69	4097.67	3908.86	3759.98	3640.81	3544.27	3465.30
250000	4522.59	4268.40	4071.73	3916.65	3792.51	3691.95	3609.69
260000	4703.50	4439.14	4234.60	4073.31	3944.21	3839.62	3754.08
270000	4884.40	4609.88	4397.47	4229.98	4095.91	3987.30	3898.47
280000	5065.30	4780.61	4560.34	4386.65	4247.61	4134.98	4042.85
290000	5246.21	4951.35	4723.21	4543.31	4399.31	4282.66	4187.24
300000	5427.11	5122.08	4886.08	4699.98	4551.01	4430.34	4331.63
310000	5608.01	5292.82	5048.95	4856.64	4702.71	4578.01	4476.02
320000	5788.92	5463.56	5211.82	5013.31	4854.41	4725.69	4620.40
330000	5969.82	5634.29	5374.69	5169.97	5006.11	4873.37	4764.79
340000	6150.73	5805.03	5537.56	5326.64	5157.81	5021.05	4909.18
350000	6331.63	5975.76	5700.43	5483.31	5309.51	5168.72	5053.57
400000	7236.15	6829.44	6514.77	6266.64	6068.01	5907.11	5775.50
450000	8140.67	7683.13	7329.12	7049.97	6826.52	6645.50	6497.44
500000	9045.18	8536.81	8143.47	7833.29	7585.02	7383.89	7219.38
550000	9949.70	9390.49	8957.81	8616.62	8343.52	8122.28	7941.32
600000	10854.22	10244.17	9772.16	9399.95	9102.02	8860.67	8663.26

15¼%

Monthly Payments
necessary to amortize a loan

AMOUNT	15 YEARS	16 YEARS	17 YEARS	18 YEARS	19 YEARS	20 YEARS	21 YEARS
100	1.42	1.39	1.38	1.36	1.35	1.34	1.33
200	2.83	2.79	2.75	2.72	2.69	2.67	2.65
500	7.08	6.97	6.88	6.80	6.73	6.68	6.63
1000	14.17	13.94	13.75	13.60	13.46	13.35	13.26
2000	28.33	27.88	27.51	27.19	26.93	26.71	26.52
5000	70.84	69.71	68.77	67.99	67.32	66.76	66.29
6000	85.00	83.65	82.53	81.58	80.79	80.12	79.55
7000	99.17	97.60	96.28	95.18	94.25	93.47	92.81
8000	113.34	111.54	110.04	108.78	107.72	106.82	106.07
9000	127.51	125.48	123.79	122.37	121.18	120.18	119.33
10000	141.67	139.42	137.55	135.97	134.65	133.53	132.58
15000	212.51	209.14	206.32	203.96	201.97	200.29	198.88
20000	283.35	278.85	275.09	271.94	269.29	267.06	265.17
25000	354.19	348.56	343.86	339.93	336.62	333.82	331.46
30000	425.02	418.27	412.64	407.92	403.94	400.59	397.75
35000	495.86	487.98	481.41	475.90	471.27	467.35	464.04
40000	566.70	557.70	550.18	543.89	538.59	534.12	530.34
45000	637.54	627.41	618.96	611.87	605.91	600.88	596.63
50000	708.37	697.12	687.73	679.86	673.24	667.65	662.92
55000	779.21	766.83	756.50	747.84	740.56	734.41	729.21
60000	850.05	836.54	825.27	815.83	807.88	801.18	795.50
65000	920.89	906.26	894.05	883.82	875.21	867.94	861.80
70000	991.72	975.97	962.82	951.80	942.53	934.71	928.09
75000	1062.56	1045.68	1031.59	1019.79	1009.86	1001.47	994.38
80000	1133.40	1115.39	1100.37	1087.77	1077.18	1068.24	1060.67
85000	1204.24	1185.10	1169.14	1155.76	1144.50	1135.00	1126.97
90000	1275.07	1254.82	1237.91	1223.75	1211.83	1201.77	1193.26
95000	1345.91	1324.53	1306.68	1291.73	1279.15	1268.53	1259.55
100000	1416.75	1394.24	1375.46	1359.72	1346.47	1335.30	1325.84
105000	1487.59	1463.95	1444.23	1427.70	1413.80	1402.06	1392.13
110000	1558.42	1533.66	1513.00	1495.69	1481.12	1468.83	1458.43
120000	1700.10	1673.09	1650.55	1631.66	1615.77	1602.36	1591.01
130000	1841.77	1812.51	1788.10	1767.63	1750.42	1735.89	1723.59
140000	1983.45	1951.93	1925.64	1903.60	1885.06	1869.42	1856.18
150000	2125.12	2091.36	2063.19	2039.58	2019.71	2002.95	1988.76
160000	2266.80	2230.78	2200.73	2175.55	2154.36	2136.48	2121.35
170000	2408.47	2370.21	2338.28	2311.52	2289.01	2270.01	2253.93
180000	2550.15	2509.63	2475.82	2447.49	2423.65	2403.54	2386.51
190000	2691.82	2649.05	2613.37	2583.46	2558.30	2537.07	2519.10
200000	2833.50	2788.48	2750.92	2719.43	2692.95	2670.60	2651.68
210000	2975.17	2927.90	2888.46	2855.41	2827.60	2804.13	2784.27
220000	3116.85	3067.33	3026.01	2991.38	2962.24	2937.66	2916.85
230000	3258.52	3206.75	3163.55	3127.35	3096.89	3071.19	3049.44
240000	3400.20	3346.17	3301.10	3263.32	3231.54	3204.72	3182.02
250000	3541.87	3485.60	3438.64	3399.29	3366.19	3338.25	3314.60
260000	3683.55	3625.02	3576.19	3535.26	3500.83	3471.78	3447.19
270000	3825.22	3764.45	3713.74	3671.24	3635.48	3605.31	3579.77
280000	3966.90	3903.87	3851.28	3807.21	3770.13	3738.84	3712.36
290000	4108.57	4043.29	3988.83	3943.18	3904.78	3872.37	3844.94
300000	4250.25	4182.72	4126.37	4079.15	4039.42	4005.90	3977.52
310000	4391.92	4322.14	4263.92	4215.12	4174.07	4139.43	4110.11
320000	4533.60	4461.57	4401.46	4351.09	4308.72	4272.96	4242.69
330000	4675.27	4600.99	4539.01	4487.07	4443.37	4406.49	4375.28
340000	4816.95	4740.41	4676.56	4623.04	4578.01	4540.02	4507.86
350000	4958.62	4879.84	4814.10	4759.01	4712.66	4673.55	4640.45
400000	5667.00	5576.96	5501.83	5438.87	5385.90	5341.19	5303.37
450000	6375.37	6274.08	6189.56	6118.73	6059.14	6008.84	5966.29
500000	7083.75	6971.20	6877.29	6798.58	6732.37	6676.49	6629.21
550000	7792.12	7668.32	7565.02	7478.44	7405.61	7344.14	7292.13
600000	8500.50	8365.43	8252.75	8158.30	8078.85	8011.79	7955.05

Monthly Payments 15¼%
necessary to amortize a loan

AMOUNT	22 YEARS	23 YEARS	24 YEARS	25 YEARS	30 YEARS	35 YEARS	40 YEARS
100	1.32	1.31	1.31	1.30	1.28	1.28	1.27
200	2.64	2.62	2.61	2.60	2.57	2.55	2.55
500	6.59	6.56	6.53	6.50	6.42	6.39	6.37
1000	13.18	13.11	13.05	13.00	12.84	12.77	12.74
2000	26.36	26.22	26.10	26.01	25.69	25.54	25.48
5000	65.89	65.55	65.26	65.01	64.22	63.86	63.69
6000	79.07	78.66	78.31	78.02	77.07	76.63	76.43
7000	92.25	91.77	91.36	91.02	89.91	89.40	89.17
8000	105.43	104.88	104.42	104.02	102.76	102.17	101.90
9000	118.60	117.99	117.47	117.02	115.60	114.95	114.64
10000	131.78	131.10	130.52	130.03	128.45	127.72	127.38
15000	197.67	196.65	195.78	195.04	192.67	191.58	191.07
20000	263.56	262.20	261.04	260.05	256.89	255.44	254.76
25000	329.46	327.75	326.30	325.06	321.11	319.30	318.45
30000	395.35	393.30	391.56	390.08	385.34	383.16	382.14
35000	461.24	458.85	456.82	455.09	449.56	447.01	445.83
40000	527.13	524.40	522.08	520.10	513.78	510.87	509.52
45000	593.02	589.95	587.34	585.12	578.01	574.73	573.21
50000	658.91	655.50	652.60	650.13	642.23	638.59	636.90
55000	724.80	721.05	717.86	715.14	706.45	702.45	700.59
60000	790.69	786.60	783.12	780.15	770.68	766.31	764.28
65000	856.58	852.15	848.38	845.17	834.90	830.17	827.97
70000	922.47	917.70	913.64	910.18	899.12	894.03	891.66
75000	988.37	983.25	978.90	975.19	963.34	957.89	955.35
80000	1054.26	1048.80	1044.16	1040.21	1027.57	1021.75	1019.04
85000	1120.15	1114.35	1109.42	1105.22	1091.79	1085.61	1082.73
90000	1186.04	1179.90	1174.68	1170.23	1156.01	1149.47	1146.42
95000	1251.93	1245.45	1239.94	1235.25	1220.24	1213.32	1210.11
100000	1317.82	1311.00	1305.20	1300.26	1284.46	1277.18	1273.80
105000	1383.71	1376.55	1370.46	1365.27	1348.68	1341.04	1337.49
110000	1449.60	1442.10	1435.72	1430.28	1412.90	1404.90	1401.18
120000	1581.38	1573.20	1566.24	1560.31	1541.35	1532.62	1528.56
130000	1713.17	1704.31	1696.76	1690.34	1669.80	1660.34	1655.94
140000	1844.95	1835.41	1827.28	1820.36	1798.24	1788.06	1783.32
150000	1976.73	1966.51	1957.80	1950.39	1926.69	1915.78	1910.70
160000	2108.51	2097.61	2088.32	2080.41	2055.13	2043.49	2038.08
170000	2240.29	2228.71	2218.85	2210.44	2183.58	2171.21	2165.46
180000	2372.08	2359.81	2349.37	2340.46	2312.03	2298.93	2292.84
190000	2503.86	2490.91	2479.89	2470.49	2440.47	2426.65	2420.22
200000	2635.64	2622.01	2610.41	2600.52	2568.92	2554.37	2547.60
210000	2767.42	2753.11	2740.93	2730.54	2697.36	2682.09	2674.98
220000	2899.21	2884.21	2871.45	2860.57	2825.81	2809.80	2802.36
230000	3030.99	3015.31	3001.97	2990.59	2954.25	2937.52	2929.75
240000	3162.77	3146.41	3132.49	3120.62	3082.70	3065.24	3057.13
250000	3294.55	3277.51	3263.01	3250.65	3211.15	3192.96	3184.51
260000	3426.33	3408.61	3393.53	3380.67	3339.59	3320.68	3311.89
270000	3558.12	3539.71	3524.05	3510.70	3468.04	3448.40	3439.27
280000	3689.90	3670.81	3654.57	3640.72	3596.48	3576.11	3566.65
290000	3821.68	3801.91	3785.09	3770.75	3724.93	3703.83	3694.03
300000	3953.46	3933.01	3915.61	3900.77	3853.38	3831.55	3821.41
310000	4085.24	4064.11	4046.13	4030.80	3981.82	3959.27	3948.79
320000	4217.03	4195.21	4176.65	4160.83	4110.27	4086.99	4076.17
330000	4348.81	4326.31	4307.17	4290.85	4238.71	4214.71	4203.55
340000	4480.59	4457.42	4437.69	4420.88	4367.16	4342.43	4330.93
350000	4612.37	4588.52	4568.21	4550.90	4495.60	4470.14	4458.31
400000	5271.28	5244.02	5220.81	5201.03	5137.83	5108.74	5095.21
450000	5930.19	5899.52	5873.41	5851.16	5780.06	5747.33	5732.11
500000	6589.10	6555.02	6526.02	6501.29	6422.29	6385.92	6369.01
550000	7248.01	7210.52	7178.62	7151.42	7064.52	7024.51	7005.91
600000	7906.92	7866.03	7831.22	7801.55	7706.75	7663.10	7642.81

15½%

Monthly Payments
necessary to amortize a loan

AMOUNT	1 YEAR	2 YEARS	3 YEARS	4 YEARS	5 YEARS	6 YEARS	7 YEARS
100	9.05	4.87	3.49	2.81	2.41	2.14	1.96
200	18.10	9.74	6.98	5.62	4.81	4.28	3.92
500	45.25	24.36	17.46	14.04	12.03	10.71	9.79
1000	90.49	48.72	34.91	28.08	24.05	21.42	19.58
2000	180.99	97.45	69.82	56.17	48.11	42.83	39.16
5000	452.47	243.62	174.55	140.42	120.27	107.09	97.89
6000	542.97	292.35	209.46	168.51	144.32	128.50	117.47
7000	633.46	341.07	244.37	196.59	168.37	149.92	137.05
8000	723.96	389.80	279.29	224.68	192.43	171.34	156.63
9000	814.45	438.52	314.20	252.76	216.48	192.76	176.21
10000	904.94	487.25	349.11	280.85	240.53	214.17	195.78
15000	1357.42	730.87	523.66	421.27	360.80	321.26	293.68
20000	1809.89	974.49	698.21	561.70	481.06	428.35	391.57
25000	2262.36	1218.11	872.77	702.12	601.33	535.44	489.46
30000	2714.83	1461.74	1047.32	842.55	721.60	642.52	587.35
35000	3167.30	1705.36	1221.87	982.97	841.86	749.61	685.24
40000	3619.78	1948.98	1396.43	1123.39	962.13	856.70	783.13
45000	4072.25	2192.60	1570.98	1263.82	1082.39	963.79	881.03
50000	4524.72	2436.23	1745.53	1404.24	1202.66	1070.87	978.92
55000	4977.19	2679.85	1920.09	1544.67	1322.93	1177.96	1076.81
60000	5429.66	2923.47	2094.64	1685.09	1443.19	1285.05	1174.70
65000	5882.14	3167.10	2269.19	1825.52	1563.46	1392.14	1272.59
70000	6334.61	3410.72	2443.75	1965.94	1683.72	1499.22	1370.48
75000	6787.08	3654.34	2618.30	2106.36	1803.99	1606.31	1468.38
80000	7239.55	3897.96	2792.85	2246.79	1924.26	1713.40	1566.27
85000	7692.03	4141.59	2967.41	2387.21	2044.52	1820.49	1664.16
90000	8144.50	4385.21	3141.96	2527.64	2164.79	1927.57	1762.05
95000	8596.97	4628.83	3316.51	2668.06	2285.05	2034.66	1859.94
100000	9049.44	4872.45	3491.07	2808.49	2405.32	2141.75	1957.83
105000	9501.91	5116.08	3665.62	2948.91	2525.59	2248.84	2055.73
110000	9954.39	5359.70	3840.17	3089.33	2645.85	2355.92	2153.62
120000	10859.33	5846.95	4189.28	3370.18	2886.38	2570.10	2349.40
130000	11764.27	6334.19	4538.39	3651.03	3126.91	2784.27	2545.19
140000	12669.22	6821.44	4887.50	3931.88	3367.45	2998.45	2740.97
150000	13574.16	7308.68	5236.60	4212.73	3607.98	3212.62	2936.75
160000	14479.11	7795.93	5585.71	4493.57	3848.51	3426.80	3132.54
170000	15384.05	8283.17	5934.82	4774.43	4089.04	3640.97	3328.32
180000	16288.99	8770.42	6283.92	5055.27	4329.57	3855.15	3524.10
190000	17193.94	9257.66	6633.03	5336.12	4570.11	4069.32	3719.89
200000	18098.88	9744.91	6982.14	5616.97	4810.64	4283.50	3915.67
210000	19003.83	10232.15	7331.24	5897.82	5051.17	4497.67	4111.45
220000	19908.77	10719.40	7680.35	6178.67	5291.70	4711.85	4307.24
230000	20813.72	11206.64	8029.46	6459.52	5532.23	4926.02	4503.02
240000	21718.66	11693.89	8378.56	6740.37	5772.77	5140.20	4698.80
250000	22623.60	12181.14	8727.67	7021.21	6013.30	5354.37	4894.59
260000	23528.55	12668.38	9076.78	7302.06	6253.83	5568.55	5090.37
270000	24433.49	13155.63	9425.88	7582.91	6494.36	5782.72	5286.15
280000	25338.44	13642.87	9774.99	7863.76	6734.89	5996.90	5481.94
290000	26243.38	14130.12	10124.10	8144.61	6975.43	6211.07	5677.72
300000	27148.32	14617.36	10473.20	8425.46	7215.96	6425.25	5873.50
310000	28053.27	15104.61	10822.31	8706.31	7456.49	6639.42	6069.29
320000	28958.21	15591.85	11171.42	8987.15	7697.02	6853.60	6265.07
330000	29863.16	16079.10	11520.52	9268.00	7937.55	7067.77	6460.85
340000	30768.10	16566.34	11869.63	9548.85	8178.08	7281.95	6656.64
350000	31673.05	17053.59	12218.74	9829.70	8418.62	7496.12	6852.42
400000	36197.77	19489.82	13964.27	11233.94	9621.28	8567.00	7831.34
450000	40722.49	21926.04	15709.81	12638.19	10823.94	9637.87	8810.26
500000	45247.21	24362.27	17455.34	14042.43	12026.60	10708.74	9789.17
550000	49771.93	26798.50	19200.87	15446.67	13229.26	11779.62	10768.09
600000	54296.65	29234.73	20946.41	16850.92	14431.91	12850.49	11747.01

Monthly Payments 15¹/₂%
necessary to amortize a loan

AMOUNT	8 YEARS	9 YEARS	10 YEARS	11 YEARS	12 YEARS	13 YEARS	14 YEARS
100	1.82	1.72	1.64	1.58	1.53	1.49	1.46
200	3.65	3.44	3.29	3.16	3.07	2.99	2.92
500	9.12	8.61	8.22	7.91	7.67	7.47	7.30
1000	18.24	17.22	16.44	15.82	15.33	14.93	14.61
2000	36.47	34.45	32.88	31.65	30.66	29.87	29.22
5000	91.18	86.12	82.21	79.12	76.66	74.67	73.04
6000	109.42	103.34	98.65	94.95	91.99	89.60	87.65
7000	127.65	120.56	115.09	110.77	107.32	104.53	102.26
8000	145.89	137.79	131.53	126.60	122.66	119.47	116.86
9000	164.12	155.01	147.97	142.42	137.99	134.40	131.47
10000	182.36	172.24	164.41	158.25	153.32	149.33	146.08
15000	273.54	258.35	246.62	237.37	229.98	224.00	219.12
20000	364.72	344.47	328.82	316.49	306.64	298.67	292.16
25000	455.90	430.59	411.03	395.62	383.30	373.34	365.20
30000	547.08	516.71	493.23	474.74	459.96	448.00	438.24
35000	638.26	602.82	575.44	553.87	536.62	522.67	511.28
40000	729.44	688.94	657.64	632.99	613.28	597.34	584.32
45000	820.62	775.06	739.85	712.11	689.94	672.01	657.36
50000	911.80	861.18	822.05	791.24	766.60	746.67	730.39
55000	1002.98	947.29	904.26	870.36	843.26	821.34	803.43
60000	1094.16	1033.41	986.46	949.48	919.92	896.01	876.47
65000	1185.33	1119.53	1068.67	1028.61	996.58	970.67	949.51
70000	1276.51	1205.65	1150.87	1107.73	1073.24	1045.34	1022.55
75000	1367.69	1291.76	1233.08	1186.86	1149.90	1120.01	1095.59
80000	1458.87	1377.88	1315.28	1265.98	1226.56	1194.68	1168.63
85000	1550.05	1464.00	1397.49	1345.10	1303.22	1269.34	1241.67
90000	1641.23	1550.12	1479.69	1424.23	1379.88	1344.01	1314.71
95000	1732.41	1636.23	1561.90	1503.35	1456.54	1418.68	1387.75
100000	1823.59	1722.35	1644.11	1582.47	1533.20	1493.35	1460.79
105000	1914.77	1808.47	1726.31	1661.60	1609.86	1568.01	1533.83
110000	2005.95	1894.59	1808.52	1740.72	1686.52	1642.68	1606.87
120000	2188.31	2066.82	1972.93	1898.97	1839.83	1792.01	1752.95
130000	2370.67	2239.06	2137.34	2057.22	1993.17	1941.35	1899.03
140000	2553.03	2411.29	2301.75	2215.46	2146.49	2090.68	2045.11
150000	2735.39	2583.53	2466.16	2373.71	2299.81	2240.02	2191.18
160000	2917.75	2755.76	2630.57	2531.96	2453.13	2389.35	2337.26
170000	3100.11	2928.00	2794.98	2690.21	2606.45	2538.69	2483.34
180000	3282.47	3100.23	2959.39	2848.45	2759.77	2688.02	2629.42
190000	3464.83	3272.47	3123.80	3006.70	2913.09	2837.36	2775.50
200000	3647.18	3444.71	3288.21	3164.95	3066.41	2986.69	2921.58
210000	3829.54	3616.94	3452.62	3323.20	3219.73	3136.03	3067.66
220000	4011.90	3789.18	3617.03	3481.44	3373.05	3285.36	3213.74
230000	4194.26	3961.41	3781.44	3639.69	3526.37	3434.69	3359.82
240000	4376.62	4133.65	3945.85	3797.94	3679.69	3584.03	3505.90
250000	4558.98	4305.88	4110.26	3956.19	3833.01	3733.36	3651.97
260000	4741.34	4478.12	4274.67	4114.43	3986.33	3882.70	3798.05
270000	4923.70	4650.35	4439.08	4272.68	4139.65	4032.03	3944.13
280000	5106.06	4822.59	4603.50	4430.93	4292.97	4181.37	4090.21
290000	5288.42	4994.82	4767.91	4589.18	4446.29	4330.70	4236.29
300000	5470.78	5167.06	4932.32	4747.42	4599.61	4480.04	4382.37
310000	5653.14	5339.29	5096.73	4905.67	4752.93	4629.37	4528.45
320000	5835.50	5511.53	5261.14	5063.92	4906.25	4778.71	4674.53
330000	6017.85	5683.76	5425.55	5222.17	5059.57	4928.04	4820.61
340000	6200.21	5856.00	5589.96	5380.41	5212.89	5077.37	4966.69
350000	6382.57	6028.23	5754.37	5538.66	5366.21	5226.71	5112.76
400000	7294.37	6889.41	6576.42	6329.90	6132.82	5973.38	5843.16
450000	8206.17	7750.59	7398.47	7121.14	6899.42	6720.06	6573.55
500000	9117.96	8611.76	8220.53	7912.37	7666.02	7466.73	7303.95
550000	10029.76	9472.94	9042.58	8703.61	8432.62	8213.40	8034.34
600000	10941.55	10334.12	9864.63	9494.85	9199.23	8960.07	8764.74

15¹/₂%

Monthly Payments
necessary to amortize a loan

AMOUNT	15 YEARS	16 YEARS	17 YEARS	18 YEARS	19 YEARS	20 YEARS	21 YEARS
100	1.43	1.41	1.39	1.38	1.36	1.35	1.34
200	2.87	2.82	2.79	2.76	2.73	2.71	2.69
500	7.17	7.06	6.97	6.89	6.82	6.77	6.72
1000	14.34	14.12	13.93	13.78	13.65	13.54	13.45
2000	28.68	28.24	27.87	27.56	27.30	27.08	26.89
5000	71.70	70.59	69.66	68.89	68.24	67.69	67.23
6000	86.04	84.71	83.60	82.67	81.89	81.23	80.68
7000	100.38	98.83	97.53	96.45	95.54	94.77	94.12
8000	114.72	112.94	111.46	110.23	109.19	108.31	107.57
9000	129.06	127.06	125.40	124.00	122.83	121.85	121.02
10000	143.40	141.18	139.33	137.78	136.48	135.39	134.46
15000	215.10	211.77	208.99	206.67	204.72	203.08	201.70
20000	286.80	282.36	278.66	275.56	272.97	270.78	268.93
25000	358.50	352.95	348.32	344.45	341.21	338.47	336.16
30000	430.20	423.54	417.99	413.35	409.45	406.16	403.39
35000	501.90	494.13	487.65	482.24	477.69	473.86	470.62
40000	573.60	564.71	557.32	551.13	545.93	541.55	537.85
45000	645.30	635.30	626.98	620.02	614.17	609.25	605.09
50000	717.00	705.89	696.65	688.91	682.41	676.94	672.32
55000	788.69	776.48	766.31	757.80	750.65	744.63	739.55
60000	860.39	847.07	835.98	826.69	818.90	812.33	806.78
65000	932.09	917.66	905.64	895.58	887.14	880.02	874.01
70000	1003.79	988.25	975.30	964.47	955.38	947.72	941.25
75000	1075.49	1058.84	1044.97	1033.36	1023.62	1015.41	1008.48
80000	1147.19	1129.43	1114.63	1102.26	1091.86	1083.10	1075.71
85000	1218.89	1200.02	1184.30	1171.15	1160.10	1150.80	1142.94
90000	1290.59	1270.61	1253.96	1240.04	1228.34	1218.49	1210.17
95000	1362.29	1341.20	1323.63	1308.93	1296.58	1286.19	1277.40
100000	1433.99	1411.79	1393.29	1377.82	1364.83	1353.88	1344.64
105000	1505.69	1482.38	1462.96	1446.71	1433.07	1421.57	1411.87
110000	1577.39	1552.97	1532.62	1515.60	1501.31	1489.27	1479.10
120000	1720.79	1694.14	1671.95	1653.38	1637.79	1624.66	1613.56
130000	1864.19	1835.32	1811.28	1791.17	1774.27	1760.04	1748.03
140000	2007.59	1976.50	1950.61	1928.95	1910.76	1895.43	1882.49
150000	2150.99	2117.68	2089.94	2066.73	2047.24	2030.82	2016.95
160000	2294.38	2258.86	2229.27	2204.51	2183.72	2166.21	2151.42
170000	2437.78	2400.04	2368.60	2342.29	2320.20	2301.60	2285.88
180000	2581.18	2541.22	2507.93	2480.08	2456.69	2436.99	2420.35
190000	2724.58	2682.39	2647.26	2617.86	2593.17	2572.37	2554.81
200000	2867.98	2823.57	2786.58	2755.64	2729.65	2707.76	2689.27
210000	3011.38	2964.75	2925.91	2893.42	2866.13	2843.15	2823.74
220000	3154.78	3105.93	3065.24	3031.20	3002.62	2978.54	2958.20
230000	3298.18	3247.11	3204.57	3168.98	3139.10	3113.93	3092.66
240000	3441.58	3388.29	3343.90	3306.77	3275.58	3249.31	3227.13
250000	3584.98	3529.47	3483.23	3444.55	3412.07	3384.70	3361.59
260000	3728.37	3670.65	3622.56	3582.33	3548.55	3520.09	3496.05
270000	3871.77	3811.82	3761.89	3720.11	3685.03	3655.48	3630.52
280000	4015.17	3953.00	3901.22	3857.89	3821.51	3790.87	3764.98
290000	4158.57	4094.18	4040.55	3995.68	3958.00	3926.25	3899.45
300000	4301.97	4235.36	4179.88	4133.46	4094.48	4061.64	4033.91
310000	4445.37	4376.54	4319.21	4271.24	4230.96	4197.03	4168.37
320000	4588.77	4517.72	4458.54	4409.02	4367.44	4332.42	4302.84
330000	4732.17	4658.90	4597.87	4546.80	4503.93	4467.81	4437.30
340000	4875.57	4800.07	4737.19	4684.59	4640.41	4603.19	4571.76
350000	5018.97	4941.25	4876.52	4822.37	4776.89	4738.58	4706.23
400000	5735.96	5647.15	5573.17	5511.28	5459.30	5415.52	5378.55
450000	6452.96	6353.04	6269.82	6200.19	6141.72	6092.46	6050.86
500000	7169.95	7058.93	6966.46	6889.10	6824.13	6769.40	6723.18
550000	7886.95	7764.83	7663.11	7578.01	7506.54	7446.34	7395.50
600000	8603.94	8470.72	8359.75	8266.92	8188.96	8123.28	8067.82

Monthly Payments 15 1/2%
necessary to amortize a loan

AMOUNT	22 YEARS	23 YEARS	24 YEARS	25 YEARS	30 YEARS	35 YEARS	40 YEARS
100	1.34	1.33	1.32	1.32	1.30	1.30	1.29
200	2.67	2.66	2.65	2.64	2.61	2.60	2.59
500	6.68	6.65	6.62	6.60	6.52	6.49	6.47
1000	13.37	13.30	13.25	13.20	13.05	12.98	12.94
2000	26.74	26.60	26.49	26.39	26.09	25.95	25.89
5000	66.84	66.51	66.23	65.99	65.23	64.88	64.72
6000	80.21	79.81	79.47	79.18	78.27	77.86	77.66
7000	93.58	93.11	92.72	92.38	91.32	90.83	90.61
8000	106.94	106.41	105.96	105.58	104.36	103.81	103.55
9000	120.31	119.72	119.21	118.78	117.41	116.78	116.50
10000	133.68	133.02	132.45	131.97	130.45	129.76	129.44
15000	200.52	199.53	198.68	197.96	195.68	194.64	194.16
20000	267.36	266.04	264.91	263.95	260.90	259.52	258.88
25000	334.20	332.54	331.13	329.94	326.13	324.40	323.60
30000	401.04	399.05	397.36	395.92	391.36	389.28	388.32
35000	467.88	465.56	463.59	461.91	456.58	454.15	453.04
40000	534.72	532.07	529.82	527.90	521.81	519.03	517.76
45000	601.57	598.58	596.04	593.89	587.03	583.91	582.48
50000	668.41	665.09	662.27	659.87	652.26	648.79	647.20
55000	735.25	731.60	728.50	725.86	717.48	713.67	711.92
60000	802.09	798.11	794.72	791.85	782.71	778.55	776.64
65000	868.93	864.61	860.95	857.83	847.94	843.43	841.36
70000	935.77	931.12	927.18	923.82	913.16	908.31	906.08
75000	1002.61	997.63	993.40	989.81	978.39	973.19	970.80
80000	1069.45	1064.14	1059.63	1055.80	1043.61	1038.07	1035.52
85000	1136.29	1130.65	1125.86	1121.78	1108.84	1102.95	1100.24
90000	1203.13	1197.16	1192.09	1187.77	1174.07	1167.83	1164.96
95000	1269.97	1263.67	1258.31	1253.76	1239.29	1232.71	1229.68
100000	1336.81	1330.18	1324.54	1319.75	1304.52	1297.58	1294.40
105000	1403.65	1396.68	1390.77	1385.73	1369.74	1362.46	1359.12
110000	1470.49	1463.19	1456.99	1451.72	1434.97	1427.34	1423.84
120000	1604.17	1596.21	1589.45	1583.69	1565.42	1557.10	1553.28
130000	1737.86	1729.23	1721.90	1715.67	1695.87	1686.86	1682.72
140000	1871.54	1862.25	1854.36	1847.64	1826.32	1816.62	1812.16
150000	2005.22	1995.26	1986.81	1979.62	1956.78	1946.38	1941.60
160000	2138.90	2128.28	2119.26	2111.59	2087.23	2076.14	2071.04
170000	2272.58	2261.30	2251.72	2243.57	2217.68	2205.89	2200.48
180000	2406.26	2394.32	2384.17	2375.54	2348.13	2335.65	2329.92
190000	2539.94	2527.33	2516.62	2507.52	2478.58	2465.41	2459.36
200000	2673.62	2660.35	2649.08	2639.49	2609.03	2595.17	2588.80
210000	2807.30	2793.37	2781.53	2771.46	2739.49	2724.93	2718.24
220000	2940.99	2926.39	2913.99	2903.44	2869.94	2854.69	2847.68
230000	3074.67	3059.40	3046.44	3035.41	3000.39	2984.44	2977.12
240000	3208.35	3192.42	3178.89	3167.39	3130.84	3114.20	3106.56
250000	3342.03	3325.44	3311.35	3299.36	3261.29	3243.96	3236.00
260000	3475.71	3458.46	3443.80	3431.34	3391.74	3373.72	3365.44
270000	3609.39	3591.47	3576.26	3563.31	3522.20	3503.48	3494.88
280000	3743.07	3724.49	3708.71	3695.29	3652.65	3633.24	3624.32
290000	3876.75	3857.51	3841.16	3827.26	3783.10	3763.00	3753.76
300000	4010.43	3990.53	3973.62	3959.24	3913.55	3892.75	3883.20
310000	4144.12	4123.54	4106.07	4091.21	4044.00	4022.51	4012.64
320000	4277.80	4256.56	4238.53	4223.18	4174.45	4152.27	4142.08
330000	4411.48	4389.58	4370.98	4355.16	4304.91	4282.03	4271.52
340000	4545.16	4522.60	4503.43	4487.13	4435.36	4411.79	4400.96
350000	4678.84	4655.62	4635.89	4619.11	4565.81	4541.55	4530.40
400000	5347.25	5320.70	5298.16	5278.98	5218.07	5190.34	5177.60
450000	6015.65	5985.79	5960.43	5938.85	5870.33	5839.13	5824.80
500000	6684.06	6650.88	6622.70	6598.73	6522.58	6487.92	6472.00
550000	7352.46	7315.97	7284.97	7258.60	7174.84	7136.72	7119.20
600000	8020.87	7981.05	7947.24	7918.47	7827.10	7785.51	7766.40

15¾%

Monthly Payments
necessary to amortize a loan

AMOUNT	1 YEAR	2 YEARS	3 YEARS	4 YEARS	5 YEARS	6 YEARS	7 YEARS
100	9.06	4.88	3.50	2.82	2.42	2.16	1.97
200	18.12	9.77	7.01	5.64	4.84	4.31	3.94
500	45.31	24.42	17.52	14.11	12.09	10.78	9.86
1000	90.61	48.84	35.03	28.21	24.19	21.55	19.72
2000	181.23	97.69	70.07	56.42	48.37	43.11	39.44
5000	453.06	244.22	175.17	141.06	120.93	107.77	98.60
6000	543.68	293.06	210.20	169.27	145.11	129.33	118.32
7000	634.29	341.91	245.24	197.49	169.30	150.88	138.04
8000	724.90	390.75	280.27	225.70	193.48	172.44	157.76
9000	815.51	439.59	315.30	253.91	217.67	193.99	177.48
10000	906.13	488.44	350.34	282.12	241.85	215.54	197.20
15000	1359.19	732.66	525.51	423.19	362.78	323.32	295.80
20000	1812.25	976.87	700.67	564.25	483.71	431.09	394.40
25000	2265.31	1221.09	875.84	705.31	604.64	538.86	493.00
30000	2718.38	1465.31	1051.01	846.37	725.56	646.63	591.60
35000	3171.44	1709.53	1226.18	987.43	846.49	754.41	690.20
40000	3624.50	1953.75	1401.35	1128.50	967.42	862.18	788.80
45000	4077.57	2197.97	1576.52	1269.56	1088.34	969.95	887.40
50000	4530.63	2442.19	1751.69	1410.62	1209.27	1077.72	986.00
55000	4983.69	2686.41	1926.86	1551.68	1330.20	1185.49	1084.60
60000	5436.76	2930.62	2102.02	1692.74	1451.13	1293.27	1183.20
65000	5889.82	3174.84	2277.19	1833.81	1572.05	1401.04	1281.80
70000	6342.88	3419.06	2452.36	1974.87	1692.98	1508.81	1380.40
75000	6795.94	3663.28	2627.53	2115.93	1813.91	1616.58	1479.00
80000	7249.01	3907.50	2802.70	2256.99	1934.83	1724.35	1577.60
85000	7702.07	4151.72	2977.87	2398.05	2055.76	1832.13	1676.19
90000	8155.13	4395.94	3153.04	2539.12	2176.69	1939.90	1774.79
95000	8608.20	4640.16	3328.20	2680.18	2297.62	2047.67	1873.39
100000	9061.26	4884.37	3503.37	2821.24	2418.54	2155.44	1971.99
105000	9514.32	5128.59	3678.54	2962.30	2539.47	2263.22	2070.59
110000	9967.39	5372.81	3853.71	3103.36	2660.40	2370.99	2169.19
120000	10873.51	5861.25	4204.05	3385.49	2902.26	2586.53	2366.39
130000	11779.64	6349.69	4554.39	3667.61	3144.11	2802.08	2563.59
140000	12685.76	6838.12	4904.72	3949.74	3385.96	3017.62	2760.79
150000	13591.89	7326.56	5255.06	4231.86	3627.81	3233.16	2957.99
160000	14498.02	7815.00	5605.40	4513.98	3869.67	3448.71	3155.19
170000	15404.14	8303.44	5955.73	4796.11	4111.52	3664.25	3352.39
180000	16310.27	8791.88	6306.07	5078.23	4353.38	3879.80	3549.59
190000	17216.39	9280.31	6656.41	5360.36	4595.23	4095.34	3746.79
200000	18122.52	9768.75	7006.75	5642.48	4837.08	4310.89	3943.99
210000	19028.64	10257.19	7357.06	5924.61	5078.94	4526.43	4141.19
220000	19934.77	10745.62	7707.42	6206.73	5320.79	4741.97	4338.39
230000	20840.90	11234.06	8057.76	6488.85	5562.65	4957.52	4535.59
240000	21747.02	11722.50	8408.10	6770.98	5804.50	5173.06	4732.79
250000	22653.15	12210.94	8758.43	7053.10	6046.36	5388.61	4929.99
260000	23559.27	12699.37	9108.77	7335.23	6288.21	5604.15	5127.18
270000	24465.40	13187.81	9459.11	7617.35	6530.06	5819.70	5324.38
280000	25371.53	13676.25	9809.45	7899.47	6771.92	6035.24	5521.58
290000	26277.65	14164.69	10159.78	8181.60	7013.77	6250.78	5718.78
300000	27183.78	14653.12	10510.12	8463.72	7255.63	6466.33	5915.98
310000	28089.90	15141.56	10860.46	8745.85	7497.48	6681.87	6113.18
320000	28996.03	15630.00	11210.79	9027.97	7739.34	6897.42	6310.38
330000	29902.16	16118.43	11561.13	9310.09	7981.19	7112.96	6507.58
340000	30808.28	16606.87	11911.47	9592.22	8223.04	7328.51	6704.78
350000	31714.41	17095.31	12261.81	9874.34	8464.90	7544.05	6901.98
400000	36245.04	19537.50	14013.49	11284.96	9674.17	8621.77	7887.98
450000	40775.67	21979.68	15765.18	12695.58	10883.44	9699.49	8873.97
500000	45306.30	24421.87	17516.87	14106.20	12092.71	10777.22	9859.97
550000	49836.93	26864.06	19268.55	15516.82	13301.98	11854.94	10845.97
600000	54367.56	29306.25	21020.24	16927.44	14511.25	12932.66	11831.96

AMOUNT	8 YEARS	9 YEARS	10 YEARS	11 YEARS	12 YEARS	13 YEARS	14 YEARS
100	1.84	1.74	1.66	1.60	1.55	1.51	1.48
200	3.68	3.47	3.32	3.20	3.10	3.02	2.96
500	9.19	8.69	8.30	7.99	7.75	7.55	7.39
1000	18.38	17.37	16.60	15.98	15.49	15.10	14.78
2000	36.76	34.75	33.19	31.97	30.99	30.20	29.56
5000	91.91	86.87	82.98	79.92	77.47	75.50	73.89
6000	110.29	104.24	99.58	95.90	92.97	90.60	88.67
7000	128.67	121.62	116.17	111.89	108.46	105.70	103.44
8000	147.06	138.99	132.77	127.87	123.96	120.80	118.22
9000	165.44	156.37	149.36	143.85	139.45	135.90	133.00
10000	183.82	173.74	165.96	159.84	154.95	151.00	147.78
15000	275.73	260.61	248.94	239.75	232.42	226.50	221.67
20000	367.64	347.48	331.92	319.67	309.90	302.00	295.56
25000	459.55	434.35	414.90	399.59	387.37	377.50	369.45
30000	551.46	521.22	497.88	479.51	464.84	453.00	443.33
35000	643.37	608.09	580.85	559.43	542.32	528.50	517.22
40000	735.28	694.96	663.83	639.34	619.79	604.00	591.11
45000	827.19	781.83	746.81	719.26	697.27	679.49	665.00
50000	919.10	868.70	829.79	799.18	774.74	754.99	738.89
55000	1011.01	955.57	912.77	879.10	852.21	830.49	812.78
60000	1102.92	1042.44	995.75	959.02	929.69	905.99	886.67
65000	1194.83	1129.31	1078.73	1038.93	1007.16	981.49	960.56
70000	1286.74	1216.19	1161.71	1118.85	1084.63	1056.99	1034.45
75000	1378.65	1303.06	1244.69	1198.77	1162.11	1132.49	1108.34
80000	1470.57	1389.93	1327.67	1278.69	1239.58	1207.99	1182.22
85000	1562.48	1476.80	1410.65	1358.61	1317.06	1283.49	1256.11
90000	1654.39	1563.67	1493.63	1438.52	1394.53	1358.99	1330.00
95000	1746.30	1650.54	1576.61	1518.44	1472.00	1434.49	1403.89
100000	1838.21	1737.41	1659.58	1598.36	1549.48	1509.99	1477.78
105000	1930.12	1824.28	1742.56	1678.28	1626.95	1585.49	1551.67
110000	2022.03	1911.15	1825.54	1758.20	1704.43	1660.99	1625.56
120000	2205.85	2084.89	1991.50	1918.03	1859.37	1811.99	1773.34
130000	2389.67	2258.63	2157.46	2077.87	2014.32	1962.98	1921.11
140000	2573.49	2432.37	2323.42	2237.71	2169.27	2113.98	2068.89
150000	2757.31	2606.11	2489.38	2397.54	2324.22	2264.98	2216.67
160000	2941.13	2779.85	2655.34	2557.38	2479.17	2415.98	2364.45
170000	3124.95	2953.59	2821.29	2717.21	2634.11	2566.98	2512.23
180000	3308.77	3127.33	2987.25	2877.05	2789.06	2717.98	2660.00
190000	3492.59	3301.07	3153.21	3036.89	2944.01	2868.98	2807.78
200000	3676.41	3474.81	3319.17	3196.72	3098.96	3019.98	2955.56
210000	3860.23	3648.56	3485.13	3356.56	3253.90	3170.97	3103.34
220000	4044.05	3822.30	3651.09	3516.39	3408.85	3321.97	3251.12
230000	4227.87	3996.04	3817.05	3676.23	3563.80	3472.97	3398.89
240000	4411.70	4169.78	3983.00	3836.07	3718.75	3623.97	3546.67
250000	4595.52	4343.52	4148.96	3995.90	3873.70	3774.97	3694.45
260000	4779.34	4517.26	4314.92	4155.74	4028.64	3925.97	3842.23
270000	4963.16	4691.00	4480.88	4315.57	4183.59	4076.97	3990.01
280000	5146.98	4864.74	4646.84	4475.41	4338.54	4227.97	4137.78
290000	5330.80	5038.48	4812.80	4635.25	4493.49	4378.96	4285.56
300000	5514.62	5212.22	4978.75	4795.08	4648.44	4529.96	4433.34
310000	5698.44	5385.96	5144.71	4954.92	4803.38	4680.96	4581.12
320000	5882.26	5559.70	5310.67	5114.75	4958.33	4831.96	4728.90
330000	6066.08	5733.44	5476.63	5274.59	5113.28	4982.96	4876.67
340000	6249.90	5907.18	5642.59	5434.43	5268.23	5133.96	5024.45
350000	6433.72	6080.93	5808.55	5594.26	5423.17	5284.96	5172.23
400000	7352.83	6949.63	6638.34	6393.44	6197.91	6039.95	5911.12
450000	8271.93	7818.33	7468.13	7192.62	6972.65	6794.95	6650.01
500000	9191.03	8687.04	8297.92	7991.80	7747.39	7549.94	7388.90
550000	10110.13	9555.74	9127.72	8790.98	8522.13	8304.93	8127.79
600000	11029.24	10424.44	9957.51	9590.16	9296.87	9059.93	8866.68

15¾%

Monthly Payments
necessary to amortize a loan

AMOUNT	15 YEARS	16 YEARS	17 YEARS	18 YEARS	19 YEARS	20 YEARS	21 YEARS
100	1.45	1.43	1.41	1.40	1.38	1.37	1.36
200	2.90	2.86	2.82	2.79	2.77	2.75	2.73
500	7.26	7.15	7.06	6.98	6.92	6.86	6.82
1000	14.51	14.29	14.11	13.96	13.83	13.73	13.64
2000	29.03	28.59	28.22	27.92	27.67	27.45	27.27
5000	72.57	71.47	70.56	69.80	69.16	68.63	68.18
6000	87.08	85.76	84.67	83.76	83.00	82.35	81.81
7000	101.59	100.06	98.78	97.72	96.83	96.08	95.45
8000	116.10	114.35	112.90	111.68	110.66	109.80	109.08
9000	130.62	128.65	127.01	125.64	124.49	123.53	122.72
10000	145.13	142.94	141.01	139.60	138.33	137.25	136.35
15000	217.70	214.41	211.68	209.40	207.49	205.88	204.53
20000	290.26	285.88	282.24	279.20	276.65	274.51	272.70
25000	362.83	357.35	352.80	349.00	345.81	343.13	340.88
30000	435.39	428.82	423.36	418.80	414.98	411.76	409.05
35000	507.96	500.29	493.92	488.60	484.14	480.39	477.23
40000	580.52	571.76	564.48	558.40	553.30	549.01	545.40
45000	653.09	643.23	635.04	628.20	622.46	617.64	613.58
50000	725.65	714.71	705.60	698.00	691.63	686.27	681.75
55000	798.22	786.18	776.16	767.80	760.79	754.89	749.93
60000	870.78	857.65	846.72	837.60	829.95	823.52	818.10
65000	943.35	929.12	917.28	907.40	899.11	892.15	886.28
70000	1015.92	1000.59	987.84	977.20	968.28	960.77	954.45
75000	1088.48	1072.06	1058.40	1047.00	1037.44	1029.40	1022.63
80000	1161.05	1143.53	1128.96	1116.80	1106.60	1098.03	1090.80
85000	1233.61	1215.00	1199.52	1186.60	1175.76	1166.65	1158.98
90000	1306.18	1286.47	1270.08	1256.40	1244.93	1235.28	1227.15
95000	1378.74	1357.94	1340.64	1326.20	1314.09	1303.91	1295.33
100000	1451.31	1429.41	1411.20	1396.00	1383.25	1372.53	1363.50
105000	1523.87	1500.88	1481.76	1465.80	1452.41	1441.16	1431.68
110000	1596.44	1572.35	1552.32	1535.60	1521.58	1509.79	1499.85
120000	1741.57	1715.29	1693.44	1675.20	1659.90	1647.04	1636.20
130000	1886.70	1858.23	1834.56	1814.80	1798.23	1784.29	1772.55
140000	2031.83	2001.18	1975.68	1954.40	1936.53	1921.55	1908.90
150000	2176.96	2144.12	2116.80	2094.00	2074.88	2058.80	2045.25
160000	2322.09	2287.06	2257.93	2233.59	2213.20	2196.05	2181.60
170000	2467.22	2430.00	2399.05	2373.19	2351.53	2333.31	2317.95
180000	2612.35	2572.94	2540.17	2512.79	2489.85	2470.56	2454.30
190000	2757.48	2715.88	2681.29	2652.39	2628.18	2607.81	2590.65
200000	2902.62	2858.82	2822.41	2791.99	2766.50	2745.07	2727.00
210000	3047.75	3001.76	2963.53	2931.59	2904.83	2882.32	2863.35
220000	3192.88	3144.70	3104.65	3071.19	3043.15	3019.57	2999.70
230000	3338.01	3287.65	3245.77	3210.79	3181.48	3156.83	3136.05
240000	3483.14	3430.59	3386.89	3350.39	3319.80	3294.08	3272.40
250000	3628.27	3573.53	3528.01	3489.99	3458.13	3431.33	3408.75
260000	3773.40	3716.47	3669.13	3629.59	3596.45	3568.59	3545.10
270000	3918.53	3859.41	3810.25	3769.19	3734.78	3705.84	3681.45
280000	4063.66	4002.35	3951.37	3908.79	3873.10	3843.09	3817.80
290000	4208.79	4145.29	4092.49	4048.39	4011.43	3980.35	3954.15
300000	4353.92	4288.23	4233.61	4187.99	4149.75	4117.60	4090.50
310000	4499.05	4431.17	4374.73	4327.59	4288.08	4254.85	4226.85
320000	4644.18	4574.11	4515.85	4467.19	4426.40	4392.11	4363.20
330000	4789.32	4717.06	4656.97	4606.79	4564.73	4529.36	4499.55
340000	4934.45	4860.00	4798.09	4746.39	4703.05	4666.61	4635.90
350000	5079.58	5002.94	4939.21	4885.99	4841.38	4803.87	4772.25
400000	5805.23	5717.64	5644.82	5583.99	5533.00	5490.13	5454.00
450000	6530.88	6432.35	6350.41	6281.99	6224.63	6176.40	6135.75
500000	7256.54	7147.05	7056.02	6979.98	6916.25	6862.67	6817.50
550000	7982.19	7861.76	7761.62	7677.98	7607.88	7548.94	7499.25
600000	8707.85	8576.47	8467.22	8375.98	8299.50	8235.20	8181.00

Monthly Payments 15¾%
necessary to amortize a loan

AMOUNT	22 YEARS	23 YEARS	24 YEARS	25 YEARS	30 YEARS	35 YEARS	40 YEARS
100	1.36	1.35	1.34	1.34	1.32	1.32	1.32
200	2.71	2.70	2.69	2.68	2.65	2.64	2.63
500	6.78	6.75	6.72	6.70	6.62	6.59	6.58
1000	13.56	13.49	13.44	13.39	13.25	13.18	13.15
2000	27.12	26.99	26.88	26.79	26.49	26.36	26.30
5000	67.79	67.47	67.20	66.96	66.23	65.90	65.75
6000	81.35	80.96	80.64	80.36	79.48	79.08	78.90
7000	94.91	94.46	94.08	93.75	92.72	92.26	92.05
8000	108.47	107.95	107.51	107.14	105.97	105.44	105.20
9000	122.03	121.45	120.95	120.54	119.22	118.62	118.35
10000	135.58	134.94	134.39	133.93	132.46	131.80	131.50
15000	203.38	202.41	201.59	200.89	198.69	197.70	197.25
20000	271.17	269.88	268.79	267.86	264.92	263.60	263.00
25000	338.97	337.35	335.98	334.82	331.15	329.50	328.75
30000	406.76	404.82	403.18	401.79	397.39	395.40	394.50
35000	474.55	472.29	470.38	468.75	463.62	461.30	460.26
40000	542.35	539.76	537.57	535.72	529.85	527.21	526.01
45000	610.14	607.23	604.77	602.68	596.08	593.11	591.76
50000	677.93	674.71	671.97	669.64	662.31	659.01	657.51
55000	745.73	742.18	739.16	736.61	728.54	724.91	723.26
60000	813.52	809.65	806.36	803.57	794.77	790.81	789.01
65000	881.31	877.12	873.56	870.54	861.00	856.71	854.76
70000	949.11	944.59	940.76	937.50	927.23	922.61	920.51
75000	1016.90	1012.06	1007.95	1004.47	993.46	988.51	986.26
80000	1084.70	1079.53	1075.15	1071.43	1059.69	1054.41	1052.01
85000	1152.49	1147.00	1142.35	1138.40	1125.92	1120.31	1117.76
90000	1220.28	1214.47	1209.54	1205.36	1192.16	1186.21	1183.51
95000	1288.08	1281.94	1276.74	1272.33	1258.39	1252.11	1249.27
100000	1355.87	1349.41	1343.94	1339.29	1324.62	1318.01	1315.02
105000	1423.66	1416.88	1411.13	1406.25	1390.85	1383.91	1380.77
110000	1491.46	1484.35	1478.33	1473.22	1457.08	1449.82	1446.52
120000	1627.04	1619.29	1612.72	1607.15	1589.54	1581.62	1578.02
130000	1762.63	1754.23	1747.12	1741.08	1722.00	1713.42	1709.52
140000	1898.22	1889.17	1881.51	1875.01	1854.46	1845.22	1841.02
150000	2033.80	2024.12	2015.90	2008.93	1986.93	1977.02	1972.52
160000	2169.39	2159.06	2150.30	2142.86	2119.39	2108.82	2104.03
170000	2304.98	2294.00	2284.69	2276.79	2251.85	2240.62	2235.53
180000	2440.56	2428.94	2419.08	2410.72	2384.31	2372.42	2367.03
190000	2576.15	2563.88	2553.48	2544.65	2516.77	2504.23	2498.53
200000	2711.74	2698.82	2687.87	2678.58	2649.23	2636.03	2630.03
210000	2847.32	2833.76	2822.27	2812.51	2781.70	2767.83	2761.53
220000	2982.91	2968.70	2956.66	2946.44	2914.16	2899.63	2893.03
230000	3118.50	3103.64	3091.05	3080.37	3046.62	3031.43	3024.54
240000	3254.09	3238.58	3225.45	3214.29	3179.08	3163.23	3156.04
250000	3389.67	3373.53	3359.84	3348.22	3311.54	3295.03	3287.54
260000	3525.26	3508.47	3494.23	3482.15	3444.00	3426.84	3419.04
270000	3660.85	3643.41	3628.63	3616.08	3576.47	3558.64	3550.54
280000	3796.43	3778.35	3763.02	3750.01	3708.93	3690.44	3682.04
290000	3932.02	3913.29	3897.41	3883.94	3841.39	3822.24	3813.55
300000	4067.61	4048.23	4031.81	4017.87	3973.85	3954.04	3945.05
310000	4203.19	4183.17	4166.20	4151.80	4106.31	4085.84	4076.55
320000	4338.78	4318.11	4300.59	4285.73	4238.77	4217.64	4208.05
330000	4474.37	4453.05	4434.99	4419.66	4371.24	4349.45	4339.55
340000	4609.95	4587.99	4569.38	4553.58	4503.70	4481.25	4471.05
350000	4745.54	4722.94	4703.78	4687.51	4636.16	4613.05	4602.56
400000	5423.48	5397.64	5375.74	5357.16	5298.47	5272.05	5260.06
450000	6101.41	6072.35	6047.71	6026.80	5960.78	5931.06	5917.57
500000	6779.34	6747.05	6719.68	6696.45	6623.09	6590.07	6575.08
550000	7457.28	7421.76	7391.65	7366.09	7285.39	7249.08	7232.59
600000	8135.21	8096.46	8063.62	8035.74	7947.70	7908.08	7890.09

Monthly Payments
necessary to amortize a loan

AMOUNT	1 YEAR	2 YEARS	3 YEARS	4 YEARS	5 YEARS	6 YEARS	7 YEARS
100	9.07	4.90	3.52	2.83	2.43	2.17	1.99
200	18.15	9.79	7.03	5.67	4.86	4.34	3.97
500	45.37	24.48	17.58	14.17	12.16	10.85	9.93
1000	90.73	48.96	35.16	28.34	24.32	21.69	19.86
2000	181.46	97.93	70.31	56.68	48.64	43.38	39.72
5000	453.65	244.82	175.79	141.70	121.59	108.46	99.31
6000	544.39	293.78	210.94	170.04	145.91	130.15	119.17
7000	635.12	342.74	246.10	198.38	170.23	151.84	139.03
8000	725.85	391.70	281.26	226.72	194.54	173.53	158.90
9000	816.58	440.67	316.41	255.06	218.86	195.23	178.76
10000	907.31	489.63	351.57	283.40	243.18	216.92	198.62
15000	1360.96	734.45	527.36	425.10	364.77	325.38	297.93
20000	1814.62	979.26	703.14	566.81	486.36	433.84	397.24
25000	2268.27	1224.08	878.93	708.51	607.95	542.30	496.55
30000	2721.93	1468.89	1054.71	850.21	729.54	650.76	595.86
35000	3175.58	1713.71	1230.50	991.91	851.13	759.21	695.17
40000	3629.23	1958.52	1406.28	1133.61	972.72	867.67	794.48
45000	4082.89	2203.34	1582.07	1275.31	1094.31	976.13	893.79
50000	4536.54	2448.16	1757.85	1417.01	1215.90	1084.59	993.10
55000	4990.20	2692.97	1933.64	1558.72	1337.49	1193.05	1092.41
60000	5443.85	2937.79	2109.42	1700.42	1459.08	1301.51	1191.72
65000	5897.51	3182.60	2285.21	1842.12	1580.67	1409.97	1291.03
70000	6351.16	3427.42	2460.99	1983.82	1702.26	1518.43	1390.34
75000	6804.81	3672.23	2636.78	2125.52	1823.85	1626.89	1489.65
80000	7258.47	3917.05	2812.56	2267.22	1945.44	1735.35	1588.97
85000	7712.12	4161.86	2988.35	2408.92	2067.03	1843.81	1688.28
90000	8165.78	4406.68	3164.13	2550.63	2188.63	1952.27	1787.59
95000	8619.43	4651.50	3339.92	2692.33	2310.22	2060.72	1886.90
100000	9073.09	4896.31	3515.70	2834.03	2431.81	2169.18	1986.21
105000	9526.74	5141.13	3691.49	2975.73	2553.40	2277.64	2085.52
110000	9980.39	5385.94	3867.27	3117.43	2674.99	2386.10	2184.83
120000	10887.70	5875.57	4218.84	3400.83	2918.17	2603.02	2383.45
130000	11795.01	6365.20	4570.41	3684.24	3161.35	2819.94	2582.07
140000	12702.32	6854.84	4921.98	3967.64	3404.53	3036.86	2780.69
150000	13609.63	7344.47	5273.55	4251.04	3647.71	3253.78	2979.31
160000	14516.94	7834.10	5625.13	4534.44	3890.89	3470.69	3177.93
170000	15424.25	8323.73	5976.70	4817.85	4134.07	3687.61	3376.55
180000	16331.55	8813.36	6328.27	5101.25	4377.25	3904.53	3575.17
190000	17238.86	9302.99	6679.84	5384.65	4620.43	4121.45	3773.79
200000	18146.17	9792.62	7031.41	5668.06	4863.61	4338.37	3972.41
210000	19053.48	10282.25	7382.98	5951.46	5106.79	4555.29	4171.03
220000	19960.79	10771.88	7734.55	6234.86	5349.97	4772.20	4369.65
230000	20868.10	11261.52	8086.12	6518.26	5593.15	4989.12	4568.27
240000	21775.41	11751.15	8437.69	6801.67	5836.33	5206.04	4766.90
250000	22682.71	12240.78	8789.26	7085.07	6079.51	5422.96	4965.52
260000	23590.02	12730.41	9140.83	7368.47	6322.69	5639.88	5164.14
270000	24497.33	13220.04	9492.40	7651.88	6565.88	5856.80	5362.76
280000	25404.64	13709.67	9843.97	7935.28	6809.06	6073.72	5561.38
290000	26311.95	14199.30	10195.54	8218.68	7052.24	6290.63	5760.00
300000	27219.26	14688.93	10547.11	8502.08	7295.42	6507.55	5958.62
310000	28126.57	15178.56	10898.68	8785.49	7538.60	6724.47	6157.24
320000	29033.87	15668.20	11250.25	9068.89	7781.78	6941.39	6355.86
330000	29941.18	16157.83	11601.82	9352.29	8024.96	7158.31	6554.48
340000	30848.49	16647.46	11953.39	9635.70	8268.14	7375.23	6753.10
350000	31755.80	17137.09	12304.96	9919.10	8511.32	7592.14	6951.72
400000	36292.34	19585.24	14062.81	11336.11	9727.22	8676.74	7944.83
450000	40828.89	22033.40	15820.66	12753.13	10943.13	9761.33	8937.93
500000	45365.43	24481.56	17578.52	14170.14	12159.03	10845.92	9931.03
550000	49901.97	26929.71	19336.37	15587.15	13374.93	11930.51	10924.14
600000	54438.51	29377.87	21094.22	17004.17	14590.83	13015.10	11917.24

Monthly Payments 16%

necessary to amortize a loan

AMOUNT	8 YEARS	9 YEARS	10 YEARS	11 YEARS	12 YEARS	13 YEARS	14 YEARS
100	1.85	1.75	1.68	1.61	1.57	1.53	1.49
200	3.71	3.51	3.35	3.23	3.13	3.05	2.99
500	9.26	8.76	8.38	8.07	7.83	7.63	7.47
1000	18.53	17.53	16.75	16.14	15.66	15.27	14.95
2000	37.06	35.05	33.50	32.29	31.32	30.53	29.90
5000	92.64	87.63	83.76	80.72	78.29	76.34	74.74
6000	111.17	105.15	100.51	96.86	93.95	91.60	89.69
7000	129.70	122.68	117.26	113.00	109.61	106.87	104.64
8000	148.23	140.20	134.01	129.15	125.27	122.14	119.59
9000	166.76	157.73	150.76	145.29	140.92	137.40	134.54
10000	185.29	175.25	167.51	161.43	156.58	152.67	149.48
15000	277.93	262.88	251.27	242.15	234.87	229.01	224.23
20000	370.58	350.51	335.03	322.86	313.17	305.34	298.97
25000	463.22	438.13	418.78	403.58	391.46	381.68	373.71
30000	555.86	525.76	502.54	484.30	469.75	458.01	448.45
35000	648.51	613.38	586.30	565.01	548.04	534.35	523.20
40000	741.15	701.01	670.05	645.73	626.33	610.68	597.94
45000	833.80	788.64	753.81	726.44	704.62	687.02	672.68
50000	926.44	876.26	837.57	807.16	782.91	763.35	747.42
55000	1019.08	963.89	921.32	887.87	861.20	839.69	822.16
60000	1111.73	1051.52	1005.08	968.59	939.50	916.02	896.91
65000	1204.37	1139.14	1088.84	1049.31	1017.79	992.36	971.65
70000	1297.02	1226.77	1172.59	1130.02	1096.08	1068.69	1046.39
75000	1389.66	1314.39	1256.35	1210.74	1174.37	1145.03	1121.13
80000	1482.30	1402.02	1340.10	1291.45	1252.66	1221.36	1195.88
85000	1574.95	1489.65	1423.86	1372.17	1330.95	1297.70	1270.62
90000	1667.59	1577.27	1507.62	1452.89	1409.24	1374.03	1345.36
95000	1760.23	1664.90	1591.37	1533.60	1487.53	1450.37	1420.10
100000	1852.88	1752.53	1675.13	1614.32	1565.83	1526.70	1494.85
105000	1945.52	1840.15	1758.89	1695.03	1644.12	1603.04	1569.59
110000	2038.17	1927.78	1842.64	1775.75	1722.41	1679.37	1644.33
120000	2223.45	2103.03	2010.16	1937.18	1878.99	1832.05	1793.81
130000	2408.74	2278.28	2177.67	2098.61	2035.57	1984.72	1943.30
140000	2594.03	2453.54	2345.18	2260.04	2192.16	2137.39	2092.78
150000	2779.32	2628.79	2512.70	2421.48	2348.74	2290.06	2242.27
160000	2964.61	2804.04	2680.21	2582.91	2505.32	2442.73	2391.75
170000	3149.89	2979.29	2847.72	2744.34	2661.90	2595.40	2541.24
180000	3335.18	3154.55	3015.24	2905.77	2818.49	2748.07	2690.72
190000	3520.47	3329.80	3182.75	3067.20	2975.07	2900.74	2840.21
200000	3705.76	3505.05	3350.26	3228.63	3131.65	3053.41	2989.69
210000	3891.05	3680.30	3517.78	3390.07	3288.23	3206.08	3139.18
220000	4076.33	3855.56	3685.29	3551.50	3444.82	3358.75	3288.66
230000	4261.62	4030.81	3852.80	3712.93	3601.40	3511.42	3438.14
240000	4446.91	4206.06	4020.31	3874.36	3757.98	3664.09	3587.63
250000	4632.20	4381.31	4187.83	4035.79	3914.56	3816.76	3737.11
260000	4817.48	4556.57	4355.34	4197.22	4071.15	3969.43	3886.60
270000	5002.77	4731.82	4522.85	4358.66	4227.73	4122.10	4036.08
280000	5188.06	4907.07	4690.37	4520.09	4384.31	4274.77	4185.57
290000	5373.35	5082.32	4857.88	4681.52	4540.89	4427.44	4335.05
300000	5558.64	5257.58	5025.39	4842.95	4697.48	4580.11	4484.54
310000	5743.92	5432.83	5192.91	5004.38	4854.06	4732.78	4634.02
320000	5929.21	5608.08	5360.42	5165.82	5010.64	4885.45	4783.51
330000	6114.50	5783.33	5527.93	5327.25	5167.22	5038.12	4932.99
340000	6299.79	5958.59	5695.45	5488.68	5323.81	5190.80	5082.47
350000	6485.08	6133.84	5862.96	5650.11	5480.39	5343.47	5231.96
400000	7411.51	7010.10	6700.52	6457.27	6263.30	6106.82	5979.38
450000	8337.95	7886.36	7538.09	7264.43	7046.21	6870.17	6726.80
500000	9264.39	8762.63	8375.66	8071.59	7829.13	7633.52	7474.23
550000	10190.83	9638.89	9213.22	8878.74	8612.04	8396.87	8221.65
600000	11117.27	10515.15	10050.79	9685.90	9394.95	9160.23	8969.07

16%

Monthly Payments
necessary to amortize a loan

AMOUNT	15 YEARS	16 YEARS	17 YEARS	18 YEARS	19 YEARS	20 YEARS	21 YEARS
100	1.47	1.45	1.43	1.41	1.40	1.39	1.38
200	2.94	2.89	2.86	2.83	2.80	2.78	2.76
500	7.34	7.24	7.15	7.07	7.01	6.96	6.91
1000	14.69	14.47	14.29	14.14	14.02	13.91	13.82
2000	29.37	28.94	28.58	28.28	28.03	27.83	27.65
5000	73.44	72.36	71.46	70.71	70.09	69.56	69.12
6000	88.12	86.83	85.75	84.85	84.10	83.48	82.95
7000	102.81	101.30	100.04	99.00	98.12	97.39	96.77
8000	117.50	115.77	114.34	113.14	112.14	111.30	110.59
9000	132.18	130.24	128.63	127.28	126.16	125.21	124.42
10000	146.87	144.71	142.92	141.42	140.17	139.13	138.24
15000	220.31	217.07	214.38	212.14	210.26	208.69	207.36
20000	293.74	289.42	285.84	282.85	280.35	278.25	276.49
25000	367.18	361.78	357.30	353.56	350.44	347.81	345.61
30000	440.61	434.13	428.76	424.27	420.52	417.38	414.73
35000	514.05	506.49	500.22	494.99	490.61	486.94	483.85
40000	587.48	578.84	571.68	565.70	560.70	556.50	552.97
45000	660.92	651.20	643.13	636.41	630.79	626.07	622.09
50000	734.35	723.56	714.59	707.12	700.87	695.63	691.22
55000	807.79	795.91	786.05	777.84	770.96	765.19	760.34
60000	881.22	868.27	857.51	848.55	841.05	834.75	829.46
65000	954.66	940.62	928.97	919.26	911.14	904.32	898.58
70000	1028.09	1012.98	1000.43	989.97	981.22	973.88	967.70
75000	1101.53	1085.33	1071.89	1060.69	1051.31	1043.44	1036.82
80000	1174.96	1157.69	1143.35	1131.40	1121.40	1113.00	1105.94
85000	1248.40	1230.04	1214.81	1202.11	1191.48	1182.57	1175.07
90000	1321.83	1302.40	1286.27	1272.82	1261.57	1252.13	1244.19
95000	1395.27	1374.75	1357.73	1343.53	1331.66	1321.69	1313.31
100000	1468.70	1447.11	1429.19	1414.25	1401.75	1391.26	1382.43
105000	1542.14	1519.47	1500.65	1484.96	1471.83	1460.82	1451.55
110000	1615.57	1591.82	1572.11	1555.67	1541.92	1530.38	1520.67
120000	1762.44	1736.53	1715.03	1697.10	1682.10	1669.51	1658.92
130000	1909.31	1881.24	1857.94	1838.52	1822.27	1808.63	1797.16
140000	2056.18	2025.95	2000.86	1979.95	1962.44	1947.76	1935.40
150000	2203.05	2170.67	2143.78	2121.37	2102.62	2086.88	2073.65
160000	2349.92	2315.38	2286.70	2262.80	2242.79	2226.01	2211.89
170000	2496.79	2460.09	2429.62	2404.22	2382.97	2365.14	2350.13
180000	2643.66	2604.80	2572.54	2545.64	2523.14	2504.26	2488.37
190000	2790.53	2749.51	2715.46	2687.07	2663.32	2643.39	2626.62
200000	2937.40	2894.22	2858.38	2828.49	2803.49	2782.51	2764.86
210000	3084.27	3038.93	3001.30	2969.92	2943.67	2921.64	2903.10
220000	3231.14	3183.64	3144.21	3111.34	3083.84	3060.76	3041.35
230000	3378.01	3328.35	3287.13	3252.77	3224.02	3199.89	3179.59
240000	3524.88	3473.06	3430.05	3394.19	3364.19	3339.01	3317.83
250000	3671.75	3617.78	3572.97	3535.62	3504.37	3478.14	3456.08
260000	3818.62	3762.49	3715.89	3677.04	3644.54	3617.27	3594.32
270000	3965.49	3907.20	3858.81	3818.47	3784.72	3756.39	3732.56
280000	4112.36	4051.91	4001.73	3959.89	3924.89	3895.52	3870.81
290000	4259.23	4196.62	4144.65	4101.32	4065.06	4034.64	4009.05
300000	4406.10	4341.33	4287.56	4242.74	4205.24	4173.77	4147.29
310000	4552.97	4486.04	4430.48	4384.17	4345.41	4312.89	4285.53
320000	4699.84	4630.75	4573.40	4525.59	4485.59	4452.02	4423.78
330000	4846.71	4775.46	4716.32	4667.02	4625.76	4591.14	4562.02
340000	4993.58	4920.18	4859.24	4808.44	4765.94	4730.27	4700.26
350000	5140.45	5064.89	5002.16	4949.86	4906.11	4869.40	4838.51
400000	5874.80	5788.44	5716.75	5656.99	5606.99	5565.02	5529.72
450000	6609.15	6512.00	6431.35	6364.11	6307.86	6260.65	6220.94
500000	7343.50	7235.55	7145.94	7071.24	7008.73	6956.28	6912.15
550000	8077.85	7959.11	7860.54	7778.36	7709.60	7651.91	7603.37
600000	8812.20	8682.66	8575.13	8485.48	8410.48	8347.54	8294.58

Monthly Payments 16%

necessary to amortize a loan

AMOUNT	22 YEARS	23 YEARS	24 YEARS	25 YEARS	30 YEARS	35 YEARS	40 YEARS
100	1.37	1.37	1.36	1.36	1.34	1.34	1.34
200	2.75	2.74	2.73	2.72	2.69	2.68	2.67
500	6.87	6.84	6.82	6.79	6.72	6.69	6.68
1000	13.75	13.69	13.63	13.59	13.45	13.38	13.36
2000	27.50	27.37	27.27	27.18	26.90	26.77	26.71
5000	68.75	68.44	68.17	67.94	67.24	66.92	66.78
6000	82.50	82.12	81.80	81.53	80.69	80.31	80.14
7000	96.25	95.81	95.44	95.12	94.13	93.69	93.50
8000	110.00	109.50	109.07	108.71	107.58	107.08	106.85
9000	123.75	123.18	122.71	122.30	121.03	120.46	120.21
10000	137.50	136.87	136.34	135.89	134.48	133.85	133.56
15000	206.25	205.31	204.51	203.83	201.71	200.77	200.35
20000	275.00	273.74	272.68	271.78	268.95	267.69	267.13
25000	343.75	342.18	340.85	339.72	336.19	334.62	333.91
30000	412.50	410.61	409.02	407.67	403.43	401.54	400.69
35000	481.25	479.05	477.19	475.61	470.66	468.46	467.48
40000	550.00	547.48	545.36	543.56	537.90	535.39	534.26
45000	618.75	615.92	613.53	611.50	605.14	602.31	601.04
50000	687.50	684.35	681.70	679.44	672.38	669.23	667.82
55000	756.24	752.79	749.86	747.39	739.62	736.16	734.61
60000	824.99	821.22	818.03	815.33	806.85	803.08	801.39
65000	893.74	889.66	886.20	883.28	874.09	870.01	868.17
70000	962.49	958.09	954.37	951.22	941.33	936.93	934.95
75000	1031.24	1026.53	1022.54	1019.17	1008.57	1003.85	1001.74
80000	1099.99	1094.96	1090.71	1087.11	1075.81	1070.78	1068.52
85000	1168.74	1163.40	1158.88	1155.06	1143.04	1137.70	1135.30
90000	1237.49	1231.84	1227.05	1223.00	1210.28	1204.62	1202.08
95000	1306.24	1300.27	1295.22	1290.94	1277.52	1271.55	1268.87
100000	1374.99	1368.71	1363.39	1358.89	1344.76	1338.47	1335.65
105000	1443.74	1437.14	1431.56	1426.83	1411.99	1405.39	1402.43
110000	1512.49	1505.58	1499.73	1494.78	1479.23	1472.32	1469.21
120000	1649.99	1642.45	1636.07	1630.67	1613.71	1606.16	1602.78
130000	1787.49	1779.32	1772.41	1766.56	1748.18	1740.01	1736.34
140000	1924.99	1916.19	1908.75	1902.44	1882.66	1873.86	1869.91
150000	2062.49	2053.06	2045.09	2038.33	2017.14	2007.70	2003.47
160000	2199.98	2189.93	2181.42	2174.22	2151.61	2141.55	2137.04
170000	2337.48	2326.80	2317.76	2310.11	2286.09	2275.40	2270.60
180000	2474.98	2463.67	2454.10	2446.00	2420.56	2409.24	2404.17
190000	2612.48	2600.54	2590.44	2581.89	2555.04	2543.09	2537.73
200000	2749.98	2737.41	2726.78	2717.78	2689.51	2676.94	2671.30
210000	2887.48	2874.28	2863.12	2853.67	2823.99	2810.79	2804.86
220000	3024.98	3011.15	2999.46	2989.56	2958.47	2944.63	2938.43
230000	3162.48	3148.02	3135.80	3125.44	3092.94	3078.48	3071.99
240000	3299.98	3284.89	3272.14	3261.33	3227.42	3212.33	3205.56
250000	3437.48	3421.76	3408.48	3397.22	3361.89	3346.17	3339.12
260000	3574.97	3558.64	3544.82	3533.11	3496.37	3480.02	3472.69
270000	3712.47	3695.51	3681.15	3669.00	3630.84	3613.87	3606.25
280000	3849.97	3832.38	3817.49	3804.89	3765.32	3747.71	3739.82
290000	3987.47	3969.25	3953.83	3940.78	3899.80	3881.56	3873.38
300000	4124.97	4106.12	4090.17	4076.67	4034.27	4015.41	4006.95
310000	4262.47	4242.99	4226.51	4212.56	4168.75	4149.26	4140.51
320000	4399.97	4379.86	4362.85	4348.44	4303.22	4283.10	4274.08
330000	4537.47	4516.73	4499.19	4484.33	4437.70	4416.95	4407.64
340000	4674.97	4653.60	4635.53	4620.22	4572.17	4550.80	4541.20
350000	4812.47	4790.47	4771.87	4756.11	4706.65	4684.64	4674.77
400000	5499.96	5474.82	5453.56	5435.56	5379.03	5353.88	5342.59
450000	6187.45	6159.18	6135.26	6115.00	6051.41	6023.11	6010.42
500000	6874.95	6843.53	6816.95	6794.44	6723.78	6692.35	6678.24
550000	7562.45	7527.88	7498.65	7473.89	7396.16	7361.58	7346.07
600000	8249.94	8212.24	8180.34	8153.33	8068.54	8030.82	8013.89

16¼%

Monthly Payments
necessary to amortize a loan

AMOUNT	1 YEAR	2 YEARS	3 YEARS	4 YEARS	5 YEARS	6 YEARS	7 YEARS
100	9.08	4.91	3.53	2.85	2.45	2.18	2.00
200	18.17	9.82	7.06	5.69	4.89	4.37	4.00
500	45.42	24.54	17.64	14.23	12.23	10.91	10.00
1000	90.85	49.08	35.28	28.47	24.45	21.83	20.00
2000	181.70	98.17	70.56	56.94	48.90	43.66	40.01
5000	454.25	245.41	176.40	142.34	122.26	109.15	100.02
6000	545.10	294.50	211.68	170.81	146.71	130.98	120.03
7000	635.94	343.58	246.96	199.28	171.16	152.81	140.03
8000	726.79	392.66	282.24	227.75	195.61	174.64	160.04
9000	817.64	441.74	317.53	256.22	220.06	196.47	180.04
10000	908.49	490.83	352.81	284.68	244.51	218.30	200.05
15000	1362.74	736.24	529.21	427.03	366.77	327.45	300.07
20000	1816.98	981.65	705.61	569.37	489.02	436.59	400.09
25000	2271.23	1227.07	882.01	711.71	611.28	545.74	500.12
30000	2725.48	1472.48	1058.42	854.05	733.53	654.89	600.14
35000	3179.72	1717.89	1234.82	996.40	855.79	764.04	700.16
40000	3633.97	1963.31	1411.22	1138.74	978.04	873.19	800.19
45000	4088.21	2208.72	1587.63	1281.08	1100.30	982.34	900.21
50000	4542.46	2454.13	1764.03	1423.42	1222.55	1091.49	1000.24
55000	4996.71	2699.55	1940.43	1565.77	1344.81	1200.63	1100.26
60000	5450.95	2944.96	2116.83	1708.11	1467.07	1309.78	1200.28
65000	5905.20	3190.37	2293.24	1850.45	1589.32	1418.93	1300.31
70000	6359.44	3435.79	2469.64	1992.79	1711.58	1528.08	1400.33
75000	6813.69	3681.20	2646.04	2135.14	1833.83	1637.23	1500.35
80000	7267.94	3926.61	2822.45	2277.48	1956.09	1746.38	1600.38
85000	7722.18	4172.02	2998.85	2419.82	2078.34	1855.53	1700.40
90000	8176.43	4417.44	3175.25	2562.16	2200.60	1964.67	1800.42
95000	8630.67	4662.85	3351.66	2704.51	2322.85	2073.82	1900.45
100000	9084.92	4908.26	3528.06	2846.85	2445.11	2182.97	2000.47
105000	9539.17	5153.68	3704.46	2989.19	2567.36	2292.12	2100.49
110000	9993.41	5399.09	3880.86	3131.53	2689.62	2401.27	2200.52
120000	10901.90	5889.92	4233.67	3416.22	2934.13	2619.57	2400.57
130000	11810.40	6380.74	4586.48	3700.90	3178.64	2837.86	2600.61
140000	12718.89	6871.57	4939.28	3985.59	3423.15	3056.16	2800.66
150000	13627.38	7362.40	5292.09	4270.27	3667.66	3274.46	3000.71
160000	14535.87	7853.22	5644.89	4554.96	3912.17	3492.75	3200.75
170000	15444.36	8344.05	5997.70	4839.64	4156.69	3711.05	3400.80
180000	16352.86	8834.88	6350.50	5124.33	4401.20	3929.35	3600.85
190000	17261.35	9325.70	6703.31	5409.01	4645.71	4147.65	3800.90
200000	18169.84	9816.53	7056.12	5693.70	4890.22	4365.94	4000.94
210000	19078.33	10307.36	7408.92	5978.38	5134.73	4584.24	4200.99
220000	19986.83	10798.18	7761.73	6263.07	5379.24	4802.54	4401.04
230000	20895.32	11289.01	8114.53	6547.75	5623.75	5020.83	4601.08
240000	21803.81	11779.84	8467.34	6832.44	5868.26	5239.13	4801.13
250000	22712.30	12270.66	8820.15	7117.12	6112.77	5457.43	5001.18
260000	23620.79	12761.49	9172.95	7401.81	6357.28	5675.73	5201.23
270000	24529.29	13252.31	9525.76	7686.49	6601.79	5894.02	5401.27
280000	25437.78	13743.14	9878.56	7971.18	6846.31	6112.32	5601.32
290000	26346.27	14233.97	10231.37	8255.86	7090.82	6330.62	5801.37
300000	27254.76	14724.79	10584.17	8540.54	7335.33	6548.92	6001.41
310000	28163.25	15215.62	10936.98	8825.23	7579.84	6767.21	6201.46
320000	29071.75	15706.45	11289.79	9109.91	7824.35	6985.51	6401.51
330000	29980.24	16197.27	11642.59	9394.60	8068.86	7203.81	6601.56
340000	30888.73	16688.10	11995.40	9679.28	8313.37	7422.10	6801.60
350000	31797.22	17178.93	12348.20	9963.97	8557.88	7640.40	7001.65
400000	36339.68	19633.06	14112.23	11387.39	9780.44	8731.89	8001.89
450000	40882.14	22087.19	15876.26	12810.82	11002.99	9823.37	9002.12
500000	45424.60	24541.32	17640.29	14234.24	12225.54	10914.86	10002.36
550000	49967.06	26995.46	19404.32	15657.67	13448.10	12006.34	11002.59
600000	54509.52	29449.59	21168.35	17081.09	14670.65	13097.83	12002.83

Monthly Payments 16¼%
necessary to amortize a loan

AMOUNT	8 YEARS	9 YEARS	10 YEARS	11 YEARS	12 YEARS	13 YEARS	14 YEARS
100	1.87	1.77	1.69	1.63	1.58	1.54	1.51
200	3.74	3.54	3.38	3.26	3.16	3.09	3.02
500	9.34	8.84	8.45	8.15	7.91	7.72	7.56
1000	18.68	17.68	16.91	16.30	15.82	15.43	15.12
2000	37.35	35.35	33.81	32.61	31.64	30.87	30.24
5000	93.38	88.39	84.54	81.52	79.11	77.17	75.60
6000	112.06	106.06	101.44	97.82	94.93	92.61	90.72
7000	130.73	123.74	118.35	114.12	110.76	108.04	105.84
8000	149.41	141.42	135.26	130.43	126.58	123.48	120.96
9000	168.08	159.09	152.17	146.73	142.40	138.91	136.08
10000	186.76	176.77	169.07	163.03	158.22	154.35	151.20
15000	280.14	265.16	253.61	244.55	237.34	231.52	226.80
20000	373.52	353.54	338.15	326.07	316.45	308.70	302.40
25000	466.90	441.93	422.69	407.57	395.56	385.87	378.00
30000	560.28	530.31	507.22	489.10	474.67	463.05	453.60
35000	653.66	618.70	591.76	570.62	553.79	540.22	529.19
40000	747.04	707.08	676.30	652.14	632.90	617.40	604.79
45000	840.42	795.47	760.83	733.65	712.01	694.57	680.39
50000	933.80	883.85	845.37	815.17	791.12	771.75	755.99
55000	1027.18	972.24	929.91	896.69	870.23	848.92	831.59
60000	1120.57	1060.62	1014.45	978.21	949.35	926.10	907.19
65000	1213.95	1149.01	1098.98	1059.72	1028.46	1003.27	982.79
70000	1307.33	1237.39	1183.52	1141.24	1107.57	1080.45	1058.39
75000	1400.71	1325.78	1268.06	1222.76	1186.68	1157.62	1133.99
80000	1494.09	1414.16	1352.60	1304.27	1265.80	1234.80	1209.59
85000	1587.47	1502.55	1437.13	1385.79	1344.91	1311.97	1285.19
90000	1680.85	1590.93	1521.67	1467.31	1424.02	1389.15	1360.79
95000	1774.23	1679.32	1606.21	1548.83	1503.13	1466.32	1436.39
100000	1867.61	1767.71	1690.74	1630.34	1582.24	1543.49	1511.99
105000	1960.99	1856.09	1775.28	1711.86	1661.36	1620.67	1587.58
110000	2054.37	1944.48	1859.82	1793.38	1740.47	1697.84	1663.18
120000	2241.13	2121.25	2028.89	1956.41	1898.69	1852.19	1814.38
130000	2427.89	2298.02	2197.97	2119.45	2056.92	2006.54	1965.58
140000	2614.65	2474.79	2367.04	2282.48	2215.14	2160.89	2116.78
150000	2801.41	2651.56	2536.12	2445.51	2373.37	2315.24	2267.98
160000	2988.17	2828.33	2705.19	2608.55	2531.59	2469.59	2419.18
170000	3174.94	3005.10	2874.27	2771.58	2689.81	2623.94	2570.37
180000	3361.70	3181.87	3043.34	2934.62	2848.04	2778.29	2721.57
190000	3548.46	3358.64	3212.41	3097.65	3006.26	2932.64	2872.77
200000	3735.22	3535.41	3381.49	3260.69	3164.49	3086.99	3023.97
210000	3921.98	3712.18	3550.56	3423.72	3322.71	3241.34	3175.17
220000	4108.74	3888.95	3719.64	3586.76	3480.94	3395.69	3326.37
230000	4295.50	4065.72	3888.71	3749.79	3639.16	3550.04	3477.57
240000	4482.26	4242.49	4057.79	3912.82	3797.39	3704.39	3628.76
250000	4669.02	4419.26	4226.86	4075.86	3955.61	3858.74	3779.96
260000	4855.79	4596.03	4395.93	4238.89	4113.83	4013.09	3931.16
270000	5042.54	4772.80	4565.01	4401.93	4272.06	4167.44	4082.36
280000	5229.31	4949.58	4734.08	4564.96	4430.28	4321.78	4233.56
290000	5416.07	5126.35	4903.16	4728.00	4588.51	4476.13	4384.76
300000	5602.83	5303.12	5072.23	4891.03	4746.73	4630.48	4535.96
310000	5789.59	5479.89	5241.31	5054.06	4904.96	4784.83	4687.15
320000	5976.35	5656.66	5410.38	5217.10	5063.18	4939.18	4838.35
330000	6163.11	5833.43	5579.46	5380.13	5221.40	5093.53	4989.55
340000	6349.87	6010.20	5748.53	5543.17	5379.63	5247.88	5140.75
350000	6536.63	6186.97	5917.60	5706.20	5537.85	5402.23	5291.95
400000	7470.44	7070.82	6762.98	6521.37	6328.98	6173.98	6047.94
450000	8404.24	7954.67	7608.35	7336.54	7120.10	6945.73	6803.93
500000	9338.04	8838.53	8453.72	8151.72	7911.22	7717.47	7559.93
550000	10271.85	9722.38	9299.09	8966.89	8702.34	8489.22	8315.92
600000	11205.65	10606.23	10144.46	9782.06	9493.46	9260.97	9071.91

16¼%

Monthly Payments
necessary to amortize a loan

AMOUNT	15 YEARS	16 YEARS	17 YEARS	18 YEARS	19 YEARS	20 YEARS	21 YEARS
100	1.49	1.46	1.45	1.43	1.42	1.41	1.40
200	2.97	2.93	2.89	2.87	2.84	2.82	2.80
500	7.43	7.32	7.24	7.16	7.10	7.05	7.01
1000	14.86	14.65	14.47	14.33	14.20	14.10	14.01
2000	29.72	29.30	28.94	28.65	28.41	28.20	28.03
5000	74.31	73.24	72.36	71.63	71.02	70.50	70.07
6000	89.17	87.89	86.83	85.95	85.22	84.60	84.09
7000	104.03	102.54	101.31	100.28	99.42	98.70	98.10
8000	118.89	117.19	115.78	114.61	113.62	112.80	112.11
9000	133.76	131.84	130.25	128.93	127.83	126.90	126.13
10000	148.62	146.49	144.72	143.26	142.03	141.00	140.14
15000	222.93	219.73	217.09	214.89	213.05	211.51	210.21
20000	297.23	292.98	289.45	286.51	284.06	282.01	280.29
25000	371.54	366.22	361.81	358.14	355.08	352.51	350.36
30000	445.85	439.47	434.17	429.77	426.09	423.01	420.43
35000	520.16	512.71	506.54	501.40	497.11	493.52	490.50
40000	594.47	585.95	578.90	573.03	568.12	564.02	560.57
45000	668.78	659.20	651.26	644.66	639.14	634.52	630.64
50000	743.08	732.44	723.62	716.28	710.16	705.02	700.71
55000	817.39	805.69	795.99	787.91	781.17	775.53	770.78
60000	891.70	878.93	868.35	859.54	852.19	846.03	840.86
65000	966.01	952.17	940.71	931.17	923.20	916.53	910.93
70000	1040.32	1025.42	1013.07	1002.80	994.22	987.03	981.00
75000	1114.63	1098.66	1085.43	1074.43	1065.23	1057.53	1051.07
80000	1188.93	1171.91	1157.80	1146.06	1136.25	1128.04	1121.14
85000	1263.24	1245.15	1230.16	1217.68	1207.26	1198.54	1191.21
90000	1337.55	1318.40	1302.52	1289.31	1278.28	1269.04	1261.28
95000	1411.86	1391.64	1374.88	1360.94	1349.30	1339.54	1331.35
100000	1486.17	1464.88	1447.25	1432.57	1420.31	1410.05	1401.43
105000	1560.48	1538.13	1519.61	1504.20	1491.33	1480.55	1471.50
110000	1634.78	1611.37	1591.97	1575.83	1562.34	1551.05	1541.57
120000	1783.40	1757.86	1736.70	1719.08	1704.37	1692.05	1681.71
130000	1932.02	1904.35	1881.42	1862.34	1846.41	1833.06	1821.85
140000	2080.64	2050.84	2026.14	2005.60	1988.44	1974.06	1962.00
150000	2229.25	2197.33	2170.87	2148.85	2130.47	2115.07	2102.14
160000	2377.87	2343.81	2315.59	2292.11	2272.50	2256.07	2242.28
170000	2526.49	2490.30	2460.32	2435.37	2414.53	2397.08	2382.42
180000	2675.10	2636.79	2605.04	2578.62	2556.56	2538.08	2522.57
190000	2823.72	2783.28	2749.77	2721.88	2698.59	2679.09	2662.71
200000	2972.34	2929.77	2894.49	2865.14	2840.62	2820.09	2802.85
210000	3120.95	3076.26	3039.22	3008.39	2982.65	2961.10	2942.99
220000	3269.57	3222.74	3183.94	3151.65	3124.69	3102.10	3083.14
230000	3418.19	3369.23	3328.67	3294.91	3266.72	3243.10	3223.28
240000	3566.80	3515.72	3473.39	3438.17	3408.75	3384.11	3363.42
250000	3715.42	3662.21	3618.12	3581.42	3550.78	3525.11	3503.56
260000	3864.04	3808.70	3762.84	3724.68	3692.81	3666.12	3643.71
270000	4012.65	3955.19	3907.56	3867.94	3834.84	3807.12	3783.85
280000	4161.27	4101.67	4052.29	4011.19	3976.87	3948.13	3923.99
290000	4309.89	4248.16	4197.01	4154.45	4118.90	4089.13	4064.13
300000	4458.50	4394.65	4341.74	4297.71	4260.94	4230.14	4204.28
310000	4607.12	4541.14	4486.46	4440.96	4402.97	4371.14	4344.42
320000	4755.74	4687.63	4631.19	4584.22	4545.00	4512.15	4484.56
330000	4904.35	4834.12	4775.91	4727.48	4687.03	4653.15	4624.70
340000	5052.97	4980.60	4920.64	4870.73	4829.06	4794.15	4764.85
350000	5201.59	5127.09	5065.36	5013.99	4971.09	4935.16	4904.99
400000	5944.67	5859.54	5788.49	5730.28	5681.25	5640.18	5605.70
450000	6687.76	6591.98	6512.61	6446.56	6391.40	6345.20	6306.42
500000	7430.84	7324.42	7236.23	7162.84	7101.56	7050.23	7007.13
550000	8173.92	8056.86	7959.85	7879.13	7811.71	7755.25	7707.84
600000	8917.01	8789.30	8683.48	8595.41	8521.87	8460.27	8408.55

Monthly Payments 16¼%
necessary to amortize a loan

AMOUNT	22 YEARS	23 YEARS	24 YEARS	25 YEARS	30 YEARS	35 YEARS	40 YEARS
100	1.39	1.39	1.38	1.38	1.36	1.36	1.36
200	2.79	2.78	2.77	2.76	2.73	2.72	2.71
500	6.97	6.94	6.91	6.89	6.82	6.79	6.78
1000	13.94	13.88	13.83	13.79	13.65	13.59	13.56
2000	27.88	27.76	27.66	27.57	27.30	27.18	27.13
5000	69.71	69.40	69.15	68.93	68.25	67.95	67.81
6000	83.65	83.28	82.97	82.71	81.90	81.54	81.38
7000	97.59	97.16	96.80	96.50	95.55	95.13	94.94
8000	111.52	111.04	110.63	110.28	109.19	108.72	108.50
9000	125.48	124.93	124.46	124.07	122.84	122.31	122.07
10000	139.42	138.81	138.29	137.85	136.49	135.89	135.63
15000	209.13	208.21	207.44	206.78	204.74	203.84	203.44
20000	278.83	277.61	276.58	275.71	272.99	271.79	271.26
25000	348.54	347.02	345.73	344.64	341.23	339.74	339.07
30000	418.25	416.42	414.87	413.56	409.48	407.68	406.89
35000	487.96	485.82	484.02	482.49	477.73	475.63	474.70
40000	557.67	555.22	553.16	551.42	545.97	543.58	542.52
45000	627.38	624.63	622.31	620.34	614.22	611.53	610.33
50000	697.09	694.03	691.45	689.27	682.47	679.47	678.15
55000	766.80	763.43	760.60	758.20	750.71	747.42	745.96
60000	836.50	832.84	829.74	827.12	818.96	815.37	813.78
65000	906.21	902.24	898.89	896.05	887.21	883.32	881.59
70000	975.92	971.64	968.03	964.98	955.45	951.26	949.41
75000	1045.63	1041.05	1037.18	1033.91	1023.70	1019.21	1017.22
80000	1115.34	1110.45	1106.32	1102.83	1091.95	1087.16	1085.04
85000	1185.05	1179.85	1175.47	1171.76	1160.19	1155.11	1152.85
90000	1254.76	1249.25	1244.61	1240.69	1228.44	1223.05	1220.67
95000	1324.46	1318.66	1313.76	1309.61	1296.69	1291.00	1288.48
100000	1394.17	1388.06	1382.90	1378.54	1364.93	1358.95	1356.30
105000	1463.88	1457.46	1452.05	1447.47	1433.18	1426.90	1424.11
110000	1533.59	1526.87	1521.19	1516.40	1501.43	1494.84	1491.93
120000	1673.01	1665.67	1659.48	1654.25	1637.92	1630.74	1627.56
130000	1812.43	1804.48	1797.77	1792.10	1774.42	1766.63	1763.19
140000	1951.84	1943.29	1936.06	1929.96	1910.91	1902.53	1898.82
150000	2091.26	2082.09	2074.35	2067.81	2047.40	2038.42	2034.45
160000	2230.68	2220.90	2212.64	2205.67	2183.90	2174.32	2170.07
170000	2370.09	2359.70	2350.93	2343.52	2320.39	2310.21	2305.70
180000	2509.51	2498.51	2489.22	2481.37	2456.88	2446.11	2441.33
190000	2648.93	2637.32	2627.51	2619.23	2593.38	2582.00	2576.96
200000	2788.35	2776.12	2765.80	2757.08	2729.87	2717.90	2712.59
210000	2927.76	2914.93	2904.09	2894.94	2866.36	2853.79	2848.22
220000	3067.18	3053.73	3042.38	3032.79	3002.86	2989.69	2983.85
230000	3206.60	3192.54	3180.67	3170.64	3139.35	3125.58	3119.48
240000	3346.02	3331.35	3318.96	3308.50	3275.84	3261.48	3255.11
250000	3485.43	3470.15	3457.25	3446.35	3412.34	3397.37	3390.74
260000	3624.85	3608.96	3595.54	3584.21	3548.83	3533.27	3526.37
270000	3764.27	3747.76	3733.83	3722.06	3685.32	3669.16	3662.00
280000	3903.69	3886.57	3872.12	3859.92	3821.82	3805.06	3797.63
290000	4043.10	4025.38	4010.41	3997.77	3958.31	3940.95	3933.26
300000	4182.52	4164.18	4148.70	4135.62	4094.80	4076.85	4068.89
310000	4321.94	4302.99	4286.99	4273.48	4231.30	4212.74	4204.52
320000	4461.35	4441.79	4425.28	4411.33	4367.79	4348.64	4340.15
330000	4600.77	4580.60	4563.57	4549.19	4504.28	4484.53	4475.78
340000	4740.19	4719.41	4701.87	4687.04	4640.78	4620.43	4611.41
350000	4879.61	4858.21	4840.16	4824.89	4777.27	4756.32	4747.04
400000	5576.69	5552.24	5531.61	5514.17	5459.74	5435.80	5425.19
450000	6273.78	6246.27	6223.06	6203.44	6142.21	6115.27	6103.34
500000	6970.87	6940.30	6914.51	6892.71	6824.67	6794.75	6781.48
550000	7667.95	7634.33	7605.96	7581.98	7507.14	7474.22	7459.63
600000	8365.04	8328.36	8297.41	8271.25	8189.61	8153.70	8137.78

16½%

Monthly Payments
necessary to amortize a loan

AMOUNT	1 YEAR	2 YEARS	3 YEARS	4 YEARS	5 YEARS	6 YEARS	7 YEARS
100	9.10	4.92	3.54	2.86	2.46	2.20	2.01
200	18.19	9.84	7.08	5.72	4.92	4.39	4.03
500	45.48	24.60	17.70	14.30	12.29	10.98	10.07
1000	90.97	49.20	35.40	28.60	24.58	21.97	20.15
2000	181.94	98.40	70.81	57.19	49.17	43.94	40.30
5000	454.84	246.01	177.02	142.99	122.92	109.84	100.74
6000	545.81	295.21	212.43	171.58	147.51	131.81	120.89
7000	636.77	344.42	247.83	200.18	172.09	153.78	141.04
8000	727.74	393.62	283.24	228.78	196.68	175.74	161.18
9000	818.71	442.82	318.64	257.37	221.26	197.71	181.33
10000	909.68	492.02	354.04	285.97	245.85	219.68	201.48
15000	1364.51	738.04	531.07	428.96	368.77	329.52	302.22
20000	1819.35	984.05	708.09	571.94	491.69	439.36	402.96
25000	2274.19	1230.06	885.11	714.93	614.61	549.20	503.70
30000	2729.03	1476.07	1062.13	857.91	737.54	659.04	604.44
35000	3183.87	1722.08	1239.15	1000.90	860.46	768.88	705.18
40000	3638.71	1968.09	1416.18	1143.88	983.38	878.72	805.92
45000	4093.54	2214.11	1593.20	1286.87	1106.30	988.56	906.66
50000	4548.38	2460.12	1770.22	1429.85	1229.23	1098.40	1007.39
55000	5003.22	2706.13	1947.24	1572.84	1352.15	1208.24	1108.13
60000	5458.06	2952.14	2124.26	1715.82	1475.07	1318.08	1208.87
65000	5912.90	3198.15	2301.28	1858.81	1597.99	1427.92	1309.61
70000	6367.73	3444.16	2478.31	2001.79	1720.92	1537.76	1410.35
75000	6822.57	3690.18	2655.33	2144.78	1843.84	1647.60	1511.09
80000	7277.41	3936.19	2832.35	2287.76	1966.76	1757.44	1611.83
85000	7732.25	4182.20	3009.37	2430.75	2089.68	1867.28	1712.57
90000	8187.09	4428.21	3186.39	2573.73	2212.61	1977.13	1813.31
95000	8641.93	4674.22	3363.42	2716.72	2335.53	2086.97	1914.05
100000	9096.76	4920.24	3540.44	2859.70	2458.45	2196.81	2014.79
105000	9551.60	5166.25	3717.46	3002.69	2581.37	2306.65	2115.53
110000	10006.44	5412.26	3894.48	3145.67	2704.30	2416.49	2216.27
120000	10916.12	5904.28	4248.53	3431.64	2950.14	2636.17	2417.75
130000	11825.79	6396.31	4602.57	3717.61	3195.99	2855.85	2619.23
140000	12735.47	6888.33	4956.61	4003.58	3441.83	3075.53	2820.70
150000	13645.15	7380.35	5310.66	4289.55	3687.68	3295.21	3022.18
160000	14554.82	7872.38	5664.70	4575.52	3933.52	3514.89	3223.66
170000	15464.50	8364.40	6018.75	4861.49	4179.37	3734.57	3425.14
180000	16374.17	8856.42	6372.79	5147.46	4425.21	3954.25	3626.62
190000	17283.85	9348.45	6726.83	5433.43	4671.06	4173.93	3828.10
200000	18193.53	9840.47	7080.88	5719.40	4916.90	4393.61	4029.58
210000	19103.20	10332.49	7434.92	6005.37	5162.75	4613.29	4231.06
220000	20012.88	10824.52	7788.96	6291.34	5408.59	4832.97	4432.54
230000	20922.56	11316.54	8143.01	6577.31	5654.44	5052.65	4634.01
240000	21832.23	11808.56	8497.05	6863.28	5900.29	5272.33	4835.49
250000	22741.91	12300.59	8851.10	7149.25	6146.13	5492.01	5036.97
260000	23651.59	12792.61	9205.14	7435.22	6391.98	5711.70	5238.45
270000	24561.26	13284.63	9559.18	7721.19	6637.82	5931.38	5439.93
280000	25470.94	13776.66	9913.23	8007.16	6883.67	6151.06	5641.41
290000	26380.61	14268.68	10267.27	8293.13	7129.51	6370.74	5842.89
300000	27290.29	14760.71	10621.31	8579.10	7375.36	6590.42	6044.37
310000	28199.97	15252.73	10975.36	8865.07	7621.20	6810.10	6245.85
320000	29109.64	15744.75	11329.40	9151.04	7867.05	7029.78	6447.32
330000	30019.32	16236.78	11683.45	9437.01	8112.89	7249.46	6648.80
340000	30929.00	16728.80	12037.49	9722.98	8358.74	7469.14	6850.28
350000	31838.67	17220.82	12391.53	10008.95	8604.58	7688.82	7051.76
400000	36387.05	19680.94	14161.75	11438.80	9833.81	8787.22	8059.16
450000	40935.44	22141.06	15931.97	12868.65	11063.03	9885.63	9066.55
500000	45483.82	24601.18	17702.19	14298.50	12292.26	10984.03	10073.94
550000	50032.20	27061.29	19472.41	15728.36	13521.49	12082.43	11081.34
600000	54580.58	29521.41	21242.63	17158.21	14750.71	13180.84	12088.73

Monthly Payments 16½%
necessary to amortize a loan

AMOUNT	8 YEARS	9 YEARS	10 YEARS	11 YEARS	12 YEARS	13 YEARS	14 YEARS
100	1.88	1.78	1.71	1.65	1.60	1.56	1.53
200	3.76	3.57	3.41	3.29	3.20	3.12	3.06
500	9.41	8.91	8.53	8.23	7.99	7.80	7.65
1000	18.82	17.83	17.06	16.46	15.99	15.60	15.29
2000	37.65	35.66	34.13	32.93	31.97	31.21	30.58
5000	94.12	89.15	85.32	82.32	79.94	78.02	76.46
6000	112.94	106.98	102.39	98.79	95.92	93.62	91.75
7000	131.77	124.81	119.45	115.25	111.91	109.22	107.04
8000	150.59	142.64	136.51	131.72	127.90	124.83	122.34
9000	169.42	160.47	153.58	148.18	143.89	140.43	137.63
10000	188.24	178.29	170.64	164.64	159.87	156.04	152.92
15000	282.35	267.44	255.96	246.97	239.81	234.05	229.38
20000	376.48	356.59	341.28	329.29	319.75	312.07	305.84
25000	470.60	445.74	426.61	411.61	399.68	390.09	382.30
30000	564.72	534.88	511.93	493.93	479.62	468.11	458.76
35000	658.84	624.03	597.25	576.25	559.56	546.12	535.22
40000	752.96	713.18	682.57	658.58	639.49	624.14	611.68
45000	847.08	802.33	767.89	740.90	719.43	702.16	688.14
50000	941.20	891.47	853.21	823.22	799.37	780.18	764.60
55000	1035.32	980.62	938.53	905.54	879.30	858.20	841.06
60000	1129.44	1069.77	1023.85	987.86	959.24	936.21	917.52
65000	1223.56	1158.92	1109.17	1070.18	1039.18	1014.23	993.98
70000	1317.68	1248.06	1194.50	1152.51	1119.11	1092.25	1070.44
75000	1411.80	1337.21	1279.82	1234.83	1199.05	1170.27	1146.90
80000	1505.92	1426.36	1365.14	1317.15	1278.99	1248.29	1223.36
85000	1600.04	1515.51	1450.46	1399.47	1358.92	1326.30	1299.82
90000	1694.16	1604.65	1535.78	1481.79	1438.86	1404.32	1376.28
95000	1788.28	1693.80	1621.10	1564.12	1518.80	1482.34	1452.74
100000	1882.40	1782.95	1706.42	1646.44	1598.73	1560.36	1529.20
105000	1976.52	1872.10	1791.74	1728.76	1678.67	1638.37	1605.66
110000	2070.64	1961.24	1877.07	1811.08	1758.61	1716.39	1682.12
120000	2258.88	2139.54	2047.71	1975.73	1918.48	1872.43	1835.04
130000	2447.12	2317.83	2218.35	2140.37	2078.35	2028.46	1987.96
140000	2635.36	2496.13	2388.99	2305.01	2238.23	2184.50	2140.88
150000	2823.60	2674.42	2559.63	2469.66	2398.10	2340.54	2293.80
160000	3011.80	2852.72	2730.28	2634.30	2557.97	2496.57	2446.72
170000	3200.08	3031.01	2900.92	2798.94	2717.85	2652.61	2599.64
180000	3388.31	3209.31	3071.56	2963.59	2877.72	2808.64	2752.56
190000	3576.55	3387.60	3242.20	3128.23	3037.59	2964.68	2905.48
200000	3764.79	3565.90	3412.85	3292.88	3197.47	3120.71	3058.40
210000	3953.03	3744.19	3583.49	3457.52	3357.34	3276.75	3211.32
220000	4141.27	3922.49	3754.13	3622.16	3517.21	3432.79	3364.23
230000	4329.51	4100.78	3924.77	3786.81	3677.09	3588.82	3517.15
240000	4517.75	4279.08	4095.42	3951.45	3836.96	3744.86	3670.07
250000	4705.99	4457.37	4266.06	4116.10	3996.83	3900.89	3822.99
260000	4894.23	4635.67	4436.70	4280.74	4156.71	4056.93	3975.91
270000	5082.47	4813.96	4607.34	4445.38	4316.58	4212.96	4128.83
280000	5270.71	4992.26	4777.98	4610.03	4476.45	4369.00	4281.75
290000	5458.95	5170.55	4948.63	4774.67	4636.33	4525.03	4434.67
300000	5647.19	5348.84	5119.27	4939.31	4796.20	4681.07	4587.59
310000	5835.43	5527.14	5289.91	5103.96	4956.07	4837.11	4740.51
320000	6023.67	5705.43	5460.55	5268.60	5115.95	4993.14	4893.43
330000	6211.91	5883.73	5631.20	5433.25	5275.82	5149.18	5046.35
340000	6400.15	6062.02	5801.84	5597.89	5435.69	5305.21	5199.27
350000	6588.39	6240.32	5972.48	5762.53	5595.57	5461.25	5352.19
400000	7529.59	7131.79	6825.69	6585.75	6394.93	6241.43	6116.79
450000	8470.79	8023.27	7678.90	7408.97	7194.30	7021.61	6881.39
500000	9411.99	8914.74	8532.11	8232.19	7993.67	7801.78	7645.99
550000	10353.18	9806.22	9385.33	9055.41	8793.03	8581.96	8410.59
600000	11294.38	10697.69	10238.54	9878.63	9592.40	9362.14	9175.19

16½%

Monthly Payments
necessary to amortize a loan

AMOUNT	15 YEARS	16 YEARS	17 YEARS	18 YEARS	19 YEARS	20 YEARS	21 YEARS
100	1.50	1.48	1.47	1.45	1.44	1.43	1.42
200	3.01	2.97	2.93	2.90	2.88	2.86	2.84
500	7.52	7.41	7.33	7.25	7.19	7.14	7.10
1000	15.04	14.83	14.65	14.51	14.39	14.29	14.20
2000	30.07	29.65	29.31	29.02	28.78	28.58	28.41
5000	75.19	74.14	73.27	72.55	71.95	71.45	71.02
6000	90.22	88.96	87.92	87.06	86.34	85.73	85.23
7000	105.26	103.79	102.58	101.57	100.73	100.02	99.43
8000	120.30	118.62	117.23	116.08	115.12	114.31	113.64
9000	135.33	133.45	131.88	130.59	129.51	128.60	127.84
10000	150.37	148.27	146.54	145.10	143.89	142.89	142.05
15000	225.56	222.41	219.81	217.64	215.84	214.34	213.07
20000	300.74	296.55	293.08	290.19	287.79	285.78	284.10
25000	375.93	370.68	366.34	362.74	359.74	357.23	355.12
30000	451.11	444.82	439.61	435.29	431.68	428.67	426.15
35000	526.30	518.96	512.88	507.84	503.63	500.12	497.17
40000	601.48	593.09	586.15	580.38	575.58	571.56	568.19
45000	676.67	667.23	659.42	652.93	647.53	643.01	639.22
50000	751.85	741.36	732.69	725.48	719.47	714.45	710.24
55000	827.04	815.50	805.96	798.03	791.42	785.90	781.27
60000	902.23	889.64	879.23	870.58	863.37	857.34	852.29
65000	977.41	963.77	952.49	943.12	935.31	928.79	923.31
70000	1052.60	1037.91	1025.76	1015.67	1007.26	1000.23	994.34
75000	1127.78	1112.05	1099.03	1088.22	1079.21	1071.68	1065.36
80000	1202.97	1186.18	1172.30	1160.77	1151.16	1143.12	1136.39
85000	1278.15	1260.32	1245.57	1233.32	1223.10	1214.57	1207.41
90000	1353.34	1334.46	1318.84	1305.86	1295.05	1286.01	1278.44
95000	1428.52	1408.59	1392.11	1378.41	1367.00	1357.46	1349.46
100000	1503.71	1482.73	1465.38	1450.96	1438.94	1428.90	1420.48
105000	1578.89	1556.87	1538.64	1523.51	1510.89	1500.35	1491.51
110000	1654.08	1631.00	1611.91	1596.06	1582.84	1571.79	1562.53
120000	1804.45	1779.28	1758.45	1741.15	1726.73	1714.68	1704.58
130000	1954.82	1927.55	1904.99	1886.25	1870.63	1857.57	1846.63
140000	2105.19	2075.82	2051.53	2031.34	2014.52	2000.46	1988.68
150000	2255.56	2224.09	2198.06	2176.44	2158.42	2143.35	2130.73
160000	2405.93	2372.37	2344.60	2321.54	2302.31	2286.24	2272.77
170000	2556.30	2520.64	2491.14	2466.63	2446.21	2429.13	2414.82
180000	2706.68	2668.91	2637.68	2611.73	2590.10	2572.02	2556.87
190000	2857.05	2817.19	2784.21	2756.83	2734.00	2714.91	2698.92
200000	3007.42	2965.46	2930.75	2901.92	2877.89	2857.80	2840.97
210000	3157.79	3113.73	3077.29	3047.02	3021.78	3000.69	2983.02
220000	3308.16	3262.01	3223.83	3192.11	3165.68	3143.58	3125.06
230000	3458.53	3410.28	3370.36	3337.21	3309.57	3286.47	3267.11
240000	3608.90	3558.55	3516.90	3482.31	3453.47	3429.36	3409.16
250000	3759.27	3706.82	3663.44	3627.40	3597.36	3572.25	3551.21
260000	3909.64	3855.10	3809.98	3772.50	3741.26	3715.14	3693.26
270000	4060.01	4003.37	3956.51	3917.59	3885.15	3858.03	3835.31
280000	4210.38	4151.64	4103.05	4062.69	4029.05	4000.92	3977.35
290000	4360.75	4299.92	4249.59	4207.79	4172.94	4143.81	4119.40
300000	4511.13	4448.19	4396.13	4352.88	4316.83	4286.70	4261.45
310000	4661.50	4596.46	4542.66	4497.98	4460.73	4429.59	4403.50
320000	4811.87	4744.74	4689.20	4643.07	4604.62	4572.48	4545.55
330000	4962.24	4893.01	4835.74	4788.17	4748.52	4715.37	4687.60
340000	5112.61	5041.28	4982.28	4933.27	4892.41	4858.26	4829.65
350000	5262.98	5189.55	5128.82	5078.36	5036.31	5001.15	4971.69
400000	6014.83	5930.92	5861.50	5803.84	5755.78	5715.60	5681.94
450000	6766.69	6672.28	6594.19	6529.32	6475.25	6430.05	6392.18
500000	7518.54	7413.65	7326.88	7254.80	7194.72	7144.50	7102.42
550000	8270.40	8155.01	8059.57	7980.28	7914.20	7858.95	7812.66
600000	9022.25	8896.38	8792.25	8705.76	8633.67	8573.40	8522.90

Monthly Payments 16½%
necessary to amortize a loan

AMOUNT	22 YEARS	23 YEARS	24 YEARS	25 YEARS	30 YEARS	35 YEARS	40 YEARS
100	1.41	1.41	1.40	1.40	1.39	1.38	1.38
200	2.83	2.81	2.80	2.80	2.77	2.76	2.75
500	7.07	7.04	7.01	6.99	6.93	6.90	6.88
1000	14.13	14.07	14.02	13.98	13.85	13.79	13.77
2000	28.27	28.15	28.05	27.96	27.70	27.59	27.54
5000	70.67	70.37	70.12	69.91	69.26	68.97	68.85
6000	84.81	84.45	84.15	83.89	83.11	82.77	82.62
7000	98.94	98.52	98.17	97.88	96.96	96.56	96.39
8000	113.07	112.60	112.20	111.86	110.81	110.36	110.16
9000	127.21	126.67	126.22	125.84	124.66	124.15	123.93
10000	141.34	140.75	140.25	139.82	138.51	137.95	137.70
15000	212.01	211.12	210.37	209.74	207.77	206.92	206.54
20000	282.68	281.49	280.49	279.65	277.03	275.89	275.39
25000	353.35	351.87	350.62	349.56	346.29	344.86	344.24
30000	424.03	422.24	420.74	419.47	415.54	413.84	413.09
35000	494.70	492.62	490.86	489.39	484.80	482.81	481.94
40000	565.37	562.99	560.99	559.30	554.06	551.78	550.78
45000	636.04	633.36	631.11	629.21	623.32	620.75	619.63
50000	706.71	703.74	701.23	699.12	692.57	689.73	688.48
55000	777.38	774.11	771.36	769.03	761.83	758.70	757.33
60000	848.05	844.48	841.48	838.95	831.09	827.67	826.18
65000	918.72	914.86	911.60	908.86	900.35	896.65	895.02
70000	989.39	985.23	981.73	978.77	969.60	965.62	963.87
75000	1060.06	1055.60	1051.85	1048.68	1038.86	1034.59	1032.72
80000	1130.73	1125.98	1121.97	1118.60	1108.12	1103.56	1101.57
85000	1201.40	1196.35	1192.10	1188.51	1177.38	1172.54	1170.42
90000	1272.08	1266.73	1262.22	1258.42	1246.63	1241.51	1239.26
95000	1342.75	1337.10	1332.34	1328.33	1315.89	1310.48	1308.11
100000	1413.42	1407.47	1402.47	1398.24	1385.15	1379.45	1376.96
105000	1484.09	1477.85	1472.59	1468.16	1454.41	1448.43	1445.81
110000	1554.76	1548.22	1542.71	1538.07	1523.66	1517.40	1514.66
120000	1696.10	1688.97	1682.96	1677.89	1662.18	1655.34	1652.35
130000	1837.44	1829.71	1823.21	1817.72	1800.69	1793.29	1790.05
140000	1978.79	1970.46	1963.45	1957.54	1939.21	1931.24	1927.74
150000	2120.13	2111.21	2103.70	2097.37	2077.72	2069.18	2065.44
160000	2261.47	2251.96	2243.95	2237.19	2216.24	2207.13	2203.13
170000	2402.81	2392.70	2384.19	2377.02	2354.75	2345.07	2340.83
180000	2544.15	2533.45	2524.44	2516.84	2493.27	2483.02	2478.53
190000	2685.49	2674.20	2664.69	2656.66	2631.78	2620.96	2616.22
200000	2826.83	2814.95	2804.93	2796.49	2770.30	2758.91	2753.92
210000	2968.18	2955.69	2945.18	2936.31	2908.81	2896.85	2891.61
220000	3109.52	3096.44	3085.43	3076.14	3047.33	3034.80	3029.31
230000	3250.86	3237.19	3225.67	3215.96	3185.84	3172.74	3167.01
240000	3392.20	3377.93	3365.92	3355.79	3324.36	3310.69	3304.70
250000	3533.54	3518.68	3506.17	3495.61	3462.87	3448.63	3442.40
260000	3674.88	3659.43	3646.41	3635.44	3601.39	3586.58	3580.09
270000	3816.23	3800.18	3786.66	3775.26	3739.90	3724.53	3717.79
280000	3957.57	3940.92	3926.91	3915.09	3878.41	3862.47	3855.49
290000	4098.91	4081.67	4067.15	4054.91	4016.93	4000.42	3993.18
300000	4240.25	4222.42	4207.40	4194.73	4155.44	4138.36	4130.88
310000	4381.59	4363.17	4347.65	4334.56	4293.96	4276.31	4268.57
320000	4522.93	4503.91	4487.89	4474.38	4432.47	4414.25	4406.27
330000	4664.28	4644.66	4628.14	4614.21	4570.99	4552.20	4543.97
340000	4805.62	4785.41	4768.39	4754.03	4709.50	4690.14	4681.66
350000	4946.96	4926.16	4908.63	4893.86	4848.02	4828.09	4819.36
400000	5653.67	5629.89	5609.87	5592.98	5540.59	5517.82	5507.84
450000	6360.38	6333.63	6311.10	6292.10	6233.17	6207.54	6196.32
500000	7067.08	7037.36	7012.33	6991.22	6925.74	6897.27	6884.80
550000	7773.79	7741.10	7713.57	7690.35	7618.31	7587.00	7573.28
600000	8480.50	8444.84	8414.80	8389.47	8310.89	8276.72	8261.76

16¾%

Monthly Payments
necessary to amortize a loan

AMOUNT	1 YEAR	2 YEARS	3 YEARS	4 YEARS	5 YEARS	6 YEARS	7 YEARS
100	9.11	4.93	3.55	2.87	2.47	2.21	2.03
200	18.22	9.86	7.11	5.75	4.94	4.42	4.06
500	45.54	24.66	17.76	14.36	12.36	11.05	10.15
1000	91.09	49.32	35.53	28.73	24.72	22.11	20.29
2000	182.17	98.64	71.06	57.45	49.44	44.21	40.58
5000	455.43	246.61	177.64	143.63	123.59	110.53	101.46
6000	546.52	295.93	213.17	172.36	148.31	132.64	121.75
7000	637.60	345.26	248.70	201.08	173.03	154.75	142.04
8000	728.69	394.58	284.23	229.81	197.75	176.85	162.33
9000	819.78	443.90	319.76	258.53	222.47	198.96	182.62
10000	910.86	493.22	355.28	287.26	247.18	221.07	202.92
15000	1366.29	739.83	532.93	430.89	370.78	331.60	304.37
20000	1821.72	986.44	710.57	574.52	494.37	442.14	405.83
25000	2277.15	1233.06	888.21	718.15	617.96	552.67	507.29
30000	2732.58	1479.67	1065.85	861.78	741.55	663.21	608.75
35000	3188.02	1726.28	1243.50	1005.41	865.14	773.74	710.21
40000	3643.45	1972.89	1421.14	1149.03	988.73	884.27	811.66
45000	4098.88	2219.50	1598.78	1292.66	1112.33	994.81	913.12
50000	4554.31	2466.11	1776.42	1436.29	1235.92	1105.34	1014.58
55000	5009.74	2712.72	1954.06	1579.92	1359.51	1215.88	1116.04
60000	5465.17	2959.33	2131.71	1723.55	1483.10	1326.41	1217.50
65000	5920.60	3205.94	2309.35	1867.18	1606.69	1436.95	1318.95
70000	6376.03	3452.56	2486.99	2010.81	1730.28	1547.48	1420.41
75000	6831.46	3699.17	2664.63	2154.44	1853.88	1658.01	1521.87
80000	7286.89	3945.78	2842.27	2298.07	1977.47	1768.55	1623.33
85000	7742.32	4192.39	3019.92	2441.70	2101.06	1879.08	1724.78
90000	8197.75	4439.00	3197.56	2585.33	2224.65	1989.62	1826.24
95000	8653.18	4685.61	3375.20	2728.96	2348.24	2100.15	1927.70
100000	9108.62	4932.22	3552.84	2872.59	2471.84	2210.69	2029.16
105000	9564.05	5178.83	3730.49	3016.22	2595.43	2321.22	2130.62
110000	10019.48	5425.44	3908.13	3159.84	2719.02	2431.76	2232.07
120000	10930.34	5918.67	4263.41	3447.10	2966.20	2652.82	2434.99
130000	11841.20	6411.89	4618.70	3734.36	3213.39	2873.89	2637.91
140000	12752.06	6905.11	4973.98	4021.62	3460.57	3094.96	2840.82
150000	13662.92	7398.33	5329.26	4308.88	3707.75	3316.03	3043.74
160000	14573.78	7891.56	5684.55	4596.14	3954.94	3537.10	3246.65
170000	15484.65	8384.78	6039.83	4883.40	4202.12	3758.17	3449.57
180000	16395.51	8878.00	6395.12	5170.66	4449.30	3979.24	3652.49
190000	17306.37	9371.22	6750.40	5457.91	4696.49	4200.30	3855.40
200000	18217.23	9864.44	7105.69	5745.17	4943.67	4421.37	4058.32
210000	19128.09	10357.67	7460.97	6032.43	5190.85	4642.44	4261.23
220000	20038.95	10850.89	7816.25	6319.69	5438.04	4863.51	4464.15
230000	20949.82	11344.11	8171.54	6606.95	5685.22	5084.58	4667.06
240000	21860.68	11837.33	8526.82	6894.21	5932.40	5305.65	4869.98
250000	22771.54	12330.56	8882.11	7181.47	6179.59	5526.72	5072.90
260000	23682.40	12823.78	9237.39	7468.72	6426.77	5747.78	5275.81
270000	24593.26	13317.00	9592.68	7755.98	6673.95	5968.85	5478.73
280000	25504.12	13810.22	9947.96	8043.24	6921.14	6189.92	5681.64
290000	26414.98	14303.44	10303.24	8330.50	7168.32	6410.99	5884.56
300000	27325.85	14796.67	10658.53	8617.76	7415.51	6632.06	6087.48
310000	28236.71	15289.89	11013.81	8905.02	7662.69	6853.13	6290.39
320000	29147.57	15783.11	11369.10	9192.28	7909.87	7074.20	6493.31
330000	30058.43	16276.33	11724.38	9479.53	8157.06	7295.27	6696.22
340000	30969.29	16769.56	12079.67	9766.79	8404.24	7516.33	6899.14
350000	31880.15	17262.78	12434.95	10054.05	8651.42	7737.40	7102.06
400000	36434.46	19728.89	14211.37	11490.35	9887.34	8842.75	8116.63
450000	40988.77	22195.00	15987.79	12926.64	11123.26	9948.09	9131.21
500000	45543.08	24661.11	17764.22	14362.93	12359.18	11053.43	10145.79
550000	50097.38	27127.22	19540.64	15799.22	13595.09	12158.78	11160.37
600000	54651.69	29593.33	21317.06	17235.52	14831.01	13264.12	12174.95

Monthly Payments 16¾%
necessary to amortize a loan

AMOUNT	8 YEARS	9 YEARS	10 YEARS	11 YEARS	12 YEARS	13 YEARS	14 YEARS
100	1.90	1.80	1.72	1.66	1.62	1.58	1.55
200	3.79	3.60	3.44	3.33	3.23	3.15	3.09
500	9.49	8.99	8.61	8.31	8.08	7.89	7.73
1000	18.97	17.98	17.22	16.63	16.15	15.77	15.46
2000	37.94	35.97	34.44	33.25	32.31	31.55	30.93
5000	94.86	89.91	86.11	83.13	80.76	78.86	77.32
6000	113.83	107.90	103.33	99.76	96.92	94.64	92.79
7000	132.81	125.88	120.55	116.38	113.07	110.41	108.25
8000	151.78	143.86	137.77	133.01	129.22	126.18	123.72
9000	170.75	161.84	155.00	149.63	145.38	141.96	139.18
10000	189.72	179.83	172.22	166.26	161.53	157.73	154.65
15000	284.59	269.74	258.33	249.39	242.29	236.59	231.97
20000	379.45	359.65	344.43	332.52	323.06	315.46	309.30
25000	474.31	449.56	430.54	415.65	403.82	394.32	386.62
30000	569.17	539.48	516.65	498.78	484.59	473.19	463.94
35000	664.03	629.39	602.76	581.91	565.35	552.05	541.27
40000	758.90	719.30	688.87	665.04	646.12	630.92	618.59
45000	853.76	809.21	774.98	748.17	726.88	709.78	695.92
50000	948.62	899.13	861.08	831.30	807.65	788.65	773.24
55000	1043.48	989.04	947.19	914.43	888.41	867.51	850.57
60000	1138.35	1078.95	1033.30	997.56	969.18	946.37	927.89
65000	1233.21	1168.86	1119.41	1080.69	1049.94	1025.24	1005.21
70000	1328.07	1258.78	1205.52	1163.82	1130.71	1104.10	1082.54
75000	1422.93	1348.69	1291.63	1246.95	1211.47	1182.97	1159.86
80000	1517.79	1438.60	1377.73	1330.08	1292.23	1261.83	1237.19
85000	1612.66	1528.51	1463.84	1413.21	1373.00	1340.70	1314.51
90000	1707.52	1618.43	1549.95	1496.34	1453.76	1419.56	1391.83
95000	1802.38	1708.34	1636.06	1579.47	1534.53	1498.43	1469.16
100000	1897.24	1798.25	1722.17	1662.60	1615.29	1577.29	1546.48
105000	1992.10	1888.17	1808.28	1745.73	1696.06	1656.16	1623.81
110000	2086.97	1978.08	1894.38	1828.86	1776.82	1735.02	1701.13
120000	2276.69	2157.90	2066.60	1995.12	1938.35	1892.75	1855.78
130000	2466.42	2337.73	2238.82	2161.38	2099.88	2050.48	2010.43
140000	2656.14	2517.55	2411.03	2327.64	2261.41	2208.21	2165.08
150000	2845.86	2697.38	2583.25	2493.90	2422.94	2365.94	2319.72
160000	3035.59	2877.20	2755.47	2660.16	2584.47	2523.67	2474.37
170000	3225.31	3057.03	2927.68	2826.42	2746.00	2681.39	2629.02
180000	3415.03	3236.86	3099.90	2992.68	2907.53	2839.12	2783.67
190000	3604.76	3416.68	3272.12	3158.94	3069.06	2996.85	2938.32
200000	3794.49	3596.51	3444.33	3325.20	3230.59	3154.58	3092.96
210000	3984.21	3776.33	3616.55	3491.46	3392.12	3312.31	3247.61
220000	4173.93	3956.16	3788.77	3657.72	3553.65	3470.04	3402.26
230000	4363.66	4135.98	3960.98	3823.98	3715.18	3627.77	3556.91
240000	4553.38	4315.81	4133.20	3990.24	3876.70	3785.50	3711.56
250000	4743.11	4495.63	4305.42	4156.50	4038.23	3943.23	3866.21
260000	4932.83	4675.46	4477.63	4322.76	4199.76	4100.96	4020.85
270000	5122.56	4855.28	4649.85	4489.02	4361.29	4258.69	4175.50
280000	5312.28	5035.11	4822.07	4655.28	4522.82	4416.41	4330.15
290000	5502.00	5214.93	4994.29	4821.54	4684.35	4574.14	4484.80
300000	5691.73	5394.76	5166.50	4987.80	4845.88	4731.87	4639.45
310000	5881.45	5574.58	5338.72	5154.06	5007.41	4889.60	4794.10
320000	6071.18	5754.41	5510.94	5320.32	5168.94	5047.33	4948.74
330000	6260.90	5934.23	5683.15	5486.58	5330.47	5205.06	5103.39
340000	6450.63	6114.06	5855.37	5652.84	5492.00	5362.79	5258.04
350000	6640.35	6293.88	6027.59	5819.10	5653.53	5520.52	5412.69
400000	7588.97	7193.01	6888.67	6650.41	6461.17	6309.16	6185.93
450000	8537.59	8092.14	7749.75	7481.71	7268.82	7097.81	6959.17
500000	9486.21	8991.26	8610.84	8313.01	8076.47	7886.45	7732.41
550000	10434.83	9890.39	9471.92	9144.31	8884.11	8675.10	8505.65
600000	11383.46	10789.52	10333.00	9975.61	9691.76	9463.74	9278.89

193

16¾%

Monthly Payments
necessary to amortize a loan

AMOUNT	15 YEARS	16 YEARS	17 YEARS	18 YEARS	19 YEARS	20 YEARS	21 YEARS
100	1.52	1.50	1.48	1.47	1.46	1.45	1.44
200	3.04	3.00	2.97	2.94	2.92	2.90	2.88
500	7.61	7.50	7.42	7.35	7.29	7.24	7.20
1000	15.21	15.01	14.84	14.69	14.58	14.48	14.40
2000	30.43	30.01	29.67	29.39	29.15	28.96	28.79
5000	76.07	75.03	74.18	73.47	72.88	72.39	71.98
6000	91.28	90.04	89.01	88.17	87.46	86.87	86.38
7000	106.49	105.05	103.85	102.86	102.04	101.35	100.77
8000	121.71	120.05	118.69	117.55	116.61	115.83	115.17
9000	136.92	135.06	133.52	132.25	131.19	130.30	129.56
10000	152.13	150.06	148.36	146.94	145.76	144.78	143.96
15000	228.20	225.10	222.54	220.41	218.65	217.17	215.94
20000	304.26	300.13	296.72	293.88	291.53	289.56	287.92
25000	380.33	375.16	370.89	367.36	364.41	361.95	359.90
30000	456.40	450.19	445.07	440.83	437.29	434.35	431.88
35000	532.46	525.22	519.25	514.30	510.18	506.74	503.86
40000	608.53	600.26	593.43	587.77	583.06	579.13	575.84
45000	684.59	675.29	667.61	661.24	655.94	651.52	647.82
50000	760.66	750.32	741.79	734.71	728.82	723.91	719.80
55000	836.73	825.36	815.97	808.18	801.70	796.30	791.78
60000	912.79	900.39	890.15	881.65	874.59	868.69	863.76
65000	988.86	975.42	964.32	955.12	947.47	941.08	935.74
70000	1064.92	1050.45	1038.50	1028.59	1020.35	1013.47	1007.72
75000	1140.99	1125.49	1112.68	1102.07	1093.23	1085.86	1079.70
80000	1217.06	1200.52	1186.86	1175.54	1166.12	1158.26	1151.68
85000	1293.12	1275.55	1261.04	1249.01	1239.00	1230.65	1223.66
90000	1369.19	1350.58	1335.22	1322.48	1311.88	1303.04	1295.64
95000	1445.26	1425.61	1409.40	1395.95	1384.76	1375.43	1367.62
100000	1521.32	1500.65	1483.58	1469.42	1457.64	1447.82	1439.60
105000	1597.39	1575.68	1557.75	1542.89	1530.53	1520.21	1511.58
110000	1673.45	1650.71	1631.93	1616.36	1603.41	1592.60	1583.56
120000	1825.59	1800.78	1780.29	1763.30	1749.17	1737.38	1727.52
130000	1977.72	1950.84	1928.65	1910.25	1894.94	1882.17	1871.48
140000	2129.85	2100.91	2077.01	2057.19	2040.70	2026.95	2015.44
150000	2281.98	2250.97	2225.36	2204.13	2186.47	2171.73	2159.40
160000	2434.11	2401.04	2373.72	2351.07	2332.23	2316.51	2303.37
170000	2586.25	2551.10	2522.08	2498.02	2478.00	2461.29	2447.33
180000	2738.38	2701.16	2670.44	2644.96	2623.76	2606.08	2591.29
190000	2890.51	2851.23	2818.79	2791.90	2769.52	2750.86	2735.25
200000	3042.64	3001.29	2967.15	2938.84	2915.29	2895.64	2879.21
210000	3194.77	3151.36	3115.51	3085.78	3061.05	3040.42	3023.17
220000	3346.91	3301.42	3263.87	3232.73	3206.82	3185.20	3167.13
230000	3499.04	3451.49	3412.22	3379.67	3352.58	3329.98	3311.09
240000	3651.17	3601.55	3560.58	3526.61	3498.35	3474.77	3455.05
250000	3803.30	3751.62	3708.94	3673.55	3644.11	3619.55	3599.01
260000	3955.43	3901.68	3857.30	3820.49	3789.88	3764.33	3742.97
270000	4107.57	4051.75	4005.65	3967.44	3935.64	3909.11	3886.93
280000	4259.70	4201.81	4154.01	4114.38	4081.40	4053.89	4030.89
290000	4411.83	4351.88	4302.37	4261.32	4227.17	4198.68	4174.85
300000	4563.96	4501.94	4450.73	4408.26	4372.93	4343.46	4318.81
310000	4716.10	4652.01	4599.08	4555.20	4518.70	4488.24	4462.77
320000	4868.23	4802.07	4747.44	4702.15	4664.46	4633.02	4606.73
330000	5020.36	4952.13	4895.80	4849.09	4810.23	4777.80	4750.69
340000	5172.49	5102.20	5044.16	4996.03	4955.99	4922.59	4894.65
350000	5324.62	5252.26	5192.51	5142.97	5101.76	5067.37	5038.61
400000	6085.28	6002.59	5934.30	5877.68	5830.58	5791.28	5758.41
450000	6845.94	6752.91	6676.09	6612.39	6559.40	6515.19	6478.21
500000	7606.61	7503.23	7417.88	7347.10	7288.22	7239.10	7198.02
550000	8367.27	8253.56	8159.66	8081.81	8017.04	7963.01	7917.82
600000	9127.93	9003.88	8901.45	8816.52	8745.87	8686.92	8637.62

Monthly Payments 16¾%
necessary to amortize a loan

AMOUNT	22 YEARS	23 YEARS	24 YEARS	25 YEARS	30 YEARS	35 YEARS	40 YEARS
100	1.43	1.43	1.42	1.42	1.41	1.40	1.40
200	2.87	2.85	2.84	2.84	2.81	2.80	2.80
500	7.16	7.13	7.11	7.09	7.03	7.00	6.99
1000	14.33	14.27	14.22	14.18	14.05	14.00	13.98
2000	28.65	28.54	28.44	28.36	28.11	28.00	27.95
5000	71.64	71.35	71.10	70.90	70.27	70.00	69.88
6000	85.96	85.62	85.33	85.08	84.32	84.00	83.86
7000	100.29	99.89	99.55	99.26	98.38	98.00	97.83
8000	114.62	114.16	113.77	113.44	112.43	112.00	111.81
9000	128.94	128.42	127.99	127.62	126.49	126.00	125.79
10000	143.27	142.69	142.21	141.80	140.54	140.00	139.76
15000	214.91	214.04	213.31	212.70	210.81	210.00	209.65
20000	286.54	285.39	284.42	283.60	281.08	280.00	279.53
25000	358.18	356.74	355.52	354.50	351.35	349.99	349.41
30000	429.82	428.08	426.63	425.40	421.62	419.99	419.29
35000	501.45	499.43	497.73	496.30	491.89	489.99	489.17
40000	573.09	570.78	568.83	567.20	562.16	559.99	559.05
45000	644.72	642.12	639.94	638.10	632.43	629.99	628.94
50000	716.36	713.47	711.04	709.00	702.70	699.99	698.82
55000	788.00	784.82	782.15	779.90	772.97	769.99	768.70
60000	859.63	856.16	853.25	850.80	843.24	839.99	838.58
65000	931.27	927.51	924.35	921.70	913.51	909.99	908.46
70000	1002.90	998.86	995.46	992.60	983.78	979.99	978.34
75000	1074.54	1070.21	1066.56	1063.50	1054.05	1049.98	1048.23
80000	1146.17	1141.55	1137.67	1134.40	1124.32	1119.98	1118.11
85000	1217.81	1212.90	1208.77	1205.30	1194.59	1189.98	1187.99
90000	1289.45	1284.25	1279.88	1276.20	1264.86	1259.98	1257.87
95000	1361.08	1355.59	1350.98	1347.10	1335.13	1329.98	1327.75
100000	1432.72	1426.94	1422.08	1418.00	1405.40	1399.98	1397.64
105000	1504.35	1498.29	1493.19	1488.90	1475.67	1469.98	1467.52
110000	1575.99	1569.63	1564.29	1559.80	1545.94	1539.98	1537.40
120000	1719.26	1712.33	1706.50	1701.60	1686.47	1679.98	1677.16
130000	1862.53	1855.02	1848.71	1843.40	1827.01	1819.97	1816.93
140000	2005.81	1997.72	1990.92	1985.20	1967.55	1959.97	1956.69
150000	2149.08	2140.41	2133.13	2127.00	2108.09	2099.97	2096.45
160000	2292.35	2283.10	2275.33	2268.80	2248.63	2239.97	2236.22
170000	2435.62	2425.80	2417.54	2410.59	2389.17	2379.97	2375.98
180000	2578.89	2568.49	2559.75	2552.39	2529.71	2519.96	2515.74
190000	2722.17	2711.19	2701.96	2694.19	2670.25	2659.96	2655.51
200000	2865.44	2853.88	2844.17	2835.99	2810.79	2799.96	2795.27
210000	3008.71	2996.57	2986.38	2977.79	2951.33	2939.96	2935.03
220000	3151.98	3139.27	3128.58	3119.59	3091.87	3079.96	3074.80
230000	3295.25	3281.96	3270.79	3261.39	3232.41	3219.95	3214.56
240000	3438.52	3424.66	3413.00	3403.19	3372.95	3359.95	3354.32
250000	3581.80	3567.35	3555.21	3544.99	3513.49	3499.95	3494.09
260000	3725.07	3710.04	3697.42	3686.79	3654.03	3639.95	3633.85
270000	3868.34	3852.74	3839.63	3828.59	3794.57	3779.95	3773.62
280000	4011.61	3995.43	3981.83	3970.39	3935.11	3919.94	3913.38
290000	4154.88	4138.13	4124.04	4112.19	4075.65	4059.94	4053.14
300000	4298.16	4280.82	4266.25	4253.99	4216.19	4199.94	4192.91
310000	4441.43	4423.51	4408.46	4395.79	4356.73	4339.94	4332.67
320000	4584.70	4566.21	4550.67	4537.59	4497.27	4479.94	4472.43
330000	4727.97	4708.90	4692.88	4679.39	4637.81	4619.93	4612.20
340000	4871.24	4851.60	4835.08	4821.19	4778.34	4759.93	4751.96
350000	5014.51	4994.29	4977.29	4962.99	4918.88	4899.93	4891.72
400000	5730.87	5707.76	5688.33	5671.99	5621.58	5599.92	5590.54
450000	6447.23	6421.23	6399.38	6380.99	6324.28	6299.91	6289.36
500000	7163.59	7134.70	7110.42	7089.99	7026.98	6999.90	6988.18
550000	7879.95	7848.17	7821.46	7798.98	7729.68	7699.89	7686.99
600000	8596.31	8561.64	8532.50	8507.98	8432.37	8399.88	8385.81

Monthly Payments
necessary to amortize a loan

AMOUNT	1 YEAR	2 YEARS	3 YEARS	4 YEARS	5 YEARS	6 YEARS	7 YEARS
100	9.12	4.94	3.57	2.89	2.49	2.22	2.04
200	18.24	9.89	7.13	5.77	4.97	4.45	4.09
500	45.60	24.72	17.83	14.43	12.43	11.12	10.22
1000	91.20	49.44	35.65	28.86	24.85	22.25	20.44
2000	182.41	98.88	71.31	57.71	49.71	44.49	40.87
5000	456.02	247.21	178.26	144.28	124.26	111.23	102.18
6000	547.23	296.65	213.92	173.13	149.12	133.48	122.61
7000	638.43	346.10	249.57	201.99	173.97	155.72	143.05
8000	729.64	395.54	285.22	230.84	198.82	177.97	163.49
9000	820.84	444.98	320.87	259.70	223.67	200.22	183.92
10000	912.05	494.42	356.53	288.55	248.53	222.46	204.36
15000	1368.07	741.63	534.79	432.83	372.79	333.69	306.54
20000	1824.10	988.85	713.05	577.10	497.05	444.92	408.72
25000	2280.12	1236.06	891.32	721.38	621.31	556.15	510.90
30000	2736.14	1483.27	1069.58	865.65	745.58	667.38	613.07
35000	3192.17	1730.48	1247.85	1009.93	869.84	778.61	715.25
40000	3648.19	1977.69	1426.11	1154.20	994.10	889.85	817.43
45000	4104.21	2224.90	1604.37	1298.48	1118.37	1001.08	919.61
50000	4560.24	2472.11	1782.64	1442.75	1242.63	1112.31	1021.79
55000	5016.26	2719.32	1960.90	1587.03	1366.89	1223.54	1123.97
60000	5472.29	2966.54	2139.16	1731.30	1491.15	1334.77	1226.15
65000	5928.31	3213.75	2317.43	1875.58	1615.42	1446.00	1328.33
70000	6384.33	3460.96	2495.69	2019.85	1739.68	1557.23	1430.51
75000	6840.36	3708.17	2673.95	2164.13	1863.94	1668.46	1532.69
80000	7296.38	3955.38	2852.22	2308.40	1988.21	1779.69	1634.86
85000	7752.40	4202.59	3030.48	2452.68	2112.47	1890.92	1737.04
90000	8208.43	4449.80	3208.75	2596.95	2236.73	2002.15	1839.22
95000	8664.45	4697.02	3387.01	2741.23	2360.99	2113.38	1941.40
100000	9120.48	4944.23	3565.27	2885.50	2485.26	2224.61	2043.58
105000	9576.50	5191.44	3743.54	3029.78	2609.52	2335.84	2145.76
110000	10032.52	5438.65	3921.80	3174.05	2733.78	2447.07	2247.94
120000	10944.57	5933.07	4278.33	3462.61	2982.31	2669.54	2452.30
130000	11856.62	6427.49	4634.85	3751.16	3230.83	2892.00	2656.65
140000	12768.67	6921.92	4991.38	4039.71	3479.36	3114.46	2861.01
150000	13680.71	7416.34	5347.91	4328.26	3727.89	3336.92	3065.37
160000	14592.76	7910.76	5704.44	4616.81	3976.41	3559.38	3269.73
170000	15504.81	8405.18	6060.96	4905.36	4224.94	3781.84	3474.09
180000	16416.86	8899.61	6417.49	5193.91	4473.46	4004.30	3678.44
190000	17328.90	9394.03	6774.02	5482.46	4721.99	4226.76	3882.80
200000	18240.95	9888.45	7130.55	5771.01	4970.52	4449.23	4087.16
210000	19153.00	10382.88	7487.07	6059.56	5219.04	4671.69	4291.52
220000	20065.05	10877.30	7843.60	6348.11	5467.57	4894.15	4495.88
230000	20977.09	11371.72	8200.13	6636.66	5716.09	5116.61	4700.24
240000	21889.14	11866.14	8556.65	6925.21	5964.62	5339.07	4904.59
250000	22801.19	12360.57	8913.18	7213.76	6213.14	5561.53	5108.95
260000	23713.24	12854.99	9269.71	7502.30	6461.67	5783.99	5313.31
270000	24625.28	13349.41	9626.23	7790.86	6710.20	6006.46	5517.67
280000	25537.33	13843.83	9982.76	8079.41	6958.72	6228.92	5722.03
290000	26449.38	14338.26	10339.29	8367.96	7207.25	6451.38	5926.38
300000	27361.43	14832.68	10695.82	8656.51	7455.77	6673.84	6130.74
310000	28273.47	15327.10	11052.35	8945.06	7704.30	6896.30	6335.10
320000	29185.52	15821.52	11408.87	9233.61	7952.82	7118.76	6539.46
330000	30097.57	16315.95	11765.40	9522.16	8201.35	7341.22	6743.82
340000	31009.62	16810.37	12121.93	9810.71	8449.88	7563.68	6948.17
350000	31921.66	17304.79	12478.45	10099.26	8698.40	7786.15	7152.53
400000	36481.90	19776.91	14261.09	11542.02	9941.03	8898.45	8174.32
450000	41042.14	22249.02	16043.73	12984.77	11183.66	10010.76	9196.11
500000	45602.38	24721.13	17826.36	14427.52	12426.29	11123.07	10217.90
550000	50162.61	27193.25	19609.00	15870.27	13668.92	12235.37	11239.69
600000	54722.85	29665.36	21391.64	17313.03	14911.55	13347.68	12261.48

AMOUNT	8 YEARS	9 YEARS	10 YEARS	11 YEARS	12 YEARS	13 YEARS	14 YEARS
100	1.91	1.81	1.74	1.68	1.63	1.59	1.56
200	3.82	3.63	3.48	3.36	3.26	3.19	3.13
500	9.56	9.07	8.69	8.39	8.16	7.97	7.82
1000	19.12	18.14	17.38	16.79	16.32	15.94	15.64
2000	38.24	36.27	34.76	33.58	32.64	31.89	31.28
5000	95.61	90.68	86.90	83.94	81.60	79.71	78.19
6000	114.73	108.82	104.28	100.73	97.92	95.66	93.83
7000	133.85	126.95	121.66	117.52	114.23	111.60	109.47
8000	152.97	145.09	139.04	134.31	130.55	127.54	125.11
9000	172.09	163.23	156.42	151.09	146.87	143.49	140.75
10000	191.21	181.36	173.80	167.88	163.19	159.43	156.38
15000	286.82	272.04	260.70	251.82	244.79	239.14	234.58
20000	382.43	362.72	347.60	335.77	326.38	318.86	312.77
25000	478.04	453.40	434.49	419.71	407.98	398.57	390.96
30000	573.64	544.09	521.39	503.65	489.58	478.29	469.15
35000	669.25	634.77	608.29	587.59	571.17	558.00	547.34
40000	764.86	725.45	695.19	671.53	652.77	637.72	625.54
45000	860.47	816.13	782.09	755.47	734.37	717.43	703.73
50000	956.07	906.81	868.99	839.42	815.96	797.15	781.92
55000	1051.68	997.49	955.89	923.36	897.56	876.86	860.11
60000	1147.29	1088.17	1042.79	1007.30	979.15	956.58	938.30
65000	1242.89	1178.85	1129.68	1091.24	1060.75	1036.29	1016.49
70000	1338.50	1269.53	1216.58	1175.18	1142.35	1116.01	1094.69
75000	1434.11	1360.21	1303.48	1259.12	1223.94	1195.72	1172.88
80000	1529.72	1450.90	1390.38	1343.07	1305.54	1275.44	1251.07
85000	1625.32	1541.58	1477.28	1427.01	1387.13	1355.15	1329.26
90000	1720.93	1632.26	1564.18	1510.95	1468.73	1434.87	1407.45
95000	1816.54	1722.94	1651.08	1594.89	1550.33	1514.58	1485.65
100000	1912.15	1813.62	1737.98	1678.83	1631.92	1594.30	1563.84
105000	2007.75	1904.30	1824.88	1762.77	1713.52	1674.01	1642.03
110000	2103.36	1994.98	1911.77	1846.72	1795.12	1753.72	1720.22
120000	2294.57	2176.34	2085.57	2014.60	1958.31	1913.15	1876.61
130000	2485.79	2357.70	2259.37	2182.48	2121.50	2072.58	2032.99
140000	2677.00	2539.07	2433.17	2350.36	2284.69	2232.01	2189.37
150000	2868.22	2720.43	2606.96	2518.25	2447.88	2391.44	2345.76
160000	3059.43	2901.79	2780.76	2686.13	2611.08	2550.87	2502.14
170000	3250.65	3083.15	2954.56	2854.01	2774.27	2710.30	2658.53
180000	3441.86	3264.51	3128.36	3021.90	2937.46	2869.73	2814.91
190000	3633.08	3445.88	3302.16	3189.78	3100.65	3029.16	2971.29
200000	3824.29	3627.24	3475.95	3357.66	3263.85	3188.59	3127.68
210000	4015.51	3808.60	3649.75	3525.55	3427.04	3348.02	3284.06
220000	4206.72	3989.96	3823.55	3693.43	3590.23	3507.45	3440.44
230000	4397.93	4171.32	3997.35	3861.31	3753.42	3666.88	3596.83
240000	4589.15	4352.69	4171.14	4029.20	3916.62	3826.31	3753.21
250000	4780.36	4534.05	4344.94	4197.08	4079.81	3985.74	3909.60
260000	4971.58	4715.41	4518.74	4364.96	4243.00	4145.17	4065.98
270000	5162.79	4896.77	4692.54	4532.85	4406.19	4304.60	4222.36
280000	5354.01	5078.13	4866.33	4700.73	4569.38	4464.03	4378.75
290000	5545.22	5259.49	5040.13	4868.61	4732.58	4623.46	4535.13
300000	5736.44	5440.86	5213.93	5036.50	4895.77	4782.89	4691.51
310000	5927.65	5622.22	5387.73	5204.38	5058.96	4942.32	4847.90
320000	6118.87	5803.58	5561.52	5372.26	5222.15	5101.74	5004.28
330000	6310.08	5984.94	5735.32	5540.15	5385.35	5261.17	5160.67
340000	6501.29	6166.30	5909.12	5708.03	5548.54	5420.60	5317.05
350000	6692.51	6347.67	6082.92	5875.91	5711.73	5580.03	5473.43
400000	7648.58	7254.48	6951.91	6715.33	6527.69	6377.18	6255.35
450000	8604.65	8161.28	7820.89	7554.74	7343.65	7174.33	7037.27
500000	9560.73	9068.09	8689.88	8394.16	8159.61	7971.48	7819.19
550000	10516.80	9974.90	9558.87	9233.58	8975.58	8768.62	8601.11
600000	11472.87	10881.71	10427.86	10072.99	9791.54	9565.77	9383.03

17%

Monthly Payments
necessary to amortize a loan

AMOUNT	15 YEARS	16 YEARS	17 YEARS	18 YEARS	19 YEARS	20 YEARS	21 YEARS
100	1.54	1.52	1.50	1.49	1.48	1.47	1.46
200	3.08	3.04	3.00	2.98	2.95	2.93	2.92
500	7.70	7.59	7.51	7.44	7.38	7.33	7.29
1000	15.39	15.19	15.02	14.88	14.76	14.67	14.59
2000	30.78	30.37	30.04	29.76	29.53	29.34	29.18
5000	76.95	75.93	75.09	74.40	73.82	73.34	72.94
6000	92.34	91.12	90.11	89.28	88.58	88.01	87.53
7000	107.73	106.30	105.13	104.16	103.35	102.68	102.11
8000	123.12	121.49	120.15	119.04	118.11	117.34	116.70
9000	138.51	136.68	135.17	133.92	132.88	132.01	131.29
10000	153.90	151.86	150.18	148.79	147.64	146.68	145.88
15000	230.85	227.80	225.28	223.19	221.46	220.02	218.82
20000	307.80	303.73	300.37	297.59	295.28	293.36	291.76
25000	384.75	379.66	375.46	371.99	369.10	366.70	364.70
30000	461.70	455.59	450.55	446.38	442.92	440.04	437.63
35000	538.65	531.52	525.65	520.78	516.74	513.38	510.57
40000	615.60	607.45	600.74	595.18	590.56	586.72	583.51
45000	692.55	683.39	675.83	669.58	664.38	660.06	656.45
50000	769.50	759.32	750.92	743.97	738.20	733.40	729.39
55000	846.45	835.25	826.01	818.37	812.02	806.74	802.33
60000	923.40	911.18	901.11	892.77	885.85	880.08	875.27
65000	1000.35	987.11	976.20	967.17	959.67	953.42	948.21
70000	1077.30	1063.04	1051.29	1041.56	1033.49	1026.76	1021.15
75000	1154.25	1138.98	1126.38	1115.96	1107.31	1100.10	1094.09
80000	1231.20	1214.91	1201.47	1190.36	1181.13	1173.44	1167.03
85000	1308.15	1290.84	1276.57	1264.76	1254.95	1246.78	1239.96
90000	1385.10	1366.77	1351.66	1339.15	1328.77	1320.12	1312.90
95000	1462.05	1442.70	1426.75	1413.55	1402.59	1393.46	1385.84
100000	1539.00	1518.63	1501.84	1487.95	1476.41	1466.80	1458.78
105000	1615.95	1594.57	1576.94	1562.34	1550.23	1540.14	1531.72
110000	1692.90	1670.50	1652.03	1636.74	1624.05	1613.48	1604.66
120000	1846.81	1822.36	1802.21	1785.54	1771.69	1760.16	1750.54
130000	2000.71	1974.22	1952.40	1934.33	1919.33	1906.84	1896.42
140000	2154.61	2126.09	2102.58	2083.13	2066.97	2053.52	2042.29
150000	2308.51	2277.95	2252.77	2231.92	2214.61	2200.20	2188.17
160000	2462.41	2429.81	2402.95	2380.72	2362.25	2346.88	2334.05
170000	2616.31	2581.68	2553.13	2529.51	2509.89	2493.56	2479.93
180000	2770.21	2733.54	2703.32	2678.31	2657.54	2640.24	2625.81
190000	2924.11	2885.40	2853.50	2827.10	2805.18	2786.92	2771.69
200000	3078.01	3037.27	3003.69	2975.89	2952.82	2933.60	2917.56
210000	3231.91	3189.13	3153.87	3124.69	3100.46	3080.28	3063.44
220000	3385.81	3340.99	3304.06	3273.48	3248.10	3226.96	3209.32
230000	3539.71	3492.86	3454.24	3422.28	3395.74	3373.64	3355.20
240000	3693.61	3644.72	3604.42	3571.07	3543.38	3520.32	3501.08
250000	3847.51	3796.59	3754.61	3719.87	3691.02	3667.00	3646.95
260000	4001.41	3948.45	3904.79	3868.66	3838.66	3813.68	3792.83
270000	4155.31	4100.31	4054.98	4017.46	3986.30	3960.36	3938.71
280000	4309.21	4252.18	4205.16	4166.25	4133.94	4107.04	4084.59
290000	4463.11	4404.04	4355.35	4315.05	4281.58	4253.72	4230.47
300000	4617.01	4555.90	4505.53	4463.84	4429.23	4400.40	4376.35
310000	4770.91	4707.77	4655.71	4612.64	4576.87	4547.08	4522.22
320000	4924.81	4859.63	4805.90	4761.43	4724.51	4693.76	4668.10
330000	5078.71	5011.49	4956.08	4910.23	4872.15	4840.44	4813.98
340000	5232.61	5163.36	5106.27	5059.02	5019.79	4987.12	4959.86
350000	5386.52	5315.22	5256.45	5207.82	5167.43	5133.80	5105.74
400000	6156.02	6074.54	6007.37	5951.79	5905.63	5867.20	5835.13
450000	6925.52	6833.85	6758.30	6695.76	6643.84	6600.60	6564.52
500000	7695.02	7593.17	7509.22	7439.74	7382.04	7334.00	7293.91
550000	8464.52	8352.49	8260.14	8183.71	8120.25	8067.40	8023.30
600000	9234.03	9111.80	9011.06	8927.68	8858.45	8800.80	8752.69

Monthly Payments **17%**
necessary to amortize a loan

AMOUNT	22 YEARS	23 YEARS	24 YEARS	25 YEARS	30 YEARS	35 YEARS	40 YEARS
100	1.45	1.45	1.44	1.44	1.43	1.42	1.42
200	2.90	2.89	2.88	2.88	2.85	2.84	2.84
500	7.26	7.23	7.21	7.19	7.13	7.10	7.09
1000	14.52	14.46	14.42	14.38	14.26	14.21	14.18
2000	29.04	28.93	28.84	28.76	28.51	28.41	28.37
5000	72.60	72.32	72.09	71.89	71.28	71.03	70.92
6000	87.12	86.79	86.51	86.27	85.54	85.23	85.10
7000	101.65	101.25	100.92	100.65	99.80	99.44	99.28
8000	116.17	115.72	115.34	115.02	114.05	113.64	113.47
9000	130.69	130.18	129.76	129.40	128.31	127.85	127.65
10000	145.21	144.65	144.18	143.78	142.57	142.05	141.83
15000	217.81	216.97	216.26	215.67	213.85	213.08	212.75
20000	290.42	289.29	288.35	287.56	285.14	284.11	283.66
25000	363.02	361.62	360.44	359.45	356.42	355.13	354.58
30000	435.62	433.94	432.53	431.34	427.70	426.16	425.50
35000	508.23	506.26	504.61	503.23	498.99	497.18	496.41
40000	580.83	578.58	576.70	575.12	570.27	568.21	567.33
45000	653.43	650.91	648.79	647.01	641.55	639.24	638.25
50000	726.04	723.23	720.88	718.90	712.84	710.26	709.16
55000	798.64	795.55	792.96	790.79	784.12	781.29	780.08
60000	871.25	867.88	865.05	862.68	855.41	852.32	850.99
65000	943.85	940.20	937.14	934.57	926.69	923.34	921.91
70000	1016.45	1012.52	1009.23	1006.46	997.97	994.37	992.83
75000	1089.06	1084.85	1081.31	1078.35	1069.26	1065.39	1063.74
80000	1161.66	1157.17	1153.40	1150.24	1140.54	1136.42	1134.66
85000	1234.27	1229.49	1225.49	1222.13	1211.82	1207.45	1205.58
90000	1306.87	1301.81	1297.58	1294.02	1283.11	1278.47	1276.49
95000	1379.47	1374.14	1369.66	1365.91	1354.39	1349.50	1347.41
100000	1452.08	1446.46	1441.75	1437.80	1425.68	1420.53	1418.32
105000	1524.68	1518.78	1513.84	1509.69	1496.96	1491.55	1489.24
110000	1597.28	1591.11	1585.93	1581.58	1568.24	1562.58	1560.16
120000	1742.49	1735.75	1730.10	1725.36	1710.81	1704.63	1701.99
130000	1887.70	1880.40	1874.28	1869.14	1853.38	1846.68	1843.82
140000	2032.91	2025.05	2018.45	2012.92	1995.95	1988.74	1985.65
150000	2178.11	2169.69	2162.63	2156.69	2138.51	2130.79	2127.49
160000	2323.32	2314.34	2306.80	2300.47	2281.08	2272.84	2269.32
170000	2468.53	2458.98	2450.98	2444.25	2423.65	2414.89	2411.15
180000	2613.74	2603.63	2595.15	2588.03	2566.22	2556.95	2552.98
190000	2758.95	2748.28	2739.33	2731.81	2708.78	2699.00	2694.81
200000	2904.15	2892.92	2883.50	2875.59	2851.35	2841.05	2836.65
210000	3049.36	3037.57	3027.68	3019.37	2993.92	2983.10	2978.48
220000	3194.57	3182.21	3171.85	3163.15	3136.49	3125.16	3120.31
230000	3339.78	3326.86	3316.03	3306.93	3279.05	3267.21	3262.14
240000	3484.98	3471.51	3460.20	3450.71	3421.62	3409.26	3403.98
250000	3630.19	3616.15	3604.38	3594.49	3564.19	3551.32	3545.81
260000	3775.40	3760.80	3748.55	3738.27	3706.76	3693.37	3687.64
270000	3920.61	3905.44	3892.73	3882.05	3849.32	3835.42	3829.47
280000	4065.81	4050.09	4036.90	4025.83	3991.89	3977.47	3971.31
290000	4211.02	4194.73	4181.08	4169.61	4134.46	4119.53	4113.14
300000	4356.23	4339.38	4325.25	4313.39	4277.03	4261.58	4254.97
310000	4501.44	4484.03	4469.43	4457.17	4419.59	4403.63	4396.80
320000	4646.65	4628.67	4613.60	4600.95	4562.16	4545.68	4538.64
330000	4791.85	4773.32	4757.78	4744.73	4704.73	4687.74	4680.47
340000	4937.06	4917.97	4901.95	4888.51	4847.30	4829.79	4822.30
350000	5082.27	5062.61	5046.13	5032.29	4989.86	4971.84	4964.13
400000	5808.31	5785.84	5767.00	5751.19	5702.70	5682.10	5673.29
450000	6534.34	6509.07	6487.88	6470.08	6415.54	6392.37	6382.46
500000	7260.38	7232.30	7208.76	7188.98	7128.38	7102.63	7091.62
550000	7986.42	7955.53	7929.63	7907.88	7841.21	7812.89	7800.78
600000	8712.46	8678.76	8650.51	8626.78	8554.05	8523.16	8509.94

17¼%

Monthly Payments
necessary to amortize a loan

AMOUNT	1 YEAR	2 YEARS	3 YEARS	4 YEARS	5 YEARS	6 YEARS	7 YEARS
100	9.13	4.96	3.58	2.90	2.50	2.24	2.06
200	18.26	9.91	7.16	5.80	5.00	4.48	4.12
500	45.66	24.78	17.89	14.49	12.49	11.19	10.29
1000	91.32	49.56	35.78	28.98	24.99	22.39	20.58
2000	182.65	99.12	71.55	57.97	49.97	44.77	41.16
5000	456.62	247.81	178.89	144.92	124.94	111.93	102.90
6000	547.94	297.37	214.66	173.91	149.92	134.32	123.48
7000	639.26	346.94	250.44	202.89	174.91	156.70	144.06
8000	730.59	396.50	286.22	231.88	199.90	179.09	164.64
9000	821.91	446.06	322.00	260.86	224.88	201.47	185.22
10000	913.23	495.62	357.77	289.85	249.87	223.86	205.81
15000	1369.85	743.44	536.66	434.77	374.81	335.79	308.71
20000	1826.47	991.25	715.55	579.69	499.74	447.72	411.61
25000	2283.09	1239.06	894.43	724.61	624.68	559.65	514.51
30000	2739.70	1486.87	1073.32	869.54	749.62	671.58	617.42
35000	3196.32	1734.69	1252.20	1014.46	874.55	783.51	720.32
40000	3652.94	1982.50	1431.09	1159.38	999.49	895.43	823.22
45000	4109.55	2230.31	1609.98	1304.30	1124.42	1007.36	926.12
50000	4566.17	2478.12	1788.86	1449.23	1249.36	1119.29	1029.03
55000	5022.79	2725.94	1967.75	1594.15	1374.30	1231.22	1131.93
60000	5479.41	2973.75	2146.64	1739.07	1499.23	1343.15	1234.83
65000	5936.02	3221.56	2325.52	1884.00	1624.17	1455.08	1337.74
70000	6392.64	3469.37	2504.41	2028.92	1749.10	1567.01	1440.64
75000	6849.26	3717.19	2683.30	2173.84	1874.04	1678.94	1543.54
80000	7305.87	3965.00	2862.18	2318.76	1998.98	1790.87	1646.44
85000	7762.49	4212.81	3041.07	2463.69	2123.91	1902.80	1749.35
90000	8219.11	4460.62	3219.95	2608.61	2248.85	2014.73	1852.25
95000	8675.73	4708.43	3398.84	2753.53	2373.78	2126.66	1955.15
100000	9132.34	4956.25	3577.73	2898.45	2498.72	2238.59	2058.05
105000	9588.96	5204.06	3756.61	3043.38	2623.66	2350.52	2160.96
110000	10045.58	5451.87	3935.50	3188.30	2748.59	2462.44	2263.86
120000	10958.81	5947.50	4293.27	3478.15	2998.46	2686.30	2469.66
130000	11872.05	6443.12	4651.05	3767.99	3248.34	2910.16	2675.47
140000	12785.28	6938.75	5008.82	4057.84	3498.21	3134.02	2881.28
150000	13698.52	7434.37	5366.59	4347.68	3748.08	3357.88	3087.08
160000	14611.75	7930.00	5724.36	4637.53	3997.95	3581.74	3292.89
170000	15524.98	8425.62	6082.14	4927.37	4247.82	3805.60	3498.69
180000	16438.22	8921.24	6439.91	5217.22	4497.70	4029.45	3704.50
190000	17351.45	9416.87	6797.68	5507.06	4747.57	4253.31	3910.30
200000	18264.69	9912.49	7155.45	5796.91	4997.44	4477.17	4116.11
210000	19177.92	10408.12	7513.23	6086.75	5247.31	4701.03	4321.91
220000	20091.16	10903.74	7871.00	6376.60	5497.18	4924.89	4527.72
230000	21004.39	11399.37	8228.77	6666.45	5747.06	5148.75	4733.52
240000	21917.62	11894.99	8586.55	6956.29	5996.93	5372.61	4939.33
250000	22830.86	12390.62	8944.32	7246.14	6246.80	5596.46	5145.14
260000	23744.09	12886.24	9302.09	7535.98	6496.67	5820.32	5350.94
270000	24657.33	13381.87	9659.86	7825.83	6746.54	6044.18	5556.75
280000	25570.56	13877.49	10017.64	8115.67	6996.42	6268.04	5762.55
290000	26483.80	14373.12	10375.41	8405.52	7246.29	6491.90	5968.36
300000	27397.03	14868.74	10733.18	8695.36	7496.16	6715.76	6174.16
310000	28310.27	15364.37	11090.95	8985.21	7746.03	6939.62	6379.97
320000	29223.50	15859.99	11448.73	9275.05	7995.90	7163.47	6585.77
330000	30136.73	16355.62	11806.50	9564.90	8245.78	7387.33	6791.58
340000	31049.97	16851.24	12164.27	9854.75	8495.65	7611.19	6997.38
350000	31963.20	17346.87	12522.05	10144.59	8745.52	7835.05	7203.19
400000	36529.37	19824.99	14310.91	11593.82	9994.88	8954.34	8232.22
450000	41095.55	22303.11	16099.77	13043.05	11244.24	10073.64	9261.24
500000	45661.72	24781.24	17888.64	14492.27	12493.60	11192.93	10290.27
550000	50227.89	27259.36	19677.50	15941.50	13742.96	12312.22	11319.30
600000	54794.06	29737.48	21466.36	17390.73	14992.32	13431.52	12348.32

Monthly Payments 17¼%
necessary to amortize a loan

AMOUNT	8 YEARS	9 YEARS	10 YEARS	11 YEARS	12 YEARS	13 YEARS	14 YEARS
100	1.93	1.83	1.75	1.70	1.65	1.61	1.58
200	3.85	3.66	3.51	3.39	3.30	3.22	3.16
500	9.64	9.15	8.77	8.48	8.24	8.06	7.91
1000	19.27	18.29	17.54	16.95	16.49	16.11	15.81
2000	38.54	36.58	35.08	33.90	32.97	32.23	31.63
5000	96.36	91.45	87.69	84.76	82.43	80.57	79.06
6000	115.63	109.74	105.23	101.71	98.92	96.68	94.88
7000	134.90	128.03	122.77	118.66	115.40	112.80	110.69
8000	154.17	146.32	140.31	135.61	131.89	128.91	126.50
9000	173.44	164.61	157.85	152.56	148.38	145.02	142.31
10000	192.71	182.90	175.39	169.51	164.86	161.14	158.13
15000	289.07	274.36	263.08	254.27	247.29	241.71	237.19
20000	385.42	365.81	350.77	339.03	329.72	322.27	316.25
25000	481.78	457.26	438.46	423.78	412.16	402.84	395.32
30000	578.13	548.71	526.16	508.54	494.59	483.41	474.38
35000	674.49	640.17	613.85	593.30	577.02	563.98	553.44
40000	770.84	731.62	701.54	678.05	659.45	644.55	632.51
45000	867.20	823.07	789.23	762.81	741.88	725.12	711.57
50000	963.55	914.52	876.93	847.56	824.31	805.68	790.63
55000	1059.91	1005.98	964.62	932.32	906.74	886.25	869.70
60000	1156.26	1097.43	1052.31	1017.08	989.17	966.82	948.76
65000	1252.62	1188.88	1140.00	1101.83	1071.60	1047.39	1027.82
70000	1348.97	1280.33	1227.70	1186.59	1154.03	1127.96	1106.88
75000	1445.33	1371.78	1315.39	1271.35	1236.47	1208.53	1185.95
80000	1541.68	1463.24	1403.08	1356.10	1318.90	1289.10	1265.01
85000	1638.04	1554.69	1490.77	1440.86	1401.33	1369.66	1344.07
90000	1734.39	1646.14	1578.47	1525.62	1483.76	1450.23	1423.14
95000	1830.75	1737.59	1666.16	1610.37	1566.19	1530.80	1502.20
100000	1927.10	1829.05	1753.85	1695.13	1648.62	1611.37	1581.26
105000	2023.46	1920.50	1841.54	1779.89	1731.05	1691.94	1660.33
110000	2119.82	2011.95	1929.24	1864.64	1813.48	1772.51	1739.39
120000	2312.53	2194.85	2104.62	2034.16	1978.35	1933.64	1897.52
130000	2505.24	2377.76	2280.01	2203.67	2143.21	2094.78	2055.64
140000	2697.95	2560.66	2455.39	2373.18	2308.07	2255.92	2213.77
150000	2890.66	2743.57	2630.78	2542.69	2472.93	2417.05	2371.90
160000	3083.37	2926.47	2806.16	2712.21	2637.79	2578.19	2530.02
170000	3276.08	3109.38	2981.55	2881.72	2802.66	2739.33	2688.15
180000	3468.79	3292.28	3156.93	3051.23	2967.52	2900.47	2846.28
190000	3661.50	3475.19	3332.32	3220.75	3132.38	3061.60	3004.40
200000	3854.21	3658.09	3507.70	3390.26	3297.24	3222.74	3162.53
210000	4046.92	3841.00	3683.09	3559.77	3462.10	3383.88	3320.65
220000	4239.63	4023.90	3858.47	3729.29	3626.97	3545.01	3478.78
230000	4432.34	4206.81	4033.86	3898.80	3791.83	3706.15	3636.91
240000	4625.05	4389.71	4209.24	4068.31	3956.69	3867.29	3795.03
250000	4817.76	4572.61	4384.63	4237.82	4121.55	4028.42	3953.16
260000	5010.47	4755.52	4560.01	4407.34	4286.41	4189.56	4111.29
270000	5203.18	4938.42	4735.40	4576.85	4451.28	4350.70	4269.41
280000	5395.89	5121.33	4910.78	4746.36	4616.14	4511.83	4427.54
290000	5588.60	5304.23	5086.17	4915.88	4781.00	4672.97	4585.67
300000	5781.31	5487.14	5261.55	5085.39	4945.86	4834.11	4743.79
310000	5974.03	5670.04	5436.94	5254.90	5110.73	4995.25	4901.92
320000	6166.74	5852.95	5612.32	5424.42	5275.59	5156.38	5060.04
330000	6359.45	6035.85	5787.71	5593.93	5440.45	5317.52	5218.17
340000	6552.16	6218.76	5963.09	5763.44	5605.31	5478.66	5376.30
350000	6744.87	6401.66	6138.48	5932.95	5770.17	5639.79	5534.42
400000	7708.42	7316.18	7015.40	6780.52	6594.48	6445.48	6325.06
450000	8671.97	8230.71	7892.33	7628.08	7418.79	7251.16	7115.69
500000	9635.52	9145.23	8769.25	8475.65	8243.11	8056.85	7906.32
550000	10599.08	10059.75	9646.18	9323.21	9067.42	8862.53	8696.95
600000	11562.63	10974.27	10523.10	10170.78	9891.73	9668.22	9487.58

17¼%

Monthly Payments
necessary to amortize a loan

AMOUNT	15 YEARS	16 YEARS	17 YEARS	18 YEARS	19 YEARS	20 YEARS	21 YEARS
100	1.56	1.54	1.52	1.51	1.50	1.49	1.48
200	3.11	3.07	3.04	3.01	2.99	2.97	2.96
500	7.78	7.68	7.60	7.53	7.48	7.43	7.39
1000	15.57	15.37	15.20	15.07	14.95	14.86	14.78
2000	31.14	30.73	30.40	30.13	29.90	29.72	29.56
5000	77.84	76.83	76.01	75.33	74.76	74.29	73.90
6000	93.41	92.20	91.21	90.39	89.71	89.15	88.68
7000	108.97	107.57	106.41	105.46	104.67	104.01	103.46
8000	124.54	122.94	121.61	120.52	119.62	118.87	118.24
9000	140.11	138.30	136.82	135.59	134.57	133.73	133.02
10000	155.68	153.67	152.02	150.65	149.52	148.58	147.80
15000	233.51	230.50	228.03	225.98	224.29	222.88	221.70
20000	311.35	307.34	304.04	301.31	299.05	297.17	295.60
25000	389.19	384.17	380.04	376.63	373.81	371.46	369.50
30000	467.03	461.01	456.05	451.96	448.57	445.75	443.41
35000	544.86	537.84	532.06	527.29	523.33	520.04	517.31
40000	622.70	614.68	608.07	602.62	598.09	594.34	591.21
45000	700.54	691.51	684.08	677.94	672.86	668.63	665.11
50000	778.38	768.34	760.09	753.27	747.62	742.92	739.01
55000	856.22	845.18	836.10	828.60	822.38	817.21	812.91
60000	934.05	922.01	912.11	903.92	897.14	891.51	886.81
65000	1011.89	998.85	988.12	979.25	971.90	965.80	960.71
70000	1089.73	1075.68	1064.13	1054.58	1046.66	1040.09	1034.61
75000	1167.57	1152.52	1140.13	1129.90	1121.43	1114.38	1108.51
80000	1245.41	1229.35	1216.14	1205.23	1196.19	1188.67	1182.41
85000	1323.24	1306.19	1292.15	1280.56	1270.95	1262.97	1256.32
90000	1401.08	1383.02	1368.16	1355.89	1345.71	1337.26	1330.22
95000	1478.92	1459.86	1444.17	1431.21	1420.47	1411.55	1404.12
100000	1556.76	1536.69	1520.18	1506.54	1495.24	1485.84	1478.02
105000	1634.59	1613.52	1596.19	1581.87	1570.00	1560.13	1551.92
110000	1712.43	1690.36	1672.20	1657.19	1644.76	1634.43	1625.82
120000	1868.11	1844.03	1824.21	1807.85	1794.28	1783.01	1773.62
130000	2023.78	1997.70	1976.23	1958.50	1943.81	1931.59	1921.42
140000	2179.46	2151.37	2128.25	2109.16	2093.33	2080.18	2069.23
150000	2335.14	2305.03	2280.27	2259.81	2242.85	2228.76	2217.03
160000	2490.81	2458.70	2432.29	2410.46	2392.38	2377.35	2364.83
170000	2646.49	2612.37	2584.30	2561.12	2541.90	2525.93	2512.63
180000	2802.16	2766.04	2736.32	2711.77	2691.42	2674.52	2660.43
190000	2957.84	2919.71	2888.34	2862.42	2840.95	2823.10	2808.23
200000	3113.51	3073.38	3040.36	3013.08	2990.47	2971.68	2956.04
210000	3269.19	3227.05	3192.38	3163.73	3139.99	3120.27	3103.84
220000	3424.87	3380.72	3344.39	3314.39	3289.52	3268.85	3251.64
230000	3580.54	3534.39	3496.41	3465.04	3439.04	3417.44	3399.44
240000	3736.22	3688.06	3648.43	3615.69	3588.57	3566.02	3547.24
250000	3891.89	3841.72	3800.45	3766.35	3738.09	3714.60	3695.05
260000	4047.57	3995.39	3952.46	3917.00	3887.61	3863.19	3842.85
270000	4203.24	4149.06	4104.48	4067.66	4037.14	4011.77	3990.65
280000	4358.92	4302.73	4256.50	4218.31	4186.66	4160.36	4138.45
290000	4514.60	4456.40	4408.52	4368.96	4336.18	4308.94	4286.25
300000	4670.27	4610.07	4560.54	4519.62	4485.71	4457.53	4434.05
310000	4825.95	4763.74	4712.55	4670.27	4635.23	4606.11	4581.86
320000	4981.62	4917.41	4864.57	4820.93	4784.75	4754.69	4729.66
330000	5137.30	5071.08	5016.59	4971.58	4934.28	4903.28	4877.46
340000	5292.97	5224.75	5168.61	5122.23	5083.80	5051.86	5025.26
350000	5448.65	5378.41	5320.63	5272.89	5233.32	5200.45	5173.06
400000	6227.03	6146.76	6080.71	6026.16	5980.94	5943.37	5912.07
450000	7005.41	6915.10	6840.80	6779.43	6728.56	6686.29	6651.08
500000	7783.79	7683.45	7600.89	7532.70	7476.18	7429.21	7390.09
550000	8562.16	8451.79	8360.98	8285.97	8223.80	8172.13	8129.10
600000	9340.54	9220.14	9121.07	9039.24	8971.41	8915.05	8868.11

202

Monthly Payments 17¼%

necessary to amortize a loan

AMOUNT	22 YEARS	23 YEARS	24 YEARS	25 YEARS	30 YEARS	35 YEARS	40 YEARS
100	1.47	1.47	1.46	1.46	1.45	1.44	1.44
200	2.94	2.93	2.92	2.92	2.89	2.88	2.88
500	7.36	7.33	7.31	7.29	7.23	7.21	7.20
1000	14.71	14.66	14.61	14.58	14.46	14.41	14.39
2000	29.43	29.32	29.23	29.15	28.92	28.82	28.78
5000	73.57	73.30	73.07	72.88	72.30	72.05	71.95
6000	88.29	87.96	87.69	87.46	86.76	86.47	86.34
7000	103.00	102.62	102.30	102.03	101.22	100.88	100.73
8000	117.72	117.28	116.92	116.61	115.68	115.29	115.12
9000	132.43	131.94	131.53	131.19	130.14	129.70	129.51
10000	147.15	146.60	146.15	145.76	144.60	144.11	143.90
15000	220.72	219.90	219.22	218.65	216.90	216.16	215.85
20000	294.30	293.21	292.29	291.53	289.20	288.22	287.80
25000	367.87	366.51	365.37	364.41	361.50	360.27	359.76
30000	441.45	439.81	438.44	437.29	433.80	432.33	431.71
35000	515.02	513.11	511.51	510.17	506.10	504.38	503.66
40000	588.60	586.41	584.59	583.06	578.39	576.44	575.61
45000	662.17	659.71	657.66	655.94	650.69	648.49	647.56
50000	735.74	733.02	730.73	728.82	722.99	720.55	719.51
55000	809.32	806.32	803.81	801.70	795.29	792.60	791.46
60000	882.89	879.62	876.88	874.58	867.59	864.66	863.41
65000	956.47	952.92	949.95	947.47	939.89	936.71	935.37
70000	1030.04	1026.22	1023.03	1020.35	1012.19	1008.76	1007.32
75000	1103.62	1099.52	1096.10	1093.23	1084.49	1080.82	1079.27
80000	1177.19	1172.83	1169.17	1166.11	1156.79	1152.87	1151.22
85000	1250.77	1246.13	1242.25	1239.00	1229.09	1224.93	1223.17
90000	1324.34	1319.43	1315.32	1311.88	1301.39	1296.98	1295.12
95000	1397.91	1392.73	1388.39	1384.76	1373.69	1369.04	1367.07
100000	1471.49	1466.03	1461.47	1457.64	1445.99	1441.09	1439.02
105000	1545.06	1539.33	1534.54	1530.52	1518.29	1513.15	1510.97
110000	1618.64	1612.64	1607.61	1603.41	1590.58	1585.20	1582.93
120000	1765.79	1759.24	1753.76	1749.17	1735.18	1729.31	1726.83
130000	1912.94	1905.84	1899.91	1894.93	1879.78	1873.42	1870.73
140000	2060.09	2052.45	2046.05	2040.70	2024.38	2017.53	2014.63
150000	2207.23	2199.05	2192.20	2186.46	2168.98	2161.64	2158.53
160000	2354.38	2345.65	2338.35	2332.23	2313.58	2305.75	2302.44
170000	2501.53	2492.26	2484.49	2477.99	2458.18	2449.86	2446.34
180000	2648.68	2638.86	2630.64	2623.75	2602.77	2593.97	2590.24
190000	2795.83	2785.46	2776.79	2769.52	2747.37	2738.07	2734.14
200000	2942.98	2932.07	2922.93	2915.28	2891.97	2882.18	2878.05
210000	3090.13	3078.67	3069.08	3061.05	3036.57	3026.29	3021.95
220000	3237.28	3225.27	3215.23	3206.81	3181.17	3170.40	3165.85
230000	3384.43	3371.88	3361.37	3352.58	3325.77	3314.51	3309.75
240000	3531.57	3518.48	3507.52	3498.34	3470.37	3458.62	3453.66
250000	3678.72	3665.08	3653.67	3644.10	3614.96	3602.73	3597.56
260000	3825.87	3811.69	3799.81	3789.87	3759.56	3746.84	3741.46
270000	3973.02	3958.29	3945.96	3935.63	3904.16	3890.95	3885.36
280000	4120.17	4104.89	4092.11	4081.40	4048.76	4035.06	4029.27
290000	4267.32	4251.50	4238.25	4227.16	4193.36	4179.17	4173.17
300000	4414.47	4398.10	4384.40	4372.92	4337.96	4323.28	4317.07
310000	4561.62	4544.70	4530.55	4518.69	4482.56	4467.38	4460.97
320000	4708.77	4691.31	4676.69	4664.45	4627.15	4611.49	4604.87
330000	4855.91	4837.91	4822.84	4810.22	4771.75	4755.60	4748.78
340000	5003.06	4984.51	4968.99	4955.98	4916.35	4899.71	4892.68
350000	5150.21	5131.12	5115.13	5101.74	5060.95	5043.82	5036.58
400000	5885.96	5864.13	5845.87	5830.57	5783.94	5764.37	5756.09
450000	6621.70	6597.15	6576.60	6559.39	6506.94	6484.91	6475.60
500000	7357.45	7330.17	7307.33	7288.21	7229.93	7205.46	7195.12
550000	8093.19	8063.18	8038.07	8017.03	7952.92	7926.00	7914.63
600000	8828.94	8796.20	8768.80	8745.85	8675.91	8646.55	8634.14

17¹/₂%

Monthly Payments
necessary to amortize a loan

AMOUNT	1 YEAR	2 YEARS	3 YEARS	4 YEARS	5 YEARS	6 YEARS	7 YEARS
100	9.14	4.97	3.59	2.91	2.51	2.25	2.07
200	18.29	9.94	7.18	5.82	5.02	4.51	4.15
500	45.72	24.84	17.95	14.56	12.56	11.26	10.36
1000	91.44	49.68	35.90	29.11	25.12	22.53	20.73
2000	182.88	99.37	71.80	58.23	50.24	45.05	41.45
5000	457.21	248.41	179.51	145.57	125.61	112.63	103.63
6000	548.65	298.10	215.41	174.69	150.73	135.16	124.35
7000	640.10	347.78	251.31	203.80	175.86	157.68	145.08
8000	731.54	397.46	287.22	232.91	200.98	180.21	165.81
9000	822.98	447.15	323.12	262.03	226.10	202.73	186.53
10000	914.42	496.83	359.02	291.14	251.22	225.26	207.26
15000	1371.63	745.24	538.53	436.72	376.83	337.89	310.89
20000	1828.84	993.66	718.04	582.29	502.44	450.52	414.52
25000	2286.06	1242.07	897.55	727.86	628.06	563.15	518.14
30000	2743.27	1490.49	1077.06	873.43	753.67	675.78	621.77
35000	3200.48	1738.90	1256.57	1019.00	879.28	788.41	725.40
40000	3657.69	1987.31	1436.08	1164.57	1004.89	901.04	829.03
45000	4114.90	2235.73	1615.59	1310.15	1130.50	1013.67	932.66
50000	4572.11	2484.14	1795.10	1455.72	1256.11	1126.30	1036.29
55000	5029.32	2732.56	1974.61	1601.29	1381.72	1238.93	1139.92
60000	5486.53	2980.97	2154.12	1746.86	1507.33	1351.56	1243.55
65000	5943.74	3229.39	2333.63	1892.43	1632.94	1464.19	1347.18
70000	6400.95	3477.80	2513.14	2038.01	1758.55	1576.82	1450.81
75000	6858.17	3726.21	2692.65	2183.58	1884.17	1689.45	1554.43
80000	7315.38	3974.63	2872.17	2329.15	2009.78	1802.08	1658.06
85000	7772.59	4223.04	3051.68	2474.72	2135.39	1914.71	1761.69
90000	8229.80	4471.46	3231.19	2620.29	2261.00	2027.34	1865.32
95000	8687.01	4719.87	3410.70	2765.87	2386.61	2139.97	1968.95
100000	9144.22	4968.28	3590.21	2911.44	2512.22	2252.60	2072.58
105000	9601.43	5216.70	3769.72	3057.01	2637.83	2365.23	2176.21
110000	10058.64	5465.11	3949.23	3202.58	2763.44	2477.87	2279.84
120000	10973.06	5961.94	4308.25	3493.72	3014.67	2703.13	2487.10
130000	11887.49	6458.77	4667.27	3784.87	3265.89	2928.39	2694.35
140000	12801.91	6955.60	5026.29	4076.01	3517.11	3153.65	2901.61
150000	13716.33	7452.43	5385.31	4367.16	3768.33	3378.91	3108.87
160000	14630.75	7949.26	5744.33	4658.30	4019.55	3604.17	3316.13
170000	15545.17	8446.08	6103.35	4949.44	4270.78	3829.43	3523.38
180000	16459.60	8942.91	6462.37	5240.59	4522.00	4054.69	3730.64
190000	17374.02	9439.74	6821.39	5531.73	4773.22	4279.95	3937.90
200000	18288.44	9936.57	7180.41	5822.87	5024.44	4505.21	4145.16
210000	19202.86	10433.40	7539.43	6114.02	5275.66	4730.47	4352.42
220000	20117.28	10930.23	7898.45	6405.16	5526.89	4955.73	4559.67
230000	21031.71	11427.06	8257.48	6696.31	5778.11	5180.99	4766.93
240000	21946.13	11923.88	8616.50	6987.45	6029.33	5406.25	4974.19
250000	22860.55	12420.71	8975.52	7278.59	6280.55	5631.51	5181.45
260000	23774.97	12917.54	9334.54	7569.74	6531.78	5856.77	5388.71
270000	24689.40	13414.37	9693.56	7860.88	6783.00	6082.03	5595.96
280000	25603.82	13911.20	10052.58	8152.02	7034.22	6307.29	5803.22
290000	26518.24	14408.03	10411.60	8443.17	7285.44	6532.55	6010.48
300000	27432.66	14904.85	10770.62	8734.31	7536.66	6757.81	6217.74
310000	28347.08	15401.68	11129.64	9025.46	7787.89	6983.07	6425.00
320000	29261.51	15898.51	11488.66	9316.60	8039.11	7208.33	6632.25
330000	30175.93	16395.34	11847.68	9607.74	8290.33	7433.60	6839.51
340000	31090.35	16892.17	12206.70	9898.89	8541.55	7658.86	7046.77
350000	32004.77	17389.00	12565.72	10190.03	8792.77	7884.12	7254.03
400000	36576.88	19873.14	14360.83	11645.75	10048.89	9010.42	8290.32
450000	41148.99	22357.28	16155.93	13101.47	11305.00	10136.72	9326.61
500000	45721.10	24841.42	17951.03	14557.19	12561.11	11263.02	10362.90
550000	50293.21	27325.57	19746.14	16012.91	13817.22	12389.33	11399.19
600000	54865.32	29809.71	21541.24	17468.62	15073.33	13515.63	12435.48

Monthly Payments 17½%
necessary to amortize a loan

AMOUNT	8 YEARS	9 YEARS	10 YEARS	11 YEARS	12 YEARS	13 YEARS	14 YEARS
100	1.94	1.84	1.77	1.71	1.67	1.63	1.60
200	3.88	3.69	3.54	3.42	3.33	3.26	3.20
500	9.71	9.22	8.85	8.56	8.33	8.14	7.99
1000	19.42	18.45	17.70	17.11	16.65	16.29	15.99
2000	38.84	36.89	35.40	34.23	33.31	32.57	31.98
5000	97.11	92.23	88.49	85.57	83.27	81.43	79.94
6000	116.53	110.67	106.19	102.69	99.92	97.71	95.93
7000	135.95	129.12	123.89	119.80	116.58	114.00	111.91
8000	155.37	147.56	141.58	136.92	133.23	130.28	127.90
9000	174.79	166.01	159.28	154.03	149.88	146.57	143.89
10000	194.21	184.45	176.98	171.15	166.54	162.85	159.88
15000	291.32	276.68	265.47	256.72	249.81	244.28	239.81
20000	388.42	368.91	353.96	342.30	333.08	325.70	319.75
25000	485.53	461.13	442.45	427.87	416.35	407.13	399.69
30000	582.64	553.36	530.94	513.45	499.62	488.55	479.63
35000	679.74	645.59	619.43	599.02	582.89	569.98	559.57
40000	776.85	737.81	707.92	684.60	666.15	651.40	639.50
45000	873.95	830.04	796.40	770.17	749.42	732.83	719.44
50000	971.06	922.27	884.89	855.75	832.69	814.26	799.38
55000	1068.17	1014.49	973.38	941.32	915.96	895.68	879.32
60000	1165.27	1106.72	1061.87	1026.90	999.23	977.11	959.26
65000	1262.38	1198.95	1150.36	1112.47	1082.50	1058.53	1039.19
70000	1359.48	1291.17	1238.85	1198.05	1165.77	1139.96	1119.13
75000	1456.59	1383.40	1327.34	1283.62	1249.04	1221.38	1199.07
80000	1553.70	1475.63	1415.83	1369.19	1332.31	1302.81	1279.01
85000	1650.80	1567.85	1504.32	1454.77	1415.58	1384.24	1358.94
90000	1747.91	1660.08	1592.81	1540.34	1498.85	1465.66	1438.88
95000	1845.01	1752.31	1681.30	1625.92	1582.12	1547.09	1518.82
100000	1942.12	1844.53	1769.79	1711.49	1665.39	1628.51	1598.76
105000	2039.23	1936.76	1858.28	1797.07	1748.66	1709.94	1678.70
110000	2136.33	2028.99	1946.77	1882.64	1831.93	1791.36	1758.63
120000	2330.55	2213.44	2123.75	2053.79	1998.46	1954.21	1918.51
130000	2524.76	2397.89	2300.72	2224.94	2165.00	2117.07	2078.39
140000	2718.97	2582.35	2477.70	2396.09	2331.54	2279.92	2238.26
150000	2913.18	2766.80	2654.68	2567.24	2498.08	2442.77	2398.14
160000	3107.39	2951.25	2831.66	2738.39	2664.62	2605.62	2558.01
170000	3301.61	3135.71	3008.64	2909.54	2831.16	2768.47	2717.89
180000	3495.82	3320.16	3185.62	3080.69	2997.70	2931.32	2877.77
190000	3690.03	3504.61	3362.60	3251.84	3164.24	3094.17	3037.64
200000	3884.24	3689.07	3539.58	3422.99	3330.77	3257.02	3197.52
210000	4078.45	3873.52	3716.55	3594.14	3497.31	3419.88	3357.39
220000	4272.67	4057.97	3893.53	3765.29	3663.85	3582.73	3517.27
230000	4466.88	4242.43	4070.51	3936.44	3830.39	3745.58	3677.14
240000	4661.09	4426.88	4247.49	4107.58	3996.93	3908.43	3837.02
250000	4855.30	4611.33	4424.47	4278.73	4163.47	4071.28	3996.90
260000	5049.51	4795.79	4601.45	4449.88	4330.01	4234.13	4156.77
270000	5243.73	4980.24	4778.43	4621.03	4496.54	4396.98	4316.65
280000	5437.94	5164.69	4955.41	4792.18	4663.08	4559.83	4476.52
290000	5632.15	5349.15	5132.38	4963.33	4829.62	4722.69	4636.40
300000	5826.36	5533.60	5309.36	5134.48	4996.16	4885.54	4796.28
310000	6020.58	5718.05	5486.34	5305.63	5162.70	5048.39	4956.15
320000	6214.79	5902.51	5663.32	5476.78	5329.24	5211.24	5116.03
330000	6409.00	6086.96	5840.30	5647.93	5495.78	5374.09	5275.90
340000	6603.21	6271.41	6017.28	5819.08	5662.32	5536.94	5435.78
350000	6797.42	6455.87	6194.26	5990.23	5828.85	5699.79	5595.66
400000	7768.48	7378.13	7079.15	6845.97	6661.55	6514.05	6395.03
450000	8739.54	8300.40	7964.04	7701.72	7494.24	7328.31	7194.41
500000	9710.61	9222.67	8848.94	8557.47	8326.94	8142.56	7993.79
550000	10681.67	10144.93	9733.83	9413.22	9159.63	8956.82	8793.17
600000	11652.73	11067.20	10618.73	10268.96	9992.32	9771.07	9592.55

17½%

Monthly Payments
necessary to amortize a loan

AMOUNT	15 YEARS	16 YEARS	17 YEARS	18 YEARS	19 YEARS	20 YEARS	21 YEARS
100	1.57	1.55	1.54	1.53	1.51	1.50	1.50
200	3.15	3.11	3.08	3.05	3.03	3.01	2.99
500	7.87	7.77	7.69	7.63	7.57	7.52	7.49
1000	15.75	15.55	15.39	15.25	15.14	15.05	14.97
2000	31.49	31.10	30.77	30.50	30.28	30.10	29.95
5000	78.73	77.74	76.93	76.26	75.71	75.25	74.87
6000	94.47	93.29	92.31	91.51	90.85	90.30	89.84
7000	110.22	108.84	107.70	106.76	105.99	105.35	104.81
8000	125.97	124.39	123.09	122.02	121.13	120.40	119.78
9000	141.71	139.93	138.47	137.27	136.27	135.44	134.76
10000	157.46	155.48	153.86	152.52	151.41	150.49	149.73
15000	236.19	233.22	230.79	228.78	227.12	225.74	224.60
20000	314.92	310.96	307.72	305.04	302.82	300.99	299.46
25000	393.64	388.70	384.64	381.30	378.53	376.24	374.33
30000	472.37	466.44	461.57	457.56	454.24	451.48	449.19
35000	551.10	544.18	538.50	533.82	529.94	526.73	524.06
40000	629.83	621.93	615.43	610.08	605.65	601.98	598.92
45000	708.56	699.67	692.36	686.34	681.36	677.22	673.79
50000	787.29	777.41	769.29	762.60	757.06	752.47	748.66
55000	866.02	855.15	846.22	838.86	832.77	827.72	823.52
60000	944.75	932.89	923.15	915.12	908.47	902.97	898.39
65000	1023.48	1010.63	1000.08	991.38	984.18	978.21	973.25
70000	1102.20	1088.37	1077.01	1067.64	1059.89	1053.46	1048.12
75000	1180.93	1166.11	1153.93	1143.90	1135.59	1128.71	1122.98
80000	1259.66	1243.85	1230.86	1220.16	1211.30	1203.95	1197.85
85000	1338.39	1321.59	1307.79	1296.42	1287.01	1279.20	1272.71
90000	1417.12	1399.33	1384.72	1372.68	1362.71	1354.45	1347.58
95000	1495.85	1477.07	1461.65	1448.94	1438.42	1429.69	1422.44
100000	1574.58	1554.81	1538.58	1525.19	1514.12	1504.94	1497.31
105000	1653.31	1632.55	1615.51	1601.45	1589.83	1580.19	1572.18
110000	1732.04	1710.29	1692.44	1677.71	1665.54	1655.44	1647.04
120000	1889.49	1865.78	1846.30	1830.23	1816.95	1805.93	1796.77
130000	2046.95	2021.26	2000.15	1982.75	1968.36	1956.42	1946.50
140000	2204.41	2176.74	2154.01	2135.27	2119.77	2106.92	2096.23
150000	2361.87	2332.22	2307.87	2287.79	2271.19	2257.41	2245.97
160000	2519.33	2487.70	2461.73	2440.31	2422.60	2407.91	2395.70
170000	2676.78	2643.18	2615.59	2592.83	2574.01	2558.40	2545.43
180000	2834.24	2798.66	2769.44	2745.35	2725.42	2708.90	2695.16
190000	2991.70	2954.14	2923.30	2897.87	2876.84	2859.39	2844.89
200000	3149.16	3109.63	3077.16	3050.39	3028.25	3009.88	2994.62
210000	3306.61	3265.11	3231.02	3202.91	3179.66	3160.38	3144.35
220000	3464.07	3420.59	3384.87	3355.43	3331.07	3310.87	3294.08
230000	3621.53	3576.07	3538.73	3507.95	3482.48	3461.37	3443.81
240000	3778.99	3731.55	3692.59	3660.47	3633.90	3611.86	3593.54
250000	3936.45	3887.03	3846.45	3812.99	3785.31	3762.35	3743.28
260000	4093.90	4042.51	4000.31	3965.51	3936.72	3912.85	3893.01
270000	4251.36	4197.99	4154.16	4118.03	4088.13	4063.34	4042.74
280000	4408.82	4353.48	4308.02	4270.55	4239.55	4213.84	4192.47
290000	4566.28	4508.96	4461.88	4423.07	4390.96	4364.33	4342.20
300000	4723.73	4664.44	4615.74	4575.58	4542.37	4514.83	4491.93
310000	4881.19	4819.92	4769.60	4728.10	4693.78	4665.32	4641.66
320000	5038.65	4975.40	4923.45	4880.62	4845.20	4815.81	4791.39
330000	5196.11	5130.88	5077.31	5033.14	4996.61	4966.31	4941.12
340000	5353.57	5286.36	5231.17	5185.66	5148.02	5116.80	5090.85
350000	5511.02	5441.84	5385.03	5338.18	5299.43	5267.30	5240.59
400000	6298.31	6219.25	6154.32	6100.78	6056.50	6019.77	5989.24
450000	7085.60	6996.66	6923.61	6863.38	6813.56	6772.24	6737.90
500000	7872.89	7774.06	7692.90	7625.97	7570.62	7524.71	7486.55
550000	8660.18	8551.47	8462.19	8388.57	8327.68	8277.18	8235.21
600000	9447.47	9328.88	9231.48	9151.17	9084.74	9029.65	8983.86

Monthly Payments

necessary to amortize a loan

17¹/₂%

AMOUNT	22 YEARS	23 YEARS	24 YEARS	25 YEARS	30 YEARS	35 YEARS	40 YEARS
100	1.49	1.49	1.48	1.48	1.47	1.46	1.46
200	2.98	2.97	2.96	2.96	2.93	2.92	2.92
500	7.45	7.43	7.41	7.39	7.33	7.31	7.30
1000	14.91	14.86	14.81	14.78	14.66	14.62	14.60
2000	29.82	29.71	29.62	29.55	29.33	29.23	29.19
5000	74.55	74.28	74.06	73.88	73.32	73.08	72.99
6000	89.46	89.14	88.87	88.65	87.98	87.70	87.58
7000	104.37	104.00	103.69	103.43	102.64	102.32	102.18
8000	119.28	118.85	118.50	118.20	117.31	116.93	116.78
9000	134.19	133.71	133.31	132.98	131.97	131.55	131.38
10000	149.10	148.57	148.12	147.75	146.63	146.17	145.97
15000	223.64	222.85	222.18	221.63	219.95	219.25	218.96
20000	298.19	297.13	296.25	295.51	293.27	292.34	291.95
25000	372.74	371.41	370.31	369.38	366.58	365.42	364.93
30000	447.29	445.70	444.37	443.26	439.90	438.50	437.92
35000	521.83	519.98	518.43	517.14	513.21	511.59	510.91
40000	596.38	594.26	592.49	591.01	586.53	584.67	583.89
45000	670.93	668.54	666.55	664.89	659.85	657.75	656.88
50000	745.48	742.83	740.61	738.76	733.16	730.84	729.87
55000	820.03	817.11	814.68	812.64	806.48	803.92	802.85
60000	894.57	891.39	888.74	886.52	879.80	877.01	875.84
65000	969.12	965.68	962.80	960.39	953.11	950.09	948.83
70000	1043.67	1039.96	1036.86	1034.27	1026.43	1023.17	1021.81
75000	1118.22	1114.24	1110.92	1108.15	1099.74	1096.26	1094.80
80000	1192.76	1188.52	1184.98	1182.02	1173.06	1169.34	1167.79
85000	1267.31	1262.81	1259.04	1255.90	1246.38	1242.42	1240.77
90000	1341.86	1337.09	1333.11	1329.78	1319.69	1315.51	1313.76
95000	1416.41	1411.37	1407.17	1403.65	1393.01	1388.59	1386.75
100000	1490.95	1485.65	1481.23	1477.53	1466.33	1461.68	1459.73
105000	1565.50	1559.94	1555.29	1551.41	1539.64	1534.76	1532.72
110000	1640.05	1634.22	1629.35	1625.28	1612.96	1607.84	1605.71
120000	1789.15	1782.79	1777.48	1773.04	1759.59	1754.01	1751.68
130000	1938.24	1931.35	1925.60	1920.79	1906.22	1900.18	1897.65
140000	2087.34	2079.92	2073.72	2068.54	2052.86	2046.35	2043.63
150000	2236.43	2228.48	2221.84	2216.29	2199.49	2192.51	2189.60
160000	2385.53	2377.05	2369.97	2364.05	2346.12	2338.68	2335.57
170000	2534.62	2525.61	2518.09	2511.80	2492.75	2484.85	2481.55
180000	2683.72	2674.18	2666.21	2659.55	2639.39	2631.02	2627.52
190000	2832.81	2822.74	2814.34	2807.31	2786.02	2777.18	2773.49
200000	2981.91	2971.31	2962.46	2955.06	2932.65	2923.35	2919.47
210000	3131.01	3119.88	3110.58	3102.81	3079.28	3069.52	3065.44
220000	3280.10	3268.44	3258.70	3250.57	3225.92	3215.69	3211.41
230000	3429.20	3417.01	3406.83	3398.32	3372.55	3361.85	3357.39
240000	3578.29	3565.57	3554.95	3546.07	3519.18	3508.02	3503.36
250000	3727.39	3714.14	3703.07	3693.82	3665.81	3654.19	3649.33
260000	3876.48	3862.70	3851.20	3841.58	3812.45	3800.36	3795.31
270000	4025.58	4011.27	3999.32	3989.33	3959.08	3946.52	3941.28
280000	4174.67	4159.83	4147.44	4137.08	4105.71	4092.69	4087.25
290000	4323.77	4308.40	4295.56	4284.84	4252.34	4238.86	4233.23
300000	4472.86	4456.96	4443.69	4432.59	4398.98	4385.03	4379.20
310000	4621.96	4605.53	4591.81	4580.34	4545.61	4531.19	4525.17
320000	4771.06	4754.10	4739.93	4728.10	4692.24	4677.36	4671.15
330000	4920.15	4902.66	4888.06	4875.85	4838.87	4823.53	4817.12
340000	5069.25	5051.23	5036.18	5023.60	4985.51	4969.70	4963.09
350000	5218.34	5199.79	5184.30	5171.35	5132.14	5115.86	5109.07
400000	5963.82	5942.62	5924.92	5910.12	5865.30	5846.70	5838.93
450000	6709.30	6685.45	6665.53	6648.88	6598.46	6577.54	6568.80
500000	7454.67	7428.27	7406.15	7387.65	7331.63	7308.38	7298.67
550000	8200.25	8171.10	8146.76	8126.41	8064.79	8039.21	8028.53
600000	8945.73	8913.93	8887.38	8865.18	8797.95	8770.05	8758.40

17¾%

Monthly Payments
necessary to amortize a loan

AMOUNT	1 YEAR	2 YEARS	3 YEARS	4 YEARS	5 YEARS	6 YEARS	7 YEARS
100	9.16	4.98	3.60	2.92	2.53	2.27	2.09
200	18.31	9.96	7.21	5.85	5.05	4.53	4.17
500	45.78	24.90	18.01	14.62	12.63	11.33	10.44
1000	91.56	49.80	36.03	29.24	25.26	22.67	20.87
2000	183.12	99.61	72.05	58.49	50.52	45.33	41.74
5000	457.81	249.02	180.14	146.22	126.29	113.33	104.36
6000	549.37	298.82	216.16	175.47	151.55	136.00	125.23
7000	640.93	348.62	252.19	204.71	176.80	158.67	146.10
8000	732.49	398.43	288.22	233.96	202.06	181.33	166.97
9000	824.05	448.23	324.24	263.20	227.32	204.00	187.84
10000	915.61	498.03	360.27	292.45	252.58	226.67	208.72
15000	1373.42	747.05	540.41	438.67	378.86	340.00	313.07
20000	1831.22	996.07	720.54	584.89	505.15	453.33	417.43
25000	2289.03	1245.08	900.68	731.11	631.44	566.67	521.79
30000	2746.83	1494.10	1080.81	877.34	757.73	680.00	626.15
35000	3204.64	1743.12	1260.95	1023.56	884.02	793.33	730.50
40000	3662.44	1992.14	1441.08	1169.78	1010.30	906.67	834.86
45000	4120.25	2241.15	1621.22	1316.00	1136.59	1020.00	939.22
50000	4578.05	2490.17	1801.36	1462.23	1262.88	1133.33	1043.58
55000	5035.86	2739.19	1981.49	1608.45	1389.17	1246.67	1147.94
60000	5493.66	2988.20	2161.63	1754.67	1515.46	1360.00	1252.29
65000	5951.47	3237.22	2341.76	1900.89	1641.75	1473.34	1356.65
70000	6409.27	3486.24	2521.90	2047.12	1768.03	1586.67	1461.01
75000	6867.08	3735.25	2702.03	2193.34	1894.32	1700.00	1565.37
80000	7324.88	3984.27	2882.17	2339.56	2020.61	1813.34	1669.72
85000	7782.69	4233.29	3062.30	2485.78	2146.90	1926.67	1774.08
90000	8240.50	4482.31	3242.44	2632.01	2273.19	2040.00	1878.44
95000	8698.30	4731.32	3422.58	2778.23	2399.47	2153.34	1982.80
100000	9156.11	4980.34	3602.71	2924.45	2525.76	2266.67	2087.16
105000	9613.91	5229.36	3782.85	3070.68	2652.05	2380.00	2191.51
110000	10071.72	5478.37	3962.98	3216.90	2778.34	2493.34	2295.87
120000	10987.33	5976.41	4323.25	3509.34	3030.91	2720.00	2504.59
130000	11902.94	6474.44	4683.52	3801.79	3283.49	2946.67	2713.30
140000	12818.55	6972.47	5043.79	4094.23	3536.07	3173.34	2922.02
150000	13734.16	7470.51	5404.07	4386.68	3788.64	3400.00	3130.73
160000	14649.77	7968.54	5764.34	4679.12	4041.22	3626.67	3339.45
170000	15565.38	8466.58	6124.61	4971.57	4293.80	3853.34	3548.17
180000	16480.99	8964.61	6484.88	5264.01	4546.37	4080.00	3756.88
190000	17396.60	9462.64	6845.15	5556.46	4798.95	4306.67	3965.60
200000	18312.21	9960.68	7205.42	5848.91	5051.52	4533.34	4174.31
210000	19227.82	10458.71	7565.69	6141.35	5304.10	4760.01	4383.03
220000	20143.43	10956.75	7925.96	6433.80	5556.68	4986.67	4591.74
230000	21059.04	11454.78	8286.23	6726.24	5809.25	5213.34	4800.46
240000	21974.65	11952.81	8646.51	7018.69	6061.83	5440.01	5009.17
250000	22890.26	12450.85	9006.78	7311.13	6314.41	5666.67	5217.89
260000	23805.87	12948.88	9367.05	7603.58	6566.98	5893.34	5426.61
270000	24721.49	13446.92	9727.32	7896.02	6819.56	6120.01	5635.32
280000	25637.10	13944.95	10087.59	8188.47	7072.13	6346.67	5844.04
290000	26552.71	14442.98	10447.86	8480.91	7324.71	6573.34	6052.75
300000	27468.32	14941.02	10808.13	8773.36	7577.29	6800.01	6261.47
310000	28383.93	15439.05	11168.40	9065.80	7829.86	7026.67	6470.18
320000	29299.54	15937.09	11528.67	9358.25	8082.44	7253.34	6678.90
330000	30215.15	16435.12	11888.95	9650.69	8335.02	7480.01	6887.61
340000	31130.76	16933.15	12249.22	9943.14	8587.59	7706.67	7096.33
350000	32046.37	17431.19	12609.49	10235.58	8840.17	7933.34	7305.05
400000	36624.42	19921.36	14410.84	11697.81	10103.05	9066.68	8348.62
450000	41202.48	22411.53	16212.20	13160.04	11365.93	10200.01	9392.20
500000	45780.53	24901.70	18013.55	14622.26	12628.81	11333.35	10435.78
550000	50358.58	27391.87	19814.91	16084.49	13891.69	12466.68	11479.36
600000	54936.63	29882.03	21616.26	17546.72	15154.57	13600.01	12522.94

Monthly Payments 17¾%
necessary to amortize a loan

AMOUNT	8 YEARS	9 YEARS	10 YEARS	11 YEARS	12 YEARS	13 YEARS	14 YEARS
100	1.96	1.86	1.79	1.73	1.68	1.65	1.62
200	3.91	3.72	3.57	3.46	3.36	3.29	3.23
500	9.79	9.30	8.93	8.64	8.41	8.23	8.08
1000	19.57	18.60	17.86	17.28	16.82	16.46	16.16
2000	39.14	37.20	35.72	34.56	33.64	32.91	32.33
5000	97.86	93.00	89.29	86.40	84.11	82.29	80.82
6000	117.43	111.60	107.15	103.68	100.93	98.74	96.98
7000	137.00	130.21	125.01	120.95	117.76	115.20	113.14
8000	156.58	148.81	142.86	138.23	134.58	131.66	129.31
9000	176.15	167.41	160.72	155.51	151.40	148.12	145.47
10000	195.72	186.01	178.58	172.79	168.22	164.57	161.63
15000	293.58	279.01	267.87	259.19	252.33	246.86	242.45
20000	391.44	372.02	357.16	345.58	336.44	329.14	323.26
25000	489.30	465.02	446.45	431.98	420.56	411.43	404.08
30000	587.16	558.02	535.74	518.38	504.67	493.72	484.90
35000	685.02	651.03	625.03	604.77	588.78	576.00	565.71
40000	782.88	744.03	714.32	691.17	672.89	658.29	646.53
45000	880.74	837.04	803.60	777.57	757.00	740.58	727.34
50000	978.60	930.04	892.89	863.96	841.11	822.86	808.16
55000	1076.46	1023.04	982.18	950.36	925.22	905.15	888.98
60000	1174.32	1116.05	1071.47	1036.75	1009.33	987.43	969.79
65000	1272.18	1209.05	1160.76	1123.15	1093.44	1069.72	1050.61
70000	1370.04	1302.06	1250.05	1209.55	1177.55	1152.01	1131.42
75000	1467.89	1395.06	1339.34	1295.94	1261.67	1234.29	1212.24
80000	1565.75	1488.06	1428.63	1382.34	1345.78	1316.58	1293.06
85000	1663.61	1581.07	1517.92	1468.73	1429.89	1398.86	1373.87
90000	1761.47	1674.07	1607.21	1555.13	1514.00	1481.15	1454.69
95000	1859.33	1767.08	1696.50	1641.53	1598.11	1563.44	1535.51
100000	1957.19	1860.08	1785.79	1727.92	1682.22	1645.72	1616.32
105000	2055.05	1953.09	1875.08	1814.32	1766.33	1728.01	1697.14
110000	2152.91	2046.09	1964.37	1900.72	1850.44	1810.30	1777.95
120000	2348.63	2232.10	2142.95	2073.51	2018.66	1974.87	1939.59
130000	2544.35	2418.11	2321.52	2246.30	2186.89	2139.44	2101.22
140000	2740.07	2604.11	2500.10	2419.09	2355.11	2304.01	2262.85
150000	2935.79	2790.12	2678.68	2591.88	2523.33	2468.58	2424.48
160000	3131.51	2976.13	2857.26	2764.68	2691.55	2633.16	2586.11
170000	3327.23	3162.14	3035.84	2937.47	2859.77	2797.73	2747.75
180000	3522.95	3348.15	3214.42	3110.26	3028.00	2962.30	2909.38
190000	3718.67	3534.15	3393.00	3283.05	3196.22	3126.87	3071.01
200000	3914.39	3720.16	3571.58	3455.85	3364.44	3291.45	3232.64
210000	4110.11	3906.17	3750.16	3628.64	3532.66	3456.02	3394.27
220000	4305.83	4092.18	3928.73	3801.43	3700.88	3620.59	3555.91
230000	4501.54	4278.19	4107.31	3974.22	3869.11	3785.16	3717.54
240000	4697.26	4464.19	4285.89	4147.02	4037.33	3949.74	3879.17
250000	4892.98	4650.20	4464.47	4319.81	4205.55	4114.31	4040.80
260000	5088.70	4836.21	4643.05	4492.60	4373.77	4278.88	4202.43
270000	5284.42	5022.22	4821.63	4665.39	4541.99	4443.45	4364.07
280000	5480.14	5208.23	5000.21	4838.19	4710.22	4608.02	4525.70
290000	5675.86	5394.24	5178.79	5010.98	4878.44	4772.60	4687.33
300000	5871.58	5580.24	5357.37	5183.77	5046.66	4937.17	4848.96
310000	6067.30	5766.25	5535.94	5356.56	5214.88	5101.74	5010.60
320000	6263.02	5952.26	5714.52	5529.35	5383.10	5266.31	5172.23
330000	6458.74	6138.27	5893.10	5702.15	5551.33	5430.89	5333.86
340000	6654.46	6324.28	6071.68	5874.94	5719.55	5595.46	5495.49
350000	6850.18	6510.28	6250.26	6047.73	5887.77	5760.03	5657.12
400000	7828.77	7440.32	7143.15	6911.69	6728.88	6582.89	6465.28
450000	8807.37	8370.37	8036.05	7775.65	7569.99	7405.75	7273.44
500000	9785.97	9300.41	8928.94	8639.62	8411.10	8228.62	8081.61
550000	10764.56	10230.45	9821.84	9503.58	9252.21	9051.48	8889.77
600000	11743.16	11160.49	10714.73	10367.54	10093.32	9874.34	9697.93

17³/₄%   Monthly Payments
necessary to amortize a loan

AMOUNT	15 YEARS	16 YEARS	17 YEARS	18 YEARS	19 YEARS	20 YEARS	21 YEARS
100	1.59	1.57	1.56	1.54	1.53	1.52	1.52
200	3.18	3.15	3.11	3.09	3.07	3.05	3.03
500	7.96	7.87	7.79	7.72	7.67	7.62	7.58
1000	15.92	15.73	15.57	15.44	15.33	15.24	15.17
2000	31.85	31.46	31.14	30.88	30.66	30.48	30.33
5000	79.62	78.65	77.85	77.20	76.65	76.20	75.83
6000	95.55	94.38	93.42	92.63	91.98	91.45	91.00
7000	111.47	110.11	108.99	108.07	107.32	106.69	106.17
8000	127.40	125.84	124.56	123.51	122.65	121.93	121.33
9000	143.32	141.57	140.13	138.95	137.98	137.17	136.50
10000	159.25	157.30	155.70	154.39	153.31	152.41	151.67
15000	238.87	235.95	233.56	231.59	229.96	228.61	227.50
20000	318.49	314.60	311.41	308.78	306.61	304.82	303.33
25000	398.12	393.25	389.26	385.98	383.27	381.02	379.16
30000	477.74	471.90	467.11	463.17	459.92	457.23	455.00
35000	557.36	550.55	544.97	540.37	536.58	533.43	530.83
40000	636.99	629.20	622.82	617.57	613.23	609.64	606.66
45000	716.61	707.85	700.67	694.76	689.88	685.84	682.50
50000	796.23	786.50	778.52	771.96	766.54	762.05	758.33
55000	875.86	865.15	856.37	849.15	843.19	838.25	834.16
60000	955.48	943.80	934.23	926.35	919.84	914.46	909.99
65000	1035.10	1022.45	1012.08	1003.54	996.50	990.66	985.83
70000	1114.73	1101.10	1089.93	1080.74	1073.15	1066.87	1061.66
75000	1194.35	1179.75	1167.78	1157.93	1149.80	1143.07	1137.49
80000	1273.97	1258.40	1245.64	1235.13	1226.46	1219.28	1213.32
85000	1353.60	1337.05	1323.49	1312.33	1303.11	1295.48	1289.16
90000	1433.22	1415.70	1401.34	1389.52	1379.76	1371.69	1364.99
95000	1512.84	1494.35	1479.19	1466.72	1456.42	1447.89	1440.82
100000	1592.47	1573.00	1557.04	1543.91	1533.07	1524.10	1516.66
105000	1672.09	1651.65	1634.90	1621.11	1609.73	1600.30	1592.49
110000	1751.71	1730.30	1712.75	1698.30	1686.38	1676.51	1668.32
120000	1910.96	1887.60	1868.45	1852.70	1839.69	1828.92	1819.99
130000	2070.21	2044.90	2024.16	2007.09	1992.99	1981.33	1971.65
140000	2229.45	2202.20	2179.86	2161.48	2146.30	2133.74	2123.32
150000	2388.70	2359.50	2335.57	2315.87	2299.61	2286.15	2274.98
160000	2547.95	2516.80	2491.27	2470.26	2452.92	2438.56	2426.65
170000	2707.19	2674.10	2646.98	2624.65	2606.22	2590.97	2578.32
180000	2866.44	2831.40	2802.68	2779.04	2759.53	2743.38	2729.98
190000	3025.69	2988.70	2958.38	2933.43	2912.84	2895.79	2881.65
200000	3184.93	3146.00	3114.09	3087.83	3066.14	3048.20	3033.31
210000	3344.18	3303.30	3269.79	3242.22	3219.45	3200.61	3184.98
220000	3503.43	3460.60	3425.50	3396.61	3372.76	3353.02	3336.64
230000	3662.67	3617.90	3581.20	3551.00	3526.07	3505.43	3488.31
240000	3821.92	3775.20	3736.91	3705.39	3679.37	3657.84	3639.97
250000	3981.17	3932.50	3892.61	3859.78	3832.68	3810.25	3791.64
260000	4140.41	4089.80	4048.32	4014.17	3985.99	3962.66	3943.31
270000	4299.66	4247.11	4204.02	4168.56	4139.29	4115.07	4094.97
280000	4458.91	4404.41	4359.73	4322.96	4292.60	4267.48	4246.64
290000	4618.15	4561.71	4515.43	4477.35	4445.91	4419.89	4398.30
300000	4777.40	4719.01	4671.13	4631.74	4599.22	4572.30	4549.97
310000	4936.65	4876.31	4826.84	4786.13	4752.52	4724.71	4701.63
320000	5095.89	5033.61	4982.54	4940.52	4905.83	4877.12	4853.30
330000	5255.14	5190.91	5138.25	5094.91	5059.14	5029.53	5004.97
340000	5414.39	5348.21	5293.95	5249.30	5212.44	5181.94	5156.63
350000	5573.63	5505.51	5449.66	5403.69	5365.75	5334.35	5308.30
400000	6369.87	6292.01	6228.18	6175.65	6132.29	6096.40	6066.62
450000	7166.10	7078.51	7006.70	6947.61	6898.82	6858.45	6824.95
500000	7962.33	7865.01	7785.22	7719.56	7665.36	7620.50	7583.28
550000	8758.57	8651.51	8563.75	8491.52	8431.90	8382.54	8341.61
600000	9554.80	9438.01	9342.27	9263.48	9198.43	9144.59	9099.94

Monthly Payments 17¾%
necessary to amortize a loan

AMOUNT	22 YEARS	23 YEARS	24 YEARS	25 YEARS	30 YEARS	35 YEARS	40 YEARS
100	1.51	1.51	1.50	1.50	1.49	1.48	1.48
200	3.02	3.01	3.00	2.99	2.97	2.96	2.96
500	7.55	7.53	7.51	7.49	7.43	7.41	7.40
1000	15.10	15.05	15.01	14.97	14.87	14.82	14.80
2000	30.21	30.11	30.02	29.95	29.73	29.65	29.61
5000	75.52	75.27	75.05	74.87	74.33	74.11	74.02
6000	90.63	90.32	90.06	89.85	89.20	88.94	88.83
7000	105.73	105.37	105.07	104.82	104.07	103.76	103.63
8000	120.84	120.43	120.08	119.80	118.94	118.58	118.44
9000	135.94	135.48	135.09	134.77	133.80	133.40	133.24
10000	151.05	150.53	150.10	149.75	148.67	148.23	148.05
15000	226.57	225.80	225.16	224.62	223.00	222.34	222.07
20000	302.09	301.06	300.21	299.49	297.34	296.46	296.09
25000	377.62	376.33	375.26	374.36	371.67	370.57	370.11
30000	453.14	451.60	450.31	449.24	446.01	444.68	444.14
35000	528.67	526.86	525.36	524.11	520.34	518.80	518.16
40000	604.19	602.13	600.41	598.98	594.68	592.91	592.18
45000	679.71	677.40	675.47	673.86	669.01	667.02	666.20
50000	755.24	752.66	750.52	748.73	743.35	741.14	740.23
55000	830.76	827.93	825.57	823.60	817.68	815.25	814.25
60000	906.28	903.19	900.62	898.48	892.02	889.37	888.27
65000	981.81	978.46	975.67	973.35	966.35	963.48	962.29
70000	1057.33	1053.73	1050.73	1048.22	1040.68	1037.59	1036.32
75000	1132.85	1128.99	1125.78	1123.09	1115.02	1111.71	1110.34
80000	1208.38	1204.26	1200.83	1197.97	1189.35	1185.82	1184.36
85000	1283.90	1279.53	1275.88	1272.84	1263.69	1259.93	1258.39
90000	1359.42	1354.79	1350.93	1347.71	1338.02	1334.05	1332.41
95000	1434.95	1430.06	1425.98	1422.59	1412.36	1408.16	1406.43
100000	1510.47	1505.32	1501.04	1497.46	1486.69	1482.28	1480.45
105000	1586.00	1580.59	1576.09	1572.33	1561.03	1556.39	1554.48
110000	1661.52	1655.86	1651.14	1647.21	1635.36	1630.50	1628.50
120000	1812.57	1806.39	1801.24	1796.95	1784.03	1778.73	1776.54
130000	1963.61	1956.92	1951.35	1946.70	1932.70	1926.96	1924.59
140000	2114.66	2107.45	2101.45	2096.44	2081.37	2075.19	2072.63
150000	2265.71	2257.99	2251.55	2246.19	2230.04	2223.41	2220.68
160000	2416.75	2408.52	2401.66	2395.94	2378.71	2371.64	2368.72
170000	2567.80	2559.05	2551.76	2545.68	2527.38	2519.87	2516.77
180000	2718.85	2709.58	2701.87	2695.43	2676.05	2668.10	2664.82
190000	2869.90	2860.12	2851.97	2845.17	2824.72	2816.32	2812.86
200000	3020.94	3010.65	3002.07	2994.92	2973.38	2964.55	2960.91
210000	3171.99	3161.18	3152.18	3144.67	3122.05	3112.78	3108.95
220000	3323.04	3311.71	3302.28	3294.41	3270.72	3261.01	3257.00
230000	3474.08	3462.25	3452.38	3444.16	3419.39	3409.23	3405.04
240000	3625.13	3612.78	3602.49	3593.90	3568.06	3557.46	3553.09
250000	3776.18	3763.31	3752.59	3743.65	3716.73	3705.69	3701.13
260000	3927.23	3913.84	3902.70	3893.40	3865.40	3853.92	3849.18
270000	4078.27	4064.38	4052.80	4043.14	4014.07	4002.14	3997.22
280000	4229.32	4214.91	4202.90	4192.89	4162.74	4150.37	4145.27
290000	4380.37	4365.44	4353.01	4342.63	4311.41	4298.60	4293.31
300000	4531.41	4515.97	4503.11	4492.38	4460.08	4446.83	4441.36
310000	4682.46	4666.51	4653.21	4642.13	4608.75	4595.05	4589.41
320000	4833.51	4817.04	4803.32	4791.87	4757.42	4743.28	4737.45
330000	4984.56	4967.57	4953.42	4941.62	4906.08	4891.51	4885.50
340000	5135.60	5118.10	5103.52	5091.36	5054.75	5039.74	5033.54
350000	5286.65	5268.64	5253.63	5241.11	5203.42	5187.97	5181.59
400000	6041.89	6021.30	6004.15	5989.84	5946.77	5929.10	5921.81
450000	6797.12	6773.96	6754.66	6738.57	6690.12	6670.24	6662.04
500000	7552.36	7526.62	7505.18	7487.30	7433.46	7411.38	7402.27
550000	8307.59	8279.29	8255.70	8236.03	8176.81	8152.52	8142.49
600000	9062.83	9031.95	9006.22	8984.76	8920.15	8893.65	8882.72

18%

Monthly Payments
necessary to amortize a loan

AMOUNT	1 YEAR	2 YEARS	3 YEARS	4 YEARS	5 YEARS	6 YEARS	7 YEARS
100	9.17	4.99	3.62	2.94	2.54	2.28	2.10
200	18.34	9.98	7.23	5.87	5.08	4.56	4.20
500	45.84	24.96	18.08	14.69	12.70	11.40	10.51
1000	91.68	49.92	36.15	29.37	25.39	22.81	21.02
2000	183.36	99.85	72.30	58.75	50.79	45.62	42.04
5000	458.40	249.62	180.76	146.87	126.97	114.04	105.09
6000	550.08	299.54	216.91	176.25	152.36	136.85	126.11
7000	641.76	349.47	253.07	205.62	177.75	159.65	147.12
8000	733.44	399.39	289.22	235.00	203.15	182.46	168.14
9000	825.12	449.32	325.37	264.37	228.54	205.27	189.16
10000	916.80	499.24	361.52	293.75	253.93	228.08	210.18
15000	1375.20	748.86	542.29	440.62	380.90	342.12	315.27
20000	1833.60	998.48	723.05	587.50	507.87	456.16	420.36
25000	2292.00	1248.10	903.81	734.37	634.84	570.19	525.45
30000	2750.40	1497.72	1084.57	881.25	761.80	684.23	630.54
35000	3208.80	1747.34	1265.33	1028.12	888.77	798.27	735.62
40000	3667.20	1996.96	1446.10	1175.00	1015.74	912.31	840.71
45000	4125.60	2246.58	1626.86	1321.87	1142.70	1026.35	945.80
50000	4584.00	2496.21	1807.62	1468.75	1269.67	1140.39	1050.89
55000	5042.40	2745.83	1988.38	1615.62	1396.64	1254.43	1155.98
60000	5500.80	2995.45	2169.14	1762.50	1523.61	1368.47	1261.07
65000	5959.20	3245.07	2349.91	1909.37	1650.57	1482.51	1366.16
70000	6417.60	3494.69	2530.67	2056.25	1777.54	1596.55	1471.25
75000	6876.00	3744.31	2711.43	2203.12	1904.51	1710.58	1576.34
80000	7334.40	3993.93	2892.19	2350.00	2031.47	1824.62	1681.43
85000	7792.80	4243.55	3072.95	2496.87	2158.44	1938.66	1786.52
90000	8251.20	4493.17	3253.72	2643.75	2285.41	2052.70	1891.61
95000	8709.60	4742.79	3434.48	2790.62	2412.38	2166.74	1996.69
100000	9168.00	4992.41	3615.24	2937.50	2539.34	2280.78	2101.78
105000	9626.40	5242.03	3796.00	3084.37	2666.31	2394.82	2206.87
110000	10084.80	5491.65	3976.76	3231.25	2793.28	2508.86	2311.96
120000	11001.60	5990.89	4338.29	3525.00	3047.21	2736.93	2522.14
130000	11918.40	6490.13	4699.81	3818.75	3301.15	2965.01	2732.32
140000	12835.20	6939.37	5061.34	4112.50	3555.08	3193.09	2942.50
150000	13752.00	7488.62	5422.86	4406.25	3809.01	3421.17	3152.68
160000	14668.80	7987.86	5784.38	4700.00	4062.95	3649.25	3362.85
170000	15585.60	8487.10	6145.91	4993.75	4316.88	3877.32	3573.03
180000	16502.40	8986.34	6507.43	5287.50	4570.82	4105.40	3783.21
190000	17419.20	9485.58	6868.96	5581.25	4824.75	4333.48	3993.39
200000	18336.00	9984.82	7230.48	5875.00	5078.69	4561.56	4203.57
210000	19252.80	10484.06	7592.00	6168.75	5332.62	4789.64	4413.75
220000	20169.60	10983.30	7953.53	6462.50	5586.55	5017.71	4623.92
230000	21086.40	11482.54	8315.05	6756.25	5840.49	5245.79	4834.10
240000	22003.20	11981.78	8676.57	7050.00	6094.42	5473.87	5044.28
250000	22920.00	12481.03	9038.10	7343.75	6348.36	5701.95	5254.46
260000	23836.80	12980.27	9399.62	7637.50	6602.29	5930.03	5464.64
270000	24753.60	13479.51	9761.15	7931.25	6856.23	6158.10	5674.82
280000	25670.40	13978.75	10122.67	8225.00	7110.16	6386.18	5884.99
290000	26587.20	14477.99	10484.19	8518.75	7364.09	6614.26	6095.17
300000	27504.00	14977.23	10845.72	8812.50	7618.03	6842.34	6305.35
310000	28420.80	15476.47	11207.24	9106.25	7871.96	7070.42	6515.53
320000	29337.60	15975.71	11568.77	9400.00	8125.90	7298.49	6725.71
330000	30254.40	16474.95	11930.29	9693.75	8379.83	7526.57	6935.89
340000	31171.20	16974.19	12291.81	9987.50	8633.77	7754.65	7146.06
350000	32088.00	17473.44	12653.34	10281.25	8887.70	7982.73	7356.24
400000	36672.00	19969.64	14460.96	11750.00	10157.37	9123.12	8407.14
450000	41256.00	22465.85	16268.58	13218.75	11427.04	10263.51	9458.03
500000	45840.00	24962.05	18076.20	14687.50	12696.71	11403.90	10508.92
550000	50424.00	27458.26	19883.82	16156.25	13966.39	12544.29	11559.81
600000	55008.00	29954.46	21691.44	17625.00	15236.06	13684.67	12610.70

Monthly Payments **18%**
necessary to amortize a loan

AMOUNT	8 YEARS	9 YEARS	10 YEARS	11 YEARS	12 YEARS	13 YEARS	14 YEARS
100	1.97	1.88	1.80	1.74	1.70	1.66	1.63
200	3.94	3.75	3.60	3.49	3.40	3.33	3.27
500	9.86	9.38	9.01	8.72	8.50	8.32	8.17
1000	19.72	18.76	18.02	17.44	16.99	16.63	16.34
2000	39.45	37.51	36.04	34.89	33.98	33.26	32.68
5000	98.62	93.78	90.09	87.22	84.96	83.15	81.70
6000	118.34	112.54	108.11	104.67	101.95	99.78	98.04
7000	138.06	131.30	126.13	122.11	118.94	116.41	114.38
8000	157.79	150.06	144.15	139.55	135.93	133.04	130.72
9000	177.51	168.81	162.17	157.00	152.92	149.67	147.06
10000	197.23	187.57	180.19	174.44	169.91	166.30	163.40
15000	295.85	281.35	270.28	261.66	254.87	249.45	245.09
20000	394.46	375.14	360.37	348.88	339.82	332.60	326.79
25000	493.08	468.92	450.46	436.10	424.78	415.75	408.49
30000	591.70	562.71	540.56	523.33	509.74	498.90	490.19
35000	690.31	656.49	630.65	610.55	594.69	582.05	571.88
40000	788.93	750.28	720.74	697.77	679.65	665.20	653.58
45000	887.54	844.06	810.83	784.99	764.60	748.35	735.28
50000	986.16	937.84	900.93	872.21	849.56	831.50	816.98
55000	1084.78	1031.63	991.02	959.43	934.52	914.65	898.67
60000	1183.39	1125.41	1081.11	1046.65	1019.47	997.80	980.37
65000	1282.01	1219.20	1171.20	1133.87	1104.43	1080.95	1062.07
70000	1380.62	1312.98	1261.30	1221.09	1189.38	1164.10	1143.77
75000	1479.24	1406.77	1351.39	1308.31	1274.34	1247.25	1225.46
80000	1577.86	1500.55	1441.48	1395.53	1359.30	1330.40	1307.16
85000	1676.47	1594.34	1531.57	1482.75	1444.25	1413.55	1388.86
90000	1775.09	1688.12	1621.67	1569.98	1529.21	1496.70	1470.56
95000	1873.71	1781.90	1711.76	1657.20	1614.16	1579.85	1552.25
100000	1972.32	1875.69	1801.85	1744.42	1699.12	1663.00	1633.95
105000	2070.94	1969.47	1891.94	1831.64	1784.08	1746.15	1715.65
110000	2169.55	2063.26	1982.04	1918.86	1869.03	1829.30	1797.35
120000	2366.79	2250.83	2162.22	2093.30	2038.94	1995.60	1960.74
130000	2564.02	2438.40	2342.41	2267.74	2208.86	2161.90	2124.14
140000	2761.25	2625.96	2522.59	2442.19	2378.77	2328.20	2287.53
150000	2958.48	2813.53	2702.78	2616.63	2548.68	2494.50	2450.93
160000	3155.71	3001.10	2882.96	2791.07	2718.59	2660.80	2614.32
170000	3352.95	3188.67	3063.15	2965.51	2888.50	2827.10	2777.72
180000	3550.18	3376.24	3243.33	3139.95	3058.42	2993.40	2941.11
190000	3747.41	3563.81	3423.52	3314.39	3228.33	3159.70	3104.51
200000	3944.64	3751.38	3603.70	3488.84	3398.24	3326.00	3267.90
210000	4141.87	3938.95	3783.89	3663.28	3568.15	3492.30	3431.30
220000	4339.11	4126.52	3964.07	3837.72	3738.06	3658.60	3594.69
230000	4536.34	4314.08	4144.26	4012.16	3907.97	3824.90	3758.09
240000	4733.57	4501.65	4324.44	4186.60	4077.89	3991.20	3921.48
250000	4930.80	4689.22	4504.63	4361.04	4247.80	4157.50	4084.88
260000	5128.04	4876.79	4684.82	4535.49	4417.71	4323.80	4248.27
270000	5325.27	5064.36	4865.00	4709.93	4587.62	4490.10	4411.67
280000	5522.50	5251.93	5045.19	4884.37	4757.53	4656.40	4575.06
290000	5719.73	5439.50	5225.37	5058.81	4927.45	4822.70	4738.46
300000	5916.96	5627.07	5405.56	5233.25	5097.36	4989.00	4901.85
310000	6114.20	5814.64	5585.74	5407.70	5267.27	5155.30	5065.25
320000	6311.43	6002.20	5765.93	5582.14	5437.18	5321.60	5228.64
330000	6508.66	6189.77	5946.12	5756.58	5607.09	5487.90	5392.04
340000	6705.89	6377.34	6126.30	5931.02	5777.01	5654.20	5555.43
350000	6903.12	6564.91	6306.49	6105.46	5946.92	5820.50	5718.83
400000	7889.29	7502.76	7207.41	6977.67	6796.48	6652.00	6535.80
450000	8875.45	8440.60	8108.33	7849.89	7646.04	7483.50	7352.78
500000	9861.61	9378.44	9009.26	8722.09	8495.60	8315.00	8169.75
550000	10847.77	10316.29	9910.19	9594.30	9345.16	9146.50	8986.73
600000	11833.93	11254.13	10811.11	10466.51	10194.72	9978.01	9803.70

18%

Monthly Payments
necessary to amortize a loan

AMOUNT	15 YEARS	16 YEARS	17 YEARS	18 YEARS	19 YEARS	20 YEARS	21 YEARS
100	1.61	1.59	1.58	1.56	1.55	1.54	1.54
200	3.22	3.18	3.15	3.13	3.10	3.09	3.07
500	8.05	7.96	7.88	7.81	7.76	7.72	7.68
1000	16.10	15.91	15.76	15.63	15.52	15.43	15.36
2000	32.21	31.83	31.51	31.25	31.04	30.87	30.72
5000	80.52	79.56	78.78	78.13	77.60	77.17	76.80
6000	96.63	95.48	94.53	93.76	93.12	92.60	92.16
7000	112.73	111.39	110.29	109.39	108.65	108.03	107.52
8000	128.83	127.30	126.05	125.02	124.17	123.46	122.88
9000	144.94	143.21	141.80	140.64	139.69	138.90	138.24
10000	161.04	159.13	157.56	156.27	155.21	154.33	153.61
15000	241.56	238.69	236.34	234.40	232.81	231.50	230.41
20000	322.08	318.25	315.11	312.54	310.42	308.66	307.21
25000	402.61	397.81	393.89	390.67	388.02	385.83	384.01
30000	483.13	477.38	472.67	468.81	465.62	462.99	460.82
35000	563.65	556.94	551.45	546.94	543.23	540.16	537.62
40000	644.17	636.50	630.23	625.08	620.83	617.32	614.42
45000	724.69	716.07	709.01	703.21	698.44	694.49	691.22
50000	805.21	795.63	787.79	781.35	776.04	771.66	768.03
55000	885.73	875.19	866.57	859.48	853.64	848.82	844.83
60000	966.25	954.75	945.34	937.61	931.25	925.99	921.63
65000	1046.77	1034.32	1024.12	1015.75	1008.85	1003.15	998.44
70000	1127.29	1113.88	1102.90	1093.88	1086.45	1080.32	1075.24
75000	1207.82	1193.44	1181.68	1172.02	1164.06	1157.48	1152.04
80000	1288.34	1273.00	1260.46	1250.15	1241.66	1234.65	1228.84
85000	1368.86	1352.57	1339.24	1328.29	1319.27	1311.81	1305.65
90000	1449.38	1432.13	1418.02	1406.42	1396.87	1388.98	1382.45
95000	1529.90	1511.69	1496.79	1484.56	1474.47	1466.15	1459.25
100000	1610.42	1591.26	1575.57	1562.69	1552.08	1543.31	1536.05
105000	1690.94	1670.82	1654.35	1640.83	1629.68	1620.48	1612.86
110000	1771.46	1750.38	1733.13	1718.96	1707.29	1697.64	1689.66
120000	1932.51	1909.51	1890.69	1875.23	1862.49	1851.97	1843.27
130000	2093.55	2068.63	2048.24	2031.50	2017.70	2006.30	1996.87
140000	2254.59	2227.76	2205.80	2187.77	2172.91	2160.64	2150.48
150000	2415.63	2386.88	2363.36	2344.04	2328.12	2314.97	2304.08
160000	2576.67	2546.01	2520.92	2500.31	2483.33	2469.30	2457.69
170000	2737.72	2705.13	2678.47	2656.58	2638.53	2623.63	2611.29
180000	2898.76	2864.26	2836.03	2812.84	2793.74	2777.96	2764.90
190000	3059.80	3023.39	2993.59	2969.11	2948.95	2932.29	2918.50
200000	3220.84	3182.51	3151.15	3125.38	3104.16	3086.62	3072.11
210000	3381.88	3341.64	3308.70	3281.65	3259.36	3240.95	3225.72
220000	3542.93	3500.76	3466.26	3437.92	3414.57	3395.29	3379.32
230000	3703.97	3659.89	3623.82	3594.19	3569.78	3549.62	3532.93
240000	3865.01	3819.01	3781.37	3750.46	3724.99	3703.95	3686.53
250000	4026.05	3978.14	3938.93	3906.73	3880.20	3858.28	3840.14
260000	4187.09	4137.26	4096.49	4063.00	4035.40	4012.61	3993.74
270000	4348.14	4296.39	4254.05	4219.27	4190.61	4166.94	4147.35
280000	4509.18	4455.52	4411.60	4375.54	4345.82	4321.27	4300.95
290000	4670.22	4614.64	4569.16	4531.81	4501.03	4475.60	4454.56
300000	4831.26	4773.77	4726.72	4688.07	4656.23	4629.93	4608.16
310000	4992.31	4932.89	4884.28	4844.34	4811.44	4784.27	4761.77
320000	5153.35	5092.02	5041.83	5000.61	4966.65	4938.60	4915.38
330000	5314.39	5251.14	5199.39	5156.88	5121.86	5092.93	5068.98
340000	5475.43	5410.27	5356.95	5313.15	5277.07	5247.26	5222.59
350000	5636.47	5569.39	5514.51	5469.42	5432.27	5401.59	5376.19
400000	6441.68	6365.02	6302.29	6250.77	6208.31	6173.25	6144.22
450000	7246.89	7160.65	7090.08	7032.11	6984.35	6944.90	6912.25
500000	8052.11	7956.28	7877.86	7813.46	7760.39	7716.56	7680.27
550000	8857.32	8751.91	8665.65	8594.80	8536.43	8488.21	8448.30
600000	9662.53	9547.53	9453.44	9376.15	9312.47	9259.87	9216.33

Monthly Payments   18%
necessary to amortize a loan

AMOUNT	22 YEARS	23 YEARS	24 YEARS	25 YEARS	30 YEARS	35 YEARS	40 YEARS
100	1.53	1.53	1.52	1.52	1.51	1.50	1.50
200	3.06	3.05	3.04	3.03	3.01	3.01	3.00
500	7.65	7.63	7.60	7.59	7.54	7.51	7.51
1000	15.30	15.25	15.21	15.17	15.07	15.03	15.01
2000	30.60	30.50	30.42	30.35	30.14	30.06	30.02
5000	76.50	76.25	76.04	75.87	75.35	75.14	75.06
6000	91.80	91.50	91.25	91.05	90.43	90.17	90.07
7000	107.10	106.75	106.46	106.22	105.50	105.20	105.08
8000	122.40	122.00	121.67	121.39	120.57	120.23	120.09
9000	137.70	137.25	136.88	136.57	135.64	135.26	135.11
10000	153.00	152.50	152.09	151.74	150.71	150.29	150.12
15000	229.51	228.76	228.13	227.61	226.06	225.43	225.18
20000	306.01	305.01	304.18	303.49	301.42	300.58	300.24
25000	382.51	381.26	380.22	379.36	376.77	375.72	375.30
30000	459.01	457.51	456.27	455.23	452.13	450.87	450.35
35000	535.51	533.76	532.31	531.10	527.48	526.01	525.41
40000	612.02	610.02	608.35	606.97	602.83	601.16	600.47
45000	688.52	686.27	684.40	682.84	678.19	676.30	675.53
50000	765.02	762.52	760.44	758.71	753.54	751.45	750.59
55000	841.52	838.77	836.49	834.59	828.90	826.59	825.65
60000	918.02	915.02	912.53	910.46	904.25	901.74	900.71
65000	994.52	991.28	988.58	986.33	979.61	976.88	975.77
70000	1071.03	1067.53	1064.62	1062.20	1054.96	1052.02	1050.83
75000	1147.53	1143.78	1140.67	1138.07	1130.31	1127.17	1125.89
80000	1224.03	1220.03	1216.71	1213.94	1205.67	1202.31	1200.95
85000	1300.53	1296.28	1292.75	1289.82	1281.02	1277.46	1276.00
90000	1377.03	1372.54	1368.80	1365.69	1356.38	1352.60	1351.06
95000	1453.54	1448.79	1444.84	1441.56	1431.73	1427.75	1426.12
100000	1530.04	1525.04	1520.89	1517.43	1507.09	1502.89	1501.18
105000	1606.54	1601.29	1596.93	1593.30	1582.44	1578.04	1576.24
110000	1683.04	1677.55	1672.98	1669.17	1657.79	1653.18	1651.30
120000	1836.05	1830.05	1825.06	1820.92	1808.50	1803.47	1801.42
130000	1989.05	1982.55	1977.15	1972.66	1959.21	1953.76	1951.54
140000	2142.05	2135.06	2129.24	2124.40	2109.92	2104.05	2101.66
150000	2295.06	2287.56	2281.33	2276.14	2260.63	2254.34	2251.77
160000	2448.06	2440.07	2433.42	2427.89	2411.34	2404.63	2401.89
170000	2601.06	2592.57	2585.51	2579.63	2562.05	2554.92	2552.01
180000	2754.07	2745.07	2737.60	2731.37	2712.75	2705.21	2702.13
190000	2907.07	2897.58	2889.69	2883.12	2863.46	2855.49	2852.25
200000	3060.08	3050.08	3041.77	3034.86	3014.17	3005.78	3002.36
210000	3213.08	3202.59	3193.86	3186.60	3164.88	3156.07	3152.48
220000	3366.08	3355.09	3345.95	3338.35	3315.59	3306.36	3302.60
230000	3519.09	3507.59	3498.04	3490.09	3466.30	3456.65	3452.72
240000	3672.09	3660.10	3650.13	3641.83	3617.00	3606.94	3602.84
250000	3825.09	3812.60	3802.22	3793.57	3767.71	3757.23	3752.96
260000	3978.10	3965.11	3954.31	3945.32	3918.42	3907.52	3903.07
270000	4131.10	4117.61	4106.39	4097.06	4069.13	4057.81	4053.19
280000	4284.11	4270.12	4258.48	4248.80	4219.84	4208.10	4203.31
290000	4437.11	4422.62	4410.57	4400.55	4370.55	4358.39	4353.43
300000	4590.11	4575.12	4562.66	4552.29	4521.26	4508.68	4503.55
310000	4743.12	4727.63	4714.75	4704.03	4671.96	4658.97	4653.67
320000	4896.12	4880.13	4866.84	4855.78	4822.67	4809.25	4803.78
330000	5049.12	5032.64	5018.93	5007.52	4973.38	4959.54	4953.90
340000	5202.13	5185.14	5171.02	5159.26	5124.09	5109.83	5104.02
350000	5355.13	5337.64	5323.10	5311.00	5274.80	5260.12	5254.14
400000	6120.15	6100.16	6083.55	6069.72	6028.34	6011.57	6004.73
450000	6885.17	6862.69	6843.99	6828.43	6781.88	6763.01	6755.32
500000	7650.19	7625.21	7604.44	7587.15	7535.43	7514.46	7505.91
550000	8415.21	8387.73	8364.88	8345.86	8288.97	8265.91	8256.50
600000	9180.23	9150.25	9125.32	9104.58	9042.51	9017.35	9007.09

18¼% Monthly Payments
necessary to amortize a loan

AMOUNT	1 YEAR	2 YEARS	3 YEARS	4 YEARS	5 YEARS	6 YEARS	7 YEARS
100	9.18	5.00	3.63	2.95	2.55	2.29	2.12
200	18.36	10.01	7.26	5.90	5.11	4.59	4.23
500	45.90	25.02	18.14	14.75	12.76	11.47	10.58
1000	91.80	50.04	36.28	29.51	25.53	22.95	21.16
2000	183.60	100.09	72.56	59.01	51.06	45.90	42.33
5000	459.00	250.22	181.39	147.53	127.65	114.75	105.82
6000	550.79	300.27	217.67	177.03	153.18	137.70	126.99
7000	642.59	350.31	253.95	206.54	178.71	160.65	148.15
8000	734.39	400.36	290.22	236.05	204.24	183.59	169.32
9000	826.19	450.40	326.50	265.55	229.77	206.54	190.48
10000	917.99	500.45	362.78	295.06	255.30	229.49	211.65
15000	1376.99	750.67	544.17	442.59	382.94	344.24	317.47
20000	1835.98	1000.90	725.56	590.12	510.59	458.99	423.29
25000	2294.98	1251.12	906.95	737.64	638.24	573.73	529.12
30000	2753.97	1501.35	1088.34	885.17	765.89	688.48	634.94
35000	3212.97	1751.57	1269.73	1032.70	893.54	803.23	740.76
40000	3671.96	2001.80	1451.12	1180.23	1021.18	917.97	846.59
45000	4130.96	2252.02	1632.51	1327.76	1148.83	1032.72	952.41
50000	4589.95	2502.25	1813.90	1475.29	1276.48	1147.47	1058.23
55000	5048.95	2752.47	1995.29	1622.82	1404.13	1262.21	1164.05
60000	5507.94	3002.70	2176.68	1770.35	1531.78	1376.96	1269.88
65000	5966.94	3252.92	2358.07	1917.88	1659.43	1491.71	1375.70
70000	6425.93	3503.15	2539.46	2065.41	1787.07	1606.45	1481.52
75000	6884.93	3753.37	2720.84	2212.93	1914.72	1721.20	1587.35
80000	7343.92	4003.60	2902.23	2360.46	2042.37	1835.95	1693.17
85000	7802.92	4253.82	3083.62	2507.99	2170.02	1950.69	1798.99
90000	8261.91	4504.05	3265.01	2655.52	2297.67	2065.44	1904.82
95000	8720.91	4754.27	3446.40	2803.05	2425.31	2180.19	2010.64
100000	9179.90	5004.50	3627.79	2950.58	2552.96	2294.93	2116.46
105000	9638.90	5254.72	3809.18	3098.11	2680.61	2409.68	2222.29
110000	10097.89	5504.95	3990.57	3245.64	2808.26	2524.43	2328.11
120000	11015.88	6005.40	4353.35	3540.70	3063.55	2753.92	2539.76
130000	11933.87	6505.85	4716.13	3835.75	3318.85	2983.42	2751.40
140000	12851.86	7006.30	5078.91	4130.81	3574.15	3212.91	2963.05
150000	13769.85	7506.75	5441.69	4425.87	3829.44	3442.40	3174.69
160000	14687.84	8007.20	5804.47	4720.93	4084.74	3671.90	3386.34
170000	15605.83	8507.65	6167.25	5015.99	4340.04	3901.39	3597.99
180000	16523.82	9008.10	6530.03	5311.04	4595.33	4130.88	3809.63
190000	17441.81	9508.55	6892.81	5606.10	4850.63	4360.38	4021.28
200000	18359.80	10009.00	7255.59	5901.16	5105.92	4589.87	4232.93
210000	19277.79	10509.45	7618.37	6196.22	5361.22	4819.36	4444.57
220000	20195.78	11009.90	7981.14	6491.28	5616.52	5048.86	4656.22
230000	21113.77	11510.35	8343.92	6786.33	5871.81	5278.35	4867.86
240000	22031.76	12010.80	8706.70	7081.39	6127.11	5507.84	5079.51
250000	22949.75	12511.25	9069.48	7376.45	6382.41	5737.34	5291.16
260000	23867.74	13011.69	9432.26	7671.51	6637.70	5966.83	5502.80
270000	24785.73	13512.14	9795.04	7966.57	6893.00	6196.32	5714.45
280000	25703.72	14012.59	10157.82	8261.62	7148.29	6425.82	5926.10
290000	26621.71	14513.04	10520.60	8556.68	7403.59	6655.31	6137.74
300000	27539.70	15013.49	10883.38	8851.74	7658.89	6884.80	6349.39
310000	28457.69	15513.94	11246.16	9146.80	7914.18	7114.30	6561.03
320000	29375.68	16014.39	11608.94	9441.85	8169.48	7343.79	6772.68
330000	30293.67	16514.84	11971.72	9736.91	8424.78	7573.28	6984.33
340000	31211.66	17015.29	12334.50	10031.97	8680.07	7802.78	7195.97
350000	32129.65	17515.74	12697.28	10327.03	8935.37	8032.27	7407.62
400000	36719.61	20017.99	14511.17	11802.32	10211.85	9179.74	8465.85
450000	41309.56	22520.24	16325.07	13277.61	11488.33	10327.21	9524.08
500000	45899.51	25022.49	18138.97	14752.90	12764.81	11474.67	10582.31
550000	50489.46	27524.74	19952.86	16228.19	14041.29	12622.14	11640.54
600000	55079.41	30026.99	21766.76	17703.48	15317.77	13769.61	12698.78

216

Monthly Payments 18¼%

necessary to amortize a loan

AMOUNT	8 YEARS	9 YEARS	10 YEARS	11 YEARS	12 YEARS	13 YEARS	14 YEARS
100	1.99	1.89	1.82	1.76	1.72	1.68	1.65
200	3.98	3.78	3.64	3.52	3.43	3.36	3.30
500	9.94	9.46	9.09	8.80	8.58	8.40	8.26
1000	19.88	18.91	18.18	17.61	17.16	16.80	16.52
2000	39.75	37.83	36.36	35.22	34.32	33.61	33.03
5000	99.38	94.57	90.90	88.05	85.80	84.02	82.58
6000	119.25	113.48	109.08	105.66	102.97	100.82	99.10
7000	139.13	132.39	127.26	123.27	120.13	117.62	115.62
8000	159.00	151.31	145.44	140.88	137.29	134.43	132.13
9000	178.88	170.22	163.62	158.49	154.45	151.23	148.65
10000	198.75	189.14	181.80	176.10	171.61	168.03	165.16
15000	298.13	283.70	272.70	264.15	257.41	252.05	247.75
20000	397.50	378.27	363.60	352.20	343.22	336.07	330.33
25000	496.88	472.84	454.49	440.24	429.02	420.09	412.91
30000	596.25	567.41	545.39	528.29	514.83	504.10	495.49
35000	695.63	661.97	636.29	616.34	600.63	588.12	578.08
40000	795.00	756.54	727.19	704.39	686.43	672.14	660.66
45000	894.38	851.11	818.09	792.44	772.24	756.16	743.24
50000	993.75	945.68	908.99	880.49	858.04	840.17	825.82
55000	1093.13	1040.25	999.89	968.54	943.85	924.19	908.40
60000	1192.50	1134.81	1090.79	1056.59	1029.65	1008.21	990.99
65000	1291.88	1229.38	1181.69	1144.63	1115.45	1092.22	1073.57
70000	1391.25	1323.95	1272.58	1232.68	1201.26	1176.24	1156.15
75000	1490.63	1418.52	1363.48	1320.73	1287.06	1260.26	1238.73
80000	1590.00	1513.08	1454.38	1408.78	1372.87	1344.28	1321.32
85000	1689.38	1607.65	1545.28	1496.83	1458.67	1428.29	1403.90
90000	1788.75	1702.22	1636.18	1584.88	1544.48	1512.31	1486.48
95000	1888.13	1796.79	1727.08	1672.93	1630.28	1596.33	1569.06
100000	1987.51	1891.36	1817.98	1760.98	1716.08	1680.34	1651.65
105000	2086.88	1985.92	1908.88	1849.03	1801.89	1764.36	1734.23
110000	2186.26	2080.49	1999.78	1937.07	1887.69	1848.38	1816.81
120000	2385.01	2269.63	2181.57	2113.17	2059.30	2016.41	1981.97
130000	2583.76	2458.76	2363.37	2289.27	2230.91	2184.45	2147.14
140000	2782.51	2647.90	2545.17	2465.37	2402.52	2352.48	2312.30
150000	2981.26	2837.03	2726.97	2641.47	2574.13	2520.52	2477.47
160000	3180.01	3026.17	2908.76	2817.56	2745.74	2688.55	2642.63
170000	3378.76	3215.30	3090.56	2993.66	2917.34	2856.59	2807.80
180000	3577.51	3404.44	3272.36	3169.76	3088.95	3024.62	2972.96
190000	3776.26	3593.58	3454.16	3345.86	3260.56	3192.65	3138.13
200000	3975.01	3782.71	3635.96	3521.95	3432.17	3360.69	3303.29
210000	4173.76	3971.85	3817.75	3698.05	3603.78	3528.72	3468.46
220000	4372.51	4160.98	3999.55	3874.15	3775.39	3696.76	3633.62
230000	4571.26	4350.12	4181.35	4050.25	3946.99	3864.79	3798.78
240000	4770.01	4539.25	4363.15	4226.34	4118.60	4032.83	3963.95
250000	4968.76	4728.39	4544.94	4402.44	4290.21	4200.86	4129.11
260000	5167.51	4917.52	4726.74	4578.54	4461.82	4368.90	4294.28
270000	5366.26	5106.66	4908.54	4754.64	4633.43	4536.93	4459.44
280000	5565.01	5295.80	5090.34	4930.73	4805.04	4704.96	4624.61
290000	5763.76	5484.93	5272.14	5106.83	4976.65	4873.00	4789.77
300000	5962.52	5674.07	5453.93	5282.93	5148.25	5041.03	4954.94
310000	6161.27	5863.20	5635.73	5459.03	5319.86	5209.07	5120.10
320000	6360.02	6052.34	5817.53	5635.13	5491.47	5377.10	5285.27
330000	6558.77	6241.47	5999.33	5811.22	5663.08	5545.14	5450.43
340000	6757.52	6430.61	6181.12	5987.32	5834.69	5713.17	5615.59
350000	6956.27	6619.74	6362.92	6163.42	6006.30	5881.21	5780.76
400000	7950.02	7565.42	7271.91	7043.91	6864.34	6721.38	6606.58
450000	8943.77	8511.10	8180.90	7924.40	7722.38	7561.55	7432.40
500000	9937.53	9456.78	9089.89	8804.88	8580.42	8401.72	8258.23
550000	10931.28	10402.46	9998.88	9685.37	9438.46	9241.89	9084.05
600000	11925.03	11348.13	10907.87	10565.86	10296.51	10082.07	9909.87

18¹/₄%

Monthly Payments
necessary to amortize a loan

AMOUNT	15 YEARS	16 YEARS	17 YEARS	18 YEARS	19 YEARS	20 YEARS	21 YEARS
100	1.63	1.61	1.59	1.58	1.57	1.56	1.56
200	3.26	3.22	3.19	3.16	3.14	3.13	3.11
500	8.14	8.05	7.97	7.91	7.86	7.81	7.78
1000	16.28	16.10	15.94	15.82	15.71	15.63	15.56
2000	32.57	32.19	31.88	31.63	31.42	31.25	31.11
5000	81.42	80.48	79.71	79.08	78.56	78.13	77.78
6000	97.71	96.57	95.65	94.89	94.27	93.75	93.33
7000	113.99	112.67	111.59	110.71	109.98	109.38	108.89
8000	130.28	128.77	127.53	126.52	125.69	125.01	124.44
9000	146.56	144.86	143.47	142.34	141.40	140.63	140.00
10000	162.84	160.96	159.42	158.15	157.11	156.26	155.55
15000	244.27	241.44	239.12	237.23	235.67	234.39	233.33
20000	325.69	321.91	318.83	316.31	314.23	312.52	311.10
25000	407.11	402.39	398.54	395.38	392.79	390.64	388.88
30000	488.53	482.87	478.25	474.46	471.34	468.77	466.65
35000	569.95	563.35	557.96	553.54	549.90	546.90	544.43
40000	651.38	643.83	637.67	632.61	628.46	625.03	622.20
45000	732.80	724.31	717.37	711.69	707.01	703.16	699.98
50000	814.22	804.79	797.08	790.76	785.57	781.29	777.75
55000	895.64	885.27	876.79	869.84	864.13	859.42	855.53
60000	977.06	965.74	956.50	948.92	942.68	937.55	933.30
65000	1058.49	1046.22	1036.21	1027.99	1021.24	1015.68	1011.08
70000	1139.91	1126.70	1115.91	1107.07	1099.80	1093.80	1088.85
75000	1221.33	1207.18	1195.62	1186.15	1178.36	1171.93	1166.63
80000	1302.75	1287.66	1275.33	1265.22	1256.91	1250.06	1244.40
85000	1384.17	1368.14	1355.04	1344.30	1335.47	1328.19	1322.18
90000	1465.60	1448.62	1434.75	1423.38	1414.03	1406.32	1399.95
95000	1547.02	1529.09	1514.45	1502.45	1492.58	1484.45	1477.73
100000	1628.44	1609.57	1594.16	1581.53	1571.14	1562.58	1555.50
105000	1709.86	1690.05	1673.87	1660.61	1649.70	1640.71	1633.28
110000	1791.28	1770.53	1753.58	1739.68	1728.26	1718.84	1711.05
120000	1954.13	1931.49	1913.00	1897.84	1885.37	1875.09	1866.61
130000	2116.97	2092.44	2072.41	2055.99	2042.48	2031.35	2022.16
140000	2279.82	2253.40	2231.83	2214.14	2199.60	2187.61	2177.71
150000	2442.66	2414.36	2391.24	2372.29	2356.71	2343.87	2333.26
160000	2605.50	2575.32	2550.66	2530.45	2513.83	2500.12	2488.81
170000	2768.35	2736.27	2710.08	2688.60	2670.94	2656.38	2644.36
180000	2931.19	2897.23	2869.49	2846.75	2828.05	2812.64	2799.91
190000	3094.04	3058.19	3028.91	3004.91	2985.17	2968.90	2955.46
200000	3256.88	3219.15	3188.33	3163.06	3142.28	3125.16	3111.01
210000	3419.72	3380.10	3347.74	3321.21	3299.40	3281.41	3266.56
220000	3582.57	3541.06	3507.16	3479.36	3456.51	3437.67	3422.11
230000	3745.41	3702.02	3666.57	3637.52	3613.62	3593.93	3577.66
240000	3908.26	3862.97	3825.99	3795.67	3770.74	3750.19	3733.21
250000	4071.10	4023.93	3985.41	3953.82	3927.85	3906.44	3888.76
260000	4233.94	4184.89	4144.82	4111.98	4084.97	4062.70	4044.31
270000	4396.79	4345.85	4304.24	4270.13	4242.08	4218.96	4199.86
280000	4559.63	4506.80	4463.66	4428.28	4399.20	4375.22	4355.41
290000	4722.48	4667.76	4623.07	4586.43	4556.31	4531.48	4510.96
300000	4885.32	4828.72	4782.49	4744.59	4713.42	4687.73	4666.51
310000	5048.17	4989.68	4941.90	4902.74	4870.54	4843.99	4822.06
320000	5211.01	5150.63	5101.32	5060.89	5027.65	5000.25	4977.61
330000	5373.85	5311.59	5260.74	5219.05	5184.77	5156.51	5133.16
340000	5536.70	5472.55	5420.15	5377.20	5341.88	5312.76	5288.72
350000	5699.54	5633.51	5579.57	5535.35	5498.99	5469.02	5444.27
400000	6513.76	6438.29	6376.65	6326.12	6284.56	6250.31	6222.02
450000	7327.98	7243.08	7173.73	7116.88	7070.14	7031.60	6999.77
500000	8142.20	8047.86	7970.81	7907.65	7855.71	7812.89	7777.52
550000	8956.42	8852.65	8767.89	8698.41	8641.28	8594.18	8555.27
600000	9770.64	9657.44	9564.98	9489.18	9426.85	9375.47	9333.03

Monthly Payments 18¼%
necessary to amortize a loan

AMOUNT	22 YEARS	23 YEARS	24 YEARS	25 YEARS	30 YEARS	35 YEARS	40 YEARS
100	1.55	1.54	1.54	1.54	1.53	1.52	1.52
200	3.10	3.09	3.08	3.07	3.06	3.05	3.04
500	7.75	7.72	7.70	7.69	7.64	7.62	7.61
1000	15.50	15.45	15.41	15.37	15.28	15.24	15.22
2000	30.99	30.90	30.82	30.75	30.55	30.47	30.44
5000	77.48	77.24	77.04	76.87	76.38	76.18	76.10
6000	92.98	92.69	92.45	92.25	91.65	91.41	91.32
7000	108.48	108.14	107.85	107.62	106.93	106.65	106.53
8000	123.97	123.58	123.26	123.00	122.20	121.88	121.75
9000	139.47	139.03	138.67	138.37	137.48	137.12	136.97
10000	154.97	154.48	154.08	153.74	152.75	152.35	152.19
15000	232.45	231.72	231.12	230.62	229.13	228.53	228.29
20000	309.93	308.96	308.16	307.49	305.50	304.70	304.38
25000	387.41	386.20	385.19	384.36	381.88	380.88	380.48
30000	464.90	463.44	462.23	461.23	458.25	457.06	456.58
35000	542.38	540.68	539.27	538.10	534.63	533.23	532.67
40000	619.86	617.92	616.31	614.98	611.00	609.41	608.77
45000	697.34	695.16	693.35	691.85	687.38	685.59	684.86
50000	774.83	772.40	770.39	768.72	763.75	761.76	760.96
55000	852.31	849.64	847.43	845.59	840.13	837.94	837.06
60000	929.79	926.88	924.47	922.46	916.50	914.11	913.15
65000	1007.27	1004.12	1001.51	999.34	992.88	990.29	989.25
70000	1084.76	1081.36	1078.55	1076.21	1069.25	1066.47	1065.34
75000	1162.24	1158.60	1155.58	1153.08	1145.63	1142.64	1141.44
80000	1239.72	1235.84	1232.62	1229.95	1222.00	1218.82	1217.54
85000	1317.20	1313.08	1309.66	1306.82	1298.38	1294.99	1293.63
90000	1394.69	1390.32	1386.70	1383.69	1374.75	1371.17	1369.73
95000	1472.17	1467.56	1463.74	1460.57	1451.13	1447.35	1445.82
100000	1549.65	1544.80	1540.78	1537.44	1527.50	1523.52	1521.92
105000	1627.13	1622.04	1617.82	1614.31	1603.88	1599.70	1598.02
110000	1704.62	1699.28	1694.86	1691.18	1680.25	1675.88	1674.11
120000	1859.58	1853.76	1848.93	1844.93	1833.00	1828.23	1826.30
130000	2014.55	2008.24	2003.01	1998.67	1985.75	1980.58	1978.50
140000	2169.51	2162.72	2157.09	2152.41	2138.50	2132.93	2130.69
150000	2324.48	2317.20	2311.17	2306.16	2291.25	2285.28	2282.88
160000	2479.44	2471.68	2465.25	2459.90	2444.01	2437.64	2435.07
170000	2634.41	2626.16	2619.32	2613.65	2596.76	2589.99	2587.26
180000	2789.37	2780.64	2773.40	2767.39	2749.51	2742.34	2739.46
190000	2944.34	2935.12	2927.48	2921.13	2902.26	2894.69	2891.65
200000	3099.30	3089.60	3081.56	3074.88	3055.01	3047.05	3043.84
210000	3254.27	3244.08	3235.64	3228.62	3207.76	3199.40	3196.03
220000	3409.23	3398.56	3389.71	3382.36	3360.51	3351.75	3348.22
230000	3564.20	3553.04	3543.79	3536.11	3513.26	3504.10	3500.41
240000	3719.16	3707.52	3697.87	3689.85	3666.01	3656.45	3652.61
250000	3874.13	3862.01	3851.95	3843.60	3818.76	3808.81	3804.80
260000	4029.09	4016.49	4006.03	3997.34	3971.51	3961.16	3956.99
270000	4184.06	4170.97	4160.10	4151.08	4124.26	4113.51	4109.18
280000	4339.02	4325.45	4314.18	4304.83	4277.01	4265.86	4261.37
290000	4493.99	4479.93	4468.26	4458.57	4429.76	4418.22	4413.57
300000	4648.95	4634.41	4622.34	4612.32	4582.51	4570.57	4565.76
310000	4803.92	4788.89	4776.42	4766.06	4735.26	4722.92	4717.95
320000	4958.89	4943.37	4930.49	4919.80	4888.01	4875.27	4870.14
330000	5113.85	5097.85	5084.57	5073.55	5040.76	5027.63	5022.33
340000	5268.82	5252.33	5238.65	5227.29	5193.51	5179.98	5174.53
350000	5423.78	5406.81	5392.73	5381.04	5346.26	5332.33	5326.72
400000	6198.61	6179.21	6163.12	6149.75	6110.01	6094.09	6087.68
450000	6973.43	6951.61	6933.51	6918.47	6873.76	6855.85	6848.64
500000	7748.26	7724.01	7703.90	7687.19	7637.52	7617.61	7609.60
550000	8523.08	8496.41	8474.28	8455.91	8401.27	8379.38	8370.56
600000	9297.91	9268.81	9244.67	9224.63	9165.02	9141.14	9131.52

18½%

Monthly Payments
necessary to amortize a loan

AMOUNT	1 YEAR	2 YEARS	3 YEARS	4 YEARS	5 YEARS	6 YEARS	7 YEARS
100	9.19	5.02	3.64	2.96	2.57	2.31	2.13
200	18.38	10.03	7.28	5.93	5.13	4.62	4.26
500	45.96	25.08	18.20	14.82	12.83	11.55	10.66
1000	91.92	50.17	36.40	29.64	25.67	23.09	21.31
2000	183.84	100.33	72.81	59.27	51.33	46.18	42.62
5000	459.59	250.83	182.02	148.18	128.33	115.46	106.56
6000	551.51	301.00	218.42	177.82	154.00	138.55	127.87
7000	643.43	351.16	254.83	207.46	179.66	161.64	149.18
8000	735.34	401.33	291.23	237.10	205.33	184.73	170.50
9000	827.26	451.49	327.63	266.73	231.00	207.82	191.81
10000	919.18	501.66	364.04	296.37	256.66	230.91	213.12
15000	1378.77	752.49	546.06	444.55	384.99	346.37	319.68
20000	1838.36	1003.32	728.07	592.74	513.32	461.83	426.24
25000	2297.95	1254.15	910.09	740.92	641.66	577.28	532.80
30000	2757.54	1504.98	1092.11	889.11	769.99	692.74	639.36
35000	3217.13	1755.81	1274.13	1037.29	898.32	808.20	745.92
40000	3676.72	2006.64	1456.15	1185.48	1026.65	923.65	852.48
45000	4136.32	2257.47	1638.17	1333.66	1154.98	1039.11	959.04
50000	4595.91	2508.30	1820.19	1481.85	1283.31	1154.57	1065.60
55000	5055.50	2759.13	2002.20	1630.03	1411.64	1270.02	1172.16
60000	5515.09	3009.96	2184.22	1778.21	1539.97	1385.48	1278.72
65000	5974.68	3260.79	2366.24	1926.40	1668.30	1500.94	1385.27
70000	6434.27	3511.62	2548.26	2074.58	1796.63	1616.39	1491.83
75000	6893.86	3762.45	2730.28	2222.77	1924.97	1731.85	1598.39
80000	7353.45	4013.28	2912.30	2370.95	2053.30	1847.31	1704.95
85000	7813.04	4264.11	3094.32	2519.14	2181.63	1962.77	1811.51
90000	8272.63	4514.94	3276.33	2667.32	2309.96	2078.22	1918.07
95000	8732.22	4765.77	3458.35	2815.51	2438.29	2193.68	2024.63
100000	9191.81	5016.60	3640.37	2963.69	2566.62	2309.14	2131.19
105000	9651.40	5267.43	3822.39	3111.88	2694.95	2424.59	2237.75
110000	10110.99	5518.26	4004.41	3260.06	2823.28	2540.05	2344.30
120000	11030.17	6019.92	4368.45	3556.43	3079.95	2770.96	2557.43
130000	11949.36	6521.58	4732.48	3852.80	3336.61	3001.88	2770.55
140000	12868.54	7023.24	5096.52	4149.17	3593.27	3232.79	2983.67
150000	13787.72	7524.90	5460.56	4445.54	3849.93	3463.70	3196.79
160000	14706.90	8026.56	5824.59	4741.91	4106.59	3694.62	3409.91
170000	15626.08	8528.22	6188.63	5038.28	4363.26	3925.53	3623.03
180000	16545.26	9029.88	6552.67	5334.64	4619.92	4156.44	3836.15
190000	17464.44	9531.54	6916.71	5631.01	4876.58	4387.36	4049.26
200000	18383.62	10033.21	7280.74	5927.38	5133.24	4618.27	4262.38
210000	19302.80	10534.87	7644.78	6223.75	5389.90	4849.18	4475.50
220000	20221.99	11036.53	8008.82	6520.12	5646.57	5080.10	4688.62
230000	21141.17	11538.19	8372.85	6816.49	5903.23	5311.01	4901.74
240000	22060.35	12039.85	8736.89	7112.86	6159.89	5541.93	5114.86
250000	22979.53	12541.51	9100.93	7409.23	6416.55	5772.84	5327.98
260000	23898.71	13043.17	9464.97	7705.60	6673.21	6003.75	5541.10
270000	24817.89	13544.83	9829.00	8001.97	6929.88	6234.67	5754.22
280000	25737.07	14046.49	10193.04	8298.34	7186.54	6465.58	5967.34
290000	26656.25	14548.15	10557.08	8594.71	7443.20	6696.49	6180.46
300000	27575.44	15049.81	10921.11	8891.07	7699.86	6927.41	6393.58
310000	28494.62	15551.47	11285.15	9187.44	7956.52	7158.32	6606.69
320000	29413.80	16053.13	11649.19	9483.81	8213.19	7389.23	6819.81
330000	30332.98	16554.79	12013.23	9780.18	8469.85	7620.15	7032.93
340000	31252.16	17056.45	12377.26	10076.55	8726.51	7851.06	7246.05
350000	32171.34	17558.11	12741.30	10372.92	8983.17	8081.97	7459.17
400000	36767.25	20066.41	14561.49	11854.77	10266.48	9236.54	8524.77
450000	41363.15	22574.71	16381.67	13336.61	11549.79	10391.11	9590.36
500000	45959.06	25083.01	18201.86	14818.46	12833.10	11545.68	10655.96
550000	50554.96	27591.31	20022.04	16300.30	14116.42	12700.24	11721.56
600000	55150.87	30099.62	21842.23	17782.15	15399.73	13854.81	12787.15

AMOUNT	8 YEARS	9 YEARS	10 YEARS	11 YEARS	12 YEARS	13 YEARS	14 YEARS
100	2.00	1.91	1.83	1.78	1.73	1.70	1.67
200	4.01	3.81	3.67	3.56	3.47	3.40	3.34
500	10.01	9.54	9.17	8.89	8.67	8.49	8.35
1000	20.03	19.07	18.34	17.78	17.33	16.98	16.69
2000	40.05	38.14	36.68	35.55	34.66	33.96	33.39
5000	100.14	95.35	91.71	88.88	86.66	84.89	83.47
6000	120.16	114.42	110.05	106.66	103.99	101.87	100.16
7000	140.19	133.50	128.39	124.43	121.32	118.84	116.86
8000	160.22	152.57	146.73	142.21	138.65	135.82	133.55
9000	180.25	171.64	165.07	159.98	155.98	152.80	150.25
10000	200.27	190.71	183.42	177.76	173.31	169.78	166.94
15000	300.41	286.06	275.12	266.64	259.97	254.66	250.41
20000	400.55	381.42	366.83	355.52	346.62	339.55	333.88
25000	500.69	476.77	458.54	444.40	433.28	424.44	417.35
30000	600.82	572.12	550.25	533.28	519.93	509.33	500.82
35000	700.96	667.48	641.96	622.16	606.59	594.21	584.29
40000	801.10	762.83	733.67	711.04	693.25	679.10	667.76
45000	901.23	858.19	825.37	799.92	779.90	763.99	751.23
50000	1001.37	953.54	917.08	888.80	866.56	848.88	834.70
55000	1101.51	1048.89	1008.79	977.68	953.21	933.76	918.17
60000	1201.65	1144.25	1100.50	1066.56	1039.87	1018.65	1001.64
65000	1301.78	1239.60	1192.21	1155.44	1126.52	1103.54	1085.11
70000	1401.92	1334.96	1283.92	1244.32	1213.18	1188.43	1168.58
75000	1502.06	1430.31	1375.62	1333.20	1299.84	1273.31	1252.05
80000	1602.20	1525.67	1467.33	1422.08	1386.49	1358.20	1335.52
85000	1702.33	1621.02	1559.04	1510.96	1473.15	1443.09	1418.99
90000	1802.47	1716.37	1650.75	1599.84	1559.80	1527.98	1502.46
95000	1902.61	1811.73	1742.46	1688.72	1646.46	1612.87	1585.93
100000	2002.74	1907.08	1834.17	1777.60	1733.11	1697.76	1669.41
105000	2102.88	2002.44	1925.87	1866.48	1819.77	1782.64	1752.88
110000	2203.02	2097.79	2017.58	1955.36	1906.43	1867.53	1836.35
120000	2403.29	2288.50	2201.00	2133.12	2079.74	2037.30	2003.29
130000	2603.57	2479.21	2384.42	2310.88	2253.05	2207.08	2170.23
140000	2803.84	2669.91	2567.83	2488.64	2426.36	2376.85	2337.17
150000	3004.12	2860.62	2751.25	2666.40	2599.67	2546.63	2504.11
160000	3204.39	3051.33	2934.66	2844.16	2772.98	2716.41	2671.05
170000	3404.66	3242.04	3118.08	3021.92	2946.29	2886.18	2837.99
180000	3604.94	3432.75	3301.50	3199.68	3119.61	3055.96	3004.93
190000	3805.21	3623.45	3484.91	3377.44	3292.92	3225.73	3171.87
200000	4005.49	3814.16	3668.33	3555.20	3466.23	3395.51	3338.81
210000	4205.76	4004.87	3851.75	3732.96	3639.54	3565.28	3505.75
220000	4406.04	4195.58	4035.16	3910.72	3812.85	3735.06	3672.69
230000	4606.31	4386.29	4218.58	4088.48	3986.16	3904.83	3839.63
240000	4806.59	4577.00	4402.00	4266.24	4159.47	4074.61	4006.57
250000	5006.86	4767.70	4585.41	4444.00	4332.79	4244.38	4173.51
260000	5207.13	4958.41	4768.83	4621.76	4506.10	4414.16	4340.45
270000	5407.41	5149.12	4952.25	4799.52	4679.41	4583.93	4507.39
280000	5607.68	5339.83	5135.66	4977.28	4852.72	4753.71	4674.33
290000	5807.96	5530.54	5319.08	5155.04	5026.03	4923.48	4841.27
300000	6008.23	5721.24	5502.50	5332.80	5199.34	5093.26	5008.22
310000	6208.51	5911.95	5685.91	5510.56	5372.65	5263.04	5175.16
320000	6408.78	6102.66	5869.33	5688.32	5545.97	5432.81	5342.10
330000	6609.06	6293.37	6052.75	5866.08	5719.28	5602.59	5509.04
340000	6809.33	6484.08	6236.16	6043.84	5892.59	5772.36	5675.98
350000	7009.60	6674.79	6419.58	6221.60	6065.90	5942.14	5842.92
400000	8010.98	7628.33	7336.66	7110.40	6932.46	6791.01	6677.62
450000	9012.35	8581.87	8253.74	7999.20	7799.01	7639.89	7512.32
500000	10013.72	9535.41	9170.83	8888.00	8665.57	8488.77	8347.03
550000	11015.09	10488.95	10087.91	9776.80	9532.13	9337.64	9181.73
600000	12016.46	11442.49	11004.99	10665.60	10398.69	10186.52	10016.43

18½%

Monthly Payments
necessary to amortize a loan

AMOUNT	15 YEARS	16 YEARS	17 YEARS	18 YEARS	19 YEARS	20 YEARS	21 YEARS
100	1.65	1.63	1.61	1.60	1.59	1.58	1.58
200	3.29	3.26	3.23	3.20	3.18	3.16	3.15
500	8.23	8.14	8.06	8.00	7.95	7.91	7.88
1000	16.47	16.28	16.13	16.00	15.90	15.82	15.75
2000	32.93	32.56	32.26	32.01	31.81	31.64	31.50
5000	82.33	81.40	80.64	80.02	79.51	79.09	78.75
6000	98.79	97.68	96.77	96.03	95.42	94.91	94.50
7000	115.26	113.96	112.90	112.03	111.32	110.73	110.25
8000	131.72	130.24	129.02	128.03	127.22	126.55	126.00
9000	148.19	146.52	145.15	144.04	143.12	142.37	141.75
10000	164.65	162.80	161.28	160.04	159.03	158.19	157.50
15000	246.98	244.19	241.92	240.06	238.54	237.28	236.25
20000	329.30	325.59	322.56	320.08	318.05	316.38	315.00
25000	411.63	406.99	403.20	400.11	397.56	395.47	393.75
30000	493.96	488.39	483.84	480.13	477.08	474.57	472.50
35000	576.28	569.78	564.48	560.15	556.59	553.66	551.25
40000	658.61	651.18	645.12	640.17	636.10	632.76	630.00
45000	740.94	732.58	725.77	720.19	715.62	711.85	708.75
50000	823.26	813.98	806.41	800.21	795.13	790.95	787.50
55000	905.59	895.37	887.05	880.23	874.64	870.04	866.25
60000	987.91	976.77	967.69	960.25	954.16	949.14	945.00
65000	1070.24	1058.17	1048.33	1040.28	1033.67	1028.23	1023.75
70000	1152.57	1139.57	1128.97	1120.30	1113.18	1107.33	1102.50
75000	1234.89	1220.96	1209.61	1200.32	1192.69	1186.42	1181.25
80000	1317.22	1302.36	1290.25	1280.34	1272.21	1265.52	1260.00
85000	1399.54	1383.76	1370.89	1360.36	1351.72	1344.61	1338.75
90000	1481.87	1465.16	1451.53	1440.38	1431.23	1423.71	1417.50
95000	1564.20	1546.55	1532.17	1520.40	1510.75	1502.80	1496.25
100000	1646.52	1627.95	1612.81	1600.42	1590.26	1581.90	1575.00
105000	1728.85	1709.35	1693.45	1680.45	1669.77	1660.99	1653.75
110000	1811.18	1790.75	1774.09	1760.47	1749.29	1740.09	1732.50
120000	1975.83	1953.54	1935.37	1920.51	1908.31	1898.28	1890.00
130000	2140.48	2116.34	2096.66	2080.55	2067.34	2056.47	2047.50
140000	2305.13	2279.13	2257.94	2240.59	2226.36	2214.66	2205.00
150000	2469.79	2441.93	2419.22	2400.64	2385.39	2372.84	2362.50
160000	2634.44	2604.72	2580.50	2560.68	2544.41	2531.03	2520.01
170000	2799.09	2767.52	2741.78	2720.72	2703.44	2689.22	2677.51
180000	2963.74	2930.31	2903.06	2880.76	2862.47	2847.41	2835.01
190000	3128.39	3093.11	3064.34	3040.81	3021.49	3005.60	2992.51
200000	3293.05	3255.90	3225.62	3200.85	3180.52	3163.79	3150.01
210000	3457.70	3418.70	3386.91	3360.89	3339.54	3321.98	3307.51
220000	3622.35	3581.50	3548.19	3520.93	3498.57	3480.17	3465.01
230000	3787.00	3744.29	3709.47	3680.98	3657.60	3638.36	3622.51
240000	3951.66	3907.09	3870.75	3841.02	3816.62	3796.55	3780.01
250000	4116.31	4069.88	4032.03	4001.06	3975.65	3954.74	3937.51
260000	4280.96	4232.68	4193.31	4161.10	4134.67	4112.93	4095.01
270000	4445.61	4395.47	4354.59	4321.15	4293.70	4271.12	4252.51
280000	4610.27	4558.27	4515.87	4481.19	4452.73	4429.31	4410.01
290000	4774.92	4721.06	4677.16	4641.23	4611.75	4587.50	4567.51
300000	4939.57	4883.86	4838.44	4801.27	4770.78	4745.69	4725.01
310000	5104.22	5046.65	4999.72	4961.32	4929.80	4903.88	4882.51
320000	5268.87	5209.45	5161.00	5121.36	5088.83	5062.07	5040.01
330000	5433.53	5372.24	5322.28	5281.40	5247.86	5220.26	5197.51
340000	5598.18	5535.04	5483.56	5441.44	5406.88	5378.45	5355.01
350000	5762.83	5697.83	5644.84	5601.49	5565.91	5536.64	5512.51
400000	6586.09	6511.81	6451.25	6401.70	6361.04	6327.59	6300.01
450000	7409.36	7325.79	7257.66	7201.91	7156.17	7118.53	7087.51
500000	8232.62	8139.76	8064.06	8002.12	7951.30	7909.48	7875.02
550000	9055.88	8953.74	8870.47	8802.34	8746.43	8700.43	8662.52
600000	9879.14	9767.71	9676.87	9602.55	9541.56	9491.38	9450.02

Monthly Payments 18½%
necessary to amortize a loan

AMOUNT	22 YEARS	23 YEARS	24 YEARS	25 YEARS	30 YEARS	35 YEARS	40 YEARS
100	1.57	1.56	1.56	1.56	1.55	1.54	1.54
200	3.14	3.13	3.12	3.11	3.10	3.09	3.09
500	7.85	7.82	7.80	7.79	7.74	7.72	7.71
1000	15.69	15.65	15.61	15.57	15.48	15.44	15.43
2000	31.39	31.29	31.21	31.15	30.96	30.88	30.85
5000	78.47	78.23	78.04	77.87	77.40	77.21	77.13
6000	94.16	93.88	93.64	93.45	92.88	92.65	92.56
7000	109.85	109.52	109.25	109.02	108.36	108.09	107.99
8000	125.54	125.17	124.86	124.60	123.84	123.53	123.41
9000	141.24	140.81	140.46	140.17	139.32	138.98	138.84
10000	156.93	156.46	156.07	155.75	154.79	154.42	154.27
15000	235.40	234.69	234.11	233.62	232.19	231.63	231.40
20000	313.86	312.92	312.14	311.50	309.59	308.83	308.53
25000	392.33	391.15	390.18	389.37	386.99	386.04	385.67
30000	470.79	469.38	468.21	467.25	464.38	463.25	462.80
35000	549.26	547.61	546.25	545.12	541.78	540.46	539.93
40000	627.72	625.84	624.28	622.99	619.18	617.67	617.07
45000	706.19	704.07	702.32	700.87	696.58	694.88	694.20
50000	784.66	782.30	780.36	778.74	773.97	772.08	771.33
55000	863.12	860.53	858.39	856.62	851.37	849.29	848.47
60000	941.59	938.76	936.43	934.49	928.77	926.50	925.60
65000	1020.05	1016.99	1014.46	1012.36	1006.16	1003.71	1002.73
70000	1098.52	1095.22	1092.50	1090.24	1083.56	1080.92	1079.87
75000	1176.98	1173.45	1170.53	1168.11	1160.96	1158.13	1157.00
80000	1255.45	1251.68	1248.57	1245.99	1238.36	1235.33	1234.13
85000	1333.91	1329.92	1326.60	1323.86	1315.75	1312.54	1311.26
90000	1412.38	1408.15	1404.64	1401.74	1393.15	1389.75	1388.40
95000	1490.85	1486.38	1482.68	1479.61	1470.55	1466.96	1465.53
100000	1569.31	1564.61	1560.71	1557.48	1547.94	1544.17	1542.66
105000	1647.78	1642.84	1638.75	1635.36	1625.34	1621.38	1619.80
110000	1726.24	1721.07	1716.78	1713.23	1702.74	1698.58	1696.93
120000	1883.17	1877.53	1872.85	1868.98	1857.53	1853.00	1851.20
130000	2040.11	2033.99	2028.92	2024.73	2012.33	2007.42	2005.46
140000	2197.04	2190.45	2185.00	2180.48	2167.12	2161.83	2159.73
150000	2353.97	2346.91	2341.07	2336.23	2321.92	2316.25	2314.00
160000	2510.90	2503.37	2497.14	2491.97	2476.71	2470.67	2468.26
170000	2667.83	2659.83	2653.21	2647.72	2631.51	2625.08	2622.53
180000	2824.76	2816.29	2809.28	2803.47	2786.30	2779.50	2776.80
190000	2981.69	2972.75	2965.35	2959.22	2941.09	2933.92	2931.06
200000	3138.62	3129.21	3121.42	3114.97	3095.89	3088.34	3085.33
210000	3295.55	3285.67	3277.49	3270.72	3250.68	3242.75	3239.60
220000	3452.49	3442.13	3433.56	3426.47	3405.48	3397.17	3393.86
230000	3609.42	3598.59	3589.64	3582.21	3560.27	3551.59	3548.13
240000	3766.35	3755.05	3745.71	3737.96	3715.07	3706.00	3702.39
250000	3923.28	3911.52	3901.78	3893.71	3869.86	3860.42	3856.66
260000	4080.21	4067.98	4057.85	4049.46	4024.66	4014.84	4010.93
270000	4237.14	4224.44	4213.92	4205.21	4179.45	4169.25	4165.19
280000	4394.07	4380.90	4369.99	4360.96	4334.24	4323.67	4319.46
290000	4551.00	4537.36	4526.06	4516.70	4489.04	4478.09	4473.73
300000	4707.94	4693.82	4682.13	4672.45	4643.83	4632.50	4627.99
310000	4864.87	4850.28	4838.20	4828.20	4798.63	4786.92	4782.26
320000	5021.80	5006.74	4994.28	4983.95	4953.42	4941.34	4936.53
330000	5178.73	5163.20	5150.35	5139.70	5108.22	5095.75	5090.79
340000	5335.66	5319.66	5306.42	5295.45	5263.01	5250.17	5245.06
350000	5492.59	5476.12	5462.49	5451.19	5417.81	5404.59	5399.33
400000	6277.25	6258.42	6242.84	6229.94	6191.78	6176.67	6170.66
450000	7061.90	7040.73	7023.20	7008.68	6965.75	6948.75	6941.99
500000	7846.56	7823.03	7803.56	7787.42	7739.72	7720.84	7713.32
550000	8631.21	8605.33	8583.91	8566.16	8513.69	8492.92	8484.65
600000	9415.87	9387.64	9364.27	9344.90	9287.67	9265.01	9255.99

18¾%

Monthly Payments
necessary to amortize a loan

AMOUNT	1 YEAR	2 YEARS	3 YEARS	4 YEARS	5 YEARS	6 YEARS	7 YEARS
100	9.20	5.03	3.65	2.98	2.58	2.32	2.15
200	18.41	10.06	7.31	5.95	5.16	4.65	4.29
500	46.02	25.14	18.26	14.88	12.90	11.62	10.73
1000	92.04	50.29	36.53	29.77	25.80	23.23	21.46
2000	184.07	100.57	73.06	59.54	51.61	46.47	42.92
5000	460.19	251.44	182.65	148.84	129.02	116.17	107.30
6000	552.22	301.72	219.18	178.61	154.82	139.40	128.76
7000	644.26	352.01	255.71	208.38	180.62	162.64	150.22
8000	736.30	402.30	292.24	238.15	206.43	185.87	171.68
9000	828.34	452.59	328.77	267.92	232.23	209.10	193.14
10000	920.37	502.87	365.30	297.68	258.03	232.34	214.60
15000	1380.56	754.31	547.95	446.53	387.05	348.51	321.90
20000	1840.75	1005.74	730.59	595.37	516.06	464.68	429.19
25000	2300.93	1257.18	913.24	744.21	645.08	580.85	536.49
30000	2761.12	1508.62	1095.89	893.05	774.10	697.01	643.79
35000	3221.31	1760.05	1278.54	1041.89	903.11	813.18	751.09
40000	3681.49	2011.49	1461.19	1190.73	1032.13	929.35	858.39
45000	4141.68	2262.93	1643.84	1339.58	1161.14	1045.52	965.69
50000	4601.87	2514.36	1826.49	1488.42	1290.16	1161.69	1072.99
55000	5062.05	2765.80	2009.14	1637.26	1419.18	1277.86	1180.28
60000	5522.24	3017.23	2191.78	1786.10	1548.19	1394.03	1287.58
65000	5982.42	3268.67	2374.43	1934.94	1677.21	1510.20	1394.88
70000	6442.61	3520.11	2557.08	2083.78	1806.22	1626.37	1502.18
75000	6902.80	3771.54	2739.73	2232.63	1935.24	1742.54	1609.48
80000	7362.98	4022.98	2922.38	2381.47	2064.25	1858.71	1716.78
85000	7823.17	4274.42	3105.03	2530.31	2193.27	1974.87	1824.08
90000	8283.36	4525.85	3287.68	2679.15	2322.29	2091.04	1931.37
95000	8743.54	4777.29	3470.33	2827.99	2451.30	2207.21	2038.67
100000	9203.73	5028.72	3652.97	2976.84	2580.32	2323.38	2145.97
105000	9663.92	5280.16	3835.62	3125.68	2709.33	2439.55	2253.27
110000	10124.10	5531.60	4018.27	3274.52	2838.35	2555.72	2360.57
120000	11044.48	6034.47	4383.57	3572.20	3096.38	2788.06	2575.17
130000	11964.85	6537.34	4748.87	3869.89	3354.41	3020.40	2789.76
140000	12885.22	7040.21	5114.16	4167.57	3612.45	3252.73	3004.36
150000	13805.60	7543.09	5479.46	4465.25	3870.48	3485.07	3218.96
160000	14725.97	8045.96	5844.76	4762.94	4128.51	3717.41	3433.55
170000	15646.34	8548.83	6210.06	5060.62	4386.54	3949.75	3648.15
180000	16566.72	9051.70	6575.35	5358.30	4644.57	4182.09	3862.75
190000	17487.09	9554.58	6940.65	5655.99	4902.61	4414.42	4077.35
200000	18407.46	10057.45	7305.95	5953.67	5160.64	4646.76	4291.94
210000	19327.83	10560.32	7671.25	6251.35	5418.67	4879.10	4506.54
220000	20248.21	11063.19	8036.54	6549.04	5676.70	5111.44	4721.14
230000	21168.58	11566.06	8401.84	6846.72	5934.73	5343.78	4935.74
240000	22088.95	12068.94	8767.14	7144.41	6192.76	5576.12	5150.33
250000	23009.33	12571.81	9132.44	7442.09	6450.80	5808.45	5364.93
260000	23929.70	13074.68	9497.73	7739.77	6708.83	6040.79	5579.53
270000	24850.07	13577.55	9863.03	8037.46	6966.86	6273.13	5794.12
280000	25770.45	14080.43	10228.33	8335.14	7224.89	6505.47	6008.72
290000	26690.82	14583.30	10593.63	8632.82	7482.92	6737.81	6223.32
300000	27611.19	15086.17	10958.92	8930.51	7740.96	6970.14	6437.92
310000	28531.56	15589.04	11324.22	9228.19	7998.99	7202.48	6652.51
320000	29451.94	16091.92	11689.52	9525.87	8257.02	7434.82	6867.11
330000	30372.31	16594.79	12054.82	9823.56	8515.05	7667.16	7081.71
340000	31292.68	17097.66	12420.11	10121.24	8773.08	7899.50	7296.30
350000	32213.06	17600.53	12785.41	10418.92	9031.11	8131.83	7510.90
400000	36814.92	20114.90	14611.90	11907.34	10321.27	9293.53	8583.89
450000	41416.78	22629.26	16438.38	13395.76	11611.43	10455.22	9656.87
500000	46018.65	25143.62	18264.87	14884.18	12901.59	11616.91	10729.86
550000	50620.52	27657.98	20091.36	16372.60	14191.75	12778.60	11802.84
600000	55222.38	30172.34	21917.85	17861.01	15481.91	13940.29	12875.83

Monthly Payments 18¾%
necessary to amortize a loan

AMOUNT	8 YEARS	9 YEARS	10 YEARS	11 YEARS	12 YEARS	13 YEARS	14 YEARS
100	2.02	1.92	1.85	1.79	1.75	1.72	1.69
200	4.04	3.85	3.70	3.59	3.50	3.43	3.37
500	10.09	9.61	9.25	8.97	8.75	8.58	8.44
1000	20.18	19.23	18.50	17.94	17.50	17.15	16.87
2000	40.36	38.46	37.01	35.89	35.00	34.30	33.74
5000	100.90	96.14	92.52	89.71	87.51	85.76	84.36
6000	121.08	115.37	111.02	107.66	105.01	102.91	101.23
7000	141.26	134.60	129.53	125.60	122.51	120.07	118.11
8000	161.44	153.83	148.03	143.54	140.02	137.22	134.98
9000	181.62	173.06	166.54	161.49	157.52	154.37	151.85
10000	201.80	192.29	185.04	179.43	175.02	171.52	168.72
15000	302.71	288.43	277.56	269.14	262.53	257.28	253.08
20000	403.61	384.57	370.08	358.86	350.04	343.05	337.45
25000	504.51	480.72	462.60	448.57	437.55	428.81	421.81
30000	605.41	576.86	555.12	538.29	525.06	514.57	506.17
35000	706.31	673.00	647.64	628.00	612.57	600.33	590.53
40000	807.22	769.15	740.17	717.71	700.08	686.09	674.89
45000	908.12	865.29	832.69	807.43	787.59	771.85	759.25
50000	1009.02	961.43	925.21	897.14	875.10	857.61	843.61
55000	1109.92	1057.58	1017.73	986.86	962.61	943.37	927.98
60000	1210.82	1153.72	1110.25	1076.57	1050.12	1029.14	1012.34
65000	1311.72	1249.86	1202.77	1166.29	1137.64	1114.90	1096.70
70000	1412.63	1346.01	1295.29	1256.00	1225.15	1200.66	1181.06
75000	1513.53	1442.15	1387.81	1345.71	1312.66	1286.42	1265.42
80000	1614.43	1538.29	1480.33	1435.43	1400.17	1372.18	1349.78
85000	1715.33	1634.44	1572.85	1525.14	1487.68	1457.94	1434.14
90000	1816.23	1730.58	1665.37	1614.86	1575.19	1543.70	1518.51
95000	1917.14	1826.72	1757.89	1704.57	1662.70	1629.46	1602.87
100000	2018.04	1922.87	1850.41	1794.28	1750.21	1715.23	1687.23
105000	2118.94	2019.01	1942.93	1884.00	1837.72	1800.99	1771.59
110000	2219.84	2115.15	2035.46	1973.71	1925.23	1886.75	1855.95
120000	2421.65	2307.44	2220.50	2153.14	2100.25	2058.27	2024.67
130000	2623.45	2499.73	2405.54	2332.57	2275.27	2229.79	2193.40
140000	2825.25	2692.01	2590.58	2512.00	2450.29	2401.32	2362.12
150000	3027.06	2884.30	2775.62	2691.43	2625.31	2572.84	2530.84
160000	3228.86	3076.59	2960.66	2870.86	2800.33	2744.36	2699.57
170000	3430.66	3268.87	3145.70	3050.28	2975.35	2915.88	2868.29
180000	3632.47	3461.16	3330.75	3229.71	3150.37	3087.41	3037.01
190000	3834.27	3653.45	3515.79	3409.14	3325.39	3258.93	3205.73
200000	4036.08	3845.73	3700.83	3588.57	3500.42	3430.45	3374.46
210000	4237.88	4038.02	3885.87	3768.00	3675.44	3601.98	3543.18
220000	4439.68	4230.30	4070.91	3947.43	3850.46	3773.50	3711.90
230000	4641.49	4422.59	4255.95	4126.85	4025.48	3945.02	3880.63
240000	4843.29	4614.88	4440.99	4306.28	4200.50	4116.54	4049.35
250000	5045.09	4807.16	4626.04	4485.71	4375.52	4288.07	4218.07
260000	5246.90	4999.45	4811.08	4665.14	4550.54	4459.59	4386.79
270000	5448.70	5191.74	4996.12	4844.57	4725.56	4631.11	4555.52
280000	5650.51	5384.02	5181.16	5024.00	4900.58	4802.63	4724.24
290000	5852.31	5576.31	5366.20	5203.43	5075.60	4974.16	4892.96
300000	6054.11	5768.60	5551.24	5382.85	5250.62	5145.68	5061.69
310000	6255.92	5960.88	5736.28	5562.28	5425.64	5317.20	5230.41
320000	6457.72	6153.17	5921.33	5741.71	5600.67	5488.72	5399.13
330000	6659.53	6345.46	6106.37	5921.14	5775.69	5660.25	5567.85
340000	6861.33	6537.74	6291.41	6100.57	5950.71	5831.77	5736.58
350000	7063.13	6730.03	6476.45	6280.00	6125.73	6003.29	5905.30
400000	8072.15	7691.46	7401.66	7177.14	7000.83	6860.91	6748.91
450000	9081.17	8652.90	8326.86	8074.28	7875.94	7718.52	7592.53
500000	10090.19	9614.33	9252.07	8971.42	8751.04	8576.13	8436.14
550000	11099.21	10575.76	10177.28	9868.57	9626.14	9433.74	9279.76
600000	12108.23	11537.20	11102.48	10765.71	10501.25	10291.36	10123.37

18¾%

Monthly Payments
necessary to amortize a loan

AMOUNT	15 YEARS	16 YEARS	17 YEARS	18 YEARS	19 YEARS	20 YEARS	21 YEARS
100	1.66	1.65	1.63	1.62	1.61	1.60	1.59
200	3.33	3.29	3.26	3.24	3.22	3.20	3.19
500	8.32	8.23	8.16	8.10	8.05	8.01	7.97
1000	16.65	16.46	16.32	16.19	16.09	16.01	15.95
2000	33.29	32.93	32.63	32.39	32.19	32.03	31.89
5000	83.23	82.32	81.58	80.97	80.47	80.06	79.73
6000	99.88	98.78	97.89	97.16	96.57	96.08	95.67
7000	116.53	115.25	114.21	113.36	112.66	112.09	111.62
8000	133.17	131.71	130.52	129.55	128.75	128.10	127.56
9000	149.82	148.18	146.84	145.74	144.85	144.11	143.51
10000	166.47	164.64	163.15	161.94	160.94	160.13	159.45
15000	249.70	246.96	244.73	242.91	241.41	240.19	239.18
20000	332.93	329.28	326.30	323.88	321.89	320.25	318.91
25000	416.17	411.60	407.88	404.84	402.36	400.32	398.64
30000	499.40	493.92	489.46	485.81	482.83	480.38	478.36
35000	582.63	576.24	571.03	566.78	563.30	560.44	558.09
40000	665.87	658.56	652.61	647.75	643.77	640.51	637.82
45000	749.10	740.88	734.18	728.72	724.24	720.57	717.55
50000	832.33	823.20	815.76	809.69	804.72	800.63	797.27
55000	915.57	905.52	897.34	890.66	885.19	880.70	877.00
60000	998.80	987.84	978.91	971.63	965.66	960.76	956.73
65000	1082.03	1070.16	1060.49	1052.60	1046.13	1040.82	1036.46
70000	1165.27	1152.47	1142.06	1133.56	1126.60	1120.89	1116.18
75000	1248.50	1234.79	1223.64	1214.53	1207.07	1200.95	1195.91
80000	1331.74	1317.11	1305.22	1295.50	1287.54	1281.01	1275.64
85000	1414.97	1399.43	1386.79	1376.47	1368.02	1361.08	1355.37
90000	1498.20	1481.75	1468.37	1457.44	1448.49	1441.14	1435.09
95000	1581.44	1564.07	1549.95	1538.41	1528.96	1521.20	1514.82
100000	1664.67	1646.39	1631.52	1619.38	1609.43	1601.27	1594.55
105000	1747.90	1728.71	1713.10	1700.35	1689.90	1681.33	1674.28
110000	1831.14	1811.03	1794.67	1781.31	1770.37	1761.39	1754.00
120000	1997.60	1975.67	1957.83	1943.25	1931.32	1921.52	1913.46
130000	2164.07	2140.31	2120.98	2105.19	2092.26	2081.65	2072.91
140000	2330.54	2304.95	2284.13	2267.13	2253.20	2241.77	2232.37
150000	2497.00	2469.59	2447.28	2429.07	2414.15	2401.90	2391.82
160000	2663.47	2634.23	2610.43	2591.00	2575.09	2562.03	2551.28
170000	2829.94	2798.87	2773.59	2752.94	2736.03	2722.15	2710.73
180000	2996.40	2963.51	2936.74	2914.88	2896.98	2882.28	2870.19
190000	3162.87	3128.15	3099.89	3076.82	3057.92	3042.41	3029.64
200000	3329.34	3292.79	3263.04	3238.75	3218.86	3202.53	3189.10
210000	3495.80	3457.42	3426.19	3400.69	3379.81	3362.66	3348.55
220000	3662.27	3622.06	3589.35	3562.63	3540.75	3522.79	3508.01
230000	3828.74	3786.70	3752.50	3724.57	3701.69	3682.91	3667.46
240000	3995.21	3951.34	3915.65	3886.51	3862.63	3843.04	3826.92
250000	4161.67	4115.98	4078.80	4048.44	4023.58	4003.17	3986.37
260000	4328.14	4280.62	4241.96	4210.38	4184.52	4163.29	4145.83
270000	4494.61	4445.26	4405.11	4372.32	4345.46	4323.42	4305.28
280000	4661.07	4609.90	4568.26	4534.26	4506.41	4483.54	4464.74
290000	4827.54	4774.54	4731.41	4696.19	4667.35	4643.67	4624.19
300000	4994.01	4939.18	4894.56	4858.13	4828.29	4803.80	4783.65
310000	5160.47	5103.82	5057.72	5020.07	4989.24	4963.92	4943.10
320000	5326.94	5268.46	5220.87	5182.01	5150.18	5124.05	5102.56
330000	5493.41	5433.10	5384.02	5343.94	5311.12	5284.18	5262.01
340000	5659.87	5597.74	5547.17	5505.88	5472.07	5444.30	5421.47
350000	5826.34	5762.37	5710.32	5667.82	5633.01	5604.43	5580.92
400000	6658.68	6585.57	6526.08	6477.51	6437.72	6405.06	6378.23
450000	7491.01	7408.77	7341.85	7287.20	7242.44	7205.70	7175.47
500000	8323.34	8231.96	8157.61	8096.89	8047.16	8006.33	7972.75
550000	9155.68	9055.16	8973.37	8906.57	8851.87	8806.96	8770.02
600000	9988.01	9878.36	9789.13	9716.26	9656.59	9607.60	9567.30

Monthly Payments 18¾%
necessary to amortize a loan

AMOUNT	22 YEARS	23 YEARS	24 YEARS	25 YEARS	30 YEARS	35 YEARS	40 YEARS
100	1.59	1.58	1.58	1.58	1.57	1.56	1.56
200	3.18	3.17	3.16	3.16	3.14	3.13	3.13
500	7.95	7.92	7.90	7.89	7.84	7.82	7.82
1000	15.89	15.84	15.81	15.78	15.68	15.65	15.63
2000	31.78	31.69	31.61	31.55	31.37	31.30	31.27
5000	79.45	79.22	79.03	78.88	78.42	78.24	78.17
6000	95.34	95.07	94.84	94.65	94.10	93.89	93.80
7000	111.23	110.91	110.65	110.43	109.79	109.54	109.44
8000	127.12	126.76	126.45	126.21	125.47	125.19	125.07
9000	143.01	142.60	142.26	141.98	141.16	140.83	140.71
10000	158.90	158.45	158.07	157.76	156.84	156.48	156.34
15000	238.35	237.67	237.10	236.63	235.26	234.72	234.51
20000	317.80	316.89	316.14	315.51	313.68	312.97	312.68
25000	397.25	396.11	395.17	394.39	392.10	391.21	390.85
30000	476.70	475.34	474.20	473.27	470.52	469.45	469.02
35000	556.16	554.56	553.24	552.15	548.94	547.69	547.20
40000	635.61	633.78	632.27	631.03	627.36	625.93	625.37
45000	715.06	713.00	711.31	709.90	705.78	704.17	703.54
50000	794.51	792.23	790.34	788.78	784.20	782.41	781.71
55000	873.96	871.45	869.37	867.66	862.62	860.65	859.88
60000	953.41	950.67	948.41	946.54	941.04	938.90	938.05
65000	1032.86	1029.89	1027.44	1025.42	1019.47	1017.14	1016.22
70000	1112.31	1109.12	1106.48	1104.30	1097.89	1095.38	1094.39
75000	1191.76	1188.34	1185.51	1183.17	1176.31	1173.62	1172.56
80000	1271.21	1267.56	1264.55	1262.05	1254.73	1251.86	1250.73
85000	1350.66	1346.78	1343.58	1340.93	1333.15	1330.10	1328.90
90000	1430.11	1426.01	1422.61	1419.81	1411.57	1408.34	1407.07
95000	1509.57	1505.23	1501.65	1498.69	1489.99	1486.58	1485.25
100000	1589.02	1584.45	1580.68	1577.57	1568.41	1564.83	1563.42
105000	1668.47	1663.67	1659.72	1656.44	1646.83	1643.07	1641.59
110000	1747.92	1742.90	1738.75	1735.32	1725.25	1721.31	1719.76
120000	1906.82	1901.34	1896.82	1893.08	1882.09	1877.79	1876.10
130000	2065.72	2059.79	2054.89	2050.83	2038.93	2034.27	2032.44
140000	2224.62	2218.23	2212.95	2208.59	2195.77	2190.76	2188.78
150000	2383.52	2376.68	2371.02	2366.35	2352.61	2347.24	2345.12
160000	2542.43	2535.12	2529.09	2524.10	2509.45	2503.72	2501.47
170000	2701.33	2693.57	2687.16	2681.86	2666.29	2660.20	2657.81
180000	2860.23	2852.01	2845.23	2839.62	2823.13	2816.69	2814.15
190000	3019.13	3010.46	3003.29	2997.37	2979.98	2973.17	2970.49
200000	3178.03	3168.90	3161.36	3155.13	3136.82	3129.65	3126.83
210000	3336.93	3327.35	3319.43	3312.89	3293.66	3286.13	3283.17
220000	3495.84	3485.79	3477.50	3470.64	3450.50	3442.62	3439.52
230000	3654.74	3644.24	3635.57	3628.40	3607.34	3599.10	3595.86
240000	3813.64	3802.68	3793.64	3786.16	3764.18	3755.58	3752.20
250000	3972.54	3961.13	3951.70	3943.91	3921.02	3912.06	3908.54
260000	4131.44	4119.57	4109.77	4101.67	4077.86	4068.55	4064.88
270000	4290.34	4278.02	4267.84	4259.43	4234.70	4225.03	4221.22
280000	4449.25	4436.46	4425.91	4417.18	4391.54	4381.51	4377.57
290000	4608.15	4594.91	4583.98	4574.94	4548.38	4537.99	4533.91
300000	4767.05	4753.35	4742.04	4732.70	4705.22	4694.48	4690.25
310000	4925.95	4911.80	4900.11	4890.45	4862.06	4850.96	4846.59
320000	5084.85	5070.24	5058.18	5048.21	5018.91	5007.44	5002.93
330000	5243.75	5228.69	5216.25	5205.96	5175.75	5163.92	5159.27
340000	5402.66	5387.14	5374.32	5363.72	5332.59	5320.41	5315.62
350000	5561.56	5545.58	5532.39	5521.48	5489.43	5476.89	5471.96
400000	6356.07	6337.81	6322.73	6310.26	6273.63	6259.30	6253.67
450000	7150.57	7130.03	7113.07	7099.04	7057.84	7041.71	7035.37
500000	7945.08	7922.26	7903.41	7887.83	7842.04	7824.13	7817.08
550000	8739.59	8714.48	8693.75	8676.61	8626.24	8606.54	8598.79
600000	9534.10	9506.71	9484.09	9465.39	9410.45	9388.95	9380.50

19%

Monthly Payments
necessary to amortize a loan

AMOUNT	1 YEAR	2 YEARS	3 YEARS	4 YEARS	5 YEARS	6 YEARS	7 YEARS
100	9.22	5.04	3.67	2.99	2.59	2.34	2.16
200	18.43	10.08	7.33	5.98	5.19	4.68	4.32
500	46.08	25.20	18.33	14.95	12.97	11.69	10.80
1000	92.16	50.41	36.66	29.90	25.94	23.38	21.61
2000	184.31	100.82	73.31	59.80	51.88	46.75	43.22
5000	460.78	252.04	183.28	149.50	129.70	116.88	108.04
6000	552.94	302.45	219.94	179.40	155.64	140.26	129.65
7000	645.10	352.86	256.59	209.30	181.58	163.64	151.26
8000	737.25	403.27	293.25	239.20	207.52	187.01	172.86
9000	829.41	453.68	329.90	269.10	233.46	210.39	194.47
10000	921.57	504.09	366.56	299.00	259.41	233.77	216.08
15000	1382.35	756.13	549.84	448.50	389.11	350.65	324.12
20000	1843.13	1008.17	733.12	598.00	518.81	467.53	432.16
25000	2303.91	1260.22	916.40	747.50	648.51	584.42	540.20
30000	2764.70	1512.26	1099.68	897.00	778.22	701.30	648.24
35000	3225.48	1764.30	1282.96	1046.50	907.92	818.19	756.28
40000	3686.26	2016.34	1466.24	1196.00	1037.62	935.07	864.32
45000	4147.05	2268.39	1649.52	1345.51	1167.32	1051.95	972.36
50000	4607.83	2520.43	1832.80	1495.01	1297.03	1168.84	1080.40
55000	5068.61	2772.47	2016.08	1644.51	1426.73	1285.72	1188.44
60000	5529.39	3024.52	2199.36	1794.01	1556.43	1402.60	1296.48
65000	5990.18	3276.56	2382.64	1943.51	1686.14	1519.49	1404.52
70000	6450.96	3528.60	2565.92	2093.01	1815.84	1636.37	1512.56
75000	6911.74	3780.65	2749.20	2242.51	1945.54	1753.25	1620.60
80000	7372.53	4032.69	2932.48	2392.01	2075.24	1870.14	1728.64
85000	7833.31	4284.73	3115.76	2541.51	2204.95	1987.02	1836.68
90000	8294.09	4536.78	3299.04	2691.01	2334.65	2103.91	1944.72
95000	8754.87	4788.82	3482.32	2840.51	2464.35	2220.79	2052.76
100000	9215.66	5040.86	3665.60	2990.01	2594.06	2337.67	2160.80
105000	9676.44	5292.90	3848.88	3139.51	2723.76	2454.56	2268.84
110000	10137.22	5544.95	4032.16	3289.01	2853.46	2571.44	2376.88
120000	11058.79	6049.03	4398.72	3588.01	3112.87	2805.21	2592.96
130000	11980.36	6553.12	4765.28	3887.02	3372.27	3038.97	2809.04
140000	12901.92	7057.21	5131.84	4186.02	3631.68	3272.74	3025.12
150000	13823.49	7561.29	5498.40	4485.02	3891.08	3506.51	3241.20
160000	14745.05	8065.38	5864.96	4784.02	4150.49	3740.28	3457.28
170000	15666.62	8569.46	6231.52	5083.02	4409.89	3974.04	3673.36
180000	16588.18	9073.55	6598.08	5382.02	4669.30	4207.81	3889.44
190000	17509.75	9577.64	6964.64	5681.02	4928.70	4441.58	4105.52
200000	18431.32	10081.72	7331.20	5980.02	5188.11	4675.34	4321.60
210000	19352.88	10585.81	7697.76	6279.02	5447.52	4909.11	4537.68
220000	20274.45	11089.90	8064.32	6578.03	5706.92	5142.88	4753.76
230000	21196.01	11593.98	8430.88	6877.03	5966.33	5376.65	4969.84
240000	22117.58	12098.07	8797.44	7176.03	6225.73	5610.41	5185.92
250000	23039.14	12602.15	9164.01	7475.03	6485.14	5844.18	5402.00
260000	23960.71	13106.24	9530.57	7774.03	6744.54	6077.95	5618.08
270000	24882.28	13610.33	9897.13	8073.03	7003.95	6311.72	5834.17
280000	25803.84	14114.41	10263.69	8372.03	7263.35	6545.48	6050.25
290000	26725.41	14618.50	10630.25	8671.03	7522.76	6779.25	6266.33
300000	27646.97	15122.59	10996.81	8970.04	7782.17	7013.02	6482.41
310000	28568.54	15626.67	11363.37	9269.04	8041.57	7246.78	6698.49
320000	29490.11	16130.76	11729.93	9568.04	8300.98	7480.55	6914.57
330000	30411.67	16634.84	12096.49	9867.04	8560.38	7714.32	7130.65
340000	31333.24	17138.93	12463.05	10166.04	8819.79	7948.09	7346.73
350000	32254.80	17643.02	12829.61	10465.04	9079.19	8181.85	7562.81
400000	36862.63	20163.45	14662.41	11960.05	10376.22	9350.69	8643.21
450000	41470.46	22683.88	16495.21	13455.05	11673.25	10519.53	9723.61
500000	46078.29	25204.31	18328.01	14950.06	12970.28	11688.36	10804.01
550000	50686.12	27724.74	20160.81	16445.07	14267.30	12857.20	11884.41
600000	55293.95	30245.17	21993.61	17940.07	15564.33	14026.03	12964.81

Monthly Payments 19%
necessary to amortize a loan

AMOUNT	8 YEARS	9 YEARS	10 YEARS	11 YEARS	12 YEARS	13 YEARS	14 YEARS
100	2.03	1.94	1.87	1.81	1.77	1.73	1.71
200	4.07	3.88	3.73	3.62	3.53	3.47	3.41
500	10.17	9.69	9.33	9.06	8.84	8.66	8.53
1000	20.33	19.39	18.67	18.11	17.67	17.33	17.05
2000	40.67	38.77	37.33	36.22	35.35	34.66	34.10
5000	101.67	96.94	93.34	90.55	88.37	86.64	85.26
6000	122.00	116.32	112.00	108.66	106.04	103.97	102.31
7000	142.34	135.71	130.67	126.77	123.72	121.29	119.36
8000	162.67	155.10	149.34	144.88	141.39	138.62	136.41
9000	183.00	174.48	168.01	162.99	159.06	155.95	153.46
10000	203.34	193.87	186.67	181.10	176.74	173.28	170.51
15000	305.01	290.81	280.01	271.65	265.10	259.91	255.77
20000	406.68	387.74	373.34	362.21	353.47	346.55	341.02
25000	508.35	484.68	466.68	452.76	441.84	433.19	426.28
30000	610.02	581.61	560.02	543.31	530.21	519.83	511.53
35000	711.69	678.55	653.35	633.86	618.58	606.47	596.79
40000	813.35	775.48	746.69	724.41	706.95	693.10	682.05
45000	915.02	872.42	840.03	814.96	795.31	779.74	767.30
50000	1016.69	969.35	933.36	905.52	883.68	866.38	852.56
55000	1118.36	1066.29	1026.70	996.07	972.05	953.02	937.81
60000	1220.03	1163.22	1120.03	1086.62	1060.42	1039.66	1023.07
65000	1321.70	1260.16	1213.37	1177.17	1148.79	1126.30	1108.32
70000	1423.37	1357.10	1306.71	1267.72	1237.16	1212.93	1193.58
75000	1525.04	1454.03	1400.04	1358.27	1325.52	1299.57	1278.84
80000	1626.71	1550.97	1493.38	1448.83	1413.89	1386.21	1364.09
85000	1728.38	1647.90	1586.72	1539.38	1502.26	1472.85	1449.35
90000	1830.05	1744.84	1680.05	1629.93	1590.63	1559.49	1534.60
95000	1931.72	1841.77	1773.39	1720.48	1679.00	1646.12	1619.86
100000	2033.39	1938.71	1866.72	1811.03	1767.36	1732.76	1705.11
105000	2135.06	2035.64	1960.06	1901.58	1855.73	1819.40	1790.37
110000	2236.73	2132.58	2053.40	1992.14	1944.10	1906.04	1875.63
120000	2440.06	2326.45	2240.07	2173.24	2120.84	2079.31	2046.14
130000	2643.40	2520.32	2426.74	2354.34	2297.57	2252.59	2216.65
140000	2846.74	2714.19	2613.41	2535.45	2474.31	2425.87	2387.16
150000	3050.08	2908.06	2800.09	2716.55	2651.05	2599.14	2557.67
160000	3253.42	3101.93	2986.76	2897.65	2827.78	2772.42	2728.18
170000	3456.76	3295.80	3173.43	3078.76	3004.52	2945.70	2898.69
180000	3660.10	3489.67	3360.10	3259.86	3181.26	3118.97	3069.21
190000	3863.43	3683.55	3546.77	3440.96	3357.99	3292.25	3239.72
200000	4066.77	3877.42	3733.45	3622.07	3534.73	3465.52	3410.23
210000	4270.11	4071.29	3920.12	3803.17	3711.47	3638.80	3580.74
220000	4473.45	4265.16	4106.79	3984.27	3888.20	3812.08	3751.25
230000	4676.79	4459.03	4293.46	4165.37	4064.94	3985.35	3921.76
240000	4880.13	4652.90	4480.14	4346.48	4241.68	4158.63	4092.27
250000	5083.47	4846.77	4666.81	4527.58	4418.41	4331.91	4262.79
260000	5286.80	5040.64	4853.48	4708.68	4595.15	4505.18	4433.30
270000	5490.14	5234.51	5040.15	4889.79	4771.88	4678.46	4603.81
280000	5693.48	5428.38	5226.83	5070.89	4948.62	4851.73	4774.32
290000	5896.82	5622.25	5413.50	5251.99	5125.36	5025.01	4944.83
300000	6100.16	5816.12	5600.17	5433.10	5302.09	5198.29	5115.34
310000	6303.50	6010.00	5786.84	5614.20	5478.83	5371.56	5285.86
320000	6506.84	6203.87	5973.52	5795.30	5655.57	5544.84	5456.37
330000	6710.18	6397.74	6160.19	5976.41	5832.30	5718.12	5626.88
340000	6913.51	6591.61	6346.86	6157.51	6009.04	5891.39	5797.39
350000	7116.85	6785.48	6533.53	6338.61	6185.78	6064.67	5967.90
400000	8133.55	7754.83	7466.89	7244.13	7069.46	6931.05	6820.46
450000	9150.24	8724.19	8400.26	8149.65	7953.14	7797.43	7673.02
500000	10166.93	9693.54	9333.62	9055.16	8836.82	8663.81	8525.57
550000	11183.63	10662.90	10266.98	9960.68	9720.51	9530.19	9378.13
600000	12200.32	11632.25	11200.34	10866.20	10604.19	10396.57	10230.69

19%

Monthly Payments
necessary to amortize a loan

AMOUNT	15 YEARS	16 YEARS	17 YEARS	18 YEARS	19 YEARS	20 YEARS	21 YEARS
100	1.68	1.66	1.65	1.64	1.63	1.62	1.61
200	3.37	3.33	3.30	3.28	3.26	3.24	3.23
500	8.41	8.32	8.25	8.19	8.14	8.10	8.07
1000	16.83	16.65	16.50	16.38	16.29	16.21	16.14
2000	33.66	33.30	33.01	32.77	32.57	32.41	32.28
5000	84.14	83.24	82.51	81.92	81.43	81.03	80.71
6000	100.97	99.89	99.02	98.30	97.72	97.24	96.85
7000	117.80	116.54	115.52	114.69	114.01	113.45	112.99
8000	134.63	133.19	132.02	131.07	130.29	129.65	129.13
9000	151.46	149.84	148.53	147.45	146.58	145.86	145.27
10000	168.29	166.49	165.03	163.84	162.87	162.07	161.41
15000	252.43	249.73	247.54	245.76	244.30	243.10	242.12
20000	336.58	332.98	330.06	327.68	325.73	324.14	322.83
25000	420.72	416.22	412.57	409.60	407.16	405.17	403.54
30000	504.86	499.47	495.09	491.52	488.60	486.21	484.24
35000	589.01	582.71	577.60	573.43	570.03	567.24	564.95
40000	673.15	665.96	660.12	655.35	651.46	648.27	645.66
45000	757.29	749.20	742.63	737.27	732.89	729.31	726.36
50000	841.44	832.45	825.14	819.19	814.33	810.34	807.07
55000	925.58	915.69	907.66	901.11	895.76	891.38	887.78
60000	1009.73	998.94	990.17	983.03	977.19	972.41	968.49
65000	1093.87	1082.18	1072.69	1064.95	1058.63	1053.45	1049.19
70000	1178.01	1165.42	1155.20	1146.87	1140.06	1134.48	1129.90
75000	1262.16	1248.67	1237.72	1228.79	1221.49	1215.51	1210.61
80000	1346.30	1331.91	1320.23	1310.71	1302.92	1296.55	1291.31
85000	1430.44	1415.16	1402.74	1392.63	1384.36	1377.58	1372.02
90000	1514.59	1498.40	1485.26	1474.55	1465.79	1458.62	1452.73
95000	1598.73	1581.65	1567.77	1556.47	1547.22	1539.65	1533.44
100000	1682.88	1664.89	1650.29	1638.38	1628.66	1620.68	1614.14
105000	1767.02	1748.14	1732.80	1720.30	1710.09	1701.72	1694.85
110000	1851.16	1831.38	1815.32	1802.22	1791.52	1782.75	1775.56
120000	2019.45	1997.87	1980.35	1966.06	1954.39	1944.82	1936.97
130000	2187.74	2164.36	2145.37	2129.90	2117.25	2106.89	2098.39
140000	2356.03	2330.85	2310.40	2293.74	2280.12	2268.96	2259.80
150000	2524.31	2497.34	2475.43	2457.58	2442.98	2431.03	2421.21
160000	2692.60	2663.83	2640.46	2621.41	2605.85	2593.10	2582.63
170000	2860.89	2830.32	2805.49	2785.25	2768.71	2755.16	2744.04
180000	3029.18	2996.81	2970.52	2949.09	2931.58	2917.23	2905.46
190000	3197.46	3163.30	3135.55	3112.93	3094.44	3079.30	3066.87
200000	3365.75	3329.79	3300.58	3276.77	3257.31	3241.37	3228.29
210000	3534.04	3496.27	3465.60	3440.61	3420.18	3403.44	3389.70
220000	3702.33	3662.76	3630.63	3604.45	3583.04	3565.51	3551.11
230000	3870.61	3829.25	3795.66	3768.28	3745.91	3727.58	3712.53
240000	4038.90	3995.74	3960.69	3932.12	3908.77	3889.64	3873.94
250000	4207.19	4162.23	4125.72	4095.96	4071.64	4051.71	4035.36
260000	4375.48	4328.72	4290.75	4259.80	4234.50	4213.78	4196.77
270000	4543.77	4495.21	4455.78	4423.64	4397.37	4375.85	4358.19
280000	4712.05	4661.70	4620.81	4587.48	4560.23	4537.92	4519.60
290000	4880.34	4828.19	4785.83	4751.31	4723.10	4699.99	4681.01
300000	5048.63	4994.68	4950.86	4915.15	4885.97	4862.05	4842.43
310000	5216.92	5161.17	5115.89	5078.99	5048.83	5024.12	5003.84
320000	5385.20	5327.66	5280.92	5242.83	5211.70	5186.19	5165.26
330000	5553.49	5494.15	5445.95	5406.67	5374.56	5348.26	5326.67
340000	5721.78	5660.64	5610.98	5570.51	5537.43	5510.33	5488.09
350000	5890.07	5827.12	5776.01	5734.34	5700.29	5672.40	5649.50
400000	6731.50	6659.57	6601.15	6553.54	6514.62	6482.74	6456.57
450000	7572.94	7492.02	7426.29	7372.73	7328.95	7293.08	7263.64
500000	8414.38	8324.46	8251.44	8191.92	8143.28	8103.42	8070.71
550000	9255.82	9156.91	9076.58	9011.11	8957.60	8913.77	8877.78
600000	10097.26	9989.36	9901.73	9830.31	9771.93	9724.11	9684.86

Monthly Payments **19%**
necessary to amortize a loan

AMOUNT	22 YEARS	23 YEARS	24 YEARS	25 YEARS	30 YEARS	35 YEARS	40 YEARS
100	1.61	1.60	1.60	1.60	1.59	1.59	1.58
200	3.22	3.21	3.20	3.20	3.18	3.17	3.17
500	8.04	8.02	8.00	7.99	7.94	7.93	7.92
1000	16.09	16.04	16.01	15.98	15.89	15.85	15.84
2000	32.18	32.09	32.01	31.95	31.78	31.71	31.68
5000	80.44	80.22	80.03	79.88	79.44	79.27	79.21
6000	96.53	96.26	96.04	95.86	95.33	95.13	95.05
7000	112.61	112.30	112.05	111.84	111.22	110.98	110.89
8000	128.70	128.35	128.06	127.81	127.11	126.84	126.73
9000	144.79	144.39	144.06	143.79	143.00	142.69	142.58
10000	160.88	160.43	160.07	159.77	158.89	158.55	158.42
15000	241.31	240.65	240.10	239.65	238.33	237.82	237.63
20000	321.75	320.87	320.14	319.54	317.78	317.10	316.83
25000	402.19	401.08	400.17	399.42	397.22	396.37	396.04
30000	482.63	481.30	480.21	479.30	476.67	475.65	475.25
35000	563.07	561.52	560.24	559.19	556.11	554.92	554.46
40000	643.51	641.73	640.28	639.07	635.56	634.20	633.67
45000	723.94	721.95	720.31	718.96	715.00	713.47	712.88
50000	804.38	802.17	800.34	798.84	794.45	792.75	792.09
55000	884.82	882.39	880.38	878.72	873.89	872.02	871.30
60000	965.26	962.60	960.41	958.61	953.34	951.30	950.50
65000	1045.70	1042.82	1040.45	1038.49	1032.78	1030.57	1029.71
70000	1126.14	1123.04	1120.48	1118.38	1112.22	1109.85	1108.92
75000	1206.57	1203.25	1200.52	1198.26	1191.67	1189.12	1188.13
80000	1287.01	1283.47	1280.55	1278.14	1271.11	1268.40	1267.34
85000	1367.45	1363.69	1360.59	1358.03	1350.56	1347.67	1346.55
90000	1447.89	1443.90	1440.62	1437.91	1430.00	1426.95	1425.76
95000	1528.33	1524.12	1520.65	1517.80	1509.45	1506.22	1504.97
100000	1608.76	1604.34	1600.69	1597.68	1588.89	1585.49	1584.17
105000	1689.20	1684.55	1680.72	1677.56	1668.34	1664.77	1663.38
110000	1769.64	1764.77	1760.76	1757.45	1747.78	1744.04	1742.59
120000	1930.52	1925.20	1920.83	1917.22	1906.67	1902.59	1901.01
130000	2091.39	2085.64	2080.90	2076.98	2065.56	2061.14	2059.43
140000	2252.27	2246.07	2240.96	2236.75	2224.45	2219.69	2217.84
150000	2413.15	2406.51	2401.03	2396.52	2383.34	2378.24	2376.26
160000	2574.02	2566.94	2561.10	2556.29	2542.23	2536.79	2534.68
170000	2734.90	2727.37	2721.17	2716.06	2701.12	2695.34	2693.10
180000	2895.78	2887.81	2881.24	2875.82	2860.01	2853.89	2851.51
190000	3056.65	3048.24	3041.31	3035.59	3018.90	3012.44	3009.93
200000	3217.53	3208.67	3201.38	3195.36	3177.78	3170.99	3168.35
210000	3378.41	3369.11	3361.45	3355.13	3336.67	3329.54	3326.77
220000	3539.28	3529.54	3521.52	3514.90	3495.56	3488.09	3485.18
230000	3700.16	3689.98	3681.58	3674.66	3654.45	3646.64	3643.60
240000	3861.03	3850.41	3841.65	3834.43	3813.34	3805.19	3802.02
250000	4021.91	4010.84	4001.72	3994.20	3972.23	3963.74	3960.44
260000	4182.79	4171.28	4161.79	4153.97	4131.12	4122.29	4118.85
270000	4343.66	4331.71	4321.86	4313.74	4290.01	4280.84	4277.27
280000	4504.54	4492.14	4481.93	4473.50	4448.90	4439.39	4435.69
290000	4665.42	4652.58	4642.00	4633.27	4607.79	4597.93	4594.11
300000	4826.29	4813.01	4802.07	4793.04	4766.68	4756.48	4752.52
310000	4987.17	4973.44	4962.14	4952.81	4925.57	4915.03	4910.94
320000	5148.05	5133.88	5122.20	5112.58	5084.46	5073.58	5069.36
330000	5308.92	5294.31	5282.27	5272.34	5243.35	5232.13	5227.78
340000	5469.80	5454.75	5442.34	5432.11	5402.23	5390.68	5386.19
350000	5630.68	5615.18	5602.41	5591.88	5561.12	5549.23	5544.61
400000	6435.06	6417.35	6402.76	6390.72	6355.57	6341.98	6336.70
450000	7239.44	7219.52	7203.10	7189.56	7150.02	7134.73	7128.79
500000	8043.82	8021.69	8003.44	7988.40	7944.46	7927.47	7920.87
550000	8848.20	8823.85	8803.79	8787.24	8738.91	8720.22	8712.96
600000	9652.59	9626.02	9604.13	9586.08	9533.35	9512.97	9505.05

19¼%

Monthly Payments
necessary to amortize a loan

AMOUNT	1 YEAR	2 YEARS	3 YEARS	4 YEARS	5 YEARS	6 YEARS	7 YEARS
100	9.23	5.05	3.68	3.00	2.61	2.35	2.18
200	18.46	10.11	7.36	6.01	5.22	4.70	4.35
500	46.14	25.27	18.39	15.02	13.04	11.76	10.88
1000	92.28	50.53	36.78	30.03	26.08	23.52	21.76
2000	184.55	101.06	73.57	60.06	52.16	47.04	43.51
5000	461.38	252.65	183.91	150.16	130.39	117.60	108.78
6000	553.66	303.18	220.70	180.19	156.47	141.12	130.54
7000	645.93	353.71	257.48	210.23	182.55	164.64	152.30
8000	738.21	404.24	294.26	240.26	208.63	188.16	174.05
9000	830.48	454.77	331.04	270.29	234.70	211.68	195.81
10000	922.76	505.30	367.83	300.32	260.78	235.20	217.57
15000	1384.14	757.95	551.74	450.48	391.17	352.80	326.35
20000	1845.52	1010.60	735.65	600.64	521.57	470.40	435.14
25000	2306.90	1263.25	919.56	750.81	651.96	588.00	543.92
30000	2768.28	1515.90	1103.48	900.97	782.35	705.60	652.70
35000	3229.66	1768.56	1287.39	1051.13	912.74	823.20	761.49
40000	3691.04	2021.21	1471.30	1201.29	1043.13	940.80	870.27
45000	4152.42	2273.86	1655.21	1351.45	1173.52	1058.40	979.06
50000	4613.80	2526.51	1839.13	1501.61	1303.92	1176.00	1087.84
55000	5075.18	2779.16	2023.04	1651.77	1434.31	1293.60	1196.63
60000	5536.56	3031.81	2206.95	1801.93	1564.70	1411.20	1305.41
65000	5997.94	3284.46	2390.87	1952.09	1695.09	1528.81	1414.19
70000	6459.32	3537.11	2574.78	2102.25	1825.48	1646.41	1522.98
75000	6920.70	3789.76	2758.69	2252.42	1955.87	1764.01	1631.76
80000	7382.07	4042.41	2942.60	2402.58	2086.26	1881.61	1740.55
85000	7843.45	4295.06	3126.52	2552.74	2216.66	1999.21	1849.33
90000	8304.83	4547.71	3310.43	2702.90	2347.05	2116.81	1958.11
95000	8766.21	4800.37	3494.34	2853.06	2477.44	2234.41	2066.90
100000	9227.59	5053.02	3678.25	3003.22	2607.83	2352.01	2175.68
105000	9688.97	5305.67	3862.17	3153.38	2738.22	2469.61	2284.47
110000	10150.35	5558.32	4046.08	3303.54	2868.61	2587.21	2393.25
120000	11073.11	6063.62	4413.91	3603.86	3129.40	2822.41	2610.82
130000	11995.87	6568.92	4781.73	3904.19	3390.18	3057.61	2828.39
140000	12918.63	7074.22	5149.56	4204.51	3650.96	3292.81	3045.95
150000	13841.39	7579.52	5517.38	4504.83	3911.75	3528.01	3263.52
160000	14764.15	8084.83	5885.21	4805.15	4172.53	3763.21	3481.09
170000	15686.91	8590.13	6253.03	5105.47	4433.31	3998.41	3698.66
180000	16609.67	9095.43	6620.86	5405.80	4694.09	4233.61	3916.23
190000	17532.43	9600.73	6988.68	5706.12	4954.88	4468.82	4133.80
200000	18455.19	10106.03	7356.51	6006.44	5215.66	4704.02	4351.36
210000	19377.95	10611.33	7724.33	6306.76	5476.44	4939.22	4568.93
220000	20300.71	11116.64	8092.16	6607.08	5737.23	5174.42	4786.50
230000	21223.46	11621.94	8459.98	6907.41	5998.01	5409.62	5004.07
240000	22146.22	12127.24	8827.81	7207.73	6258.79	5644.82	5221.64
250000	23068.98	12632.54	9195.64	7508.05	6519.58	5880.02	5439.21
260000	23991.74	13137.84	9563.46	7808.37	6780.36	6115.22	5656.77
270000	24914.50	13643.14	9931.29	8108.69	7041.14	6350.42	5874.34
280000	25837.26	14148.45	10299.11	8409.02	7301.93	6585.62	6091.91
290000	26760.02	14653.75	10666.94	8709.34	7562.71	6820.82	6309.48
300000	27682.78	15159.05	11034.76	9009.66	7823.49	7056.02	6527.05
310000	28605.54	15664.35	11402.59	9309.98	8084.27	7291.22	6744.61
320000	29528.30	16169.65	11770.41	9610.30	8345.06	7526.43	6962.18
330000	30451.06	16674.95	12138.24	9910.63	8605.84	7761.63	7179.75
340000	31373.82	17180.26	12506.06	10210.95	8866.62	7996.83	7397.32
350000	32296.58	17685.56	12873.89	10511.27	9127.41	8232.03	7614.89
400000	36910.37	20212.07	14713.02	12012.88	10431.32	9408.03	8702.73
450000	41524.17	22738.57	16552.14	13514.49	11735.24	10584.04	9790.57
500000	46137.97	25265.08	18391.27	15016.10	13039.15	11760.04	10878.41
550000	50751.76	27791.59	20230.40	16517.71	14343.07	12936.04	11966.25
600000	55365.56	30318.10	22069.53	18019.32	15646.98	14112.05	13054.09

AMOUNT	8 YEARS	9 YEARS	10 YEARS	11 YEARS	12 YEARS	13 YEARS	14 YEARS
100	2.05	1.95	1.88	1.83	1.78	1.75	1.72
200	4.10	3.91	3.77	3.66	3.57	3.50	3.45
500	10.24	9.77	9.42	9.14	8.92	8.75	8.62
1000	20.49	19.55	18.83	18.28	17.85	17.50	17.23
2000	40.98	39.09	37.66	36.56	35.69	35.01	34.46
5000	102.44	97.73	94.15	91.39	89.23	87.52	86.15
6000	122.93	117.28	112.99	109.67	107.08	105.02	103.38
7000	143.42	136.82	131.82	127.95	124.92	122.53	120.61
8000	163.90	156.37	150.65	146.23	142.77	140.03	137.84
9000	184.39	175.91	169.48	164.51	160.61	157.53	155.08
10000	204.88	195.46	188.31	182.78	178.46	175.04	172.31
15000	307.32	293.19	282.46	274.18	267.69	262.55	258.46
20000	409.76	390.92	376.62	365.57	356.92	350.07	344.61
25000	512.20	488.65	470.77	456.96	446.15	437.59	430.77
30000	614.64	586.38	564.93	548.35	535.38	525.11	516.92
35000	717.08	684.11	659.08	639.74	624.60	612.63	603.07
40000	819.52	781.84	753.24	731.14	713.83	700.14	689.22
45000	921.96	879.57	847.39	822.53	803.06	787.66	775.38
50000	1024.39	977.30	941.55	913.92	892.29	875.18	861.53
55000	1126.83	1075.03	1035.70	1005.31	981.52	962.70	947.68
60000	1229.27	1172.77	1129.86	1096.71	1070.75	1050.22	1033.84
65000	1331.71	1270.50	1224.01	1188.10	1159.98	1137.73	1119.99
70000	1434.15	1368.23	1318.17	1279.49	1249.21	1225.25	1206.14
75000	1536.59	1465.96	1412.32	1370.88	1338.44	1312.77	1292.30
80000	1639.03	1563.69	1506.47	1462.27	1427.67	1400.29	1378.45
85000	1741.47	1661.42	1600.63	1553.67	1516.90	1487.81	1464.60
90000	1843.91	1759.15	1694.78	1645.06	1606.13	1575.32	1550.76
95000	1946.35	1856.88	1788.94	1736.45	1695.35	1662.84	1636.91
100000	2048.79	1954.61	1883.09	1827.84	1784.58	1750.36	1723.06
105000	2151.23	2052.34	1977.25	1919.23	1873.81	1837.88	1809.22
110000	2253.67	2150.07	2071.40	2010.63	1963.04	1925.40	1895.37
120000	2458.55	2345.53	2259.71	2193.41	2141.50	2100.43	2067.67
130000	2663.43	2540.99	2448.02	2376.19	2319.96	2275.47	2239.98
140000	2868.30	2736.45	2636.33	2558.98	2498.42	2450.51	2412.29
150000	3073.18	2931.91	2824.64	2741.76	2676.88	2625.54	2584.59
160000	3278.06	3127.37	3012.95	2924.55	2855.33	2800.58	2756.90
170000	3482.94	3322.83	3201.26	3107.33	3033.79	2975.61	2929.21
180000	3687.82	3518.30	3389.57	3290.12	3212.25	3150.65	3101.51
190000	3892.70	3713.76	3577.88	3472.90	3390.71	3325.69	3273.82
200000	4097.58	3909.22	3766.19	3655.68	3569.17	3500.72	3446.12
210000	4302.46	4104.68	3954.50	3838.47	3747.63	3675.76	3618.43
220000	4507.34	4300.14	4142.80	4021.25	3926.08	3850.79	3790.74
230000	4712.22	4495.60	4331.11	4204.04	4104.54	4025.83	3963.04
240000	4917.09	4691.06	4519.42	4386.82	4283.00	4200.87	4135.35
250000	5121.97	4886.52	4707.73	4569.61	4461.46	4375.90	4307.66
260000	5326.85	5081.98	4896.04	4752.39	4639.92	4550.94	4479.96
270000	5531.73	5277.44	5084.35	4935.17	4818.38	4725.97	4652.27
280000	5736.61	5472.90	5272.66	5117.96	4996.84	4901.01	4824.57
290000	5941.49	5668.36	5460.97	5300.74	5175.29	5076.05	4996.88
300000	6146.37	5863.83	5649.28	5483.53	5353.75	5251.08	5169.19
310000	6351.25	6059.29	5837.59	5666.31	5532.21	5426.12	5341.49
320000	6556.13	6254.75	6025.90	5849.09	5710.67	5601.16	5513.80
330000	6761.00	6450.21	6214.21	6031.88	5889.13	5776.19	5686.11
340000	6965.88	6645.67	6402.52	6214.66	6067.59	5951.23	5858.41
350000	7170.76	6841.13	6590.83	6397.45	6246.04	6126.26	6030.72
400000	8195.16	7818.43	7532.37	7311.37	7138.34	7001.44	6892.25
450000	9219.55	8795.74	8473.92	8225.29	8030.63	7876.62	7753.78
500000	10243.95	9773.04	9415.47	9139.21	8922.92	8751.81	8615.31
550000	11268.34	10750.35	10357.01	10053.13	9815.21	9626.99	9476.84
600000	12292.74	11727.65	11298.56	10967.05	10707.50	10502.17	10338.37

19¼% Monthly Payments
necessary to amortize a loan

AMOUNT	15 YEARS	16 YEARS	17 YEARS	18 YEARS	19 YEARS	20 YEARS	21 YEARS
100	1.70	1.68	1.67	1.66	1.65	1.64	1.63
200	3.40	3.37	3.34	3.31	3.30	3.28	3.27
500	8.51	8.42	8.35	8.29	8.24	8.20	8.17
1000	17.01	16.83	16.69	16.57	16.48	16.40	16.34
2000	34.02	33.67	33.38	33.15	32.96	32.80	32.68
5000	85.06	84.17	83.46	82.87	82.40	82.01	81.69
6000	102.07	101.01	100.15	99.45	98.88	98.41	98.03
7000	119.08	117.84	116.84	116.02	115.36	114.81	114.36
8000	136.09	134.68	133.53	132.60	131.83	131.21	130.70
9000	153.10	151.51	150.22	149.17	148.31	147.61	147.04
10000	170.11	168.35	166.91	165.74	164.79	164.02	163.38
15000	255.17	252.52	250.37	248.62	247.19	246.02	245.07
20000	340.23	336.69	333.82	331.49	329.59	328.03	326.76
25000	425.29	420.86	417.28	414.36	411.98	410.04	408.45
30000	510.34	505.04	500.73	497.23	494.38	492.05	490.13
35000	595.40	589.21	584.19	580.11	576.78	574.05	571.82
40000	680.46	673.38	667.64	662.98	659.17	656.06	653.51
45000	765.51	757.55	751.10	745.85	741.57	738.07	735.20
50000	850.57	841.73	834.56	828.72	823.97	820.08	816.89
55000	935.63	925.90	918.01	911.59	906.36	902.08	898.58
60000	1020.69	1010.07	1001.47	994.47	988.76	984.09	980.27
65000	1105.74	1094.24	1084.92	1077.34	1071.15	1066.10	1061.96
70000	1190.80	1178.42	1168.38	1160.21	1153.55	1148.11	1143.65
75000	1275.86	1262.59	1251.83	1243.08	1235.95	1230.11	1225.34
80000	1360.91	1346.76	1335.29	1325.96	1318.34	1312.12	1307.02
85000	1445.97	1430.93	1418.74	1408.83	1400.74	1394.13	1388.71
90000	1531.03	1515.11	1502.20	1491.70	1483.14	1476.14	1470.40
95000	1616.09	1599.28	1585.65	1574.57	1565.53	1558.14	1552.09
100000	1701.14	1683.45	1669.11	1657.45	1647.93	1640.15	1633.78
105000	1786.20	1767.62	1752.57	1740.32	1730.33	1722.16	1715.47
110000	1871.26	1851.80	1836.02	1823.19	1812.72	1804.17	1797.16
120000	2041.37	2020.14	2002.93	1988.93	1977.52	1968.18	1960.54
130000	2211.49	2188.49	2169.84	2154.68	2142.31	2132.20	2123.91
140000	2381.60	2356.83	2336.75	2320.42	2307.10	2296.21	2287.29
150000	2551.72	2525.18	2503.67	2486.17	2471.90	2460.23	2450.67
160000	2721.83	2693.52	2670.58	2651.91	2636.69	2624.24	2614.05
170000	2891.94	2861.87	2837.49	2817.66	2801.48	2788.26	2777.43
180000	3062.06	3030.21	3004.40	2983.40	2966.27	2952.27	2940.80
190000	3232.17	3198.56	3171.31	3149.15	3131.07	3116.29	3104.18
200000	3402.29	3366.90	3338.22	3314.89	3295.86	3280.30	3267.56
210000	3572.40	3535.25	3505.13	3480.63	3460.65	3444.32	3430.94
220000	3742.52	3703.59	3672.04	3646.38	3625.45	3608.33	3594.32
230000	3912.63	3871.94	3838.95	3812.12	3790.24	3772.35	3757.69
240000	4082.74	4040.28	4005.86	3977.87	3955.03	3936.36	3921.07
250000	4252.86	4208.63	4172.78	4143.61	4119.83	4100.38	4084.45
260000	4422.97	4376.97	4339.69	4309.36	4284.62	4264.39	4247.83
270000	4593.09	4545.32	4506.60	4475.10	4449.41	4428.41	4411.21
280000	4763.20	4713.66	4673.51	4640.85	4614.20	4592.42	4574.58
290000	4933.32	4882.01	4840.42	4806.59	4779.00	4756.44	4737.96
300000	5103.43	5050.35	5007.33	4972.34	4943.79	4920.45	4901.34
310000	5273.54	5218.70	5174.24	5138.08	5108.58	5084.47	5064.72
320000	5443.66	5387.04	5341.15	5303.82	5273.38	5248.48	5228.10
330000	5613.77	5555.39	5508.06	5469.57	5438.17	5412.50	5391.47
340000	5783.89	5723.73	5674.97	5635.31	5602.96	5576.52	5554.85
350000	5954.00	5892.08	5841.89	5801.06	5767.76	5740.53	5718.23
400000	6804.57	6733.81	6676.44	6629.78	6591.72	6560.61	6535.12
450000	7655.15	7575.53	7511.00	7458.50	7415.69	7380.68	7352.01
500000	8505.72	8417.26	8345.55	8287.23	8239.65	8200.76	8168.90
550000	9356.29	9258.98	9180.11	9115.95	9063.62	9020.83	8985.79
600000	10206.86	10100.71	10014.66	9944.67	9887.58	9840.91	9802.68

Monthly Payments 19¼%
necessary to amortize a loan

AMOUNT	22 YEARS	23 YEARS	24 YEARS	25 YEARS	30 YEARS	35 YEARS	40 YEARS
100	1.63	1.62	1.62	1.62	1.61	1.61	1.60
200	3.26	3.25	3.24	3.24	3.22	3.21	3.21
500	8.14	8.12	8.10	8.09	8.05	8.03	8.02
1000	16.29	16.24	16.21	16.18	16.09	16.06	16.05
2000	32.57	32.49	32.41	32.36	32.19	32.12	32.10
5000	81.43	81.21	81.04	80.89	80.47	80.31	80.25
6000	97.71	97.46	97.24	97.07	96.56	96.37	96.30
7000	114.00	113.70	113.45	113.25	112.66	112.43	112.35
8000	130.28	129.94	129.66	129.43	128.75	128.49	128.40
9000	146.57	146.18	145.87	145.60	144.85	144.56	144.44
10000	162.86	162.43	162.07	161.78	160.94	160.62	160.49
15000	244.28	243.64	243.11	242.67	241.41	240.93	240.74
20000	325.71	324.85	324.15	323.57	321.88	321.24	320.99
25000	407.14	406.07	405.18	404.46	402.35	401.54	401.23
30000	488.57	487.28	486.22	485.35	482.82	481.85	481.48
35000	569.99	568.49	567.26	566.24	563.29	562.16	561.73
40000	651.42	649.70	648.29	647.13	643.76	642.47	641.98
45000	732.85	730.92	729.33	728.02	724.23	722.78	722.22
50000	814.28	812.13	810.37	808.91	804.70	803.09	802.47
55000	895.70	893.34	891.40	889.81	885.17	883.40	882.72
60000	977.13	974.56	972.44	970.70	965.64	963.71	962.96
65000	1058.56	1055.77	1053.48	1051.59	1046.11	1044.01	1043.21
70000	1139.99	1136.98	1134.51	1132.48	1126.58	1124.32	1123.46
75000	1221.42	1218.20	1215.55	1213.37	1207.05	1204.63	1203.70
80000	1302.84	1299.41	1296.59	1294.26	1287.52	1284.94	1283.95
85000	1384.27	1380.62	1377.62	1375.15	1367.99	1365.25	1364.20
90000	1465.70	1461.84	1458.66	1456.04	1448.46	1445.56	1444.45
95000	1547.13	1543.05	1539.70	1536.94	1528.93	1525.87	1524.69
100000	1628.55	1624.26	1620.73	1617.83	1609.40	1606.18	1604.94
105000	1709.98	1705.47	1701.77	1698.72	1689.87	1686.48	1685.19
110000	1791.41	1786.69	1782.80	1779.61	1770.34	1766.79	1765.43
120000	1954.26	1949.11	1944.88	1941.39	1931.28	1927.41	1925.93
130000	2117.12	2111.54	2106.95	2103.18	2092.22	2088.03	2086.42
140000	2279.98	2273.97	2269.02	2264.96	2253.16	2248.65	2246.91
150000	2442.83	2436.39	2431.10	2426.74	2414.10	2409.26	2407.41
160000	2605.69	2598.82	2593.17	2588.52	2575.03	2569.88	2567.90
170000	2768.54	2761.24	2755.24	2750.31	2735.97	2730.50	2728.40
180000	2931.40	2923.67	2917.32	2912.09	2896.91	2891.12	2888.89
190000	3094.25	3086.10	3079.39	3073.87	3057.85	3051.73	3049.38
200000	3257.11	3248.52	3241.46	3235.65	3218.79	3212.35	3209.88
210000	3419.96	3410.95	3403.54	3397.44	3379.73	3372.97	3370.37
220000	3582.82	3573.37	3565.61	3559.22	3540.67	3533.59	3530.87
230000	3745.67	3735.80	3727.68	3721.00	3701.61	3694.20	3691.36
240000	3908.53	3898.23	3889.76	3882.79	3862.55	3854.82	3851.85
250000	4071.38	4060.65	4051.83	4044.57	4023.49	4015.44	4012.35
260000	4234.24	4223.08	4213.90	4206.35	4184.43	4176.06	4172.84
270000	4397.10	4385.51	4375.98	4368.13	4345.37	4336.67	4333.34
280000	4559.95	4547.93	4538.05	4529.92	4506.31	4497.29	4493.83
290000	4722.81	4710.36	4700.12	4691.70	4667.25	4657.91	4654.32
300000	4885.66	4872.78	4862.20	4853.48	4828.19	4818.53	4814.82
310000	5048.52	5035.21	5024.27	5015.27	4989.13	4979.14	4975.31
320000	5211.37	5197.64	5186.34	5177.05	5150.07	5139.76	5135.81
330000	5374.23	5360.06	5348.41	5338.83	5311.01	5300.38	5296.30
340000	5537.08	5522.49	5510.49	5500.61	5471.95	5461.00	5456.79
350000	5699.94	5684.91	5672.56	5662.40	5632.89	5621.61	5617.29
400000	6514.22	6497.04	6482.93	6471.31	6437.59	6424.70	6419.76
450000	7328.49	7309.18	7293.29	7280.22	7242.92	7227.79	7222.23
500000	8142.77	8121.31	8103.66	8089.14	8046.58	8030.88	8024.70
550000	8957.05	8933.44	8914.02	8898.05	8851.68	8833.97	8827.17
600000	9771.32	9745.57	9724.39	9706.96	9656.38	9637.05	9629.64

235

19½%

Monthly Payments
necessary to amortize a loan

AMOUNT	1 YEAR	2 YEARS	3 YEARS	4 YEARS	5 YEARS	6 YEARS	7 YEARS
100	9.24	5.07	3.69	3.02	2.62	2.37	2.19
200	18.48	10.13	7.38	6.03	5.24	4.73	4.38
500	46.20	25.33	18.45	15.08	13.11	11.83	10.95
1000	92.40	50.65	36.91	30.16	26.22	23.66	21.91
2000	184.79	101.30	73.82	60.33	52.43	47.33	43.81
5000	461.98	253.26	184.55	150.82	131.08	118.32	109.53
6000	554.37	303.91	221.46	180.99	157.30	141.98	131.44
7000	646.77	354.56	258.37	211.15	183.52	165.65	153.34
8000	739.16	405.22	295.27	241.32	209.73	189.31	175.25
9000	831.56	455.87	332.18	271.48	235.95	212.97	197.16
10000	923.95	506.52	369.09	301.65	262.16	236.64	219.06
15000	1385.93	759.78	553.64	452.47	393.25	354.96	328.59
20000	1847.91	1013.04	738.19	603.29	524.33	473.28	438.12
25000	2309.88	1266.30	922.73	754.12	655.41	591.60	547.65
30000	2771.86	1519.56	1107.28	904.94	786.49	709.92	657.18
35000	3233.84	1772.82	1291.83	1055.76	917.58	828.24	766.71
40000	3695.81	2026.08	1476.37	1206.58	1048.66	946.56	876.24
45000	4157.79	2279.33	1660.92	1357.41	1179.74	1064.87	985.78
50000	4619.77	2532.59	1845.47	1508.23	1310.82	1183.19	1095.31
55000	5081.75	2785.85	2030.01	1659.05	1441.90	1301.51	1204.84
60000	5543.72	3039.11	2214.56	1809.88	1572.99	1419.83	1314.37
65000	6005.70	3292.37	2399.11	1960.70	1704.07	1538.15	1423.90
70000	6467.68	3545.63	2583.65	2111.52	1835.15	1656.47	1533.43
75000	6929.65	3798.89	2768.20	2262.35	1966.23	1774.79	1642.96
80000	7391.63	4052.15	2952.74	2413.17	2097.32	1893.11	1752.49
85000	7853.61	4305.41	3137.29	2563.99	2228.40	2011.43	1862.02
90000	8315.58	4558.67	3321.84	2714.81	2359.48	2129.75	1971.55
95000	8777.56	4811.93	3506.38	2865.64	2490.56	2248.07	2081.08
100000	9239.54	5065.19	3690.93	3016.46	2621.64	2366.39	2190.61
105000	9701.51	5318.45	3875.48	3167.28	2752.73	2484.71	2300.14
110000	10163.49	5571.71	4060.02	3318.11	2883.81	2603.03	2409.67
120000	11087.44	6078.23	4429.12	3619.75	3145.97	2839.67	2628.73
130000	12011.40	6584.74	4798.21	3921.40	3408.14	3076.30	2847.80
140000	12935.35	7091.26	5167.30	4223.04	3670.30	3312.94	3066.86
150000	13859.31	7597.78	5536.40	4524.69	3932.47	3549.58	3285.92
160000	14783.26	8104.30	5905.49	4826.34	4194.63	3786.22	3504.98
170000	15707.21	8610.82	6274.58	5127.98	4456.80	4022.86	3724.04
180000	16631.17	9117.34	6643.68	5429.63	4718.96	4259.50	3943.10
190000	17555.12	9623.86	7012.77	5731.27	4981.12	4496.14	4162.16
200000	18479.07	10130.38	7381.86	6032.92	5243.29	4732.78	4381.22
210000	19403.03	10636.89	7750.96	6334.57	5505.45	4969.42	4600.28
220000	20326.98	11143.41	8120.05	6636.21	5767.62	5206.05	4819.35
230000	21250.94	11649.93	8489.14	6937.86	6029.78	5442.69	5038.41
240000	22174.89	12156.45	8858.23	7239.50	6291.95	5679.33	5257.47
250000	23098.84	12662.97	9227.33	7541.15	6554.11	5915.97	5476.53
260000	24022.80	13169.49	9596.42	7842.80	6816.28	6152.61	5695.59
270000	24946.75	13676.01	9965.51	8144.44	7078.44	6389.25	5914.65
280000	25870.70	14182.53	10334.61	8446.09	7340.60	6625.89	6133.71
290000	26794.66	14689.04	10703.70	8747.73	7602.77	6862.53	6352.77
300000	27718.61	15195.56	11072.79	9049.38	7864.93	7099.17	6571.84
310000	28642.57	15702.08	11441.89	9351.03	8127.10	7335.80	6790.90
320000	29566.52	16208.60	11810.98	9652.67	8389.26	7572.44	7009.96
330000	30490.47	16715.12	12180.07	9954.32	8651.43	7809.08	7229.02
340000	31414.43	17221.64	12549.17	10255.96	8913.59	8045.72	7448.08
350000	32338.38	17728.16	12918.26	10557.61	9175.76	8282.36	7667.14
400000	36958.15	20260.75	14763.72	12065.84	10486.58	9465.55	8762.45
450000	41577.92	22793.34	16609.19	13574.07	11797.40	10648.75	9857.75
500000	46197.69	25325.94	18454.66	15082.30	13108.22	11831.94	10953.06
550000	50817.46	27858.53	20300.12	16590.53	14419.04	13015.14	12048.37
600000	55437.22	30391.13	22145.59	18098.76	15729.87	14198.33	13143.67

Monthly Payments 19½%
necessary to amortize a loan

AMOUNT	8 YEARS	9 YEARS	10 YEARS	11 YEARS	12 YEARS	13 YEARS	14 YEARS
100	2.06	1.97	1.90	1.84	1.80	1.77	1.74
200	4.13	3.94	3.80	3.69	3.60	3.54	3.48
500	10.32	9.85	9.50	9.22	9.01	8.84	8.71
1000	20.64	19.71	19.00	18.45	18.02	17.68	17.41
2000	41.28	39.41	37.99	36.89	36.04	35.36	34.82
5000	103.21	98.53	94.98	92.24	90.09	88.40	87.05
6000	123.85	118.23	113.97	110.68	108.11	106.08	104.46
7000	144.50	137.94	132.97	129.13	126.13	123.76	121.87
8000	165.14	157.65	151.96	147.58	144.15	141.44	139.29
9000	185.78	177.35	170.96	166.02	162.17	159.12	156.70
10000	206.42	197.06	189.95	184.47	180.19	176.80	174.11
15000	309.64	295.58	284.93	276.71	270.28	265.20	261.16
20000	412.85	394.11	379.90	368.94	360.37	353.60	348.21
25000	516.06	492.64	474.88	461.18	450.47	442.01	435.27
30000	619.27	591.17	569.86	553.41	540.56	530.41	522.32
35000	722.49	689.70	664.83	645.65	630.65	618.81	609.37
40000	825.70	788.23	759.81	737.89	720.75	707.21	696.43
45000	928.91	886.75	854.78	830.12	810.84	795.61	783.48
50000	1032.12	985.28	949.76	922.36	900.93	884.01	870.54
55000	1135.34	1083.81	1044.74	1014.59	991.03	972.41	957.59
60000	1238.55	1182.34	1139.71	1106.83	1081.12	1060.81	1044.64
65000	1341.76	1280.87	1234.69	1199.06	1171.21	1149.21	1131.70
70000	1444.97	1379.40	1329.67	1291.30	1261.31	1237.61	1218.75
75000	1548.18	1477.92	1424.64	1383.53	1351.40	1326.02	1305.80
80000	1651.40	1576.45	1519.62	1475.77	1441.49	1414.42	1392.86
85000	1754.61	1674.98	1614.59	1568.01	1531.59	1502.82	1479.91
90000	1857.82	1773.51	1709.57	1660.24	1621.68	1591.22	1566.96
95000	1961.03	1872.04	1804.55	1752.48	1711.77	1679.62	1654.02
100000	2064.25	1970.57	1899.52	1844.71	1801.86	1768.02	1741.07
105000	2167.46	2069.09	1994.50	1936.95	1891.96	1856.42	1828.12
110000	2270.67	2167.62	2089.47	2029.18	1982.05	1944.82	1915.18
120000	2477.10	2364.68	2279.43	2213.66	2162.24	2121.63	2089.28
130000	2683.52	2561.74	2469.38	2398.13	2342.42	2298.43	2263.39
140000	2889.94	2758.79	2659.33	2582.60	2522.61	2475.23	2437.50
150000	3096.37	2955.85	2849.28	2767.07	2702.80	2652.03	2611.61
160000	3302.79	3152.91	3039.24	2951.54	2882.98	2828.83	2785.71
170000	3509.22	3349.96	3229.19	3136.01	3063.17	3005.64	2959.82
180000	3715.64	3547.02	3419.14	3320.48	3243.36	3182.44	3133.93
190000	3922.07	3744.07	3609.09	3504.95	3423.54	3359.24	3308.03
200000	4128.49	3941.13	3799.04	3689.43	3603.73	3536.04	3482.14
210000	4334.92	4138.19	3989.00	3873.90	3783.92	3712.84	3656.25
220000	4541.34	4335.24	4178.95	4058.37	3964.10	3889.65	3830.36
230000	4747.77	4532.30	4368.90	4242.84	4144.29	4066.45	4004.46
240000	4954.19	4729.36	4558.85	4427.31	4324.48	4243.25	4178.57
250000	5160.62	4926.41	4748.81	4611.78	4504.66	4420.05	4352.68
260000	5367.04	5123.47	4938.76	4796.25	4684.85	4596.86	4526.78
270000	5573.46	5320.53	5128.71	4980.72	4865.04	4773.66	4700.89
280000	5779.89	5517.58	5318.66	5165.20	5045.22	4950.46	4875.00
290000	5986.31	5714.64	5508.61	5349.67	5225.41	5127.26	5049.10
300000	6192.74	5911.70	5698.57	5534.14	5405.59	5304.06	5223.21
310000	6399.16	6108.75	5888.52	5718.61	5585.78	5480.87	5397.32
320000	6605.59	6305.81	6078.47	5903.08	5765.97	5657.67	5571.43
330000	6812.01	6502.87	6268.42	6087.55	5946.15	5834.47	5745.53
340000	7018.44	6699.92	6458.38	6272.02	6126.34	6011.27	5919.64
350000	7224.86	6896.98	6648.33	6456.49	6306.53	6188.07	6093.75
400000	8256.98	7882.26	7598.09	7378.85	7207.46	7072.08	6964.28
450000	9289.11	8867.55	8547.85	8301.21	8108.39	7956.10	7834.82
500000	10321.23	9852.83	9497.61	9223.56	9009.32	8840.11	8705.35
550000	11353.35	10838.11	10447.37	10145.92	9910.26	9724.12	9575.89
600000	12385.48	11823.39	11397.13	11068.28	10811.19	10608.13	10446.42

Monthly Payments
necessary to amortize a loan

AMOUNT	15 YEARS	16 YEARS	17 YEARS	18 YEARS	19 YEARS	20 YEARS	21 YEARS
100	1.72	1.70	1.69	1.68	1.67	1.66	1.65
200	3.44	3.40	3.38	3.35	3.33	3.32	3.31
500	8.60	8.51	8.44	8.38	8.34	8.30	8.27
1000	17.19	17.02	16.88	16.77	16.67	16.60	16.53
2000	34.39	34.04	33.76	33.53	33.35	33.19	33.07
5000	85.97	85.10	84.40	83.83	83.36	82.98	82.67
6000	103.17	102.12	101.28	100.59	100.04	99.58	99.21
7000	120.36	119.14	118.16	117.36	116.71	116.18	115.74
8000	137.56	136.17	135.04	134.12	133.38	132.77	132.28
9000	154.75	153.19	151.92	150.89	150.05	149.37	148.81
10000	171.95	170.21	168.80	167.66	166.73	165.97	165.35
15000	257.92	255.31	253.20	251.48	250.09	248.95	248.02
20000	343.89	340.41	337.60	335.31	333.45	331.93	330.69
25000	429.87	425.52	422.00	419.14	416.81	414.92	413.37
30000	515.84	510.62	506.40	502.97	500.18	497.90	496.04
35000	601.81	595.72	590.80	586.80	583.54	580.88	578.71
40000	687.79	680.83	675.20	670.62	666.90	663.87	661.38
45000	773.76	765.93	759.59	754.45	750.26	746.85	744.06
50000	859.74	851.03	843.99	838.28	833.63	829.83	826.73
55000	945.71	936.14	928.39	922.11	916.99	912.82	909.40
60000	1031.68	1021.24	1012.79	1005.93	1000.35	995.80	992.08
65000	1117.66	1106.34	1097.19	1089.76	1083.72	1078.78	1074.75
70000	1203.63	1191.45	1181.59	1173.59	1167.08	1161.77	1157.42
75000	1289.60	1276.55	1265.99	1257.42	1250.44	1244.75	1240.10
80000	1375.58	1361.65	1350.39	1341.25	1333.80	1327.73	1322.77
85000	1461.55	1446.76	1434.79	1425.07	1417.17	1410.71	1405.44
90000	1547.52	1531.86	1519.19	1508.90	1500.53	1493.70	1488.12
95000	1633.50	1616.96	1603.59	1592.73	1583.89	1576.68	1570.79
100000	1719.47	1702.07	1687.99	1676.56	1667.25	1659.66	1653.46
105000	1805.44	1787.17	1772.39	1760.39	1750.62	1742.65	1736.13
110000	1891.42	1872.27	1856.79	1844.21	1833.98	1825.63	1818.81
120000	2063.36	2042.48	2025.59	2011.87	2000.71	1991.60	1984.15
130000	2235.31	2212.69	2194.38	2179.53	2167.43	2157.56	2149.50
140000	2407.26	2382.89	2363.18	2347.18	2334.16	2323.53	2314.85
150000	2579.21	2553.10	2531.98	2514.84	2500.88	2489.50	2480.19
160000	2751.15	2723.31	2700.78	2682.49	2667.61	2655.46	2645.54
170000	2923.10	2893.51	2869.58	2850.15	2834.33	2821.43	2810.88
180000	3095.05	3063.72	3038.38	3017.80	3001.06	2987.40	2976.23
190000	3266.99	3233.93	3207.18	3185.46	3167.78	3153.36	3141.58
200000	3438.94	3404.13	3375.98	3353.12	3334.51	3319.33	3306.92
210000	3610.89	3574.34	3544.77	3520.77	3501.23	3485.30	3472.27
220000	3782.83	3744.55	3713.57	3688.43	3667.96	3651.26	3637.61
230000	3954.78	3914.75	3882.37	3856.08	3834.69	3817.23	3802.96
240000	4126.73	4084.96	4051.17	4023.74	4001.41	3983.20	3968.31
250000	4298.68	4255.17	4219.97	4191.40	4168.14	4149.16	4133.65
260000	4470.62	4425.37	4388.77	4359.05	4334.86	4315.13	4299.00
270000	4642.57	4595.58	4557.57	4526.71	4501.59	4481.09	4464.35
280000	4814.52	4765.79	4726.37	4694.36	4668.31	4647.06	4629.69
290000	4986.46	4935.99	4895.16	4862.02	4835.04	4813.03	4795.04
300000	5158.41	5106.20	5063.96	5029.67	5001.76	4978.99	4960.38
310000	5330.36	5276.41	5232.76	5197.33	5168.49	5144.96	5125.73
320000	5502.30	5446.61	5401.56	5364.99	5335.21	5310.93	5291.08
330000	5674.25	5616.82	5570.36	5532.64	5501.94	5476.89	5456.42
340000	5846.20	5787.03	5739.16	5700.30	5668.67	5642.86	5621.77
350000	6018.15	5957.24	5907.96	5867.95	5835.39	5808.83	5787.11
400000	6877.88	6808.27	6751.95	6706.23	6669.02	6638.66	6613.84
450000	7737.02	7659.30	7595.94	7544.51	7502.65	7468.49	7440.58
500000	8597.35	8510.34	8439.94	8382.79	8336.27	8298.32	8267.31
550000	9457.09	9361.37	9283.93	9221.07	9169.90	9128.16	9094.04
600000	10316.82	10212.40	10127.93	10059.35	10003.53	9957.99	9920.77

Monthly Payments

19¹/₂%

necessary to amortize a loan

AMOUNT	22 YEARS	23 YEARS	24 YEARS	25 YEARS	30 YEARS	35 YEARS	40 YEARS
100	1.65	1.64	1.64	1.64	1.63	1.63	1.63
200	3.30	3.29	3.28	3.28	3.26	3.25	3.25
500	8.24	8.22	8.20	8.19	8.15	8.13	8.13
1000	16.48	16.44	16.41	16.38	16.30	16.27	16.26
2000	32.97	32.88	32.82	32.76	32.60	32.54	32.51
5000	82.42	82.21	82.04	81.90	81.50	81.34	81.29
6000	98.90	98.65	98.45	98.28	97.80	97.61	97.54
7000	115.39	115.10	114.86	114.66	114.09	113.88	113.80
8000	131.87	131.54	131.26	131.04	130.39	130.15	130.06
9000	148.35	147.98	147.67	147.42	146.69	146.42	146.31
10000	164.84	164.42	164.08	163.80	162.99	162.69	162.57
15000	247.26	246.63	246.12	245.70	244.49	244.03	243.86
20000	329.68	328.84	328.16	327.60	325.98	325.37	325.14
25000	412.10	411.06	410.20	409.50	407.48	406.72	406.43
30000	494.52	493.27	492.24	491.40	488.98	488.06	487.71
35000	576.93	575.48	574.28	573.30	570.47	569.40	569.00
40000	659.35	657.69	656.32	655.20	651.97	650.75	650.28
45000	741.77	739.90	738.36	737.10	733.46	732.09	731.57
50000	824.19	822.11	820.40	819.00	814.96	813.43	812.85
55000	906.61	904.32	902.44	900.90	896.46	894.78	894.14
60000	989.03	986.53	984.49	982.80	977.95	976.12	975.43
65000	1071.45	1068.74	1066.53	1064.70	1059.45	1057.46	1056.71
70000	1153.87	1150.96	1148.57	1146.60	1140.94	1138.81	1138.00
75000	1236.29	1233.17	1230.61	1228.50	1222.44	1220.15	1219.28
80000	1318.71	1315.38	1312.65	1310.40	1303.94	1301.49	1300.57
85000	1401.13	1397.59	1394.69	1392.31	1385.43	1382.84	1381.85
90000	1483.55	1479.80	1476.73	1474.21	1466.93	1464.18	1463.14
95000	1565.96	1562.01	1558.77	1556.11	1548.42	1545.52	1544.42
100000	1648.38	1644.22	1640.81	1638.01	1629.92	1626.87	1625.71
105000	1730.80	1726.43	1722.85	1719.91	1711.42	1708.21	1706.99
110000	1813.22	1808.64	1804.89	1801.81	1792.91	1789.55	1788.28
120000	1978.06	1973.07	1968.97	1965.61	1955.90	1952.24	1950.85
130000	2142.90	2137.49	2133.05	2129.41	2118.90	2114.93	2113.42
140000	2307.74	2301.91	2297.13	2293.21	2281.89	2277.61	2275.99
150000	2472.58	2466.33	2461.21	2457.01	2444.88	2440.30	2438.56
160000	2637.41	2630.76	2625.29	2620.81	2607.87	2602.99	2601.13
170000	2802.25	2795.18	2789.37	2784.61	2770.86	2765.67	2763.71
180000	2967.09	2959.60	2953.46	2948.41	2933.86	2928.36	2926.28
190000	3131.93	3124.02	3117.54	3112.21	3096.85	3091.05	3088.85
200000	3296.77	3288.44	3281.62	3276.01	3259.84	3253.73	3251.42
210000	3461.61	3452.87	3445.70	3439.81	3422.83	3416.42	3413.99
220000	3626.44	3617.29	3609.78	3603.61	3585.82	3579.11	3576.56
230000	3791.28	3781.71	3773.86	3767.41	3748.82	3741.79	3739.13
240000	3956.12	3946.13	3937.94	3931.21	3911.81	3904.48	3901.70
250000	4120.96	4110.56	4102.02	4095.02	4074.80	4067.17	4064.27
260000	4285.80	4274.98	4266.10	4258.82	4237.79	4229.85	4226.84
270000	4450.64	4439.40	4430.18	4422.62	4400.78	4392.54	4389.41
280000	4615.47	4603.82	4594.26	4586.42	4563.78	4555.23	4551.99
290000	4780.31	4768.24	4758.35	4750.22	4726.77	4717.91	4714.56
300000	4945.15	4932.67	4922.43	4914.02	4889.76	4880.60	4877.13
310000	5109.99	5097.09	5086.51	5077.82	5052.75	5043.29	5039.70
320000	5274.83	5261.51	5250.59	5241.62	5215.74	5205.97	5202.27
330000	5439.67	5425.93	5414.67	5405.42	5378.74	5368.66	5364.84
340000	5604.50	5590.36	5578.75	5569.22	5541.73	5531.35	5527.41
350000	5769.34	5754.78	5742.83	5733.02	5704.72	5694.03	5689.98
400000	6593.53	6576.89	6563.23	6552.02	6519.68	6507.47	6502.84
450000	7417.73	7399.00	7383.64	7371.03	7334.64	7320.90	7315.69
500000	8241.92	8221.11	8204.04	8190.03	8149.60	8134.33	8128.55
550000	9066.11	9043.22	9024.45	9009.03	8964.56	8947.77	8941.40
600000	9890.30	9865.33	9844.85	9828.04	9779.52	9761.20	9754.26

19¾%

Monthly Payments
necessary to amortize a loan

AMOUNT	1 YEAR	2 YEARS	3 YEARS	4 YEARS	5 YEARS	6 YEARS	7 YEARS
100	9.25	5.08	3.70	3.03	2.64	2.38	2.21
200	18.50	10.15	7.41	6.06	5.27	4.76	4.41
500	46.26	25.39	18.52	15.15	13.18	11.90	11.03
1000	92.51	50.77	37.04	30.30	26.35	23.81	22.06
2000	185.03	101.55	74.07	60.59	52.71	47.62	44.11
5000	462.57	253.87	185.18	151.49	131.77	119.04	110.28
6000	555.09	304.64	222.22	181.78	158.13	142.85	132.34
7000	647.60	355.42	259.25	212.08	184.48	166.66	154.39
8000	740.12	406.19	296.29	242.38	210.84	190.47	176.45
9000	832.63	456.96	333.33	272.68	237.19	214.27	198.50
10000	925.15	507.74	370.36	302.97	263.55	238.08	220.56
15000	1387.72	761.61	555.54	454.46	395.32	357.12	330.84
20000	1850.30	1015.48	740.73	605.95	527.10	476.16	441.12
25000	2312.87	1269.34	925.91	757.43	658.87	595.20	551.40
30000	2775.45	1523.21	1111.09	908.92	790.65	714.24	661.68
35000	3238.02	1777.08	1296.27	1060.41	922.42	833.28	771.96
40000	3700.60	2030.95	1481.45	1211.89	1054.20	952.33	882.24
45000	4163.17	2284.82	1666.63	1363.38	1185.97	1071.37	992.52
50000	4625.74	2538.69	1851.82	1514.87	1317.75	1190.41	1102.80
55000	5088.32	2792.56	2037.00	1666.35	1449.52	1309.45	1213.08
60000	5550.89	3046.43	2222.18	1817.84	1581.30	1428.49	1323.36
65000	6013.47	3300.29	2407.36	1969.33	1713.07	1547.53	1433.63
70000	6476.04	3554.16	2592.54	2120.81	1844.85	1666.57	1543.91
75000	6938.62	3808.03	2777.72	2272.30	1976.62	1785.61	1654.19
80000	7401.19	4061.90	2962.91	2423.79	2108.40	1904.65	1764.47
85000	7863.77	4315.77	3148.09	2575.27	2240.17	2023.69	1874.75
90000	8326.34	4569.64	3333.27	2726.76	2371.95	2142.73	1985.03
95000	8788.92	4823.51	3518.45	2878.25	2503.72	2261.77	2095.31
100000	9251.49	5077.38	3703.63	3029.73	2635.50	2380.81	2205.59
105000	9714.06	5331.24	3888.81	3181.22	2767.27	2499.85	2315.87
110000	10176.64	5585.11	4074.00	3332.71	2899.05	2618.89	2426.15
120000	11101.79	6092.85	4444.36	3635.68	3162.60	2856.98	2646.71
130000	12026.94	6600.59	4814.72	3938.65	3426.15	3095.06	2867.27
140000	12952.09	7108.33	5185.09	4241.63	3689.70	3333.14	3087.83
150000	13877.23	7616.06	5555.45	4544.60	3953.25	3571.22	3308.39
160000	14802.38	8123.80	5925.81	4847.57	4216.80	3809.30	3528.95
170000	15727.53	8631.54	6296.18	5150.54	4480.35	4047.38	3749.51
180000	16652.68	9139.28	6666.54	5453.52	4743.89	4285.46	3970.06
190000	17577.83	9647.01	7036.90	5756.49	5007.44	4523.55	4190.62
200000	18502.98	10154.75	7407.26	6059.46	5270.99	4761.63	4411.18
210000	19428.13	10662.49	7777.63	6362.44	5534.54	4999.71	4631.74
220000	20353.28	11170.23	8147.99	6665.41	5798.09	5237.79	4852.30
230000	21278.43	11677.96	8518.35	6968.38	6061.64	5475.87	5072.86
240000	22203.58	12185.70	8888.72	7271.36	6325.19	5713.95	5293.42
250000	23128.72	12693.44	9259.08	7574.33	6588.74	5952.03	5513.98
260000	24053.87	13201.18	9629.44	7877.30	6852.29	6190.11	5734.54
270000	24979.02	13708.91	9999.81	8180.28	7115.84	6428.20	5955.10
280000	25904.17	14216.65	10370.17	8483.25	7379.39	6666.28	6175.66
290000	26829.32	14724.39	10740.53	8786.22	7642.94	6904.36	6396.21
300000	27754.47	15232.13	11110.90	9089.20	7906.49	7142.44	6616.77
310000	28679.62	15739.86	11481.26	9392.17	8170.04	7380.52	6837.33
320000	29604.77	16247.60	11851.62	9695.14	8433.59	7618.60	7057.89
330000	30529.92	16755.34	12221.99	9998.12	8697.14	7856.68	7278.45
340000	31455.07	17263.08	12592.35	10301.09	8960.69	8094.77	7499.01
350000	32380.21	17770.81	12962.71	10604.06	9224.24	8332.85	7719.57
400000	37005.96	20309.50	14814.53	12118.93	10541.99	9523.25	8822.37
450000	41631.70	22848.19	16666.35	13633.80	11859.74	10713.66	9925.16
500000	46257.45	25386.88	18518.16	15148.66	13177.49	11904.07	11027.96
550000	50883.19	27925.57	20369.98	16663.53	14495.23	13094.47	12130.75
600000	55508.94	30464.25	22221.79	18178.39	15812.98	14284.88	13233.55

Monthly Payments 19¾%
necessary to amortize a loan

AMOUNT	8 YEARS	9 YEARS	10 YEARS	11 YEARS	12 YEARS	13 YEARS	14 YEARS
100	2.08	1.99	1.92	1.86	1.82	1.79	1.76
200	4.16	3.97	3.83	3.72	3.64	3.57	3.52
500	10.40	9.93	9.58	9.31	9.10	8.93	8.80
1000	20.80	19.87	19.16	18.62	18.19	17.86	17.59
2000	41.60	39.73	38.32	37.23	36.38	35.71	35.18
5000	103.99	99.33	95.80	93.08	90.96	89.29	87.96
6000	124.79	119.19	114.96	111.70	109.15	107.14	105.55
7000	145.58	139.06	134.12	130.32	127.34	125.00	123.14
8000	166.38	158.93	153.28	148.93	145.54	142.86	140.73
9000	187.18	178.79	172.44	167.55	163.73	160.72	158.32
10000	207.98	198.66	191.60	186.16	181.92	178.57	175.91
15000	311.96	297.99	287.40	279.25	272.88	267.86	263.87
20000	415.95	397.32	383.20	372.33	363.84	357.15	351.83
25000	519.94	496.64	479.00	465.41	454.80	446.44	439.78
30000	623.93	595.97	574.80	558.49	545.76	535.72	527.74
35000	727.91	695.30	670.60	651.58	636.72	625.01	615.70
40000	831.90	794.63	766.40	744.66	727.68	714.30	703.66
45000	935.89	893.96	862.20	837.74	818.64	803.58	791.61
50000	1039.88	993.29	958.01	930.82	909.60	892.87	879.57
55000	1143.87	1092.62	1053.81	1023.90	1000.56	982.16	967.53
60000	1247.85	1191.95	1149.61	1116.99	1091.52	1071.45	1055.48
65000	1351.84	1291.28	1245.41	1210.07	1182.48	1160.73	1143.44
70000	1455.83	1390.61	1341.21	1303.15	1273.44	1250.02	1231.40
75000	1559.82	1489.93	1437.01	1396.23	1364.41	1339.31	1319.35
80000	1663.81	1589.26	1532.81	1489.31	1455.37	1428.59	1407.31
85000	1767.79	1688.59	1628.61	1582.40	1546.33	1517.88	1495.27
90000	1871.78	1787.92	1724.41	1675.48	1637.29	1607.17	1583.22
95000	1975.77	1887.25	1820.21	1768.56	1728.25	1696.45	1671.18
100000	2079.76	1986.58	1916.01	1861.64	1819.21	1785.74	1759.14
105000	2183.74	2085.91	2011.81	1954.73	1910.17	1875.03	1847.10
110000	2287.73	2185.24	2107.61	2047.81	2001.13	1964.32	1935.05
120000	2495.71	2383.90	2299.21	2233.97	2183.05	2142.89	2110.97
130000	2703.68	2582.55	2490.81	2420.14	2364.97	2321.46	2286.88
140000	2911.66	2781.21	2682.41	2606.30	2546.89	2500.04	2462.79
150000	3119.63	2979.87	2874.02	2792.47	2728.81	2678.61	2638.71
160000	3327.61	3178.53	3065.62	2978.63	2910.73	2857.19	2814.62
170000	3535.59	3377.19	3257.22	3164.79	3092.65	3035.76	2990.54
180000	3743.56	3575.84	3448.82	3350.96	3274.57	3214.34	3166.45
190000	3951.54	3774.50	3640.42	3537.12	3456.49	3392.91	3342.36
200000	4159.51	3973.16	3832.02	3723.29	3638.41	3571.48	3518.28
210000	4367.49	4171.82	4023.62	3909.45	3820.33	3750.06	3694.19
220000	4575.46	4370.48	4215.22	4095.62	4002.25	3928.63	3870.11
230000	4783.44	4569.13	4406.82	4281.78	4184.18	4107.21	4046.02
240000	4991.42	4767.79	4598.42	4467.94	4366.10	4285.78	4221.93
250000	5199.39	4966.45	4790.03	4654.11	4548.02	4464.35	4397.85
260000	5407.37	5165.11	4981.63	4840.27	4729.94	4642.93	4573.76
270000	5615.34	5363.77	5173.23	5026.44	4911.86	4821.50	4749.67
280000	5823.32	5562.42	5364.83	5212.60	5093.78	5000.08	4925.59
290000	6031.29	5761.08	5556.43	5398.77	5275.70	5178.65	5101.50
300000	6239.27	5959.74	5748.03	5584.93	5457.62	5357.23	5277.42
310000	6447.24	6158.40	5939.63	5771.09	5639.54	5535.80	5453.33
320000	6655.22	6357.06	6131.23	5957.26	5821.46	5714.37	5629.24
330000	6863.20	6555.71	6322.83	6143.42	6003.38	5892.95	5805.16
340000	7071.17	6754.37	6514.43	6329.59	6185.30	6071.52	5981.07
350000	7279.15	6953.03	6706.04	6515.75	6367.22	6250.10	6156.99
400000	8319.03	7946.32	7664.04	7446.57	7276.83	7142.97	7036.55
450000	9358.90	8939.61	8622.05	8377.40	8186.43	8035.84	7916.12
500000	10398.78	9932.90	9580.05	9308.22	9096.03	8928.71	8795.69
550000	11438.66	10926.19	10538.06	10239.04	10005.64	9821.58	9675.26
600000	12478.54	11919.48	11496.06	11169.86	10915.24	10714.45	10554.83

19¾%

Monthly Payments
necessary to amortize a loan

AMOUNT	15 YEARS	16 YEARS	17 YEARS	18 YEARS	19 YEARS	20 YEARS	21 YEARS
100	1.74	1.72	1.71	1.70	1.69	1.68	1.67
200	3.48	3.44	3.41	3.39	3.37	3.36	3.35
500	8.69	8.60	8.53	8.48	8.43	8.40	8.37
1000	17.38	17.21	17.07	16.96	16.87	16.79	16.73
2000	34.76	34.41	34.14	33.91	33.73	33.58	33.46
5000	86.89	86.04	85.35	84.79	84.33	83.96	83.66
6000	104.27	103.24	102.42	101.74	101.20	100.75	100.39
7000	121.65	120.45	119.48	118.70	118.06	117.55	117.12
8000	139.03	137.66	136.55	135.66	134.93	134.34	133.85
9000	156.41	154.87	153.62	152.62	151.80	151.13	150.59
10000	173.79	172.07	170.69	169.57	168.66	167.92	167.32
15000	260.68	258.11	256.04	254.36	252.99	251.88	250.98
20000	347.57	344.15	341.38	339.14	337.33	335.84	334.64
25000	434.46	430.18	426.73	423.93	421.66	419.81	418.30
30000	521.36	516.22	512.08	508.72	505.99	503.77	501.96
35000	608.25	602.26	597.42	593.50	590.32	587.73	585.61
40000	695.14	688.30	682.77	678.29	674.65	671.69	669.27
45000	782.03	774.33	768.11	763.08	758.98	755.65	752.93
50000	868.93	860.37	853.46	847.86	843.31	839.61	836.59
55000	955.82	946.41	938.81	932.65	927.64	923.57	920.25
60000	1042.71	1032.44	1024.15	1017.43	1011.98	1007.53	1003.91
65000	1129.61	1118.48	1109.50	1102.22	1096.31	1091.49	1087.57
70000	1216.50	1204.52	1194.84	1187.01	1180.64	1175.46	1171.23
75000	1303.39	1290.55	1280.19	1271.79	1264.97	1259.42	1254.89
80000	1390.28	1376.59	1365.54	1356.58	1349.30	1343.38	1338.55
85000	1477.18	1462.63	1450.88	1441.36	1433.63	1427.34	1422.21
90000	1564.07	1548.67	1536.23	1526.15	1517.96	1511.30	1505.87
95000	1650.96	1634.70	1621.57	1610.94	1602.30	1595.26	1589.52
100000	1737.85	1720.74	1706.92	1695.72	1686.63	1679.22	1673.18
105000	1824.75	1806.78	1792.26	1780.51	1770.96	1763.18	1756.84
110000	1911.64	1892.81	1877.61	1865.29	1855.29	1847.15	1840.50
120000	2085.43	2064.89	2048.30	2034.87	2023.95	2015.07	2007.82
130000	2259.21	2236.96	2218.99	2204.44	2192.62	2182.99	2175.14
140000	2433.00	2409.03	2389.69	2374.01	2361.28	2350.91	2342.46
150000	2606.78	2581.11	2560.38	2543.58	2529.94	2518.83	2509.78
160000	2780.57	2753.18	2731.07	2713.16	2698.60	2686.76	2677.09
170000	2954.35	2925.26	2901.76	2882.73	2867.27	2854.68	2844.41
180000	3128.14	3097.33	3072.45	3052.30	3035.93	3022.60	3011.73
190000	3301.92	3269.40	3243.15	3221.87	3204.59	3190.52	3179.05
200000	3475.71	3441.48	3413.84	3391.44	3373.25	3358.45	3346.37
210000	3649.49	3613.55	3584.53	3561.02	3541.92	3526.37	3513.69
220000	3823.28	3785.63	3755.22	3730.59	3710.58	3694.29	3681.01
230000	3997.07	3957.70	3925.91	3900.16	3879.24	3862.21	3848.32
240000	4170.85	4129.77	4096.61	4069.73	4047.91	4030.13	4015.64
250000	4344.64	4301.85	4267.30	4239.31	4216.57	4198.06	4182.96
260000	4518.42	4473.92	4437.99	4408.88	4385.23	4365.98	4350.28
270000	4692.21	4646.00	4608.68	4578.45	4553.89	4533.90	4517.60
280000	4865.99	4818.07	4779.37	4748.02	4722.56	4701.82	4684.92
290000	5039.78	4990.14	4950.06	4917.59	4891.22	4869.75	4852.23
300000	5213.56	5162.22	5120.76	5087.17	5059.88	5037.67	5019.55
310000	5387.35	5334.29	5291.45	5256.74	5228.54	5205.59	5186.87
320000	5561.14	5506.37	5462.14	5426.31	5397.21	5373.51	5354.19
330000	5734.92	5678.44	5632.83	5595.88	5565.87	5541.44	5521.51
340000	5908.71	5850.51	5803.52	5765.46	5734.53	5709.36	5688.83
350000	6082.49	6022.59	5974.22	5935.03	5903.20	5877.28	5856.14
400000	6951.42	6882.96	6827.68	6782.89	6746.51	6716.89	6692.74
450000	7820.35	7743.33	7681.13	7630.75	7589.82	7556.50	7529.33
500000	8689.27	8603.70	8534.59	8478.61	8433.14	8396.11	8365.92
550000	9558.20	9464.07	9388.05	9326.47	9276.45	9235.73	9202.51
600000	10427.13	10324.43	10241.51	10174.33	10119.76	10075.34	10039.10

Monthly Payments 19³/₄%

necessary to amortize a loan

AMOUNT	22 YEARS	23 YEARS	24 YEARS	25 YEARS	30 YEARS	35 YEARS	40 YEARS
100	1.67	1.66	1.66	1.66	1.65	1.65	1.65
200	3.34	3.33	3.32	3.32	3.30	3.30	3.29
500	8.34	8.32	8.30	8.29	8.25	8.24	8.23
1000	16.68	16.64	16.61	16.58	16.50	16.48	16.46
2000	33.37	33.28	33.22	33.16	33.01	32.95	32.93
5000	83.41	83.21	83.05	82.91	82.52	82.38	82.32
6000	100.10	99.85	99.66	99.49	99.03	98.85	98.79
7000	116.78	116.50	116.26	116.08	115.53	115.33	115.25
8000	133.46	133.14	132.87	132.66	132.04	131.81	131.72
9000	150.14	149.78	149.48	149.24	148.54	148.28	148.18
10000	166.83	166.42	166.09	165.82	165.05	164.76	164.65
15000	250.24	249.63	249.14	248.73	247.57	247.14	246.97
20000	333.65	332.84	332.18	331.64	330.09	329.51	329.30
25000	417.06	416.05	415.23	414.55	412.62	411.89	411.62
30000	500.48	499.27	498.28	497.46	495.14	494.27	493.95
35000	583.89	582.48	581.32	580.38	577.66	576.65	576.27
40000	667.30	665.69	664.37	663.29	660.18	659.03	658.59
45000	750.71	748.90	747.41	746.20	742.71	741.41	740.92
50000	834.13	832.11	830.46	829.11	825.23	823.78	823.24
55000	917.54	915.32	913.51	912.02	907.75	906.16	905.57
60000	1000.95	998.53	996.55	994.93	990.28	988.54	987.89
65000	1084.36	1081.74	1079.60	1077.84	1072.80	1070.92	1070.21
70000	1167.78	1164.95	1162.64	1160.75	1155.32	1153.30	1152.54
75000	1251.19	1248.16	1245.69	1243.66	1237.85	1235.68	1234.86
80000	1334.60	1331.38	1328.73	1326.57	1320.37	1318.05	1317.19
85000	1418.01	1414.59	1411.78	1409.48	1402.89	1400.43	1399.51
90000	1501.43	1497.80	1494.83	1492.39	1485.41	1482.81	1481.84
95000	1584.84	1581.01	1577.87	1575.30	1567.94	1565.19	1564.16
100000	1668.25	1664.22	1660.92	1658.21	1650.46	1647.57	1646.48
105000	1751.66	1747.43	1743.96	1741.13	1732.98	1729.95	1728.81
110000	1835.08	1830.64	1827.01	1824.04	1815.51	1812.32	1811.13
120000	2001.90	1997.06	1993.10	1989.86	1980.55	1977.08	1975.78
130000	2168.73	2163.49	2159.19	2155.68	2145.60	2141.84	2140.43
140000	2335.55	2329.91	2325.29	2321.50	2310.65	2306.60	2305.08
150000	2502.38	2496.33	2491.38	2487.32	2475.69	2471.35	2469.73
160000	2669.20	2662.75	2657.47	2653.14	2640.74	2636.11	2634.37
170000	2836.03	2829.17	2823.56	2818.96	2805.78	2800.87	2799.02
180000	3002.85	2995.59	2989.65	2984.79	2970.83	2965.62	2963.67
190000	3169.68	3162.02	3155.75	3150.61	3135.88	3130.38	3128.32
200000	3336.50	3328.44	3321.84	3316.43	3300.92	3295.14	3292.97
210000	3503.33	3494.86	3487.93	3482.25	3465.97	3459.89	3457.62
220000	3670.15	3661.28	3654.02	3648.07	3631.01	3624.65	3622.27
230000	3836.98	3827.70	3820.11	3813.89	3796.06	3789.41	3786.91
240000	4003.81	3994.13	3986.20	3979.72	3961.11	3954.16	3951.56
250000	4170.63	4160.55	4152.30	4145.54	4126.15	4118.92	4116.21
260000	4337.46	4326.97	4318.39	4311.36	4291.20	4283.68	4280.86
270000	4504.28	4493.39	4484.48	4477.18	4456.24	4448.43	4445.51
280000	4671.11	4659.81	4650.57	4643.00	4621.29	4613.19	4610.16
290000	4837.93	4826.24	4816.66	4808.82	4786.34	4777.95	4774.80
300000	5004.76	4992.66	4982.76	4974.64	4951.38	4942.70	4939.45
310000	5171.58	5159.08	5148.85	5140.47	5116.43	5107.46	5104.10
320000	5338.41	5325.50	5314.94	5306.29	5281.47	5272.22	5268.75
330000	5505.23	5491.92	5481.03	5472.11	5446.52	5436.97	5433.40
340000	5672.06	5658.35	5647.12	5637.93	5611.57	5601.73	5598.05
350000	5838.88	5824.77	5813.21	5803.75	5776.61	5766.49	5762.70
400000	6673.01	6656.88	6643.67	6632.86	6601.84	6590.27	6585.94
450000	7507.13	7488.99	7474.13	7461.97	7427.07	7414.06	7409.18
500000	8341.26	8321.10	8304.59	8291.07	8252.30	8237.84	8232.42
550000	9175.39	9153.21	9135.05	9120.18	9077.54	9061.62	9055.66
600000	10009.51	9985.32	9965.51	9949.29	9902.77	9885.41	9878.91

20%

Monthly Payments
necessary to amortize a loan

AMOUNT	1 YEAR	2 YEARS	3 YEARS	4 YEARS	5 YEARS	6 YEARS	7 YEARS
100	9.26	5.09	3.72	3.04	2.65	2.40	2.22
200	18.53	10.18	7.43	6.09	5.30	4.79	4.44
500	46.32	25.45	18.58	15.22	13.25	11.98	11.10
1000	92.63	50.90	37.16	30.43	26.49	23.95	22.21
2000	185.27	101.79	74.33	60.86	52.99	47.91	44.41
5000	463.17	254.48	185.82	152.15	132.47	119.76	111.03
6000	555.81	305.37	222.98	182.58	158.96	143.72	133.24
7000	648.44	356.27	260.15	213.01	185.46	167.67	155.44
8000	741.08	407.17	297.31	243.44	211.95	191.62	177.65
9000	833.71	458.06	334.47	273.87	238.44	215.58	199.86
10000	926.35	508.96	371.64	304.30	264.94	239.53	222.06
15000	1389.52	763.44	557.45	456.46	397.41	359.29	333.09
20000	1852.69	1017.92	743.27	608.61	529.88	479.06	444.12
25000	2315.86	1272.40	929.09	760.76	662.35	598.82	555.15
30000	2779.04	1526.87	1114.91	912.91	794.82	718.58	666.19
35000	3242.21	1781.35	1300.73	1065.06	927.29	838.35	777.22
40000	3705.38	2035.83	1486.54	1217.21	1059.76	958.11	888.25
45000	4168.55	2290.31	1672.36	1369.37	1192.22	1077.88	999.28
50000	4631.73	2544.79	1858.18	1521.52	1324.69	1197.64	1110.31
55000	5094.90	2799.27	2044.00	1673.67	1457.16	1317.41	1221.34
60000	5558.07	3053.75	2229.82	1825.82	1589.63	1437.17	1332.37
65000	6021.24	3308.23	2415.63	1977.97	1722.10	1556.93	1443.40
70000	6484.42	3562.71	2601.45	2130.13	1854.57	1676.70	1554.43
75000	6947.59	3817.19	2787.27	2282.28	1987.04	1796.46	1665.46
80000	7410.76	4071.66	2973.09	2434.43	2119.51	1916.23	1776.50
85000	7873.93	4326.14	3158.90	2586.58	2251.98	2035.99	1887.53
90000	8337.11	4580.62	3344.72	2738.73	2384.45	2155.75	1998.56
95000	8800.28	4835.10	3530.54	2890.88	2516.92	2275.52	2109.59
100000	9263.45	5089.58	3716.36	3043.04	2649.39	2395.28	2220.62
105000	9726.62	5344.06	3902.18	3195.19	2781.86	2515.05	2331.65
110000	10189.80	5598.54	4087.99	3347.34	2914.33	2634.81	2442.68
120000	11116.14	6107.50	4459.63	3651.64	3179.27	2874.34	2664.74
130000	12042.49	6616.45	4831.27	3955.95	3444.20	3113.87	2886.81
140000	12968.83	7125.41	5202.90	4260.25	3709.14	3353.40	3108.87
150000	13895.18	7634.37	5574.54	4564.55	3974.08	3592.92	3330.93
160000	14821.52	8143.33	5946.17	4868.86	4239.02	3832.45	3552.99
170000	15747.87	8652.29	6317.81	5173.16	4503.96	4071.98	3775.05
180000	16674.21	9161.24	6689.45	5477.47	4768.90	4311.51	3997.12
190000	17600.56	9670.20	7061.08	5781.77	5033.84	4551.04	4219.18
200000	18526.90	10179.16	7432.72	6086.07	5298.78	4790.57	4441.24
210000	19453.25	10688.12	7804.35	6390.38	5563.72	5030.09	4663.30
220000	20379.59	11197.08	8175.99	6694.68	5828.65	5269.62	4885.36
230000	21305.94	11706.03	8547.62	6998.98	6093.59	5509.15	5107.43
240000	22232.28	12214.99	8919.26	7303.29	6358.53	5748.68	5329.49
250000	23158.63	12723.95	9290.90	7607.59	6623.47	5988.21	5551.55
260000	24084.97	13232.91	9662.53	7911.89	6888.41	6227.73	5773.61
270000	25011.32	13741.87	10034.17	8216.20	7153.35	6467.26	5995.67
280000	25937.66	14250.82	10405.80	8520.50	7418.29	6706.79	6217.74
290000	26864.01	14759.78	10777.44	8824.81	7683.23	6946.32	6439.80
300000	27790.35	15268.74	11149.08	9129.11	7948.17	7185.85	6661.86
310000	28716.70	15777.70	11520.71	9433.41	8213.10	7425.38	6883.92
320000	29643.04	16286.66	11892.35	9737.72	8478.04	7664.90	7105.98
330000	30569.39	16795.61	12263.98	10042.02	8742.98	7904.43	7328.05
340000	31495.73	17304.57	12635.62	10346.32	9007.92	8143.96	7550.11
350000	32422.08	17813.53	13007.25	10650.63	9272.86	8383.49	7772.17
400000	37053.80	20358.32	14865.43	12172.14	10597.55	9581.13	8882.48
450000	41685.53	22903.11	16723.61	13693.66	11922.25	10778.77	9992.79
500000	46317.25	25447.90	18581.79	15215.18	13246.94	11976.41	11103.10
550000	50948.98	27992.69	20439.97	16736.70	14571.64	13174.05	12213.41
600000	55580.70	30537.48	22298.15	18258.22	15896.33	14371.70	13323.72

Monthly Payments 20%
necessary to amortize a loan

AMOUNT	8 YEARS	9 YEARS	10 YEARS	11 YEARS	12 YEARS	13 YEARS	14 YEARS
100	2.10	2.00	1.93	1.88	1.84	1.80	1.78
200	4.19	4.01	3.87	3.76	3.67	3.61	3.55
500	10.48	10.01	9.66	9.39	9.18	9.02	8.89
1000	20.95	20.03	19.33	18.79	18.37	18.04	17.77
2000	41.91	40.05	38.65	37.57	36.73	36.07	35.55
5000	104.77	100.13	96.63	93.93	91.83	90.18	88.86
6000	125.72	120.16	115.95	112.72	110.20	108.21	106.64
7000	146.67	140.19	135.28	131.50	128.56	126.25	124.41
8000	167.63	160.21	154.60	150.29	146.93	144.28	142.18
9000	188.58	180.24	173.93	169.08	165.29	162.32	159.95
10000	209.53	200.27	193.26	187.86	183.66	180.35	177.73
15000	314.30	300.40	289.88	281.80	275.49	270.53	266.59
20000	419.06	400.53	386.51	375.73	367.32	360.70	355.45
25000	523.83	500.66	483.14	469.66	459.15	450.88	444.32
30000	628.60	600.80	579.77	563.59	550.98	541.06	533.18
35000	733.36	700.93	676.39	657.52	642.81	631.23	622.04
40000	838.13	801.06	773.02	751.45	734.64	721.41	710.91
45000	942.89	901.19	869.65	845.39	826.47	811.58	799.77
50000	1047.66	1001.33	966.28	939.32	918.30	901.76	888.63
55000	1152.43	1101.46	1062.91	1033.25	1010.13	991.94	977.50
60000	1257.19	1201.59	1159.53	1127.18	1101.97	1082.11	1066.36
65000	1361.96	1301.72	1256.16	1221.11	1193.80	1172.29	1155.22
70000	1466.72	1401.86	1352.79	1315.04	1285.63	1262.47	1244.09
75000	1571.49	1501.99	1449.42	1408.98	1377.46	1352.64	1332.95
80000	1676.26	1602.12	1546.05	1502.91	1469.29	1442.82	1421.81
85000	1781.02	1702.25	1642.67	1596.84	1561.12	1532.99	1510.68
90000	1885.79	1802.39	1739.30	1690.77	1652.95	1623.17	1599.54
95000	1990.55	1902.52	1835.93	1784.70	1744.78	1713.35	1688.40
100000	2095.32	2002.65	1932.56	1878.63	1836.61	1803.52	1777.27
105000	2200.09	2102.78	2029.18	1972.57	1928.44	1893.70	1866.13
110000	2304.85	2202.92	2125.81	2066.50	2020.27	1983.87	1954.99
120000	2514.38	2403.18	2319.07	2254.36	2203.93	2164.23	2132.72
130000	2723.92	2603.45	2512.32	2442.22	2387.59	2344.58	2310.44
140000	2933.45	2803.71	2705.58	2630.09	2571.25	2524.93	2488.17
150000	3142.98	3003.98	2898.84	2817.95	2754.91	2705.28	2665.90
160000	3352.51	3204.24	3092.09	3005.81	2938.57	2885.64	2843.62
170000	3562.04	3404.51	3285.35	3193.68	3122.23	3065.99	3021.35
180000	3771.58	3604.77	3478.60	3381.54	3305.90	3246.34	3199.08
190000	3981.11	3805.04	3671.86	3569.40	3489.56	3426.69	3376.80
200000	4190.64	4005.30	3865.11	3757.27	3673.22	3607.04	3554.53
210000	4400.17	4205.57	4058.37	3945.13	3856.88	3787.40	3732.26
220000	4609.70	4405.83	4251.62	4132.99	4040.54	3967.75	3909.98
230000	4819.24	4606.10	4444.88	4320.86	4224.20	4148.10	4087.71
240000	5028.77	4806.36	4638.14	4508.72	4407.86	4328.45	4265.44
250000	5238.30	5006.63	4831.39	4696.59	4591.52	4508.81	4443.16
260000	5447.83	5206.89	5024.65	4884.45	4775.18	4689.16	4620.89
270000	5657.36	5407.16	5217.90	5072.31	4958.84	4869.51	4798.62
280000	5866.90	5607.42	5411.16	5260.18	5142.50	5049.86	4976.34
290000	6076.43	5807.69	5604.41	5448.04	5326.16	5230.21	5154.07
300000	6285.96	6007.95	5797.67	5635.90	5509.83	5410.57	5331.80
310000	6495.49	6208.22	5990.93	5823.77	5693.49	5590.92	5509.52
320000	6705.02	6408.48	6184.18	6011.63	5877.15	5771.27	5687.25
330000	6914.56	6608.75	6377.44	6199.49	6060.81	5951.62	5864.98
340000	7124.09	6809.01	6570.69	6387.36	6244.47	6131.98	6042.70
350000	7333.62	7009.28	6763.95	6575.22	6428.13	6312.33	6220.43
400000	8381.28	8010.60	7730.23	7514.54	7346.43	7214.09	7109.06
450000	9428.94	9011.93	8696.51	8453.85	8264.74	8115.85	7997.69
500000	10476.60	10013.25	9662.78	9393.17	9183.04	9017.61	8886.33
550000	11524.26	11014.58	10629.06	10332.49	10101.35	9919.37	9774.96
600000	12571.92	12015.90	11595.34	11271.80	11019.65	10821.13	10663.59

20%

Monthly Payments
necessary to amortize a loan

AMOUNT	15 YEARS	16 YEARS	17 YEARS	18 YEARS	19 YEARS	20 YEARS	21 YEARS
100	1.76	1.74	1.73	1.71	1.71	1.70	1.69
200	3.51	3.48	3.45	3.43	3.41	3.40	3.39
500	8.78	8.70	8.63	8.57	8.53	8.49	8.46
1000	17.56	17.39	17.26	17.15	17.06	16.99	16.93
2000	35.13	34.79	34.52	34.30	34.12	33.98	33.86
5000	87.81	86.97	86.30	85.75	85.30	84.94	84.65
6000	105.38	104.37	103.55	102.90	102.36	101.93	101.58
7000	122.94	121.76	120.81	120.05	119.42	118.92	118.51
8000	140.50	139.16	138.07	137.19	136.48	135.91	135.44
9000	158.07	156.55	155.33	154.34	153.54	152.89	152.37
10000	175.63	173.95	172.59	171.49	170.60	169.88	169.29
15000	263.44	260.92	258.89	257.24	255.91	254.82	253.94
20000	351.26	347.89	345.18	342.99	341.21	339.76	338.59
25000	439.07	434.87	431.48	428.73	426.51	424.71	423.24
30000	526.89	521.84	517.77	514.48	511.81	509.65	507.88
35000	614.70	608.81	604.07	600.23	597.12	594.59	592.53
40000	702.52	695.79	690.36	685.97	682.42	679.53	677.18
45000	790.33	782.76	776.66	771.72	767.72	764.47	761.83
50000	878.15	869.73	862.95	857.47	853.02	849.41	846.47
55000	965.96	956.71	949.25	943.21	938.33	934.35	931.12
60000	1053.78	1043.68	1035.54	1028.96	1023.63	1019.29	1015.77
65000	1141.59	1130.65	1121.84	1114.71	1108.93	1104.24	1100.42
70000	1229.41	1217.63	1208.13	1200.46	1194.23	1189.18	1185.06
75000	1317.22	1304.60	1294.43	1286.20	1279.53	1274.12	1269.71
80000	1405.04	1391.57	1380.72	1371.95	1364.84	1359.06	1354.36
85000	1492.85	1478.55	1467.02	1457.70	1450.14	1444.00	1439.01
90000	1580.67	1565.52	1553.31	1543.44	1535.44	1528.94	1523.65
95000	1668.48	1652.49	1639.61	1629.19	1620.74	1613.88	1608.30
100000	1756.30	1739.47	1725.90	1714.94	1706.05	1698.82	1692.95
105000	1844.11	1826.44	1812.20	1800.68	1791.35	1783.77	1777.59
110000	1931.93	1913.41	1898.49	1886.43	1876.65	1868.71	1862.24
120000	2107.56	2087.36	2071.08	2057.92	2047.26	2038.59	2031.54
130000	2283.19	2261.31	2243.67	2229.42	2217.86	2208.47	2200.83
140000	2458.82	2435.25	2416.26	2400.91	2388.47	2378.35	2370.13
150000	2634.44	2609.20	2588.85	2572.40	2559.07	2548.24	2539.42
160000	2810.07	2783.15	2761.44	2743.90	2729.67	2718.12	2708.72
170000	2985.70	2957.09	2934.03	2915.39	2900.28	2888.00	2878.01
180000	3161.33	3131.04	3106.62	3086.89	3070.88	3057.88	3047.31
190000	3336.96	3304.99	3279.21	3258.38	3241.49	3227.77	3216.60
200000	3512.59	3478.93	3451.81	3429.87	3412.09	3397.65	3385.90
210000	3688.22	3652.88	3624.40	3601.37	3582.70	3567.53	3555.19
220000	3863.85	3826.83	3796.99	3772.86	3753.30	3737.41	3724.48
230000	4039.48	4000.77	3969.58	3944.35	3923.91	3907.30	3893.78
240000	4215.11	4174.72	4142.17	4115.85	4094.51	4077.18	4063.07
250000	4390.74	4348.67	4314.76	4287.34	4265.12	4247.06	4232.37
260000	4566.37	4522.61	4487.35	4458.83	4435.72	4416.94	4401.66
270000	4742.00	4696.56	4659.94	4630.33	4606.33	4586.83	4570.96
280000	4917.63	4870.50	4832.53	4801.82	4776.93	4756.71	4740.25
290000	5093.26	5044.45	5005.12	4973.32	4947.53	4926.59	4909.55
300000	5268.89	5218.40	5177.71	5144.81	5118.14	5096.47	5078.84
310000	5444.52	5392.34	5350.30	5316.30	5288.74	5266.36	5248.14
320000	5620.15	5566.29	5522.89	5487.80	5459.35	5436.24	5417.43
330000	5795.78	5740.24	5695.48	5659.29	5629.95	5606.12	5586.73
340000	5971.41	5914.18	5868.07	5830.78	5800.56	5776.00	5756.02
350000	6147.04	6088.13	6040.66	6002.28	5971.16	5945.89	5925.32
400000	7025.19	6957.86	6903.61	6859.75	6824.19	6795.30	6771.79
450000	7903.33	7827.60	7766.56	7717.21	7677.21	7644.71	7618.26
500000	8781.48	8697.33	8629.51	8574.68	8530.23	8494.12	8464.74
550000	9659.63	9567.06	9492.46	9432.15	9383.26	9343.54	9311.21
600000	10537.78	10436.80	10355.42	10289.62	10236.28	10192.95	10157.69

Monthly Payments 20%
necessary to amortize a loan

AMOUNT	22 YEARS	23 YEARS	24 YEARS	25 YEARS	30 YEARS	35 YEARS	40 YEARS
100	1.69	1.68	1.68	1.68	1.67	1.67	1.67
200	3.38	3.37	3.36	3.36	3.34	3.34	3.33
500	8.44	8.42	8.41	8.39	8.36	8.34	8.34
1000	16.88	16.84	16.81	16.78	16.71	16.68	16.67
2000	33.76	33.69	33.62	33.57	33.42	33.37	33.35
5000	84.41	84.21	84.05	83.92	83.55	83.41	83.36
6000	101.29	101.06	100.86	100.71	100.26	100.10	100.04
7000	118.17	117.90	117.67	117.49	116.97	116.78	116.71
8000	135.05	134.74	134.48	134.28	133.68	133.46	133.38
9000	151.93	151.58	151.30	151.06	150.39	150.15	150.05
10000	168.82	168.43	168.11	167.85	167.10	166.83	166.73
15000	253.22	252.64	252.16	251.77	250.65	250.24	250.09
20000	337.63	336.85	336.21	335.69	334.20	333.66	333.45
25000	422.04	421.06	420.26	419.61	417.75	417.07	416.82
30000	506.45	505.28	504.32	503.54	501.31	500.48	500.18
35000	590.86	589.49	588.37	587.46	584.86	583.90	583.54
40000	675.26	673.70	672.42	671.38	668.41	667.31	666.91
45000	759.67	757.91	756.48	755.30	751.96	750.73	750.27
50000	844.08	842.13	840.53	839.23	835.51	834.14	833.63
55000	928.49	926.34	924.58	923.15	919.06	917.55	917.00
60000	1012.89	1010.55	1008.64	1007.07	1002.61	1000.97	1000.36
65000	1097.30	1094.76	1092.69	1090.99	1086.16	1084.38	1083.72
70000	1181.71	1178.98	1176.74	1174.92	1169.71	1167.79	1167.08
75000	1266.12	1263.19	1260.79	1258.84	1253.26	1251.21	1250.45
80000	1350.53	1347.40	1344.85	1342.76	1336.81	1334.62	1333.81
85000	1434.93	1431.61	1428.90	1426.68	1420.37	1418.04	1417.17
90000	1519.34	1515.83	1512.95	1510.61	1503.92	1501.45	1500.54
95000	1603.75	1600.04	1597.01	1594.53	1587.47	1584.86	1583.90
100000	1688.16	1684.25	1681.06	1678.45	1671.02	1668.28	1667.26
105000	1772.57	1768.46	1765.11	1762.37	1754.57	1751.69	1750.63
110000	1856.97	1852.68	1849.17	1846.30	1838.12	1835.11	1833.99
120000	2025.79	2021.10	2017.27	2014.14	2005.22	2001.93	2000.72
130000	2194.61	2189.53	2185.38	2181.99	2172.32	2168.76	2167.44
140000	2363.42	2357.95	2353.48	2349.83	2339.43	2335.59	2334.17
150000	2532.24	2526.38	2521.59	2517.68	2506.53	2502.42	2500.90
160000	2701.05	2694.80	2689.70	2685.52	2673.63	2669.25	2667.62
170000	2869.87	2863.23	2857.80	2853.37	2840.73	2836.07	2834.35
180000	3038.68	3031.65	3025.91	3021.21	3007.83	3002.90	3001.08
190000	3207.50	3200.08	3194.01	3189.06	3174.94	3169.73	3167.80
200000	3376.32	3368.50	3362.12	3356.90	3342.04	3336.56	3334.53
210000	3545.13	3536.93	3530.23	3524.75	3509.14	3503.38	3501.25
220000	3713.95	3705.35	3698.33	3692.59	3676.24	3670.21	3667.98
230000	3882.76	3873.78	3866.44	3860.44	3843.34	3837.04	3834.71
240000	4051.58	4042.20	4034.54	4028.28	4010.44	4003.87	4001.43
250000	4220.40	4210.63	4202.65	4196.13	4177.55	4170.70	4168.16
260000	4389.21	4379.05	4370.76	4363.97	4344.65	4337.52	4334.89
270000	4558.03	4547.48	4538.86	4531.82	4511.75	4504.35	4501.61
280000	4726.84	4715.90	4706.97	4699.66	4678.85	4671.18	4668.34
290000	4895.66	4884.33	4875.07	4867.51	4845.95	4838.01	4835.07
300000	5064.47	5052.75	5043.18	5035.36	5013.06	5004.83	5001.79
310000	5233.29	5221.18	5211.28	5203.20	5180.16	5171.66	5168.52
320000	5402.11	5389.60	5379.39	5371.05	5347.26	5338.49	5335.25
330000	5570.92	5558.03	5547.50	5538.89	5514.36	5505.32	5501.97
340000	5739.74	5726.45	5715.60	5706.74	5681.46	5672.15	5668.70
350000	5908.55	5894.88	5883.71	5874.58	5848.57	5838.97	5835.42
400000	6752.63	6737.00	6724.24	6713.81	6684.07	6673.11	6669.06
450000	7596.71	7579.13	7564.77	7553.03	7519.58	7507.25	7502.69
500000	8440.79	8421.25	8405.30	8392.26	8355.09	8341.39	8336.32
550000	9284.87	9263.38	9245.83	9231.48	9190.60	9175.53	9169.95
600000	10128.95	10105.50	10086.36	10070.71	10026.11	10009.67	10003.58

20¼%

Monthly Payments
necessary to amortize a loan

AMOUNT	1 YEAR	2 YEARS	3 YEARS	4 YEARS	5 YEARS	6 YEARS	7 YEARS
100	9.28	5.10	3.73	3.06	2.66	2.41	2.24
200	18.55	10.20	7.46	6.11	5.33	4.82	4.47
500	46.38	25.51	18.65	15.28	13.32	12.05	11.18
1000	92.75	51.02	37.29	30.56	26.63	24.10	22.36
2000	185.51	102.04	74.58	61.13	53.27	48.20	44.71
5000	463.77	255.09	186.46	152.82	133.17	120.49	111.78
6000	556.53	306.11	223.75	183.38	159.80	144.59	134.14
7000	649.28	357.13	261.04	213.95	186.43	168.69	156.50
8000	742.03	408.14	298.33	244.51	213.07	192.78	178.86
9000	834.79	459.16	335.62	275.07	239.70	216.88	201.21
10000	927.54	510.18	372.91	305.64	266.33	240.98	223.57
15000	1391.31	765.27	559.37	458.46	399.50	361.47	335.35
20000	1855.08	1020.36	745.82	611.27	532.66	481.96	447.14
25000	2318.85	1275.45	932.28	764.09	665.83	602.45	558.92
30000	2782.63	1530.54	1118.73	916.91	799.00	722.94	670.71
35000	3246.40	1785.63	1305.19	1069.73	932.16	843.43	782.49
40000	3710.17	2040.72	1491.64	1222.55	1065.33	963.92	894.28
45000	4173.94	2295.81	1678.10	1375.37	1198.49	1084.41	1006.06
50000	4637.71	2550.90	1864.55	1528.19	1331.66	1204.90	1117.85
55000	5101.48	2805.99	2051.01	1681.00	1464.82	1325.39	1229.63
60000	5565.25	3061.08	2237.47	1833.82	1597.99	1445.88	1341.42
65000	6029.02	3316.17	2423.92	1986.64	1731.16	1566.37	1453.20
70000	6492.79	3571.26	2610.38	2139.46	1864.32	1686.86	1564.99
75000	6956.56	3826.35	2796.83	2292.28	1997.49	1807.35	1676.77
80000	7420.34	4081.44	2983.29	2445.10	2130.65	1927.84	1788.56
85000	7884.11	4336.53	3169.74	2597.92	2263.82	2048.33	1900.34
90000	8347.88	4591.62	3356.20	2750.73	2396.99	2168.82	2012.13
95000	8811.65	4846.71	3542.65	2903.55	2530.15	2289.31	2123.91
100000	9275.42	5101.80	3729.11	3056.37	2663.32	2409.80	2235.70
105000	9739.19	5356.89	3915.56	3209.19	2796.48	2530.29	2347.48
110000	10202.96	5611.98	4102.02	3362.01	2929.65	2650.78	2459.27
120000	11130.50	6122.16	4474.93	3667.65	3195.98	2891.76	2682.84
130000	12058.05	6632.34	4847.84	3973.28	3462.31	3132.73	2906.41
140000	12985.59	7142.52	5220.75	4278.92	3728.65	3373.71	3129.98
150000	13913.13	7652.70	5593.66	4584.56	3994.98	3614.69	3353.55
160000	14840.67	8162.88	5966.57	4890.20	4261.31	3855.67	3577.12
170000	15768.21	8673.06	6339.48	5195.83	4527.64	4096.65	3800.69
180000	16695.76	9183.24	6712.40	5501.47	4793.97	4337.63	4024.26
190000	17623.30	9693.42	7085.31	5807.11	5060.31	4578.61	4247.83
200000	18550.84	10203.60	7458.22	6112.74	5326.64	4819.59	4471.40
210000	19478.38	10713.78	7831.13	6418.38	5592.97	5060.57	4694.97
220000	20405.92	11223.96	8204.04	6724.02	5859.30	5301.55	4918.53
230000	21333.47	11734.14	8576.95	7029.66	6125.63	5542.53	5142.10
240000	22261.01	12244.32	8949.86	7335.29	6391.96	5783.51	5365.67
250000	23188.55	12754.50	9322.77	7640.93	6658.29	6024.49	5589.24
260000	24116.09	13264.68	9695.68	7946.57	6924.63	6265.47	5812.81
270000	25043.63	13774.86	10068.59	8252.20	7190.96	6506.45	6036.38
280000	25971.18	14285.04	10441.50	8557.84	7457.29	6747.43	6259.95
290000	26898.72	14795.22	10814.42	8863.48	7723.62	6988.41	6483.52
300000	27826.26	15305.40	11187.33	9169.12	7989.95	7229.39	6707.09
310000	28753.80	15815.58	11560.24	9474.75	8256.29	7470.37	6930.66
320000	29681.34	16325.76	11933.15	9780.39	8522.62	7711.35	7154.23
330000	30608.89	16835.95	12306.06	10086.03	8788.95	7952.33	7377.80
340000	31536.43	17346.13	12678.97	10391.66	9055.28	8193.31	7601.37
350000	32463.97	17856.31	13051.88	10697.30	9321.61	8434.29	7824.94
400000	37101.68	20407.21	14916.44	12225.49	10653.27	9639.18	8942.79
450000	41739.39	22958.11	16780.99	13753.67	11984.93	10844.08	10060.64
500000	46377.10	25509.01	18645.54	15281.86	13316.59	12048.98	11178.49
550000	51014.81	28059.91	20510.10	16810.05	14648.25	13253.88	12296.34
600000	55652.52	30610.81	22374.65	18338.23	15979.91	14458.78	13414.19

248

Monthly Payments 20¼%
necessary to amortize a loan

AMOUNT	8 YEARS	9 YEARS	10 YEARS	11 YEARS	12 YEARS	13 YEARS	14 YEARS
100	2.11	2.02	1.95	1.90	1.85	1.82	1.80
200	4.22	4.04	3.90	3.79	3.71	3.64	3.59
500	10.55	10.09	9.75	9.48	9.27	9.11	8.98
1000	21.11	20.19	19.49	18.96	18.54	18.21	17.95
2000	42.22	40.38	38.98	37.91	37.08	36.43	35.91
5000	105.55	100.94	97.46	94.78	92.70	91.07	89.77
6000	126.66	121.13	116.95	113.74	111.24	109.28	107.73
7000	147.77	141.31	136.44	132.70	129.78	127.50	125.68
8000	168.87	161.50	155.93	151.65	148.33	145.71	143.64
9000	189.98	181.69	175.42	170.61	166.87	163.92	161.59
10000	211.09	201.88	194.92	189.57	185.41	182.14	179.54
15000	316.64	302.82	292.37	284.35	278.11	273.20	269.32
20000	422.19	403.76	389.83	379.14	370.81	364.27	359.09
25000	527.73	504.69	487.29	473.92	463.52	455.34	448.86
30000	633.28	605.63	584.75	568.71	556.22	546.41	538.63
35000	738.83	706.57	682.21	663.49	648.92	637.48	628.41
40000	844.37	807.51	779.66	758.27	741.63	728.54	718.18
45000	949.92	908.45	877.12	853.06	834.33	819.61	807.95
50000	1055.47	1009.39	974.58	947.84	927.03	910.68	897.72
55000	1161.02	1110.33	1072.04	1042.63	1019.74	1001.75	987.50
60000	1266.56	1211.27	1169.50	1137.41	1112.44	1092.82	1077.27
65000	1372.11	1312.20	1266.95	1232.19	1205.15	1183.88	1167.04
70000	1477.66	1413.14	1364.41	1326.98	1297.85	1274.95	1256.81
75000	1583.20	1514.08	1461.87	1421.76	1390.55	1366.02	1346.59
80000	1688.75	1615.02	1559.33	1516.55	1483.26	1457.09	1436.36
85000	1794.30	1715.96	1656.79	1611.33	1575.96	1548.16	1526.13
90000	1899.84	1816.90	1754.25	1706.12	1668.66	1639.23	1615.90
95000	2005.39	1917.84	1851.70	1800.90	1761.37	1730.29	1705.68
100000	2110.94	2018.78	1949.16	1895.68	1854.07	1821.36	1795.45
105000	2216.48	2119.72	2046.62	1990.47	1946.77	1912.43	1885.22
110000	2322.03	2220.65	2144.08	2085.25	2039.48	2003.50	1974.99
120000	2533.12	2422.53	2338.99	2274.82	2224.88	2185.63	2154.54
130000	2744.22	2624.41	2533.91	2464.39	2410.29	2367.77	2334.08
140000	2955.31	2826.29	2728.83	2653.96	2595.70	2549.91	2513.63
150000	3166.40	3028.16	2923.74	2843.53	2781.10	2732.04	2693.17
160000	3377.50	3230.04	3118.66	3033.09	2966.51	2914.18	2872.72
170000	3588.59	3431.92	3313.57	3222.66	3151.92	3096.31	3052.26
180000	3799.69	3633.80	3508.49	3412.23	3337.33	3278.45	3231.81
190000	4010.78	3835.68	3703.41	3601.80	3522.73	3460.59	3411.35
200000	4221.87	4037.55	3898.32	3791.37	3708.14	3642.72	3590.90
210000	4432.97	4239.43	4093.24	3980.94	3893.55	3824.86	3770.44
220000	4644.06	4441.31	4288.15	4170.50	4078.95	4006.99	3949.99
230000	4855.15	4643.19	4483.07	4360.07	4264.36	4189.13	4129.53
240000	5066.25	4845.06	4677.99	4549.64	4449.77	4371.27	4309.08
250000	5277.34	5046.94	4872.90	4739.21	4635.17	4553.40	4488.62
260000	5488.44	5248.82	5067.82	4928.78	4820.58	4735.54	4668.17
270000	5699.53	5450.70	5262.74	5118.35	5005.99	4917.68	4847.71
280000	5910.62	5652.57	5457.65	5307.91	5191.40	5099.81	5027.26
290000	6121.72	5854.45	5652.57	5497.48	5376.80	5281.95	5206.80
300000	6332.81	6056.33	5847.48	5687.05	5562.21	5464.08	5386.35
310000	6543.90	6258.21	6042.40	5876.62	5747.62	5646.22	5565.89
320000	6755.00	6460.08	6237.32	6066.19	5933.02	5828.36	5745.44
330000	6966.09	6661.96	6432.23	6255.76	6118.43	6010.49	5924.98
340000	7177.18	6863.84	6627.15	6445.32	6303.84	6192.63	6104.53
350000	7388.28	7065.72	6822.06	6634.89	6489.24	6374.76	6284.07
400000	8443.75	8075.11	7796.64	7582.73	7416.28	7285.45	7181.80
450000	9499.21	9084.49	8771.23	8530.58	8343.31	8196.13	8079.52
500000	10554.68	10093.88	9745.81	9478.42	9270.35	9106.81	8977.25
550000	11610.15	11103.27	10720.39	10426.26	10197.38	10017.49	9874.97
600000	12665.62	12112.66	11694.97	11374.10	11124.42	10928.17	10772.70

20¼%

Monthly Payments
necessary to amortize a loan

AMOUNT	15 YEARS	16 YEARS	17 YEARS	18 YEARS	19 YEARS	20 YEARS	21 YEARS
100	1.77	1.76	1.74	1.73	1.73	1.72	1.71
200	3.55	3.52	3.49	3.47	3.45	3.44	3.43
500	8.87	8.79	8.72	8.67	8.63	8.59	8.56
1000	17.75	17.58	17.45	17.34	17.26	17.18	17.13
2000	35.50	35.16	34.90	34.68	34.51	34.37	34.26
5000	88.74	87.91	87.25	86.71	86.28	85.92	85.64
6000	106.49	105.49	104.70	104.05	103.53	103.11	102.77
7000	124.24	123.08	122.15	121.39	120.79	120.29	119.89
8000	141.98	140.66	139.60	138.74	138.04	137.48	137.02
9000	159.73	158.24	157.04	156.08	155.30	154.66	154.15
10000	177.48	175.82	174.49	173.42	172.55	171.85	171.28
15000	266.22	263.74	261.74	260.13	258.83	257.77	256.91
20000	354.96	351.65	348.99	346.84	345.10	343.69	342.55
25000	443.70	439.56	436.23	433.55	431.38	429.62	428.19
30000	532.44	527.47	523.48	520.26	517.65	515.54	513.83
35000	621.18	615.39	610.73	606.97	603.93	601.46	599.46
40000	709.92	703.30	697.98	693.68	690.20	687.39	685.10
45000	798.66	791.21	785.22	780.39	776.48	773.31	770.74
50000	887.40	879.12	872.47	867.10	862.76	859.23	856.38
55000	976.14	967.04	959.72	953.81	949.03	945.16	942.01
60000	1064.88	1054.95	1046.96	1040.52	1035.31	1031.08	1027.65
65000	1153.62	1142.86	1134.21	1127.23	1121.58	1117.00	1113.29
70000	1242.36	1230.77	1221.46	1213.94	1207.86	1202.93	1198.93
75000	1331.10	1318.69	1308.70	1300.65	1294.13	1288.85	1284.56
80000	1419.84	1406.60	1395.95	1387.36	1380.41	1374.78	1370.20
85000	1508.58	1494.51	1483.20	1474.07	1466.68	1460.70	1455.84
90000	1597.31	1582.42	1570.44	1560.78	1552.96	1546.62	1541.48
95000	1686.05	1670.33	1657.69	1647.49	1639.24	1632.55	1627.11
100000	1774.79	1758.25	1744.94	1734.20	1725.51	1718.47	1712.75
105000	1863.53	1846.16	1832.18	1820.91	1811.79	1804.39	1798.39
110000	1952.27	1934.07	1919.43	1907.62	1898.06	1890.32	1884.03
120000	2129.75	2109.90	2093.93	2081.04	2070.61	2062.16	2055.30
130000	2307.23	2285.72	2268.42	2254.46	2243.16	2234.01	2226.58
140000	2484.71	2461.55	2442.91	2427.88	2415.72	2405.86	2397.85
150000	2662.19	2637.37	2617.41	2601.30	2588.27	2577.70	2569.13
160000	2839.67	2813.19	2791.90	2774.72	2760.82	2749.55	2740.40
170000	3017.15	2989.02	2966.39	2948.14	2933.37	2921.40	2911.68
180000	3194.63	3164.84	3140.89	3121.56	3105.92	3093.24	3082.95
190000	3372.11	3340.67	3315.38	3294.98	3278.47	3265.09	3254.23
200000	3549.58	3516.49	3489.88	3468.40	3451.02	3436.94	3425.50
210000	3727.07	3692.32	3664.37	3641.82	3623.57	3608.78	3596.78
220000	3904.55	3868.14	3838.86	3815.24	3796.12	3780.63	3768.05
230000	4082.03	4043.97	4013.36	3988.66	3968.68	3952.48	3939.33
240000	4259.51	4219.79	4187.85	4162.08	4141.23	4124.33	4110.60
250000	4436.99	4395.62	4362.34	4335.50	4313.78	4296.17	4281.88
260000	4614.46	4571.44	4536.84	4508.92	4486.33	4468.02	4453.15
270000	4791.94	4747.27	4711.33	4682.34	4658.88	4639.87	4624.43
280000	4969.42	4923.09	4885.83	4855.76	4831.43	4811.71	4795.70
290000	5146.90	5098.92	5060.32	5029.18	5003.98	4983.56	4966.98
300000	5324.38	5274.74	5234.81	5202.60	5176.53	5155.41	5138.25
310000	5501.86	5450.56	5409.31	5376.02	5349.08	5327.25	5309.53
320000	5679.34	5626.39	5583.80	5549.44	5521.64	5499.10	5480.80
330000	5856.82	5802.21	5758.29	5722.86	5694.19	5670.95	5652.08
340000	6034.30	5978.04	5932.79	5896.28	5866.74	5842.79	5823.35
350000	6211.78	6153.86	6107.28	6069.70	6039.29	6014.64	5994.63
400000	7099.18	7032.99	6979.75	6936.79	6902.04	6873.88	6851.00
450000	7986.57	7912.11	7852.22	7803.89	7764.80	7733.11	7707.38
500000	8873.97	8791.23	8724.69	8670.99	8627.56	8592.34	8563.75
550000	9761.37	9670.36	9597.16	9538.09	9490.31	9451.58	9420.13
600000	10648.77	10549.48	10469.63	10405.19	10353.07	10310.81	10276.50

Monthly Payments 20¼%
necessary to amortize a loan

AMOUNT	22 YEARS	23 YEARS	24 YEARS	25 YEARS	30 YEARS	35 YEARS	40 YEARS
100	1.71	1.70	1.70	1.70	1.69	1.69	1.69
200	3.42	3.41	3.40	3.40	3.38	3.38	3.38
500	8.54	8.52	8.51	8.49	8.46	8.44	8.44
1000	17.08	17.04	17.01	16.99	16.92	16.89	16.88
2000	34.16	34.09	34.02	33.97	33.83	33.78	33.76
5000	85.41	85.22	85.06	84.94	84.58	84.45	84.40
6000	102.49	102.26	102.07	101.92	101.50	101.34	101.28
7000	119.57	119.30	119.09	118.91	118.41	118.23	118.16
8000	136.65	136.35	136.10	135.90	135.33	135.12	135.04
9000	153.73	153.39	153.11	152.88	152.24	152.01	151.92
10000	170.81	170.43	170.12	169.87	169.16	168.90	168.80
15000	256.22	255.65	255.18	254.81	253.74	253.35	253.21
20000	341.62	340.86	340.25	339.74	338.32	337.80	337.61
25000	427.03	426.08	425.31	424.68	422.90	422.25	422.01
30000	512.43	511.29	510.37	509.61	507.48	506.70	506.41
35000	597.84	596.51	595.43	594.55	592.06	591.15	590.82
40000	683.24	681.73	680.49	679.49	676.64	675.60	675.22
45000	768.65	766.94	765.55	764.42	761.22	760.05	759.62
50000	854.05	852.16	850.62	849.36	845.80	844.50	844.02
55000	939.46	937.37	935.68	934.29	930.38	928.95	928.43
60000	1024.86	1022.59	1020.74	1019.23	1014.96	1013.40	1012.83
65000	1110.27	1107.80	1105.80	1104.17	1099.54	1097.85	1097.23
70000	1195.67	1193.02	1190.86	1189.10	1184.11	1182.30	1181.63
75000	1281.08	1278.24	1275.92	1274.04	1268.69	1266.75	1266.04
80000	1366.48	1363.45	1360.98	1358.97	1353.27	1351.20	1350.44
85000	1451.89	1448.67	1446.05	1443.91	1437.85	1435.65	1434.84
90000	1537.29	1533.88	1531.11	1528.84	1522.43	1520.10	1519.24
95000	1622.70	1619.10	1616.17	1613.78	1607.01	1604.55	1603.65
100000	1708.10	1704.32	1701.23	1698.72	1691.59	1689.00	1688.05
105000	1793.51	1789.53	1786.29	1783.65	1776.17	1773.45	1772.45
110000	1878.91	1874.75	1871.35	1868.59	1860.75	1857.90	1856.85
120000	2049.72	2045.18	2041.48	2038.46	2029.91	2026.80	2025.66
130000	2220.53	2215.61	2211.60	2208.33	2199.07	2195.70	2194.46
140000	2391.34	2386.04	2381.72	2378.20	2368.23	2364.60	2363.27
150000	2562.15	2556.47	2551.85	2548.07	2537.39	2533.50	2532.07
160000	2732.96	2726.90	2721.97	2717.95	2706.55	2702.40	2700.88
170000	2903.77	2897.34	2892.09	2887.82	2875.71	2871.30	2869.68
180000	3074.58	3067.77	3062.22	3057.69	3044.87	3040.19	3038.49
190000	3245.39	3238.20	3232.34	3227.56	3214.03	3209.09	3207.29
200000	3416.20	3408.63	3402.46	3397.43	3383.18	3377.99	3376.10
210000	3587.01	3579.06	3572.59	3567.30	3552.34	3546.89	3544.90
220000	3757.82	3749.49	3742.71	3737.18	3721.50	3715.79	3713.71
230000	3928.63	3919.92	3912.83	3907.05	3890.66	3884.69	3882.51
240000	4099.44	4090.36	4082.95	4076.92	4059.82	4053.59	4051.32
250000	4270.25	4260.79	4253.08	4246.79	4228.98	4222.49	4220.12
260000	4441.06	4431.22	4423.20	4416.66	4398.14	4391.39	4388.93
270000	4611.87	4601.65	4593.32	4586.53	4567.30	4560.29	4557.73
280000	4782.68	4772.08	4763.45	4756.41	4736.46	4729.19	4726.54
290000	4953.49	4942.51	4933.57	4926.28	4905.62	4898.09	4895.34
300000	5124.30	5112.95	5103.69	5096.15	5074.78	5066.99	5064.14
310000	5295.11	5283.38	5273.82	5266.02	5243.94	5235.89	5232.95
320000	5465.92	5453.81	5443.94	5435.89	5413.10	5404.79	5401.75
330000	5636.73	5624.24	5614.06	5605.76	5582.25	5573.69	5570.56
340000	5807.54	5794.67	5784.19	5775.64	5751.41	5742.59	5739.36
350000	5978.35	5965.10	5954.31	5945.51	5920.57	5911.49	5908.17
400000	6832.40	6817.26	6804.92	6794.87	6766.37	6755.99	6752.19
450000	7686.45	7669.42	7655.54	7644.22	7612.17	7600.49	7596.22
500000	8540.50	8521.58	8506.16	8493.58	8457.96	8444.99	8440.24
550000	9394.55	9373.73	9356.77	9342.94	9303.76	9289.48	9284.27
600000	10248.60	10225.89	10207.39	10192.30	10149.55	10133.98	10128.29

20½%

Monthly Payments
necessary to amortize a loan

AMOUNT	1 YEAR	2 YEARS	3 YEARS	4 YEARS	5 YEARS	6 YEARS	7 YEARS
100	9.29	5.11	3.74	3.07	2.68	2.42	2.25
200	18.57	10.23	7.48	6.14	5.35	4.85	4.50
500	46.44	25.57	18.71	15.35	13.39	12.12	11.25
1000	92.87	51.14	37.42	30.70	26.77	24.24	22.51
2000	185.75	102.28	74.84	61.39	53.55	48.49	45.02
5000	464.37	255.70	187.09	153.49	133.86	121.21	112.54
6000	557.24	306.84	224.51	184.18	160.64	145.46	135.05
7000	650.12	357.98	261.93	214.88	187.41	169.70	157.56
8000	742.99	409.12	299.35	245.58	214.18	193.95	180.07
9000	835.87	460.26	336.77	276.28	240.96	218.19	202.57
10000	928.74	511.40	374.19	306.97	267.73	242.44	225.08
15000	1393.11	767.11	561.28	460.46	401.59	363.65	337.62
20000	1857.48	1022.81	748.38	613.95	535.46	484.87	450.16
25000	2321.85	1278.51	935.47	767.43	669.32	606.09	562.71
30000	2786.22	1534.21	1122.57	920.92	803.19	727.31	675.25
35000	3250.59	1789.91	1309.66	1074.41	937.05	848.52	787.79
40000	3714.96	2045.62	1496.75	1227.90	1070.91	969.74	900.33
45000	4179.33	2301.32	1683.85	1381.38	1204.78	1090.96	1012.87
50000	4643.70	2557.02	1870.94	1534.87	1338.64	1212.18	1125.41
55000	5108.07	2812.72	2058.04	1688.36	1472.51	1333.39	1237.95
60000	5572.44	3068.42	2245.13	1841.84	1606.37	1454.61	1350.49
65000	6036.81	3324.13	2432.22	1995.33	1740.24	1575.83	1463.04
70000	6501.18	3579.83	2619.32	2148.82	1874.10	1697.05	1575.58
75000	6965.55	3835.53	2806.41	2302.30	2007.96	1818.27	1688.12
80000	7429.92	4091.23	2993.51	2455.79	2141.83	1939.48	1800.66
85000	7894.29	4346.93	3180.60	2609.28	2275.69	2060.70	1913.20
90000	8358.66	4602.64	3367.70	2762.77	2409.56	2181.92	2025.74
95000	8823.03	4858.34	3554.79	2916.25	2543.42	2303.14	2138.28
100000	9287.40	5114.04	3741.88	3069.74	2677.29	2424.35	2250.82
105000	9751.77	5369.74	3928.98	3223.23	2811.15	2545.57	2363.37
110000	10216.14	5625.44	4116.07	3376.71	2945.01	2666.79	2475.91
120000	11144.88	6136.85	4490.26	3683.69	3212.74	2909.22	2700.99
130000	12073.62	6648.25	4864.45	3990.66	3480.47	3151.66	2926.07
140000	13002.36	7159.66	5238.64	4297.64	3748.20	3394.09	3151.15
150000	13931.10	7671.06	5612.83	4604.61	4015.93	3636.53	3376.24
160000	14859.84	8182.46	5987.01	4911.58	4283.66	3878.97	3601.32
170000	15788.58	8693.87	6361.20	5218.56	4551.39	4121.40	3826.40
180000	16717.32	9205.27	6735.39	5525.53	4819.11	4363.84	4051.48
190000	17646.05	9716.67	7109.58	5832.51	5086.84	4606.27	4276.57
200000	18574.79	10228.08	7483.77	6139.48	5354.57	4848.71	4501.65
210000	19503.53	10739.48	7857.96	6446.45	5622.30	5091.14	4726.73
220000	20432.27	11250.89	8232.14	6753.43	5890.03	5333.58	4951.81
230000	21361.01	11762.29	8606.33	7060.40	6157.76	5576.01	5176.90
240000	22289.75	12273.69	8980.52	7367.37	6425.49	5818.45	5401.98
250000	23218.49	12785.10	9354.71	7674.35	6693.21	6060.88	5627.06
260000	24147.23	13296.50	9728.90	7981.32	6960.94	6303.32	5852.14
270000	25075.97	13807.91	10103.09	8288.30	7228.67	6545.75	6077.23
280000	26004.71	14319.31	10477.27	8595.27	7496.40	6788.19	6302.31
290000	26933.45	14830.71	10851.46	8902.24	7764.13	7030.62	6527.39
300000	27862.19	15342.12	11225.65	9209.22	8031.86	7273.06	6752.47
310000	28790.93	15853.52	11599.84	9516.19	8299.59	7515.50	6977.55
320000	29719.67	16364.93	11974.03	9823.17	8567.31	7757.93	7202.64
330000	30648.41	16876.33	12348.22	10130.14	8835.04	8000.37	7427.72
340000	31577.15	17387.73	12722.40	10437.11	9102.77	8242.80	7652.80
350000	32505.89	17899.14	13096.59	10744.09	9370.50	8485.24	7877.88
400000	37149.59	20456.16	14967.53	12278.96	10709.14	9697.41	9003.30
450000	41793.29	23013.18	16838.48	13813.83	12047.79	10909.59	10128.71
500000	46436.99	25570.20	18709.42	15348.70	13386.43	12121.77	11254.12
550000	51080.68	28127.22	20580.36	16883.57	14725.07	13333.94	12379.53
600000	55724.38	30684.24	22451.30	18418.44	16063.71	14546.12	13504.94

AMOUNT	8 YEARS	9 YEARS	10 YEARS	11 YEARS	12 YEARS	13 YEARS	14 YEARS
100	2.13	2.03	1.97	1.91	1.87	1.84	1.81
200	4.25	4.07	3.93	3.83	3.74	3.68	3.63
500	10.63	10.17	9.83	9.56	9.36	9.20	9.07
1000	21.27	20.35	19.66	19.13	18.72	18.39	18.14
2000	42.53	40.70	39.32	38.26	37.43	36.79	36.27
5000	106.33	101.75	98.29	95.64	93.58	91.96	90.68
6000	127.60	122.10	117.95	114.77	112.30	110.36	108.82
7000	148.86	142.45	137.61	133.90	131.01	128.75	126.96
8000	170.13	162.80	157.27	153.02	149.73	147.14	145.10
9000	191.39	183.15	176.92	172.15	168.44	165.53	163.23
10000	212.66	203.50	196.58	191.28	187.16	183.93	181.37
15000	318.99	305.24	294.87	286.92	280.74	275.89	272.05
20000	425.32	406.99	393.16	382.56	374.32	367.85	362.74
25000	531.65	508.74	491.46	478.20	467.90	459.81	453.42
30000	637.98	610.49	589.75	573.84	561.48	551.78	544.11
35000	744.31	712.24	688.04	669.48	655.06	643.74	634.79
40000	850.64	813.98	786.33	765.12	748.64	735.70	725.48
45000	956.97	915.73	884.62	860.76	842.22	827.67	816.16
50000	1063.30	1017.48	982.91	956.40	935.79	919.63	906.85
55000	1169.63	1119.23	1081.20	1052.04	1029.37	1011.59	997.53
60000	1275.96	1220.98	1179.49	1147.67	1122.95	1103.56	1088.21
65000	1382.29	1322.72	1277.78	1243.31	1216.53	1195.52	1178.90
70000	1488.62	1424.47	1376.08	1338.95	1310.11	1287.48	1269.58
75000	1594.95	1526.22	1474.37	1434.59	1403.69	1379.44	1360.27
80000	1701.28	1627.97	1572.66	1530.23	1497.27	1471.41	1450.95
85000	1807.62	1729.71	1670.95	1625.87	1590.85	1563.37	1541.64
90000	1913.95	1831.46	1769.24	1721.51	1684.43	1655.33	1632.32
95000	2020.28	1933.21	1867.53	1817.15	1778.01	1747.30	1723.01
100000	2126.61	2034.96	1965.82	1912.79	1871.59	1839.26	1813.69
105000	2232.94	2136.71	2064.11	2008.43	1965.17	1931.22	1904.38
110000	2339.27	2238.45	2162.41	2104.07	2058.75	2023.18	1995.06
120000	2551.93	2441.95	2358.99	2295.35	2245.91	2207.11	2176.43
130000	2764.59	2645.45	2555.57	2486.63	2433.07	2391.04	2357.80
140000	2977.25	2848.94	2752.15	2677.91	2620.23	2574.96	2539.17
150000	3189.91	3052.44	2948.73	2869.19	2807.38	2758.89	2720.54
160000	3402.57	3255.93	3145.32	3060.47	2994.54	2942.81	2901.91
170000	3615.23	3459.43	3341.90	3251.75	3181.70	3126.74	3083.27
180000	3827.89	3662.93	3538.48	3443.02	3368.86	3310.67	3264.64
190000	4040.55	3866.42	3735.06	3634.30	3556.02	3494.59	3446.01
200000	4253.21	4069.92	3931.65	3825.58	3743.18	3678.52	3627.38
210000	4465.87	4273.41	4128.23	4016.86	3930.34	3862.44	3808.75
220000	4678.53	4476.91	4324.81	4208.14	4117.50	4046.37	3990.12
230000	4891.19	4680.40	4521.39	4399.42	4304.66	4230.29	4171.49
240000	5103.85	4883.90	4717.98	4590.70	4491.81	4414.22	4352.86
250000	5316.51	5087.40	4914.56	4781.98	4678.97	4598.15	4534.23
260000	5529.18	5290.89	5111.14	4973.26	4866.13	4782.07	4715.60
270000	5741.84	5494.39	5307.72	5164.54	5053.29	4966.00	4896.96
280000	5954.50	5697.88	5504.30	5355.82	5240.45	5149.92	5078.33
290000	6167.16	5901.38	5700.89	5547.10	5427.61	5333.85	5259.70
300000	6379.82	6104.88	5897.47	5738.37	5614.77	5517.78	5441.07
310000	6592.48	6308.37	6094.05	5929.65	5801.93	5701.70	5622.44
320000	6805.14	6511.87	6290.63	6120.93	5989.09	5885.63	5803.81
330000	7017.80	6715.36	6487.22	6312.21	6176.24	6069.55	5985.18
340000	7230.46	6918.86	6683.80	6503.49	6363.40	6253.48	6166.55
350000	7443.12	7122.35	6880.38	6694.77	6550.56	6437.40	6347.92
400000	8506.42	8139.83	7863.29	7651.17	7486.36	7357.03	7254.76
450000	9569.73	9157.31	8846.20	8607.56	8422.15	8276.66	8161.61
500000	10633.03	10174.79	9829.12	9563.96	9357.95	9196.29	9068.45
550000	11696.33	11192.27	10812.03	10520.35	10293.74	10115.92	9975.30
600000	12759.64	12209.75	11794.94	11476.75	11229.54	11035.55	10882.14

20½%

Monthly Payments
necessary to amortize a loan

AMOUNT	15 YEARS	16 YEARS	17 YEARS	18 YEARS	19 YEARS	20 YEARS	21 YEARS
100	1.79	1.78	1.76	1.75	1.75	1.74	1.73
200	3.59	3.55	3.53	3.51	3.49	3.48	3.47
500	8.97	8.89	8.82	8.77	8.73	8.69	8.66
1000	17.93	17.77	17.64	17.54	17.45	17.38	17.33
2000	35.87	35.54	35.28	35.07	34.90	34.76	34.65
5000	89.67	88.85	88.20	87.68	87.25	86.91	86.63
6000	107.60	106.62	105.84	105.21	104.70	104.29	103.96
7000	125.53	124.40	123.48	122.75	122.15	121.67	121.28
8000	143.47	142.17	141.12	140.28	139.60	139.05	138.61
9000	161.40	159.94	158.76	157.82	157.05	156.43	155.93
10000	179.33	177.71	176.40	175.35	174.50	173.82	173.26
15000	269.00	266.56	264.60	263.03	261.75	260.72	259.89
20000	358.67	355.42	352.80	350.70	349.00	347.63	346.52
25000	448.34	444.27	441.01	438.38	436.26	434.54	433.15
30000	538.00	533.12	529.21	526.05	523.51	521.45	519.78
35000	627.67	621.98	617.41	613.73	610.76	608.35	606.41
40000	717.34	710.83	705.61	701.40	698.01	695.26	693.04
45000	807.01	799.69	793.81	789.08	785.26	782.17	779.67
50000	896.67	888.54	882.01	876.75	872.51	869.08	866.30
55000	986.34	977.39	970.21	964.43	959.76	955.98	952.93
60000	1076.01	1066.25	1058.41	1052.10	1047.01	1042.89	1039.55
65000	1165.68	1155.10	1146.61	1139.78	1134.26	1129.80	1126.18
70000	1255.01	1243.96	1234.82	1227.46	1221.51	1216.71	1212.81
75000	1345.01	1332.81	1323.02	1315.13	1308.77	1303.62	1299.44
80000	1434.68	1421.66	1411.22	1402.81	1396.02	1390.52	1386.07
85000	1524.34	1510.52	1499.42	1490.48	1483.27	1477.43	1472.70
90000	1614.01	1599.37	1587.62	1578.16	1570.52	1564.34	1559.33
95000	1703.68	1688.23	1675.82	1665.83	1657.77	1651.25	1645.96
100000	1793.35	1777.08	1764.02	1753.51	1745.02	1738.15	1732.59
105000	1883.01	1865.93	1852.22	1841.18	1832.27	1825.06	1819.22
110000	1972.68	1954.79	1940.42	1928.86	1919.52	1911.97	1905.85
120000	2152.02	2132.50	2116.83	2104.21	2094.02	2085.78	2079.11
130000	2331.35	2310.20	2293.23	2279.56	2268.53	2259.60	2252.37
140000	2510.69	2487.91	2469.63	2454.91	2443.03	2433.42	2425.63
150000	2690.03	2665.62	2646.03	2630.26	2617.53	2607.23	2598.89
160000	2869.35	2843.33	2822.44	2805.61	2792.03	2781.05	2772.15
170000	3048.69	3021.04	2998.84	2980.96	2966.53	2954.86	2945.40
180000	3228.02	3198.74	3175.24	3156.31	3141.04	3128.68	3118.66
190000	3407.36	3376.45	3351.64	3331.67	3315.54	3302.49	3291.92
200000	3586.69	3554.16	3528.04	3507.02	3490.04	3476.31	3465.18
210000	3766.03	3731.87	3704.45	3682.37	3664.54	3650.12	3638.44
220000	3945.36	3909.58	3880.85	3857.72	3839.04	3823.94	3811.70
230000	4124.70	4087.28	4057.25	4033.07	4013.55	3997.75	3984.96
240000	4304.03	4264.99	4233.65	4208.42	4188.05	4171.57	4158.22
250000	4483.37	4442.70	4410.06	4383.77	4362.55	4345.39	4331.48
260000	4662.70	4620.41	4586.46	4559.12	4537.05	4519.20	4504.74
270000	4842.04	4798.12	4762.86	4734.47	4711.55	4693.02	4678.00
280000	5021.37	4975.82	4939.26	4909.82	4886.06	4866.83	4851.25
290000	5200.71	5153.53	5115.67	5085.17	5060.56	5040.65	5024.51
300000	5380.05	5331.24	5292.07	5260.52	5235.06	5214.46	5197.77
310000	5559.37	5508.95	5468.47	5435.88	5409.56	5388.28	5371.03
320000	5738.71	5686.66	5644.87	5611.23	5584.06	5562.09	5544.29
330000	5918.04	5864.36	5821.27	5786.58	5758.57	5735.91	5717.55
340000	6097.38	6042.07	5997.68	5961.93	5933.07	5909.72	5890.81
350000	6276.71	6219.78	6174.08	6137.28	6107.57	6083.54	6064.07
400000	7173.39	7108.32	7056.09	7014.03	6980.05	6952.62	6930.36
450000	8070.06	7996.86	7938.10	7890.79	7852.59	7821.69	7796.66
500000	8966.73	8885.40	8820.11	8767.54	8725.10	8690.77	8662.95
550000	9863.41	9773.94	9702.12	9644.29	9597.61	9559.85	9529.25
600000	10760.08	10662.48	10584.13	10521.05	10470.12	10428.92	10395.55

Monthly Payments 20½%
necessary to amortize a loan

AMOUNT	22 YEARS	23 YEARS	24 YEARS	25 YEARS	30 YEARS	35 YEARS	40 YEARS
100	1.73	1.72	1.72	1.72	1.71	1.71	1.71
200	3.46	3.45	3.44	3.44	3.42	3.42	3.42
500	8.64	8.62	8.61	8.60	8.56	8.55	8.54
1000	17.28	17.24	17.21	17.19	17.12	17.10	17.09
2000	34.56	34.49	34.43	34.38	34.24	34.19	34.18
5000	86.40	86.22	86.07	85.95	85.61	85.49	85.44
6000	103.68	103.46	103.29	103.14	102.73	102.58	102.53
7000	120.97	120.71	120.50	120.33	119.85	119.68	119.62
8000	138.25	137.95	137.71	137.52	136.97	136.78	136.71
9000	155.53	155.20	154.93	154.71	154.10	153.88	153.80
10000	172.81	172.44	172.14	171.90	171.22	170.97	170.88
15000	259.21	258.66	258.21	257.85	256.83	256.46	256.33
20000	345.62	344.88	344.29	343.80	342.44	341.94	341.77
25000	432.02	431.10	430.36	429.75	428.05	427.43	427.21
30000	518.42	517.32	516.43	515.70	513.65	512.92	512.65
35000	604.83	603.54	602.50	601.65	599.26	598.40	598.09
40000	691.23	689.76	688.57	687.60	684.87	683.89	683.53
45000	777.63	775.99	774.64	773.55	770.48	769.38	768.98
50000	864.04	862.21	860.72	859.50	856.09	854.86	854.42
55000	950.44	948.43	946.79	945.45	941.70	940.35	939.86
60000	1036.85	1034.65	1032.86	1031.40	1027.31	1025.83	1025.30
65000	1123.25	1120.87	1118.93	1117.35	1112.92	1111.32	1110.74
70000	1209.65	1207.09	1205.00	1203.30	1198.53	1196.81	1196.19
75000	1296.06	1293.31	1291.07	1289.26	1284.14	1282.29	1281.63
80000	1382.46	1379.53	1377.15	1375.21	1369.74	1367.78	1367.07
85000	1468.87	1465.75	1463.22	1461.16	1455.35	1453.27	1452.51
90000	1555.27	1551.97	1549.29	1547.11	1540.96	1538.75	1537.95
95000	1641.67	1638.19	1635.36	1633.06	1626.57	1624.24	1623.39
100000	1728.08	1724.41	1721.43	1719.01	1712.18	1709.72	1708.84
105000	1814.48	1810.63	1807.50	1804.96	1797.79	1795.21	1794.28
110000	1900.89	1896.85	1893.57	1890.91	1883.40	1880.70	1879.72
120000	2073.69	2069.29	2065.72	2062.81	2054.62	2051.67	2050.60
130000	2246.50	2241.73	2237.86	2234.71	2225.84	2222.64	2221.49
140000	2419.31	2414.18	2410.00	2406.61	2397.05	2393.61	2392.37
150000	2592.12	2586.62	2582.15	2578.51	2568.27	2564.59	2563.25
160000	2764.92	2759.06	2754.29	2750.41	2739.49	2735.56	2734.14
170000	2937.73	2931.50	2926.43	2922.31	2910.71	2906.53	2905.02
180000	3110.54	3103.94	3098.58	3094.21	3081.93	3077.50	3075.91
190000	3283.35	3276.38	3270.72	3266.11	3253.14	3248.48	3246.79
200000	3456.15	3448.82	3442.86	3438.01	3424.36	3419.45	3417.67
210000	3628.96	3621.26	3615.01	3609.91	3595.58	3590.42	3588.56
220000	3801.77	3793.71	3787.15	3781.82	3766.80	3761.39	3759.44
230000	3974.58	3966.15	3959.29	3953.72	3938.02	3932.36	3930.32
240000	4147.39	4138.59	4131.44	4125.62	4109.23	4103.34	4101.21
250000	4320.19	4311.03	4303.58	4297.52	4280.45	4274.31	4272.09
260000	4493.00	4483.47	4475.72	4469.42	4451.67	4445.28	4442.97
270000	4665.81	4655.91	4647.86	4641.32	4622.89	4616.25	4613.86
280000	4838.62	4828.35	4820.01	4813.22	4794.11	4787.23	4784.74
290000	5011.42	5000.79	4992.15	4985.12	4965.32	4958.20	4955.63
300000	5184.23	5173.23	5164.29	5157.02	5136.54	5129.17	5126.51
310000	5357.04	5345.68	5336.44	5328.92	5307.76	5300.14	5297.39
320000	5529.85	5518.12	5508.58	5500.82	5478.98	5471.12	5468.28
330000	5702.66	5690.56	5680.72	5672.72	5650.20	5642.09	5639.16
340000	5875.46	5863.00	5852.87	5844.62	5821.42	5813.06	5810.04
350000	6048.27	6035.44	6025.01	6016.52	5992.63	5984.03	5980.93
400000	6912.31	6897.65	6885.73	6876.03	6848.72	6838.90	6835.35
450000	7776.35	7759.85	7746.44	7735.53	7704.81	7693.76	7689.76
500000	8640.39	8622.06	8607.16	8595.04	8560.90	8548.62	8544.18
550000	9504.43	9484.26	9467.87	9454.54	9417.00	9403.48	9398.60
600000	10368.46	10346.47	10328.59	10314.04	10273.09	10258.34	10253.02

20¾%

Monthly Payments
necessary to amortize a loan

AMOUNT	1 YEAR	2 YEARS	3 YEARS	4 YEARS	5 YEARS	6 YEARS	7 YEARS
100	9.30	5.13	3.75	3.08	2.69	2.44	2.27
200	18.60	10.25	7.51	6.17	5.38	4.88	4.53
500	46.50	25.63	18.77	15.42	13.46	12.19	11.33
1000	92.99	51.26	37.55	30.83	26.91	24.39	22.66
2000	185.99	102.53	75.09	61.66	53.83	48.78	45.32
5000	464.97	256.31	187.73	154.16	134.56	121.95	113.30
6000	557.96	307.58	225.28	184.99	161.48	146.34	135.96
7000	650.96	358.84	262.83	215.82	188.39	170.73	158.62
8000	743.95	410.10	300.37	246.65	215.30	195.12	181.28
9000	836.94	461.37	337.92	277.48	242.22	219.51	203.94
10000	929.94	512.63	375.47	308.31	269.13	243.90	226.60
15000	1394.91	768.94	563.20	462.47	403.69	365.84	339.90
20000	1859.88	1025.26	750.94	616.63	538.26	487.79	453.20
25000	2324.85	1281.57	938.67	770.78	672.82	609.74	566.50
30000	2789.81	1537.89	1126.40	924.94	807.39	731.69	679.80
35000	3254.78	1794.20	1314.14	1079.10	941.95	853.63	793.10
40000	3719.75	2050.52	1501.87	1233.26	1076.52	975.58	906.40
45000	4184.72	2306.83	1689.61	1387.41	1211.08	1097.53	1019.70
50000	4649.69	2563.15	1877.34	1541.57	1345.65	1219.48	1133.00
55000	5114.66	2819.46	2065.08	1695.73	1480.21	1341.43	1246.30
60000	5579.63	3075.78	2252.81	1849.88	1614.78	1463.37	1359.60
65000	6044.60	3332.09	2440.54	2004.04	1749.34	1585.32	1472.90
70000	6509.57	3588.41	2628.28	2158.20	1883.90	1707.27	1586.20
75000	6974.54	3844.72	2816.01	2312.35	2018.47	1829.22	1699.50
80000	7439.51	4101.04	3003.75	2466.51	2153.03	1951.16	1812.80
85000	7904.48	4357.35	3191.48	2620.67	2287.60	2073.11	1926.10
90000	8369.44	4613.66	3379.21	2774.82	2422.16	2195.06	2039.40
95000	8834.41	4869.98	3566.95	2928.98	2556.73	2317.01	2152.70
100000	9299.38	5126.29	3754.68	3083.14	2691.29	2438.95	2266.00
105000	9764.35	5382.61	3942.42	3237.30	2825.86	2560.90	2379.30
110000	10229.32	5638.92	4130.15	3391.45	2960.42	2682.85	2492.60
120000	11159.26	6151.55	4505.62	3699.77	3229.55	2926.75	2719.20
130000	12089.20	6664.18	4881.09	4008.08	3498.68	3170.64	2945.80
140000	13019.14	7176.81	5256.56	4316.39	3767.81	3414.54	3172.40
150000	13949.07	7689.44	5632.02	4624.71	4036.94	3658.43	3399.00
160000	14879.01	8202.07	6007.49	4933.02	4306.07	3902.33	3625.60
170000	15808.95	8714.70	6382.96	5241.34	4575.20	4146.22	3852.20
180000	16738.89	9227.33	6758.43	5549.65	4844.33	4390.12	4078.80
190000	17668.83	9739.96	7133.90	5857.96	5113.45	4634.01	4305.40
200000	18598.77	10252.59	7509.37	6166.28	5382.58	4877.91	4532.00
210000	19528.70	10765.22	7884.83	6474.59	5651.71	5121.80	4758.60
220000	20458.64	11277.85	8260.30	6782.91	5920.84	5365.70	4985.20
230000	21388.58	11790.48	8635.77	7091.22	6189.97	5609.60	5211.80
240000	22318.52	12303.11	9011.24	7399.53	6459.10	5853.49	5438.40
250000	23248.46	12815.73	9386.71	7707.85	6728.23	6097.39	5665.00
260000	24178.40	13328.36	9762.18	8016.16	6997.36	6341.28	5891.60
270000	25108.33	13840.99	10137.64	8324.47	7266.49	6585.18	6118.20
280000	26038.27	14353.62	10513.11	8632.79	7535.62	6829.07	6344.80
290000	26968.21	14866.25	10888.58	8941.10	7804.75	7072.97	6571.40
300000	27898.15	15378.88	11264.05	9249.42	8073.88	7316.86	6798.00
310000	28828.09	15891.51	11639.52	9557.73	8343.00	7560.76	7024.60
320000	29758.03	16404.14	12014.99	9866.04	8612.13	7804.66	7251.20
330000	30687.96	16916.77	12390.45	10174.36	8881.26	8048.55	7477.80
340000	31617.90	17429.40	12765.92	10482.67	9150.39	8292.45	7704.40
350000	32547.84	17942.03	13141.39	10790.99	9419.52	8536.34	7931.00
400000	37197.53	20505.18	15018.73	12332.55	10765.17	9755.82	9064.00
450000	41847.22	23068.32	16896.07	13874.12	12110.81	10975.30	10197.00
500000	46496.92	25631.47	18773.41	15415.69	13456.46	12194.77	11330.00
550000	51146.61	28194.62	20650.76	16957.26	14802.11	13414.25	12463.00
600000	55796.30	30757.76	22528.10	18498.83	16147.75	14633.73	13596.00

Monthly Payments 20³/₄%
necessary to amortize a loan

AMOUNT	8 YEARS	9 YEARS	10 YEARS	11 YEARS	12 YEARS	13 YEARS	14 YEARS
100	2.14	2.05	1.98	1.93	1.89	1.86	1.83
200	4.28	4.10	3.97	3.86	3.78	3.71	3.66
500	10.71	10.26	9.91	9.65	9.45	9.29	9.16
1000	21.42	20.51	19.83	19.30	18.89	18.57	18.32
2000	42.85	41.02	39.65	38.60	37.78	37.14	36.64
5000	107.12	102.56	99.13	96.50	94.46	92.86	91.60
6000	128.54	123.07	118.95	115.80	113.35	111.43	109.92
7000	149.96	143.58	138.78	135.10	132.24	130.00	128.24
8000	171.39	164.10	158.60	154.40	151.13	148.58	146.56
9000	192.81	184.61	178.43	173.70	170.03	167.15	164.88
10000	214.23	205.12	198.25	193.00	188.92	185.72	183.20
15000	321.35	307.68	297.38	289.49	283.38	278.58	274.80
20000	428.47	410.24	396.51	385.99	377.83	371.44	366.40
25000	535.58	512.80	495.64	482.49	472.29	464.30	458.00
30000	642.70	615.36	594.76	578.99	566.75	557.16	549.60
35000	749.82	717.92	693.89	675.49	661.21	650.02	641.20
40000	856.93	820.48	793.02	771.98	755.67	742.89	732.79
45000	964.05	923.04	892.14	868.48	850.13	835.75	824.39
50000	1071.16	1025.60	991.27	964.98	944.58	928.61	915.99
55000	1178.28	1128.16	1090.40	1061.48	1039.04	1021.47	1007.59
60000	1285.40	1230.72	1189.53	1157.97	1133.50	1114.33	1099.19
65000	1392.51	1333.28	1288.65	1254.47	1227.96	1207.19	1190.79
70000	1499.63	1435.84	1387.78	1350.97	1322.42	1300.05	1282.39
75000	1606.75	1538.40	1486.91	1447.47	1416.88	1392.91	1373.99
80000	1713.86	1640.96	1586.03	1543.97	1511.33	1485.77	1465.59
85000	1820.98	1743.52	1685.16	1640.46	1605.79	1578.63	1557.19
90000	1928.09	1846.08	1784.29	1736.96	1700.25	1671.49	1648.79
95000	2035.21	1948.64	1883.41	1833.46	1794.71	1764.35	1740.39
100000	2142.33	2051.20	1982.54	1929.96	1889.17	1857.21	1831.99
105000	2249.44	2153.76	2081.67	2026.46	1983.63	1950.07	1923.59
110000	2356.56	2256.31	2180.80	2122.95	2078.08	2042.93	2015.19
120000	2570.79	2461.43	2379.05	2315.95	2267.00	2228.66	2198.38
130000	2785.03	2666.55	2577.30	2508.94	2455.92	2414.38	2381.58
140000	2999.26	2871.67	2775.56	2701.94	2644.83	2600.10	2564.78
150000	3213.49	3076.79	2973.81	2894.94	2833.75	2785.82	2747.98
160000	3427.72	3281.91	3172.07	3087.93	3022.67	2971.54	2931.18
170000	3641.96	3487.03	3370.32	3280.93	3211.58	3157.26	3114.38
180000	3856.19	3692.15	3568.58	3473.92	3400.50	3342.98	3297.58
190000	4070.42	3897.27	3766.83	3666.92	3589.42	3528.70	3480.78
200000	4284.65	4102.39	3965.08	3859.91	3778.33	3714.43	3663.97
210000	4498.89	4307.51	4163.34	4052.91	3967.25	3900.15	3847.17
220000	4713.12	4512.63	4361.59	4245.91	4156.17	4085.87	4030.37
230000	4927.35	4717.75	4559.85	4438.90	4345.08	4271.59	4213.57
240000	5141.59	4922.87	4758.10	4631.90	4534.00	4457.31	4396.77
250000	5355.82	5127.99	4956.35	4824.89	4722.92	4643.03	4579.97
260000	5570.05	5333.11	5154.61	5017.89	4911.83	4828.75	4763.17
270000	5784.28	5538.23	5352.86	5210.88	5100.75	5014.47	4946.37
280000	5998.52	5743.35	5551.12	5403.88	5289.67	5200.20	5129.56
290000	6212.75	5948.47	5749.37	5596.88	5478.58	5385.92	5312.76
300000	6426.98	6153.59	5947.63	5789.87	5667.50	5571.64	5495.96
310000	6641.22	6358.71	6145.88	5982.87	5856.42	5757.36	5679.16
320000	6855.45	6563.82	6344.13	6175.86	6045.33	5943.08	5862.36
330000	7069.68	6768.94	6542.39	6368.86	6234.25	6128.80	6045.56
340000	7283.91	6974.06	6740.64	6561.85	6423.17	6314.52	6228.76
350000	7498.15	7179.18	6938.90	6754.85	6612.08	6500.24	6411.96
400000	8569.31	8204.78	7930.17	7719.83	7556.67	7428.85	7327.95
450000	9640.47	9230.38	8921.44	8684.81	8501.25	8357.46	8243.94
500000	10711.64	10255.98	9912.71	9649.79	9445.83	9286.06	9159.94
550000	11782.80	11281.57	10903.98	10614.77	10390.42	10214.67	10075.93
600000	12853.96	12307.17	11895.25	11579.74	11335.00	11143.28	10991.92

20³/₄%

Monthly Payments
necessary to amortize a loan

AMOUNT	15 YEARS	16 YEARS	17 YEARS	18 YEARS	19 YEARS	20 YEARS	21 YEARS
100	1.81	1.80	1.78	1.77	1.76	1.76	1.75
200	3.62	3.59	3.57	3.55	3.53	3.52	3.50
500	9.06	8.98	8.92	8.86	8.82	8.79	8.76
1000	18.12	17.96	17.83	17.73	17.65	17.58	17.52
2000	36.24	35.92	35.66	35.46	35.29	35.16	35.05
5000	90.60	89.80	89.16	88.64	88.23	87.89	87.62
6000	108.72	107.76	106.99	106.37	105.87	105.47	105.15
7000	126.84	125.72	124.82	124.10	123.52	123.05	122.67
8000	144.96	143.68	142.65	141.83	141.17	140.63	140.20
9000	163.08	161.64	160.48	159.56	158.81	158.21	157.72
10000	181.20	179.60	178.32	177.29	176.46	175.79	175.25
15000	271.79	269.39	267.47	265.93	264.69	263.68	262.87
20000	362.39	359.19	356.63	354.57	352.91	351.58	350.49
25000	452.99	448.99	445.79	443.22	441.14	439.47	438.12
30000	543.59	538.79	534.95	531.86	529.37	527.36	525.74
35000	634.18	628.59	624.10	620.50	617.60	615.26	613.36
40000	724.78	718.39	713.26	709.15	705.83	703.15	700.99
45000	815.38	808.18	802.42	797.79	794.06	791.05	788.61
50000	905.98	897.98	891.58	886.43	882.29	878.94	876.23
55000	996.57	987.78	980.74	975.07	970.51	966.83	963.86
60000	1087.17	1077.58	1069.89	1063.72	1058.74	1054.73	1051.48
65000	1177.77	1167.38	1159.05	1152.36	1146.97	1142.62	1139.10
70000	1268.37	1257.18	1248.21	1241.00	1235.20	1230.52	1226.73
75000	1358.96	1346.97	1337.37	1329.65	1323.43	1318.41	1314.35
80000	1449.56	1436.77	1426.53	1418.29	1411.66	1406.30	1401.97
85000	1540.16	1526.57	1515.68	1506.93	1499.89	1494.20	1489.60
90000	1630.76	1616.37	1604.84	1595.58	1588.11	1582.09	1577.22
95000	1721.36	1706.17	1694.00	1684.22	1676.34	1669.99	1664.84
100000	1811.95	1795.96	1783.16	1772.86	1764.57	1757.88	1752.47
105000	1902.55	1885.76	1872.31	1861.51	1852.80	1845.77	1840.09
110000	1993.15	1975.56	1961.47	1950.15	1941.03	1933.67	1927.72
120000	2174.34	2155.16	2139.79	2127.44	2117.49	2109.46	2102.96
130000	2355.54	2334.75	2318.10	2304.72	2293.94	2285.24	2278.21
140000	2536.73	2514.35	2496.42	2482.01	2470.40	2461.03	2453.46
150000	2717.93	2693.95	2674.73	2659.30	2646.86	2636.82	2628.70
160000	2899.13	2873.54	2853.05	2836.58	2823.32	2812.61	2803.95
170000	3080.32	3053.14	3031.37	3013.87	2999.77	2988.39	2979.20
180000	3261.52	3232.74	3209.68	3191.15	3176.23	3164.18	3154.44
190000	3442.71	3412.33	3388.00	3368.44	3352.69	3339.97	3329.69
200000	3623.91	3591.93	3566.31	3545.73	3529.14	3515.76	3504.94
210000	3805.10	3771.53	3744.63	3723.01	3705.60	3691.55	3680.18
220000	3986.30	3951.12	3922.94	3900.30	3882.06	3867.33	3855.43
230000	4167.49	4130.72	4101.26	4077.59	4058.52	4043.12	4030.68
240000	4348.69	4310.32	4279.58	4254.87	4234.97	4218.91	4205.92
250000	4529.88	4489.91	4457.89	4432.16	4411.43	4394.70	4381.17
260000	4711.08	4669.51	4636.21	4609.45	4587.89	4570.49	4556.42
270000	4892.27	4849.10	4814.52	4786.73	4764.34	4746.27	4731.66
280000	5073.47	5028.70	4992.84	4964.02	4940.80	4922.06	4906.91
290000	5254.66	5208.30	5171.15	5141.30	5117.26	5097.85	5082.16
300000	5435.86	5387.89	5349.47	5318.59	5293.72	5273.64	5257.41
310000	5617.05	5567.49	5527.78	5495.88	5470.17	5449.43	5432.65
320000	5798.25	5747.09	5706.10	5673.16	5646.63	5625.21	5607.90
330000	5979.45	5926.68	5884.42	5850.45	5823.09	5801.00	5783.15
340000	6160.64	6106.28	6062.73	6027.74	5999.54	5976.79	5958.39
350000	6341.84	6285.88	6241.05	6205.02	6176.00	6152.58	6133.64
400000	7247.81	7183.86	7132.63	7091.45	7058.29	7031.52	7009.87
450000	8153.79	8081.84	8024.20	7977.89	7940.57	7910.46	7886.11
500000	9059.77	8979.82	8915.78	8864.32	8822.86	8789.40	8762.34
550000	9965.74	9877.81	9807.36	9750.75	9705.15	9668.34	9638.58
600000	10871.72	10775.79	10698.94	10637.18	10587.43	10547.28	10514.81

Monthly Payments 20¾%
necessary to amortize a loan

AMOUNT	22 YEARS	23 YEARS	24 YEARS	25 YEARS	30 YEARS	35 YEARS	40 YEARS
100	1.75	1.74	1.74	1.74	1.73	1.73	1.73
200	3.50	3.49	3.48	3.48	3.47	3.46	3.46
500	8.74	8.72	8.71	8.70	8.66	8.65	8.65
1000	17.48	17.45	17.42	17.39	17.33	17.30	17.30
2000	34.96	34.89	34.83	34.79	34.66	34.61	34.59
5000	87.40	87.23	87.08	86.97	86.64	86.52	86.48
6000	104.89	104.67	104.50	104.36	103.97	103.83	103.78
7000	122.37	122.12	121.92	121.75	121.29	121.13	121.07
8000	139.85	139.56	139.33	139.15	138.62	138.44	138.37
9000	157.33	157.01	156.75	156.54	155.95	155.74	155.67
10000	174.81	174.45	174.17	173.93	173.28	173.05	172.96
15000	262.21	261.68	261.25	260.90	259.92	259.57	259.44
20000	349.62	348.91	348.33	347.86	346.56	346.09	345.93
25000	437.02	436.13	435.41	434.83	433.20	432.61	432.41
30000	524.43	523.36	522.50	521.80	519.84	519.14	518.89
35000	611.83	610.59	609.58	608.76	606.47	605.66	605.37
40000	699.24	697.82	696.66	695.73	693.11	692.18	691.85
45000	786.64	785.04	783.75	782.70	779.75	778.71	778.33
50000	874.04	872.27	870.83	869.66	866.39	865.23	864.81
55000	961.45	959.50	957.91	956.63	953.03	951.75	951.30
60000	1048.85	1046.72	1045.00	1043.59	1039.67	1038.27	1037.78
65000	1136.26	1133.95	1132.08	1130.56	1126.31	1124.80	1124.26
70000	1223.66	1221.18	1219.16	1217.53	1212.95	1211.32	1210.74
75000	1311.07	1308.40	1306.24	1304.49	1299.59	1297.84	1297.22
80000	1398.47	1395.63	1393.33	1391.46	1386.23	1384.37	1383.70
85000	1485.87	1482.86	1480.41	1478.42	1472.87	1470.89	1470.18
90000	1573.28	1570.09	1567.49	1565.39	1559.51	1557.41	1556.67
95000	1660.68	1657.31	1654.58	1652.36	1646.14	1643.94	1643.15
100000	1748.09	1744.54	1741.66	1739.32	1732.78	1730.46	1729.63
105000	1835.49	1831.77	1828.74	1826.29	1819.42	1816.98	1816.11
110000	1922.90	1918.99	1915.83	1913.26	1906.06	1903.50	1902.59
120000	2097.71	2093.45	2089.99	2087.19	2079.34	2076.55	2075.55
130000	2272.51	2267.90	2264.16	2261.12	2252.62	2249.60	2248.52
140000	2447.32	2442.35	2438.32	2435.05	2425.90	2422.64	2421.48
150000	2622.13	2616.81	2612.49	2608.98	2599.18	2595.69	2594.44
160000	2796.94	2791.26	2786.66	2782.92	2772.45	2768.73	2767.40
170000	2971.75	2965.72	2960.82	2956.85	2945.73	2941.78	2940.37
180000	3146.56	3140.17	3134.99	3130.78	3119.01	3114.82	3113.33
190000	3321.37	3314.62	3309.15	3304.71	3292.29	3287.87	3286.29
200000	3496.18	3489.08	3483.32	3478.65	3465.57	3460.92	3459.26
210000	3670.99	3663.53	3657.49	3652.58	3638.85	3633.96	3632.22
220000	3845.80	3837.98	3831.65	3826.51	3812.12	3807.01	3805.18
230000	4020.60	4012.44	4005.82	4000.44	3985.40	3980.05	3978.14
240000	4195.41	4186.89	4179.98	4174.38	4158.68	4153.10	4151.11
250000	4370.22	4361.35	4354.15	4348.31	4331.96	4326.15	4324.07
260000	4545.03	4535.80	4528.31	4522.24	4505.24	4499.19	4497.03
270000	4719.84	4710.25	4702.48	4696.17	4678.52	4672.24	4670.00
280000	4894.65	4884.71	4876.65	4870.10	4851.79	4845.28	4842.96
290000	5069.46	5059.16	5050.81	5044.04	5025.07	5018.33	5015.92
300000	5244.26	5233.62	5224.98	5217.97	5198.35	5191.37	5188.88
310000	5419.07	5408.07	5399.14	5391.90	5371.63	5364.42	5361.85
320000	5593.88	5582.52	5573.31	5565.83	5544.91	5537.47	5534.81
330000	5768.69	5756.98	5747.48	5739.77	5718.19	5710.51	5707.77
340000	5943.50	5931.43	5921.64	5913.70	5891.47	5883.56	5880.74
350000	6118.31	6105.88	6095.81	6087.63	6064.74	6056.60	6053.70
400000	6992.35	6978.15	6966.64	6957.29	6931.14	6921.83	6918.51
450000	7866.40	7850.42	7837.47	7826.95	7797.53	7787.06	7783.33
500000	8740.44	8722.69	8708.30	8696.61	8663.92	8652.29	8648.14
550000	9614.48	9594.96	9579.13	9566.28	9530.31	9517.52	9512.95
600000	10488.53	10467.23	10449.96	10435.94	10396.70	10382.75	10377.77

21% Monthly Payments
necessary to amortize a loan

AMOUNT	1 YEAR	2 YEARS	3 YEARS	4 YEARS	5 YEARS	6 YEARS	7 YEARS
100	9.31	5.14	3.77	3.10	2.71	2.45	2.28
200	18.62	10.28	7.54	6.19	5.41	4.91	4.56
500	46.56	25.69	18.84	15.48	13.53	12.27	11.41
1000	93.11	51.39	37.68	30.97	27.05	24.54	22.81
2000	186.23	102.77	75.35	61.93	54.11	49.07	45.62
5000	465.57	256.93	188.38	154.83	135.27	122.68	114.06
6000	558.68	308.31	226.05	185.79	162.32	147.22	136.87
7000	651.80	359.70	263.73	216.76	189.37	171.75	159.69
8000	744.91	411.09	301.40	247.73	216.43	196.29	182.50
9000	838.02	462.47	339.08	278.69	243.48	220.82	205.31
10000	931.14	513.86	376.75	309.66	270.53	245.36	228.12
15000	1396.71	770.78	565.13	464.49	405.80	368.04	342.18
20000	1862.28	1027.71	753.50	619.31	541.07	490.72	456.24
25000	2327.84	1284.64	941.88	774.14	676.33	613.40	570.31
30000	2793.41	1541.57	1130.25	928.97	811.60	736.08	684.37
35000	3258.98	1798.50	1318.63	1083.80	946.87	858.76	798.43
40000	3724.55	2055.43	1507.00	1238.63	1082.13	981.44	912.49
45000	4190.12	2312.35	1695.38	1393.46	1217.40	1104.12	1026.55
50000	4655.69	2569.28	1883.75	1548.28	1352.67	1226.80	1140.61
55000	5121.26	2826.21	2072.13	1703.11	1487.93	1349.48	1254.67
60000	5586.83	3083.14	2260.50	1857.94	1623.20	1472.16	1368.73
65000	6052.40	3340.07	2448.88	2012.77	1758.47	1594.84	1482.79
70000	6517.96	3597.00	2637.25	2167.60	1893.74	1717.52	1596.86
75000	6983.53	3853.92	2825.63	2322.43	2029.00	1840.20	1710.92
80000	7449.10	4110.85	3014.01	2477.26	2164.27	1962.88	1824.98
85000	7914.67	4367.78	3202.38	2632.08	2299.54	2085.56	1939.04
90000	8380.24	4624.71	3390.76	2786.91	2434.80	2208.24	2053.10
95000	8845.81	4881.64	3579.13	2941.74	2570.07	2330.92	2167.16
100000	9311.38	5138.57	3767.51	3096.57	2705.34	2453.60	2281.22
105000	9776.95	5395.49	3955.88	3251.40	2840.60	2576.28	2395.28
110000	10242.52	5652.42	4144.26	3406.23	2975.87	2698.96	2509.34
120000	11173.65	6166.28	4521.01	3715.88	3246.40	2944.32	2737.47
130000	12104.79	6680.13	4897.76	4025.54	3516.94	3189.68	2965.59
140000	13035.93	7193.99	5274.51	4335.20	3787.47	3435.04	3193.71
150000	13967.07	7707.85	5651.26	4644.85	4058.00	3680.40	3421.83
160000	14898.20	8221.70	6028.01	4954.51	4328.54	3925.76	3649.96
170000	15829.34	8735.56	6404.76	5264.17	4599.07	4171.12	3878.08
180000	16760.48	9249.42	6781.51	5573.83	4869.60	4416.48	4106.20
190000	17691.62	9763.27	7158.26	5883.48	5140.14	4661.84	4334.32
200000	18622.75	10277.13	7535.01	6193.14	5410.67	4907.20	4562.45
210000	19553.89	10790.99	7911.76	6502.80	5681.21	5152.56	4790.57
220000	20485.03	11304.84	8288.51	6812.45	5951.74	5397.92	5018.69
230000	21416.17	11818.70	8665.27	7122.11	6222.27	5643.28	5246.81
240000	22347.31	12332.56	9042.02	7431.77	6492.81	5888.64	5474.93
250000	23278.44	12846.41	9418.77	7741.42	6763.34	6134.00	5703.06
260000	24209.58	13360.27	9795.52	8051.08	7033.87	6379.36	5931.18
270000	25140.72	13874.13	10172.27	8360.74	7304.41	6624.72	6159.30
280000	26071.86	14387.98	10549.02	8670.39	7574.94	6870.08	6387.42
290000	27002.99	14901.84	10925.77	8980.05	7845.47	7115.44	6615.55
300000	27934.13	15415.70	11302.52	9289.71	8116.01	7360.80	6843.67
310000	28865.27	15929.55	11679.27	9599.37	8386.54	7606.16	7071.79
320000	29796.41	16443.41	12056.02	9909.02	8657.08	7851.52	7299.91
330000	30727.55	16957.26	12432.77	10218.68	8927.61	8096.88	7528.03
340000	31658.68	17471.12	12809.52	10528.34	9198.14	8342.24	7756.16
350000	32589.82	17984.98	13186.27	10837.99	9468.68	8587.60	7984.28
400000	37245.51	20554.26	15070.03	12386.28	10821.34	9814.40	9124.89
450000	41901.20	23123.54	16953.78	13934.56	12174.01	11041.20	10265.50
500000	46556.88	25692.83	18837.53	15482.85	13526.68	12268.00	11406.11
550000	51212.58	28262.11	20721.29	17031.13	14879.35	13494.80	12546.72
600000	55868.26	30831.39	22605.04	18579.42	16232.02	14721.60	13687.34

Monthly Payments

21%

necessary to amortize a loan

AMOUNT	8 YEARS	9 YEARS	10 YEARS	11 YEARS	12 YEARS	13 YEARS	14 YEARS
100	2.16	2.07	2.00	1.95	1.91	1.88	1.85
200	4.32	4.13	4.00	3.89	3.81	3.75	3.70
500	10.79	10.34	10.00	9.74	9.53	9.38	9.25
1000	21.58	20.67	19.99	19.47	19.07	18.75	18.50
2000	43.16	41.35	39.99	38.94	38.14	37.50	37.01
5000	107.91	103.37	99.97	97.36	95.34	93.76	92.52
6000	129.49	124.05	119.96	116.83	114.41	112.51	111.02
7000	151.07	144.72	139.95	136.30	133.48	131.27	129.52
8000	172.65	165.40	159.95	155.77	152.54	150.02	148.03
9000	194.23	186.07	179.94	175.25	171.61	168.77	166.53
10000	215.81	206.75	199.93	194.72	190.68	187.52	185.03
15000	323.72	310.12	299.90	292.08	286.02	281.28	277.55
20000	431.62	413.50	399.86	389.44	381.36	375.04	370.07
25000	539.53	516.87	499.83	486.80	476.70	468.81	462.58
30000	647.43	620.25	599.80	584.15	572.04	562.57	555.10
35000	755.34	723.62	699.76	681.51	667.38	656.33	647.62
40000	863.24	826.99	799.73	778.87	762.72	750.09	740.14
45000	971.15	930.37	899.69	876.23	858.06	843.85	832.65
50000	1079.05	1033.74	999.66	973.59	953.40	937.61	925.17
55000	1186.96	1137.12	1099.62	1070.95	1048.74	1031.37	1017.69
60000	1294.86	1240.49	1199.59	1168.31	1144.08	1125.13	1110.20
65000	1402.77	1343.87	1299.56	1265.67	1239.42	1218.89	1202.72
70000	1510.67	1447.24	1399.52	1363.03	1334.76	1312.66	1295.24
75000	1618.58	1550.62	1499.49	1460.39	1430.10	1406.42	1387.75
80000	1726.48	1653.99	1599.45	1557.74	1525.44	1500.18	1480.27
85000	1834.39	1757.36	1699.42	1655.10	1620.78	1593.94	1572.79
90000	1942.29	1860.74	1799.39	1752.46	1716.12	1687.70	1665.30
95000	2050.20	1964.11	1899.35	1849.82	1811.46	1781.46	1757.82
100000	2158.10	2067.49	1999.32	1947.18	1906.80	1875.22	1850.34
105000	2266.01	2170.86	2099.28	2044.54	2002.14	1968.98	1942.86
110000	2373.91	2274.24	2199.25	2141.90	2097.48	2062.75	2035.37
120000	2589.72	2480.98	2399.18	2336.62	2288.16	2250.27	2220.41
130000	2805.53	2687.73	2599.11	2531.33	2478.84	2437.79	2405.44
140000	3021.34	2894.48	2799.04	2726.05	2669.52	2625.31	2590.47
150000	3237.15	3101.23	2998.98	2920.77	2860.20	2812.83	2775.51
160000	3452.96	3307.98	3198.91	3115.49	3050.88	3000.36	2960.54
170000	3668.77	3514.73	3398.84	3310.21	3241.56	3187.88	3145.58
180000	3884.58	3721.48	3598.77	3504.92	3432.24	3375.40	3330.61
190000	4100.39	3928.22	3798.70	3699.64	3622.92	3562.92	3515.64
200000	4316.20	4134.97	3998.63	3894.36	3813.60	3750.45	3700.68
210000	4532.01	4341.72	4198.57	4089.08	4004.28	3937.97	3885.71
220000	4747.82	4548.47	4398.50	4283.80	4194.96	4125.49	4070.75
230000	4963.63	4755.22	4598.43	4478.51	4385.64	4313.01	4255.78
240000	5179.44	4961.97	4798.36	4673.23	4576.32	4500.53	4440.81
250000	5395.25	5168.72	4998.29	4867.95	4767.00	4688.06	4625.85
260000	5611.06	5375.47	5198.22	5062.67	4957.68	4875.58	4810.88
270000	5826.87	5582.21	5398.16	5257.39	5148.36	5063.10	4995.91
280000	6042.68	5788.96	5598.09	5452.10	5339.04	5250.62	5180.95
290000	6258.49	5995.71	5798.02	5646.82	5529.72	5438.15	5365.98
300000	6474.30	6202.46	5997.95	5841.54	5720.40	5625.67	5551.02
310000	6690.11	6409.21	6197.88	6036.26	5911.08	5813.19	5736.05
320000	6905.92	6615.96	6397.81	6230.98	6101.76	6000.71	5921.08
330000	7121.73	6822.71	6597.75	6425.69	6292.44	6188.24	6106.12
340000	7337.54	7029.45	6797.68	6620.41	6483.12	6375.76	6291.15
350000	7553.35	7236.20	6997.61	6815.13	6673.80	6563.28	6476.19
400000	8632.40	8269.95	7997.27	7788.72	7627.20	7500.89	7401.36
450000	9711.45	9303.69	8996.93	8762.31	8580.61	8438.50	8326.52
500000	10790.50	10337.43	9996.55	9735.90	9534.01	9376.11	9251.69
550000	11869.56	11371.18	10996.24	10709.49	10487.41	10313.73	10176.86
600000	12948.61	12404.92	11995.90	11683.08	11440.81	11251.34	11102.03

21% Monthly Payments
necessary to amortize a loan

AMOUNT	15 YEARS	16 YEARS	17 YEARS	18 YEARS	19 YEARS	20 YEARS	21 YEARS
100	1.83	1.81	1.80	1.79	1.78	1.78	1.77
200	3.66	3.63	3.60	3.58	3.57	3.56	3.54
500	9.15	9.07	9.01	8.96	8.92	8.89	8.86
1000	18.31	18.15	18.02	17.92	17.84	17.78	17.72
2000	36.61	36.30	36.05	35.85	35.68	35.55	35.45
5000	91.53	90.74	90.12	89.61	89.21	88.88	88.62
6000	109.84	108.89	108.14	107.54	107.05	106.66	106.34
7000	128.14	127.04	126.16	125.46	124.89	124.44	124.07
8000	146.45	145.19	144.19	143.38	142.73	142.21	141.79
9000	164.76	163.34	162.21	161.30	160.57	159.99	159.51
10000	183.06	181.49	180.23	179.23	178.42	177.77	177.24
15000	274.59	272.23	270.35	268.84	267.62	266.65	265.86
20000	366.12	362.98	360.47	358.45	356.83	355.53	354.48
25000	457.65	453.72	450.58	448.07	446.04	444.41	443.10
30000	549.18	544.47	540.70	537.68	535.25	533.29	531.71
35000	640.71	635.21	630.82	627.29	624.46	622.18	620.33
40000	732.24	725.96	720.94	716.91	713.67	711.06	708.95
45000	823.78	816.70	811.05	806.52	802.87	799.94	797.57
50000	915.31	907.45	901.17	896.13	892.08	888.82	886.19
55000	1006.84	998.19	991.29	985.75	981.29	977.70	974.81
60000	1098.37	1088.94	1081.40	1075.36	1070.50	1066.59	1063.43
65000	1189.90	1179.68	1171.52	1164.97	1159.71	1155.47	1152.05
70000	1281.43	1270.43	1261.64	1254.58	1248.92	1244.35	1240.67
75000	1372.96	1361.17	1351.75	1344.20	1338.12	1333.23	1329.29
80000	1464.49	1451.92	1441.87	1433.81	1427.33	1422.11	1417.90
85000	1556.02	1542.66	1531.99	1523.42	1516.54	1511.00	1506.52
90000	1647.55	1633.41	1622.10	1613.04	1605.75	1599.88	1595.14
95000	1739.08	1724.15	1712.22	1702.65	1694.96	1688.76	1683.76
100000	1830.61	1814.90	1802.34	1792.26	1784.17	1777.64	1772.38
105000	1922.14	1905.64	1892.45	1881.88	1873.37	1866.53	1861.00
110000	2013.67	1996.39	1982.57	1971.49	1962.58	1955.41	1949.62
120000	2196.73	2177.88	2162.81	2150.72	2141.00	2133.17	2126.86
130000	2379.80	2359.37	2343.04	2329.94	2319.42	2310.94	2304.10
140000	2562.86	2540.86	2523.27	2509.17	2497.83	2488.70	2481.33
150000	2745.92	2722.35	2703.51	2688.40	2676.25	2666.46	2658.57
160000	2928.98	2903.84	2883.74	2867.62	2854.66	2844.23	2835.81
170000	3112.04	3085.33	3063.97	3046.85	3033.08	3021.99	3013.05
180000	3295.10	3266.82	3244.21	3226.07	3211.50	3199.76	3190.29
190000	3478.16	3448.31	3424.44	3405.30	3389.91	3377.52	3367.52
200000	3661.22	3629.80	3604.68	3584.53	3568.33	3555.29	3544.76
210000	3844.29	3811.29	3784.91	3763.75	3746.75	3733.05	3722.00
220000	4027.35	3992.78	3965.14	3942.98	3925.16	3910.81	3899.24
230000	4210.41	4174.27	4145.38	4122.21	4103.58	4088.58	4076.48
240000	4393.47	4355.76	4325.61	4301.43	4282.00	4266.34	4253.71
250000	4576.53	4537.25	4505.84	4480.66	4460.41	4444.11	4430.95
260000	4759.59	4718.74	4686.08	4659.89	4638.83	4621.87	4608.19
270000	4942.65	4900.23	4866.31	4839.11	4817.25	4799.64	4785.43
280000	5125.71	5081.72	5046.55	5018.34	4995.66	4977.40	4962.67
290000	5308.78	5263.21	5226.78	5197.56	5174.08	5155.16	5139.91
300000	5491.84	5444.70	5407.01	5376.79	5352.50	5332.93	5317.14
310000	5674.90	5626.19	5587.25	5556.02	5530.91	5510.69	5494.38
320000	5857.96	5807.68	5767.48	5735.24	5709.33	5688.46	5671.62
330000	6041.02	5989.17	5947.71	5914.47	5887.75	5866.22	5848.86
340000	6224.08	6170.66	6127.95	6093.70	6066.16	6043.99	6026.10
350000	6407.14	6352.15	6308.18	6272.92	6244.58	6221.75	6203.33
400000	7322.45	7259.60	7209.35	7169.05	7136.66	7110.57	7089.52
450000	8237.76	8167.05	8110.52	8065.19	8028.74	7999.39	7975.72
500000	9153.06	9074.50	9011.69	8961.32	8920.83	8888.21	8861.91
550000	10068.37	9981.95	9912.86	9857.45	9812.91	9777.04	9748.10
600000	10983.67	10889.40	10814.03	10753.58	10704.99	10665.86	10634.29

Monthly Payments 21%
necessary to amortize a loan

AMOUNT	22 YEARS	23 YEARS	24 YEARS	25 YEARS	30 YEARS	35 YEARS	40 YEARS
100	1.77	1.76	1.76	1.76	1.75	1.75	1.75
200	3.54	3.53	3.52	3.52	3.51	3.50	3.50
500	8.84	8.82	8.81	8.80	8.77	8.76	8.75
1000	17.68	17.65	17.62	17.60	17.53	17.51	17.50
2000	35.36	35.29	35.24	35.19	35.07	35.02	35.01
5000	88.41	88.23	88.10	87.98	87.67	87.56	87.52
6000	106.09	105.88	105.71	105.58	105.20	105.07	105.03
7000	123.77	123.53	123.33	123.18	122.74	122.58	122.53
8000	141.45	141.18	140.95	140.77	140.27	140.10	140.03
9000	159.13	158.82	158.57	158.37	157.80	157.61	157.54
10000	176.81	176.47	176.19	175.97	175.34	175.12	175.04
15000	265.22	264.70	264.29	263.95	263.01	262.68	262.56
20000	353.63	352.94	352.38	351.93	350.67	350.24	350.08
25000	442.03	441.17	440.48	439.92	438.35	437.80	437.61
30000	530.44	529.41	528.57	527.90	526.02	525.36	525.13
35000	618.85	617.64	616.67	615.88	613.69	612.92	612.65
40000	707.25	705.88	704.77	703.87	701.36	700.48	700.17
45000	795.66	794.11	792.86	791.85	789.03	788.04	787.69
50000	884.07	882.35	880.96	879.83	876.70	875.60	875.21
55000	972.47	970.58	969.05	967.81	964.37	963.16	962.73
60000	1060.88	1058.82	1057.15	1055.80	1052.04	1050.72	1050.25
65000	1149.29	1147.05	1145.24	1143.78	1139.71	1138.28	1137.78
70000	1237.69	1235.29	1233.34	1231.76	1227.38	1225.84	1225.30
75000	1326.10	1323.52	1321.44	1319.75	1315.05	1313.40	1312.82
80000	1414.51	1411.76	1409.53	1407.73	1402.72	1400.96	1400.34
85000	1502.91	1499.99	1497.63	1495.71	1490.39	1488.52	1487.86
90000	1591.32	1588.23	1585.72	1583.70	1578.06	1576.08	1575.38
95000	1679.72	1676.46	1673.82	1671.68	1665.73	1663.64	1662.90
100000	1768.13	1764.70	1761.91	1759.66	1753.40	1751.20	1750.42
105000	1856.54	1852.93	1850.01	1847.65	1841.07	1838.76	1837.94
110000	1944.94	1941.16	1938.11	1935.63	1928.74	1926.32	1925.47
120000	2121.76	2117.63	2114.30	2111.60	2104.08	2101.44	2100.51
130000	2298.57	2294.10	2290.49	2287.56	2279.42	2276.56	2275.55
140000	2475.38	2470.57	2466.68	2463.53	2454.76	2451.68	2450.59
150000	2652.20	2647.04	2642.87	2639.49	2630.10	2626.80	2625.63
160000	2829.01	2823.51	2819.06	2815.46	2805.44	2801.92	2800.68
170000	3005.82	2999.98	2995.25	2991.43	2980.78	2977.04	2975.72
180000	3182.64	3176.45	3171.45	3167.39	3156.12	3152.16	3150.76
190000	3359.45	3352.92	3347.64	3343.36	3331.46	3327.28	3325.80
200000	3536.26	3529.39	3523.83	3519.33	3506.80	3502.40	3500.85
210000	3713.08	3705.86	3700.02	3695.29	3682.14	3677.52	3675.89
220000	3889.89	3882.33	3876.21	3871.26	3857.48	3852.64	3850.93
230000	4066.70	4058.80	4052.40	4047.22	4032.82	4027.76	4025.97
240000	4243.52	4235.27	4228.59	4223.19	4208.16	4202.88	4201.02
250000	4420.33	4411.74	4404.79	4399.16	4383.50	4378.00	4376.06
260000	4597.14	4588.21	4580.98	4575.12	4558.84	4553.12	4551.10
270000	4773.95	4764.68	4757.17	4751.09	4734.18	4728.24	4726.14
280000	4950.77	4941.15	4933.36	4927.06	4909.52	4903.36	4901.19
290000	5127.58	5117.62	5109.55	5103.02	5084.86	5078.48	5076.23
300000	5304.39	5294.09	5285.74	5278.99	5260.20	5253.60	5251.27
310000	5481.21	5470.55	5461.93	5454.95	5435.54	5428.72	5426.31
320000	5658.02	5647.02	5638.13	5630.92	5610.88	5603.84	5601.35
330000	5834.83	5823.49	5814.32	5806.89	5786.22	5778.96	5776.40
340000	6011.65	5999.96	5990.51	5982.85	5961.56	5954.08	5951.44
350000	6188.46	6176.43	6166.70	6158.82	6136.90	6129.20	6126.48
400000	7072.53	7058.78	7047.66	7038.65	7013.60	7004.80	7001.69
450000	7956.59	7941.13	7928.61	7918.48	7890.30	7880.40	7876.90
500000	8840.66	8823.48	8809.57	8798.31	8767.00	8756.00	8752.12
550000	9724.72	9705.82	9690.53	9678.15	9643.70	9631.60	9627.33
600000	10608.79	10588.17	10571.49	10557.98	10520.40	10507.20	10502.54

21¼% Monthly Payments
necessary to amortize a loan

AMOUNT	1 YEAR	2 YEARS	3 YEARS	4 YEARS	5 YEARS	6 YEARS	7 YEARS
100	9.32	5.15	3.78	3.11	2.72	2.47	2.30
200	18.65	10.30	7.56	6.22	5.44	4.94	4.59
500	46.62	25.75	18.90	15.55	13.60	12.34	11.48
1000	93.23	51.51	37.80	31.10	27.19	24.68	22.96
2000	186.47	103.02	75.61	62.20	54.39	49.37	45.93
5000	466.17	257.54	189.02	155.50	135.97	123.41	114.82
6000	559.40	309.05	226.82	186.60	163.17	148.10	137.79
7000	652.64	360.56	264.62	217.70	190.36	172.78	160.75
8000	745.87	412.07	302.43	248.80	217.55	197.46	183.72
9000	839.10	463.58	340.23	279.90	244.75	222.15	206.68
10000	932.34	515.09	378.04	311.00	271.94	246.83	229.65
15000	1398.51	772.63	567.05	466.50	407.91	370.24	344.47
20000	1864.68	1030.17	756.07	622.01	543.88	493.66	459.30
25000	2330.84	1287.71	945.09	777.51	679.85	617.07	574.12
30000	2797.01	1545.26	1134.11	933.01	815.83	740.49	688.95
35000	3263.18	1802.80	1323.12	1088.51	951.80	863.90	803.77
40000	3729.35	2060.34	1512.14	1244.01	1087.77	987.32	918.60
45000	4195.52	2317.88	1701.16	1399.51	1223.74	1110.73	1033.42
50000	4661.69	2575.43	1890.18	1555.02	1359.71	1234.14	1148.25
55000	5127.86	2832.97	2079.20	1710.52	1495.68	1357.56	1263.07
60000	5594.03	3090.51	2268.21	1866.02	1631.65	1480.97	1377.90
65000	6060.20	3348.05	2457.23	2021.52	1767.62	1604.39	1492.72
70000	6526.37	3605.60	2646.25	2177.02	1903.59	1727.80	1607.55
75000	6992.53	3863.14	2835.27	2332.52	2039.56	1851.22	1722.37
80000	7458.70	4120.68	3024.28	2488.03	2175.53	1974.63	1837.20
85000	7924.87	4378.22	3213.30	2643.53	2311.51	2098.04	1952.02
90000	8391.04	4635.77	3402.32	2799.03	2447.48	2221.46	2066.84
95000	8857.21	4893.31	3591.34	2954.53	2583.45	2344.87	2181.67
100000	9323.38	5150.85	3780.35	3110.03	2719.42	2468.29	2296.49
105000	9789.55	5408.40	3969.37	3265.53	2855.39	2591.70	2411.32
110000	10255.72	5665.94	4158.39	3421.04	2991.36	2715.12	2526.14
120000	11188.06	6181.02	4536.43	3732.04	3263.30	2961.95	2755.79
130000	12120.39	6696.11	4914.46	4043.04	3535.24	3208.77	2985.44
140000	13052.73	7211.19	5292.50	4354.04	3807.19	3455.60	3215.09
150000	13985.07	7726.28	5670.53	4665.05	4079.13	3702.43	3444.74
160000	14917.41	8241.36	6048.57	4976.05	4351.07	3949.26	3674.39
170000	15849.75	8756.45	6426.60	5287.05	4623.01	4196.09	3904.04
180000	16782.08	9271.54	6804.64	5598.06	4894.95	4442.92	4133.69
190000	17714.42	9786.62	7182.67	5909.06	5166.89	4689.75	4363.34
200000	18646.76	10301.71	7560.71	6220.06	5438.84	4936.58	4592.99
210000	19579.10	10816.79	7938.75	6531.07	5710.78	5183.40	4822.64
220000	20511.44	11331.88	8316.78	6842.07	5982.72	5430.23	5052.29
230000	21443.77	11846.96	8694.82	7153.07	6254.66	5677.06	5281.94
240000	22376.11	12362.05	9072.85	7464.08	6526.60	5923.89	5511.59
250000	23308.45	12877.13	9450.89	7775.08	6798.55	6170.72	5741.24
260000	24240.79	13392.22	9828.92	8086.08	7070.49	6417.55	5970.88
270000	25173.13	13907.30	10206.96	8397.09	7342.43	6664.38	6200.53
280000	26105.46	14422.39	10584.99	8708.09	7614.37	6911.21	6430.18
290000	27037.80	14937.47	10963.03	9019.09	7886.31	7158.04	6659.83
300000	27970.14	15452.56	11341.06	9330.10	8158.25	7404.86	6889.48
310000	28902.48	15967.64	11719.10	9641.10	8430.20	7651.69	7119.13
320000	29834.82	16482.73	12097.14	9952.10	8702.14	7898.52	7348.78
330000	30767.15	16997.81	12475.17	10263.11	8974.08	8145.35	7578.43
340000	31699.49	17512.90	12853.21	10574.11	9246.02	8392.18	7808.08
350000	32631.83	18027.98	13231.24	10885.11	9517.96	8639.01	8037.73
400000	37293.52	20603.41	15121.42	12440.13	10877.67	9873.15	9185.98
450000	41955.21	23178.84	17011.60	13995.14	12237.38	11107.30	10334.22
500000	46616.90	25754.26	18901.77	15550.16	13597.09	12341.44	11482.47
550000	51278.59	28329.69	20791.95	17105.18	14956.80	13575.58	12630.72
600000	55940.28	30905.12	22682.13	18660.19	16316.51	14809.73	13778.96

Monthly Payments 21¼%
necessary to amortize a loan

AMOUNT	8 YEARS	9 YEARS	10 YEARS	11 YEARS	12 YEARS	13 YEARS	14 YEARS
100	2.17	2.08	2.02	1.96	1.92	1.89	1.87
200	4.35	4.17	4.03	3.93	3.85	3.79	3.74
500	10.87	10.42	10.08	9.82	9.62	9.47	9.34
1000	21.74	20.84	20.16	19.64	19.24	18.93	18.69
2000	43.48	41.68	40.32	39.29	38.49	37.87	37.37
5000	108.70	104.19	100.81	98.22	96.22	94.66	93.44
6000	130.44	125.03	120.97	117.87	115.47	113.60	112.12
7000	152.17	145.87	141.13	137.51	134.71	132.53	130.81
8000	173.91	166.71	161.29	157.16	153.96	151.46	149.50
9000	195.65	187.54	181.45	176.80	173.20	170.40	168.19
10000	217.39	208.38	201.61	196.45	192.45	189.33	186.87
15000	326.09	312.57	302.42	294.67	288.67	283.99	280.31
20000	434.79	416.77	403.23	392.89	384.90	378.66	373.75
25000	543.48	520.96	504.04	491.11	481.12	473.32	467.19
30000	652.18	625.15	604.84	589.34	577.35	567.99	560.62
35000	760.87	729.34	705.65	687.56	673.57	662.65	654.06
40000	869.57	833.53	806.46	785.78	769.80	757.32	747.50
45000	978.27	937.72	907.27	884.01	866.02	851.98	840.93
50000	1086.96	1041.92	1008.07	982.23	962.25	946.64	934.37
55000	1195.65	1146.11	1108.88	1080.45	1058.47	1041.31	1027.81
60000	1304.36	1250.30	1209.69	1178.68	1154.70	1135.97	1121.25
65000	1413.05	1354.49	1310.50	1276.90	1250.92	1230.64	1214.68
70000	1521.75	1458.68	1411.30	1375.12	1347.14	1325.30	1308.12
75000	1630.44	1562.87	1512.11	1473.34	1443.37	1419.97	1401.56
80000	1739.14	1667.07	1612.92	1571.57	1539.59	1514.63	1495.00
85000	1847.84	1771.26	1713.73	1669.79	1635.82	1609.30	1588.43
90000	1956.53	1875.45	1814.53	1768.01	1732.04	1703.96	1681.87
95000	2065.23	1979.64	1915.34	1866.24	1828.27	1798.62	1775.31
100000	2173.93	2083.83	2016.15	1964.46	1924.49	1893.29	1868.74
105000	2282.62	2188.02	2116.95	2062.68	2020.72	1987.95	1962.18
110000	2391.32	2292.22	2217.76	2160.91	2116.94	2082.62	2055.62
120000	2608.71	2500.60	2419.38	2357.35	2309.39	2271.95	2242.49
130000	2826.10	2708.98	2620.99	2553.80	2501.84	2461.28	2429.37
140000	3043.50	2917.37	2822.61	2750.24	2694.29	2650.60	2616.24
150000	3260.89	3125.75	3024.22	2946.69	2886.74	2839.93	2803.12
160000	3478.28	3334.13	3225.84	3143.13	3079.19	3029.26	2989.99
170000	3695.67	3542.52	3427.45	3339.58	3271.64	3218.59	3176.86
180000	3913.07	3750.90	3629.07	3536.03	3464.09	3407.92	3363.74
190000	4130.46	3959.28	3830.68	3732.47	3656.53	3597.25	3550.61
200000	4347.85	4167.66	4032.29	3928.92	3848.98	3786.58	3737.49
210000	4565.24	4376.05	4233.91	4125.36	4041.43	3975.91	3924.36
220000	4782.64	4584.43	4435.52	4321.81	4233.88	4165.23	4111.24
230000	5000.03	4792.81	4637.14	4518.26	4426.33	4354.56	4298.11
240000	5217.42	5001.20	4838.75	4714.70	4618.78	4543.89	4484.99
250000	5434.82	5209.58	5040.37	4911.15	4811.23	4733.22	4671.86
260000	5652.21	5417.96	5241.98	5107.59	5003.68	4922.55	4858.73
270000	5869.60	5626.35	5443.60	5304.04	5196.13	5111.88	5045.61
280000	6086.99	5834.73	5645.21	5500.49	5388.58	5301.20	5232.48
290000	6304.39	6043.11	5846.83	5696.93	5581.03	5490.54	5419.36
300000	6521.78	6251.50	6048.44	5893.38	5773.48	5679.87	5606.23
310000	6739.17	6459.88	6250.06	6089.82	5965.92	5869.19	5793.11
320000	6956.56	6668.26	6451.67	6286.27	6158.37	6058.52	5979.98
330000	7173.96	6876.65	6653.29	6482.72	6350.82	6247.85	6166.86
340000	7391.35	7085.03	6854.90	6679.16	6543.27	6437.18	6353.73
350000	7608.74	7293.41	7056.52	6875.61	6735.72	6626.51	6540.60
400000	8695.70	8335.33	8064.59	7857.84	7697.97	7573.15	7474.98
450000	9782.67	9377.25	9072.66	8840.07	8660.21	8519.80	8409.35
500000	10869.63	10419.16	10080.74	9822.30	9622.46	9466.44	9343.72
550000	11956.59	11461.08	11088.81	10804.53	10584.70	10413.09	10278.09
600000	13043.56	12502.99	12096.88	11786.76	11546.95	11359.73	11212.46

21¼%

Monthly Payments
necessary to amortize a loan

AMOUNT	15 YEARS	16 YEARS	17 YEARS	18 YEARS	19 YEARS	20 YEARS	21 YEARS
100	1.85	1.83	1.82	1.81	1.80	1.80	1.79
200	3.70	3.67	3.64	3.62	3.61	3.59	3.58
500	9.25	9.17	9.11	9.06	9.02	8.99	8.96
1000	18.49	18.34	18.22	18.12	18.04	17.97	17.92
2000	36.99	36.68	36.43	36.23	36.08	35.95	35.85
5000	92.47	91.69	91.08	90.59	90.19	89.87	89.62
6000	110.96	110.03	109.29	108.70	108.23	107.85	107.54
7000	129.45	128.37	127.51	126.82	126.27	125.82	125.46
8000	147.95	146.71	145.73	144.94	144.30	143.80	143.39
9000	166.44	165.05	163.94	163.05	162.34	161.77	161.31
10000	184.93	183.39	182.16	181.17	180.38	179.74	179.23
15000	277.40	275.08	273.23	271.76	270.57	269.62	268.85
20000	369.86	366.78	364.31	362.34	360.76	359.49	358.47
25000	462.33	458.47	455.39	452.93	450.95	449.36	448.08
30000	554.80	550.17	546.47	543.51	541.14	539.23	537.70
35000	647.26	641.86	637.55	634.10	631.33	629.11	627.31
40000	739.73	733.55	728.63	724.68	721.52	718.98	716.93
45000	832.20	825.25	819.70	815.27	811.71	808.85	806.55
50000	924.66	916.94	910.78	905.85	901.90	898.72	896.16
55000	1017.13	1008.64	1001.86	996.44	992.09	988.59	985.78
60000	1109.59	1100.33	1092.94	1087.02	1082.28	1078.47	1075.40
65000	1202.06	1192.02	1184.02	1177.61	1172.47	1168.34	1165.01
70000	1294.53	1283.72	1275.10	1268.20	1262.66	1258.21	1254.63
75000	1386.99	1375.41	1366.17	1358.78	1352.85	1348.08	1344.25
80000	1479.46	1467.11	1457.25	1449.37	1443.04	1437.96	1433.86
85000	1571.92	1558.80	1548.33	1539.95	1533.23	1527.83	1523.48
90000	1664.39	1650.50	1639.41	1630.54	1623.42	1617.70	1613.10
95000	1756.86	1742.19	1730.49	1721.12	1713.61	1707.57	1702.71
100000	1849.32	1833.88	1821.57	1811.71	1803.80	1797.44	1792.33
105000	1941.79	1925.58	1912.64	1902.29	1893.99	1887.32	1881.94
110000	2034.26	2017.27	2003.72	1992.88	1984.18	1977.19	1971.56
120000	2219.19	2200.66	2185.88	2174.05	2164.56	2156.93	2150.79
130000	2404.12	2384.05	2368.04	2355.22	2344.94	2336.68	2330.03
140000	2589.05	2567.44	2550.19	2536.39	2525.32	2516.42	2509.26
150000	2773.98	2750.83	2732.35	2717.56	2705.70	2696.17	2688.49
160000	2958.92	2934.23	2914.51	2898.73	2886.08	2875.91	2867.73
170000	3143.85	3117.60	3096.66	3079.90	3066.46	3055.65	3046.96
180000	3328.78	3300.99	3278.82	3261.07	3246.84	3235.40	3226.19
190000	3513.71	3484.38	3460.97	3442.24	3427.23	3415.14	3405.42
200000	3698.65	3667.77	3643.13	3623.41	3607.60	3594.89	3584.66
210000	3883.58	3851.16	3825.29	3804.59	3787.98	3774.63	3763.89
220000	4068.51	4034.55	4007.44	3985.76	3968.36	3954.38	3943.12
230000	4253.44	4217.93	4189.60	4166.93	4148.74	4134.12	4122.36
240000	4438.38	4401.32	4371.76	4348.10	4329.12	4313.87	4301.59
250000	4623.31	4584.71	4553.91	4529.27	4509.50	4493.61	4480.82
260000	4808.24	4768.10	4736.07	4710.44	4689.88	4673.35	4660.05
270000	4993.17	4951.49	4918.23	4891.61	4870.26	4853.10	4839.29
280000	5178.10	5134.88	5100.38	5072.78	5050.64	5032.84	5018.52
290000	5363.04	5318.26	5282.54	5253.95	5231.02	5212.59	5197.75
300000	5547.97	5501.65	5464.70	5435.12	5411.40	5392.33	5376.99
310000	5732.90	5685.04	5646.85	5616.29	5591.78	5572.08	5556.22
320000	5917.83	5868.43	5829.01	5797.46	5772.16	5751.82	5735.45
330000	6102.77	6051.82	6011.17	5978.63	5952.54	5931.57	5914.68
340000	6287.70	6235.21	6193.32	6159.81	6132.92	6111.31	6093.92
350000	6472.63	6418.60	6375.48	6340.98	6313.30	6291.05	6273.15
400000	7397.29	7335.54	7286.26	7246.83	7215.20	7189.78	7169.31
450000	8321.95	8252.48	8197.05	8152.68	8117.10	8088.50	8065.48
500000	9246.62	9169.42	9107.83	9058.54	9019.00	8987.22	8961.64
550000	10171.28	10086.36	10018.61	9964.39	9920.90	9885.94	9857.81
600000	11095.94	11003.31	10929.39	10870.24	10822.80	10784.66	10753.97

AMOUNT	22 YEARS	23 YEARS	24 YEARS	25 YEARS	30 YEARS	35 YEARS	40 YEARS
100	1.79	1.78	1.78	1.78	1.77	1.77	1.77
200	3.58	3.57	3.56	3.56	3.55	3.54	3.54
500	8.94	8.92	8.91	8.90	8.87	8.86	8.86
1000	17.88	17.85	17.82	17.80	17.74	17.72	17.71
2000	35.76	35.70	35.64	35.60	35.48	35.44	35.42
5000	89.41	89.24	89.11	89.00	88.70	88.60	88.56
6000	107.29	107.09	106.93	106.80	106.44	106.32	106.27
7000	125.17	124.94	124.75	124.60	124.18	124.04	123.99
8000	143.06	142.79	142.58	142.40	141.92	141.76	141.70
9000	160.94	160.64	160.40	160.20	159.66	159.48	159.41
10000	178.82	178.49	178.22	178.00	177.40	177.19	177.12
15000	268.23	267.73	267.33	267.00	266.10	265.79	265.68
20000	357.64	356.98	356.44	356.01	354.81	354.39	354.24
25000	447.05	446.22	445.55	445.01	443.51	442.99	442.81
30000	536.46	535.46	534.66	534.01	532.21	531.58	531.37
35000	625.87	624.71	623.77	623.01	620.91	620.18	619.93
40000	715.28	713.95	712.88	712.01	709.61	708.78	708.49
45000	804.69	803.20	801.99	801.01	798.31	797.38	797.05
50000	894.10	892.44	891.10	890.01	887.01	885.97	885.61
55000	983.51	981.68	980.21	979.01	975.72	974.57	974.17
60000	1072.92	1070.93	1069.32	1068.02	1064.42	1063.17	1062.73
65000	1162.33	1160.17	1158.43	1157.02	1153.12	1151.77	1151.29
70000	1251.74	1249.42	1247.54	1246.02	1241.82	1240.36	1239.86
75000	1341.15	1338.66	1336.65	1335.02	1330.52	1328.96	1328.42
80000	1430.56	1427.90	1425.76	1424.02	1419.22	1417.56	1416.98
85000	1519.97	1517.15	1514.87	1513.02	1507.92	1506.15	1505.54
90000	1609.39	1606.39	1603.98	1602.02	1596.63	1594.75	1594.10
95000	1698.80	1695.64	1693.09	1691.02	1685.33	1683.35	1682.66
100000	1788.21	1784.88	1782.19	1780.03	1774.03	1771.95	1771.22
105000	1877.62	1874.12	1871.30	1869.03	1862.73	1860.54	1859.78
110000	1967.03	1963.37	1960.41	1958.03	1951.43	1949.14	1948.34
120000	2145.85	2141.86	2138.63	2136.03	2128.83	2126.34	2125.47
130000	2324.67	2320.34	2316.85	2314.03	2306.24	2303.53	2302.59
140000	2503.49	2498.83	2495.07	2492.04	2483.64	2480.73	2479.71
150000	2682.31	2677.32	2673.29	2670.04	2661.04	2657.92	2656.83
160000	2861.13	2855.81	2851.51	2848.04	2838.45	2835.11	2833.95
170000	3039.95	3034.30	3029.73	3026.04	3015.85	3012.31	3011.08
180000	3218.77	3212.78	3207.95	3204.05	3193.25	3189.50	3188.20
190000	3397.59	3391.27	3386.17	3382.05	3370.66	3366.70	3365.32
200000	3576.41	3569.76	3564.39	3560.05	3548.06	3543.89	3542.44
210000	3755.23	3748.25	3742.61	3738.05	3725.46	3721.09	3719.57
220000	3934.05	3926.74	3920.83	3916.06	3902.86	3898.28	3896.69
230000	4112.87	4105.22	4099.05	4094.06	4080.27	4075.48	4073.81
240000	4291.69	4283.71	4277.27	4272.06	4257.67	4252.67	4250.93
250000	4470.51	4462.20	4455.49	4450.06	4435.07	4429.87	4428.05
260000	4649.34	4640.69	4633.71	4628.07	4612.48	4607.06	4605.18
270000	4828.16	4819.18	4811.93	4806.07	4789.88	4784.26	4782.30
280000	5006.98	4997.66	4990.15	4984.07	4967.28	4961.45	4959.42
290000	5185.80	5176.15	5168.37	5162.07	5144.68	5138.65	5136.54
300000	5364.62	5354.64	5346.58	5340.08	5322.09	5315.84	5313.66
310000	5543.44	5533.13	5524.80	5518.08	5499.49	5493.03	5490.79
320000	5722.26	5711.62	5703.02	5696.08	5676.89	5670.23	5667.91
330000	5901.08	5890.10	5881.24	5874.08	5854.30	5847.42	5845.03
340000	6079.90	6068.59	6059.46	6052.09	6031.70	6024.62	6022.15
350000	6258.72	6247.08	6237.68	6230.09	6209.10	6201.81	6199.28
400000	7152.82	7139.52	7128.78	7120.10	7096.12	7087.79	7084.89
450000	8046.93	8031.96	8019.88	8010.12	7983.13	7973.76	7970.50
500000	8941.03	8924.40	8910.97	8900.13	8870.15	8859.73	8856.11
550000	9835.13	9816.84	9802.07	9790.14	9757.16	9745.71	9741.72
600000	10729.23	10709.28	10693.17	10680.15	10644.17	10631.68	10627.33

21½%

Monthly Payments
necessary to amortize a loan

AMOUNT	1 YEAR	2 YEARS	3 YEARS	4 YEARS	5 YEARS	6 YEARS	7 YEARS
100	9.34	5.16	3.79	3.12	2.73	2.48	2.31
200	18.67	10.33	7.59	6.25	5.47	4.97	4.62
500	46.68	25.82	18.97	15.62	13.67	12.42	11.56
1000	93.35	51.63	37.93	31.24	27.34	24.83	23.12
2000	186.71	103.26	75.86	62.47	54.67	49.66	46.24
5000	466.77	258.16	189.66	156.18	136.68	124.15	115.59
6000	560.12	309.79	227.59	187.41	164.01	148.98	138.71
7000	653.48	361.42	265.53	218.65	191.35	173.81	161.83
8000	746.83	413.05	303.46	249.88	218.68	198.64	184.95
9000	840.19	464.68	341.39	281.12	246.02	223.47	208.06
10000	933.54	516.32	379.32	312.35	273.35	248.30	231.18
15000	1400.31	774.47	568.98	468.53	410.03	372.45	346.77
20000	1867.08	1032.63	758.65	624.71	546.71	496.60	462.36
25000	2333.85	1290.79	948.31	780.88	683.38	620.75	577.95
30000	2800.62	1548.95	1137.97	937.06	820.06	744.91	693.54
35000	3267.39	1807.10	1327.63	1093.23	956.74	869.06	809.13
40000	3734.16	2065.26	1517.29	1249.41	1093.42	993.21	924.73
45000	4200.93	2323.42	1706.95	1405.59	1230.09	1117.36	1040.32
50000	4667.70	2581.58	1896.61	1561.76	1366.77	1241.51	1155.91
55000	5134.47	2839.74	2086.28	1717.94	1503.45	1365.66	1271.50
60000	5601.23	3097.89	2275.94	1874.12	1640.12	1489.81	1387.09
65000	6068.01	3356.05	2465.60	2030.29	1776.80	1613.96	1502.68
70000	6534.77	3614.21	2655.26	2186.47	1913.48	1738.11	1618.27
75000	7001.54	3872.37	2844.92	2342.64	2050.15	1862.26	1733.86
80000	7468.31	4130.53	3034.58	2498.82	2186.83	1986.42	1849.45
85000	7935.08	4388.68	3224.24	2655.00	2323.51	2110.57	1965.04
90000	8401.85	4646.84	3413.90	2811.17	2460.18	2234.72	2080.63
95000	8868.62	4905.00	3603.57	2967.35	2596.86	2358.87	2196.22
100000	9335.39	5163.16	3793.23	3123.53	2733.54	2483.02	2311.81
105000	9802.16	5421.31	3982.89	3279.70	2870.21	2607.17	2427.40
110000	10268.93	5679.47	4172.55	3435.88	3006.89	2731.32	2542.99
120000	11202.47	6195.79	4551.87	3748.23	3280.25	2979.62	2774.18
130000	12136.01	6712.10	4931.20	4060.58	3553.60	3227.93	3005.36
140000	13069.55	7228.42	5310.52	4372.94	3826.95	3476.23	3236.54
150000	14003.09	7744.74	5689.84	4685.29	4100.31	3724.53	3467.72
160000	14936.63	8261.05	6069.16	4997.64	4373.66	3972.83	3698.90
170000	15870.16	8777.37	6448.49	5309.99	4647.01	4221.13	3930.08
180000	16803.70	9293.68	6827.81	5622.35	4920.37	4469.44	4161.26
190000	17737.24	9810.00	7207.13	5934.70	5193.72	4717.74	4392.45
200000	18670.78	10326.31	7586.45	6247.05	5467.08	4966.04	4623.63
210000	19604.32	10842.63	7965.78	6559.40	5740.43	5214.34	4854.81
220000	20537.86	11358.95	8345.10	6871.76	6013.78	5462.64	5085.99
230000	21471.40	11875.26	8724.42	7184.11	6287.14	5710.95	5317.17
240000	22404.94	12391.58	9103.75	7496.46	6560.49	5959.25	5548.35
250000	23338.48	12907.89	9483.07	7808.81	6833.85	6207.55	5779.53
260000	24272.02	13424.21	9862.39	8121.17	7107.20	6455.85	6010.71
270000	25205.56	13940.52	10241.71	8433.52	7380.55	6704.15	6241.90
280000	26139.09	14456.84	10621.04	8745.87	7653.91	6952.46	6473.08
290000	27072.63	14973.16	11000.36	9058.22	7927.26	7200.76	6704.26
300000	28006.17	15489.47	11379.68	9370.58	8200.61	7449.06	6935.44
310000	28939.71	16005.79	11759.00	9682.93	8473.97	7697.36	7166.62
320000	29873.25	16522.10	12138.33	9995.28	8747.32	7945.66	7397.80
330000	30806.79	17038.42	12517.65	10307.63	9020.68	8193.97	7628.98
340000	31740.33	17554.73	12896.97	10619.99	9294.03	8442.27	7860.17
350000	32673.87	18071.05	13276.30	10932.34	9567.38	8690.57	8091.35
400000	37341.56	20652.63	15172.91	12494.10	10934.15	9932.08	9247.25
450000	42009.26	23234.21	17069.52	14055.87	12300.92	11173.59	10403.16
500000	46676.95	25815.79	18966.14	15617.63	13667.69	12415.10	11559.07
550000	51344.65	28397.36	20862.75	17179.39	15034.46	13656.61	12714.97
600000	56012.35	30978.94	22759.36	18741.15	16401.23	14898.12	13870.88

Monthly Payments 21½%
necessary to amortize a loan

AMOUNT	8 YEARS	9 YEARS	10 YEARS	11 YEARS	12 YEARS	13 YEARS	14 YEARS
100	2.19	2.10	2.03	1.98	1.94	1.91	1.89
200	4.38	4.20	4.07	3.96	3.88	3.82	3.77
500	10.95	10.50	10.17	9.91	9.71	9.56	9.44
1000	21.90	21.00	20.33	19.82	19.42	19.11	18.87
2000	43.80	42.00	40.66	39.64	38.84	38.23	37.74
5000	109.49	105.01	101.65	99.09	97.11	95.57	94.36
6000	131.39	126.01	121.98	118.91	116.53	114.68	113.23
7000	153.29	147.02	142.31	138.73	135.96	133.80	132.10
8000	175.18	168.02	162.64	158.54	155.38	152.91	150.98
9000	197.08	189.02	182.97	178.36	174.80	172.03	169.85
10000	218.98	210.02	203.30	198.18	194.22	191.14	188.72
15000	328.47	315.03	304.96	297.27	291.34	286.71	283.08
20000	437.96	420.05	406.61	396.36	388.45	382.28	377.44
25000	547.45	525.06	508.26	495.45	485.56	477.85	471.80
30000	656.94	630.07	609.91	594.54	582.67	573.42	566.16
35000	766.43	735.08	711.56	693.63	679.78	668.99	660.52
40000	875.92	840.09	813.21	792.72	776.90	764.56	754.88
45000	985.41	945.10	914.87	891.81	874.01	860.13	849.24
50000	1094.90	1050.12	1016.52	990.90	971.12	955.70	943.60
55000	1204.39	1155.13	1118.17	1089.99	1068.23	1051.27	1037.96
60000	1313.88	1260.14	1219.82	1189.08	1165.34	1146.85	1132.32
65000	1423.37	1365.15	1321.47	1288.17	1262.45	1242.42	1226.68
70000	1532.86	1470.16	1423.12	1387.26	1359.57	1337.99	1321.04
75000	1642.35	1575.17	1524.78	1486.35	1456.68	1433.56	1415.40
80000	1751.84	1680.19	1626.43	1585.44	1553.79	1529.13	1509.76
85000	1861.33	1785.20	1728.08	1684.52	1650.90	1624.70	1604.12
90000	1970.82	1890.21	1829.73	1783.61	1748.01	1720.27	1698.48
95000	2080.31	1995.22	1931.38	1882.70	1845.13	1815.84	1792.84
100000	2189.80	2100.23	2033.03	1981.79	1942.24	1911.41	1887.20
105000	2299.29	2205.24	2134.69	2080.88	2039.35	2006.98	1981.56
110000	2408.78	2310.26	2236.34	2179.97	2136.46	2102.55	2075.92
120000	2627.76	2520.28	2439.64	2378.15	2330.69	2293.69	2264.64
130000	2846.74	2730.30	2642.94	2576.33	2524.91	2484.83	2453.36
140000	3065.72	2940.32	2846.25	2774.51	2719.13	2675.97	2642.08
150000	3284.70	3150.35	3049.55	2972.69	2913.36	2867.11	2830.80
160000	3503.68	3360.37	3252.85	3170.87	3107.58	3058.25	3019.52
170000	3722.66	3570.39	3456.16	3369.05	3301.80	3249.39	3208.24
180000	3941.64	3780.42	3659.46	3567.23	3496.03	3440.54	3396.96
190000	4160.62	3990.44	3862.76	3765.41	3690.25	3631.68	3585.68
200000	4379.61	4200.46	4066.07	3963.59	3884.48	3822.82	3774.40
210000	4598.59	4410.49	4269.37	4161.77	4078.70	4013.96	3963.12
220000	4817.57	4620.51	4472.67	4359.95	4272.92	4205.10	4151.84
230000	5036.55	4830.53	4675.98	4558.13	4467.15	4396.24	4340.56
240000	5255.53	5040.56	4879.28	4756.31	4661.37	4587.38	4529.29
250000	5474.51	5250.58	5082.58	4954.49	4855.59	4778.52	4718.01
260000	5693.49	5460.60	5285.89	5152.66	5049.82	4969.66	4906.73
270000	5912.47	5670.63	5489.19	5350.84	5244.04	5160.80	5095.45
280000	6131.45	5880.65	5692.49	5549.02	5438.27	5351.94	5284.17
290000	6350.43	6090.67	5895.80	5747.20	5632.49	5543.09	5472.89
300000	6569.41	6300.70	6099.10	5945.38	5826.71	5734.23	5661.61
310000	6788.39	6510.72	6302.40	6143.56	6020.94	5925.37	5850.33
320000	7007.37	6720.74	6505.71	6341.74	6215.16	6116.51	6039.05
330000	7226.35	6930.77	6709.01	6539.92	6409.39	6307.65	6227.77
340000	7445.33	7140.79	6912.31	6738.10	6603.61	6498.79	6416.49
350000	7664.31	7350.81	7115.62	6936.28	6797.83	6689.93	6605.21
400000	8759.21	8400.93	8132.13	7927.18	7768.95	7645.63	7548.81
450000	9854.11	9451.04	9148.65	8918.07	8740.07	8601.34	8492.41
500000	10949.01	10501.16	10165.17	9908.97	9711.19	9557.04	9436.01
550000	12043.91	11551.28	11181.68	10899.87	10682.31	10512.75	10379.61
600000	13138.82	12601.39	12198.20	11890.76	11653.43	11468.45	11323.21

21½%

Monthly Payments
necessary to amortize a loan

AMOUNT	15 YEARS	16 YEARS	17 YEARS	18 YEARS	19 YEARS	20 YEARS	21 YEARS
100	1.87	1.85	1.84	1.83	1.82	1.82	1.81
200	3.74	3.71	3.68	3.66	3.65	3.63	3.62
500	9.34	9.26	9.20	9.16	9.12	9.09	9.06
1000	18.68	18.53	18.41	18.31	18.23	18.17	18.12
2000	37.36	37.06	36.82	36.62	36.47	36.35	36.25
5000	93.40	92.65	92.04	91.56	91.17	90.86	90.62
6000	112.09	111.18	110.45	109.87	109.41	109.04	108.74
7000	130.77	129.70	128.86	128.18	127.64	127.21	126.86
8000	149.45	148.23	147.27	146.50	145.88	145.38	144.98
9000	168.13	166.76	165.68	164.81	164.11	163.56	163.11
10000	186.81	185.29	184.08	183.12	182.35	181.73	181.23
15000	280.21	277.94	276.13	274.68	273.52	272.59	271.85
20000	373.62	370.58	368.17	366.24	364.69	363.46	362.46
25000	467.02	463.23	460.21	457.80	455.87	454.32	453.08
30000	560.43	555.88	552.25	549.36	547.04	545.18	543.69
35000	653.83	648.52	644.29	640.92	638.22	636.05	634.31
40000	747.23	741.17	736.34	732.48	729.39	726.91	724.92
45000	840.64	833.81	828.38	824.04	820.56	817.78	815.54
50000	934.04	926.46	920.42	915.60	911.74	908.64	906.15
55000	1027.45	1019.10	1012.46	1007.16	1002.91	999.50	996.77
60000	1120.85	1111.75	1104.50	1098.72	1094.08	1090.37	1087.39
65000	1214.26	1204.40	1196.55	1190.28	1185.26	1181.23	1178.00
70000	1307.66	1297.04	1288.59	1281.84	1276.43	1272.10	1268.62
75000	1401.06	1389.69	1380.63	1373.40	1367.60	1362.96	1359.23
80000	1494.47	1482.33	1472.67	1464.95	1458.78	1453.83	1449.85
85000	1587.87	1574.98	1564.71	1556.51	1549.95	1544.69	1540.46
90000	1681.28	1667.63	1656.76	1648.07	1641.13	1635.55	1631.08
95000	1774.68	1760.27	1748.80	1739.63	1732.30	1726.42	1721.69
100000	1868.08	1852.92	1840.84	1831.19	1823.47	1817.28	1812.31
105000	1961.49	1945.56	1932.88	1922.75	1914.65	1908.15	1902.92
110000	2054.89	2038.21	2024.92	2014.31	2005.82	1999.01	1993.54
120000	2241.70	2223.50	2209.01	2197.43	2188.17	2180.74	2174.77
130000	2428.51	2408.79	2393.09	2380.55	2370.51	2362.47	2356.00
140000	2615.32	2594.08	2577.17	2563.67	2552.86	2544.19	2537.23
150000	2802.13	2779.38	2761.26	2746.79	2735.21	2725.92	2718.46
160000	2988.94	2964.67	2945.34	2929.91	2917.56	2907.65	2899.69
170000	3175.74	3149.96	3129.43	3113.03	3099.90	3089.38	3080.92
180000	3362.55	3335.25	3313.51	3296.15	3282.25	3271.11	3262.16
190000	3549.36	3520.54	3497.59	3479.27	3464.60	3452.83	3443.39
200000	3736.17	3705.83	3681.68	3662.39	3646.95	3634.56	3624.62
210000	3922.98	3891.13	3865.76	3845.51	3829.29	3816.29	3805.85
220000	4109.79	4076.42	4049.85	4028.63	4011.64	3998.02	3987.08
230000	4296.59	4261.71	4233.93	4211.75	4193.99	4179.75	4168.31
240000	4483.40	4447.00	4418.01	4394.86	4376.33	4361.48	4349.54
250000	4670.21	4632.29	4602.10	4577.98	4558.68	4543.20	4530.77
260000	4857.02	4817.58	4786.18	4761.10	4741.03	4724.93	4712.00
270000	5043.83	5002.88	4970.27	4944.22	4923.38	4906.66	4893.23
280000	5230.64	5188.17	5154.35	5127.34	5105.72	5088.39	5074.46
290000	5417.45	5373.46	5338.43	5310.46	5288.07	5270.12	5255.70
300000	5604.25	5558.75	5522.52	5493.58	5470.42	5451.84	5436.93
310000	5791.06	5744.04	5706.60	5676.70	5652.77	5633.57	5618.16
320000	5977.87	5929.33	5890.69	5859.82	5835.11	5815.30	5799.39
330000	6164.68	6114.63	6074.77	6042.94	6017.46	5997.03	5980.62
340000	6351.49	6299.92	6258.85	6226.06	6199.81	6178.76	6161.85
350000	6538.30	6485.21	6442.94	6409.18	6382.16	6360.48	6343.08
400000	7472.34	7411.67	7363.36	7324.77	7293.89	7269.13	7249.23
450000	8406.38	8338.13	8283.78	8240.37	8205.63	8177.77	8155.39
500000	9340.42	9264.59	9204.20	9155.97	9117.36	9086.41	9061.54
550000	10274.47	10191.04	10124.62	10071.57	10029.10	9995.05	9967.70
600000	11208.51	11117.50	11045.03	10987.16	10940.84	10903.69	10873.85

Monthly Payments 21½%
necessary to amortize a loan

AMOUNT	22 YEARS	23 YEARS	24 YEARS	25 YEARS	30 YEARS	35 YEARS	40 YEARS
100	1.81	1.81	1.80	1.80	1.79	1.79	1.79
200	3.62	3.61	3.60	3.60	3.59	3.59	3.58
500	9.04	9.03	9.01	9.00	8.97	8.96	8.96
1000	18.08	18.05	18.02	18.00	17.95	17.93	17.92
2000	36.17	36.10	36.05	36.01	35.89	35.85	35.84
5000	90.42	90.25	90.12	90.02	89.73	89.64	89.60
6000	108.50	108.31	108.15	108.02	107.68	107.56	107.52
7000	126.58	126.36	126.17	126.03	125.63	125.49	125.44
8000	144.66	144.41	144.20	144.03	143.57	143.42	143.36
9000	162.75	162.46	162.22	162.04	161.52	161.34	161.28
10000	180.83	180.51	180.25	180.04	179.47	179.27	179.20
15000	271.25	270.76	270.37	270.06	269.20	268.91	268.80
20000	361.66	361.02	360.50	360.08	358.93	358.54	358.40
25000	452.08	451.27	450.62	450.10	448.67	448.18	448.01
30000	542.49	541.53	540.75	540.12	538.40	537.81	537.61
35000	632.91	631.78	630.87	630.14	628.13	627.45	627.21
40000	723.32	722.04	721.00	720.16	717.87	717.08	716.81
45000	813.74	812.29	811.12	810.18	807.60	806.72	806.41
50000	904.16	902.55	901.25	900.21	897.33	896.35	896.01
55000	994.57	992.80	991.37	990.23	987.07	985.99	985.61
60000	1084.99	1083.06	1081.50	1080.25	1076.80	1075.62	1075.21
65000	1175.40	1173.31	1171.62	1170.27	1166.54	1165.26	1164.81
70000	1265.82	1263.56	1261.75	1260.29	1256.27	1254.89	1254.42
75000	1356.23	1353.82	1351.87	1350.31	1346.00	1344.53	1344.02
80000	1446.65	1444.07	1442.00	1440.33	1435.74	1434.16	1433.62
85000	1537.06	1534.33	1532.12	1530.35	1525.47	1523.80	1523.22
90000	1627.48	1624.58	1622.25	1620.37	1615.20	1613.43	1612.82
95000	1717.89	1714.84	1712.37	1710.39	1704.94	1703.07	1702.42
100000	1808.31	1805.09	1802.50	1800.41	1794.67	1792.70	1792.02
105000	1898.73	1895.35	1892.62	1890.43	1884.40	1882.34	1881.62
110000	1989.14	1985.60	1982.75	1980.45	1974.14	1971.97	1971.22
120000	2169.97	2166.11	2163.00	2160.49	2153.60	2151.24	2150.43
130000	2350.80	2346.62	2343.25	2340.53	2333.07	2330.51	2329.63
140000	2531.63	2527.13	2523.50	2520.57	2512.54	2509.78	2508.83
150000	2712.47	2707.64	2703.75	2700.62	2692.00	2689.05	2688.03
160000	2893.30	2888.15	2884.00	2880.66	2871.47	2868.32	2867.24
170000	3074.13	3068.66	3064.25	3060.70	3050.94	3047.59	3046.44
180000	3254.96	3249.17	3244.50	3240.74	3230.41	3226.86	3225.64
190000	3435.79	3429.67	3424.75	3420.78	3409.87	3406.13	3404.84
200000	3616.62	3610.18	3605.00	3600.82	3589.34	3585.40	3584.05
210000	3797.45	3790.69	3785.25	3780.86	3768.81	3764.67	3763.25
220000	3978.28	3971.20	3965.50	3960.90	3948.27	3943.94	3942.45
230000	4159.11	4151.71	4145.75	4140.94	4127.74	4123.21	4121.65
240000	4339.94	4332.22	4326.00	4320.99	4307.21	4302.48	4300.85
250000	4520.78	4512.73	4506.25	4501.03	4486.67	4481.75	4480.06
260000	4701.61	4693.24	4686.50	4681.07	4666.14	4661.02	4659.26
270000	4882.44	4873.75	4866.75	4861.11	4845.61	4840.29	4838.46
280000	5063.27	5054.26	5047.00	5041.15	5025.08	5019.56	5017.66
290000	5244.10	5234.77	5227.25	5221.19	5204.54	5198.83	5196.87
300000	5424.93	5415.28	5407.50	5401.23	5384.01	5378.10	5376.07
310000	5605.76	5595.79	5587.75	5581.27	5563.48	5557.37	5555.27
320000	5786.59	5776.29	5768.00	5761.31	5742.94	5736.64	5734.47
330000	5967.42	5956.80	5948.25	5941.35	5922.41	5915.91	5913.67
340000	6148.25	6137.31	6128.50	6121.40	6101.88	6095.18	6092.88
350000	6329.09	6317.82	6308.75	6301.44	6281.34	6274.45	6272.08
400000	7233.24	7220.37	7210.00	7201.64	7178.68	7170.80	7168.09
450000	8137.40	8122.91	8111.25	8101.85	8076.01	8067.15	8064.10
500000	9041.55	9025.46	9012.50	9002.05	8973.35	8963.50	8960.11
550000	9945.71	9928.01	9913.75	9902.26	9870.68	9859.85	9856.12
600000	10849.86	10830.55	10815.00	10802.46	10768.02	10756.20	10752.14

Monthly Payments
necessary to amortize a loan

AMOUNT	1 YEAR	2 YEARS	3 YEARS	4 YEARS	5 YEARS	6 YEARS	7 YEARS
100	9.35	5.18	3.81	3.14	2.75	2.50	2.33
200	18.69	10.35	7.61	6.27	5.50	5.00	4.65
500	46.74	25.88	19.03	15.69	13.74	12.49	11.64
1000	93.47	51.75	38.06	31.37	27.48	24.98	23.27
2000	186.95	103.51	76.12	62.74	54.95	49.96	46.54
5000	467.37	258.77	190.31	156.85	137.38	124.89	116.36
6000	560.84	310.53	228.37	188.22	164.86	149.87	139.63
7000	654.32	362.28	266.43	219.59	192.34	174.85	162.90
8000	747.79	414.04	304.49	250.96	219.82	199.82	186.17
9000	841.27	465.79	342.55	282.33	247.29	224.80	209.45
10000	934.74	517.55	380.61	313.71	274.77	249.78	232.72
15000	1402.11	776.32	570.92	470.56	412.15	374.67	349.08
20000	1869.48	1035.10	761.22	627.41	549.54	499.56	465.44
25000	2336.85	1293.87	951.53	784.26	686.92	624.45	581.80
30000	2804.22	1552.64	1141.84	941.12	824.31	749.34	698.15
35000	3271.59	1811.42	1332.14	1097.97	961.69	874.23	814.51
40000	3738.96	2070.19	1522.45	1254.82	1099.08	999.12	930.87
45000	4206.33	2328.97	1712.76	1411.67	1236.46	1124.01	1047.23
50000	4673.71	2587.74	1903.06	1568.53	1373.85	1248.90	1163.59
55000	5141.08	2846.51	2093.37	1725.38	1511.23	1373.79	1279.95
60000	5608.45	3105.29	2283.67	1882.23	1648.62	1498.68	1396.31
65000	6075.82	3364.06	2473.98	2039.08	1786.00	1623.57	1512.67
70000	6543.19	3622.83	2664.29	2195.94	1923.39	1748.46	1629.03
75000	7010.56	3881.61	2854.59	2352.79	2060.77	1873.35	1745.39
80000	7477.93	4140.38	3044.90	2509.64	2198.16	1998.24	1861.74
85000	7945.30	4399.16	3235.21	2666.49	2335.54	2123.13	1978.10
90000	8412.67	4657.93	3425.51	2823.35	2472.93	2248.02	2094.46
95000	8880.04	4916.70	3615.82	2980.20	2610.31	2372.91	2210.82
100000	9347.41	5175.48	3806.12	3137.05	2747.70	2497.79	2327.18
105000	9814.78	5434.25	3996.43	3293.90	2885.08	2622.68	2443.54
110000	10282.15	5693.03	4186.74	3450.76	3022.47	2747.57	2559.90
120000	11216.89	6210.57	4567.35	3764.46	3297.23	2997.35	2792.62
130000	12151.63	6728.12	4947.96	4078.17	3572.00	3247.13	3025.33
140000	13086.37	7245.67	5328.57	4391.87	3846.77	3496.91	3258.05
150000	14021.12	7763.22	5709.19	4705.58	4121.54	3746.69	3490.77
160000	14955.86	8280.76	6089.80	5019.28	4396.31	3996.47	3723.49
170000	15890.60	8798.31	6470.41	5332.99	4671.08	4246.25	3956.21
180000	16825.34	9315.86	6851.02	5646.69	4945.85	4496.03	4188.92
190000	17760.08	9833.41	7231.64	5960.40	5220.62	4745.81	4421.64
200000	18694.82	10350.96	7612.25	6274.10	5495.39	4995.59	4654.36
210000	19629.56	10868.50	7992.86	6587.81	5770.16	5245.37	4887.08
220000	20564.30	11386.05	8373.47	6901.51	6044.93	5495.15	5119.80
230000	21499.04	11903.60	8754.09	7215.22	6319.70	5744.93	5352.51
240000	22433.78	12421.15	9134.70	7528.92	6594.47	5994.71	5585.23
250000	23368.53	12938.70	9515.31	7842.63	6869.24	6244.49	5817.95
260000	24303.27	13456.24	9895.92	8156.33	7144.01	6494.27	6050.67
270000	25238.01	13973.79	10276.54	8470.04	7418.78	6744.05	6283.39
280000	26172.75	14491.34	10657.15	8783.74	7693.55	6993.83	6516.10
290000	27107.49	15008.89	11037.76	9097.45	7968.32	7243.60	6748.82
300000	28042.23	15526.43	11418.37	9411.15	8243.09	7493.38	6981.54
310000	28976.97	16043.98	11798.99	9724.86	8517.86	7743.16	7214.26
320000	29911.71	16561.53	12179.60	10038.56	8792.63	7992.94	7446.98
330000	30846.45	17079.08	12560.21	10352.27	9067.40	8242.72	7679.69
340000	31781.19	17596.63	12940.82	10665.97	9342.17	8492.50	7912.41
350000	32715.94	18114.17	13321.43	10979.68	9616.94	8742.28	8145.13
400000	37389.64	20701.91	15224.50	12548.20	10990.78	9991.18	9308.72
450000	42063.35	23289.65	17127.56	14116.73	12364.63	11240.08	10472.31
500000	46737.05	25877.39	19030.62	15685.26	13738.48	12488.97	11635.90
550000	51410.76	28465.13	20933.68	17253.78	15112.33	13737.87	12799.49
600000	56084.46	31052.87	22836.75	18822.31	16486.17	14986.77	13963.08

Monthly Payments 21¾%
necessary to amortize a loan

AMOUNT	8 YEARS	9 YEARS	10 YEARS	11 YEARS	12 YEARS	13 YEARS	14 YEARS
100	2.21	2.12	2.05	2.00	1.96	1.93	1.91
200	4.41	4.23	4.10	4.00	3.92	3.86	3.81
500	11.03	10.58	10.25	10.00	9.80	9.65	9.53
1000	22.06	21.17	20.50	19.99	19.60	19.30	19.06
2000	44.11	42.33	41.00	39.98	39.20	38.59	38.11
5000	110.29	105.83	102.50	99.96	98.00	96.48	95.29
6000	132.34	127.00	123.00	119.95	117.60	115.77	114.34
7000	154.40	148.17	143.50	139.94	137.20	135.07	133.40
8000	176.46	169.33	164.00	159.93	156.80	154.37	152.46
9000	198.52	190.50	184.50	179.93	176.40	173.66	171.51
10000	220.57	211.67	205.00	199.92	196.00	192.96	190.57
15000	330.86	317.50	307.50	299.88	294.01	289.44	285.86
20000	441.15	423.34	409.99	399.84	392.01	385.92	381.14
25000	551.43	529.17	512.49	499.80	490.01	482.40	476.43
30000	661.72	635.01	614.99	599.76	588.01	578.87	571.71
35000	772.01	740.84	717.49	699.71	686.01	675.35	667.00
40000	882.29	846.67	819.99	799.67	784.02	771.83	762.28
45000	992.58	952.51	922.49	899.63	882.02	868.31	857.57
50000	1102.86	1058.34	1024.99	999.59	980.02	964.79	952.86
55000	1213.15	1164.18	1127.49	1099.55	1078.02	1061.27	1048.14
60000	1323.44	1270.01	1229.98	1199.51	1176.02	1157.75	1143.43
65000	1433.72	1375.84	1332.48	1299.47	1274.03	1254.23	1238.71
70000	1544.01	1481.68	1434.98	1399.43	1372.03	1350.71	1334.00
75000	1654.30	1587.51	1537.48	1499.39	1470.03	1447.19	1429.28
80000	1764.58	1693.35	1639.98	1599.35	1568.03	1543.67	1524.57
85000	1874.87	1799.18	1742.48	1699.31	1666.03	1640.15	1619.86
90000	1985.16	1905.02	1844.98	1799.27	1764.03	1736.62	1715.14
95000	2095.44	2010.85	1947.48	1899.22	1862.04	1833.10	1810.43
100000	2205.73	2116.68	2049.97	1999.18	1960.04	1929.58	1905.71
105000	2316.02	2222.52	2152.47	2099.14	2058.04	2026.06	2001.00
110000	2426.30	2328.35	2254.97	2199.10	2156.04	2122.54	2096.28
120000	2646.88	2540.02	2459.97	2398.98	2352.05	2315.50	2286.85
130000	2867.46	2751.69	2664.97	2598.94	2548.05	2508.46	2477.43
140000	3088.02	2963.36	2869.96	2798.86	2744.05	2701.42	2668.00
150000	3308.59	3175.03	3074.96	2998.78	2940.06	2894.37	2858.57
160000	3529.17	3386.70	3279.96	3198.69	3136.06	3087.33	3049.14
170000	3749.74	3598.36	3484.96	3398.61	3332.07	3280.29	3239.71
180000	3970.31	3810.03	3689.95	3598.53	3528.07	3473.25	3430.28
190000	4190.89	4021.70	3894.95	3798.45	3724.07	3666.21	3620.85
200000	4411.46	4233.37	4099.95	3998.37	3920.08	3859.16	3811.42
210000	4632.03	4445.04	4304.95	4198.29	4116.08	4052.12	4002.00
220000	4852.61	4656.71	4509.94	4398.21	4312.09	4245.08	4192.57
230000	5073.18	4868.37	4714.94	4598.12	4508.09	4438.04	4383.14
240000	5293.75	5080.04	4919.94	4798.04	4704.09	4631.00	4573.71
250000	5514.32	5291.71	5124.94	4997.96	4900.10	4823.96	4764.28
260000	5734.90	5503.38	5329.93	5197.88	5096.10	5016.91	4954.85
270000	5955.47	5715.05	5534.93	5397.80	5292.10	5209.87	5145.42
280000	6176.04	5926.72	5739.93	5597.72	5488.11	5402.83	5335.99
290000	6396.62	6138.39	5944.92	5797.63	5684.11	5595.79	5526.57
300000	6617.19	6350.05	6149.92	5997.55	5880.12	5788.75	5717.14
310000	6837.76	6561.72	6354.92	6197.47	6076.12	5981.71	5907.71
320000	7058.34	6773.39	6559.92	6397.39	6272.12	6174.66	6098.28
330000	7278.91	6985.06	6764.91	6597.31	6468.13	6367.62	6288.85
340000	7499.48	7196.73	6969.91	6797.23	6664.13	6560.58	6479.42
350000	7720.05	7408.40	7174.91	6997.14	6860.14	6753.54	6669.99
400000	8822.92	8466.74	8199.90	7996.74	7840.15	7718.33	7622.85
450000	9925.78	9525.08	9224.88	8996.33	8820.17	8683.12	8575.70
500000	11028.65	10583.42	10249.87	9995.92	9800.19	9647.91	9528.56
550000	12131.51	11641.77	11274.86	10995.51	10780.21	10612.70	10481.42
600000	13234.38	12700.11	12299.84	11995.10	11760.23	11577.49	11434.27

21¾%

Monthly Payments
necessary to amortize a loan

AMOUNT	15 YEARS	16 YEARS	17 YEARS	18 YEARS	19 YEARS	20 YEARS	21 YEARS
100	1.89	1.87	1.86	1.85	1.84	1.84	1.83
200	3.77	3.74	3.72	3.70	3.69	3.67	3.66
500	9.43	9.36	9.30	9.25	9.22	9.19	9.16
1000	18.87	18.72	18.60	18.51	18.43	18.37	18.32
2000	37.74	37.44	37.20	37.01	36.86	36.74	36.65
5000	94.34	93.60	93.01	92.54	92.16	91.86	91.62
6000	113.21	112.32	111.61	111.04	110.59	110.23	109.94
7000	132.08	131.04	130.21	129.55	129.02	128.60	128.26
8000	150.95	149.76	148.81	148.06	147.45	146.97	146.59
9000	169.82	168.48	167.41	166.56	165.89	165.34	164.91
10000	188.69	187.20	186.02	185.07	184.32	183.72	183.23
15000	283.03	280.80	279.02	277.61	276.48	275.57	274.85
20000	377.38	374.40	372.03	370.14	368.64	367.43	366.46
25000	471.72	468.00	465.04	462.68	460.80	459.29	458.08
30000	566.07	561.60	558.05	555.22	552.96	551.15	549.70
35000	660.41	655.20	651.05	647.75	645.11	643.00	641.31
40000	754.76	748.80	744.06	740.29	737.27	734.86	732.93
45000	849.10	842.40	837.07	832.82	829.43	826.72	824.54
50000	943.45	936.00	930.07	925.36	921.59	918.58	916.16
55000	1037.79	1029.60	1023.09	1017.90	1013.75	1010.43	1007.78
60000	1132.14	1123.20	1116.09	1110.43	1105.91	1102.29	1099.39
65000	1226.48	1216.80	1209.10	1202.97	1198.07	1194.15	1191.01
70000	1320.83	1310.40	1302.11	1295.50	1290.23	1286.01	1282.62
75000	1415.17	1404.00	1395.12	1388.04	1382.39	1377.87	1374.24
80000	1509.52	1497.60	1488.13	1480.58	1474.55	1469.72	1465.86
85000	1603.86	1591.20	1581.13	1573.11	1566.71	1561.58	1557.47
90000	1698.21	1684.80	1674.14	1665.65	1658.87	1653.44	1649.09
95000	1792.55	1778.40	1767.15	1758.19	1751.03	1745.30	1740.70
100000	1886.90	1872.00	1860.16	1850.72	1843.18	1837.15	1832.32
105000	1981.24	1965.60	1953.16	1943.26	1935.34	1929.01	1923.94
110000	2075.59	2059.20	2046.17	2035.79	2027.50	2020.87	2015.55
120000	2264.28	2246.40	2232.19	2220.87	2211.82	2204.58	2198.79
130000	2452.96	2433.60	2418.20	2405.94	2396.14	2388.30	2382.02
140000	2641.65	2620.80	2604.22	2591.01	2580.46	2572.02	2565.25
150000	2830.34	2808.00	2790.24	2776.08	2764.78	2755.73	2748.48
160000	3019.03	2995.19	2976.25	2961.15	2949.10	2939.45	2931.71
170000	3207.72	3182.39	3162.27	3146.23	3133.41	3123.16	3114.95
180000	3396.41	3369.59	3348.28	3331.30	3317.73	3306.88	3298.18
190000	3585.10	3556.79	3534.30	3516.37	3502.05	3490.59	3481.41
200000	3773.79	3743.99	3720.31	3701.44	3686.37	3674.31	3664.64
210000	3962.48	3931.19	3906.33	3886.51	3870.69	3858.02	3847.87
220000	4151.17	4118.39	4092.34	4071.59	4055.01	4041.74	4031.11
230000	4339.86	4305.59	4278.36	4256.66	4239.32	4225.45	4214.34
240000	4528.55	4492.79	4464.38	4441.73	4423.64	4409.17	4397.57
250000	4717.24	4679.99	4650.39	4626.80	4607.96	4592.88	4580.80
260000	4905.93	4867.19	4836.41	4811.87	4792.28	4776.60	4764.03
270000	5094.62	5054.39	5022.42	4996.95	4976.60	4960.31	4947.27
280000	5283.31	5241.59	5208.44	5182.02	5160.92	5144.03	5130.50
290000	5472.00	5428.79	5394.45	5367.09	5345.23	5327.75	5313.73
300000	5660.69	5615.99	5580.47	5552.16	5529.55	5511.46	5496.96
310000	5849.38	5803.19	5766.49	5737.24	5713.87	5695.18	5680.19
320000	6038.07	5990.39	5952.50	5922.31	5898.19	5878.89	5863.43
330000	6226.76	6177.59	6138.52	6107.38	6082.51	6062.61	6046.66
340000	6415.45	6364.79	6324.53	6292.45	6266.83	6246.32	6229.89
350000	6604.14	6551.60	6510.55	6477.52	6451.15	6430.04	6413.12
400000	7547.58	7487.99	7440.63	7402.88	7372.74	7348.61	7329.28
450000	8491.03	8423.99	8370.71	8328.24	8294.33	8267.19	8245.44
500000	9434.48	9359.98	9300.78	9253.61	9215.92	9185.77	9161.60
550000	10377.93	10295.98	10230.86	10178.97	10137.51	10104.35	10077.77
600000	11321.38	11231.98	11160.94	11104.33	11059.11	11022.92	10993.93

Monthly Payments 21¾%
necessary to amortize a loan

AMOUNT	22 YEARS	23 YEARS	24 YEARS	25 YEARS	30 YEARS	35 YEARS	40 YEARS
100	1.83	1.83	1.82	1.82	1.82	1.81	1.81
200	3.66	3.65	3.65	3.64	3.63	3.63	3.63
500	9.14	9.13	9.11	9.10	9.08	9.07	9.06
1000	18.28	18.25	18.23	18.21	18.15	18.13	18.13
2000	36.57	36.51	36.46	36.42	36.31	36.27	36.26
5000	91.42	91.27	91.14	91.04	90.77	90.67	90.64
6000	109.71	109.52	109.37	109.25	108.92	108.81	108.77
7000	127.99	127.77	127.60	127.46	127.07	126.94	126.90
8000	146.28	146.03	145.83	145.67	145.23	145.08	145.03
9000	164.56	164.28	164.05	163.87	163.38	163.21	163.15
10000	182.84	182.53	182.28	182.08	181.53	181.35	181.28
15000	274.27	273.80	273.42	273.12	272.30	272.02	271.92
20000	365.69	365.07	364.57	364.16	363.06	362.69	362.57
25000	457.11	456.33	455.71	455.20	453.83	453.36	453.21
30000	548.53	547.60	546.85	546.24	544.60	544.04	543.85
35000	639.96	638.87	637.99	637.28	635.36	634.71	634.49
40000	731.38	730.13	729.13	728.33	726.13	725.38	725.13
45000	822.80	821.40	820.27	819.37	816.89	816.06	815.77
50000	914.22	912.67	911.41	910.41	907.66	906.73	906.41
55000	1005.64	1003.93	1002.56	1001.45	998.43	997.40	997.05
60000	1097.07	1095.20	1093.70	1092.49	1089.19	1088.08	1087.70
65000	1188.49	1186.46	1184.84	1183.53	1179.96	1178.75	1178.34
70000	1279.91	1277.73	1275.98	1274.57	1270.73	1269.42	1268.98
75000	1371.33	1369.00	1367.12	1365.61	1361.49	1360.09	1359.62
80000	1462.76	1460.26	1458.26	1456.65	1452.26	1450.77	1450.26
85000	1554.18	1551.53	1549.40	1547.69	1543.02	1541.44	1540.90
90000	1645.60	1642.80	1640.55	1638.73	1633.79	1632.11	1631.54
95000	1737.02	1734.06	1731.69	1729.78	1724.56	1722.79	1722.19
100000	1828.44	1825.33	1822.83	1820.82	1815.32	1813.46	1812.83
105000	1919.87	1916.60	1913.97	1911.86	1906.09	1904.13	1903.47
110000	2011.29	2007.86	2005.11	2002.90	1996.85	1994.81	1994.11
120000	2194.13	2190.40	2187.39	2184.98	2178.39	2176.15	2175.39
130000	2376.98	2372.93	2369.68	2367.06	2359.92	2357.50	2356.67
140000	2559.82	2555.46	2551.96	2549.14	2541.45	2538.84	2537.96
150000	2742.67	2738.00	2734.24	2731.22	2722.98	2720.19	2719.24
160000	2925.51	2920.53	2916.53	2913.31	2904.52	2901.54	2900.52
170000	3108.35	3103.06	3098.81	3095.39	3086.05	3082.88	3081.80
180000	3291.20	3285.59	3281.09	3277.47	3267.58	3264.23	3263.09
190000	3474.04	3468.13	3463.37	3459.55	3449.11	3445.57	3444.37
200000	3656.89	3650.66	3645.66	3641.63	3630.64	3626.92	3625.65
210000	3839.73	3833.19	3827.94	3823.71	3812.18	3808.26	3806.94
220000	4022.58	4015.73	4010.22	4005.80	3993.71	3989.61	3988.22
230000	4205.42	4198.26	4192.51	4187.88	4175.24	4170.96	4169.50
240000	4388.27	4380.79	4374.79	4369.96	4356.77	4352.30	4350.78
250000	4571.11	4563.33	4557.07	4552.04	4538.31	4533.65	4532.07
260000	4753.95	4745.86	4739.35	4734.12	4719.84	4714.99	4713.35
270000	4936.80	4928.39	4921.64	4916.20	4901.37	4896.34	4894.63
280000	5119.64	5110.92	5103.92	5098.29	5082.90	5077.69	5075.91
290000	5302.49	5293.46	5286.20	5280.37	5264.43	5259.03	5257.20
300000	5485.33	5475.99	5468.48	5462.45	5445.97	5440.38	5438.48
310000	5668.18	5658.52	5650.77	5644.53	5627.50	5621.72	5619.76
320000	5851.02	5841.06	5833.05	5826.61	5809.03	5803.07	5801.04
330000	6033.86	6023.59	6015.33	6008.69	5990.56	5984.42	5982.33
340000	6216.71	6206.12	6197.62	6190.78	6172.09	6165.76	6163.61
350000	6399.55	6388.66	6379.90	6372.86	6353.63	6347.11	6344.89
400000	7313.78	7301.32	7291.31	7283.27	7261.29	7253.84	7251.31
450000	8228.00	8213.99	8202.73	8193.67	8168.95	8160.57	8157.72
500000	9142.22	9126.65	9114.14	9104.08	9076.61	9067.30	9064.13
550000	10056.44	10039.32	10025.56	10014.49	9984.27	9974.03	9970.55
600000	10970.66	10951.98	10936.97	10924.90	10891.93	10880.76	10876.96

Annual Amortization Schedules

Annual amortization schedules are rarely seen but are very important when a mortgage holder really wants to understand the underlying concepts of a mortgage loan. The schedules display (1) the progress made each year by a mortgage holder toward the repayment of the loan principal and (2) the interest charges that have been paid during any year. The schedules are based on a mortgage loan of $10,000 and on annual interest rates that vary from 5% to 21% in increments of $\frac{1}{4}$%. At every interest rate, schedules for both 25-year and 30-year mortgages are given.

The first column shows the interest paid during the year and the second column shows the principal paid during the year. These two amounts add up to the annual payment (or the sum of twelve monthly payments). The third column in each schedule shows the remaining balance of the mortgage at the end of each year. Note that, at the end of the complete term on each schedule, the remaining balance is zero. You may also note that from the first year of payments to the last year the interest paid during the year decreases as the years go by. The payment toward the principal increases over the years.

Here are some illustrative situations to help you understand and use the schedules:

Situation 1

Mr. Brown holds a 30-year conventional mortgage for an original principal of $30,000.00 at an annual interest rate of 9%. He has just completed his tenth year of monthly payments. For tax and other reasons the following questions arise: What interest charges were paid during the tenth year? How much principal has been paid during the tenth year? What is left to be paid on the principal?

The answers are found by first locating, on the 9% page of the annual amortization schedules, the 30-year schedule. Note that the schedule is based on a principal of $10,000.00, and because Mr. Brown's original principal was $30,000.00, all amounts on this schedule must be multiplied by 3. Looking down the schedule to the 10-year line you will notice that (1) the interest paid during the tenth year is $812.41, (2) the amount paid toward the principal during the year is $153.11, and (3) the remaining balance of the principal at the end of the year is $8,942.97. Multiplying by 3 provides Mr. Brown with these answers:

$2,437.23	(interest charges paid during the tenth year)
$459.33	(principal paid during the tenth year)
$26,828.91	(portion of principal still to be paid)

Situation 2

Mrs. Jones holds a 25-year conventional mortgage for an original principal of $40,000.00 at an annual interest rate of 8% and has just completed her twentieth year of monthly payments. For comparative purposes she wants to know how much of the principal is left unpaid. To find the answer, she must first locate the page that shows the 8% schedules. Using the schedule for the 25-year mortgage, she must look down to the 20-year line and then across to the last column showing the mortgage balance at the end of the twentieth year. The amount shown, $3,806.48, is based on a mortgage principal of $10,000.00. Since Mrs. Jones' original mortgage was 4 times as great she must multiply this amount by 4 to get $15,225.92 as the answer.

Annual Amortization

Based on mortgage of $10,000

5%

25-YEAR TERM
MONTHLY PAYMENT: 58.46
ANNUAL PAYMENT: 701.52

30-YEAR TERM
MONTHLY PAYMENT: 53.68
ANNUAL PAYMENT: 644.16

YR	INTEREST PD DUR YR	PRINCIPAL PD DUR YR	MORTG BAL END OF YR	INTEREST PD DUR YR	PRINCIPAL PD DUR YR	MORTG BAL END OF YR
1	495.33	206.19	9793.81	496.62	147.54	9852.46
2	484.78	216.74	9577.07	489.08	155.08	9697.38
3	473.69	227.83	9349.24	481.14	163.02	9534.36
4	462.04	239.48	9109.76	472.80	171.36	9363.00
5	449.78	251.74	8858.02	464.03	180.13	9182.87
6	436.90	264.62	8593.40	454.82	189.34	8993.53
7	423.37	278.15	8315.25	445.13	199.03	8794.50
8	409.13	292.39	8022.86	434.95	209.21	8585.29
9	394.18	307.34	7715.52	424.24	219.92	8365.37
10	378.45	323.07	7392.45	412.99	231.17	8134.21
11	361.92	339.60	7052.85	401.17	242.99	7891.21
12	344.55	356.97	6695.88	388.73	255.43	7635.79
13	326.28	375.24	6320.64	375.67	268.49	7367.29
14	307.09	394.43	5926.21	361.93	282.23	7085.06
15	286.91	414.61	5511.58	347.49	296.67	6788.39
16	265.69	435.83	5075.77	332.31	311.85	6476.54
17	243.40	458.12	4617.64	316.36	327.80	6148.74
18	219.96	481.56	4136.08	299.59	344.57	5804.16
19	195.32	506.20	3629.88	281.96	362.20	5441.96
20	169.42	532.10	3097.78	263.43	380.73	5061.23
21	142.20	559.32	2538.46	243.95	400.21	4661.01
22	113.58	587.94	1950.53	223.47	420.69	4240.32
23	83.50	618.02	1332.51	201.95	442.21	3798.11
24	51.88	649.64	682.87	179.32	464.84	3333.27
25	18.65	682.87	0.00	155.54	488.62	2844.66
26				130.54	513.62	2331.04
27				104.26	539.90	1791.14
28				76.64	567.52	1223.63
29				47.61	596.55	627.07
30				17.09	627.07	0.00

5¼%

25-YEAR TERM
MONTHLY PAYMENT: 59.95
ANNUAL PAYMENT: 719.04

30-YEAR TERM
MONTHLY PAYMENT: 55.22
ANNUAL PAYMENT: 662.64

YR	INTEREST PD DUR YR	PRINCIPAL PD DUR YR	MORTG BAL END OF YR	INTEREST PD DUR YR	PRINCIPAL PD DUR YR	MORTG BAL END OF YR
1	520.20	198.84	9801.16	521.63	141.01	9858.99
2	509.51	209.53	9591.63	514.05	148.59	9710.41
3	498.24	220.80	9370.83	506.06	156.58	9553.83
4	486.37	232.67	9138.16	497.64	165.00	9388.82
5	473.85	245.19	8892.97	488.76	173.88	9214.95
6	460.67	258.37	8634.60	479.41	183.23	9031.72
7	446.77	272.27	8362.33	469.56	193.08	8838.64
8	432.13	286.91	8075.41	459.17	203.47	8635.18
9	416.70	302.34	7773.07	448.23	214.41	8420.77
10	400.43	318.61	7454.46	436.70	225.94	8194.83
11	383.30	335.74	7118.72	424.55	238.09	7956.74
12	365.24	353.80	6764.93	411.74	250.90	7705.84
13	346.22	372.82	6392.10	398.25	264.39	7441.45
14	326.16	392.88	5999.23	384.03	278.61	7162.84
15	305.03	414.01	5585.22	369.05	293.59	6869.25
16	282.77	436.27	5148.95	353.26	309.38	6559.87
17	259.30	459.74	4689.21	336.62	326.02	6233.84
18	234.58	484.46	4204.75	319.08	343.56	5890.29
19	208.52	510.52	3694.24	300.61	362.03	5528.26
20	181.07	537.97	3156.26	281.14	381.50	5146.75
21	152.13	566.91	2589.36	260.62	402.02	4744.73
22	121.65	597.39	1991.96	239.00	423.64	4321.09
23	89.52	629.52	1362.44	216.21	446.43	3874.66
24	55.66	663.38	699.06	192.20	470.44	3404.22
25	19.98	699.06	0.00	166.90	495.74	2908.48
26				140.24	522.40	2386.08
27				112.14	550.50	1835.58
28				82.54	580.10	1255.48
29				51.34	611.30	644.18
30				18.46	644.18	0.00

Annual Amortization
Based on mortgage of $10,000

5½%

	25-YEAR TERM MONTHLY PAYMENT: 61.41 ANNUAL PAYMENT: 736.92			30-YEAR TERM MONTHLY PAYMENT: 56.78 ANNUAL PAYMENT: 681.31		
YR	INTEREST PD DUR YR	PRINCIPAL PD DUR YR	MORTG BAL END OF YR	INTEREST PD DUR YR	PRINCIPAL PD DUR YR	MORTG BAL END OF YR
1	545.23	191.69	9808.31	546.65	134.71	9865.29
2	534.42	202.50	9605.81	539.05	142.31	9722.98
3	523.00	213.92	9391.88	531.03	150.33	9572.65
4	510.93	225.99	9165.89	522.55	158.81	9413.83
5	498.18	238.74	8927.15	513.59	167.77	9246.06
6	484.71	252.21	8674.95	504.12	177.24	9068.82
7	470.49	266.43	8408.51	494.13	187.23	8881.59
8	455.46	281.46	8127.05	483.56	197.80	8683.79
9	439.58	297.34	7829.71	472.41	208.95	8474.84
10	422.81	314.11	7515.60	460.62	220.74	8254.10
11	405.09	331.83	7183.77	448.17	233.19	8020.91
12	386.37	350.55	6833.23	435.01	246.35	7774.56
13	366.60	370.32	6462.91	421.12	260.24	7514.32
14	345.71	391.21	6071.70	406.44	274.92	7239.40
15	323.64	413.28	5658.42	390.93	290.43	6948.97
16	300.33	436.59	5221.83	374.55	306.81	6642.16
17	275.70	461.22	4760.62	357.24	324.12	6318.04
18	249.69	487.23	4273.39	338.96	342.40	5975.64
19	222.20	514.72	3758.67	319.65	361.71	5613.93
20	193.17	543.75	3214.92	299.24	382.12	5231.81
21	162.50	574.42	2640.50	277.69	403.67	4828.14
22	130.10	606.82	2033.68	254.92	426.44	4401.70
23	95.87	641.05	1392.63	230.86	450.50	3951.20
24	59.71	677.21	715.41	205.45	475.91	3475.29
25	21.51	715.41	0.00	178.61	502.75	2972.54
26				150.25	531.11	2441.42
27				120.29	561.07	1880.35
28				88.64	592.72	1287.63
29				55.20	626.16	661.48
30				19.88	661.48	0.00

5¾%

	25-YEAR TERM MONTHLY PAYMENT: 62.91 ANNUAL PAYMENT: 754.92			30-YEAR TERM MONTHLY PAYMENT: 58.36 ANNUAL PAYMENT: 700.32		
YR	INTEREST PD DUR YR	PRINCIPAL PD DUR YR	MORTG BAL END OF YR	INTEREST PD DUR YR	PRINCIPAL PD DUR YR	MORTG BAL END OF YR
1	570.17	184.75	9815.25	571.68	128.64	9871.36
2	559.27	195.65	9619.60	564.08	136.24	9735.12
3	547.72	207.20	9412.40	556.04	144.28	9590.84
4	535.48	219.44	9192.96	547.52	152.80	9438.04
5	522.53	232.39	8960.56	538.50	161.82	9276.22
6	508.81	246.11	8714.45	528.95	171.37	9104.84
7	494.24	260.64	8453.80	518.83	181.49	8923.35
8	478.89	276.03	8177.77	508.11	192.21	8731.14
9	462.59	292.33	7885.44	496.76	203.56	8527.59
10	445.33	309.59	7575.85	484.75	215.57	8312.01
11	427.05	327.87	7247.98	472.02	228.30	8083.71
12	407.70	347.22	6900.76	458.54	241.78	7841.93
13	387.20	367.72	6533.04	444.27	256.05	7585.88
14	365.48	389.44	6143.60	429.15	271.17	7314.71
15	342.49	412.43	5731.17	413.14	287.18	7027.53
16	318.14	436.78	5294.40	396.18	304.14	6723.39
17	292.36	462.56	4831.83	378.23	322.09	6401.30
18	265.05	489.87	4341.96	359.21	341.11	6060.19
19	236.12	518.80	3823.16	339.07	361.25	5698.94
20	205.49	549.43	3273.74	317.74	382.58	5316.36
21	173.04	581.86	2691.87	295.16	405.16	4911.20
22	138.70	616.22	2075.66	271.24	429.08	4482.11
23	102.32	652.60	1423.06	245.90	454.42	4027.70
24	63.79	691.13	731.93	219.07	481.25	3546.45
25	22.99	731.93	0.00	190.66	509.66	3036.79
26				160.57	539.75	2497.04
27				128.70	571.62	1925.42
28				94.96	605.36	1320.06
29				59.22	641.10	678.96
30				21.36	678.96	0.00

Annual Amortization
Based on mortgage of $10,000

6%

	25-YEAR TERM MONTHLY PAYMENT: 64.43 ANNUAL PAYMENT: 773.16			30-YEAR TERM MONTHLY PAYMENT: 59.96 ANNUAL PAYMENT: 719.52		
YR	INTEREST PD DUR YR	PRINCIPAL PD DUR YR	MORTG BAL END OF YR	INTEREST PD DUR YR	PRINCIPAL PD DUR YR	MORTG BAL END OF YR
1	595.16	178.00	9822.00	596.72	122.80	9877.20
2	584.18	188.98	9633.01	589.14	130.38	9746.82
3	572.52	200.64	9432.37	581.10	138.42	9608.41
4	560.15	213.01	9219.36	572.57	146.95	9461.45
5	547.01	226.15	8993.21	563.50	156.02	9305.44
6	533.06	240.10	8753.11	553.88	165.64	9139.80
7	518.25	254.91	8498.20	543.66	175.86	8963.94
8	502.53	270.63	8227.57	532.82	186.70	8777.24
9	485.84	287.32	7940.24	521.30	198.22	8579.02
10	468.11	305.05	7635.20	509.08	210.44	8368.57
11	449.30	323.86	7311.34	496.10	223.42	8145.15
12	429.33	343.83	6967.50	482.32	237.20	7907.94
13	408.12	365.04	6602.46	467.69	251.83	7656.11
14	385.60	387.56	6214.91	452.15	267.37	7388.74
15	361.70	411.46	5803.45	435.66	283.86	7104.88
16	336.32	436.84	5366.61	418.15	301.37	6803.52
17	309.38	463.78	4902.83	399.57	319.95	6483.57
18	280.77	492.39	4410.44	379.83	339.69	6143.88
19	250.40	522.76	3887.68	358.88	360.64	5783.24
20	218.16	555.00	3332.69	336.64	382.88	5400.36
21	183.93	589.23	2743.46	313.02	406.50	4993.86
22	147.59	625.57	2117.88	287.95	431.57	4562.29
23	109.00	664.16	1453.73	261.33	458.19	4104.11
24	68.04	705.12	748.61	233.07	486.45	3617.66
25	24.55	748.61	0.00	203.07	516.45	3101.21
26				171.22	548.30	2552.91
27				137.40	582.12	1970.78
28				101.49	618.03	1352.76
29				63.38	656.14	696.61
30				22.91	696.61	0.00

6¼%

	25-YEAR TERM MONTHLY PAYMENT: 65.97 ANNUAL PAYMENT: 738.84			30-YEAR TERM MONTHLY PAYMENT: 61.57 ANNUAL PAYMENT: 738.84		
YR	INTEREST PD DUR YR	PRINCIPAL PD DUR YR	MORTG BAL END OF YR	INTEREST PD DUR YR	PRINCIPAL PD DUR YR	MORTG BAL END OF YR
1	620.18	171.46	9828.54	621.66	117.18	9882.82
2	609.15	182.49	9646.05	614.12	124.72	9758.10
3	597.41	194.23	9451.83	606.10	132.74	9625.36
4	584.92	206.72	9245.11	597.56	141.28	9484.09
5	571.62	220.02	9025.09	588.48	150.36	9333.72
6	557.47	234.17	8790.92	578.80	160.04	9173.69
7	542.41	249.23	8541.69	568.51	170.33	9003.36
8	526.38	265.26	8276.43	557.55	181.29	8822.07
9	509.32	282.32	7994.11	545.89	192.95	8629.13
10	491.16	300.48	7693.63	533.48	205.36	8423.77
11	471.81	319.81	7373.82	520.27	218.57	8205.21
12	451.26	340.38	7033.44	506.22	232.62	7972.58
13	429.37	362.27	6671.17	491.25	247.59	7725.00
14	406.06	385.58	6285.59	475.33	263.51	7461.48
15	381.26	410.38	5875.21	458.38	280.46	7181.02
16	354.87	436.77	5438.44	440.34	298.50	6882.52
17	326.77	464.87	4973.57	421.14	317.70	6564.82
18	296.87	494.77	4478.80	400.70	338.14	6226.68
19	265.05	526.59	3952.21	378.95	359.89	5866.80
20	231.18	560.46	3391.75	355.81	383.03	5483.76
21	195.13	596.51	2795.23	331.17	407.67	5076.09
22	156.76	634.88	2160.35	304.95	433.89	4642.19
23	115.92	675.72	1484.63	277.04	461.80	4180.39
24	72.46	719.18	765.44	247.33	491.51	3688.88
25	26.20	765.44	0.00	215.72	523.12	3165.76
26				182.07	556.77	2608.99
27				146.26	592.58	2016.41
28				108.14	630.70	1385.71
29				67.57	671.27	714.44
30				24.40	714.44	0.00

Annual Amortization
Based on mortgage of $10,000

6½%

	25-YEAR TERM MONTHLY PAYMENT: 67.52 ANNUAL PAYMENT: 810.24			30-YEAR TERM MONTHLY PAYMENT: 63.21 ANNUAL PAYMENT: 758.52		
YR	INTEREST PD DUR YR	PRINCIPAL PD DUR YR	MORTG BAL END OF YR	INTEREST PD DUR YR	PRINCIPAL PD DUR YR	MORTG BAL END OF YR
1	645.13	165.11	9834.89	646.75	111.77	9888.23
2	634.07	176.17	9658.72	639.26	119.26	9768.97
3	622.27	187.97	9470.76	631.27	127.25	9641.72
4	609.69	200.55	9270.20	622.75	135.77	9505.96
5	596.25	213.99	9056.22	613.66	144.86	9361.10
6	581.92	228.32	8827.90	603.96	154.56	9206.54
7	566.63	243.61	8584.29	593.61	164.91	9041.62
8	550.32	259.92	8324.37	582.56	175.96	8865.67
9	532.91	277.33	8047.04	570.78	187.74	8677.93
10	514.34	295.90	7751.14	558.21	200.31	8477.61
11	494.52	315.72	7435.42	544.79	213.73	8263.88
12	473.38	336.86	7098.55	530.48	228.04	8035.84
13	450.81	359.43	6739.13	515.20	243.32	7792.52
14	426.74	383.50	6355.63	498.91	259.61	7532.91
15	401.06	409.18	5946.45	481.52	277.00	7255.91
16	373.66	436.58	5509.86	462.97	295.55	6960.37
17	344.42	465.82	5044.04	443.18	315.34	6645.02
18	313.22	497.02	4547.02	422.06	336.46	6308.56
19	279.91	530.31	4016.72	399.52	359.00	5949.57
20	244.42	565.82	3450.89	375.48	383.04	5566.53
21	206.52	603.72	2847.18	349.83	408.69	5157.84
22	166.09	644.15	2203.03	322.46	436.06	4721.78
23	122.95	687.29	1515.74	293.26	465.26	4256.51
24	76.92	733.32	782.43	262.10	496.42	3760.09
25	27.81	782.43	0.00	228.85	529.67	3230.42
26				193.38	565.14	2665.27
27				155.53	602.99	2062.28
28				115.14	643.38	1418.90
29				72.06	686.46	732.44
30				26.08	732.44	0.00

6¾%

	25-YEAR TERM MONTHLY PAYMENT: 69.09 ANNUAL PAYMENT: 829.08			30-YEAR TERM MONTHLY PAYMENT: 64.86 ANNUAL PAYMENT: 778.32		
YR	INTEREST PD DUR YR	PRINCIPAL PD DUR YR	MORTG BAL END OF YR	INTEREST PD DUR YR	PRINCIPAL PD DUR YR	MORTG BAL END OF YR
1	670.13	158.95	9841.05	671.75	106.57	9893.43
2	659.06	170.02	9671.03	664.32	114.00	9779.43
3	647.22	181.86	9489.17	656.39	121.93	9657.50
4	634.56	194.52	9294.65	647.90	130.42	9527.07
5	621.02	208.06	9086.59	638.82	139.50	9387.57
6	606.59	222.49	8864.04	629.10	149.22	9238.35
7	591.03	238.05	8625.99	618.71	159.61	9078.75
8	574.46	254.62	8371.37	607.60	170.72	8908.03
9	556.73	272.35	8099.02	595.71	182.61	8725.42
10	537.77	291.31	7807.71	583.00	195.32	8530.10
11	517.48	311.60	7496.11	569.40	208.92	8321.18
12	495.79	333.29	7162.82	554.85	223.47	8097.71
13	472.58	356.50	6806.32	539.29	239.03	7858.68
14	447.76	381.32	6425.00	522.65	255.67	7603.01
15	421.21	407.87	6017.13	504.85	273.47	7329.54
16	392.81	436.27	5580.86	485.81	292.51	7037.03
17	362.43	466.65	5114.21	465.44	312.88	6724.15
18	329.94	499.14	4615.07	443.65	334.67	6389.48
19	295.19	533.89	4081.18	420.35	357.97	6031.51
20	258.01	571.07	3510.11	395.43	382.89	5648.62
21	218.25	610.83	2899.28	368.77	409.55	5239.07
22	175.72	653.36	2245.92	340.25	438.07	4801.00
23	130.23	698.85	1547.07	309.75	468.57	4332.43
24	81.57	747.51	799.56	277.12	501.20	3831.24
25	29.52	799.56	0.00	242.23	536.09	3295.14
26				204.90	573.42	2721.72
27				164.97	613.35	2108.38
28				122.27	656.05	1452.32
29				76.59	701.73	750.59
30				27.73	750.59	0.00

Annual Amortization
Based on mortgage of $10,000

7%

YR	INTEREST PD DUR YR	PRINCIPAL PD DUR YR	MORTG BAL END OF YR	INTEREST PD DUR YR	PRINCIPAL PD DUR YR	MORTG BAL END OF YR
1	695.18	152.98	9847.02	696.78	101.58	9898.42
2	684.04	164.04	9682.98	689.44	108.92	9789.49
3	672.26	175.90	9507.08	681.56	116.80	9672.70
4	659.55	188.61	9318.46	673.12	125.24	9547.45
5	645.91	202.25	9116.22	664.06	134.30	9413.16
6	631.29	216.87	8899.35	654.36	144.00	9269.16
7	615.61	232.55	8666.80	643.95	154.41	9114.74
8	598.80	249.36	8417.44	632.78	165.58	8949.17
9	580.78	267.38	8150.05	620.81	177.55	8771.62
10	561.45	286.71	7863.34	607.98	190.38	8581.24
11	540.72	307.44	7555.90	594.22	204.14	8377.09
12	518.49	329.67	7226.23	579.46	218.90	8158.19
13	494.66	353.50	6872.74	563.63	234.73	7923.47
14	469.11	379.05	6493.68	546.67	251.69	7671.78
15	441.71	406.45	6087.23	528.47	269.89	7401.89
16	412.32	435.84	5651.40	508.96	289.40	7112.49
17	380.82	467.34	5184.05	488.04	310.32	6802.17
18	347.03	501.13	4682.93	465.61	332.75	6469.42
19	310.81	537.35	4145.57	441.55	356.81	6112.61
20	271.96	576.20	3569.38	415.76	382.60	5730.01
21	230.31	617.85	2951.52	388.10	410.26	5319.75
22	185.64	662.52	2289.01	358.44	439.92	4879.83
23	137.75	710.41	1578.60	326.64	471.72	4408.11
24	86.39	761.77	816.83	292.54	505.82	3902.29
25	31.33	816.83	0.00	255.98	542.38	3359.91
26				216.77	581.59	2778.32
27				174.72	623.64	2154.68
28				129.64	668.72	1485.96
29				81.30	717.06	768.90
30				29.46	768.90	0.00

7¼%

YR	INTEREST PD DUR YR	PRINCIPAL PD DUR YR	MORTG BAL END OF YR	INTEREST PD DUR YR	PRINCIPAL PD DUR YR	MORTG BAL END OF YR
1	720.16	147.20	9852.80	721.85	96.79	9903.21
2	709.13	158.23	9694.58	714.60	104.04	9799.17
3	697.27	170.09	9524.49	706.80	111.84	9687.33
4	684.52	182.84	9341.65	698.42	120.22	9567.11
5	670.82	196.54	9145.10	689.41	129.23	9437.88
6	656.08	211.28	8933.82	679.72	138.92	9298.96
7	640.25	227.11	8706.71	669.31	149.33	9149.62
8	623.22	244.14	8462.57	658.11	160.53	8989.09
9	604.92	262.44	8200.13	646.08	172.56	8816.53
10	585.25	282.11	7918.02	633.14	185.50	8631.04
11	564.10	303.26	7614.77	619.24	199.40	8431.63
12	541.37	325.99	7288.78	604.29	214.35	8217.29
13	516.94	350.42	6938.35	588.23	230.41	7986.87
14	490.67	376.69	6561.66	570.95	247.69	7739.19
15	462.43	404.93	6156.73	552.39	266.25	7472.93
16	432.08	435.28	5721.45	532.43	286.21	7186.72
17	399.45	467.91	5253.54	510.98	307.66	6879.06
18	364.38	502.98	4750.56	487.91	330.73	6548.33
19	326.68	540.68	4209.88	463.12	355.52	6192.82
20	286.15	581.21	3628.66	436.47	382.17	5810.65
21	242.58	624.78	3003.88	407.83	410.81	5399.84
22	195.75	671.61	2332.27	377.03	441.61	4958.23
23	145.40	721.96	1610.32	343.93	474.71	4483.52
24	91.29	776.07	834.24	308.35	510.29	3973.23
25	33.11	834.24	0.00	270.10	548.54	3424.69
26				228.98	589.66	2835.03
27				184.78	633.86	2201.17
28				137.27	681.37	1519.80
29				86.19	732.45	787.35
30				31.29	787.35	0.00

Annual Amortization
Based on mortgage of $10,000

7½%

	25-YEAR TERM MONTHLY PAYMENT: 73.90 ANNUAL PAYMENT: 886.80			30-YEAR TERM MONTHLY PAYMENT: 73.90 ANNUAL PAYMENT: 839.04		
YR	INTEREST PD DUR YR	PRINCIPAL PD DUR YR	MORTG BAL END OF YR	INTEREST PD DUR YR	PRINCIPAL PD DUR YR	MORTG BAL END OF YR
1	745.21	141.59	9858.41	746.86	92.18	9907.82
2	734.22	152.58	9705.83	739.70	99.34	9808.48
3	722.37	164.43	9541.40	731.99	107.05	9701.42
4	709.61	177.19	9364.20	723.68	115.36	9586.06
5	695.85	190.95	9173.25	714.72	124.32	9461.74
6	681.03	205.77	8967.48	705.07	133.97	9327.77
7	665.05	221.75	8745.73	694.67	144.37	9183.40
8	647.84	238.96	8506.77	683.46	155.58	9027.83
9	629.29	257.51	8249.26	671.38	167.66	8860.17
10	609.29	277.51	7971.75	658.37	180.67	8679.50
11	587.75	299.05	7672.70	644.34	194.70	8484.80
12	564.53	322.27	7350.44	629.23	209.81	8274.99
13	539.52	347.28	7003.15	612.94	226.10	8048.89
14	512.56	374.24	6628.91	595.39	243.65	7805.24
15	483.50	403.30	6225.61	576.47	262.57	7542.67
16	452.19	434.61	5791.01	556.09	282.95	7259.71
17	418.45	468.35	5322.66	534.12	304.92	6954.79
18	382.10	504.70	4817.95	510.45	328.59	6626.20
19	342.91	543.89	4274.07	484.94	354.10	6272.10
20	300.69	586.11	3687.96	457.45	381.59	5890.51
21	255.15	631.61	3056.35	427.83	411.21	5479.30
22	206.16	680.64	2375.70	395.90	443.14	5036.16
23	153.32	733.48	1642.22	361.50	477.54	4558.63
24	96.37	790.43	851.79	324.43	514.61	4044.01
25	35.01	851.79	0.00	284.48	554.56	3489.45
26				241.43	597.61	2891.84
27				195.03	644.01	2247.83
28				145.04	694.00	1553.82
29				91.16	747.88	805.94
30				33.10	805.94	0.00

7¾%

	25-YEAR TERM MONTHLY PAYMENT: 75.53 ANNUAL PAYMENT: 906.36			30-YEAR TERM MONTHLY PAYMENT: 71.64 ANNUAL PAYMENT: 859.68		
YR	INTEREST PD DUR YR	PRINCIPAL PD DUR YR	MORTG BAL END OF YR	INTEREST PD DUR YR	PRINCIPAL PD DUR YR	MORTG BAL END OF YR
1	770.20	136.16	9863.84	771.91	87.77	9912.23
2	759.26	147.10	9716.74	764.86	94.82	9817.41
3	747.45	158.91	9557.82	757.25	102.43	9714.98
4	734.68	171.68	9386.15	749.02	110.66	9604.32
5	720.90	185.46	9200.68	740.13	119.55	9484.77
6	706.00	200.36	9000.32	730.53	129.15	9355.63
7	689.91	216.45	8783.87	720.16	139.52	9216.11
8	672.53	233.83	8550.04	708.95	150.73	9065.38
9	653.75	252.61	8297.42	696.85	162.83	8902.55
10	633.46	272.90	8024.52	683.77	175.91	8726.64
11	611.54	294.82	7729.70	669.64	190.04	8536.60
12	587.86	318.50	7411.20	654.38	205.30	8331.31
13	562.28	344.08	7067.13	637.89	221.79	8109.52
14	534.65	371.71	6695.41	620.08	239.60	7869.92
15	504.80	401.56	6293.85	600.84	258.84	7611.08
16	472.54	433.82	5860.03	580.05	279.63	7331.45
17	437.70	468.66	5391.38	557.59	302.09	7029.36
18	400.06	506.30	4885.08	533.33	326.35	6703.01
19	359.40	546.96	4338.12	507.12	352.56	6350.45
20	315.47	590.89	3747.24	478.80	380.88	5969.57
21	268.02	638.34	3108.89	448.22	411.46	5558.11
22	216.75	689.61	2419.28	415.17	444.51	5113.60
23	161.37	744.99	1674.29	379.47	480.21	4633.39
24	101.53	804.83	869.46	340.90	518.78	4114.61
25	36.90	869.46	0.00	299.24	560.44	3554.17
26				254.23	605.45	2948.72
27				205.60	654.08	2294.64
28				153.07	706.61	1588.03
29				96.32	763.36	824.67
30				35.01	824.67	0.00

Annual Amortization
Based on mortgage of $10,000

8%

25-YEAR TERM
MONTHLY PAYMENT: $77.18
ANNUAL PAYMENT: $926.16

30-YEAR TERM
MONTHLY PAYMENT: $73.38
ANNUAL PAYMENT: $880.56

YR	INTEREST PD DUR YR	PRINCIPAL PD DUR YR	MORTG BAL AT YR END	INTEREST PD DUR YR	PRINCIPAL PD DUR YR	MORTG BAL AT YR END
1	795.25	130.91	9869.09	797.02	83.54	9916.46
2	784.38	141.78	9727.31	790.09	90.47	9825.99
3	772.62	153.54	9573.77	782.58	97.98	9728.01
4	759.87	166.29	9407.48	774.45	106.11	9621.90
5	746.07	180.09	9227.39	765.64	114.92	9506.99
6	731.12	195.04	9032.36	756.10	124.46	9382.53
7	714.94	211.22	8821.13	745.77	134.79	9247.74
8	697.40	228.76	8592.38	734.59	145.97	9101.77
9	678.42	247.74	8344.64	722.47	158.09	8943.68
10	657.86	268.30	8076.33	709.35	171.21	8772.47
11	635.59	290.57	7785.76	695.14	185.42	8587.05
12	611.47	314.69	7471.07	679.75	200.81	8386.24
13	585.35	340.81	7130.25	663.08	217.48	8168.76
14	557.06	369.10	6761.16	645.03	235.53	7933.23
15	526.43	399.73	6361.42	625.48	255.08	7678.16
16	493.25	432.91	5928.51	604.31	276.25	7401.90
17	457.32	468.84	5459.67	581.38	299.18	7102.73
18	418.40	507.76	4951.92	556.55	324.01	6778.72
19	376.26	549.90	4402.02	529.66	350.90	6427.82
20	330.62	595.54	3806.48	500.53	380.03	6047.80
21	281.19	644.97	3161.51	468.99	411.57	5636.23
22	227.66	698.50	2463.00	434.83	445.73	5190.50
23	169.68	756.48	1706.53	397.84	482.72	4707.78
24	106.90	819.26	887.26	357.77	522.79	4184.99
25	38.90	887.26	0.00	314.38	566.18	3618.81
26				267.39	613.17	3005.64
27				216.50	664.06	2341.58
28				161.38	719.18	1622.39
29				101.69	778.87	843.52
30				37.04	843.52	0.00

8¼%

25-YEAR TERM
MONTHLY PAYMENT: $78.85
ANNUAL PAYMENT: $946.20

30-YEAR TERM
MONTHLY PAYMENT: $75.13
ANNUAL PAYMENT: $901.56

YR	INTEREST PD DUR YR	PRINCIPAL PD DUR YR	MORTG BAL AT YR END	INTEREST PD DUR YR	PRINCIPAL PD DUR YR	MORTG BAL AT YR END
1	820.37	125.83	9874.17	822.08	79.48	9920.52
2	809.59	136.61	9737.56	815.27	86.29	9834.23
3	797.88	148.32	9589.25	807.87	93.69	9740.54
4	785.17	161.03	9428.22	799.85	101.71	9638.83
5	771.38	174.82	9253.40	791.13	110.43	9528.40
6	756.39	189.81	9063.59	781.67	119.89	9408.50
7	740.13	206.07	8857.52	771.39	130.17	9278.34
8	722.47	223.73	8633.79	760.24	141.32	9137.02
9	703.30	242.90	8390.89	748.13	153.43	8983.58
10	682.48	263.72	8127.18	734.98	166.58	8817.00
11	659.89	286.31	7840.86	720.71	180.85	8636.15
12	635.35	310.85	7530.01	705.21	196.35	8439.80
13	608.71	337.49	7192.53	688.38	213.18	8226.62
14	579.79	366.41	6826.12	670.11	231.45	7995.17
15	548.40	397.80	6428.32	650.28	251.28	7743.90
16	514.31	431.89	5996.43	628.75	272.81	7471.08
17	477.30	468.90	5527.52	605.37	296.19	7174.90
18	437.12	509.08	5018.44	579.99	321.57	6853.33
19	393.49	552.71	4465.73	552.43	349.13	6504.20
20	346.13	600.07	3865.66	522.52	379.04	6125.16
21	294.71	651.49	3214.17	490.04	411.52	5713.63
22	238.88	707.32	2506.85	454.77	446.79	5266.84
23	178.27	767.93	1738.92	416.49	485.07	4781.77
24	112.46	833.74	905.18	374.92	526.64	4255.13
25	41.02	905.18	0.00	329.79	571.77	3683.36
26				280.79	620.77	3062.59
27				227.60	673.96	2388.63
28				169.84	731.72	1656.91
29				107.14	794.42	862.49
30				39.07	862.49	0.00

Annual Amortization
Based on mortgage of $10,000

8 1/2 %

	25-YEAR TERM MONTHLY PAYMENT: $80.52 ANNUAL PAYMENT: $966.24			30-YEAR TERM MONTHLY PAYMENT: $76.89 ANNUAL PAYMENT: $922.68		
YR	INTEREST PD DUR YR	PRINCIPAL PD DUR YR	MORTG BAL AT YR END	INTEREST PD DUR YR	PRINCIPAL PD DUR YR	MORTG BAL AT YR END
1	845.33	120.91	9879.09	847.08	75.60	9924.40
2	834.64	131.60	9747.49	840.40	82.28	9842.13
3	823.01	143.23	9604.26	833.13	89.55	9752.57
4	810.35	155.89	9448.37	825.21	97.47	9655.11
5	796.57	169.67	9278.70	816.60	106.08	9549.03
6	781.57	184.67	9094.03	807.22	115.46	9433.57
7	765.25	200.99	8893.04	797.02	125.66	9307.90
8	747.48	218.76	8674.29	785.91	136.77	9171.13
9	728.15	238.09	8436.19	773.82	148.86	9022.27
10	707.10	259.14	8177.06	760.66	162.02	8860.25
11	684.20	282.04	7895.01	746.34	176.34	8683.92
12	659.27	306.97	7588.04	730.75	191.93	8491.99
13	632.13	334.11	7253.93	713.79	208.89	8283.10
14	602.60	363.64	6890.30	695.33	227.35	8055.74
15	570.46	395.78	6494.52	675.23	247.45	7808.29
16	535.48	430.76	6063.75	653.36	269.32	7538.97
17	497.40	468.84	5594.91	629.55	293.13	7245.84
18	455.96	510.28	5084.63	603.64	319.04	6926.80
19	410.86	555.38	4529.25	575.44	347.24	6579.56
20	361.76	604.48	3924.77	544.75	377.93	6201.63
21	308.33	657.91	3266.87	511.34	411.34	5790.29
22	250.18	716.06	2550.81	474.98	447.70	5342.60
23	186.89	779.35	1771.46	435.41	487.27	4855.33
24	118.00	848.24	923.22	392.34	530.34	4324.99
25	43.02	923.22	0.00	345.46	577.22	3747.78
26				294.44	628.24	3119.54
27				238.91	683.77	2435.77
28				178.47	744.21	1691.57
29				112.69	809.99	881.58
30				41.10	881.58	0.00

8 3/4 %

	25-YEAR TERM MONTHLY PAYMENT: $82.21 ANNUAL PAYMENT: $986.52			30-YEAR TERM MONTHLY PAYMENT: $78.67 ANNUAL PAYMENT: $944.04		
YR	INTEREST PD DUR YR	PRINCIPAL PD DUR YR	MORTG BAL AT YR END	INTEREST PD DUR YR	PRINCIPAL PD DUR YR	MORTG BAL AT YR END
1	870.36	116.16	9883.84	872.16	71.88	9928.12
2	859.78	126.74	9757.10	865.61	78.43	9849.70
3	848.24	138.28	9618.82	858.47	85.57	9764.13
4	835.64	150.88	9467.94	850.68	93.36	9670.76
5	821.89	164.63	9303.31	842.17	101.87	9568.89
6	806.90	179.62	9123.69	832.89	111.15	9457.74
7	790.53	195.99	8927.70	822.76	121.28	9336.47
8	772.68	213.84	8713.86	811.72	132.32	9204.14
9	753.20	233.32	8480.55	799.66	144.38	9059.77
10	731.95	254.57	8225.97	786.51	157.53	8902.24
11	708.76	277.76	7948.21	772.16	171.88	8730.36
12	683.45	303.07	7645.14	756.50	187.54	8542.82
13	655.84	330.68	7314.47	739.42	204.62	8338.20
14	625.72	360.80	6953.67	720.78	223.26	8114.94
15	592.85	393.67	6560.00	700.44	243.60	7871.34
16	556.99	429.53	6130.47	678.25	265.79	7605.55
17	517.86	468.66	5661.82	654.04	290.00	7315.55
18	475.17	511.35	5150.47	627.62	316.42	6999.13
19	428.59	557.93	4592.54	598.80	345.24	6653.89
20	377.77	608.75	3983.79	567.35	376.69	6277.19
21	322.31	664.21	3319.58	533.03	411.01	5866.18
22	261.80	724.72	2594.86	495.59	448.45	5417.73
23	195.79	790.73	1804.13	454.74	489.30	4928.43
24	123.75	862.77	941.36	410.16	533.88	4394.55
25	45.16	941.36	0.00	361.53	582.51	3812.04
26				308.47	635.57	3176.47
27				250.57	693.47	2483.00
28				187.39	756.65	1726.35
29				118.47	825.57	900.78
30				43.26	900.78	0.00

Annual Amortization

Based on mortgage of $10,000

9%

25-YEAR TERM
MONTHLY PAYMENT: $83.92
ANNUAL PAYMENT: $1007.04

30-YEAR TERM
MONTHLY PAYMENT: $80.46
ANNUAL PAYMENT: $965.52

YR	INTEREST PD DUR YR	PRINCIPAL PD DUR YR	MORTG BAL AT YR END	INTEREST PD DUR YR	PRINCIPAL PD DUR YR	MORTG BAL AT YR END
1	895.48	111.56	9888.44	897.20	68.32	9931.68
2	885.01	122.03	9766.41	890.79	74.73	9856.95
3	873.56	133.48	9632.93	883.78	81.74	9775.21
4	861.04	146.00	9486.94	876.11	89.41	9685.81
5	847.35	159.69	9327.24	867.73	97.79	9588.01
6	832.37	174.67	9152.57	858.55	106.97	9481.05
7	815.98	191.06	8961.51	848.52	117.00	9364.05
8	798.06	208.98	8752.53	837.54	127.98	9236.07
9	778.46	228.58	8523.95	825.54	139.98	9096.09
10	757.01	250.03	8273.92	812.41	153.11	8942.97
11	733.56	273.48	8000.44	798.04	167.48	8775.50
12	707.90	299.14	7701.31	782.33	183.19	8592.31
13	679.84	327.20	7374.11	765.15	200.37	8391.94
14	649.15	357.89	7016.22	746.35	219.17	8172.77
15	615.58	391.46	6624.76	725.79	239.73	7933.05
16	578.86	428.18	6196.57	703.31	262.21	7670.83
17	538.69	468.35	5728.22	678.71	286.81	7384.02
18	494.75	512.29	5215.94	651.80	313.72	7070.31
19	446.70	560.34	4655.60	622.37	343.15	6727.16
20	394.13	612.90	4042.69	590.19	375.33	6351.83
21	336.64	670.40	3372.29	554.98	410.54	5941.28
22	273.75	733.29	2639.00	516.46	449.06	5492.23
23	204.96	802.08	1836.93	474.34	491.18	5001.05
24	129.72	877.32	959.61	428.26	537.26	4463.79
25	47.43	959.61	0.00	377.87	587.65	3876.14
26				322.74	642.78	3233.36
27				262.44	703.08	2530.28
28				196.49	769.03	1761.25
29				124.35	841.17	920.08
30				45.44	920.08	0.00

9¼%

25-YEAR TERM
MONTHLY PAYMENT: $85.64
ANNUAL PAYMENT: $1027.68

30-YEAR TERM
MONTHLY PAYMENT: $82.27
ANNUAL PAYMENT: $987.24

YR	INTEREST PD DUR YR	PRINCIPAL PD DUR YR	MORTG BAL AT YR END	INTEREST PD DUR YR	PRINCIPAL PD DUR YR	MORTG BAL AT YR END
1	920.56	107.12	9892.88	922.32	64.92	9935.08
2	910.22	117.46	9775.41	916.06	71.18	9863.90
3	898.88	128.80	9646.61	909.19	78.05	9785.85
4	886.44	141.24	9505.37	901.65	85.59	9700.26
5	827.81	154.87	9350.51	893.39	93.85	9606.41
6	857.86	169.82	9180.69	884.33	102.91	9503.50
7	841.47	186.21	8994.48	874.40	112.84	9390.66
8	823.50	204.18	8790.30	863.51	123.73	9266.93
9	803.79	223.89	8566.41	851.56	135.68	9131.25
10	782.18	245.50	8320.91	838.47	148.77	8982.48
11	758.48	269.20	8051.72	824.11	163.13	8819.35
12	732.50	295.18	7756.53	808.36	178.88	8640.47
13	704.01	323.67	7432.86	791.10	196.14	8444.32
14	672.76	354.92	7077.95	772.16	215.08	8229.25
15	638.51	389.17	6688.77	751.40	235.84	7993.41
16	600.94	426.74	6262.04	728.64	258.60	7734.81
17	559.75	467.93	5794.11	703.68	283.56	7451.24
18	514.59	513.09	5281.01	676.31	310.93	7140.31
19	465.06	562.62	4718.39	646.29	340.95	6799.36
20	410.75	616.93	4101.47	613.38	373.86	6425.51
21	351.20	676.48	3424.99	577.30	409.94	6015.57
22	285.91	741.77	2683.22	537.73	449.51	5566.06
23	214.31	813.37	1869.85	494.34	492.90	5073.16
24	135.80	891.88	977.97	446.76	540.48	4532.68
25	49.71	977.97	0.00	394.59	592.65	3940.04
26				337.39	649.85	3290.19
27				274.66	712.58	2577.61
28				205.88	781.36	1796.25
29				130.46	856.78	939.48
30				47.76	939.48	0.00

Annual Amortization

Based on mortgage of $10,000

9½%

25-YEAR TERM
MONTHLY PAYMENT: $87.37
ANNUAL PAYMENT: $1048.44

30-YEAR TERM
MONTHLY PAYMENT: $84.09
ANNUAL PAYMENT: $1009.08

YR	INTEREST PD DUR YR	PRINCIPAL PD DUR YR	MORTG BAL AT YR END	INTEREST PD DUR YR	PRINCIPAL PD DUR YR	MORTG BAL AT YR END
1	945.60	102.84	9897.16	947.42	61.66	9938.34
2	935.40	113.04	9784.12	941.30	67.78	9870.55
3	924.18	124.26	9659.86	934.57	74.51	9796.04
4	911.84	136.60	9523.28	927.17	81.91	9714.10
5	898.29	150.15	9373.11	919.04	90.04	9624.10
6	883.39	165.05	9208.05	910.11	98.97	9525.13
7	867.00	181.44	9026.62	900.29	108.79	9416.33
8	849.00	199.44	8827.17	889.49	119.59	9296.74
9	829.20	219.24	8607.94	877.62	131.46	9165.28
10	807.44	241.00	8366.94	864.57	144.51	9020.77
11	783.53	264.91	8102.03	850.23	158.85	8861.92
12	757.23	291.21	7810.83	834.46	174.62	8687.31
13	728.33	320.11	7490.71	817.13	191.95	8495.36
14	696.56	351.88	7138.83	798.08	211.00	8284.36
15	661.64	386.80	6752.03	777.14	231.94	8052.43
16	623.25	425.19	6326.84	754.12	254.96	7797.47
17	581.05	467.39	5859.45	728.82	280.26	7517.21
18	534.66	513.78	5345.68	701.00	308.08	7209.13
19	483.67	564.77	4780.91	670.43	338.65	6870.48
20	427.62	620.82	4160.09	636.82	372.26	6498.22
21	366.01	682.43	3477.66	599.87	409.21	6089.02
22	298.28	750.16	2727.49	559.26	449.82	5639.20
23	223.82	824.62	1902.88	514.62	494.46	5144.73
24	141.98	906.46	996.42	465.54	543.54	4601.20
25	52.02	996.42	0.00	411.60	597.48	4003.71
26				352.30	656.78	3346.93
27				287.11	721.97	2624.97
28				215.46	793.62	1831.35
29				136.70	872.38	958.97
30				50.11	958.97	0.00

9¾%

25-YEAR TERM
MONTHLY PAYMENT: $89.11
ANNUAL PAYMENT: $1069.32

30-YEAR TERM
MONTHLY PAYMENT: $85.92
ANNUAL PAYMENT: $1031.04

YR	INTEREST PD DUR YR	PRINCIPAL PD DUR YR	MORTG BAL AT YR END	INTEREST PD DUR YR	PRINCIPAL PD DUR YR	MORTG BAL AT YR END
1	970.62	98.70	9901.30	972.48	58.56	9941.44
2	960.56	108.76	9792.54	966.51	64.53	9876.92
3	949.47	119.85	9672.68	959.93	71.11	9805.81
4	937.24	132.08	9540.61	952.68	78.36	9727.45
5	923.77	145.55	9395.06	944.69	86.35	9641.10
6	908.93	160.39	9234.67	935.88	95.16	9545.94
7	892.58	176.74	9057.93	926.18	104.86	9441.08
8	874.55	194.77	8863.16	915.49	115.55	9325.53
9	854.69	214.63	8648.53	903.70	127.34	9198.19
10	832.80	236.52	8412.01	890.72	140.32	9057.87
11	808.68	260.64	8151.38	876.41	154.63	8903.24
12	782.10	287.22	7864.16	860.64	170.40	8732.84
13	752.82	316.50	7547.66	843.26	187.78	8545.06
14	720.54	348.78	7198.88	824.11	206.93	8338.14
15	684.97	384.35	6814.53	803.01	228.03	8110.11
16	645.78	423.54	6390.98	779.76	251.28	7858.82
17	602.58	466.74	5924.25	754.13	276.91	7581.92
18	554.99	514.33	5409.92	725.89	305.15	7276.77
19	502.54	566.78	4843.13	694.78	336.26	6940.51
20	444.74	624.58	4218.55	660.49	370.55	6569.95
21	381.05	688.27	3530.28	622.70	408.34	6161.61
22	310.86	758.46	2771.82	581.06	449.98	5711.63
23	233.51	835.81	1936.01	535.17	495.87	5215.75
24	148.28	921.04	1014.97	484.60	546.44	4669.31
25	54.35	1014.97	0.00	428.88	602.16	4067.15
26				367.47	663.57	3403.58
27				299.80	731.24	2672.34
28				225.23	805.81	1866.52
29				143.05	887.99	978.54
30				52.50	978.54	0.00

Annual Amortization

Based on mortgage of $10,000

10%

25-YEAR TERM
MONTHLY PAYMENT: $90.87
ANNUAL PAYMENT: $1090.44

30-YEAR TERM
MONTHLY PAYMENT: $87.76
ANNUAL PAYMENT: $1053.12

YR	INTEREST PD DUR YR	PRINCIPAL PD DUR YR	MORTG BAL AT YR END	INTEREST PD DUR YR	PRINCIPAL PD DUR YR	MORTG BAL AT YR END
1	995.74	94.70	9905.30	997.53	55.59	9944.41
2	985.82	104.62	9800.68	991.71	61.41	9883.00
3	974.86	115.58	9685.10	985.28	67.84	9815.16
4	962.76	127.68	9557.42	978.18	74.94	9740.22
5	949.39	141.05	9416.38	970.33	82.79	9657.43
6	934.62	155.82	9260.56	961.66	91.46	9565.97
7	918.31	172.13	9088.43	952.08	101.04	9464.94
8	900.28	190.16	8898.27	941.50	111.62	9353.32
9	880.37	210.07	8688.20	929.82	123.30	9230.02
10	858.37	232.07	8456.14	916.90	136.22	9093.80
11	834.07	256.37	8199.77	902.64	150.48	8943.32
12	807.23	283.21	7916.56	886.88	166.24	8777.09
13	777.57	312.87	7603.69	869.48	183.64	8593.44
14	744.81	345.63	7258.06	850.25	202.87	8390.57
15	708.62	381.82	6876.24	829.00	224.12	8166.46
16	668.64	421.80	6454.44	805.54	247.58	7918.87
17	624.47	465.97	5988.47	779.61	273.51	7645.36
18	575.68	514.76	5473.71	750.97	302.15	7343.21
19	521.77	568.67	4905.05	719.33	333.79	7009.43
20	462.23	628.21	4276.83	684.38	368.74	6640.69
21	396.45	693.99	3582.84	645.77	407.35	6233.33
22	323.78	766.66	2816.18	603.11	450.01	5783.33
23	243.50	846.94	1969.23	555.99	497.13	5286.20
24	154.81	935.63	1033.60	503.94	549.18	4737.01
25	56.84	1033.60	0.00	446.43	606.69	4130.32
26				382.90	670.22	3460.10
27				312.72	740.40	2719.70
28				235.19	817.93	1901.77
29				149.54	903.58	998.19
30				54.93	998.19	0.00

10¼%

25-YEAR TERM
MONTHLY PAYMENT: $92.64
ANNUAL PAYMENT: $1111.68

30-YEAR TERM
MONTHLY PAYMENT: $89.61
ANNUAL PAYMENT: $1075.32

YR	INTEREST PD DUR YR	PRINCIPAL PD DUR YR	MORTG BAL AT YR END	INTEREST PD DUR YR	PRINCIPAL PD DUR YR	MORTG BAL AT YR END
1	1020.83	90.85	9909.15	1022.57	52.75	9947.25
2	1011.07	100.61	9808.54	1016.90	58.42	9888.82
3	1000.26	111.42	9697.12	1010.62	64.70	9824.12
4	988.28	123.40	9573.72	1003.67	71.65	9752.47
5	975.02	136.66	9437.07	995.97	79.35	9673.12
6	960.34	151.34	9285.73	987.44	87.88	9585.24
7	944.08	167.60	9118.12	978.00	97.32	9487.91
8	926.07	185.61	8932.51	967.54	107.78	9380.13
9	906.12	205.56	8726.96	955.96	119.36	9260.77
10	884.04	227.64	8499.31	943.13	132.19	9128.58
11	859.57	252.11	8247.21	928.93	146.39	8982.19
12	832.48	279.20	7968.01	913.20	162.12	8820.07
13	802.48	309.20	7658.81	895.78	179.54	8640.52
14	769.26	342.42	7316.39	876.48	198.84	8441.69
15	732.46	379.22	6937.17	855.12	220.20	8221.48
16	691.71	419.97	6517.21	831.46	243.87	7977.62
17	646.59	465.09	6052.11	805.25	270.07	7707.55
18	596.61	515.07	5537.05	776.23	299.09	7408.46
19	541.26	570.42	4966.63	744.09	331.23	7077.23
20	479.97	631.71	4334.92	708.50	366.82	6710.41
21	412.09	699.59	3635.33	669.08	406.24	6304.17
22	336.91	774.77	2860.56	625.43	449.89	5854.28
23	253.66	858.02	2002.54	577.09	498.23	5356.05
24	161.46	950.22	1052.32	523.55	551.77	4804.28
25	59.36	1052.32	0.00	464.26	611.06	4193.22
26				398.60	676.72	3516.49
27				325.88	749.44	2767.05
28				245.35	829.97	1937.08
29				156.16	919.16	1017.92
30				57.40	1017.92	0.00

Annual Amortization
Based on mortgage of $10,000

10 1/2 %

	25-YEAR TERM MONTHLY PAYMENT: $94.42 ANNUAL PAYMENT: $1133.04			30-YEAR TERM MONTHLY PAYMENT: $91.47 ANNUAL PAYMENT: $1097.64		
YR	INTEREST PD DUR YR	PRINCIPAL PD DUR YR	MORTG BAL AT YR END	INTEREST PD DUR YR	PRINCIPAL PD DUR YR	MORTG BAL AT YR END
1	1045.91	87.13	9912.87	1047.59	50.05	9949.95
2	1036.31	96.73	9816.13	1042.07	55.57	9894.38
3	1025.65	107.39	9708.74	1035.95	61.69	9832.69
4	1013.81	119.23	9589.51	1029.15	68.49	9764.21
5	1000.67	132.37	9457.14	1021.60	76.04	9688.17
6	986.08	146.96	9310.18	1013.22	84.42	9603.75
7	969.89	163.15	9147.03	1003.92	93.72	9510.04
8	951.91	181.13	8965.90	993.59	104.05	9405.99
9	931.95	201.09	8764.80	982.13	115.51	9290.48
10	909.78	223.26	8541.55	969.40	128.24	9162.24
11	885.18	247.86	8293.69	955.27	142.37	9019.86
12	857.87	275.17	8018.51	939.58	158.06	8861.80
13	827.54	305.50	7713.02	922.16	175.48	8686.31
14	793.87	339.17	7373.85	902.82	194.82	8491.49
15	756.50	376.54	6997.31	881.35	216.29	8275.20
16	715.00	418.04	6579.27	857.51	240.13	8035.07
17	668.93	464.11	6115.16	831.05	266.59	7768.47
18	617.79	515.25	5599.91	801.67	295.97	7472.50
19	561.00	572.04	5027.87	769.05	328.59	7143.91
20	497.96	635.08	4392.79	732.84	364.80	6779.11
21	427.97	705.07	3687.72	692.64	405.00	6374.11
22	350.27	782.77	2904.96	648.00	449.64	5924.47
23	264.01	869.03	2035.93	598.45	499.19	5425.28
24	168.24	964.80	1071.12	543.44	554.20	4871.08
25	61.92	1071.12	0.00	482.37	615.27	4255.81
26				414.56	683.08	3572.73
27				339.28	758.36	2814.37
28				255.71	841.93	1972.44
29				162.92	934.72	1037.72
30				59.92	1037.72	0.00

10 3/4 %

	25-YEAR TERM MONTHLY PAYMENT: $96.21 ANNUAL PAYMENT: $1154.52			30-YEAR TERM MONTHLY PAYMENT: $93.35 ANNUAL PAYMENT: $1120.20		
YR	INTEREST PD DUR YR	PRINCIPAL PD DUR YR	MORTG BAL AT YR END	INTEREST PD DUR YR	PRINCIPAL PD DUR YR	MORTG BAL AT YR END
1	1070.97	83.55	9916.45	1072.73	47.47	9952.53
2	1061.53	92.99	9823.47	1067.37	52.83	9899.69
3	1051.03	103.49	9719.98	1061.40	58.80	9840.89
4	1039.34	115.18	9604.80	1054.76	65.44	9775.45
5	1026.33	128.19	9476.61	1047.36	72.84	9702.61
6	1011.85	142.67	9333.94	1039.14	81.06	9621.55
7	995.73	158.79	9175.15	1029.98	90.22	9531.33
8	977.80	176.72	8998.43	1019.79	100.41	9430.92
9	957.84	196.68	8801.75	1008.45	111.75	9319.16
10	935.62	218.90	8582.85	995.82	124.38	9194.79
11	910.89	243.63	8339.22	981.77	138.43	9056.36
12	883.37	271.15	8068.08	966.14	154.06	8902.30
13	852.75	301.77	7766.30	948.73	171.47	8730.83
14	818.66	335.86	7430.44	929.37	190.83	8540.00
15	780.72	373.80	7056.64	907.81	212.39	8327.61
16	738.50	416.02	6640.61	883.82	236.38	8091.22
17	691.59	463.02	6177.60	857.12	263.08	7828.14
18	639.20	515.32	5662.28	827.40	292.80	7535.34
19	580.99	573.53	5088.75	794.33	325.87	7209.47
20	516.21	638.31	4450.43	757.52	362.68	6846.78
21	444.10	710.42	3740.02	716.55	403.65	6443.13
22	363.86	790.66	2949.35	670.95	449.25	5993.88
23	274.54	879.98	2069.38	620.21	499.99	5493.89
24	175.14	979.38	1090.00	563.73	556.47	4937.41
25	64.52	1090.00	0.00	500.87	619.33	4318.08
26				430.91	689.29	3628.79
27				353.05	767.15	2861.64
28				266.39	853.81	2007.84
29				169.95	950.25	1057.59
30				62.61	1057.59	0.00

Annual Amortization
Based on mortgage of $10,000

11%

	25-YEAR TERM			30-YEAR TERM		
	MONTHLY PAYMENT: $98.01			**MONTHLY PAYMENT: $95.23**		
	ANNUAL PAYMENT: $1176.12			**ANNUAL PAYMENT: $1142.76**		
	INTEREST	PRINCIPAL	MORTG BAL	INTEREST	PRINCIPAL	MORTG BAL
YR	PD DUR YR	PD DUR YR	AT YR END	PD DUR YR	PD DUR YR	AT YR END
1	1096.03	80.09	9919.91	1097.75	45.01	9954.99
2	1086.76	89.36	9830.54	1092.54	50.22	9904.77
3	1076.42	99.70	9730.84	1086.73	56.03	9848.73
4	1064.88	111.24	9619.60	1080.24	62.52	9786.22
5	1052.01	124.11	9495.49	1073.01	69.75	9716.46
6	1037.64	138.48	9357.01	1064.94	77.82	9638.64
7	1021.62	154.50	9202.51	1055.93	86.83	9551.81
8	1003.74	172.38	9030.13	1045.88	96.88	9454.94
9	983.79	192.33	8837.81	1034.67	108.09	9346.85
10	961.54	214.58	8623.22	1022.17	120.59	9226.26
11	936.71	239.41	8383.81	1008.21	134.55	9091.71
12	909.00	267.12	8116.69	992.64	150.12	8941.59
13	878.09	298.03	7818.67	975.27	167.49	8774.10
14	843.60	332.52	7486.15	955.89	186.87	8587.22
15	805.13	370.99	7115.16	934.26	208.50	8378.73
16	762.20	413.92	6701.23	910.14	232.62	8146.10
17	714.30	461.82	6239.41	883.22	259.54	7886.56
18	660.85	515.27	5724.14	853.18	289.58	7596.98
19	601.23	574.89	5149.25	819.67	323.09	7273.89
20	534.70	641.42	4507.84	782.29	360.47	6913.42
21	460.48	715.64	3792.20	740.57	402.19	6511.23
22	377.67	798.45	2993.74	694.03	448.73	6062.50
23	285.27	890.85	2102.89	642.10	500.66	5561.85
24	182.18	993.94	1108.96	584.17	558.59	5003.25
25	67.16	1108.96	0.00	519.53	623.23	4380.02
26				447.41	695.35	3684.67
27				366.95	775.81	2908.86
28				277.17	865.59	2043.27
29				177.00	965.76	1077.51
30				65.25	1077.51	0.00

11¼%

	25-YEAR TERM			30-YEAR TERM		
	MONTHLY PAYMENT: $99.82			**MONTHLY PAYMENT: $97.13**		
	ANNUAL PAYMENT: $1197.84			**ANNUAL PAYMENT: $1165.56**		
	INTEREST	PRINCIPAL	MORTG BAL	INTEREST	PRINCIPAL	MORTG BAL
YR	PD DUR YR	PD DUR YR	AT YR END	PD DUR YR	PD DUR YR	AT YR END
1	1121.07	76.77	9923.23	1122.89	42.67	9957.33
2	1111.98	85.86	9837.37	1117.83	47.73	9909.61
3	1101.81	96.03	9741.34	1112.18	53.38	9856.23
4	1090.43	107.41	9633.92	1105.86	59.70	9796.52
5	1077.90	120.14	9513.78	1098.78	66.78	9729.74
6	1063.46	134.38	9379.41	1090.87	74.69	9655.05
7	1047.54	150.30	9229.11	1082.02	83.54	9571.51
8	1029.73	168.11	9061.01	1072.12	93.44	9478.07
9	1009.82	188.02	8872.98	1061.05	104.51	9373.56
10	987.54	210.30	8662.68	1048.67	116.89	9256.67
11	962.62	235.22	8427.46	1034.82	130.74	9125.92
12	934.75	263.09	8164.37	1019.32	146.24	8979.69
13	903.58	294.26	7870.11	1002.00	163.56	8816.13
14	868.71	329.13	7540.99	982.62	182.94	8633.18
15	829.72	368.12	7172.86	960.94	204.62	8428.57
16	786.10	411.74	6761.12	936.70	228.86	8199.71
17	737.31	460.53	6300.59	909.58	255.98	7943.73
18	682.75	515.09	5785.50	879.25	286.31	7657.42
19	621.72	576.12	5209.37	845.33	320.23	7337.18
20	553.45	644.39	4564.99	807.38	358.18	6979.01
21	477.10	720.74	3844.25	764.95	400.61	6578.40
22	391.70	806.14	3038.11	717.48	448.08	6130.31
23	296.19	901.65	2136.46	664.39	501.17	5629.14
24	189.36	1008.48	1127.98	605.01	560.55	5068.59
25	69.86	1127.98	0.00	538.59	626.97	4441.61
26				464.30	701.26	3740.35
27				381.21	784.35	2956.00
28				288.28	877.28	2078.72
29				184.33	981.23	1097.49
30				68.07	1097.49	0.00

Annual Amortization

Based on mortgage of $10,000

11½%

25-YEAR TERM
MONTHLY PAYMENT: $101.65
ANNUAL PAYMENT: $1219.80

30-YEAR TERM
MONTHLY PAYMENT: $99.03
ANNUAL PAYMENT: $1188.36

YR	INTEREST PD DUR YR	PRINCIPAL PD DUR YR	MORTG BAL AT YR END	INTEREST PD DUR YR	PRINCIPAL PD DUR YR	MORTG BAL AT YR END
1	1146.24	73.56	9926.44	1147.92	40.44	9959.56
2	1137.32	82.48	9843.96	1143.02	45.34	9914.22
3	1127.32	92.48	9751.48	1137.52	50.84	9863.38
4	1116.10	103.70	9647.78	1131.36	57.00	9806.38
5	1103.53	116.27	9531.51	1124.44	63.92	9742.47
6	1089.43	130.37	9401.15	1116.69	71.67	9670.80
7	1073.62	146.18	9254.97	1108.00	80.36	9590.44
8	1055.90	163.90	9091.07	1098.26	90.10	9500.35
9	1036.02	183.78	8907.29	1087.34	101.02	9399.34
10	1013.74	206.06	8701.23	1075.08	113.28	9286.05
11	988.75	231.05	8470.18	1061.35	127.01	9159.04
12	960.74	259.06	8211.12	1045.95	142.41	9016.62
13	929.32	290.48	7920.64	1028.68	159.68	8856.94
14	894.10	325.70	7594.94	1009.32	179.04	8677.90
15	854.60	365.20	7229.74	987.61	200.75	8477.14
16	810.32	409.48	6820.26	963.26	225.10	8252.05
17	760.67	459.13	6361.13	935.97	252.39	7999.65
18	704.99	514.81	5846.32	905.36	283.00	7716.66
19	642.57	577.23	5269.09	871.05	317.31	7399.34
20	572.57	647.23	4621.87	832.57	355.79	7043.55
21	494.09	725.71	3896.16	789.43	398.93	6644.62
22	406.09	813.71	3082.45	741.05	447.31	6197.31
23	307.42	912.38	2170.07	686.81	501.55	5695.76
24	196.79	1023.01	1147.06	625.99	562.37	5133.40
25	72.74	1147.06	0.00	557.80	630.56	4502.84
26				481.34	707.02	3795.82
27				395.61	792.75	3003.07
28				299.48	888.88	2114.19
29				191.69	996.67	1117.52
30				70.84	1117.52	0.00

11¾%

25-YEAR TERM
MONTHLY PAYMENT: $103.48
ANNUAL PAYMENT: $1241.76

30-YEAR TERM
MONTHLY PAYMENT: $100.94
ANNUAL PAYMENT: $1211.28

YR	INTEREST PD DUR YR	PRINCIPAL PD DUR YR	MORTG BAL AT YR END	INTEREST PD DUR YR	PRINCIPAL PD DUR YR	MORTG BAL AT YR END
1	1171.29	70.47	9929.53	1172.97	38.31	9961.69
2	1162.55	79.21	9850.31	1168.22	43.06	9918.63
3	1152.72	89.04	9761.27	1162.88	48.41	9870.22
4	1141.68	100.08	9661.19	1156.87	54.41	9815.81
5	1129.26	112.50	9548.69	1150.12	61.16	9754.65
6	1115.31	126.45	9422.24	1142.54	68.74	9685.91
7	1099.62	142.14	9280.10	1134.01	77.27	9608.64
8	1081.99	159.77	9120.33	1124.42	86.86	9521.78
9	1062.17	179.59	8940.74	1113.65	97.63	9424.15
10	1039.90	201.86	8738.88	1101.54	109.74	9314.42
11	1014.86	226.90	8511.98	1087.93	123.35	9191.06
12	986.71	255.05	8256.93	1072.63	138.65	9052.41
13	955.08	286.68	7970.25	1055.43	155.85	8896.56
14	919.52	322.24	7648.01	1036.10	175.18	8721.38
15	879.55	362.21	7285.80	1014.37	196.91	8524.47
16	834.62	407.14	6878.66	989.95	221.33	8303.14
17	784.12	457.64	6421.02	962.49	248.79	8054.35
18	727.35	514.41	5906.61	931.63	279.65	7774.70
19	663.55	578.21	5328.40	896.95	314.33	7460.37
20	591.83	649.93	4678.47	857.96	353.32	7107.04
21	511.21	730.55	3947.92	814.13	397.15	6709.89
22	420.59	821.17	3126.75	764.87	446.41	6263.48
23	318.74	923.02	2203.72	709.49	501.79	5761.70
24	204.24	1037.52	1166.21	647.25	564.03	5197.67
25	75.55	1166.21	0.00	577.29	633.99	4563.68
26				498.65	712.63	3851.05
27				410.26	801.02	3050.03
28				310.90	900.38	2149.66
29				199.22	1012.06	1137.60
30				73.68	1137.60	0.00

Annual Amortization
Based on mortgage of $10,000

12%

	25-YEAR TERM			30-YEAR TERM		
	MONTHLY PAYMENT: $105.32			**MONTHLY PAYMENT: $102.86**		
	ANNUAL PAYMENT: $1263.84			**ANNUAL PAYMENT: $1234.32**		
	INTEREST	PRINCIPAL	MORTG BAL	INTEREST	PRINCIPAL	MORTG BAL
YR	PD DUR YR	PD DUR YR	AT YR END	PD DUR YR	PD DUR YR	AT YR END
1	1196.34	67.50	9932.50	1198.03	36.29	9963.71
2	1187.78	76.06	9856.44	1193.43	40.89	9922.82
3	1178.13	85.71	9770.73	1188.24	46.08	9876.75
4	1167.26	96.58	9674.15	1182.40	51.92	9824.83
5	1155.01	108.83	9565.32	1175.82	58.50	9766.32
6	1141.21	122.63	9442.69	1168.40	65.92	9700.40
7	1125.66	138.18	9304.51	1160.04	74.29	9626.11
8	1108.13	155.71	9148.80	1150.61	83.71	9542.41
9	1088.39	175.45	8973.35	1140.00	94.32	9448.08
10	1066.13	197.71	8775.64	1128.04	106.28	9341.80
11	1041.06	222.78	8552.86	1114.56	119.76	9222.04
12	1012.80	251.04	8301.82	1099.37	134.95	9087.08
13	980.97	282.87	8018.95	1082.25	152.07	8935.01
14	945.09	318.75	7700.20	1062.97	171.35	8763.66
15	904.67	359.17	7341.03	1041.23	193.09	8570.57
16	859.11	404.73	6936.30	1016.74	217.58	8353.00
17	807.87	456.06	6480.25	989.15	245.17	8107.83
18	749.95	513.89	5966.35	958.06	276.26	7831.56
19	684.77	579.07	5387.28	923.02	311.30	7520.26
20	611.33	652.51	4734.77	883.54	350.78	7169.48
21	528.58	735.26	3999.51	839.05	395.27	6774.22
22	435.33	828.51	3171.00	788.92	445.40	6328.82
23	330.25	933.59	2237.40	732.43	501.89	5826.93
24	211.85	1051.99	1185.41	668.78	565.54	5261.39
25	78.43	1185.41	0.00	597.06	637.26	4624.13
26				516.24	718.08	3906.05
27				425.17	809.15	3096.90
28				322.55	911.77	2185.12
29				206.91	1027.41	1157.71
30				76.61	1157.71	0.00

12¼%

	25-YEAR TERM			30-YEAR TERM		
	MONTHLY PAYMENT: $107.17			**MONTHLY PAYMENT: $104.79**		
	ANNUAL PAYMENT: $1286.04			**ANNUAL PAYMENT: $1257.48**		
	INTEREST	PRINCIPAL	MORTG BAL	INTEREST	PRINCIPAL	MORTG BAL
YR	PD DUR YR	PD DUR YR	AT YR END	PD DUR YR	PD DUR YR	AT YR END
1	1221.40	64.64	9935.36	1223.12	34.36	9965.64
2	1213.02	73.02	9862.34	1218.66	38.82	9926.82
3	1203.55	82.49	9779.85	1213.63	43.85	9882.97
4	1192.86	93.18	9686.67	1207.95	49.53	9833.44
5	1180.79	105.25	9581.42	1201.53	55.95	9777.49
6	1167.14	118.90	9462.52	1194.28	63.20	9714.29
7	1151.73	134.31	9328.21	1186.08	71.40	9642.89
8	1134.32	151.72	9176.50	1176.83	80.65	9562.24
9	1114.66	171.38	9005.11	1166.38	91.10	9471.14
10	1092.44	193.60	8811.52	1154.57	102.91	9368.22
11	1067.01	218.69	8592.83	1141.23	116.25	9251.97
12	1039.00	247.04	8345.79	1126.16	131.32	9120.65
13	1006.98	279.06	8066.74	1109.14	148.34	8972.31
14	970.81	315.23	7751.51	1089.91	167.57	8804.74
15	929.95	356.09	7395.42	1068.19	189.29	8615.45
16	883.80	402.24	6993.18	1043.66	213.82	8401.63
17	831.66	454.38	6538.81	1015.94	241.54	8160.09
18	772.77	513.27	6025.53	984.63	272.85	7887.24
19	706.24	579.80	5445.73	949.27	308.21	7579.03
20	631.09	654.95	4790.78	909.32	348.16	7230.87
21	546.19	739.85	4050.93	864.19	393.29	6837.58
22	450.29	835.75	3215.18	813.21	444.27	6393.31
23	341.97	944.07	2271.11	755.63	501.85	5891.46
24	219.60	1066.44	1204.67	690.58	566.90	5324.56
25	81.37	1204.67	0.00	617.10	640.38	4684.18
26				534.09	723.39	3960.79
27				440.33	817.15	3143.64
28				334.41	923.07	2220.58
29				214.77	1042.71	1177.86
30				79.62	1177.86	0.00

Annual Amortization
Based on mortgage of $10,000

12½%

	25-YEAR TERM MONTHLY PAYMENT: $109.04 ANNUAL PAYMENT: $1308.48			30-YEAR TERM MONTHLY PAYMENT: $106.73 ANNUAL PAYMENT: $1280.76		
YR	INTEREST PD DUR YR	PRINCIPAL PD DUR YR	MORTG BAL AT YR END	INTEREST PD DUR YR	PRINCIPAL PD DUR YR	MORTG BAL AT YR END
1	1246.59	61.89	9938.11	1248.23	32.53	9967.47
2	1238.39	70.09	9868.02	1243.92	36.84	9930.63
3	1229.11	79.37	9788.65	1239.04	41.72	9888.91
4	1218.60	89.88	9698.78	1233.52	47.24	9841.67
5	1206.70	101.78	9597.00	1227.26	53.50	9788.18
6	1193.23	115.25	9481.75	1220.18	60.58	9727.60
7	1177.96	130.52	9351.23	1212.16	68.60	9658.99
8	1160.68	147.80	9203.43	1203.07	77.69	9581.31
9	1141.11	167.37	9036.06	1192.79	87.97	9493.33
10	1118.95	189.53	8846.53	1181.14	99.62	9393.71
11	1093.85	214.63	8631.90	1167.95	112.81	9280.90
12	1065.43	243.05	8388.85	1153.01	127.75	9153.15
13	1033.25	275.23	8113.62	1136.09	144.67	9008.48
14	996.80	311.68	7801.94	1116.94	163.82	8844.65
15	955.53	352.95	7448.99	1095.24	185.52	8659.14
16	908.79	399.69	7049.30	1070.68	210.08	8449.05
17	855.87	452.61	6596.69	1042.86	237.90	8211.15
18	795.94	512.54	6084.15	1011.36	269.40	7941.75
19	728.07	580.41	5503.73	975.68	305.08	7636.67
20	651.21	657.27	4846.46	935.29	345.47	7291.20
21	564.18	744.30	4102.16	889.54	391.22	6899.98
22	465.62	842.86	3259.30	837.74	443.02	6456.96
23	354.01	954.47	2304.83	779.07	501.69	5955.27
24	227.63	1080.85	1223.98	712.64	568.12	5387.15
25	84.50	1223.98	0.00	637.41	643.35	4743.80
26				552.22	728.54	4015.27
27				455.75	825.01	3190.26
28				346.51	934.25	2256.01
29				222.80	1057.96	1198.05
30				82.71	1198.05	0.00

12¾%

	25-YEAR TERM MONTHLY PAYMENT: $110.91 ANNUAL PAYMENT: $1330.92			30-YEAR TERM MONTHLY PAYMENT: $108.67 ANNUAL PAYMENT: $1304.04		
YR	INTEREST PD DUR YR	PRINCIPAL PD DUR YR	MORTG BAL AT YR END	INTEREST PD DUR YR	PRINCIPAL PD DUR YR	MORTG BAL AT YR END
1	1271.67	59.25	9940.75	1273.25	30.79	9969.21
2	1263.66	67.26	9873.50	1269.09	34.95	9934.26
3	1254.57	76.35	9797.15	1264.36	39.68	9894.58
4	1244.24	86.68	9710.47	1258.99	45.05	9849.53
5	1232.52	98.40	9612.07	1252.90	51.14	9798.39
6	1219.22	111.70	9500.37	1245.99	58.05	9740.34
7	1204.11	126.81	9373.57	1238.14	65.90	9674.44
8	1186.97	143.95	9229.61	1229.23	74.81	9599.63
9	1167.50	163.42	9066.20	1219.11	84.93	9514.70
10	1145.40	185.52	8880.68	1207.61	96.41	9418.29
11	1120.32	210.60	8670.08	1194.59	109.45	9308.84
12	1091.84	239.08	8431.00	1179.79	124.25	9184.59
13	1059.51	271.41	8159.59	1162.99	141.05	9043.54
14	1022.81	308.11	7851.49	1143.92	160.12	8883.42
15	981.15	349.77	7501.72	1122.26	181.78	8701.64
16	933.85	397.07	7104.65	1097.68	206.36	8495.29
17	880.16	450.76	6653.89	1069.78	234.26	8261.03
18	819.21	511.71	6142.18	1038.10	265.94	7995.09
19	750.02	580.90	5561.28	1002.14	301.90	7693.20
20	671.47	659.45	4901.82	961.32	342.72	7350.48
21	582.29	748.63	4153.20	914.98	389.06	6961.42
22	481.06	849.86	3303.34	862.37	441.67	6519.75
23	366.14	964.78	2338.56	802.65	501.39	6018.35
24	235.69	1095.23	1243.33	734.85	569.19	5449.16
25	87.59	1243.33	0.00	657.88	646.16	4803.00
26				570.51	733.53	4069.47
27				471.32	832.72	3236.74
28				358.72	945.32	2291.44
29				230.89	1073.15	1218.27
30				85.77	1218.27	0.00

Annual Amortization
Based on mortgage of $10,000

13%

25-YEAR TERM
MONTHLY PAYMENT: $112.78
ANNUAL PAYMENT: $1353.36

30-YEAR TERM
MONTHLY PAYMENT: $110.62
ANNUAL PAYMENT: $1327.44

YR	INTEREST PD DUR YR	PRINCIPAL PD DUR YR	MORTG BAL AT YR END	INTEREST PD DUR YR	PRINCIPAL PD DUR YR	MORTG BAL AT YR END
1	1296.66	56.70	9943.30	1298.31	29.13	9970.87
2	1288.83	64.53	9878.77	1294.28	33.16	9937.71
3	1279.92	73.44	9805.33	1289.71	37.73	9899.98
4	1269.79	83.57	9721.76	1284.50	42.94	9857.03
5	1258.25	95.11	9626.65	1278.57	48.87	9808.17
6	1245.12	108.24	9518.42	1271.83	55.61	9752.55
7	1230.18	123.18	9395.24	1264.15	63.29	9689.26
8	1213.18	140.18	9255.06	1255.41	72.03	9617.23
9	1193.83	159.53	9095.54	1245.47	81.97	9535.26
10	1171.81	181.55	8913.99	1234.16	93.28	9441.98
11	1146.75	206.61	8707.38	1221.28	106.16	9335.82
12	1118.22	235.13	8472.26	1206.63	120.81	9215.01
13	1085.78	267.58	8204.67	1189.95	137.49	9077.52
14	1048.84	304.52	7900.16	1170.97	156.47	8921.05
15	1006.81	346.55	7553.61	1149.38	178.06	8742.99
16	958.98	394.38	7159.23	1124.80	202.64	8540.34
17	904.64	448.82	6710.41	1096.83	230.61	8309.73
18	842.59	510.77	6199.63	1064.99	262.45	8047.28
19	772.00	581.28	5618.36	1028.77	298.67	7748.61
20	691.85	661.51	4956.85	987.54	339.90	7408.71
21	600.54	752.82	4204.03	940.62	386.82	7021.89
22	496.65	856.73	3347.29	887.23	440.21	6581.68
23	378.37	974.99	2372.30	826.47	500.97	6080.70
24	243.79	1109.57	1262.73	757.32	570.12	5510.58
25	90.63	1262.73	0.00	678.62	648.82	4861.76
26				589.06	738.38	4123.38
27				487.14	840.30	3283.08
28				371.15	956.29	2326.79
29				239.15	1088.29	1238.51
30				88.93	1238.51	0.00

13¼%

25-YEAR TERM
MONTHLY PAYMENT: $114.67
ANNUAL PAYMENT: $1376.04

30-YEAR TERM
MONTHLY PAYMENT: $112.58
ANNUAL PAYMENT: $1350.96

YR	INTEREST PD DUR YR	PRINCIPAL PD DUR YR	MORTG BAL AT YR END	INTEREST PD DUR YR	PRINCIPAL PD DUR YR	MORTG BAL AT YR END
1	1321.78	54.26	9945.74	1323.40	27.56	9972.44
2	1314.14	61.90	9883.84	1319.52	31.44	9940.99
3	1305.42	70.62	9813.23	1315.09	35.87	9905.12
4	1295.48	80.56	9732.66	1310.03	40.93	9864.19
5	1284.13	91.91	9640.75	1304.27	46.69	9817.50
6	1271.18	104.86	9535.89	1297.69	53.27	9764.24
7	1256.41	119.63	9416.27	1290.19	60.77	9703.47
8	1239.56	136.48	9279.79	1281.63	69.33	9634.14
9	1220.34	155.70	9124.09	1271.87	79.09	9555.04
10	1198.41	177.63	8946.46	1260.73	90.23	9464.81
11	1173.39	202.65	8743.81	1248.02	102.94	9361.87
12	1144.85	231.19	8512.62	1233.52	117.44	9244.42
13	1112.29	263.75	8248.87	1216.97	133.99	9110.44
14	1075.14	300.90	7947.96	1198.10	152.86	8957.58
15	1032.75	343.29	7604.67	1176.57	174.39	8783.19
16	984.40	391.64	7213.03	1152.01	198.95	8584.24
17	929.24	446.80	6766.23	1123.99	226.97	8357.27
18	866.31	509.73	6256.50	1092.02	258.94	8098.33
19	794.51	581.53	5674.97	1055.55	295.41	7802.91
20	712.60	663.44	5011.53	1013.94	337.02	7465.89
21	619.16	756.88	4254.64	966.47	384.49	7081.40
22	512.55	863.49	3391.15	912.31	438.65	6642.75
23	390.92	985.12	2406.04	850.53	500.43	6142.32
24	252.17	1123.87	1282.17	780.04	570.92	5571.40
25	93.87	1282.17	0.00	699.63	651.33	4920.07
26				607.89	743.07	4177.00
27				503.23	847.73	3329.26
28				383.82	967.14	2362.13
29				247.60	1103.36	1258.77
30				92.19	1258.77	0.00

Annual Amortization
Based on mortgage of $10,000

13½%

	25-YEAR TERM			30-YEAR TERM		
	MONTHLY PAYMENT: $116.56					MONTHLY PAYMENT: $114.54
	ANNUAL PAYMENT: $1398.72					ANNUAL PAYMENT: $1374.48
YR	INTEREST PD DUR YR	PRINCIPAL PD DUR YR	MORTG BAL AT YR END	INTEREST PD DUR YR	PRINCIPAL PD DUR YR	MORTG BAL AT YR END
1	1346.81	51.91	9948.09	1348.41	26.07	9973.93
2	1339.35	59.37	9888.73	1344.67	29.81	9944.12
3	1330.82	67.89	9820.83	1340.38	34.10	9910.02
4	1321.07	77.65	9743.18	1335.48	39.00	9871.02
5	1309.91	88.81	9654.38	1329.88	44.60	9826.42
6	1297.15	101.57	9552.81	1323.47	51.01	9775.42
7	1282.56	116.16	9436.65	1316.14	58.34	9717.08
8	1265.87	132.85	9303.81	1307.76	66.72	9650.37
9	1246.79	151.93	9151.87	1298.18	76.30	9574.06
10	1224.96	173.76	8978.11	1287.22	87.26	9486.80
11	1199.99	198.73	8779.38	1274.68	99.80	9387.00
12	1171.44	227.58	8552.11	1260.34	114.14	9272.86
13	1138.79	259.93	8292.17	1243.94	130.54	9142.32
14	1101.44	297.28	7994.89	1225.18	149.30	8993.02
15	1058.73	339.99	7654.90	1203.73	170.75	8822.27
16	1009.88	388.84	7266.06	1179.20	195.28	8627.00
17	954.02	444.70	6821.36	1151.15	223.33	8403.66
18	890.12	508.60	6312.76	1119.06	255.42	8148.24
19	817.05	581.67	5731.09	1082.36	292.12	7856.12
20	733.48	665.24	5065.85	1040.39	334.09	7522.03
21	637.90	760.82	4305.03	992.39	382.09	7139.94
22	528.59	870.13	3434.91	937.49	436.99	6702.96
23	403.58	995.14	2439.76	874.71	499.77	6203.19
24	260.60	1138.12	1301.64	802.91	571.57	5631.62
25	97.08	1301.64	0.00	720.79	653.69	4977.92
26				626.87	747.61	4230.31
27				519.45	855.03	3375.28
28				396.61	977.87	2397.41
29				256.11	1118.37	1279.05
30				95.43	1279.05	0.00

13¾%

	25-YEAR TERM			30-YEAR TERM		
	MONTHLY PAYMENT: $118.47					MONTHLY PAYMENT: $116.51
	ANNUAL PAYMENT: $1421.64					ANNUAL PAYMENT: $1398.12
YR	INTEREST PD DUR YR	PRINCIPAL PD DUR YR	MORTG BAL AT YR END	INTEREST PD DUR YR	PRINCIPAL PD DUR YR	MORTG BAL AT YR END
1	1371.99	49.65	9950.35	1373.47	24.65	9975.35
2	1364.71	56.93	9893.42	1369.86	28.26	9947.09
3	1356.38	65.26	9828.16	1365.72	32.40	9914.69
4	1346.81	74.83	9753.33	1360.97	37.15	9877.54
5	1335.85	85.79	9667.54	1355.53	42.59	9834.95
6	1323.29	98.36	9569.19	1349.29	48.83	9786.11
7	1308.87	112.77	9456.42	1342.13	55.99	9730.13
8	1292.35	129.29	9327.13	1333.93	64.19	9665.94
9	1273.41	148.23	9178.90	1324.53	73.59	9592.35
10	1251.69	169.95	9008.95	1313.75	84.37	9507.98
11	1226.80	194.84	8814.11	1301.39	96.73	9411.24
12	1198.25	223.39	8590.72	1287.21	110.91	9300.34
13	1165.52	256.12	8334.60	1270.97	127.15	9173.18
14	1128.00	293.64	8040.96	1252.34	145.78	9027.40
15	1084.98	336.66	7704.30	1230.98	167.14	8860.26
16	1035.66	385.98	7318.32	1206.49	191.63	8668.63
17	979.11	442.53	6875.79	1178.42	219.70	8448.93
18	914.28	507.36	6368.43	1146.23	251.89	8197.04
19	839.95	581.69	5786.73	1109.33	288.79	7908.24
20	754.72	666.92	5119.81	1067.02	331.10	7577.14
21	657.02	764.62	4355.19	1018.51	379.61	7197.53
22	545.00	876.64	3478.55	962.89	435.23	6762.30
23	416.56	1005.08	2473.47	899.13	498.99	6263.31
24	269.31	1152.33	1321.15	826.03	572.09	5691.22
25	100.49	1321.15	0.00	742.21	655.91	5035.31
26				646.12	752.00	4283.31
27				535.95	862.17	3421.13
28				409.63	988.49	2432.65
29				264.81	1133.31	1299.34
30				98.78	1299.34	0.00

Annual Amortization
Based on mortgage of $10,000

14%

25-YEAR TERM
MONTHLY PAYMENT: $120.38
ANNUAL PAYMENT: $1444.56

30-YEAR TERM
MONTHLY PAYMENT: $118.49
ANNUAL PAYMENT: $1421.88

YR	INTEREST PD DUR YR	PRINCIPAL PD DUR YR	MORTG BAL AT YR END	INTEREST PD DUR YR	PRINCIPAL PD DUR YR	MORTG BAL AT YR END
1	1397.08	47.48	9952.52	1398.58	23.30	9976.70
2	1389.99	54.57	9897.94	1395.10	26.78	9949.91
3	1381.83	62.73	9835.22	1391.10	30.78	9919.13
4	1372.47	72.09	9763.12	1386.50	35.38	9883.75
5	1361.70	82.86	9680.26	1381.21	40.67	9843.08
6	1349.33	95.23	9585.03	1375.14	46.74	9796.34
7	1335.10	109.46	9475.58	1368.16	53.72	9742.62
8	1318.76	125.80	9349.77	1360.14	61.74	9680.88
9	1299.97	144.59	9205.18	1350.92	70.96	9609.92
10	1278.38	166.18	9039.00	1340.32	81.56	9528.36
11	1253.56	191.00	8848.00	1328.14	93.74	9434.62
12	1225.03	219.53	8628.47	1314.14	107.74	9326.89
13	1192.25	252.31	8376.16	1298.05	123.83	9203.06
14	1154.57	289.99	8086.17	1279.56	142.32	9060.74
15	1111.26	333.30	7752.87	1258.30	163.58	8897.16
16	1061.49	383.07	7369.80	1233.88	188.00	8709.16
17	1004.28	440.28	6929.52	1205.80	216.08	8493.08
18	938.52	506.04	6423.48	1173.53	248.35	8244.72
19	862.95	581.61	5841.87	1136.44	285.44	7959.28
20	776.09	668.47	5173.41	1093.81	328.07	7631.22
21	676.26	768.30	4405.11	1044.82	377.06	7254.15
22	561.52	883.04	3522.07	988.51	433.37	6820.78
23	429.65	1014.91	2507.16	923.78	498.10	6322.68
24	278.08	1166.48	1340.68	849.40	572.48	5750.20
25	103.88	1340.68	0.00	763.90	657.98	5092.23
26				665.64	756.24	4335.98
27				552.70	869.18	3466.80
28				422.90	998.98	2467.82
29				273.71	1148.17	1319.65
30				102.23	1319.65	0.00

14¼%

25-YEAR TERM
MONTHLY PAYMENT: $122.29
ANNUAL PAYMENT: $1467.48

30-YEAR TERM
MONTHLY PAYMENT: $120.47
ANNUAL PAYMENT: $1445.64

YR	INTEREST PD DUR YR	PRINCIPAL PD DUR YR	MORTG BAL AT YR END	INTEREST PD DUR YR	PRINCIPAL PD DUR YR	MORTG BAL AT YR END
1	1422.08	45.40	9954.60	1423.61	22.03	9977.97
2	1415.17	52.31	9902.29	1420.26	25.38	9952.60
3	1407.21	60.27	9842.01	1416.40	29.24	9923.36
4	1398.03	69.45	9772.57	1411.95	33.69	9889.66
5	1387.47	80.01	9692.55	1406.82	38.82	9850.85
6	1375.28	92.19	9600.36	1400.91	44.73	9806.12
7	1361.26	106.22	9494.14	1394.11	51.53	9754.59
8	1345.09	122.39	9371.75	1386.27	59.37	9695.21
9	1326.47	141.01	9230.74	1377.23	68.41	9626.80
10	1305.01	162.47	9068.26	1366.82	78.82	9547.98
11	1280.28	187.20	8881.06	1354.82	90.82	9457.17
12	1251.79	215.69	8665.38	1341.00	104.64	9352.53
13	1218.97	248.51	8416.86	1325.08	120.56	9231.97
14	1181.15	286.33	8130.53	1306.73	138.91	9093.06
15	1137.57	329.91	7800.62	1285.59	160.05	8933.01
16	1087.36	380.12	7420.50	1261.23	184.41	8748.60
17	1029.52	437.96	6982.54	1233.17	212.47	8536.13
18	962.86	504.62	6477.92	1200.83	244.81	8291.32
19	886.07	581.41	5896.51	1163.58	282.06	8009.26
20	797.59	669.89	5226.62	1120.65	324.99	7684.27
21	695.64	771.84	4454.78	1071.19	374.45	7309.82
22	578.18	889.30	3565.47	1014.21	431.43	6878.39
23	442.84	1024.64	2540.83	948.55	497.09	6381.30
24	286.90	1180.58	1360.25	872.90	572.74	5808.56
25	107.23	1360.25	0.00	785.74	659.90	5148.66
26				685.31	760.33	4388.33
27				569.60	876.04	3512.29
28				436.28	1009.36	2502.93
29				282.67	1162.97	1339.96
30				105.68	1339.96	0.00

Annual Amortization
Based on mortgage of $10,000

14¹/₂%

YR	INTEREST PD DUR YR	PRINCIPAL PD DUR YR	MORTG BAL AT YR END	INTEREST PD DUR YR	PRINCIPAL PD DUR YR	MORTG BAL AT YR END
1	1447.23	43.41	9956.59	1448.71	20.81	9979.19
2	1440.51	50.13	9906.46	1445.48	24.04	9955.14
3	1432.73	57.91	9848.55	1441.75	27.77	9927.38
4	1423.76	66.88	9781.67	1437.45	32.07	9895.30
5	1413.39	77.25	9704.41	1432.47	37.05	9858.26
6	1401.41	89.23	9615.18	1426.73	42.79	9815.47
7	1387.57	103.07	9512.12	1420.10	49.42	9766.04
8	1371.60	119.04	9393.07	1412.43	57.09	9708.96
9	1353.14	137.50	9255.57	1403.58	65.94	9643.02
10	1331.82	158.82	9096.76	1393.36	76.16	9566.86
11	1307.20	183.44	8913.32	1381.55	87.97	9478.99
12	1278.76	211.88	8701.44	1367.92	101.60	9377.29
13	1245.91	244.73	8456.71	1352.16	117.36	9259.93
14	1207.97	282.67	8174.04	1333.97	135.55	9124.38
15	1164.15	326.49	7847.55	1312.95	156.57	8967.82
16	1113.04	377.11	7470.43	1288.68	180.84	8786.98
17	1055.06	435.58	7034.86	1260.64	208.88	8578.10
18	987.63	503.11	6531.75	1228.26	241.26	8336.84
19	909.53	581.11	5950.64	1190.86	278.66	8058.18
20	819.44	671.20	5279.45	1147.65	321.87	7736.31
21	715.38	775.26	4504.19	1097.75	371.77	7364.55
22	595.19	895.45	3608.74	1040.12	429.40	6935.14
23	456.36	1034.28	2574.46	973.54	495.98	6439.17
24	296.01	1194.63	1379.84	896.65	572.87	5866.30
25	110.80	1379.84	0.00	807.84	661.68	5204.61
26				705.25	764.27	4440.34
27				586.76	882.76	3557.59
28				419.90	1019.62	2537.97
29				291.83	1177.69	1360.28
30				109.24	1360.28	0.00

14³/₄%

YR	INTEREST PD DUR YR	PRINCIPAL PD DUR YR	MORTG BAL AT YR END	INTEREST PD DUR YR	PRINCIPAL PD DUR YR	MORTG BAL AT YR END
1	1472.31	41.49	9958.51	1473.73	19.67	9980.33
2	1465.76	48.04	9910.47	1470.63	22.77	9957.56
3	1458.18	55.62	9854.85	1467.03	26.37	9931.20
4	1449.39	64.41	9790.44	1462.87	30.53	9900.67
5	1439.22	74.58	9715.87	1458.05	35.35	9865.32
6	1427.45	86.35	9629.52	1452.47	40.93	9824.39
7	1413.82	99.98	9529.53	1446.01	47.39	9777.00
8	1398.03	115.77	9413.76	1438.53	54.87	9722.13
9	1379.75	134.05	9279.71	1429.86	63.54	9658.59
10	1358.58	155.22	9124.49	1419.83	73.57	9585.02
11	1334.08	179.72	8944.77	1408.21	85.19	9499.83
12	1305.70	208.10	8736.67	1394.76	98.64	9401.19
13	1272.84	240.96	8495.71	1379.19	114.21	9286.98
14	1234.80	279.00	8216.71	1361.15	132.25	9154.73
15	1190.75	323.05	7893.66	1340.27	153.13	9001.61
16	1139.74	374.06	7519.59	1316.10	177.30	8824.31
17	1080.68	433.12	7086.47	1288.10	205.30	8619.01
18	1012.29	501.51	6584.96	1255.69	237.71	8381.30
19	933.11	580.69	6004.26	1218.15	275.25	8106.05
20	841.42	672.38	5331.88	1174.70	318.70	7787.35
21	735.25	778.55	4553.34	1124.38	369.02	7418.32
22	612.33	901.47	3651.87	1066.11	427.29	6991.03
23	469.99	1043.81	2608.06	998.64	494.76	6496.27
24	305.19	1208.61	1399.44	920.53	572.87	5923.40
25	114.36	1399.44	0.00	830.07	663.33	5260.07
26				725.34	768.06	4492.01
27				604.07	889.33	3602.68
28				463.65	1029.75	2572.93
29				301.06	1192.34	1380.60
30				112.80	1380.60	0.00

Annual Amortization
Based on mortgage of $10,000

15%

25-YEAR TERM
MONTHLY PAYMENT: $128.08
ANNUAL PAYMENT: $1536.96

30-YEAR TERM
MONTHLY PAYMENT: $126.44
ANNUAL PAYMENT: $1517.28

YR	INTEREST PD DUR YR	PRINCIPAL PD DUR YR	MORTG BAL AT YR END	INTEREST PD DUR YR	PRINCIPAL PD DUR YR	MORTG BAL AT YR END
1	1497.31	39.65	9960.35	1498.70	18.58	9981.42
2	1490.94	46.02	9914.33	1495.72	21.56	9959.86
3	1483.54	53.42	9860.91	1492.25	25.03	9934.84
4	1474.95	62.01	9798.90	1488.23	29.05	9905.78
5	1464.98	71.98	9726.92	1483.56	33.72	9872.06
6	1453.41	83.55	9643.37	1478.14	39.14	9832.92
7	1439.98	96.98	9546.39	1471.85	45.43	9787.49
8	1424.39	112.57	9433.82	1464.54	52.74	9734.75
9	1406.30	130.66	9303.16	1456.06	61.22	9673.53
10	1385.29	151.67	9151.49	1446.22	71.06	9602.48
11	1360.91	176.05	8975.44	1434.80	82.48	9520.00
12	1332.61	204.35	8771.09	1421.54	95.74	9424.26
13	1299.76	237.20	8533.88	1406.15	111.13	9313.13
14	1261.63	275.33	8258.55	1388.29	128.99	9184.14
15	1217.36	319.60	7938.95	1367.55	149.73	9034.41
16	1165.99	370.97	7567.98	1343.48	173.80	8860.61
17	1106.35	430.61	7137.37	1315.54	201.74	8658.87
18	1037.13	499.83	6637.54	1283.11	234.17	8424.70
19	956.72	580.18	6057.36	1245.47	271.81	8152.89
20	863.51	673.45	5383.92	1201.77	315.51	7837.38
21	755.25	781.71	4602.21	1151.05	366.23	7471.16
22	629.59	907.37	3694.85	1092.18	425.10	7046.06
23	483.73	1053.23	2641.62	1023.85	493.43	6552.63
24	314.42	1222.54	1419.07	944.52	572.76	5979.87
25	117.89	1419.07	0.00	852.45	664.83	5315.04
26				745.58	771.70	4543.33
27				621.52	895.76	3647.58
28				477.52	1039.76	2607.82
29				310.38	1206.90	1400.92
30				116.36	1400.92	0.00

15¼%

25-YEAR TERM
MONTHLY PAYMENT: $130.03
ANNUAL PAYMENT: $1560.36

30-YEAR TERM
MONTHLY PAYMENT: $128.45
ANNUAL PAYMENT: $1541.40

YR	INTEREST PD DUR YR	PRINCIPAL PD DUR YR	MORTG BAL AT YR END	INTEREST PD DUR YR	PRINCIPAL PD DUR YR	MORTG BAL AT YR END
1	1522.47	37.89	9962.11	1523.86	17.54	9982.46
2	1516.28	44.08	9918.03	1520.99	20.41	9962.04
3	1509.06	51.30	9866.73	1517.65	23.75	9938.29
4	1500.67	59.69	9807.04	1513.76	27.64	9910.65
5	1490.90	69.46	9737.58	1509.24	32.16	9878.49
6	1479.54	80.82	9656.76	1503.97	37.43	9841.06
7	1466.31	94.05	9562.71	1497.85	43.55	9797.51
8	1450.92	109.44	9453.28	1490.73	50.67	9746.84
9	1433.02	127.34	9325.93	1482.43	58.97	9687.87
10	1412.18	148.18	9177.76	1472.79	68.61	9619.26
11	1387.94	172.42	9005.33	1461.56	79.84	9539.42
12	1359.72	200.64	8804.69	1448.50	92.90	9446.51
13	1326.89	233.47	8571.23	1433.29	108.11	9338.41
14	1288.69	271.67	8299.56	1415.60	125.80	9212.61
15	1244.24	316.12	7983.44	1395.02	146.38	9066.23
16	1192.52	367.84	7615.60	1371.07	170.33	8895.91
17	1132.33	428.03	7187.57	1343.20	198.20	8697.71
18	1062.09	498.07	6689.51	1310.77	230.63	8467.08
19	980.80	579.56	6109.94	1273.03	268.37	8198.71
20	885.97	674.39	5435.55	1229.12	312.28	7886.43
21	775.62	784.74	4650.82	1178.03	363.37	7523.06
22	647.22	913.14	3737.68	1118.57	422.83	7100.23
23	497.81	1062.55	2675.13	1049.39	492.01	6608.22
24	323.95	1236.41	1438.72	968.88	572.52	6035.70
25	121.64	1438.72	0.00	875.20	666.20	5369.50
26				766.20	775.20	4594.30
27				639.36	902.04	3692.26
28				491.76	1049.64	2642.62
29				320.01	1221.39	1421.23
30				120.17	1421.23	0.00

Annual Amortization
Based on mortgage of $10,000

15 1/2%

	25-YEAR TERM MONTHLY PAYMENT: $131.97 ANNUAL PAYMENT: $1583.64			30-YEAR TERM MONTHLY PAYMENT: $130.45 ANNUAL PAYMENT: $1565.40		
YR	INTEREST PD DUR YR	PRINCIPAL PD DUR YR	MORTG BAL AT YR END	INTEREST PD DUR YR	PRINCIPAL PD DUR YR	MORTG BAL AT YR END
1	1547.45	36.19	9963.81	1548.84	16.56	9983.44
2	1541.42	42.22	9921.59	1546.08	19.32	9964.11
3	1534.39	49.25	9872.34	1542.86	22.54	9941.57
4	1526.19	57.45	9814.89	1539.11	26.29	9915.28
5	1516.62	67.02	9747.87	1534.73	30.67	9884.61
6	1505.47	78.17	9669.70	1529.62	35.78	9848.84
7	1492.45	91.19	9578.51	1523.67	41.73	9807.10
8	1477.27	106.37	9472.13	1516.72	48.68	9758.42
9	1459.56	124.08	9348.05	1508.61	56.79	9701.63
10	1438.90	144.74	9203.31	1499.16	66.24	9635.39
11	1414.80	168.84	9034.46	1488.13	77.27	9558.12
12	1386.68	196.96	8837.51	1475.26	90.14	9467.98
13	1353.89	229.75	8607.76	1460.25	105.15	9362.84
14	1315.64	268.00	8339.76	1442.75	122.65	9240.18
15	1271.02	312.62	8027.13	1422.33	143.07	9097.11
16	1218.96	364.68	7662.46	1398.50	166.90	8930.22
17	1158.25	425.39	7237.06	1370.72	194.68	8735.53
18	1087.42	496.22	6740.84	1338.30	227.10	8508.44
19	1004.80	578.84	6162.00	1300.49	264.91	8243.53
20	908.42	675.22	5486.78	1256.38	309.02	7934.51
21	796.00	787.64	4699.14	1204.93	360.47	7574.04
22	664.85	918.79	3780.35	1144.91	420.49	7153.56
23	511.88	1071.76	2708.58	1074.90	490.50	6663.06
24	333.43	1250.21	1458.37	993.24	572.16	6090.90
25	125.27	1458.37	0.00	897.97	667.43	5423.47
26				786.84	778.56	4644.91
27				657.22	908.18	3736.73
28				506.00	1059.40	2677.33
29				329.61	1235.79	1441.54
30				123.86	1441.54	0.00

15 3/4%

	25-YEAR TERM MONTHLY PAYMENT: $133.93 ANNUAL PAYMENT: $1607.16			30-YEAR TERM MONTHLY PAYMENT: $132.46 ANNUAL PAYMENT: $1589.52		
YR	INTEREST PD DUR YR	PRINCIPAL PD DUR YR	MORTG BAL AT YR END	INTEREST PD DUR YR	PRINCIPAL PD DUR YR	MORTG BAL AT YR END
1	1572.59	34.57	9965.43	1573.88	15.64	9984.36
2	1566.73	40.43	9925.00	1571.23	18.29	9966.08
3	1559.88	47.28	9877.72	1568.14	21.38	9944.69
4	1551.88	55.28	9822.44	1564.51	25.01	9919.69
5	1542.51	64.65	9757.79	1560.28	29.24	9890.45
6	1531.56	75.60	9682.19	1555.33	34.19	9856.25
7	1518.76	88.40	9593.79	1549.53	39.99	9816.27
8	1503.78	103.38	9490.41	1542.76	46.76	9769.51
9	1486.27	120.89	9369.52	1534.84	54.68	9714.83
10	1465.80	141.36	9228.16	1525.58	63.94	9650.89
11	1441.85	165.31	9062.85	1514.75	74.77	9576.12
12	1413.85	193.31	8869.54	1502.08	87.44	9488.68
13	1381.11	226.05	8643.49	1487.27	102.25	9386.44
14	1342.82	264.34	8379.14	1469.96	119.56	9266.87
15	1298.04	309.12	8070.03	1449.70	139.82	9127.06
16	1245.68	361.48	7708.55	1426.02	163.50	8963.56
17	1184.46	422.70	7285.85	1398.33	191.19	8772.37
18	1112.86	494.30	6791.55	1365.94	223.58	8548.79
19	1029.13	578.03	6213.52	1328.07	261.45	8287.35
20	931.23	675.93	5537.59	1283.79	305.73	7981.62
21	816.74	790.42	4747.17	1232.00	357.52	7624.10
22	682.85	924.31	3822.86	1171.45	418.07	7206.03
23	526.29	1080.87	2741.99	1100.63	488.89	6717.15
24	343.21	1263.95	1478.04	1017.83	571.69	6145.45
25	129.12	1478.04	0.00	920.99	668.53	5476.92
26				807.75	781.77	4695.16
27				675.34	914.18	3780.98
28				520.49	1069.03	2711.95
29				339.42	1250.10	1461.85
30				127.67	1461.85	0.00

Annual Amortization
Based on mortgage of $10,000

16%

25-YEAR TERM
MONTHLY PAYMENT: $135.89
ANNUAL PAYMENT: $1630.68

30-YEAR TERM
MONTHLY PAYMENT: $134.48
ANNUAL PAYMENT: $1613.76

	25-YEAR TERM			30-YEAR TERM		
YR	INTEREST PD DUR YR	PRINCIPAL PD DUR YR	MORTG BAL AT YR END	INTEREST PD DUR YR	PRINCIPAL PD DUR YR	MORTG BAL AT YR END
1	1597.66	33.02	9966.98	1599.00	14.76	9985.24
2	1591.97	38.71	9928.27	1596.46	17.30	9967.94
3	1585.31	45.37	9882.90	1593.48	20.28	9947.65
4	1577.49	53.19	9829.71	1589.98	23.78	9923.88
5	1568.33	62.35	9767.35	1585.89	28.87	9896.00
6	1557.58	73.10	9694.26	1581.08	32.68	9863.33
7	1544.99	85.69	9608.57	1575.46	38.30	9825.02
8	1530.23	100.45	9508.12	1568.86	44.90	9780.12
9	1512.92	117.76	9390.36	1561.12	52.64	9727.48
10	1492.64	138.04	9252.32	1552.05	61.71	9665.78
11	1468.86	161.82	9090.50	1541.42	72.34	9593.44
12	1440.98	189.70	8900.80	1528.96	84.80	9508.64
13	1408.30	222.38	8678.42	1514.35	99.41	9409.24
14	1369.90	260.69	8417.73	1497.23	116.53	9292.71
15	1325.08	305.60	8112.13	1477.15	136.61	9156.10
16	1272.44	358.24	7753.89	1453.62	160.14	8995.96
17	1210.72	419.96	7333.93	1426.03	187.73	8808.23
18	1138.38	492.30	6841.63	1393.69	220.07	8588.17
19	1053.57	577.11	6264.52	1355.78	257.98	8330.19
20	954.15	676.53	5587.98	1311.34	302.42	8027.77
21	837.60	793.08	4794.90	1259.24	354.52	7673.25
22	700.98	929.70	3865.20	1198.17	415.59	7257.66
23	540.81	1089.87	2775.33	1126.58	487.18	6770.48
24	353.06	1277.62	1497.71	1042.65	571.11	6199.37
25	132.97	1497.71	0.00	944.26	669.50	5529.87
26				828.93	784.83	4745.04
27				693.72	920.04	3825.00
28				535.23	1078.53	2746.47
29				349.43	1264.33	1482.14
30				131.62	1482.14	0.00

16¼%

25-YEAR TERM
MONTHLY PAYMENT: $137.85
ANNUAL PAYMENT: $1654.20

30-YEAR TERM
MONTHLY PAYMENT: $136.49
ANNUAL PAYMENT: $1637.88

	25-YEAR TERM			30-YEAR TERM		
YR	INTEREST PD DUR YR	PRINCIPAL PD DUR YR	MORTG BAL AT YR END	INTEREST PD DUR YR	PRINCIPAL PD DUR YR	MORTG BAL AT YR END
1	1622.67	31.53	9968.47	1623.95	13.93	9986.07
2	1617.15	37.05	9931.42	1621.51	16.37	9969.70
3	1610.66	43.54	9887.88	1618.64	19.24	9950.47
4	1603.02	51.17	9836.71	1615.27	22.61	9927.86
5	1594.07	60.13	9776.57	1611.32	26.56	9901.30
6	1583.53	70.67	9705.91	1606.66	31.22	9870.08
7	1571.16	83.04	9622.86	1601.19	36.69	9833.39
8	1556.61	97.59	9525.27	1594.77	43.11	9790.28
9	1539.51	114.69	9410.58	1587.22	50.66	9739.61
10	1519.43	134.77	9275.81	1578.34	59.54	9680.07
11	1495.82	158.38	9117.43	1567.91	69.97	9610.11
12	1468.07	186.13	8931.30	1555.66	82.22	9527.88
13	1435.47	218.73	8712.57	1541.25	96.63	9431.25
14	1397.16	257.04	8455.53	1524.33	113.55	9317.70
15	1352.13	302.07	8153.46	1504.44	133.44	9184.25
16	1299.12	354.98	7798.48	1481.06	156.82	9027.43
17	1237.04	417.16	7381.32	1453.59	184.29	8843.15
18	1163.67	490.23	6891.08	1421.31	216.57	8626.58
19	1078.09	576.11	6314.98	1383.37	254.51	8372.07
20	977.18	677.02	5637.95	1338.79	299.09	8072.98
21	858.59	795.61	4842.34	1286.40	351.48	7721.50
22	719.22	934.98	3907.37	1224.84	413.04	7308.46
23	555.45	1098.75	2808.61	1152.48	485.40	6823.06
24	362.98	1291.22	1517.39	1067.46	570.42	6252.64
25	136.81	1517.39	0.00	967.54	670.34	5582.31
26				850.12	787.76	4794.55
27				712.13	925.75	3868.80
28				549.97	1087.91	2780.89
29				359.41	1278.47	1502.42
30				135.46	1502.42	0.00

Annual Amortization
Based on mortgage of $10,000

16½%

25-YEAR TERM
MONTHLY PAYMENT: $139.82
ANNUAL PAYMENT: $1677.84

30-YEAR TERM
MONTHLY PAYMENT: $138.51
ANNUAL PAYMENT: $1662.12

YR	INTEREST PD DUR YR	PRINCIPAL PD DUR YR	MORTG BAL AT YR END	INTEREST PD DUR YR	PRINCIPAL PD DUR YR	MORTG BAL AT YR END
1	1647.74	30.10	9969.90	1648.98	13.14	9986.86
2	1642.38	35.46	9934.43	1646.64	15.48	9971.38
3	1636.06	41.78	9892.66	1643.88	18.24	9953.14
4	1628.62	49.22	9843.44	1640.63	21.49	9931.65
5	1619.86	57.98	9785.46	1636.81	25.31	9906.34
6	1609.53	68.31	9717.15	1632.30	29.82	9876.51
7	1597.37	80.47	9636.68	1626.99	35.13	9841.38
8	1583.04	94.80	9541.88	1620.73	41.39	9800.00
9	1566.16	111.68	9430.21	1613.36	48.76	9751.24
10	1546.28	131.56	9298.64	1604.68	57.44	9693.80
11	1522.85	154.99	9143.65	1594.45	67.67	9626.14
12	1495.25	182.59	8961.06	1582.40	79.72	9546.42
13	1462.15	215.11	8745.95	1568.21	93.91	9452.51
14	1424.43	253.41	8492.54	1551.49	110.63	9341.88
15	1379.01	298.53	8194.01	1531.79	130.33	9211.55
16	1326.15	351.69	7842.32	1508.58	153.54	9058.01
17	1263.67	414.32	7428.00	1481.24	180.88	8877.12
18	1189.75	488.09	6939.91	1449.03	213.09	8664.03
19	1102.83	575.01	6364.90	1411.08	251.04	8413.00
20	1000.47	677.40	5687.50	1366.38	295.74	8117.26
21	879.82	798.02	4889.48	1313.72	348.40	7768.86
22	737.72	940.12	3949.35	1251.68	410.44	7358.43
23	570.31	1107.53	2841.82	1178.60	483.52	6874.90
24	373.09	1304.75	1537.08	1092.50	569.62	6305.28
25	140.76	1537.08	0.00	991.07	671.05	5634.23
26				871.57	790.55	4843.68
27				730.80	931.32	3912.36
28				564.96	1097.16	2815.21
29				369.60	1292.52	1522.68
30				139.44	1522.68	0.00

16¾%

25-YEAR TERM
MONTHLY PAYMENT: $141.80
ANNUAL PAYMENT: $1701.60

30-YEAR TERM
MONTHLY PAYMENT: $140.54
ANNUAL PAYMENT: $1686.48

YR	INTEREST PD DUR YR	PRINCIPAL PD DUR YR	MORTG BAL AT YR END	INTEREST PD DUR YR	PRINCIPAL PD DUR YR	MORTG BAL AT YR END
1	1672.86	28.74	9971.26	1674.08	12.40	9987.60
2	1667.66	33.94	9937.33	1671.84	14.64	9972.96
3	1661.52	40.08	9897.25	1669.19	17.29	9955.67
4	1654.27	47.33	9849.92	1666.06	20.42	9935.25
5	1645.70	55.90	9794.02	1662.36	24.12	9911.13
6	1635.59	66.01	9728.00	1658.00	28.48	9882.65
7	1623.64	77.96	9650.04	1652.84	33.64	9849.02
8	1609.53	92.07	9557.97	1646.76	39.72	9809.29
9	1592.87	108.73	9449.24	1639.57	46.91	9762.38
10	1573.19	128.41	9320.83	1631.08	55.40	9706.98
11	1549.95	151.65	9169.18	1621.05	65.43	9641.55
12	1522.50	179.10	8990.08	1609.21	77.27	9564.28
13	1490.09	211.51	8778.57	1595.23	91.25	9473.03
14	1451.81	249.79	8528.79	1578.71	107.77	9365.26
15	1406.61	294.99	8233.79	1559.21	127.27	9237.99
16	1353.22	348.38	7885.42	1536.18	150.30	9087.69
17	1290.17	411.43	7473.99	1508.98	177.50	8910.19
18	1215.71	485.89	6988.10	1476.85	209.63	8700.58
19	1127.78	573.82	6414.28	1438.91	247.57	8452.99
20	1023.93	677.67	5736.62	1394.11	292.37	8160.62
21	901.24	800.31	4936.31	1341.20	345.28	7815.34
22	756.45	945.15	3991.16	1278.71	407.77	7407.57
23	585.40	1116.20	2874.97	1204.91	481.57	6926.00
24	383.40	1318.20	1556.76	1117.76	568.72	6357.28
25	144.84	1556.76	0.00	1014.84	671.64	5685.64
26				893.28	793.20	4892.44
27				749.73	936.75	3955.69
28				580.20	1106.28	2849.42
29				379.99	1306.49	1542.93
30				143.55	1542.93	0.00

Annual Amortization
Based on mortgage of $10,000

17%

25-YEAR TERM
MONTHLY PAYMENT: $143.78
ANNUAL PAYMENT: $1725.36

30-YEAR TERM
MONTHLY PAYMENT: $142.57
ANNUAL PAYMENT: $1710.84

YR	INTEREST PD DUR YR	PRINCIPAL PD DUR YR	MORTG BAL AT YR END	INTEREST PD DUR YR	PRINCIPAL PD DUR YR	MORTG BAL AT YR END
1	1697.93	27.43	9972.57	1699.15	11.69	9988.31
2	1692.89	32.47	9940.10	1697.00	13.84	9974.46
3	1686.92	38.44	9901.66	1694.45	16.39	9958.07
4	1679.85	45.51	9856.15	1691.44	19.40	9938.67
5	1671.48	53.88	9802.26	1687.87	22.97	9915.70
6	1661.57	63.79	9738.47	1683.64	27.20	9888.50
7	1649.84	75.52	9662.95	1678.64	32.20	9856.30
8	1635.95	89.41	9573.55	1672.72	38.12	9818.18
9	1619.51	105.85	9467.70	1665.71	45.13	9773.05
10	1600.05	125.31	9342.38	1657.41	53.43	9719.63
11	1577.00	148.36	9194.02	1647.59	63.25	9656.37
12	1549.72	175.64	9018.38	1635.96	74.88	9581.49
13	1517.42	207.94	8810.44	1622.19	88.65	9492.84
14	1479.18	246.18	8564.27	1605.88	104.96	9387.88
15	1433.91	291.45	8272.82	1586.58	124.26	9263.62
16	1380.32	345.04	7927.78	1563.73	147.11	9116.51
17	1316.67	408.69	7519.28	1536.68	174.16	8942.35
18	1241.75	483.61	7035.67	1504.65	206.19	8736.17
19	1152.82	572.54	6463.13	1466.74	244.10	8492.07
20	1047.53	677.83	5785.30	1421.85	288.99	8203.08
21	922.88	802.48	4982.83	1368.71	342.13	7860.94
22	775.32	950.04	4032.78	1305.79	405.05	7455.89
23	600.61	1124.75	2908.03	1231.31	479.53	6976.36
24	393.78	1331.58	1576.45	1143.12	567.72	6408.64
25	148.91	1576.45	0.00	1038.73	672.11	5736.53
26				915.13	795.71	4940.82
27				768.80	942.04	3998.78
28				595.57	1115.27	2883.52
29				390.48	1320.36	1563.16
30				147.68	1563.16	0.00

17¼%

25-YEAR TERM
MONTHLY PAYMENT: $145.76
ANNUAL PAYMENT: $1749.12

30-YEAR TERM
MONTHLY PAYMENT: $144.60
ANNUAL PAYMENT: $1735.20

YR	INTEREST PD DUR YR	PRINCIPAL PD DUR YR	MORTG BAL AT YR END	INTEREST PD DUR YR	PRINCIPAL PD DUR YR	MORTG BAL AT YR END
1	1722.94	26.18	9973.82	1724.17	11.03	9988.97
2	1718.05	31.07	9942.76	1722.11	13.09	9975.88
3	1712.25	36.87	9905.89	1719.67	15.53	9960.35
4	1705.36	43.76	9862.14	1716.77	18.43	9941.92
5	1697.19	51.93	9810.21	1713.32	21.88	9920.04
6	1687.49	61.63	9748.57	1709.23	25.97	9894.07
7	1675.97	73.14	9675.43	1704.38	30.82	9863.26
8	1662.31	86.81	9588.62	1698.63	36.57	9826.68
9	1646.09	103.03	9485.59	1691.79	43.41	9783.28
10	1626.85	122.27	9363.32	1683.69	51.51	9731.76
11	1604.00	145.12	9218.20	1674.06	61.14	9670.62
12	1576.89	172.23	9045.98	1662.64	72.56	9598.06
13	1544.72	204.40	8841.58	1649.08	86.12	9511.95
14	1506.54	242.58	8599.00	1633.00	102.20	9409.74
15	1461.22	287.90	8311.09	1613.90	121.30	9288.45
16	1407.40	341.69	7969.41	1591.24	143.96	9144.49
17	1343.60	405.52	7563.89	1564.35	170.85	8973.64
18	1267.85	481.27	7082.62	1532.44	202.76	8770.88
19	1177.30	571.18	6511.44	1494.56	240.64	8530.24
20	1071.23	677.89	5833.55	1449.60	285.60	8244.64
21	944.60	804.52	5029.03	1396.25	338.95	7905.68
22	794.30	954.82	4074.21	1332.93	402.27	7503.41
23	615.93	1133.19	2941.02	1257.78	477.42	7025.99
24	404.23	1344.89	1596.13	1168.59	566.61	6459.37
25	152.99	1596.13	0.00	1062.74	672.46	5786.91
26				937.11	798.09	4988.82
27				788.02	947.18	4041.63
28				611.07	1124.13	2917.50
29				401.07	1334.13	1583.37
30				151.83	1583.37	0.00

Annual Amortization

Based on mortgage of $10,000

17½%

	25-YEAR TERM MONTHLY PAYMENT: $147.75 ANNUAL PAYMENT: $1773.00			30-YEAR TERM MONTHLY PAYMENT: $146.63 ANNUAL PAYMENT: $1759.56		
YR	INTEREST PD DUR YR	PRINCIPAL PD DUR YR	MORTG BAL AT YR END	INTEREST PD DUR YR	PRINCIPAL PD DUR YR	MORTG BAL AT YR END
1	1748.02	24.98	9975.02	1749.16	10.40	9989.60
2	1743.28	29.72	9945.31	1747.19	12.37	9977.23
3	1737.65	35.35	9909.96	1744.84	14.72	9962.51
4	1730.94	42.06	9867.89	1742.05	17.51	9945.00
5	1722.96	50.04	9817.85	1738.73	20.83	9924.17
6	1713.46	59.54	9758.31	1734.77	24.79	9899.38
7	1702.17	70.83	9687.48	1730.07	29.49	9869.89
8	1688.73	84.27	9603.21	1724.47	35.09	9834.81
9	1672.74	100.26	9502.94	1717.82	41.74	9793.06
10	1653.71	119.29	9383.65	1709.90	49.66	9743.40
11	1631.08	141.92	9241.73	1700.47	59.09	9684.31
12	1604.15	168.85	9072.88	1689.26	70.30	9614.02
13	1572.11	200.89	8871.99	1675.93	83.63	9530.38
14	1533.99	239.01	8632.98	1660.06	99.50	9430.88
15	1488.64	284.36	8348.63	1641.18	118.38	9312.50
16	1434.69	338.31	8010.32	1618.71	140.85	9171.65
17	1370.50	402.50	7607.81	1591.99	167.57	9004.08
18	1294.13	478.87	7128.94	1560.19	199.37	8804.71
19	1203.26	569.74	6559.21	1522.37	237.19	8567.52
20	1095.16	677.84	5881.37	1477.36	282.20	8285.32
21	966.45	806.55	5074.91	1423.82	335.74	7949.57
22	813.53	959.47	4115.44	1360.11	399.45	7550.12
23	631.48	1141.52	2973.92	1284.32	475.24	7074.88
24	414.88	1358.12	1615.81	1194.14	565.42	6509.47
25	157.19	1615.81	0.00	1086.86	672.70	5836.77
26				959.22	800.34	5036.43
27				807.37	952.19	4084.24
28				626.68	1132.87	2951.37
29				411.74	1347.82	1603.55
30				156.01	1603.55	0.00

17¾%

	25-YEAR TERM MONTHLY PAYMENT: $149.75 ANNUAL PAYMENT: $1797.00			30-YEAR TERM MONTHLY PAYMENT: $148.67 ANNUAL PAYMENT: $1784.04		
YR	INTEREST PD DUR YR	PRINCIPAL PD DUR YR	MORTG BAL AT YR END	INTEREST PD DUR YR	PRINCIPAL PD DUR YR	MORTG BAL AT YR END
1	1773.17	23.83	9976.17	1774.24	9.80	9990.20
2	1768.58	28.42	9947.75	1772.35	11.69	9978.51
3	1763.10	33.90	9913.86	1770.10	13.94	9964.56
4	1756.57	40.43	9873.43	1767.41	16.63	9947.93
5	1748.78	48.22	9825.21	1764.20	19.84	9928.09
6	1739.49	57.51	9767.70	1760.38	23.66	9904.44
7	1728.41	68.59	9699.12	1755.82	28.22	9876.22
8	1715.20	81.80	9617.32	1750.39	33.65	9842.57
9	1699.44	97.56	9519.76	1743.90	40.14	9802.43
10	1680.64	116.36	9403.40	1736.17	47.87	9754.56
11	1658.22	138.78	9264.62	1726.95	57.09	9697.47
12	1631.48	165.52	9099.10	1715.95	68.09	9629.38
13	1599.59	197.41	8901.69	1702.83	81.21	9548.17
14	1561.55	235.45	8666.24	1687.18	96.86	9451.31
15	1516.19	280.81	8385.43	1668.52	115.52	9335.78
16	1462.08	334.92	8050.51	1646.26	137.78	9198.00
17	1397.55	399.45	7651.06	1619.71	164.33	9033.67
18	1320.59	476.41	7174.64	1588.05	195.99	8837.68
19	1228.79	568.21	6606.43	1550.29	233.75	8603.92
20	1119.31	677.69	5928.74	1505.25	278.79	8325.13
21	988.74	808.26	5120.48	1451.53	332.51	7992.62
22	833.00	964.00	4156.48	1387.46	396.58	7596.04
23	647.26	1149.74	3006.74	1311.05	472.99	7123.05
24	425.73	1371.27	1635.48	1219.92	564.12	6558.93
25	161.52	1635.48	0.00	1111.22	672.82	5886.11
26				981.59	802.45	5083.66
27				826.97	957.07	4126.60
28				642.57	1141.47	2985.12
29				422.63	1361.41	1623.72
30				160.32	1623.72	0.00

Annual Amortization
Based on mortgage of $10,000

18%

25-YEAR TERM
MONTHLY PAYMENT: $151.74
ANNUAL PAYMENT: $1820.88

30-YEAR TERM
MONTHLY PAYMENT: $150.71
ANNUAL PAYMENT: $1808.52

YR	INTEREST PD DUR YR	PRINCIPAL PD DUR YR	MORTG BAL AT YR END	INTEREST PD DUR YR	PRINCIPAL PD DUR YR	MORTG BAL AT YR END
1	1798.15	22.73	9977.27	1799.28	9.24	9990.76
2	1793.70	27.18	9950.09	1797.47	11.05	9979.71
3	1788.39	32.49	9917.60	1795.31	13.21	9966.50
4	1782.03	38.85	9878.75	1792.73	15.79	9950.71
5	1774.43	46.45	9832.30	1789.64	18.88	9931.83
6	1765.34	55.54	9776.76	1785.94	22.58	9909.25
7	1754.48	66.40	9710.36	1781.53	26.99	9882.26
8	1741.49	79.39	9630.97	1776.25	32.27	9849.99
9	1725.96	94.92	9536.05	1769.93	38.59	9811.40
10	1707.39	113.49	9422.57	1762.39	46.13	9765.27
11	1685.19	135.69	9286.88	1753.36	55.16	9710.11
12	1658.65	162.23	9124.65	1742.57	65.95	9644.16
13	1626.91	193.97	8930.68	1729.67	78.85	9565.32
14	1588.97	231.91	8698.78	1714.25	94.27	9471.04
15	1543.61	277.27	8421.50	1695.81	112.71	9358.33
16	1489.37	331.51	8089.99	1673.76	134.76	9223.57
17	1424.52	396.36	7693.62	1647.40	161.12	9062.44
18	1346.98	473.90	7219.72	1615.88	192.64	8869.80
19	1254.28	566.60	6653.12	1578.19	230.33	8639.47
20	1143.44	677.44	5975.68	1533.14	275.38	8364.09
21	1010.92	809.96	5165.72	1479.27	329.25	8034.84
22	852.48	968.40	4197.32	1414.86	393.66	7641.18
23	663.04	1157.84	3039.47	1337.85	470.67	7170.51
24	436.54	1384.34	1655.14	1245.78	562.74	6607.77
25	165.74	1655.14	0.00	1135.70	672.82	5934.94
26				1004.08	804.44	5130.50
27				846.72	961.80	4168.70
28				658.57	1149.95	3018.75
29				433.62	1374.90	1643.85
30				164.67	1643.85	0.00

18¼%

25-YEAR TERM
MONTHLY PAYMENT: $153.74
ANNUAL PAYMENT: $1844.88

30-YEAR TERM
MONTHLY PAYMENT: $152.75
ANNUAL PAYMENT: $1833.00

YR	INTEREST PD DUR YR	PRINCIPAL PD DUR YR	MORTG BAL AT YR END	INTEREST PD DUR YR	PRINCIPAL PD DUR YR	MORTG BAL AT YR END
1	1823.20	21.68	9978.32	1824.29	8.71	9991.29
2	1818.89	25.99	9952.33	1822.56	10.44	9980.85
3	1813.73	31.15	9921.19	1820.49	12.51	9968.34
4	1807.55	37.33	9883.86	1818.01	14.99	9953.35
5	1800.14	44.74	9839.12	1815.03	17.97	9935.38
6	1791.25	53.63	9785.79	1811.46	21.54	9913.84
7	1780.61	64.28	9721.21	1807.18	25.82	9888.02
8	1767.84	77.04	9644.18	1802.06	30.94	9857.08
9	1752.55	92.34	9551.84	1795.91	37.09	9819.99
10	1734.21	110.67	9441.17	1788.55	44.45	9775.53
11	1712.24	132.64	9308.53	1779.74	53.28	9722.25
12	1685.90	158.98	9149.54	1769.14	63.86	9658.39
13	1654.33	190.55	8958.99	1756.46	76.54	9581.85
14	1616.49	228.39	8730.60	1741.36	91.74	9490.12
15	1571.14	273.74	8456.86	1723.05	109.95	9380.16
16	1516.78	328.10	8128.76	1701.21	131.79	9248.37
17	1451.64	393.24	7735.52	1675.04	157.96	9090.42
18	1373.55	471.33	7264.19	1643.68	189.32	8901.10
19	1279.96	564.92	6699.27	1606.09	226.91	8674.18
20	1167.79	677.09	6022.18	1561.03	271.97	8402.21
21	1033.34	811.54	5210.63	1507.02	325.98	8076.23
22	872.19	972.69	4237.94	1442.30	390.70	7685.53
23	679.05	1165.83	3072.11	1364.72	468.28	7217.25
24	447.55	1397.33	1674.79	1271.73	561.27	6655.98
25	170.09	1674.79	0.00	1160.28	672.72	5983.26
26				1026.70	806.30	5176.96
27				866.60	966.40	4210.56
28				674.70	1158.30	3052.26
29				444.70	1388.30	1663.96
30				169.04	1663.96	0.00

Annual Amortization
Based on mortgage of $10,000

18½%

	25-YEAR TERM			30-YEAR TERM		
	MONTHLY PAYMENT: $155.75					MONTHLY PAYMENT: $154.79
	ANNUAL PAYMENT: $1869.00					ANNUAL PAYMENT: $1857.48
YR	INTEREST PD DUR YR	PRINCIPAL PD DUR YR	MORTG BAL AT YR END	INTEREST PD DUR YR	PRINCIPAL PD DUR YR	MORTG BAL AT YR END
1	1848.32	20.68	9979.32	1849.27	8.21	9991.79
2	1844.16	24.84	9954.48	1847.62	9.86	9981.93
3	1839.15	29.85	9924.63	1845.63	11.85	9970.09
4	1833.14	35.86	9888.77	1843.25	14.23	9955.85
5	1825.91	43.09	9845.68	1840.38	17.10	9938.75
6	1817.22	51.78	9793.90	1836.93	20.55	9918.20
7	1806.79	62.21	9731.69	1832.79	24.69	9893.51
8	1794.25	74.75	9656.95	1827.81	29.67	9863.84
9	1779.19	89.81	9567.14	1821.84	35.64	9828.20
10	1761.09	107.91	9459.23	1814.65	42.83	9785.37
11	1739.35	129.65	9329.58	1806.02	51.46	9733.91
12	1713.22	155.78	9173.80	1795.65	61.83	9672.08
13	1681.83	187.17	8986.62	1783.19	74.29	9597.80
14	1644.11	224.89	8761.73	1768.22	89.26	9508.54
15	1598.79	270.21	8491.51	1750.23	107.25	9401.29
16	1544.33	324.67	8166.85	1728.62	128.86	9272.43
17	1478.91	390.10	7776.74	1702.65	154.83	9117.61
18	1400.29	468.71	7308.04	1671.45	186.03	8931.58
19	1305.84	563.16	6744.88	1633.96	223.52	8708.06
20	1192.35	676.65	6068.23	1588.92	268.56	8439.50
21	1055.99	813.01	5255.22	1534.80	322.68	8116.82
22	892.15	976.85	4278.37	1469.77	387.71	7729.12
23	695.29	1173.71	3104.66	1391.64	465.84	7263.28
24	458.77	1410.23	1694.43	1297.77	559.71	6703.57
25	174.57	1694.43	0.00	1184.97	672.51	6031.06
26				1049.45	808.03	5223.03
27				886.61	970.87	4252.16
28				690.96	1166.52	3085.64
29				455.88	1401.60	1684.05
30				173.43	1684.05	0.00

18¾%

	25-YEAR TERM			30-YEAR TERM		
	MONTHLY PAYMENT: $157.76					MONTHLY PAYMENT: $156.84
	ANNUAL PAYMENT: $1893.12					ANNUAL PAYMENT: $1882.08
YR	INTEREST PD DUR YR	PRINCIPAL PD DUR YR	MORTG BAL AT YR END	INTEREST PD DUR YR	PRINCIPAL PD DUR YR	MORTG BAL AT YR END
1	1873.40	19.72	9980.28	1874.35	7.73	9992.27
2	1869.37	23.75	9956.54	1872.77	9.31	9982.96
3	1864.52	28.60	9927.93	1870.86	11.22	9971.74
4	1858.67	34.45	9893.48	1868.57	13.51	9958.23
5	1851.62	41.50	9851.99	1865.81	16.27	9941.95
6	1843.14	49.98	9802.00	1862.48	19.60	9922.35
7	1832.92	60.20	9741.80	1858.47	23.61	9898.74
8	1820.61	72.51	9669.29	1853.64	28.44	9870.31
9	1805.78	87.34	9581.95	1847.83	34.25	9836.06
10	1787.92	105.20	9476.75	1840.82	41.26	9794.80
11	1766.41	126.71	9350.04	1832.39	49.69	9745.11
12	1740.50	152.62	9197.42	1822.23	59.85	9685.26
13	1709.29	183.83	9013.59	1809.99	72.09	9613.16
14	1671.70	221.42	8792.17	1795.25	86.83	9526.33
15	1626.42	266.70	8525.47	1777.49	104.59	9421.74
16	1571.89	321.23	8204.24	1756.10	125.98	9295.77
17	1506.20	386.92	7817.32	1730.34	151.74	9144.03
18	1427.08	466.04	7351.29	1699.32	182.76	8961.27
19	1331.79	561.33	6789.95	1661.95	220.13	8741.13
20	1217.01	676.11	6113.84	1616.93	265.15	8475.98
21	1078.75	814.37	5299.47	1562.71	319.37	8156.62
22	912.23	980.89	4318.58	1497.41	384.67	7771.94
23	711.65	1181.47	3137.11	1418.75	463.33	7308.61
24	470.06	1423.06	1714.05	1324.01	558.07	6750.54
25	179.07	1714.05	0.00	1209.89	672.19	6078.35
26				1072.44	809.64	5268.71
27				906.88	975.20	4293.51
28				707.47	1174.61	3118.90
29				467.28	1414.80	1704.10
30				177.98	1704.10	0.00

Annual Amortization
Based on mortgage of $10,000

19%

25-YEAR TERM
MONTHLY PAYMENT: $159.77
ANNUAL PAYMENT: $1917.24

30-YEAR TERM
MONTHLY PAYMENT: $158.89
ANNUAL PAYMENT: $1906.68

YR	INTEREST PD DUR YR	PRINCIPAL PD DUR YR	MORTG BAL AT YR END	INTEREST PD DUR YR	PRINCIPAL PD DUR YR	MORTG BAL AT YR END
1	1898.44	18.80	9981.20	1899.40	7.28	9992.72
2	1894.54	22.70	9958.51	1897.89	8.79	9983.92
3	1889.83	27.41	9931.10	1896.06	10.62	9973.30
4	1884.15	33.09	9898.01	1893.86	12.82	9960.48
5	1877.28	39.96	9858.05	1891.20	15.48	9945.00
6	1869.00	48.24	9809.81	1887.99	18.69	9926.30
7	1858.99	58.25	9751.56	1884.11	22.57	9903.73
8	1846.90	70.34	9681.22	1879.43	27.25	9876.48
9	1832.31	84.93	9596.29	1873.77	32.91	9843.57
10	1814.68	102.55	9493.75	1866.94	39.74	9803.83
11	1793.42	123.82	9369.93	1858.70	47.98	9755.86
12	1767.73	149.51	9220.42	1848.75	57.93	9697.92
13	1736.72	180.52	9039.90	1836.73	69.95	9627.97
14	1699.27	217.97	8821.93	1822.22	84.46	9543.51
15	1654.05	263.19	8558.74	1804.70	101.98	9441.53
16	1599.45	317.79	8240.95	1783.54	123.14	9318.39
17	1533.53	383.71	7857.24	1758.00	148.68	9169.71
18	1453.92	463.32	7393.92	1727.15	179.53	8990.18
19	1357.81	559.43	6834.49	1689.91	216.77	8773.41
20	1241.75	675.49	6159.01	1644.94	261.74	8511.66
21	1101.62	815.62	5343.39	1590.64	316.04	8195.62
22	932.42	984.82	4358.57	1525.08	381.60	7814.02
23	728.12	1189.12	3169.46	1445.91	460.77	7353.25
24	481.44	1435.80	1733.66	1350.33	556.35	6796.90
25	183.58	1733.66	0.00	1234.91	671.77	6125.13
26				1095.55	811.13	5314.00
27				927.28	979.40	4334.60
28				724.10	1182.58	3152.03
29				478.78	1427.90	1724.12
30				182.56	1724.12	0.00

19¼%

25-YEAR TERM
MONTHLY PAYMENT: $161.78
ANNUAL PAYMENT: $1941.36

30-YEAR TERM
MONTHLY PAYMENT: $160.94
ANNUAL PAYMENT: $1931.28

YR	INTEREST PD DUR YR	PRINCIPAL PD DUR YR	MORTG BAL AT YR END	INTEREST PD DUR YR	PRINCIPAL PD DUR YR	MORTG BAL AT YR END
1	1923.44	17.92	9982.08	1924.42	6.86	9993.14
2	1919.67	21.69	9960.39	1922.98	8.30	9984.84
3	1915.11	26.25	9934.14	1921.23	10.05	9974.78
4	1909.58	31.78	9902.36	1919.11	12.17	9962.62
5	1902.89	38.47	9863.89	1916.55	14.73	9947.89
6	1894.80	46.56	9817.33	1913.45	17.83	9930.06
7	1885.00	56.36	9760.97	1909.70	21.58	9908.49
8	1873.14	68.22	9692.75	1905.16	26.12	9882.37
9	1858.79	82.57	9610.18	1899.67	31.61	9850.75
10	1841.41	99.95	9510.24	1893.01	38.27	9812.49
11	1820.38	120.98	9389.26	1884.96	46.32	9766.17
12	1794.44	146.44	9242.82	1875.22	56.06	9710.11
13	1764.11	177.25	9065.57	1863.42	67.86	9642.24
14	1726.81	214.55	8851.02	1849.14	82.14	9560.10
15	1681.67	259.69	8591.33	1831.85	99.43	9460.68
16	1627.02	314.34	8276.99	1810.93	120.35	9340.33
17	1560.87	380.49	7896.51	1785.61	145.67	9194.66
18	1480.81	460.55	7435.96	1754.95	176.33	9018.33
19	1383.90	557.46	6878.49	1717.85	213.43	8804.90
20	1266.59	674.77	6203.73	1672.94	258.34	8546.56
21	1124.61	816.75	5386.98	1618.58	312.70	8233.86
22	952.74	988.62	4398.36	1552.78	378.50	7855.36
23	744.71	1196.65	3201.71	1473.13	458.15	7397.21
24	492.90	1448.46	1753.25	1376.72	554.56	6842.65
25	188.11	1753.25	0.00	1260.03	671.25	6171.40
26				1118.99	812.50	5358.90
27				947.81	983.47	4375.44
28				740.87	1190.41	3185.02
29				490.37	1440.91	1744.11
30				187.17	1744.11	0.00

Annual Amortization
Based on mortgage of $10,000

19½%

25-YEAR TERM
MONTHLY PAYMENT: $163.80
ANNUAL PAYMENT: $1965.60

30-YEAR TERM
MONTHLY PAYMENT: $162.99
ANNUAL PAYMENT: $1955.88

YR	INTEREST PD DUR YR	PRINCIPAL PD DUR YR	MORTG BAL AT YR END	INTEREST PD DUR YR	PRINCIPAL PD DUR YR	MORTG BAL AT YR END
1	1948.52	17.08	9982.92	1949.42	6.46	9993.54
2	1944.87	20.73	9962.19	1948.04	7.84	9985.70
3	1940.45	25.15	9937.04	1946.37	9.51	9976.19
4	1935.08	30.52	9906.53	1944.34	11.54	9964.64
5	1928.57	37.03	9869.50	1941.87	14.01	9950.63
6	1920.67	44.93	9824.58	1938.88	17.00	9933.64
7	1911.06	54.52	9770.05	1935.26	20.62	9913.01
8	1899.45	66.15	9703.90	1930.86	25.02	9887.99
9	1885.33	80.27	9623.63	1925.51	30.37	9857.62
10	1868.20	97.40	9526.23	1919.03	36.85	9820.78
11	1847.41	118.19	9408.04	1911.17	44.71	9776.07
12	1822.07	143.41	9264.63	1901.63	54.25	9721.82
13	1791.59	174.01	9090.62	1890.05	65.83	9655.99
14	1754.45	211.15	8879.47	1876.01	79.87	9576.12
15	1709.39	256.21	8623.25	1858.96	96.92	9479.20
16	1654.71	310.89	8312.37	1838.28	117.60	9361.60
17	1588.37	377.23	7935.14	1813.18	142.70	9218.89
18	1507.86	457.74	7477.39	1782.72	173.16	9045.74
19	1410.18	555.42	6921.97	1745.77	210.11	8835.63
20	1291.64	673.96	6248.01	1700.93	254.95	8580.68
21	1147.82	817.78	5430.23	1646.53	309.35	8271.33
22	973.30	992.31	4437.92	1580.51	375.37	7895.96
23	761.52	1204.07	3233.85	1500.40	455.48	7440.48
24	504.57	1461.03	1772.82	1403.20	552.68	6887.80
25	192.78	1772.82	0.00	1285.25	670.63	6217.17
26				1142.13	813.75	5403.42
27				968.47	987.41	4416.01
28				757.75	1198.13	3217.89
29				502.06	1453.82	1764.07
30				191.81	1764.07	0.00

19¾%

25-YEAR TERM
MONTHLY PAYMENT: $165.82
ANNUAL PAYMENT: $1989.94

30-YEAR TERM
MONTHLY PAYMENT: $165.05
ANNUAL PAYMENT: $1980.60

YR	INTEREST PD DUR YR	PRINCIPAL PD DUR YR	MORTG BAL AT YR END	INTEREST PD DUR YR	PRINCIPAL PD DUR YR	MORTG BAL AT YR END
1	1973.56	16.28	9983.72	1974.52	6.08	9993.92
2	1970.04	19.80	9963.92	1973.20	7.40	9986.52
3	1965.75	24.09	9939.83	1971.60	9.00	9977.51
4	1960.54	29.30	9910.52	1969.65	10.95	9966.56
5	1954.20	35.64	9874.89	1967.28	13.32	9953.24
6	1946.49	43.35	9831.54	1964.40	16.20	9937.04
7	1937.11	52.73	9778.81	1960.89	19.71	9917.33
8	1925.70	64.14	9714.67	1956.63	23.97	9893.35
9	1911.82	78.02	9636.64	1951.44	29.16	9864.19
10	1894.93	94.91	9541.73	1945.13	35.47	9828.72
11	1874.39	115.45	9426.29	1937.45	43.15	9785.57
12	1849.41	140.43	9285.86	1928.11	52.49	9733.08
13	1819.02	170.82	9115.04	1916.76	63.84	9669.24
14	1782.06	207.78	8907.26	1902.94	77.66	9591.58
15	1737.10	252.74	8654.52	1886.14	94.46	9497.12
16	1682.40	307.44	8347.08	1865.69	114.91	9382.21
17	1615.88	373.96	7973.12	1840.83	139.77	9242.44
18	1534.90	454.89	7518.23	1810.58	170.02	9072.42
19	1436.52	553.32	6964.91	1773.79	206.81	8865.61
20	1316.78	673.06	6291.85	1729.04	251.56	8614.05
21	1171.13	818.71	5473.14	1674.60	306.00	8308.05
22	993.97	995.87	4477.27	1608.39	372.21	7935.84
23	778.46	1211.38	3265.89	1527.84	452.76	7483.08
24	516.33	1473.51	1792.38	1429.86	550.74	6932.34
25	197.46	1792.38	0.00	1310.69	669.91	6262.43
26				1165.72	814.88	5447.55
27				989.38	991.22	4456.33
28				774.89	1205.71	3250.62
29				513.98	1466.62	1783.99
30				196.61	1783.99	0.00

Annual Amortization

Based on mortgage of $10,000

20%

25-YEAR TERM
MONTHLY PAYMENT: $167.85
ANNUAL PAYMENT: $2014.20

30-YEAR TERM
MONTHLY PAYMENT: $167.10
ANNUAL PAYMENT: $2005.20

YR	INTEREST PD DUR YR	PRINCIPAL PD DUR YR	MORTG BAL AT YR END	INTEREST PD DUR YR	PRINCIPAL PD DUR YR	MORTG BAL AT YR END
1	1998.69	15.51	9984.49	1999.47	5.73	9994.27
2	1995.28	18.92	9965.57	1998.21	6.99	9987.29
3	1991.13	23.07	9942.50	1996.68	8.52	9978.77
4	1986.07	28.13	9914.38	1994.81	10.39	9968.38
5	1979.90	34.30	9880.08	1992.53	12.67	9955.71
6	1972.38	41.82	9838.25	1989.76	15.44	9940.27
7	1963.20	51.00	9787.25	1986.37	18.83	9921.44
8	1952.01	62.19	9725.07	1982.24	22.96	9898.47
9	1938.37	75.83	9649.24	1977.20	28.00	9870.47
10	1921.73	92.47	9556.77	1971.05	34.15	9836.32
11	1901.45	112.75	9444.01	1963.56	41.64	9794.68
12	1876.71	137.49	9306.52	1954.43	50.77	9743.91
13	1846.54	167.66	9138.87	1943.29	61.91	9682.00
14	1809.76	204.44	8934.43	1929.70	75.50	9606.50
15	1764.91	249.29	8685.14	1913.14	92.06	9514.45
16	1710.22	303.98	8381.15	1892.94	112.26	9402.19
17	1643.53	370.67	8010.48	1868.32	136.88	9265.31
18	1562.20	452.00	7558.48	1838.29	166.91	9098.39
19	1463.04	551.16	7007.32	1801.67	203.53	8894.86
20	1342.12	672.08	6335.24	1757.01	248.19	8646.67
21	1194.67	819.53	5515.71	1702.56	302.64	8344.04
22	1014.87	999.33	4516.39	1636.17	369.03	7975.00
23	795.63	1218.57	3297.82	1555.21	449.99	7525.01
24	528.29	1485.91	1811.91	1456.48	548.72	6976.29
25	202.29	1811.91	0.00	1336.10	669.10	6307.19
26				1189.30	815.90	5491.29
27				1010.30	994.90	4496.39
28				792.03	1213.17	3283.22
29				525.87	1479.33	1803.88
30				201.32	1803.88	0.00

20¼%

25-YEAR TERM
MONTHLY PAYMENT: $169.87
ANNUAL PAYMENT: $2038.44

30-YEAR TERM
MONTHLY PAYMENT: $169.16
ANNUAL PAYMENT: $2029.92

YR	INTEREST PD DUR YR	PRINCIPAL PD DUR YR	MORTG BAL AT YR END	INTEREST PD DUR YR	PRINCIPAL PD DUR YR	MORTG BAL AT YR END
1	2023.66	14.78	9985.22	2024.53	5.39	9994.61
2	2020.37	18.07	9967.15	2023.33	6.59	9988.01
3	2016.35	22.09	9945.06	2021.86	8.06	9979.96
4	2011.44	27.00	9918.06	2020.07	9.85	9970.10
5	2005.44	33.00	9885.06	2017.88	12.04	9958.06
6	1998.10	40.34	9844.71	2015.20	14.72	9943.34
7	1989.12	49.32	9795.40	2011.93	17.99	9925.35
8	1978.16	60.28	9735.11	2007.93	21.99	9903.35
9	1964.75	73.69	9661.42	2003.03	26.89	9876.47
10	1948.36	90.08	9571.34	1997.05	32.87	9843.60
11	1928.33	110.11	9461.23	1989.75	40.18	9803.43
12	1903.84	134.60	9326.63	1980.81	49.11	9754.32
13	1873.91	164.53	9162.10	1969.89	60.03	9694.29
14	1837.31	201.13	8960.97	1956.54	73.38	9620.90
15	1792.59	245.85	8715.11	1940.22	89.70	9531.20
16	1737.91	300.53	8414.58	1920.27	109.65	9421.55
17	1671.07	367.37	8047.22	1895.88	134.04	9287.52
18	1589.37	449.07	7598.15	1866.08	163.84	9123.67
19	1489.50	548.94	7049.21	1829.64	200.28	8923.39
20	1367.42	671.02	6378.20	1785.10	244.82	8678.57
21	1218.19	820.25	5557.95	1730.65	299.27	8379.29
22	1035.78	1002.66	4555.29	1664.09	365.83	8013.47
23	812.79	1225.65	3329.64	1582.74	447.18	7566.28
24	540.22	1498.22	1831.42	1483.29	546.63	7019.65
25	207.02	1831.42	0.00	1361.72	668.20	6351.45
26				1213.11	816.81	5534.64
27				1031.46	998.46	4536.18
28				809.41	1220.51	3315.68
29				537.98	1491.94	1823.74
30				206.18	1823.74	0.00

Annual Amortization
Based on mortgage of $10,000

20½%

	25-YEAR TERM			30-YEAR TERM		
	MONTHLY PAYMENT: $171.90			MONTHLY PAYMENT: $171.22		
	ANNUAL PAYMENT: $2062.80			ANNUAL PAYMENT: $2054.64		
YR	INTEREST PD DUR YR	PRINCIPAL PD DUR YR	MORTG BAL AT YR END	INTEREST PD DUR YR	PRINCIPAL PD DUR YR	MORTG BAL AT YR END
1	2048.72	14.08	9985.92	2049.56	5.08	9994.92
2	2045.54	17.26	9968.66	2048.42	6.22	9988.70
3	2041.65	21.15	9947.51	2047.02	7.62	9981.08
4	2036.89	25.91	9921.60	2045.30	9.34	9971.74
5	2031.04	31.76	9889.84	2043.19	11.45	9960.29
6	2023.89	38.91	9850.93	2040.61	14.03	9946.26
7	2015.12	47.68	9803.25	2037.45	17.19	9929.07
8	2004.37	58.43	9744.81	2033.58	21.06	9908.01
9	1991.20	71.60	9673.21	2028.83	25.81	9882.20
10	1975.06	87.74	9585.47	2023.01	31.63	9850.57
11	1955.28	107.52	9477.95	2015.88	38.76	9811.81
12	1931.05	131.75	9346.20	2007.15	47.49	9764.32
13	1901.35	161.45	9184.74	1996.44	58.20	9706.12
14	1864.96	197.84	8986.90	1983.32	71.32	9634.80
15	1820.36	242.44	8744.46	1967.25	87.39	9547.41
16	1765.72	297.08	8447.38	1947.55	107.09	9440.31
17	1698.75	364.05	8083.34	1923.41	131.23	9309.08
18	1616.70	446.10	7637.23	1893.83	160.81	9148.27
19	1516.15	546.65	7090.58	1857.58	197.06	8951.22
20	1392.93	669.87	6420.71	1813.17	241.47	8709.74
21	1241.94	820.86	5599.85	1758.74	295.90	8413.84
22	1056.97	1005.88	4593.96	1692.04	362.60	8051.24
23	830.19	1232.61	3361.35	1610.31	444.33	7606.91
24	552.35	1510.45	1850.90	1510.16	544.48	7062.42
25	211.90	1850.90	0.00	1387.43	667.21	6395.21
26				1237.04	817.60	5577.61
27				1052.75	1001.89	4575.72
28				826.92	1227.72	3348.00
29				550.19	1504.45	1843.55
30				211.09	1843.55	0.00

20¾%

	25-YEAR TERM			30-YEAR TERM		
	MONTHLY PAYMENT: $173.93			MONTHLY PAYMENT: $173.28		
	ANNUAL PAYMENT: $2087.16			ANNUAL PAYMENT: $2079.36		
YR	INTEREST PD DUR YR	PRINCIPAL PD DUR YR	MORTG BAL AT YR END	INTEREST PD DUR YR	PRINCIPAL PD DUR YR	MORTG BAL AT YR END
1	2073.74	13.42	9986.58	2074.58	4.78	9995.22
2	2070.68	16.48	9970.10	2073.49	5.87	9989.35
3	2066.91	20.24	9949.86	2072.15	7.21	9982.14
4	2062.29	24.87	9924.99	2070.50	8.86	9973.28
5	2056.61	30.55	9894.44	2068.48	10.88	9962.40
6	2049.63	37.53	9856.91	2065.99	13.37	9949.04
7	2041.06	46.10	9810.81	2062.94	16.42	9932.62
8	2030.53	56.63	9754.18	2059.19	20.17	9912.45
9	2017.59	69.57	9684.62	2054.58	24.78	9887.68
10	2001.70	85.46	9599.16	2048.92	30.44	9857.24
11	1982.19	104.97	9494.19	2041.97	37.39	9819.85
12	1958.21	128.95	9365.23	2033.43	45.93	9773.93
13	1928.75	158.41	9206.83	2022.94	56.42	9717.51
14	1892.57	194.59	9012.24	2010.06	69.30	9648.21
15	1848.12	239.04	8773.20	1994.23	85.13	9563.07
16	1793.92	293.24	8479.96	1974.79	104.58	9458.49
17	1726.45	360.71	8118.85	1950.89	128.47	9330.02
18	1644.06	443.10	7675.74	1921.55	157.81	9172.21
19	1542.84	544.32	7131.43	1885.50	193.86	8978.35
20	1418.51	668.65	6462.78	1841.22	238.14	8740.21
21	1265.78	821.38	5641.40	1786.82	292.53	8447.68
22	1078.17	1008.99	4632.41	1720.01	359.35	8088.32
23	847.79	1239.47	3392.94	1637.92	441.44	7646.89
24	564.58	1522.58	1870.36	1537.09	542.27	7104.62
25	216.80	1870.36	0.00	1413.23	666.13	6438.48
26				1261.07	818.29	5620.19
27				1074.16	1005.40	4614.99
28				844.55	1234.81	3380.19
29				562.50	1516.86	1863.33
30				216.03	1863.33	0.00

Annual Amortization
Based on mortgage of $10,000

21%

25-YEAR TERM
MONTHLY PAYMENT: $175.97
ANNUAL PAYMENT: $2111.64

30-YEAR TERM
MONTHLY PAYMENT: $175.34
ANNUAL PAYMENT: $2104.08

YR	INTEREST PD DUR YR	PRINCIPAL PD DUR YR	MORTG BAL AT YR END	INTEREST PD DUR YR	PRINCIPAL PD DUR YR	MORTG BAL AT YR END
1	2098.86	12.78	9987.22	2099.58	4.50	9995.50
2	2095.90	15.74	9971.48	2098.54	5.54	9989.97
3	2092.26	19.38	9952.21	2097.26	6.82	9983.15
4	2087.78	23.86	9928.24	2095.68	8.40	9974.75
5	2082.25	29.39	9898.85	2093.74	10.34	9964.41
6	2075.45	36.19	9862.67	2091.35	12.73	9951.68
7	2067.08	44.56	9818.10	2088.40	15.68	9935.99
8	2056.76	54.88	9763.22	2084.77	19.31	9916.69
9	2044.06	67.58	9695.65	2080.30	23.78	9892.91
10	2028.42	83.22	9612.43	2074.80	29.28	9863.62
11	2009.16	102.48	9509.95	2068.02	36.06	9827.56
12	1985.44	126.20	9383.75	2059.67	44.41	9783.16
13	1956.24	155.40	9228.35	2049.40	54.68	9728.48
14	1920.27	191.37	9036.98	2036.74	67.34	9661.14
15	1875.98	235.66	8801.32	2021.16	82.92	9578.22
16	1821.44	290.20	8511.12	2001.97	102.11	9476.10
17	1754.28	357.36	8153.76	1978.33	125.75	9350.36
18	1671.57	440.07	7713.68	1949.23	154.85	9195.51
19	1569.61	541.92	7171.76	1913.39	190.69	9004.82
20	1444.30	667.35	6504.42	1869.26	234.82	8770.00
21	1289.85	821.79	5682.62	1814.91	289.17	8480.83
22	1099.65	1011.99	4670.63	1747.99	356.09	8124.74
23	865.44	1246.21	3424.42	1665.57	438.51	7686.23
24	577.01	1534.63	1889.80	1564.09	539.99	7146.24
25	221.84	1889.80	0.00	1439.11	664.97	6481.27
26				1285.21	818.87	5662.40
27				1095.69	1008.39	4654.01
28				862.31	1241.77	3412.24
29				574.92	1529.16	1883.07
30				221.01	1883.07	0.00

21¼%

25-YEAR TERM
MONTHLY PAYMENT: $178.00
ANNUAL PAYMENT: $2136.00

30-YEAR TERM
MONTHLY PAYMENT: $177.40
ANNUAL PAYMENT: $2128.80

YR	INTEREST PD DUR YR	PRINCIPAL PD DUR YR	MORTG BAL AT YR END	INTEREST PD DUR YR	PRINCIPAL PD DUR YR	MORTG BAL AT YR END
1	2123.83	12.17	9987.83	2124.57	4.23	9995.77
2	2120.98	15.02	9972.80	2123.58	5.22	9990.55
3	2117.45	18.55	9954.26	2122.35	6.45	9984.10
4	2113.10	22.90	9931.36	2120.84	7.96	9976.14
5	2107.73	28.27	9903.09	2118.97	9.83	9966.31
6	2101.11	34.89	9868.20	2116.67	12.13	9954.18
7	2092.93	43.07	9825.13	2113.83	14.97	9939.21
8	2082.83	53.17	9771.95	2110.31	18.49	9920.72
9	2070.36	65.64	9706.31	2105.98	22.82	9897.90
10	2054.97	81.03	9625.28	2100.63	28.17	9869.73
11	2035.97	100.03	9525.25	2094.02	34.78	9834.96
12	2012.52	123.48	9401.77	2085.87	42.93	9792.03
13	1983.56	152.44	9249.33	2075.81	52.99	9739.03
14	1947.82	188.18	9061.15	2063.38	65.42	9673.61
15	1903.70	232.30	8828.85	2048.04	80.76	9592.86
16	1849.23	286.77	8542.08	2029.11	99.69	9493.16
17	1781.99	354.01	8188.07	2005.73	123.07	9370.09
18	1698.99	437.01	7751.06	1976.88	151.92	9218.17
19	1596.52	539.48	7211.58	1941.25	187.55	9030.62
20	1470.03	665.97	6545.61	1897.28	231.52	8799.10
21	1313.88	822.12	5723.50	1843.00	285.80	8513.30
22	1121.12	1014.88	4708.62	1775.98	352.82	8160.48
23	883.17	1252.83	3455.79	1693.26	435.54	7724.94
24	589.42	1546.58	1909.21	1591.14	537.66	7187.29
25	226.79	1909.21	0.00	1465.08	663.72	6523.56
26				1309.45	819.35	5704.21
27				1117.34	1011.46	4692.76
28				880.19	1248.61	3444.15
29				587.43	1541.37	1902.77
30				226.03	1902.77	0.00

Annual Amortization
Based on mortgage of $10,000

21½%

25-YEAR TERM
MONTHLY PAYMENT: $180.04
ANNUAL PAYMENT: $2160.48

30-YEAR TERM
MONTHLY PAYMENT: $179.47
ANNUAL PAYMENT: $2153.64

YR	INTEREST PD DUR YR	PRINCIPAL PD DUR YR	MORTG BAL AT YR END	INTEREST PD DUR YR	PRINCIPAL PD DUR YR	MORTG BAL AT YR END
1	2148.89	11.59	9988.41	2149.66	3.98	9996.02
2	2146.14	14.34	9974.07	2148.71	4.93	9991.09
3	2142.73	17.75	9956.31	2147.54	6.10	9985.00
4	2138.51	21.97	9934.35	2146.10	7.54	9977.45
5	2133.30	27.18	9907.16	2144.30	9.34	9968.11
6	2126.84	33.64	9873.53	2142.09	11.55	9956.56
7	2118.85	41.63	9831.90	2139.34	14.30	9942.26
8	2108.96	51.52	9780.38	2135.95	17.69	9924.57
9	2096.73	63.75	9716.63	2131.74	21.90	9902.67
10	2081.59	78.89	9637.73	2126.54	27.10	9875.58
11	2062.85	97.63	9540.10	2120.11	33.53	9842.04
12	2039.66	120.82	9419.29	2112.14	41.50	9800.55
13	2010.97	149.51	9269.77	2102.29	51.35	9749.19
14	1975.46	185.02	9084.75	2090.09	63.55	9685.65
15	1931.51	228.97	8855.78	2075.00	78.64	9607.00
16	1877.13	283.35	8572.44	2056.32	97.32	9509.69
17	1809.84	350.64	8221.79	2033.21	120.43	9389.25
18	1726.56	433.92	7787.87	2004.60	149.04	9240.22
19	1623.50	536.98	7250.89	1969.21	184.43	9055.78
20	1495.96	664.52	6586.37	1925.40	228.24	8827.55
21	1338.14	822.34	5764.03	1871.20	282.44	8545.10
22	1142.83	1017.65	4746.38	1804.11	349.53	8195.58
23	901.13	1259.35	3487.03	1721.10	432.54	7763.04
24	602.03	1558.45	1928.59	1618.37	535.27	7227.77
25	231.89	1928.59	0.00	1491.24	662.40	6565.37
26				1333.20	819.72	5745.66
27				1139.23	1014.41	4731.25
28				898.31	1255.33	3475.92
29				600.16	1553.48	1922.44
30				231.20	1922.44	0.00

21¾%

25-YEAR TERM
MONTHLY PAYMENT: $182.08
ANNUAL PAYMENT: $2184.96

30-YEAR TERM
MONTHLY PAYMENT: $181.53
ANNUAL PAYMENT: $2178.36

YR	INTEREST PD DUR YR	PRINCIPAL PD DUR YR	MORTG BAL AT YR END	INTEREST PD DUR YR	PRINCIPAL PD DUR YR	MORTG BAL AT YR END
1	2173.92	11.04	9988.96	2174.61	3.75	9996.25
2	2171.27	13.69	9975.27	2173.71	4.65	9991.60
3	2167.97	16.99	9958.28	2172.60	5.76	9985.84
4	2163.89	21.07	9937.21	2171.21	7.15	9978.69
5	2158.82	26.14	9911.07	2169.49	8.87	9969.82
6	2152.53	32.43	9878.64	2167.36	11.00	9958.82
7	2144.73	40.23	9838.42	2164.71	13.65	9945.17
8	2135.05	49.91	9788.51	2161.43	16.93	9928.24
9	2123.05	61.91	9726.60	2157.35	21.01	9907.23
10	2108.16	76.80	9649.80	2152.30	26.06	9881.17
11	2089.68	95.28	9554.52	2146.05	32.33	9848.84
12	2066.76	118.20	9436.32	2138.25	40.11	9808.73
13	2038.33	146.63	9289.70	2128.60	49.76	9758.97
14	2003.06	181.90	9107.80	2116.64	61.72	9697.25
15	1959.31	225.65	8882.14	2101.79	76.57	9620.68
16	1905.05	279.93	8602.20	2083.37	94.99	9525.69
17	1837.69	347.27	8254.94	2060.52	117.84	9407.85
18	1754.15	430.81	7824.13	2032.17	146.19	9261.66
19	1650.52	534.44	7289.70	1997.01	181.35	9080.31
20	1521.97	662.99	6626.70	1953.39	224.97	8855.34
21	1362.49	822.47	5804.23	1899.27	279.09	8576.25
22	1164.64	1020.32	4783.91	1832.14	346.22	8230.03
23	919.21	1265.75	3518.16	1748.85	429.51	7800.52
24	614.74	1570.22	1947.94	1645.54	532.82	7267.70
25	237.02	1947.94	0.00	1517.37	660.99	6606.71
26				1358.37	819.99	5786.71
27				1161.12	1017.24	4769.48
28				916.43	1261.93	3507.54
29				612.87	1565.49	1942.06
30				236.30	1942.06	0.00

Home Buyers Guide

Look Before You Leap . . .

Knowledge is power when you are looking at real estate. Whether you are looking for an old or new house, or a condo, the more information you have the better equipped you will be to make a satisfactory purchase. Here are some ideas that you may use in your quest for more knowledge.

Look closely at the area where you are considering to buy. Investigate the community and learn about the services the community has to offer. These would include, for example, the libraries, police and fire departments, as well as hospitals. If you need to know about schools, find out where they are located, school transportation and how the schools are rated.

Other important items may be how close you are to public transportation and local shopping. Spend some time in the neighborhood and see if you are satisfied with what you see. Be sure you learn about any vacant or nonresidential properties in the surrounding areas. You may find out that you would own property next to land that may be used for industrial purposes. See if you can get a survey of the land you are interested in.

If you are considering a resale, and possibly even if it's a new property, you may want to hire an engineer or home inspector. A full report on the property, including a roof inspection is especially helpful in determining the value of the property. Items to look for are the age of construction, type of wiring, type of plumbing, heating and possible air conditioning. Check the condition of major appliances, the windows and the doors. This is just a guideline and we hope that it sets off a light bulb in your head to find out as much as you can.

If the house is older, find out about any renovations and changes that have been made since the property was first built. Determine if the natural terrain is likely to create a water problem. The engineer's report may help you in that area. Inspect all you can. Find out if asbestos or any carcinogens were used in the building. If you can, given it the "rain test." Examine the attic and the basement during and after a heavy rain.

The engineer or home inspector's report may also point out some problems. If you can determine the cost to rectify these problems, they should be factored into the purchase price. For example, if you know that the boiler is old and will have to be replaced, the cost may be estimated and used to reduce the price of the property.

In planning your purchase and your monthly carrying costs, you should also consider the cost of utilities and taxes. Electric, gas, and oil can vary greatly from property to property. Taxes can be a major factor in your calculations of the total costs. Information on all taxes should be readily available. Other costs will be discussed later on.

If It's New . . .

If you are buying a new home that is already built, it's probably a good idea to have it inspected by an engineer or home inspector. The report may give you a better insight into what you are buying. Problems may also surface that can't easily be seen by a nonprofessional. Research the reputation of the builder. Find out what other properties he has built. Ask owners of properties that the builder completed about his workmanship and builder warranties. If the builder has been in business for some time then references should be easier to get. Find out what recourse you may have if the workmanship or the materials are substandard. Local town halls, building departments, or libraries may help you with these matters.

Building a home requires greater planning and attention. An architect and general contractor may have to be hired to execute the entire project. Research their reputation and their track record with past clients. Be sure they are familiar with local and state building codes and guidelines. Since new construction may involve dealing with additional outside parties, it is more likely that legal assistance will be required. Timing is also a consideration. You may want to set up milestones with non-performance penalties. Learn what legal recourse you may have for non-performance. A contract should cover these constraints carefully.

Legal Matters . . .

Several considerations of a legal nature will also demand your attention. Without appropriate legal advice, you can put at risk what may be your single largest investment. It may be appropriate to choose an attorney to assist you in these matters. In fact some states, such as New York, require that you have an attorney in connection with closing.

You should have confidence in any advisor. This is especially true for your attorney. In selecting an attorney to assist you in the purchase of your home, you should consider the attorney's (1) familiarity with the community in which you are buying or building, (2) his/her real estate experience, (3) prior work with you or other members of your family, (4) recommendations from others, and (5) fees.

Legal issues may arise in connection with deposits or binders, problems uncovered in engineering reports, negotiating an appropriate price or other terms of purchase, obtaining clear title, entering into a contract, and finally closing.

Engineering reports may identify possible violations of local codes covering structural, electrical, or plumbing requirements. You should coordinate the information obtained from the engineering report with that contained in the latest certificate of occupancy, making sure that the latest changes are appropriately reflected.

Prior to negotiating a final purchase price, you must make sure that you can get a marketable title. The chain of ownership must indicate that title will pass to you, clear of any encumbrance. A title guarantee company will conduct the appropriate research and will issue title insurance which may be required by the lending institution at closing. The title company should also check for violations against local building codes. Such violations should be corrected by the seller. The title company will also check appropriate sources to discover if there are any pending litigation or judgments against the seller, any easements against the property, and whether there are any Federal, State, or local tax liens. The cost of title insurance may be based on a sliding scale which takes into account the risk involved. Generally 30 to 60 days may be required to clear title. This time frame as well as the lender's time frame for approval of a mortgage will determine how soon closing can occur.

Between the binder and contract you should have an engineering report completed. This will permit you to negotiate the best possible contract.

The contract should be made subject to obtaining clear title, a favorable termite inspection, correction of, or financial consideration for, defects uncovered in the engineering report or violations noted in the title search. Include any warranties that are mutually agreeable concerning appliances that are to be left. In addition, it may be appropriate to specify in the contract satisfactory limits on a moving date for the seller.

The closing may be viewed as a "mopping-up operation." Nevertheless, several important items need to be dealt with at closing. If the property being purchased was or will be held jointly by a husband and wife, all such individuals must be present at closing. If the property was jointly held by a husband and wife and one has died prior to closing, proof of death must be brought to the closing. Clear title, and title insurance will also be required. Because at closing you generally take the property "as is," it is generally recommended that you conduct a personal inspection a day or two prior to closing. During your inspection, make sure the seller appears ready to move and has complied with the title company exceptions, and that hazardous conditions, if any, have been removed. In addition, those items which are being left should be in appropriate working order.

Lastly, you should be prepared to write a number of checks for miscellaneous items, which could add up to a substantial sum. Some of these items include your attorney's fee, escrow for local taxes, title, and other closing costs.

Money Matters . . .

Purchasing a home is a major investment involving significant immediate cost on your part as well as a significant obligation in the form of subsequent monthly payments for years to come.

To protect this investment, you may be required to secure title insurance. The mortgage lender will probably require that your homeowners insurance (which covers such areas as fire protection) is adequate to cover the value of your investment. In some jurisdictions, the seller may be required to guarantee major items (e.g., appliances, roof) for a limited period following purchase. Insurance for the seller may be available for this purpose. It is relatively inexpensive and should be considered. Insurance which extinguishes the mortgage debt on the death of the borrower should also be considered as an option.

In negotiating a purchase price, remember not to buy on emotion. The cost of correcting problems uncovered in the engineering report or title search should be taken into account. If these problems are not corrected by the seller, their cost should be taken into account in the negotiated purchase price. You need to remain objective. After all problems are corrected, the net cost of your home should be reasonably related to the market value of comparable homes in the same community.

Careful consideration also needs to be given to the great variety of mortgages which are available from the many lenders serving the local community. Your individual circumstances will dictate the type of mortgage most appropriate for you. For example, adjustable rate mortgages may have interest rates which are initially lower than fixed rate mortgages of the same amount and term. However, the interest rate on adjustable mortgages may be greater after one, two, or three years. In this case, if there is a reasonable chance that you may be moving again within a few years, a fixed rate mortgage may be financially advantageous. A comparison of your monthly carrying costs should be made under a variety of mortgages before you select one. When these comparisons are made you should also consider the possible effect of changing economic conditions on your monthly payments.

We hope that these guidelines will be helpful to you in your prospective purchase.

Glossary

acceleration clause A clause in a mortgage stipulating that, if certain defined conditions occur, any amount of money still outstanding is due and payable at once. Also called a *call-back clause*.

Adjustable Rate Mortgage (ARM) A mortgage, the interest rate of which varies during the term of the mortgage. Also called a *Variable Rate Mortgage*.

amortization The process of repaying a loan through a series of installment payments.

annual interest rate A percentage that, when multiplied by the principal, gives the amount of money that the principal will earn over the period of a year.

balloon note A note that usually calls for a final payment greater than the regular periodic payments.

blanket mortgage One mortgage that covers more than one parcel of real estate.

bridge loan A short-term loan in effect from the end of one loan to the beginning of another loan, or prior to permanent financing.

call-back clause *See* acceleration clause.

conventional mortgage A mortgage made by a bank or other private institution and not insured by a governmental agency.

discount points A charge, made by the lending institution to the borrower, that is based on the mortgage amount. A point is one percent of the principal mortgage amount.

Federal Housing Administration (FHA) mortgage A mortgage loan made by a lender and insured by the Federal Housing Administration.

first mortgage The primary mortgage on a property. If a foreclosure occurs, the first mortgage is repaid before any "junior" mortgages.

Flexible Payment Mortgage (FPM) A mortgage with payments that vary over the term of the mortgage. Usually the initial payments are lower than later payments.

Graduated Payment Mortgage (GPM) A mortgage with payments that increase in a specified manner over the term of the mortgage.

interest The amount of money earned by the principal during a specified period of time.

interest rate A percentage that, when multiplied by the principal, determines the amount of money that the principal earns over a period of time, usually one year.

junior mortgage A mortgage of lesser rank than the first mortgage. *See also* first mortgage.

mortgage A legal document that establishes real estate as the security for the loan which finances that real estate. Colloquially, the term *mortgage* is sometimes used to refer to the loan itself.

mortgage commitment A written offer of a mortgage loan by a lending institution. Often in the form of a letter, the commitment specifies the terms and conditions of the mortgage loan being offered to the prospective borrower.

mortgagee The institution or person who is the lender or creditor on a mortgage loan.

mortgagor The institution or person who is the borrower or debtor on a mortgage loan.

open-end mortgage A mortgage that provides for additional amounts to be loaned to the borrower without the need to create a new mortgage.

points *See* discount points.

prepayment clause A clause in a mortgage enabling the borrower to pay off the mortgage balance before the end of the mortgage term. This privilege sometimes involves a prepayment penalty.

Price Level Adjusted Mortgage (PLAM) A mortgage that provides for a periodic changing of the interest rate. A portion of the rate is determined by the contract rate, and an additional portion is determined by recalculating the mortgage balance based on a cost of living index.

principal Initial amount of money invested or borrowed.

Renegotiated Rate Mortgage (RRM) *See* Rollover Mortgage (ROM).

Reverse Annuity Mortgage (RAM) A type of mortgage that allows a borrower to draw on the current equity of the property.

Rollover Mortgage (ROM) A mortgage that provides for the renegotiation of the interest rate and the payment terms at specific intervals. Also called a *Renegotiated Rate Mortgage*.

Shared Appreciation Mortgage (SAM) A mortgage providing for the lender to receive a share in the appreciation of residential real estate. In return for this, the borrower is given an interest rate lower than the prevailing rate. Also called a *Shared Equity Mortgage*.

Shared Equity Mortgage (SEM) *See* Shared Appreciation Mortgage (SAM).

subject to mortgage A purchaser of mortgaged real estate having title but not being responsible for any of the mortgage debt beyond the value of his or her equity in the property.

Variable Rate Mortgage (VRM) *See* Adjustable Rate Mortgage.

Veterans Administration (VA) mortgage A mortgage made to veterans by a lender for residential real estate and insured by the Veterans Administration.

Notes

Notes

Notes

Notes

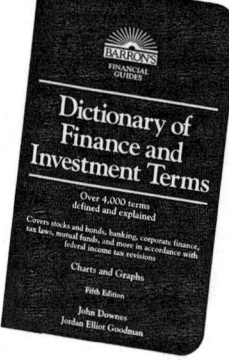

More selected BARRON'S titles:

BARRON'S ACCOUNTING HANDBOOK, 3rd ED.
Joel G. Siegel and Jae K. Shim
Provides accounting rules, guidelines, formulas and techniques, etc., to help student
business professionals work out accounting problems.
Hardcover, $35.00, Canada $48.95/ISBN 0-7641-5282-3, 880 pages

REAL ESTATE HANDBOOK, 5th ED.
Jack P. Friedman and Jack C. Harris
A dictionary/reference for everyone in real estate. Defines approximately 2000 legal,
financial, and architectural terms.
Hardcover, $35.00, Canada $49.00/ ISBN 0-7641-5263-7, approx. 780 pages

HOW TO PREPARE FOR THE REAL ESTATE LICENSING
EXAMS: SALESPERSON, BROKER, APPRAISER, 6th ED.
Bruce Lindeman and Jack P. Friedman
Reviews current exam topics and features updated model exams and supplemental exa
all with explained answers.
Paperback, $14.95, Canada $21.00/ISBN 0-7641-0773-9, 340 pages

BARRON'S FINANCE AND INVESTMENT HANDBOOK, 5th
John Downes and Jordan Elliot Goodman
This hard-working handbook of essential information defines more than 3000 key ter
and explores 30 basic investment opportunities. The investment information is thoro
up-to-date.
Hardcover, $35.00, Canada $45.95/ISBN 0-7641-5099-5, 1392 pages

FINANCIAL TABLES FOR MONEY MANAGEMENT
Stephen S. Solomon, Dr. Clifford Marshall, Martin Pepper, Jack P. Friedman, and Jack C.
Pocket-sized handbooks of interest and investment rate tables used easily by average i
and mortgage holders.
Each book: Paperback.
Adjustable Rate Mortgages, 2nd Ed., $8.95, Canada $11.50/0-8120-1529-0, 288 pp.
Canadian Mortgage Payments, 2nd Ed., Canada $8.95/0-8120-1617-3, 336 pp.
Mortgage Payments, 3rd Ed., $7.95, Canada $11.50/0-7641-1801-3, 336 pp.
Real Estate Loans, 3rd Ed., $7.95, Canada $11.50/0-7641-1800-5, 350 pp.

Books may be purchased at your bookstore or by mail from Barron's. Enclose check or money orde
total amount plus sales tax where applicable and 18% for postage and handling (minimum charge
Prices subject to change without notice.

Barron's Educational Series, Inc.
250 Wireless Blvd., Hauppauge, NY 11788
In Canada: Georgetown Book Warehouse
34 Armstrong Ave., Georgetown, Ontario L7G 4R9
www.barronseduc.com

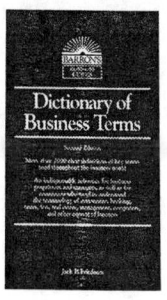

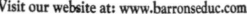